Ulrike Gretzel
Rob Law
Matthias Fuchs (eds.)

Information and
Communication Technologies
in Tourism 2010

Proceedings of the International Conference
in Lugano, Switzerland,
February 10-12, 2010

SpringerWienNewYork

Dr. Ulrike Gretzel
Laboratory for Intelligent Systems in Tourism
Texas A&M University, Texas, USA

Dr. Rob Law
School of Hotel & Tourism Management
The Hong Kong Polytechnic University, Hong Kong

Prof. Matthias Fuchs
Mid Sweden University
European Tourism Research Inst. (ETOUR), Sweden

© 2010 Springer-Verlag/Wien
Printed in Austria

SpringerWienNewYork is part of Springer Science + Business Media
springer.at

Typesetting: Camera ready by the authors
Printing: Ferdinand Berger & Söhne Gesellschaft m.b.H., 3580 Horn, Austria

Printed on acid-free and chlorine-free bleached paper

With 102 figures and 109 tables
SPIN: 12710409

Library of Congress Control Number: 2009943511

ISBN 978-3-211-99406-1 SpringerWienNewYork

Preface

Since its inauguration in 1993, ENTER has established itself as a venue that facilitates exchanges among practitioners and scholars in the fields of travel & tourism and information technologies. The discussions emerging from the research presentations, workshops, panels and keynotes not only foster the exploration of the future of eTourism but also motivate participants to actively shape it. The 2010 conference theme "eTourism Horizons" reflects the active role of ENTER in identifying and moulding future eTourism trends. It also emphasizes the far-reaching changes happening in the arena of information and communication technologies in tourism and stresses the constant emergence of new horizons. Imagining new horizons is an integral part of the activities at the conference and research plays an important role in this process.

Almost 90 research papers were submitted to the international conference and underwent a double-blind peer-review process. Only the highest quality papers are featured in the proceedings book. They not only reflect different disciplinary backgrounds but also a variety of topics and applied methodological approaches. This diversity is what makes ENTER unique as a forum for idea exchange and learning. This year's ENTER conference also includes a short paper track with papers reflecting emerging ideas and technology prototypes. The short papers are published separately and are only available in electronic form. Also new this year was the ability for researchers to propose a special topic track. As a result, the ENTER 2010 conference includes a special track on "Implementing Tracking Technologies for Tourism Research, Management and Planning" organized by Noam Shoval.

A rigorous reviewing process requires reputable and efficient reviewers. We would like to thank the Research Program Committee members for their time and effort in reviewing the papers and making valuable comments that helped the authors improve their work. Due to the large volume of papers submitted this year, we also had to rely on several ad hoc reviewers. Thus, we would like to thank Irem Arsal, Lois Burgess, Christoph Grün, Woojin Lee, Maria Teresa Linaza, Nicole Mitsche, Cristian Morosan, Niels Christian Nielsen, Bing Pan, Young A Park, Pradeep Racherla, Sofia Reino, Ahmed Seffah, and Florian Zach for their ad-hoc contributions to the review process. We would further like to acknowledge the authors as the main contributors to the success of the conference. There would be no ENTER conference without their interest in the conference and their willingness to share their ideas and research findings in the form of research papers and presentations.

Ulrike Gretzel, Rob Law, Matthias Fuchs

Lugano, February 2010

Contents

1 Technology Use by Hotels

2 ICT Adoption and Use

3 Website Evaluation

4 Mobile Technology

5 Tracking Technologies in Tourism Research, Management & Planning

6 Online Travel Shopping

7 ICTs and Destination Management Organizations

8 eSatisfaction, Dissatisfaction and Complaints

9 Online Reputation

10 Travel Distribution

11 Online Search

12 Web 2.0

13 Sustainability and Inclusion through ICTs

14 Social Media Marketing

15 Online Destinations

16 Semantics

Index of Authors

Research Programme Review Committee

Seventeenth International Conference on Information and Communication Technologies in Travel and Tourism, Lugano, Switzerland, February 10-12, 2010

SCHERTLER Walter, University of Trier, Germany
SHELDON Pauline, University of Hawaii, USA
SHOVAL, Noam, The Hebrew University of Jerusalem, Israel
SIGALA Marianna, University of the Aegean, Greece
STOCK Oliviero, FBK-irst, Trento, Italy
SUZUKI Keiji, Hokkaido University, Japan
VAN DER PIJL John, Erasmus University, Netherlands
WERTHNER Hannes, Vienna University of Technology, Austria
WÖBER Karl, MODUL University Vienna, Austria
XIANG Zheng (Phil), University of North Texas, USA
YAMAMOTO Masahito, Hokkaido University, Japan
ZANKER Markus, University of Klagenfurt, Austria
ZINS Andreas, MODUL University Vienna, Austria

Hotel Domain Name Adoption and Implementation

Peter O'Connor[a]
Jamie Murphy[b]

[a] Essec Business School, France
oconnor@essec.fr

[b] University of Western Australia Business School, Australia
jmurphy@biz.uwa.edu.au

Abstract

Registering appropriate domain names, such as Hilton.com for Hilton hotels, has become essential for companies to engage customers on the Web. By establishing if leading hotel brands have registered trade names as domain names in generic and country domains, this study benchmarks current industry practices. Diffusion of innovations theory helps investigate the relationship between three – size, market sector and country of headquarters – organisational characteristics and both domain name adoption and implementation. Findings indicate that hotels perform well in registering generic and country domains. Academically, country of headquarters and brand size but not market sector related significantly to domain name adoption. Brand size, and to a lesser extent country headquarters, related significantly to domain name implementation. Finally, the results showed a leapfrog effect whereby hotels that lagged in the adoption of domain names often led in the implementation of domain names.

Keywords: Domain Names, Diffusion of Innovations, Hotel sector, Leapfrog effects

1 Introduction

The Internet offers organisations new opportunities to reach out and communicate with customers (Baloglu and Pekcan 2006). Although initially established for research and administrative purposes, commercial use of the Internet has grown exponentially since the 1994 launch of the World Wide Web. Internet commerce continues to expand at a rapid pace, with both "pure-play" and traditional "bricks and mortar" businesses adopting e-commerce features by moving general information, catalogues, orders, transaction processing and payments online (Hanson and Kalyanam 2007). As a result, an online presence has become critical for organisations wishing to engage with this high potential market (Sharma and Sheth 2004).

To operate effectively online, businesses and brands must have an easily recognizable domain name, or, as discussed later, domain name portfolio (Hanson and Kalyanam 2007). Domain names in effect act as street signs, guiding potential customers to a particular website and enhancing corporate recognition (Murphy and Massey 1997). For example, users seeking Hilton hotels would type the domain name *hilton.com*. An ideal domain name comes readily to mind, references the business clearly and uniquely, and identifies the company's goods and services (Bagby and Ruhnka 2004). Thus organisations that want websites easily accessible to potential and existing customers should register and use domain names that closely match their corporate names and trademarks, in both top level domains (such as .com) and in the country domains (such as .fr for France, .de for Germany, etc) of the countries in which they wish to operate (Radcliffe 2002). Some commentators go so far as to claim that having branded domain names corresponding to well-known trademarks are a prerequisite for companies wishing to establish an Internet presence (Wang 2006).

Given the nominal financial outlay of about US$10 annually, many commentators advise registering multiple domain names, including company names, brand names and trademarks for legal and branding purposes. Many also advise the registration of misspellings, nicknames and sound-alike names in order to prevent misuse (Bagby and Ruhnka 2004). Failure to do so can result in third parties registering such domains, and either ransoming the domain name or setting up competitive websites to divert potential customers elsewhere (Murphy, Raffa et al. 2003).

The travel sector in particular has led the surge online (Dinlersoz and Hernández-Murillo 2005). An estimated 40 million people searched for travel information in the United States alone in 2008, leading to estimated online sales of US$ 98 billion (Burka, Carrol et al. 2008). Hotels have been quick to take advantage of the power of online distribution (O'Connor and Piccoli 2003). A hotel website brings considerable benefits by facilitating both the distribution of information to potential customers and the booking process itself (Chung and Law 2003). In a 2000 study, Mullen (2000) claimed that more than two-thirds of hospitality and tourism companies already used their websites as a marketing tool.

Murphy et al (2003) advised hotels to adopt branded domain names, such as Hilton.com, as soon as possible to prevent third parties from acquiring them, protect their on-line identity and reinforce their brand. Yet have hotels have heeded this advice? To the author's knowledge, few empirical studies have examined this issue. One study, carried out in 2006, examined 494 hotels in four Malaysian states and found that 27% of the hotels had a branded URL (Hashim and Murphy 2007). Using the Diffusion of Innovations as its theoretical base, the study also found that hotel size, star category and affiliation all related positively to adopting branded URLs.

And while to date there has been no global study of domain name adoption by hotels, regional studies (see for example Baloglu and Pekcan (2006), (Cobanoglu 2007), Murphy, Olaru et al (2003) and Sigala (2003)) suggest that hotels have adopted minimal web presence. With many hotels adopting only a superficial approach to online distribution, it seems unlikely that they would have invested the time and money, albeit minimal, to leverage their trademarks as domain names. Yet without empirical research, current industry practice is unknown.

The seemingly poor implementation and integration of the Internet into hospitality business practices may, however, be a research artefact. As new media generally take about 30 years to become standard practices (Fidler 1997), typical organisational use of the World Wide Web may be years or decades away. Similarly, the Diffusion of Innovations argues that both individuals and organisations evolve in their use of new technologies (Rogers 2003). Each user typically falls into one of five technology adopter categories, ranging from Innovators (the first to adopt) to Laggards (the last to adopt). Extant hospitality Internet studies may omit late adopter categories and focus on nascent Internet use.

To address these knowledge gaps and benchmark industry practices, this study explores branded domain name ownership by the top 100 global hotel brands. Using the diffusion of innovations theory as its base, this paper complements studies of how three organisational factors – brand size, market sector and headquarters country – associate with the *adoption* of an innovation, in this case the date of registering the .com domain name. The paper also addresses calls for research that goes beyond adopting an innovation and examines effective use of that innovation (Fichman 2004). Drawing on Rogers' (2003) adopter categories, do early adopters of domain names lead in the successful *implementation* of domain name portfolios? Or is there a leapfrog effect whereby late adopters, benefiting from the experience of their peers, outperform early adopters in the implementation of that innovation (Hobday 1995; Goldenberg and Oreg 2007)?

The paper starts by explaining the composition of a domain name and its importance as a marketing, branding and promotional tool. Diffusion of innovations theory is then introduced to frame the research study and help understand domain name adoption. Having outlined the research methodology, results of the study are then presented and implications for industry and for academia explored.

2 Background

To the user, Internet addresses comprise character strings separated by dots (Mueller 1998). Technically known as domain names, these provide a more persistent and easier to remember identifier than the underlying numerical Internet Protocol (IP) address assigned to every device connected to the Internet.

The latter typically comprises four separate groups of not more than three integers separated by a period (for example 147.252.1.34) that facilitates data transfer from one place to another. As humans are poor at remembering complicated numbers, in the early 1980s Jon Postel and others developed the Domain Name System using strings of letters instead of numbers (Harmon 1998). As a result, users can enter Coke.com rather than 147.252.1.34. Domain names thus serve as mnemonic devices that make the Internet easy to use by humans. As will be discussed, domain names also serve a marketing function. As they are easier to remember, type and promote than IP addresses, domain names play a key role in helping companies gain Internet visibility and promote their brand (Hanson and Kalyanam 2007)

Top level domains (TLDs) are the characters at the rightmost end of an Internet address (Mueller 1998). There are currently two TLD categories. Generic Top Level Domains (gTLDs) began theoretically to reflect the site purpose, such as .com for commercial sites, .org for non-profit organisations and .net for internet related companies (Mueller 1998). However, this rule never held. Additional descriptive gTLDs (including, .biz, .info, .mobi and recently .travel) were introduced to provide more options to companies wishing to register meaningful domain names. The second naming structure, country code Top Level Domains (ccTLDs), is based on political geography, and usually consists of two-letter codes for countries or territories (e.g. .uk for the United Kingdom, .de for Germany or .eu for the European Community).

Immediately to the left of the TLD is the second level name (for example in the hypothetical *www.abchotel.com*, the second level name is "abchotel"). Generally this describes the business (Ellis and Eklund 2004) and is normally a company's name, an abbreviation of that name or some aspect of its trademark (Wang 2006). The policies and procedures for registration of second level domains vary. For example, .com domain names can be any combination of 2 to 63 characters – letters, numbers or hyphens – must begin with a letter, and are assigned on a first-come first-served basis with no restrictions on who can register a combination, no review process, and the applicant need have no connection with the domain name in question. However rigid restrictions often apply in other domains. For example, a nominated trade association must certify that companies seeking .travel names operate in the travel sector (Radcliffe 2002). ccTLDs tend to impose stricter restrictions than gTLDs, having, amongst other things, residency or website hosting requirements (Tanenbaum 2003).

To obtain a domain name, an individual or organisation visits the website of a registrar of the domain in question, such as Network Solutions for the generic .com domain or AFNIC (Association Française pour le Nommage Internet en Coopération) for the French .fr domain. If searching the registry database (known as a WHOIS) shows their desired domain name is available, the applicant can register it by supplying contact and technical information and paying an annual fee (Moringiello 2004). Once registered, the applicant has the exclusive right to use that domain name in perpetuity as long as the annual registration fee is paid, and also has the right to transfer this right to a third party.

2.1 Domain Names and Branding

According to Bagby and Ruhnka (2004) domain names serve two purposes. The first is the technical mapping discussed above, matching the domain name and relevant IP address to facilitate data routing. The second is to strengthen brand image; domain names that strongly identify an organisation play a critical role in attracting e-commerce and generating repeat traffic (Degeratu, Rangaswamy et al. 2000). For many consumers, typing a brand name or a trade name followed by .com into a web browser is a first step in finding a particular brand (Murphy and Scharl 2007). Thus, as electronic commerce grows in importance, so too does the need to have a correct portfolio of domain names (Hanson and Kalyanam 2007). Companies wishing to do business online should acquire easy to remember domain names that correspond closely to the names of their products, trade names and trademarks (Maher 1996). Some commentators claim that domain names have now become more important than trademarks (Deva 2005).

In particular having a company name as a name in the .com domain has become highly desirable (Murphy, Raffa et al. 2003). However, as by their nature they are unique, "good" domain names have become a scarce commodity. Since allocation, in .com at least, is on a first-come first served basis, the use of one character combination as a domain name precludes others from adopting the same string (Mueller 1998). The first person or organisation to register a particular combination becomes the unique owner, preventing all others from using that domain name.

In the early Internet days, when educational institutions and governments were the primary users, conflicts over who owned a particular domain name caused few problems (Maher 1996). There is, after all, only one Cornell University and thus unlikely that several institutions would seek Cornell.edu. However, as Internet use grew, individuals and organisations competing for the limited number of domain names rushed to obtain commercially advantageous, i.e. recognisable, names (Murphy and Massey 1997). Many companies attempting to register desired domain names found them already registered – in some cases by legitimate companies in other sectors with a similar trade name, or as discussed below, by competitors or other individuals wishing to misuse the domain name (Wang 2006). Many disagreements ultimately ended up in court, with most arguments focusing on trademark abuse (Radcliffe 2002).

Yet there is an inherent conflict between trademark law and allocating domain names. Offline, multiple companies frequently own rights to a trademark, but are differentiated geographically or by the sector in which they operate. For example, over 15 different companies have registered the word "Apple" as a trademark in the United States alone, for goods ranging from computers to rice. While multiple users of the same trademark can exist in the offline world, only one corresponding domain name exists in each top-level domain (Radcliffe 2002). The company that acted first gained a valuable asset.

The ease of registering domain names, coupled with the first-come first-served principle, spawned other challenges (Mueller 1998). For example, speculators pre-emptively register thousands of recognisable domain names in the hope to subsequently ransom them back to companies wishing to use their brand name as their domain name (Ellis and Eklund 2004). Such name speculation, known as cyber-squatting, quickly became widespread for top level domain names, making it problematic for legitimate businesses to register their brands as domain names (Radcliffe 2002). And while cyber squatters typically register a company's name, brands, trademarks or close variants as domain names with the intent to resell them at a profit, angry employees, industry critics, customers and even competitors registered domain names to engage in cyber smearing – posting disparaging or defamatory information on official looking but bogus websites (Bagby and Ruhnka 2004).

2.2 Diffusion of Innovations

Although domain names continue to grow in importance as more businesses go online, empirical research on domain name registration and their use as a marketing /

branding tool, is limited. A partial reason for this may be the difficulty examining the issue at anything beyond the descriptive level. One theoretical approach to help understand how companies use domain names is the Diffusion of Innovations (Rogers 2003). In general, diffusion amongst individuals depends on factors such as social structures and social norms, as well as the influence of opinion leaders and change agents (Murphy, Olaru et al. 2003). Damanpour (1991) and others extended this theory to organisations, citing leadership characteristics, company structure and external factors as key influencers of organisational innovation. He noted that unlike individuals making optional decisions, organisations decide authoritatively or collectively whether to adopt innovations, regardless of the opinions of individuals within that company.

Furthermore, unlike the yes/no decision with individual adoption, organisational adoption ranges from awareness of an innovation to successful infusion and implementation of the innovation within organisational work practices and systems (Wolfe 1994). With regard to domain names, simply registering a .com domain name suggests *adoption*. Going beyond adoption and developing a domain name portfolio, registering brand names as names in multiple gTLDs and ccTLDs, suggests *implementation* of that same technology − domain names. Thus this paper operationalises adoption as the .com name registration date and operationalises implementation as the number of registered gTLD and ccTLD names. As noted, there is a dearth of studies on the organisational implementation of technologies, as well as how adopter categories relate to the implementation of technologies. Given that registering names in domains other than .com goes beyond domain name adoption and towards implementing a comprehensive domain name strategy, the following Research Question helps address this gap.

RQ: How do adopter categories relate to gTLD and ccTLD registrations?

Past hospitality research has shown that hotel size and market sector often relate positively to the adoption of new technologies. Large and upscale hotels tend to adopt Internet technologies faster than small and downscale hotels (see, for example, Siguaw, Enz et al. 2000; Murphy, Olaru et al. 2003; Hashim and Murphy 2007). Thus in line with past adoption studies and extending to add technology implementation;

Hypothesis 1: Brand size in rooms relates positively with the a) primary site's domain name age, b) number of gTLDs registered, and c) number of ccTLDs registered.

Hypothesis 2: Market sector relates positively with the a) primary site's domain name age, b) number of gTLDs registered, and c) number of ccTLDs registered.

In addition to organisational factors, Internet diffusion often relates to country-level factors such as IT infrastructure (Beilocka and Dimitrova 2003). Given that the US developed and leads in the development of the Internet (Hanson and Kalyanam 2007), it is further hypothesised that;

Hypothesis 3: Relative to non-US based hotel chains, US hotel chains will lead in the a) primary site's domain name age, b) number of gTLDs registered and c) number of ccTLDs registered.

3   Research Methodology

The top 100 hotel brands (by number of rooms), published annually by Hotels Magazine was the study population. As with Ellis and Eklund (2004), the rationale was that such companies are at the forefront of protecting their online identities, partly to protect their brand and partly because they should have the knowledge, technical resources and financial capability to do so. As well, these companies' actions should demonstrate hospitality best practices (Ellis and Eklund 2004). Note that brands, rather than hotel companies were used, as in practically all cases the brand (e.g. Sofitel, Novotel, etc), rather than the hotel company name (Accor Hotels & Resorts) is used in consumer facing marketing. The native country of each brand (by headquarter location) was also recorded to investigate differences in behaviour between US and non-US brands. Lastly, following the example of Siguaw, Enz et al (2000) each brand was assigned to an upscale, mid-scale or economy segment based on data from Smith Travel Research (in the US) or The Bench (internationally). A search for the brand name via Google.com in March 2009 noted the first .com site in the organic search results as the "primary" site. A WHOIS lookup on this domain name yielded the original registration date as well as the registrant. Then a registrant search via *Domaintools.com* gave that same registrant's number of domain name in six gTLDSs (.net, .org, .info, .biz, .mobi and .travel), and in five ccTLDs (.co.uk, .us, .de, .es, .fr). Output from this site was validated by searching for sites registered by the authors and by a local web development company. In all cases, the correct number and range of sites were returned, implying that Domaintools.com correctly assessed the number of domain names registered to a particular registrant.

4   Findings

With a mean size of 47,500 rooms, the analysed brands comprised 34% upscale brands, 38% mid-scale brands and 28% economy brands. With the hospitality industry estimated at 32.3 billon rooms, the brands surveyed thus represented 15 percent of the global lodging sector. As Table One shows, economy brands tended to be the largest, with an average size of over 56,000 rooms, followed by up-scale brands at nearly 50,000 rooms. Both economy and mid-scale brands were more likely to be headquartered in the United States than their up-scale competitors.

Table 1. Breakdown of Hotel Brands

	Proportion of Total	Average Size (Rooms)	% with US Headquarters
Economy	28%	56074	60%
Mid-Scale	38%	39476	65%
Up-Scale	34%	49422	37%

Rogers (2003) defines Innovators and Early adopters as the first 16% to adopt an innovation, followed by the Early Majority (34%), Late Majority (34%) and Laggards (16%). To investigate relationships between adopter categories and domain name registrations, this study categorized the brands based on each brand's .com registration date. Table 2 below lists the percentages of, and average gTLD and ccTLD registrations by these adopter categories.

As Table 2 shows, over seven in ten of the top 100 hotel brands registered the six target gTLDs and on average, the brands registered almost five gTLDs. The top gTLDs were .net and .mobi, both at 90% registrations. The least popular gTLD was .travel, at 71%. The average number of ccTLDs registered was 3.51. The top ccTLD was .co.uk at 82% and the least popular ccTLD was .fr at 50%.

Table 2. Domain Name Registrations

	Total	Inn/Early A.	Early Maj.	Late Maj.	Laggards
Percentage gTLD registrations					
.net	90	**100**	97.1	82.2	*68.8*
.mobi	90	*87.5*	**94.1**	88.2	*87.5*
.org	87	93.8	**97.1**	88.2	*56.3*
.info	79	87.5	**97.1**	82.4	*25*
.biz	79	87.5	**94.1**	79.4	*37.5*
.travel	71	81.3	**85.3**	67.6	*37.5*
Percentage ccTLD registrations					
.co.uk	82	93.8	**97.1**	82.4	*37.5*
.de	78	**93.8**	91.2	79.4	*31.3*
.us	78	93.8	**97.1**	73.5	*31.3*
.es	63	**81.3**	76.5	58.8	*25*
.fr	50	**68.8**	58.8	52.9	*6.3*
Average Registrations					
gTLDS	4.95	5.4	**5.7**	4.9	*3.1*
ccTLDS	**3.51**	4.3	4.2	3.5	*1.3*
Total TLDs	**8.47**	9.7	**9.8**	8.4	*4.4*

Bold for category leader and *Italics* for category laggard

The results of Chi-square tests show significant differences (p<.05) across adopter categories for all TLDs except .mobi. Suggesting a leapfrog effect, the Early Majority category often leads the Innovators/Early Adopters in domain name registrations.

4.1 Hypotheses Testing

Testing for the first and second hypotheses used correlation analysis, a one-tailed test with Pearson's and Spearman's product-moment correlation coefficient, respectively, as the test statistic. As hypothesised, brand size showed a significant positive relationship with the primary site's domain name age (r=.349, p<0.001), number of gTLDs registered (r=.317, p=.001) and number of ccTLDs registered (r=.352, p<.001). However the results for the second hypothesis − that market sector relates positively with the number of gTLDs registered − were insignificant and in the wrong direction.

Testing for the third hypothesis was via one-tailed t-tests. The results were in the hypothesised direction, significantly so for two variables. The US-based hotel brands registered their .com domain name significantly earlier (M=8 August 1997, SD=2.99 years) than did the non US-based brands (M=9 October 1998, SD=3.28 years, t(98)=1.87, p=.034). Similarly, US-based brands registered significantly more gTLDs (M=5.31, SD=1.26) than did the non US-based brands (M=4.54, SD=1.81, t(78.3)=-2.434), p=.009). There were no significant differences between ccTLD registrations by US (M=3.58, SD=1.61) and non US-based brands (M=3.44, SD=1.92).

5 Conclusions

5.1 Industry Implications

As part of a growing body of hospitality Internet research, this paper provides a useful benchmark of domain name diffusion by leading hotel brands. The majority of brands registered their trade names as domain names in each of the generic TLDs, although opportunities, or dangers depending on the perspective, still exist for many companies in the less common domains such as .info, .biz and .travel. Companies should follow the advice of Murphy, Raffa et al (2003) and register appropriate .info and .biz domain names to prevent cyber-squatting or cyber-smearing websites, or the domain name being lost to a third party. Given strict .travel registration requirements and possible low consumer acceptance of .travel domain names, registration in .travel may not merit the approximate US$ 100 annual fee.

Hotel brands have been less vigilant in registering their ccTLD names. In the French (.fr) and Spanish (.es) domains, only about half of the world's leading hotel brands have to date registered their trade names as domain names. While, as previously discussed, this may be caused by the rigid restrictions often imposed by ccTLD registrars, hotel brands in general tend to be global, and any brand that may in the future want to expand into these territories should do whatever necessary to comply with restrictions and register desired domain names before an alternative legitimate trademark holder within these countries permanently removes this opportunity.

5.2 Academic Implications

This is one of the few studies to examine leapfrogging effects. As the study results show, the leaders in adopting an innovation were not always the leaders in implementing that same innovation. Rather than the innovator/early adopter category, the early majority category often led in the implementation of a comprehensive domain name strategy, particularly with gTLD registrations.

Diffusion of innovations theory suggests that organisational characteristics relate to *adoption*, yet few diffusion studies examine the organisational *implementation* of a technology. With regard to domain name adoption, and in line with extant research, this study found that organisational size and having a US headquarter location related positively to the date of registering a branded .com name. Yet in contrast with most adoption studies, no relationship was found between market sector and .com domain name adoption. This aberrant finding may be an artefact characteristic of many hospitality Internet studies, namely examining a subset of the population, early adopters, or examining small rather than large hotel brands. Scholars should use the results in this paper for questioning and replicating Internet diffusion studies from late last century and early this century.

The findings were mixed with regard to *implementation*, registering domain name portfolios. Just one organisational factor, brand size, related positively to gTLD and ccTLD registrations. The hotel brand's market sector or company headquarter location showed no significant relationship with ccTLD registrations. US-based brands, however, registered significantly more gTLDs than did non-US brands. And albeit insignificant, hotel sector showed a negative relationship with gTLD registrations. These mixed findings highlight the need and opportunity for future research of the organisational implementation of technologies.

5.3 Limitations and Future Research

Like any research, this study has limitations and offers future research opportunities. Firstly, the study only looked at hotel brands, effectively ignoring the large segment of the market that is unbranded. As Yeung and Law (2004) point out, chain and independent properties differ greatly in their marketing expertise, and thus different results could be expected by including independent properties in a study. Broadening the study to include a representative sample of hotels would increase generalisability and help establish a true industry benchmark.

Secondly, when identifying the trade name used by the company, there was a risk that the first site to appear in the Google search results was not owned by the brand in question. However as this study focused on major brands, the risk was minimal; research shows that hotel brands of this size invest heavily in search engine optimisation and their sites normally appear first on search engine result listings (O'Connor 2007). Nevertheless, as a safety mechanism, each registrant was examined to see if it the address and email address listed was logical for the brand in question. However, if the study was to be repeated with a different sample of hotels, particularly smaller or unbranded properties, attention should be paid to insure that the site selected was an official site of the brand in question.

A presumption was also made that all domain names for a particular brand were registered using a single email address. While this would be good practice, as it would allow easily managing lifecycles, renewals and other administrative issues, there is a risk that in reality brands are not so well organised. Multiple email addresses may have been used to registered alternative domains and thus the number of domain names associated with each brand in the study may be understated.

Furthermore, the Domaintools.com tool used as a key source of data in this study may be a weak means of identifying the domains associated with a particular registrant. However the site in question was tested and at least superficially validated by the authors prior to this study, is used extensively in legal actions in relation to cyber-squatting and has been widely cited in the press as an invasion of privacy since it allows the domain names associated with an individual to be identified. However more in-depth research, along the lines of that carried out by Murphy et al (2007) to validate the WayBack Machine as a data source, should be carried out to assess the system for accuracy and reliability.

Lastly the study only examined the registration of a single trade name across multiple domains. No attempt was made to identify confusing similar sites, misspellings, gripe sites (such as ihateMarriott.com or Marriottsucks.com) or parasites that take advantage of user typing mistakes to gain traffic such as yohop.com which profits from yahoo.com. Such a study would be of interest to help industry practitioners to assess how broadly they need to think in terms of words to register as domain names. For companies truly wishing to serve a global customer base, adapting their website to take into account the language, culture and social norms of local marketplaces has become a key issue. This study benchmarks the efforts of the top fifty hotel chains to incorporate appropriate content and facilities on their website as an indicator of their commitment to servicing international markets.

References

Bagby, J. W. and J. C. Ruhnka (2004). Protecting Domain Name Assets. *CPA Journal* 74(4): 64-69.

Baloglu, S. and Y. A. Pekcan (2006). The website design and Internet site marketing practices of upscale and luxury hotels in Turkey. *Tourism Management* 27(1): 171-176.

Beilocka, R. and D. Dimitrova (2003). An Exploratory Model of Inter-country Internet Diffusion. *Telecommunications Policy* 27(3-4): 237-252.

Burka, K., W. Carrol, et al. (2008). *U.S. Online Travel Overview*. Sherman. NY, PhoCusWright Inc.

Chung, T. and R. Law (2003). Developing a performance indicator for hotel websites. *International Journal of Hospitality Management* 22(1): 119-125.

Cobanoglu, C. (2007). 6th Restaurant Web Study. *Hospitality Technology* 11(4): 3-11.

Damanpour, F. (1991). Organizational innovation: a meta analysis of effects of determinants and moderators. *Academy of Management Journal* 34: 555-9.

Degeratu, A., A. Rangaswamy, et al. (2000). Consumer Choice Behavior in Online and Traditional Supermarkets: The Effects of Brand Name, Price, and Other Search Attributes. *International Journal of Research in Marketing* 17(1): 55-78.

Deva, S. (2005). What's in a name? Disputes relating to domain names in India. *International Review of Law, Computers & Technology* 19(2): 165-181.

Dinlersoz, E. M. and R. Hernández-Murillo (2005). The Diffusion of Electronic Business in the United States. *Federal Reserve Bank of St. Louis Review* 87(1): 11-34.

Ellis, T. S. and J. Eklund (2004). Problems and Issues with the Domain Name System: A Review of Fortune 100 Companies. *Journal of Internet Commerce* 3(1): 79.

Fichman, R. G. (2004). Real Options and IT Platform Adoption: Implications for Theory and Practice. *Information Systems Research* 15(2): 132-154.

Fidler, R. F. (1997). *Mediamorphosis - Understanding New Media*. Thousand Oaks, California, Pine Forge Press.

Goldenberg, J. and S. Oreg (2007). Laggards in Disguise: Resistance to Adopt and the Leapfrogging Effect. *Technological Forecasting and Social Change* 74(8): 1272-1281.

Hanson, W. and K. Kalyanam (2007). *Internet Marketing and e-Commerce*. Mason City, OH, Thomson South-Western.

Harmon, A. (1998). We, the People Of the Internet; Cybercitizens Debate How to Form On-Line Union, Perfect or Otherwise. Retrieved 29 July, 2009, from http://www.nytimes.com/1998/06/29/business/we-people-internet-cybercitizens-debate-form-line-union-perfect-otherwise.html.

Hashim, N. H. and J. Murphy (2007). Branding on the Web: Evolving Domain Name Usage among Malaysian Hotels. *Tourism Management* 28(2): 621-624.

Hobday, M. (1995). East Asian Latecomer Firms: Learning the Technology of Electronics. *World Development* 23(7): 1171-1193.

Maher, D. (1996). Trademarks on the Internet: Who's in Charge? Retrieved 18 March 2009, from http://www.isoc.org/inet96/proceedings/f4/f4_2.htm.

Moringiello, J. M. (2004). Grasping Intangibles: Domain Names And Creditors' Rights. *Journal of Internet Law* 8(3): 3-11.

Mueller, M. L. (1998). The battle over Internet domain names: Global or national TLDs? *Telecommunications Policy* 22(2): 89-107.

Mullen, T. (2000). Travel's long journey to the web. *InternetWeek* 835: 103-106.

Murphy, J., N. Hashim, et al. (2007). Take me back: Validating the Wayback Machine. *Journal of Computer-Mediated Communication* 13(1): article 4, http://jcmc.indiana.edu/vol13/issue1/murphy.html

Murphy, J. and B. Massey (1997). Domain-Name Speculators Buy Up Web Real Estate and Toss the Dice. The New York Times on the Web.

Murphy, J., D. Olaru, et al. (2003). Swiss Hotels' Web-site and E-mail Management: The Bandwagon Effect. *Cornell Hotel and Restaurant Administration Quarterly* 44(1): 71-87.

Murphy, J., L. Raffa, et al. (2003). The Use of Domain Names in e-branding by the World's Top Brands. *Electronic Markets* 13(3): 222.

Murphy, J. and A. Scharl (2007). An investigation of global versus local online branding. *International Marketing Review* 24(3): 297-312.

O'Connor, P. (2007). An analysis of hotel trademark abuse in Pay-Per-Click search advertising. ENTER Information and Communications Technology in Tourism. M. Sigala, L. Mich and J. Murphy. Ljubljana, Slovenia, Springer: 377-388.

O'Connor, P. and G. Piccoli (2003). Global Distribution Systems: Revisited. *Cornell Hotel and Restaurant Administration Quarterly* 44(2): 105 - 114.

Radcliffe, M. (2002). Advanced domain name and trademark issues. *Journal of Internet Law* 5(7): 13.

Rogers, E. M. (2003). *Diffusion of Innovations*. New York, New York, Simon & Schuster.

Sharma, A. and J. N. Sheth (2004). Web-based marketing: The coming revolution in marketing thought and strategy. *Journal of Business Research* 57(7): 696-702.

Sigala, M. (2003). Developing and Benchmarking Internet Marketing Strategies in the Hotel Sector in Greece. *Journal of Hospitality & Tourism Research* 27(4): 375-401.

Siguaw, J. A., C. A. Enz, et al. (2000). Adoption of Information Technology in U.S. Hotels: Strategically Driven Objectives. *Journal of Travel Research* 39(2): 192-201.

Tanenbaum, W. A. (2003). Adventures with foreign domain names. *Journal of Internet Law* 6(8): 8.

Wang, F. (2006). Domain names management and legal protection. *International Journal of Information Management* 26(2): 116-127.

Wolfe, R. A. (1994). Organizational innovation: review, critique and suggested research. *Journal of Management Studies* 31(3): 405-431.

Yeung, T. A. and R. Law (2004). Extending the modified heuristic usability evaluation technique to chain and independent hotel websites. *International Journal of Hospitality Management* 23(3): 307-313.

ICT Efficiency and Effectiveness in the Hotel Sector – A Three-Stage DEA Approach

Christina Scholochow[a]
Matthias Fuchs[a/b]
Wolfram Höpken[a/c]

[a] eTourism Competence Center Austria (ECCA)
University of Innsbruck, Austria
christina.scholochow@student.uibk.ac.at

[b] European Tourism Research Institute (ETOUR)
Mid-Sweden University, Sweden
matthias.fuchs@etour.se

[c] Business Informatics Group, University of Applied Sciences Ravensburg-Weingarten, Germany
wolfram.hoepken@hs-weingarten.de

Abstract

A data envelopment analysis model is presented to investigate information and communication technology's (ICT) efficiency and effectiveness in the Austrian hotel sector. The proposed three-stage procedure allows to evaluate both, allocative efficiency of expenses devoted to ICTS, the effectiveness of ICTS to maximise the level of output, and finally, to validate the model by relating total output to total input. In order to obtain a most comprehensive picture subjective assessments about adoption conditions and efficiency gains induced by ICTS are additionally considered. Data is gathered via online surveys in 2008 by addressing the managers of 3,600 Austrian hotels. Results show that the impact of ICTS on productivity gains is positive and significant. However, results also suggest that intermediate ICT adopters show lowest allocative efficiency compared to heavy and weak ICT adopters. Similarly, ICTS' effectiveness in generating hotel revenues is proved only for heavy and weak ICT adopters.

Keywords: Three-stage DEA, allocative ICT efficiency, ICT effectiveness, hotel sector, subjective data.

1 Introduction

E-tourism literature has highlighted that information and communication technologies (ICTS) result in greater productivity, decreased costs, increased revenues and improved business operations and customer service (Armijos et al., 2002; Sigala et al., 2004; Werthner & Ricci, 2004). Hotel industry quickly identified the implementation of ICTS as vital to achieve their goals for successful description, promotion, distribution, amalgamation, organization and delivery of their services (Ham et al., 2005). However, the relationship between ICT investments and corporate performance is complex and multifaceted, thus, leading to volatile productivity effects. This situation of marginal (or stagnating) productivity gains despite significant ICT investments is also known as the ICT productivity paradox (David et al., 1996; Brynjolfsson & Hitt, 1998). For diverging results between ICT investment and productivity gains, however, a number of explanations exist:

1) *Measurement problems:* Definitions and amortization rules for ICT differ significantly between branches and countries. Thus, the manifold ICT processes (particularly in the service sector) are insufficiently represented in balance sheets, financial statements or official statistics wherefore productivity metrics cannot capture the full ICT impact from better processes or customer services (Vuorinen et al., 1998; Grönroos & Ojasalo, 2004). 2) *Time lags:* Since employees must be properly trained and barriers to use must be surmounted it can take only a few weeks to years before productivity gains induced by new ICTS can be observed (Klein, 2005). However, according to McGrath and More (2005) in an information intensive and highly competitive industry, like tourism, ICT investments typically require a relatively short time frame for capturing payoffs. Other determinants that have to be considered when explaining dynamic effects of ICT investments on firm performance are the level of the analyses (e.g. firm, sector and country), variances in the sample period and the methodology used to detect various dimensions of firm performance (Sangho & Soung, 2006). 3) *Changed processes & routines*: Adoption of new ICTS triggers dramatic organisational changes, like de- and recentralisation of decision processes or the relocation and outsourcing of work processes. Consequently, productivity gains can only be expected if ICT innovations are accompanied by organisational innovations with respect to firm-related decision and transformation processes, respectively. Put differently, only well organized firms may benefit from ICT adoption – by contrast, despite of huge ICT investments, the productivity level of poorly run firms with low profitability will continue to erode.

In order to investigate ICTS' allocative efficiency and effectiveness in the hotel sector the paper proposes a three-stage DEA model. The approach allows to evaluate both, allocative efficiency from expenses devoted to ICT, the effectiveness of ICTS to maximise hotel output and, finally, to validate the approach by relating total output to total input. Besides this three-stage approach and based on the postulate that ICT expenditures are more effective at generating revenues than other resource items we investigate the contrast between effectiveness and productivity via the returns to scale (RTS) of individual hotels (Keh et al. 2006). Finally, to obtain a comprehensive picture about ICTS' allocative efficiency and effectiveness, subjective assessments about the adoption context and perceived productivity gains induced by ICTS are considered. Data is collected via online surveys in 2008 by addressing the managers of 3,600 Austrian hotels. The paper is structured as follows: Section two provides a review of related economic and e-tourism literature and discusses productivity definitions and prior ICT productivity studies in the hotel sector. Section three presents data envelopment analysis as the method used to test the hypothesis formulated in section four. The latter section also presents the three-stage DEA procedure and discusses data gathering. Section five discusses the results from both, cluster analyses, DEA and hypothesis testing. The conclusion summarizes the results, discusses the managerial and tourism policy implications and sketches the agenda for future research on ICT efficiency and effectiveness in tourism.

2   Literature Review

Economists define ICTS as producer durable goods to substitute expensive resource inputs (e.g. labour) and to boost a firm's competitiveness (Tangen, 2004). Typically, this is achieved through process reengineering and by combining ICTS with other innovations. Moreover, in service industries (like tourism) long-term success depends on the degree of how internal efficiency (i.e. the cost effective use of resources) and external efficiency (i.e. the revenue-generating capability through convenience, punctuality, promptness, etc.) can be improved (Grönroos & Ojasalo, 2004). However, due to measurement difficulties productivity concepts are often rooted in the context of mass manufacturing and empirical research typically underestimates the ICTS' impact on productivity in the service industries (Vuorinen et al., 1998). Another likely reason for inconsistent results is the lack of considering industry characteristics, like information intensity. Thus, time lags between IT investments and payoffs vary accordingly (Sangho & Soung, 2006, p. 44).

Before presenting the proposed methodology, basic productivity concepts are briefly discussed. *Productivity* is the quotient between output(s) and one, more or all inputs used in a production process (Keh et al., 2006, p. 266). Productivity measures how well production processes transform resource inputs into outputs. Productivity gains are achieved because output increases more rapidly than inputs or because there is a decline in the use of inputs while output(s) are kept constant. By contrast, *efficiency* is purposefully connected to how input resources are utilized and is achieved when the marginal productivity per unit is equated across all resources that contribute to a firm's output (ibid, 2006, p. 266). Thus, the term emphasizes the difference between the minimum resource input theoretically required and the level of resources actually used. Finally, *effectiveness* is concerned with determining which strategy – among all possible strategies – maximises long-term ROI (ibid, 2006, p. 266). Although the latter term is strongly interlinked to customer value processes, the most effective use of resources assumes that resources are used efficiently. To sum up, Tangen (2004) describes efficiency as 'doing the things right', whereas effectiveness is about doing 'the right things' (e.g. reaching the strategic goals).

E-tourism literature provides only few studies capturing the impact of ICTS on hotel efficiency and performance (Johns et al. 1995; Tarim et al. 2000; Sigala et al. 2004). For instance, the regression-based approach conducted by Ham et al. (2005, p. 291) revealed that front- and back office applications as well as restaurant and banquet management systems significantly affected the performance of lodging operations. Similarly, research based on non-parametric methods is highlighting that the debate regarding the ICT productivity paradox has been a methodological artefact. For instance, for 3 star hotels Sigala (2003) revealed significant productivity differences among hotels without ICT, with loosely integrated ICT systems and finally, with fully integrated ICT systems. Thus, her findings confirm the impact of ICT integration on productivity and indicate synergy and complementary effects (ibid, 2003, p. 1238). Finally, Shang et al. (2008, p. 529) apply data envelopment analysis to analyze the impact of ICTS on hotel performance. By contrast to the above mentioned research, however, their study found no efficiency effects owing to a different e-commerce adoption status of hotels in Taiwan. Inspired by this research we propose a three-stage DEA approach to investigate the ICT impact on productivity gains in the Austrian hotel sector.

3 The DEA Methodology

Single input-output ratios are not sufficient to holistically evaluate operating efficiency. However, data envelopment analysis (DEA) provides a way to consider multiple in- and output factors by a ratio of weighted outputs to weighted inputs (Zhu, 2009). Previously applied to measure productivity gains from resource investments for a variety of industries, DEA is a multivariate non-parametric method that constructs a linear frontier function in a stepwise approach (Charnes et al., 1978):

$$\max h_i = \frac{\sum_{r=1}^{s} u_r y_{ri}}{\sum_{j=1}^{m} v_j x_{ji}} \quad subject \ to \quad \frac{\sum_{r=1}^{s} u_r y_{ri}}{\sum_{j=1}^{m} v_j x_{ji}} \leq 1 \quad \text{for each } i = 1, \dots, n \text{ DMUS}$$

h_i = efficiency of unit 1 to be estimated;
y_i = outputs of the i_{th} unit; x_i = inputs of the i_{th} unit
$u_r \geq 0$ for $r = 1, \dots, s$ different outputs; $v_j \geq 0$ for $j = 1, \dots, m$ different inputs

The unknown weights u_r and v_j are estimated by DEA on the base of the data in order to obtain a relative efficiency measure for each unit. For this purpose, DEA arranges optimization contingent on each decision making unit's (DMU) performance to convert inputs into outputs in relation to the performance of all other DMUS. The weights for each DMU are separately estimated such that the efficiency level can be the maximum attainable. If the DMU's input-output combination lies on the frontier isoquant the DMU is considered to be efficient showing an efficiency value of 1, suggesting 100% efficiency. By contrast, DMUS using their resources less efficiently are located above the frontier-isoquant and the efficiency score is < 1. There are two ways of carrying out DEA: input-oriented – i.e. a given level of outputs is achieved with the minimum amount of inputs, and output-oriented – i.e. the output is maximized for a given level of input. Finally, DEA is not limited to monetary measures rather it handles any type of measurement quantities. However, researchers should be aware of pitfalls when applying DEA. First of all, sample size has a major impact on efficiency scores as a higher number of DMUS increases the chance of encountering units close to the true production frontier (Brown, 2006, p. 1102). Secondly, model specification (i.e. selection of appropriate in- and outputs) is essential. Four criteria should be taken into consideration when selecting DEA factors: 1) the factors should reflect all resources used by the DMU; 2) the factors should capture all operational activity levels and relevant performance measures; 3) all DMUS should employ the same factors, and 4) environmental influence has to be assessed and if necessary, included as uncontrolled inputs (ibid, 2006). Finally, DEA is highly sensitive to outliers. In contrast to parametric approaches measuring inefficiency relative to the average unit DEA is an extreme point method. Thus, outliers or noisy data severely bias the computation of efficiency score values.

4 Three-Stage DEA Framework

The proposed approach is a three-stage DEA procedure because efficiency in services is not simply 'an engineering process where inputs are transformed into outputs stiffly via a certain production function. Rather, there is an intermediate stage buffering the service production process' (Keh et al., 2006, p. 267). Thus, the incorporation of efficiency drivers in a three-stage framework should yield superior insights than isolated DEA efficiency analyses. Moreover, in order to gain a comprehensive picture of allocative ICT efficiency and ICT effectiveness the study includes objective and subjective data gathered in the course of an online survey during winter 2008 by addressing the managers of 3,600 Austrian hotels. Following Tornatzky and Fleisher's (1990) technology organisation environment framework, subjective data is collected on perception scales (i.e. 1=completely agree, 6=completely disagree) with respect to availability of the technical equipment and factors driving the adoption and use of ICTS. Similarly, according to Zhu (2009), productivity gains induced by ICTS are measured on perceptive scales. Objective data is gathered with respect to whether (or not) the following ICTS are adopted (Kim et al., 2008): Website with booking functionality, online platform, Intranet, e-mail marketing, and systems supporting online procurement, property management, enterprise resource planning, yield management, costing & accounting, e-customer relationship management and personnel management, respectively. Finally, output (revenues, overnights) and input data (ICT budget, employees, operating and marketing expenses) is measured on an objective base and is gathered by official statistics (Herold Austria, 2009). Inspired by Keh et al. (2006) the three-stage DEA framework in figure 1 is proposed:

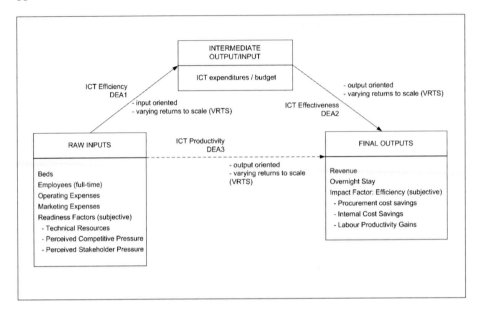

Fig. 1. Three-stage DEA framework

Stage 1 – Allocative ICT efficiency relates to a hotel's intra-organization operation, deciding what appropriate proportion of total expenses to allocate to ICT expenses (Keh et al. 2006, p. 267). Accordingly, input data comprises the number of beds and employees, operating expenses (i.e. for materials, resources and equipment) and marketing & advertising expenses. Subjective data captures technical resources (i.e. assessment of ICT system's modernity), competitive pressure (i.e. decline in competitive position due to an eventual absence of actually used ICTS) and stakeholder pressure (i.e. expectations of tourists and business partners to use latest ICTS). Finally, ICT budget is the output measure. Accordingly, input minimization and variable returns to scale (VRTS) are assumed (Brown, 2006).

Stage 2 – ICT effectiveness: In the second stage the ICT budget is used as a resource input to generate the maximal revenue from room rental and F&B operations. Thus, revenue and overnight stays are considered as output. In addition, subjective data about experienced cost savings with procurement and internal processes as well as gains of labour productivity is included. Output maximization and VRTS is assumed.

Stage 3 – ICT Productivity: Following Keh et al. (2006, p. 267), the third stage allows us to compare the ratio of outputs to inputs as an added check and, therefore, to assess if a three-stage model is indeed more informative. Again we assume output maximization and VRTS.

By treating the stages separately, the proposed framework facilitates the assessment of allocative ICT efficiency, ICT effectiveness and total productivity, respectively (ibid, 2006, p. 267). Assuming that management tries to minimize or right-size ICTS expenses while trying to maximize output, we posit that there is a negative correlation between efficiency scores obtained in the first two stages (i.e. allocative ICT efficiency and ICT effectiveness). Put differently, an efficient unit tends to keep inputs low for a given ICT budget (i.e. input minimization) while simultaneously trying to gain the maximum output (i.e. output maximization). Thus, in order to validate this model assumption, hypothesis H_{1a} is formulated.

- H_{1a}: For an individual hotel, ICT efficiency (DEA 1) is negatively correlated to ICT effectiveness (DEA 2) (ibid, 2006).

In the effectiveness stage ICT expenses directly determine what sells in what volume and price. Thus, this stage has a close relationship with the ultimate financial productivity ratio as ICT effectiveness should offer more improvement possibilities than ICT budget allocation efficiency in hotels' strategic planning (ibid, 2006). Hence, we posit:

- H_{1b}: For an individual hotel, ICT effectiveness (DEA 2) is positively correlated to productivity (DEA 3) (ibid, 2006).

Finally, we postulate that ICT expenses are more effective at generating revenues than other resource items. We investigate this contrast between effectiveness and productivity via their returns to scale which are obtainable as by-products of DEA (ibid, 2006, p. 268). Thus, hypothesis H_2 reads as:

- H_2: For an individual hotel, ICT effectiveness (DEA 2) and total productivity (DEA 3) exhibit different returns to scale (ibid, 2006).

5 Empirical Findings

In response to an online survey addressing the managers of 3,600 Austrian accommodation businesses, a totality of 700 completed questionnaires (i.e. 20%) equally distributed over the whole of Austria returned. Typically for the small-scaled hotel industry, average firm size stands at 14 employees and only 2.5% show more than 50 employees (Fuchs et al. 2009, p. 437). The average hotel company adopts 4.5 computers, usually all connected to the Internet. Furthermore, 83% of the hotel managers confirm the availability of a modern ICT system (%s are stemming from cumulated scale values < 4). The majority (i.e. 57%) dispose over an ICT budget below € 2,000 per year. Only 5% show budgets amounting above € 10,000. Furthermore, 95% agree that ICTS are indispensable for remaining competitive. Finally, 78% declare that final customers (i.e. tourists) expect from the hotel to adopt latest ICTS. Similarly, 71% consider that business partners (e.g. DMOS) strongly demand latest ICTS. In order to comply with the request of DEA (i.e. to analyse homogenous DMU sets) hotels are grouped with regard to their ICT adoption status. Hierarchical cluster analysis (i.e. squared Euclidian distance, Ward's aggregation) based on binary variables (i.e. 1=adopted, 2=not adopted) was employed. From the three emerging adopter groups (Table 1), 92% of the originally assigned cases could be correctly classified by two discriminant functions (Hair et al., 2006).

Table 1. ICT adoption status among adopter groups in the hotel sector

ICT Application	Heavy Adopters CL 1 (N=263)	Intermediate Adopters Cl 2 (N=248)	Weak Adopters Cl 3 (N=189)	TOTAL SAMPLE (N=700)
Property Management System (PMS)	99%	73%	56%	78%
Enterprise Resource Planning System (ERP)	95%	10%	8%	41%
Yield Management System (YMS)	73%	27%	17%	42%
Intranet (INTR)	77%	45%	21%	50%
Costing & Accounting System (CAS)	94%	96%	4%	78%
eCustomer Relationship Management (eCRM)	97%	71%	40%	67%
E-Mail Marketing (EMM)	98%	88%	71%	87%
Personal Information System (PIS)	73%	34%	4%	40%
Websites with booking functionality (WBOOK)	78%	76%	47%	68%
Distribution via Online Platforms (OPLA)	99%	95%	94%	96%
Online Procurement (PROC)	98%	87%	74%	88%

Cluster 1 (37%) is labelled as 'heavy ICT adopters', since with the only exception of YMS, INTR, PIS and WEBOOK all e-Business application are fully adopted. By contrast, cl. 2 (35%) are 'intermediate ICT adopters', fully adopting only CAS, OPLA and PROC. Finally, cl. 3 is labelled as 'weak ICT adopters' (27%) fully adopting only OPLA. Interestingly, OPLA, EMM and PROC are almost fully adopted by all clusters (Table 1). Contingency analysis revealed significant associations between cluster membership and hotel category (χ^2=42.899; sig=.000): A predominance of 4/5 star hotels is observed in cl. 1 (adj. res=6.4), a predominance of 3 star hotels in cl. 3 (adj. res=3.4) and a predominance of 0/1/2 and 3 star hotels in cl. 2, respectively (adj. res=1.5 and 1.7). Due to the assumed relationship between hotel category and size, the analysis further revealed associations between cluster membership and hotel size (contingency coefficient .256;, sig=.000). Following size categories are considered: Smallest hotels: < 35 beds [25%], small hotels: 35-84 beds [51%], large hotels: 86-120 beds [13%] and largest hotels: > 120 beds [12%]. Strong predominance of largest hotels (adj. res=5.2) is observed in cl. 1, whereas smallest hotels dominate cl. 2 (adj. res=2.1) and cl. 3 (adj. res=2.4), respectively.

Table 2. Median efficiency score values

	ICT Efficiency (DEA 1)	ICT Effectiveness (DEA 2)	Total Productivity (DEA 3)
Advanced ICT adopters	75.28 %	67.65 %	93.88 %
Intermediate ICT adopters	65.73 %	67.66 %	92.95 %
Weak ICT adopters	70.61 %	68.78 %	98.91 %

By including objective and subjective data, the methodological starting point was to conduct separate DEA runs for each stage and for each ICT adopter group. The obtained median efficiency score values are summarized in Table 2.

Advanced ICT adopters emerged as most efficient (i.e. 75.28 %) in appropriately allocating their ICT budget as a proportion of total expenses. Interestingly, even though the weak ICT adopters are not that efficient (70.61 %), compared to other adopter groups they show relatively high total productivity. However, if focussing on ICT resources, particularly with regard to allocative ICT efficiency (DEA 1) and ICT effectiveness (DEA 2), DEA results indicate that for all three adopter groups there is ample room for convergence towards best practice norms (Table 2).

The next methodological step aims at empirically testing the previously formulated hypotheses. In order to verify hypotheses H_{1a} and H_{1b}, DEA efficiency score values are analysed by Spearman's bivariate correlation (Table 3).

Table 3. Spearman correlation of efficiency scores

	H_{1a} DEA 1 vs DEA 2	H_{1b} DEA 2 vs DEA 3
Advanced Adopters	-.129 (sig. = .037)	.548 (sig. = .000)
Intermediate Adopters	-.159 (sig. = .012)	.575 (sig. = .000)
Weak Adopters	-.248 (sig. = .001)	.524 (sig. = .000)

As assumed by H_{1a}, efficiency score values of DEA 1 (i.e. allocative ICT efficiency) and DEA 2 (i.e. ICT effectiveness) are negatively correlated in all three adopter groups (i.e. sig. < 0.05). Thus, the obtained results provide evidence to validate the proposed three-stage DEA approach. Secondly, as presumed by hypothesis H_{1b}, a strongly significant positive correlation between ICT effectiveness (i.e. DEA 2) and total productivity (i.e. DEA 3) is observed for all three ICT adopter groups. The latter results suggest that ICT usage leads to a higher productivity level of hotel operations – thus falsifying the previously discussed assumptions relating to the ICT productivity paradox (David et al., 1996; Brynjolfsson & Hitt, 1998). In tourism, IT investments tend to require relatively shorter time frames for capturing payoffs, thereby showing relatively strong effects on firm performance (McGrath & More, 2005). With other words, our study results could be biased by lag effects. Thus, the exploration of time lag effects on the performance of hotel businesses associated with IT investments is considered as a promising area for future research (Sangho & Soung, 2006; Fuchs et al. 2010).

The final methodological step aims at testing hypothesis H_2 postulating that ICT expenses are more effective at generating revenues than other resource items. As suggested by Keh et al. (2006), this assumed contrast between ICT effectiveness and total productivity is empirically investigated by cross-tabulating the returns to scales (RTS) corresponding to the DEA stages 2 and 3, respectively (Table 4).

Table 4. Contingency table for RTS from DEA stages 2 and 3 among adopter groups

Advanced ICT adopters Chi² Pearson: 18.121 (sig. < .000)		RTS DEA 3			
		Decreasing	Constant	Increasing	Total
RTS DEA 2	Constant	0	11 (4.20 %)	0	11 (4.20 %)
	Increasing	39 (14.8 %)	91 (34.6 %)	122 (46.4 %)	252 (95.8 %)
	Total	39 (14.8 %)	102 (38.8 %)	122 (46.4 %)	263 (100 %)

Intermediate ICT adopters Chi² Pearson: 3.691 (sig.= .158)		RTS DEA 3			
		Decreasing	Constant	Increasing	Total
RTS DEA 2	Constant	1 (0.4 %)	10 (4.0 %)	5 (2.0 %)	16 (6.4 %)
	Increasing	18 (7.2 %)	89 (36.0 %)	125 (50.4 %)	232 (93.6 %)
	Total	19 (7.6 %)	99 (40.0 %)	130 (52.4 %)	248 (100 %)

Weak ICT adopters Chi² Pearson: 18.803 (sig < .000)		RTS DEA 3			
		Decreasing	Constant	Increasing	Total
RTS DEA 2	Constant	0 (0.00 %)	17 (9.0 %)	1 (0.50 %)	18 (9.51 %)
	Increasing	23 (12.2 %)	70 (37.0 %)	78 (41.2 %)	171 (90.4 %)
	Total	23 (12.2 %)	87 (46.0 %)	79 (41.8 %)	189 (100 %)

As can be seen from Table 4, the hypothesized contrast in returns to scale between ICT effectiveness and productivity (i.e. highlighting the value of ICT investments in generating hotel revenues) is observed with significance for both, advanced and weak ICT adopters. By considering that efficient DMUS per definition exhibit constant returns to scale (Brown, 2006), 14.8% of the advanced ICT adopters and 12.2% of the weak ICT adopters exhibit increasing returns to scale in DEA 2 (ICT effectiveness) although being characterized by decreasing returns to scale in DEA 3 (total productivity). The verification of H_2, at least for these two adopter groups, implies that even for relatively inefficient hotels showing decreasing returns to scale with respect to total productivity, ICT usage is able to increase returns to scale, thus, still positively contributing to hotels' total productivity.

6 Conclusion and Outlook

First of all, by considering objective and subjective in- and output data the proposed three-stage DEA framework measuring allocative ICT efficiency, ICT effectiveness and total productivity in the (i.e. Austrian) hotel sector could be empirically validated (H_{1a}). Moreover, by observing strong and positive correlations between ICT effectiveness and total productivity (H_{1b}) the often controversially discussed productivity paradox has been falsified for the (i.e. Austrian) hotel sector (David et al. 1996; Brynjolfsson & Hitt, 1998). Obviously, the biggest advantage of the proposed three-stage methodology is that one can separate in each stage the stars from the poor performers and study the derived results to acquire useful insights on hotel operations (Keh et al. 2006). For instance, both, advanced and weak ICT adopters outperformed hotels pertaining to the group of intermediate ICT adopters with respect to allocative ICT efficiency (i.e. DEA 1) and ICT effectiveness (i.e. DEA 2). This polarisation tendency has further been confirmed by the identified contrasts in scale inefficiencies (i.e. returns to scale) highlighting the value of ICT investments in generating room and F&B revenues for both heavy and weak ICT adopters, respectively (H_2). Moreover, from the conducted cluster analyses it was shown that for heavy ICT adopters (i.e. cl. 1) - characterized as relatively large 4/5 star hotels – as well as weak ICT adopters (i.e. cl. 3) - characterised as relatively small 3 star hotels – their highly differentiated and consistent channel strategies are the likely reasons for their most successful (i.e. most efficient and effective) ICT adoption practices leading to highest productivity gains (Klein 2005). Again, this finding would not have been possible from either the commonly used single ratio of hotel performance measure (i.e. RevPAR) or standard one-stage DEA investigations (Johns et al. 1997).

However, in order to improve the proposed three-stage DEA approach future research should consider ICT-induced efficiency and effectiveness gains also from external hotel business processes, thus, including subjective output data from cooperation partners, suppliers and in particular from hotel guests (e.g. guest satisfaction).

References

Armijos, A., DeFranco, A., Hamilton, M. & Skorupa, J. (2002). IT trends in the lodging industry. *International Journal of Hospitality Information Technology,* 2(2): 1-17.

Brown, R. (2006). Pitfalls and protocols for DEA studies. *European Journal of Operational Research,* 174: 1100-1116.

Brynjolfsson, E. & Hitt, L. (1998). Beyond the productivity paradox. *Communications of the ACM,* 41(8): 49-55.

Buhalis, D. (1998). Strategic use of information technologies in the tourism industry, *Tourism Management*, 19(3): 409-423.

Charnes, A., Cooper, W.W. & Rhodes, E. (1978). Measuring the efficiency of decision making units. *European Journal of Operational Research* 2(3): 429-444.

David, J. Grabski, S. & Ksavana, M. (1996). The productivity-paradox of hotel technology. *Cornell Hotel and Restaurant Administration Quarterly*, 37(2): 64-70.

Fuchs, M., Witting, Ch. & Höpken, W. (2009). E-Business Readiness, Intensity and Impact – An Austrian Hotel Study. In Höpken, W., Gretzel, U. & Law, R. (Eds.), *Information and Communication Technologies in Tourism* 2009, New York: Springer: 431-442.

Fuchs, M., Scholochow, Ch., & Höpken, W. (2010). eBusness Adoption, use and value creation – An Austrian hotel study, *Information Technology and Tourism*, 11(4): in print.

Grönroos, D. & Ojasalo, K. (2004). Service Productivity. *Journal of Business Research* 57(3): 414-423.

Hair, J., Black, W., Babin, B., Anderson H. & Tatham, R. (2006). *Multivariate data analysis, 6th edition*, New Jersey: Prentice Hall.

Ham, S., Kim, W.G. & Joeng, S. (2005). Effect of IT on performance of upscale hotels, *International Journal of Hospitality Management*, 24(2): 281-294.

24

Herold Austria (2009). http://www.herold.at (02.09.2009).

Johns, N.; Howcroft, B. & Drake, L. (1997). The use of data envelopment analysis to monitor hotel productivity. *Progress in Tourism and Hospitality Research* 3(2): 119-127.

Keh, H.T., Chu, S. & Xu, J. (2006). Efficiency, effectiveness and productivity of marketing in services. *European Journal of Operational Research,* 170: 265-276.

Kim, T.G., Lee, J.H. & Law, R. (2008). An empirical examination of the acceptance behaviour of hotel front office systems, *Tourism Management* 29(3): 500-513.

Klein, S. (2005). *ICT does matter!* Lecture held at University of Innsbruck (unpublished).

McGrath, M.G. & More, E. (2005). An extended tourism information architecture: Capturing and modelling change. In Frew, A. (Eds.) *Information and Communication Technologies in Tourism 2005*, New York: Springer: 1-12.

Sangho, L. & Soung H.K. (2006). A lag effect of IT investment on firm performance, *Information Resources Management Journal,* 19(1): 43-69.

Shang, J.-K., Hung, W.-T., Lo, C.-F. & Wang, F.-C. (2008). E-commerce and hotel performance. *The Service Industries Journal,* 28(4): 529-549.

Sigala, M. (2003). The ICT productivity impact on the UK hotel sector. *International Journal of Operations & Production Management,* 23 (10): 1224-1245.

Sigala, M., Airey, D. Jones, P. & Lockwood, A. (2004). ICT paradox lost? A stepwise DEA methodology to evaluate technology investments in tourism settings. *Journal of Travel Research* 43(2): 180-192.

Tarim, S., Dener, H. & Tarim, S.A. (2000). Efficiency measurement in the hotel industry: A DEA application, *Int. Journal of Tourism & Hospitality Research*, 11(2): 111-123.

Tangen, S. (2004). Demystifiyng productivity and performance. *International Journal of Productivity and Performance Management,* 54(1): 34-46

Tornatzky, L.G. & Fleisher, M. (1990). *The context of technological innovation*, Lexington, MA: Lexington Books

Vuorinen, I., Järvinen R. & Lehtinen U. (1998). Content and measurement of productivity in the service sector. *Int. Journal of Service Industry Management* 9(4): 377-396.

Werthner, H. & Ricci, F. (2004). E-commerce and tourism. *Communications of the ACM*, 47(12): 101-105.

Zhu, J. (2009). *Quantitative models for performance evaluation.* Springer, New York.

Acknowledgement

The research was kindly financed by the Austrian Research Promotion Agency (FFG) and the Tiroler Zukunftsstiftung, Austria.

Importance-Performance Analysis of In-Room Technology Amenities in Hotels

Ekaterina Berezina,
Cihan Cobanoglu

Hotel, Restaurant and Institutional Management Department
University of Delaware, USA
berezina@udel.edu, cihan@udel.edu

Abstract

Given that technology amenities are integral to a hotel stay, the purpose of this study is to evaluate the importance and performance of key in-room technology amenities, new and old. A random sample of 3,000 American travelers was chosen from a national database for this study. There were 534 complete responses with a response rate of 17.8%. The importance-performance analysis by gender showed that top three important technologies for male travelers are express check-in/ check-out, high speed Internet access, and easily accessible electrical outlets while for female travelers the most important technologies are easily accessible electrical outlets, guest control panel, and high speed Internet access.

Keywords: importance-performance analysis; hotels; in-room technologies; amenities.

1 Introduction

In a competitive market, hotel guests became more and more selective in their choices. (Janes & Wisnom, 2003). Uncertainty and complexity of real-world environment, as well as constantly increasing demands of travelers have made the process of managing a hospitality organization quite challenging (Janes & Wisnom, 2003; Olsen &West, 2008). As the hospitality industry becomes more competitive, industry professionals are strengthening their efforts to find competitive advantages in order to gain and retain guests. Olsen, Connolly, and Allegro (2000) identified information technology (IT) as the single greatest force driving change in the hospitality industry. Based on this finding researchers suggested that IT will continue to dominate in the lodging industry and alter the way of conducting business in the future, regardless of property size, segment, and geographic location. Several research studies have shown the necessity of learning about guests' needs and satisfaction in order to achieve this goal (Howell, Moreo & DeMicco, 1993; Skogland & Siguaw, 2004). It has been long established that technology is a critical determinant in hotel guest satisfaction (Singh & Kasavana, 2005) and hotel choice (Cobanoglu, 2001). Hotels often utilize technology as a value-added amenity to help promote differentiation, enhance guest satisfaction, and build loyalty among clientele (Cobanoglu, Ryan, & Beck, 1999). A recent American Hotel and Lodging Association survey (Brewer, Kim, Schrier, & Farrish, 2008) identified both improved guest experience and enhanced guest satisfaction as major advantages of hotel information technology applications. A recent trade journal article reported that incorrect or improper use of technology may produce guest dissatisfaction

(Cobanoglu, 2009). In this regard, it has become important to continue to identify the amenities, services, and technology applications that travelers demand from hotels and those that impact guest satisfaction. Given that technology amenities are integral to a hotel stay (Beldona & Cobanoglu, 2007), the purpose of this study is to evaluate the importance and performance of key in-room technology amenities, new and old.

2 Review of Literature

2.1 Application of technology for the hospitality industry

The adoption of information technology by the hospitality industry started in early 1970s and has been rapidly evolving ever since (Collins & Cobanoglu, 2008; Kasavana & Cahill, 2007). The hospitality industry was found to be "an excellent example of an industry that has transformed itself in response to changes in customer requirements and demands" (Lee, Barker, & Kandampully, 2003, p. 423). The adoption of technology by the industry has brought a lot of advantages and challenges. As a general principle, the larger and more complex a hospitality facility (i.e. overnight accommodations, food and beverage outlets, spa treatments, recreational activities, etc.) the greater its reliance on automation (Piccoli and Torchio, 2006; Siguaw, Enz, & Namasivayam, 2000). Technology in hotels is applied at two levels: 1. At the managerial and operational level; and, 2. For in-room guest services (Lee et al., 2003, p. 425). In addition to management oriented PMS configurations there are guest oriented technological amenities. Amenity applications are typically introduced to enhance guest satisfaction as well as the performance and functionality of hotel staff. In-room technology amenities, designed to provide a more comfortable and safe environment, may include mini-bars, electronic locks and safes, alarm clocks, desktop computers, entertainment systems, climate control systems, fire annunciator and security systems, and others (Collins & Cobanoglu, 2008). Technologies implemented in hotel rooms has not only improved in-room services, but also provided new opportunities for entertainment (Lee et al., 2003). Selected hotel in-room technology amenities are presented in the Table 1. Many hospitality industry experts emphasize the importance of in-room technologies as the traveling public continues to become more technologically savvy (Higley, 2007; Munyan, 2008; Squires, 2008).

2.2 Role of Technology Amenities for Hotel Selection

It is important to understand current value drivers and hotel guest choice-making behavior for several reasons. First and probably the most important one is that this knowledge will help hoteliers to design products or adjust existing offerings in a way that is more appealing to customers by means of meeting their requirements, demands and expectations (Kotler, Bowen, & Makens, 2003; Lazer, Dallas, & Riegel, 2006). The role and adoption rate of hospitality technology has been a focal point for several industry studies (Beldona & Cobanoglu, 2007; Ham, Kim, & Jeong, 2005; Verma, Victorino, Karniouchina, & Feickert, 2007). A review of the existing literature reveals numerous research studies that focused on the factors important for the selection of hotel accommodation (Beldona & Cobanoglu, 2007; Chu & Choi, 2000; Lockyer, 2005; Verma et al., 2002). Among the factors traditionally considered to be important for travelers, researchers named price, location and service (Verma, Plashka, Dev, & Verma, 2002). Ananth, et al. (1992) found price to be the most important factor in hotel selection. Security followed as the second most prevalent consideration with location finishing third. In a Hong Kong study of hotel selection factors researchers distinguished six groups of values being important for hotel selection: service quality, business facilities, value, room and front desk, food and recreation, and security (Chu, & Choi, 2000). Based on importance-performance analysis "value factor fell into the Concentrate Here quadrant; service quality, room and front desk and security in the Keep Up the Good Work quadrant; and business facilities and food and recreation in the Low Priority quadrant" (p. 363). Room and front desk services were found to be more important for business travelers whereas leisure travelers put the security in the first place.

Table 1. Definitions of Select Hotel In-Room Technology Amenities

Technology	Description
Voice over IP (VoIP)	Use of Internet protocols instead of analog media to transfer voice data
In-room pay per view (PPV)	Digital video, available over a television platform, available on a payment basis
Voice-mail / messaging	Phone-based service that enables a caller to leave a voice mailbox message
In-room accessible outlets	Electrical outlets conveniently located for hotel guest access and use room
High-speed Internet access (HSIA)	Internet connectivity at speeds of 1 to 100 Mega bits per second (Mbps)
In-room safe	Electronic safe that can be opened by electronic card or personalized code
In-room control panel	Console controls room amenities (e.g. lights, temperature, curtains, blinds)
Universal battery charger	Device capable of charging the batteries of various equipment and devices
Electronic locking system	Access security by electronic media (e.g. magnetic stripe, smart card, RFID, NFC)
In-room game system	Entertainment system available in a hotel guest room (e.g. Wii or Play Station)
In-room fitness system	Specialty devices for physical exercise in a hotel guest room (e.g. treadmill unit)
In-room video checkout	Television interface enabling express folio review, account settlement, and checkout

The Cobanoglu (2001) study included technology amenities in hotel selection and revealed automated devices and services were significant determinants, especially by business travelers. Verma et al. (2002) investigated the value drivers for hotel selection among leisure and business travelers. Hotel amenities, type/location, price, loyalty programs, eating options, office/technology options and customization were named among those factors. The study concluded that "core offering" of a hotel: price, room and location still account for about 70 percent of the choice criteria, about 30 percent of the choice making process is led by new value drivers such as technology, loyalty points and customization options (p.23). In regard to this conclusion, office/technology options were found to weight from five to ten percent of the overall choice-making decision of travelers. Product selection, based on need and expectation, are considered critical in determining customer satisfaction (Kotler et al, 2003). Many researchers have investigated the nature of hotel guest satisfaction (Chathoth, 2007; Shanka & Taylor, 2003; Torres and Kline, 2006). Skogland and Siguaw (2004) concluded hotel guest satisfaction is an essential component of long-term success. Kandampully and Suhartanto (2000) cited the influence of hotel image on customer loyalty and tied satisfaction to congeniality, service, cleanliness, and price. Torres and Kline (2006) postulated a workplace model based on the assumption that employees and facilities were the most influential factors contributing to guest satisfaction.

2.3 Impact of Hotel Technology on Guest Satisfaction

Despite some incongruent findings, research results support the evolving importance of technology in property selection. In a study of upscale Korean hotels, for example, guest-related interface applications (e.g. call accounting, electronic locks, energy management, in-room entertainment, in-room vending and information services) were found to have no significant effect on hotel performance (Ham et al., 2005). A similar study, conducted in Thailand, produced controversial findings as researcher's acknowledged the dominant influence of technology amenities (e.g. television, mini-bar, telephone service, etc.) on customer satisfaction, without regard to socio-demographic characteristics (Prayukvong, Sophon, Hongpukdee, & Charupas, 2007). Chathoth (2007) concluded that an important feature of hotel information technology is the delineation of significant components (i.e. reliability, responsiveness, assurance, and empathy) involved in meeting and potentially exceeding guest needs. Analysis by Beldona & Cobanoglu (2007) involved classification of guest oriented technologies into four quadrants according to expectation of importance and satisfaction of performance. The first group, including express check-in/out, remote control TV, and in-room high speed Internet access were ranked high on both dimensions (importance and performance). A second group, awarded high importance but low performance ratings, included wireless Internet access, alarm clock, easily accessible electrical outlets and on-line reservation capabilities. This group included people who considered these technologies important when selecting a hotel but judged performance low during occupancy. A third group, rated technologies at a low importance level in hotel selection but recorded high performance scores once in-house. Group three technologies included web TV, pay-per-view movies, and in-room personal computers. The fourth group indicated low ratings for both technology importance and performance. Applications in this group included videoconferencing capabilities, wireless access to hotel website, business center services, and plasma screen television. In summary, various studies have explored the role and importance of hotel guest technology amenities in hotel selection. Additional research on this topic helps delineate technologies hoteliers should consider in order to enhance guest satisfaction.

2.4 The use of importance-performance analysis in the hospitality industry

Ways to assess guest satisfaction in the hospitality industry include comment cards (O'Neill, 2001) and guest satisfaction surveys (Baumann, 1998). Also several consumer research models are used for the same purpose such as the expectancy-value theory (Fishbein & Ajzen, 1975), the importance-performance analysis (IPA) (Martilla & James, 1977), SERVQUAL (Parasuraman, Zeitmal, & Berry, 1988), and the expectancy-disconfirmation theory (Oh & Parks, 1997). Being originally introduced by Martilla & James (1977), the importance-performance analysis was designed to learn about both customer expectations and satisfaction. This model allows to evaluate the importance of particular attributes for respondents prior to actual activity, and then match it with the satisfaction achieved after actual experience. The results are normally presented in two-dimensional grid which represents importance and satisfaction on its scales (horizontal and vertical). The IPA process involves three following steps:

1. Identifying a list of attributes that describe the product/service,
2. Rating importance and performance for each attribute,
3. Interpreting and mapping the ratings on a two-dimensional grid (Figure 1).

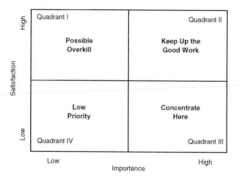

Fig. 1. Importance-Performance (Satisfaction) Grid

The four grid quadrants are identified and interpreted as follows (Martilla & James, 1977): *Quadrant I: Possible overkill* – this quadrant describes attributes with low importance but high performance characteristics. It can be suggested to relocate some resources and efforts from this quadrant to Concentrate here, however, there also could be very strong reasons to continue the practices that fall into Possible overkill. *Quadrant II: Keep up a good work* – only attributes with high importance and high satisfaction scores appear in this quadrant. It is important to keep them in this quadrant. *Quadrant III: Concentrate here* – this quadrant contains attributes that were marked by customers with high importance but performance below their expectations (low satisfaction). These attributes require most attention. *Quadrant IV: Low priority* – this quadrant includes attributes of both low importance and low performance ratings. This quadrant requires little attention as customer view the attributes included in it as of low importance. Since it has been introduced several decades ago, the importance-performance analysis has become a popular research method for hospitality and tourism industry. It is being widely used in the hotel industry (Beldona & Cobanoglu, 2007; Janes and Wisnom, 2003), tourism (Meng, Tepanon, & Uysal, 2008), recreation (Hendricks, Schneider, & Budruk, 2004), gaming and casino industry (Suh & Erdem, 2009), conventional tourism (Breiter & Milman, 2006) and airline service research areas (Chang & Yang, 2008; Leong, 2008). One of the most important advantages that the IPA provides is the possibility to service providers to identify attributes or services that are of low importance to customers and concentrate efforts and resources on those of high importance but low performance (Farnum & Hall, 2007; Hudson, Hudson & Miller, 2004; Janes & Wisnom, 2003).

3   Methodology

A random sample of 3,000 American travelers was chosen from a national database (rent-a-list.com) for this study. Selected email addresses were stratified by state population by the national database company. Each email contained an invitation and a website link to the survey. An initial email was followed by one reminder email one week later. Of the 3,000 emails in the original population, 1,332 responses were received for a response rate of 44.4%. The qualifying question for the study involved the respondent having stayed in a hotel within the immediate past 12 months. Of the 1,332 respondents, 1,172 (88%) fulfilled the qualification of a hotel stay within the last year. The remaining 160 respondents were eliminated from the study. Of the 1,172 qualified responses, 638 were incomplete and therefore deleted. The remaining 534 responses composed the population for this study (i.e. 17.8% net response rate). A web-hosted survey instrument, composed of four sections, was devised based on items identified in a review of relevant literature. The first section of the survey focused on traveler behavior, while the second section investigated technology behavior. The third section contained a list of select hotel technology amenities and the final section was concerned with guest-hotel satisfaction and demographic characteristics of respondent. A non-response analysis using wave analysis (early versus later respondents) was conducted to determine: (1) whether non-respondents and respondents differed significantly and (2) whether equivalent data from those who did not respond would have significantly altered findings. Rylander, Propst, and McMurtry (1995) suggested that late respondents and non-respondents were alike and wave analysis and respondent/non-respondent comparisons tended to yield similar results. As a result, an independent t-test was conducted to evaluate variance in early responses from late responses. The analysis indicated that there was no significant difference, concluding that this survey did not suffer from non-response bias.

4   Findings

4.1   Respondent Demographics and Travel Behavior

About 67% of the respondents were female travelers. Just over one-quarter of the respondents (25.7%) were between the ages of 36-45; 22.2% ranged between 46-55; 21% between 26-35; 12.6% were 25 or younger, 12% were between 56-65, and 6.6% were older than 66 years. About 17% were employed in professional, managerial, and related occupations; 13.7% worked in sales and office occupations, 10.4% were in service industries, and 11.8% identified as students. About 30% of the respondents had an annual income of $25,001 - $50,000; 27.9% earned $50,001 - $75,000; and 10.1% reported earning $75,001- $100,000. More than half of the respondents reported being married (55.7%), 24% were single and 12% divorced.

The most frequently reported search technique is the hotel's own website, followed by online travel agency websites e.g. Expedia, Orbitz, and Travelocity and third party review sites such as tripadvisor.com. The least utilized tool was found to be social networking sites such as MySpace and Facebook. About 41% of the respondents reported being active members of a frequent traveler program. Slightly more than one-quarter of the respondents booked their last hotel stay through an Internet travel agency such as Expedia, Orbitz, or Travelocity (26.6%). The second most frequently reported booking method was calling the hotel directly (25.3%) followed by booking through a hotel's affiliated website (e.g. Hyatt.com, Marriott.com, or Hilton.com) at 24.5%. Using a toll-free telephone reservation number was cited as the next most popular method (9.4%). Nearly one-half of the respondents reported stayed in a midscale hotel such as Courtyard, Holiday Inn Express, or Comfort Inn, while 31.3% stayed in an upscale property such as Hyatt, Hilton, or Marriott and 16.3% stayed in an economy hotel such as Ramada, EconoLodge, or Super 8. A majority of the respondents traveled for leisure while about 35% traveled for business associated purposes.

4.2 Comparing In-Room Technology Amenities' Importance and Performance by Guest Gender

For the purpose of the study an importance-performance analysis was conducted. The results are presented and described below. Figure 2a and Figure 2b show the importance-performance matrixes for male and female respectively. *Quadrant I Possible Overkill:* For male travelers, only business center technology amenity (D) fell into Quadrant I which symbolizes "Possible Overkill." However, there were no in-room technology amenities in Quadrant I for female travelers. *Quadrant II keep up a good work:* Even though, scores for individual in-room technology amenities were different for male and female business travelers, Quadrant II in-room technology amenities were exactly the same. Seven in-room technology amenities fell into Quadrant II which symbolizes "keep-up the good work." Both groups agreed that guest control panel (M), Wireless Internet access in hotel public areas (K), Alarm clock (H), easily accessible electrical outlets (I), High-speed internet access in the room (J), Express check-in/check-out (A), Phone in room (F) have high importance and performance. The fact that both high-speed internet access in the room (J) and wireless Internet access in hotel public areas (K) appeared as high importance for male and female travelers suggests that Internet as a technology amenity became an expected amenity in hotels. It is important to note that Guest control panel (M) was rated as higher importance and performance by female travelers than male travelers. *Quadrant III Concentrate here:* Quadrant III, the "concentrate here" box found no common in-room technology amenities for male and female travelers. However, in each group, a different technology appeared. For male travelers, the flat panel HD

Television (S) was rated to have higher importance than performance. For female travelers, Electronic wireless key cards (R) were rated with high importance but performance below expectation. *Quadrant IV Low Priority:* In the "low-priority" quadrant, Quadrant IV, there were 10 common in-room technology amenities for male and female travelers. These in-room technology amenities were Video-conferencing capabilities (C), Free long distance telephone calls (B), Pay per view (E), Voice-mail (G), In-room electronic safes (L), In-room gaming system (T), Wireless access to hotel website (P), Universal battery charger (N), PC in the room (O), and in-room fitness systems (U). It is important to note that several of these "low-importance" in-room technology amenities are new technologies such as video-conferencing capabilities (C),in-room gaming system (T), Wireless access to hotel website (P), Universal battery charger (N), and in-room fitness systems (U). Based on technology adoption life cycle framework, the lack of interest and performance for these new technologies makes sense as each technology goes through a life cycle that includes introduction, growth, maturity and decline. Most of these technologies are in the "introduction" stage of their product life cycle in the hotel rooms. So, it is important for hoteliers to keep an eye on these new technologies and be ready when they become a mainstream technology. The other in-room technology amenities that fell in this category tend to be old technologies such as pay per view (E), voice-mail (G), and In-room electronic safes (L). This may indicate two things for male and female travelers: 1) These technologies reached their maturity level of their product life cycle in hotels and therefore, they are rated as less important and low performance by travelers. Voice mail maybe a good example of this as travelers travel with their own cell phones which eliminated the need to use hotel voice mail systems. 2) These technologies are now part an integral part of hotels so that travelers do not even notice them but expect them to be in working order in hotels. For example, guests now expect to see a decent TV set in every hotel room. Similarly, they may expect a business center in every hotel in case there is a need for a computer or printer use. There were three in-room technology amenities that were different between male and female travelers in this Quadrant. Female travelers rated Flat panel HD Television (S) as less important and low performance. As mentioned above, this in-room technology amenity was in "Concentrate Here" quadrant for male travelers. This fact makes sense given the obvious interest of male travelers to HDTVs, especially to watch sports. The other technology that appeared in Qudrant IV for male travelers was electronic wireless key cards (R). This amenity appeared in "Concentrate Here" (Quadrant III) quadrant for female travelers. Male travelers rated Business centers (D) in the Possible Overkill Quadrant while female travelers put in Low Priority Quadrant.

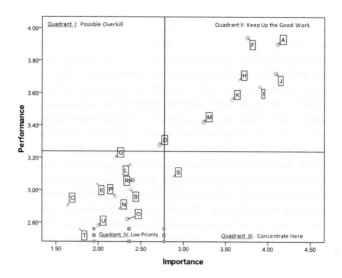

Fig. 2a. Importance-Performance Matrix for Male Travelers

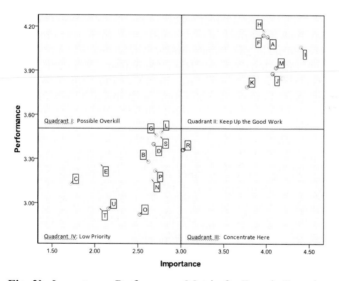

Fig. 2b. Importance-Performance Matrix for Female Travelers

A	Express check-in/check-out	K	Wireless Internet access in hotel public areas
B	Free long distance telephone calls (VoIP)	L	In-room electronic safes
C	Video-conferencing capabilities	M	Guest control panel (i.e. lights, temperature, etc.)
D	Business centers (computers, fax, copiers)	N	Universal battery charger
E	Pay per view (movie system)	O	PC in the room
F	Phone in room	P	Wireless access to hotel website (i.e. Blackberry)
G	Voice-mail	R	Electronic wireless key cards (i.e. via cell phone)
H	Alarm clock	S	Flat panel HD Television
I	Easily accessible electrical outlets	T	In-room gaming system (i.e. Wii or Play Station)
J	High-speed internet access in the room	U	In-room fitness systems

5 Conclusion

The most important sources of information for hotel selection are a hotel web site followed by on-line travel agencies web sites. More than 50% of the reservations came from on-line channels. Top three important technologies for male travelers are express check-in/ check-out, high speed Internet access, and easily accessible electrical outlets while for female travelers the most important technologies are easily accessible electrical outlets, guest control panel, and high speed Internet access. The four least important in-room technology amenities for both male and female travelers are video conferencing, in-room gaming system, pay-per-view systems and in-room fitness centers. The importance-performance analysis by gender of travelers showed that male and female travelers rated the importance and performance of the in-room technology amenities similarly with the exception of some amenities. In Cobanoglu (2001) study, there were significant differences between male and female business travelers' importance and performance scores for technology amenities. Our study showed that the gap between male and female travelers' importance for technology amenities in hotels is closing rapidly. This may be due to the fact that more female travelers travel for business purposes, therefore, demanding technology amenities that they use in their professional life. Both male and female travelers rated guest control panel, wireless Internet access in hotel public areas, alarm clock, easily accessible electrical outlets, high-speed internet access in the room, express check-in/check-out, phone in room both important and demonstrating high performance. One of the differences between male and female business travelers was in "Concentrate here" quadrant. While male travelers put High Definition TV in this quadrant, female travelers put electronic wireless key cards in this section. This makes sense given the interest of male travelers to sports and action programs in TVs while female travelers tend to focus on comfort and security aspects of technologies. Another interesting part of this study was the "Low Importance" quadrant where several old and new technologies were rated as low importance and low performance. This may be due to the fact that new technologies such as video-conferencing capabilities, in-room gaming system, wireless access to hotel website, universal battery charger, and in-room fitness systems are disruptive technologies and therefore, it does not fit in the mainstream market. Christensen (1997) has introduced the term "disruptive technology" to innovation literature. Disruptive technology, different from radical or incremental innovations, has been defined as "innovations that result in worse product performance, at least in the near-term". Disruptive technologies can be identified by its three characteristics. When they are first introduced, they are, as compared to mainstream technology in place, 1) cheaper and/or low profit margin and/or high risk; 2) less performance; 3) no established market. This may mean that hoteliers should not ignore these technologies that may not be in high demand right now. Hoteliers may not offer video conferencing capabilities, in-room gaming system, in-room fitness systems, and personal computer in every guest room as they are not mainstream technologies yet. There is a specific set of guests that may demand these amenities. They may be offered on a "demand" basis. For example, Marriott and Hilton chains offer on-demand fitness equipment for a charge to the guest room ("Hotels launch in-room fitness", 2005).

6 Limitations and Future Research

A potential threat to the representativeness of the sample is hidden in the web-based instrumentation. The sample was limited only to those people who have email addresses. In this regard the study eliminated people who do not have an email address. Above this, the responses could be received primarily from those people who are more technology-savvy or more interested in technology. Another important point to be considered about the research to be validated externally – temporal validity that identifies the extent to which the study results can be generalized across the time. Paying attention to the fast growth and development of technology one cannot assume that the results will be valid in five or ten years ahead. New technologies coming into the market can alter customers' preferences and expectations. To give an example, because of continuous technological development guests might not be satisfied with wireless internet access several years later because they may perceive the speed of wireless communication as too slow. That is why the possible suggestion would be to repeat the study on the regular basis. Otherwise, failure to consider the time variable can threaten the external validity of the study. Future studies can be conducted to assess the importance of different technology amenities for hotel selection and performance of those technologies as perceived by hotel guests. The results of the studies can be beneficial for hotel managers to develop a strategy of technology adoption and development. However, it is important to note that findings should be evaluated by each particular hotel to better meet the demands and expectations of its customers. Taking this into consideration, researchers can provide deeper analysis of the subject matter and track future potential differences in importance and performance of different technology amenities with regard to the travelers' gender, age, and travel scenario. This information will provide an opportunity to hoteliers to assess the expectations and satisfaction of customers who possess the features of their target segment.

References

Ananth, M., DeMicco, F.J., Moreo, P.J., & Howey, R.M. (1992). Marketplace lodging needs of mature travelers. *Cornell Hotel & Restaurant Administration Quarterly*, 33, 12-24.

Baumann, M. A. (1998). Surveys allow properties opportunity to improve guest retention. *Hotel & Motel Management*, 213, 40-41.

Beldona, S., & Cobanoglu, C. (2007). Importance-performance analysis of guest technologies in the lodging industry. *Cornell Hotel and Restaurant Administration Quarterly, 48*(3), 299-312.

Breiter, D., & Milman, A. (2006). Attendees' needs and service priorities in a large convention center: application of the importance-performance theory. *Tourism Management, 27*, 1354 – 1370.

Brewer, P., Kim, J., Schrier, T., & Farrish, J. (2008). Current and future technology use in the hospitality industry. American Hotel and Lodging Association. Retrieved from http://www.ahla.com/membersonly/content.aspx?id=5964

Chang, H.-L., & Yang, C.-H. (2008). Do airline self-service kiosks meet the needs of passengers? *Tourism Management*, 29, 980 – 993.

Chathoth, P. (2007). The impact of information technology on hotel operations, service management and transaction costs: A conceptual framework for full-service hotel firms. *International Journal of Hospitality Management, 26*(2), 395-408.

36

Christensen, C. M. (1997). *The innovator's dilemma*. Boston: Harvard Business School Press.

Chu, R. K. S., & Choi, T. (2000). An importance-performance analysis of hotel selection factors in the Hong Kong hotel industry: a comparison of business and leisure travelers. *Tourism Management,* 21(4), 363-377

Cobanoglu, C. (2001). Unpublished Thesis. Analysis of business travelers' hotel selection and satisfaction. Oklahoma State University.

Cobanoglu, C. (2009). Guests' Top 7 Technologies. *Hospitality Technology*, 13(2). Retrieved March 3, 2009 from: http://www.htmagazine.com/ME2/dirmod.asp?sid=783D4AA2541D483C98659D20A3 539C6E&nm=Additional&type=MultiPublishing&mod=PublishingTitles&mid=3E1967 4330734FF1BBDA3D67B50C82F1&tier=4&id=69B3BB8904A443DC9FB713C5E947 21AF

Cobanoglu, C., Ryan, B. & Beck, J. (1999). The impact of technology in lodging properties. International Council on Hotel, Restaurant, and Institutional Education Annual Convention Proceedings.

Collins, G.R., & Cobanoglu, C. (2008). Hospitality information technology: Learning how to use it (6th ed.). Dubuque, IA: Kendall/Hunt Publishing Company.

Farnum, J. O., & Hall, T.E. (2007). Exploring the utility of importance performance analysis using confidence interval and market segmentation strategies. *Journal of Park and Recreation Administration,* 25(2), 64 – 83.

Fishbein, M., & Ajzen, I. (1975). Beliefs, attitudes, intentions, and behavior: An introduction to theory and research. Reading, MA: Addison-Wesley.

Ham, S., Kim, W. G., & Jeong, S. (2005). Effect of information technology on performance in upscale hotels. *International Journal of Hospitality Management,* 24(2), 281-294.

Hendricks, W. W., Schneider, I.E., & Budruk, M. (2004). Extending importance-performance analysis with benefit-based segmentation. *Journal of Park and Recreation Administration,* 22(1), 53 – 74.

Higley, J. (2007). *Keep technology working, make guests happy* Questex Media Group.

Hotels launch in-room fitness options. Chains to provide workout equipment for busy travelers. (2005). Retrieved from http://www.msnbc.msn.com/id/6975263/

Howell, R. A., Moreo, P. J., & DeMicco, F. J. (1993). A qualitative analysis of hotel services desired by female business travelers. *Journal of Travel and Tourism Marketing,* 1(4), 115-133.

Hudson, S., Hudson, P., & Miller, G. A. (2004). The measurement of service quality in the tour operator sector: A methodological comparison. *Journal of Travel Research,* 42(2), 305-312.

Janes, P.L., & Wisnom, M.S. (2003). The use of importance performance analysis in the hospitality industry: a comparison of practices. *Journal of Quality Assurance in Hospitality & Tourism,* 4 (1/2), 23 – 45.

Kandampully, J., & Suhartanto, D. (2000). Customer loyalty in the hotel industry: The role of customer satisfaction and image. *International Journal of Contemporary Hospitality Management,* 12(6), 346-351.

Kasavana, M. L., & Cahill J.J. (2007). Managing technology in the hospitality industry (5th ed.). Lansing, MI: Educational Institute of the American Hotel and Lodging Association.

Kotler, P, Bowen, J., & Makens, J. (2003). Marketing for hospitality and tourism (3rd ed.). Upper Saddle River, NJ: Pearson Education, Inc.

Lazer, W., Dallas, M., & Riegel C. (2006). Hospitality and tourism marketing. Lansing, MI: Educational Institute of the American Hotel and Lodging Association.

Lee, S.-C., Barker, S., & Kandampully, F. (2003). Technology, service quality, and customer loyalty in hotels: Australian managerial perspectives.

Leong, C.C. (2008). An importance-performance analysis to evaluate airline service quality: the case study of a budget airline in Asia. *Journal of Quality Assurance in Hospitality & Tourism,* 8(3), 39

Lockyer, T. (2005). The perceived importance of price as one hotel selection dimension. *Tourism Management,* 26(4), 529-537.

Martilla, J. A., & James, J. C. (1977). *Importance-performance analysis*. Journal of Marketing, 41, (1), 77-79

Meng, F., Tepanon, Y., & Uysal, M. (2008). Measuring tourist satisfaction by attribute and motivation: the case of a nature-based resort. Journal of Vacation Marketing, 4(1), 41 – 56.

Munyan, R. (2008). Technology in the next generation of hotels. *Lodging Hospitality, 64*(16), 78-88.

Oh, H., & Parks, S. C. (1997). Customer satisfaction and service quality: a critical review of the literature and research implications for the hospitality industry. Hospitality Research Journal, 20(3), 35–64.

Olsen, M. D., Connolly, D. J., & Allegro, S. M. (February 2000). The Hospitality Industry and Digital Economy. International Hotel and Restaurant Association, Lausanne.

Olsen, M. D., & West J. J. (2008). Strategic Management: in the Hospitality Industry. Upper Saddle River, NJ: Pearson Education, Inc.

O'Neill, M. (2001). Service quality management in hospitality, tourism, and leisure, measuring service quality and customer satisfaction. New York, NY: The Haworth Hospitality Press.

Parasuraman, A., Zeithaml, V. A., & Berry, L. L. (1988). SERVQUAL: A multiple-item scale for measuring consumer perceptions of service quality. *Journal of Retailing*, 64(1), 12– 40.

Piccoli, G., & Torchio, P. (2006). The strategic value of information: A manager's guide to profiting from information. *Cornel Hospitality Report, 7*(6).

Prayukvong, W., Sophon, J., Hongpukdee, S., & Charupas, T. (2007). Customers' satisfaction with hotel guestrooms: A case study in ubon rachathani province, thailand. *Asia Pacific Journal of Tourism Research, 12*(2), 119-126.

Rylander, R. G., Propst, D. B., and McMurtry, T. R. (1995). Nonresponse and recall biases in a survey of traveler spending. *Journal of Travel Research*, 33 (4), 39-45.

Shanka, T., & Taylor, R. (2003). An investigation into the perceived importance of service and facility attributes of hotel satisfaction. Journal of Quality Assurance in Hospitality and Tourism, 3/4(4), 119 – 134.

Siguaw, J., Enz, C., & Namasivayam, K. (2000). The adoption of information technology in U.S. hotels: Strategically driven objectives. *Journal of Travel Research, 39*, 192.

Singh, A.J., & Kasavana, M. L. (2005). The Impact of Information Technology on Future Management of Lodging Operations, *Journal of Tourism and Hospitality Research*, 6(1), 24-37

Skogland, I., & Siguaw, J.A. (2004). Understanding switchers and stayers in the lodging industry. *Cornell Hospitality Report, 1*(4).

Squires, M. (2008). Technology changes lodging workforce. *Lodging Hospitality, 64*(16), 89-94.

Suh, E., & Erdem, M. (2009). Gap analysis as a diagnostic tool for improving the slot gaming experience. Journal of Hospitality Marketing & Management, 18, 445 – 455.

Torres, E. N. & Kline, S. F. (2006) An empirical study of customer delight in the hotel industry: preliminary findings. Proceedings of the Eleventh Annual Graduate Education and Graduate Student Research Conference in Hospitality and Tourism, Seattle, WA.

Verma, R. Plashka, G, Dev, C., & Verma A. (2002). What today's travelers want when they select a hotel. *HSMAI Marketing Review*, Fall 2002, 20-23.

Verma, R., Victorino, L., Karniouchina, K., & Feickert, J. (2007). Segmenting hotel customers based on technology readiness index. *Cornell Hospitality Report, 7*(13).

Factor Analysis of Variables Affecting e-Marketing Adoption by UK Independent Hotels

Wai Mun Lim

School of Tourism and Hospitality
University of Plymouth, U.K.
wmlim@plymouth.ac.uk

Abstract

This paper analyses the range of influences affecting the adoption of Internet technology by UK independent hotels. An extensive review of variables found in previous studies were examined together with variables found in Davis's (1989) Technology Acceptance Model. These variables were then factor analysed, resulting in two sets of factors pertinent to the understanding of the independent hotelier's decision to adopt Internet technologies: Endogenous and Exogenous factors. Seven key factors were found, they are: (1) Perceived marketing benefits of Internet technologies; (2) Perceived ease-of-use and affordability; (3) Attitude; (4) Perceived usefulness of Internet technologies; (5) Customers' pressure; (6) Competitive intensity; (7) Entrepreneurship.

Keywords: technology adoption; technology acceptance model; hotels

1 Introduction

Over the last two decades, the Internet has been aggressively adopted by hospitality enterprises as another marketing tool. It is nonetheless important to bear in mind that it is just another marketing channel where new opportunities and efficiency (Hymas, 2001) enable hoteliers to project their presence. This new mode of marketing is not only popular for business-to-business (B2B) marketing, it quickly developed into a business-to-consumer (B2C) channel enabling direct selling as the Internet became more affordable and accessible to the public. In its early days, only the resource-rich had a presence on a website, as it could prove rather costly. Since then, it has been widely claimed that the Internet could level playing fields (Sheldon, 1994). This meant that small and medium sized organisations had an equal opportunity to participate on a global level (Klein and Quelch, 1996) but not without a considerable amount of planning, strategic decision-making and financial investment continues to be pertinent. Since the appearance of the first commercial web sites in the early 1990s, they appear to have been developing in 3 directions- informational, transactional (O'Connor and O'Keefe, 1997) and promotional. The most recent DTI International Benchmarking Study (2004) revealed that the top few usages of the Internet amongst small-to-medium sized enterprises in the UK, is for anything else but marketing. Between year 2003 and 2004 the online adoption trend for marketing was shown to have slowed but the 'transactional' element of online trends in the 'payment of goods and services' and the 'promotional' element of 'placement of orders' experienced an increase of 6% and 5% respectively (DTI, 2004). As e-marketing is a phenomenon that is continually evolving to 'take advantage of the unique features of the online environment' (Dann and Dann, 2004: 35), this study aims to discover the key factors that promotes and inhibits the adoption of e-marketing by hoteliers. The literature review will first discuss what e-commerce entails in the hotel sector before exploring the theoretical underpinnings of technology adoption and evaluate the factors influencing adoption found in previous studies.

2 Literature Review

2.1 E-commerce

'Online booking' is also sometimes referred to as electronic commerce (Chen, 2005; McKay and Marshall, 2004). According to these authors, e-commerce involves selling online and must include some form of transaction which must be conducted via the Internet. Chen (2005), McKay and Marshall (2004), discussed the definition of electronic commerce and electronic business at great length, offering various authors' insights into what each should entail. While they conclude that differentiating the two is not a straightforward task, electronic commerce should result in commercial transactions via the Internet (i.e. the buying and the selling) and little else, while electronic business includes all other elements 'such as servicing customers, collaborating with partners and communicating within the organization' (Chen, 2005:3). Electronic business should also 'improve efficiencies and effectiveness along the entire supply chain, to create internal efficiencies, and thus to create value directly and indirectly for the customer' (McKay and Marshall, 2004:5).

Internet use is no longer confined to the use of the rich and young, nor is it mainly used for e-mailing. According to findings by *Which? Online 2000* documented by the English Tourism Council's Insight publication, 19% of travel products (flights/holidays) bought online by UK web users were at a high of 19% (second only to books at 23%). More specifically, GDS net reservation of hotels has been steadily increasing from 16 million reservations in 1993 to 49 million reservations in 2000 (O'Connor, 2001). According to a recent report by Davis (2007), this phenomenon has not abated, and even more interestingly while hotel bookings made via the web and the GDSs are half of what airlines receive via online, the majority of those hotel bookings are made through the hotels' own branded websites.

Hotels planning on an electronic commerce strategy should be further motivated to do so, as findings by Dresdner Kleinwort Benson/Accor revealed that total cost per reservation with an online travel intermediary can cost up to US$10.50, as opposed to only US$1.50 if reservations are made via the hotel company's website. In 2000, 70% of online spending by business travellers was on air travel, with only 20% on hotels. However, the lodging market is a far bigger industry with bookings worth US$350 billion annually. With an estimate of hotel Internet bookings at approximately US$2.6 billion in 2000 (PKFReport, 2004), the majority of the lodging market remains unexploited. Although it would appear that electronic marketing is simply a 'strategic and tactical activity' that is part and parcel of hotelier's operational strategy, these activities have forced many hotel management to re-evaluate its technological deployment in line with its e-strategies. However, it is the critical notion of a hotelier's awareness that brings us to the point of discovering how behavioural dimensions could too affect a hotelier's decision making process in relation to online strategies. To effectively examine these strategies, the next section considers an often used model to explain some of the variables that could influence hoteliers' decision of e-marketing adoption.

2.2 Technology Acceptance Model

Davis's (1989) Technology Acceptance Model closely examines the perception of adopters in relation to the technology's usefulness and its ease of use. The model expounds that external factors (variables) combined with the adopter's perceptions of usefulness and ease of use establishes the adopter's attitude towards using the examined technology. Most importantly, attitude developed by the user will further influence his/her behavioural intentions to use the system. Actual use is then predicted by behavioural intention (Malhotra and Galleta, 1999). Davis (1989) defined 'perceived usefulness' as the extent to which an individual believes that his or her performance will improve by adopting a particular technology. Igbaria, Parasuraman and Baroudi (1996) found that perceived usefulness (rather than perceived social pressure) is the main motivator for technology adoption. Conversely, the 'perceived ease of use' represents the individual's perception of the amount of effort required to adopt an innovation. According to Ranchhod and Gurau (2000), the actual use and adoption of technology requires a level of technological know-how. Both the perceptions are frequently used to measure the various constructs pertaining to technology adoption. Examples include Malhotra and Galletta's (1999) study between Microsoft exchange and schedule adoption. Similar 'perception' questions were also used in Legris, Ingham and Collerette's (2003) generic study on why individuals use technology. These studies conclude that the two perception measured, ultimately had an effect on the attitude and intention to adopt a technology. King and Gribbins (2002) suggest that managerial perspectives on the types and number of uses of an application were also paramount to the analysis of the behavioural intentions of the adopter. Yang and Yoo's (2004) study of spreadsheet software use the same constructs found in TAM. In general, the Technology Acceptance Model has been proven successful in predicting approximately 40% of technology use (Ajzen and Fishbein, 1980; Legris et. al., 2003).

2.3 Past studies of other factors found to influence technology adoption

Various models utilizing trans-disciplinary concepts were developed to form a theoretical synthesis in an attempt to explain the use of Internet technologies in relation to operational strategies within the tourism and hospitality sectors. The more prominent past examples of such studies dates as far back as Gamble's (1994) model of IT diffusion in the hotel industry, Buhalis's (1998) examination of the strategic use of technology in tourism, Sigala, Airey, Jones and Lockwood's (2000) investigation into the adoption of multimedia technology and more recently Murphy's (2004) model of diversity of diffusion.

According to an extensive study conducted by Ching and Ellis (2004), endogenous characteristics including decision maker characteristics are important in determining the likelihood of e-marketing adoption. Many studies specifically found that decision maker awareness and knowledge of new tool had an effect on a hotel's online adoption strategy (Litucy and Rail, 2000; Olsen and Connolly, 2000; Dholakia and Kshetri, 2004). More recently, a wide range of hospitality specific studies considered the perceived cost (O'Connor and Frew, 2001) and affordability (Tamilia, Senecal and Corriveau, 2002; Martin and Matlay, 2003) of the Internet influencing adoption decision. Martin and Matlay's (2003) study construed that 'what customers want' is one of the key considerations that affect the use of the Internet in SMEs. While Jeong (2004) concluded that pressure from the customer perspective had an effect on how the hospitality sector conducted their business on the Internet.

A hotel's external environment was often found to have an effect on technology adoption-performance relationships. Past studies have predominantly described the external environment in terms of certainty (Phillips, 1999). One important external environmental factor found was competitive marketing intensity, based on Ching and Ellis's (2004) investigation of competitive intensity and customers' pressure. According to Gatignon and Robertson (1989), the inclination to adopt technology was found to be correlated with intense competition with industries, as inter-firm rivalry produced an incentive to adopt innovations which could be a source of competitive advantage. Competitive intensity was also found to have a profound effect on adoption levels by Litucy and Rail (2000) where respondents highlighted key issues such as increasing business exposure and gaining a competitive edge over larger businesses, as core reasons for adoption. Using the Davis's (1989) Technology Acceptance Model as the basis of investigation, the objectives of this study are, to examine the endogenous and exogenous variables that influences the e-Marketing adoption and to ultimately collapse those variables into factors for further evaluation.

3 Methodology

With the provision of a holistic view of the phenomenon under investigation (Patton, 1980), this research aims to understand human behaviour from the hoteliers' own frame of reference (Easterby-Smith, Thorpe and Lowe, 1991). In February 2006, a random sample of 2,580 independent hotels from the AA Hotel Guide 2005 list of 4,000 independent hotels were administered surveys, via mail with a postage paid returned envelope. 408 useable responses were returned for the study. Given that the response rate is less than 20%, the extent to which the factors influence adoption behaviour remain unaffected by sampling error. To quantify the hoteliers' perception and attitude towards e-marketing, closed questions obtained and developed from relevant literature using the likert scale were included in the 4 page survey. The reliability of the survey was addressed with the computation of the cronbach's alpha where each factor registered a minimum coefficient of 0.736. In-depth interviews of a dozen hoteliers informed the development of the survey instrument, helping to ensure the validity of the survey. Given that the research seeks to identify the key factors affecting adoption, it was decided that a factor analysis was the most suitable tool to achieve that aim. A factor analysis search, explain and reviews collapsed variable items that correlate into factors (Tabachnik and Fidell, 2001).

4 Factor Analysis Findings and Discussion

To obtain the variables for the study, a series of 3 or 4 likert scale questions were obtained from past literature, measuring for example, a single factor such as the perceived ease-of-use of a technology and other external factors found in Davis's Technology Acceptance Model (TAM). It was noted that the correlation coefficients tend to be less reliable when estimating smaller samples (Tabachnik and Fidell, 2001), therefore having a sample size of 408 for this research survey is considered to be between good and very good (Comrey and Lee, 1992).There are two key sets of variables from Davis's TAM to be examined, one of which is endogenous, where perceptions of technology use is measured; the second is exogenous where external variables are considered. Section 2 of the survey (20 likert scale questions) measures the endogenous perceptions of decision makers and section 3 of the survey (12 likert scale questions) measures the exogenous assessment of decision makers. The factorability of both variable sets is tested with Kaiser's measure of sampling adequacy. Since the two sets of variables have values of 0.87 and 0.816, it can therefore be assumed that both sets are suitable for a good factor analysis (Tabachnik and Fidell, 2001).

4.1 Endogenous factors

The use of factor analysis is to determine the main dimensional factors based on the KMO (Kaiser-Meyer-Olkin) and Bartlett's test of sphericity, a scree plot which extracted a total of 4 factors and the amount of variance the variables account for (eigenvalue>1). A Direct Oblimin – an oblique rotational method with the default Delta value of 0 was used in the Principle Component Analysis (PCA). This was to ensure that a rotation requiring the factors to remain correlated is performed, because the oblique rotational method as opposed to the orthogonal rotation method often achieves greater simple structure (Darlington, 2006). The PCA also allows a large set of variables to be replaced by a smaller set which best summarizes the larger set. Following the extraction of principle components, principle factors extracted were able to estimate the number of factors, the absence of multicollinearilty, and the favourable factorability of the correlation matrices. The pattern matrix is used for interpretative reasons as 'it contains information about the unique contribution of a variable to a factor' (Field, 2005: 660). More precisely, Tabachnik and Fidell (2001) stated that as a rule of thumb, only variables with loadings of .32 and above are interpreted, where the greater the loading, the more the variable is a pure measure of the factor. The factor analysis using SPSS aggregated the 20 hoteliers' perception of Internet marketing variables into four new factors, they are assigned new labels, (1) Perceived marketing benefits of Internet technologies where the factor loadings of the 6 variables varied between .554 and .873, (2) Perceived ease of use and Affordability had 4 variables of factor loadings ranging between .609 and .846, (3) Emotional attitude is a collapsed factor made up of 3 variables with factor loadings between .817

and .912, and (4) Perceived usefulness as a factor is made up of 7 variables with factor loadings ranging from .449 to .789. The strongest factor loadings were found in the factor 'Emotional attitude' as it has the highest average factor loadings compared to the rest. While the weakest factor loadings were found in 'Perceived Usefulness' with the lowest average factor loadings. The above findings could help to explain some of the strongest or non correlations and associations in further analyses conducted.

Twenty intra organisational factors are summarised and illustrated in table 1 below, providing a good estimation of population parameters for interactions. As shown in the table, the Rotation Sums of Squared Loadings (Eigenvalues) of 7.421, 2.493, 1.543 and 1.361 respectively, accounting for 64.09% of the total cumulative variance. The loadings are not a correlation but are a measure of the unique relationship between the factor and the variables. As indicated by the reliability measure of Cronbach's Alpha, all factors were consistent and well defined by the variables. Since the recommended value for Cronbach's Alphas is at least 0.7 (Ahire, Golhar and Waller, 1996) and the lowest of the Cronbach's Alpha for the constructs was .736, the variables are therefore well defined by this factor solution. Communality values were relatively high, with a cut of .449 for inclusion of a variable in the interpretation of a factor. In relation to the hoteliers' perceptions of Internet marketing, the Kaiser-Meyer-Olkin (KMO) Measure of Sampling Adequacy (MSA) is .870, a strong value indicating that patterns of correlation are compact, yielding distinct and reliable factors in factor analysis (Field, 2005) and are greater than .06. Four factors were obtained from the 20 collapsed variables. These factors were determined by the way the variables had grouped together. For instance, Factor 1: Perceived benefits of Internet technologies for marketing, represents all variables that were in direct relation to positive marketing perceptions of the Internet and Internet technology. With factor 2: Perceived ease-of-use and affordability, two of the variables measured a respondent's ease of Internet use, while other two variables that grouped with the previous two variables measured the perception of costs in relation to the Internet. Three variables measuring attitudinal perception of Internet use grouped to create Factor 3: Emotional attitude. Finally, Factor 4: perceived usefulness arise from six variables, of which four was in relation to how and why Internet technology is being used in the respondent's hotel.

4.2 Exogenous factors

This section examines the 12 likert scale questions of exogenous variables in determining the primary dimensional factors based on the KMO and Bartlett's test of sphericity, a scree plot, extracting a total of 3 factors and the amount of variance the variables account for (eigenvalue>1). Once again, the Principle Component Analysis with Oblimin Kaiser Normalization rotation was conducted. Like the earlier factor analysis of the hoteliers' endogenous intra-organisational perceptions, an oblique rotation was also used here because relationship between the factors could exist. From the results of the pattern matrix (table 2), loadings of a minimum of .576 and a high of .892 were recorded, the findings can therefore be deemed significant.

Table 1. Results of Pattern Matrix: Endogenous factors

Qn No		Factors			
		1	2	3	4
32	Internet marketing is a beneficial marketing tool for the hotel	.873			
31	Internet marketing is a wise marketing tool for the hotel	.850			
33	Internet marketing is a valuable tool for the hotel	.815	Perceived benefits of e-Marketing		
36	The benefits of adopting Internet marketing outweigh the costs	.693			
24	Using the Internet for marketing enhances the overall effectiveness of advertising for the hotel	.556			
15	The Internet has changed the way I market my hotel	.554			
35	Internet marketing is an expensive tool to maintain		.846		
34	Internet marketing is an expensive tool to adopt		.818	PEOU and Affordability	
27	I find it takes a lot of effort to become skilful at using the Internet		.664		
26	Interacting with the Internet requires a lot of mental effort		.609		
28	Using the Internet for marketing the hotel makes me feel happy			.912	
30	Using the Internet for marketing the hotel makes me feel good	Emotional Attitude		.893	
29	Using the Internet for marketing the hotel makes me feel positive			.817	
19	We use Internet technologies in our hotel as a means of providing customer service				.789
20	We use Internet technologies in our hotel to generate revenue				.708
17	The Internet helped me to know more about guests needs and wants				.675
21	We use Internet technologies in our hotel to gather information to make decisions		Perceived Usefulnes		.606
22	We use Internet technologies in our hotel because our competitors use them				.548
18	We use Internet technologies in our hotel as a form of advertising and promotion				.459
16	The Internet has changed the way I think about markets				.449
Reliability (Cronbach's Alpha)		.901	.736	.928	.814
Eigenvalue		7.421	2.493	1.543	1.361
Cumulative % of variance		37.104	49.569	57.286	64.090

Kaiser-Meyer-Olkin Measure of
    Sampling Adequacy: 0.870
Bartlett's Test of Sphericity:
    Approx. Chi-Square   4938.559   Sig.: .000

Table 2. Results from Pattern Matrix: Exogenous Factors

Qn No		Factors		
		1	2	3
39	Our current customers demand that we communicate with them via the Internet	.838		
37	We believe that we will lose our customers to our competitors if we do not adopt the Internet for marketing	.787	Customers' pressure	
38	We believe that we will fall behind our competitors if we do not market ourselves online	.753		
40	Our current customers demand that we use the Internet for conducting transactions with them	.576		
44	A large number of new service ideas have been possible through technological breakthroughs in our industry		.803	
43	It is very difficult to forecast where technology in our industry will be in the next 2 or 3 years		.750	
45	Technological developments have had a major impact on the hotel industry		.745	
41	The technology in our industry is changing rapidly	Competitive intensity	.654	
42	Technological changes provide big opportunities in our industry		.632	
46	We believe that due to the nature of the market, wide-ranging acts are necessary to achieve our business objectives		.601	
49	In general we have a strong tendency to be ahead of others in introducing new technology	Entrepre-neurship		.892
48	Our hotel makes aggressive and intensely competitive decisions			.887
Reliability (Cronbach's Alpha)		.758	.833	.811
Eigenvalue		4.728	1.450	1.278
Cumulative % of variance		39.489	51.489	62.137

Kaiser-Meyer-Olkin Measure of Sampling Adequacy: .816

Bartlett's Test of Sphericity: Approx. Chi-Square 1949.509 Sig.: .000

The factor analysis aggregated the hoteliers' 13 perception of Internet technologies variables into three new variables, (1) Customers' pressure- made up of 4 variables recording the lowest factor loading at .576 and the highest loading at .838, (2) Competitive intensity consists of 6 variables with the weakest loading of .601 and strongest at .803 and (3) Entrepreneurship is made up of 2 variables of two equally strong factor loadings of .887 and .892. The three factors have eigenvalues of 1.278, 4.728 and 1.450 respectively, accounting for 62.137% of the cumulative variance. In relation to the hoteliers' perception of technological impacts on the industry, the Kaiser-Meyer-Olkin (KMO) Measure of Sampling Adequacy (MSA) is .816 and a significance of .000 indicating that there are distinct and reliable variables within the new factors of the factor analysis. The reliability measure of Cronbach's alpha revealed that the breakdown of the 13 variables into 3 factors were sufficiently reliable where Customers' pressure had a cronbach alpha of .758, followed by the second factor of Competitive Intensity at .833 and the Entrepreneurship factor at .811.

3 distinct factors were obtained from the 12 collapsed variables measured in section 3 of the survey. Factor 1: Customers' pressure was derived from four variables that measured customers' demands in relation to adopting the Internet for marketing. 6 variables measuring the industry's competitiveness in adopting technology collapsed to create Factor 2: Competitive intensity. Finally, Factor 3: Entrepreneurship was obtained from the two variables that measured how assertively the hoteliers react or pre-empt to the industry.

4.3 Collinearity diagnostics

It has often been reiterated that multicollinearity is a problem because its immergence will indicate that the regression coefficients may be unsound (Dimantopoulous and Schlegelmilch, 1997) and thus result in the variability of the findings to vary from one sample to another. According to Bryman and Cramer (2005), multicollinearity occurs when the tolerance statistic is low, where the closer the tolerance figures get to zero, the more likely multicollinearity will occur. Another method of diagnosing multicollinearity is by examining the VIF for each variable. The closer the value of VIF is to 10, the bigger the independent's contribution to a possible multicollinearity. Information about multicollinearity can be found in the following table 12 where values for Tolerance and the variance inflation factor (VIF) are tabulated. The tolerance statistic is the percentage of the variance in a given predictor that cannot be explained by the other predictors. As shown in table 8, the tolerances of the seven factors based on dependent variable of changes in net profitability range from 0.445 to 0.947 suggesting that multicollinearity is rather unlikely, as the high tolerances indicate that only a maximum of 55% to a minimum of 5% can be explained by the other predictors. Moreover, it is only when tolerances are close to 0 that there is high multicollinearity where the standard error of regression coefficients are inflated. This is confirmed by the very low VIF values as none of the independent variables displayed values that are even close to 10. It has been suggested that a VIF greater than 2 suggest a problem, but there are only 2 variables slightly beyond 2, where the highest is 2.247. Therefore, multicollinearity does not pose as a problem for the models tested here and all the variables used are essential to the investigation of correlations.

Table. 3 Collinearity statistics

	Collinearity Statistics	
	Tolerance	VIF
Factor 1	0.445	2.247
Factor 2	0.919	1.088
Factor 3	0.635	1.575
Factor 4	0.455	2.198
Factor 5	0.578	1.731
Factor 6	0.601	1.664
Factor 7	0.783	1.278

5 Conclusion

The primary purpose of the analysis was to collapse the 32 variables that were originally obtained from various literature reviews as being important issues relevant to the study, into a statistically manageable set of 7 factors. These 32 variables were included in the questionnaire as likert scale questions where the formation of factors derived from the factor analysis also enabled the examination of how well the findings align with previous studies. The results of the factor analysis revealed 7 factors which were used for the rest of the study's analysis, they were: (1) Perceived marketing benefits of Internet technologies; (2) Perceived ease-of-use and affordability; (3) Attitude; (4) Perceived usefulness of Internet technologies; (5) Customers' pressure; (6) Competitive intensity; (7) Entrepreneurship. Interestingly, 'perceived usefulness' was found to have one of the lowest factor loadings. This finding is not quite in line with TAM as 'perceived usefulness' is a key determinant of the adopters' attitude and subsequent actual use of technology. The 'emotional attitude' of the adopter was one of two strongest factor loadings compared to the rest of the 5 factors found. This finding is in line with Igbaria et. al.'s (1996) and Poku and Vlosky's (2004) proclamation that attitude together with subjective norms play important roles in influencing an individual's decision to adopt a particular technology. Entrepreneurship was the second factor that loaded robustly, though most studies appear to have neglected the investigation of entrepreneurship as a factor for consideration. Whilst entrepreneurship is not just about the personality traits of an individual, this research has also shown that it appears to be influenced by the external environment.

There are a wide variety of online distribution methods an hotelier could utilise, but which of the ones s/he will be employing is greatly dependent on what has been made available to the hotelier, how much an hotelier understand the various modes available and how s/he came to know about them. Attempting to understand the hotelier's process of attaining knowledge vis-à-vis the many online possibilities through its experiences and thoughts could potentially help e-marketing consultants and even hoteliers come to recognise the factors that appear to be impinging on their adoption decision, and perhaps find approaches to overcome them. Future studies could therefore develop a more robust conceptualization of key parameters, considering the hotelier's cognitive consciousness, so that their dilemmas and struggles with online channel adoption or continuation could be further explored. While hoteliers are aware of what e-marketing tools are available and which tools to use, the effectiveness of e-marketing adoption is still dependent upon the behaviour of competitors. Furthermore, an independent hotel has limited marketing and distribution resources compared to the larger chain; where the latter are often able to present their hotel property in various sales and distribution channels that are perceived to be the most productive, whether they are print ads, direct mail, public relations, sales call or electronic distribution channels. Only the most cost-effective and compelling e-marketing channels will be allocated the limited resource will in turn bring in guests and improve occupancy. It should however be noted that there could be a few explanations as to why hotels, particularly in Western European, are as not ready or are sceptical about adopting e-marketing compared to their American counterparts.

Firstly, European hotels are highly fragmented, as the majority of hotels have a comparably smaller number of rooms (average number of rooms per property in Europe is 26, compared to 78 in US). Economically, *ceteris paribus*, a larger hotel property can justify investments in e-marketing strategies more effectively than smaller ones. Secondly, of the top 50 hotel companies in the world today, 72% are in the US, while 15% are in Europe; accounting for only 2% of all hotel properties in Europe. Up to 40% of these properties hotels could be members of some chain or group, large or small. Belonging to a consortium or a larger hotel chain, makes it 'technically and organisationally' more likely to acquire a wide range of effective e-marketing tools (Marcussen, 1999).

References

Ahire, S. L., D. Y. Golhar, M.A. Waller (1996). Development and validation of TQM implementation in constructs. *Decision Sciences* 27(1): 23-56.

Ajzen, I. and M. Fishbein (1980). *Understanding attitudes and predicting social behavior.* Englewood Cliffs, NJ, Prentice Hall.

Bryman, A. and D. Cramer (2005). *Quantitative Data Analysis with SPSS 12 and 13.* East Sussex, Routledge.

Buhalis, D. (1998). Strategic use of information technologies in the tourism industry. *Tourism Management*, 19(5): 409-421.

Chen, S. (2005). *Strategic Management of e-Business.* England, John Wiley and Sons.

Ching, H.L. and P. Ellis (2004). Marketing in Cyberspace: What factors drive e-commerce adoption?, *Journal of Marketing Management*, 20: 409-429.

Comrey, A. L. and H. B. Lee (1992). *A first course in factor analysis.* New Jersey, Lawrence Earlbaum Associates.

Dann, S. and Dann, S. (2004). *Strategic Internet Marketing 2.0.* Sydney, John Wiley and Sons.

Darlington, R. (2006). Factor Analysis. http://www.psych.cornell.edu/Darlington/factor.htm Retrieved 6/08/ 2006

Davis, F. (1989). Perceived usefulness, perceived ease of use, and user acceptance of information technology. *MIS quarterly* 13(3): 319-339.

Davis, T. H. (2007). Web adds new twist to business. *Travolution.* February: 20-25.

Dholakia, R. R. and N. Kshetri (2004). Factors impacting the Adoption of the Internet among SMEs. *Small Business Economics* 23: 311-322.

Diamantopoulos, A. and Schlegelmilch (2000). *Taking the fear our of data analysis.* London, Thomson Learning.

DTI (2004). *Statistical Press Release.* London, National Statistics.

Easterby-Smith, M., R. Thorpe and A. Lowe (1991). *Management Research: An Introduction.* London, Sage.

Field, A. (2005). *Discovering statistics using SPSS.* London, Sage.

Gamble, P. (1984). *Small computers and hospitality management.* London, Nelson Thornes.

Gatignon, H. and T. S. Robertson (1989). Technology diffusion: An empirican test of competitive effects. *Journal of Marketing*, 53: 35-49.

Hymas, J. (2001). Online marketing: Segmentation and targeted customer strategies for the web. *Journal of Financial Services Marketing* 5(4): 326-331.

Igbaria, M., S. Parasuraman, JJ. Baroudi (1996). A Motivational Model of Microcomputer Usage. *Journal of Management Information Systems*, 13(1): 127-143.

Jeong, M. (2004). An exploratory study of Perceived importance of web site characteristics: The case of the bed and breakfast industry. *Journal of Hospitality and Leisure Marketing* 11(4): 29-44.

King, R. C. and M. L. Gribbins (2002). Internet Technology adoption as an organization event: An exploratory study across industries. *35th Hawaii International Conference on System Sciences*, Hawaii.

Klein, L. and J. A. Quelch (1996). The Internet and international marketing. *Sloan Management Review* 37(3): 60-75.

Legris, P., J. Ingham, P. Collerette (2003). Why do people use information technology? A critical review of the technology acceptance model. *Information and Management* 40: 191-204.

Lituchi, T. R. and A. Rail (2000). Bed and breakfasts, small inns, and the Internet: The impact of technology on the globalization of small businesses. *Journal of International Marketing* 8(2): 86-98.

Malhotra, Y. and D. F. Galletta (1999). Extending the Technology Acceptance Model to account for Social Influence: Theoretical Bases and Empirical Validation. *32nd Hawaii International Conference on System Sciences*, Hawaii, IEEE.

Marcussen, C. H. (1999). The effects of Internet distribution of travel and tourism services on the marketing mix: No frills, fair fares and fare wars in the air. *Information, Technology and Tourism* 2: 197-212.

Martin, L. M. and H. Matlay (2003). Innovative use of the Internet in established small firms: the impact of knowledge management and organisational learning in accessing new opportunities. *Qualitative Market Research* 6(1): 18-26.

McKay, J. and P. Marshall (2004). *Strategic management of eBusiness*. Queensland, John Wiley.

Murphy, H. C. (2004). The diversity of diffusion of information and communication technologies in the hospitality sector- building a contemporaneous model. *Information and communication technologies in tourism* 11: 513-524.

O'Connor, G.C. and O'Keefy, B. (1997). Viewing the Web as a marketplace: The case of small companies, *Decision Support Systems*, Vol. 21, no. 3, pp.171-183

O'Connor, P. and A. J. Frew (2001). Evaluating Electronic Channels of Distribution in the Hotel Sector-A Delphi Study. *Proceedings of the CU2 Conference in Hospitality and Tourism,* Hong Kong.

O'Connor, P. (2001). The changing face of hotel electronic distribution. *Travel and Tourism Analyst* (5): 61-78.

Olsen, M. and D. Connolly (2000). Experience based travel: How technology is changing the hospitality industry. *Cornell Hotel and Restaurant Administration Quarterly* (February): 30-40.

Patton, M. (1980). *Qualitative Evaluation Methods*. Beverly Hills, Sage Publications.

Phillips, P. A. (1999a). Hotel performance and competitive advantage: a contingency approach. *International Journal of Contemporary Hospitality Management* 11(7): 359-365.

PKFReport (2004). Shadow cast over occupancy figures for UK hoteliers. http://www.hospitalitynet.org/news/4020766.html Retrieved: 28/11/2004

Ranchhod, A. and C. Gurau (2000). Marketing on the Internet: observations within the biotechnology sector. *International Journal of Physical Distribution and Logistics,* 30(7/8): 697-709.

Sheldon, P. (1994). *Tour Operators. Tourism Marketing and Management Handbook*. L. Moutinho. London, Prentice Hall International.

Sigala, M., D. Airey, P. Jones and A.Lockwood (2000). The diffusion and application of multimedia technologies in the tourism and hospitality industries. *Information and communication technologies in tourism* 2000: 396-407.

Tabachnick, B. and I. Fidell (2001). Using multivariate statistics. Boston, Pearson.

Tamilia, R. D., S. Senecal and G. Corriveau (2002). Conventional Channels of Distribution and Electronic Intermediaries: A Functional Analysis. *Journal of Marketing Channels* 9(3/4): 27-48

Yang, H. and Y. Yoo (2004). Its all about attitude: revisiting the technology acceptance model. *Decision Support Systems* 38(1): 19-31.

Comparing Internet commerce adoption between the Finnish and the European independent accommodation companies

Juho Pesonen[a]
Outi-Maaria Palo-oja[a]

[a]Centre for Tourism Studies
University of Joensuu, Finland
{juho.pesonen; outi-maaria.palo-oja}@joensuu.fi

Abstract

Travel and tourism is an information intensive industry. Internet is often used to plan and book holidays. This means that more and more effort should be paid to Internet marketing. This study uses the extended Model of Internet Commerce Adoption (eMICA) to compare the website features and the eCommerce adoption of the Finnish and the European independent accommodation companies. The goal is to find out, how Finnish hotels can improve their websites and gain competitive advantage. The results suggest that eMICA is a useful benchmarking tool to examine industry standards but it does not clearly indicate the phase of Internet commerce adoption among the independent accommodation providers. These often small companies may be active in eCommerce even though they do not have all the features of eMICA on their websites.

Keywords: eCommerce; eMICA; Internet marketing; hotel; websites

1 Introduction

Before the Internet era, travellers had to find the hotel information elsewhere. Brochures, other travellers' expectations through word-of-mouth, magazines and television provided little information for accommodation evaluation and selection. Today the situation is completely different, thanks to the Internet. Nowadays, Internet helps the potential travellers to find and evaluate accommodation services in advance, and quite often the first impression of the hotel is based on the hotel's online presence (Musante et al., 2009). It is estimated that by the end of 2010, nearly half of all hotel bookings will be made online (Starkov & Price, 2008 [Jul 25, 2009]). Also the Finnish statistics back up this assumption According to a 2008 survey, 83 percent of the Finnish adults and 62 percent the adults in the European Union have used Internet during the last three months, In Finland, 70 percent of the Internet users had browsed travel and tourism information, and 33 percent of the users had conducted online shopping. 60 percent of the value of eCommerce in Finland comes from the travel and tourism industry. (Statistics Finland [Aug 2, 2009))

As the importance of Internet for tourism increases, it is more and more important to be present on the Internet. This is the reason why almost every major European accommodation provider has their own web pages. Because of this competition is tough and simple online presence is not enough; a good website should also provide competitive advantage. The level of Internet adoption has been proved to have significant positive relationship with competitive advantage (Teo & Pian, 2003).

Extended Model of Internet Commerce Adoption (eMICA) has been used in many occasions to measure the level of online presence, in tourism as well as in other contexts. The Model of Internet Commerce Adoption (MICA) was originally introduced by Burgess and Cooper (1998) to measure the status of Internet commerce in metal fabrication industries and it has been used by Pracy and Cooper (2000) to measure Internet commerce adoption by small and medium sized enterprises in the Illawarra, Australia. Burgess and Cooper (2000) later upgraded their model and renamed it extended MICA, or eMICA. Besides Burgess and Cooper (2000), eMICA has been used in analyzing tourism websites by Burgess et al. (2001; 2003) and Doolin et al. (2002). Lemmetyinen and Suomi (2006) used eMICA to examine, which stages of application of www-based services can be seen in the case of small businesses in the tourism industry. Lemmetyinen and Suomi (2006) criticized eMICA for its difficulty in applying it to the tourism business and suggested its terminology and operationalization to be improved. However, it has been almost ten years since the introduction of eMICA. This study aims to find out how well eMICA can be used to measure level of Internet commerce adoption in hotel industry now that some hotels or accommodation companies have websites before they even have any rooms to rent, while some hotels have had their own Internet pages for at least a decade. There has also been lack of research in the websites of independent accommodation companies, especially in Finland, where most of the tourism companies are SMEs (small and medium sized enterprises).

According to Chaffey et al. (2006), benchmarking of competitors' websites is vital in positioning a website to compete effectively with competitors that already have websites. This study uses eMICA to compare Finnish and other European websites that have high user ratings on a social media recommendation site Trivago.com. This information is then used to find out whether the Finnish accommodation companies conduct the Internet marketing differently from the European companies. Goal is to answer how websites of independent European accommodation companies differ from their Finnish counterparts and how this information can be used to develop Finnish websites. Also, we discuss our findings about the typical website features of a European independent accommodation company against Musante et al.'s (2009) findings about 5-star hotels. Thus, this study also illustrates current industry standards in website design and use of eMICA as a benchmarking tool

2 Background of the study

Hotel website design is often researched topic in travel and tourism literature. For example, Musante et al. (2009) studied how hotel class affects the attribute utilization and effectiveness of the hotel website in Singapore. They found out that especially websites of 5-star hotels differ from other hotel websites. These hotels excelled others in every attribute studied: Their websites had more company information, product offerings, transaction functions, support services, and interactive functions. On the other hand, budget hotels and especially independents did not exploit the benefits of the Internet and lagged far behind even the 3-star and 4-star hotels. Still, these budget hotels had customers enough to survive in the intense accommodation business.

Website effectiveness was also a focus in Schmidt et al.'s (2008) study. They investigated the characteristics of hotel websites and how they interacted with website effectiveness. Schmidt et al. (2008) found that promotion by informational texts, illustrative photos, and location descriptions were associated with effectiveness of hotel websites. Interestingly, the study also indicated a gap between consumer expectations for commercial transactions and the hotels' policy to encourage customers to use traditional distributions. Jeong et al. (2003) noticed that website content and information availability precedes online lodging purchases. Law and Hsu (2005) studied how each website feature is valued by the customers. The study showed that reservation information, facilities information, and contact information were the most important dimensions for those who purchased online, and the information about the surrounding area and the website management were the least rated dimensions. Nysveen et al. (2003) studied mostly valued website features in details and called them value-added services. They found that customers preferred the availability of search engines, service integration, and website personalisation but did not value as much social interaction in customer communities. In general, company websites did not coincide with customer preferences at all. Service integration, i.e. a bundle of complementary services and information, was the only value-added service in accordance with preferences. Nysveen et al. (2003) determined also companies' plans to fill the gap between customer preferences and current offerings. Hashim, Murphy and Law (2007) have reviewed hospitality website design frameworks. According to their review, there are five dimensions of website quality: information and process, value added, relationships, trust, and design and usability. These dimensions are reflected by 74 website features. There are also a few models to analyse website content. For example von Dran et al. (1999) have applied Kano's Model of Quality to the Web environment to explain which website features fill a certain user expectations. However, there are some models that do not necessitate subjective analysis but are only commit themselves on existence or non-existence of the certain website features. One of them is eMICA (Burgess & Cooper 2000).

2.1 The extended model of Internet Commerce Adoption (eMICA)

Burgess and Cooper (2000) presented the extended model of Internet Commerce Adoption that illustrates how organisations typically start by simply establishing a presence on the Internet. The functionality of the website increases over time as the expertise of the use of Internet technologies increases. The model consists of three stages: promotion, provision of information and services, and transaction processing. As sites move from promotion to processing through provision, layers of complexity and functionality are added to the site (Burgess et al. 2003). This is the transition from a static website to a dynamic site to add value through information management and rich functionality (Timmers, 1998). eMICA incorporates many layers of complexity, ranging from very simple to highly sophisticated, within the identified main stages of the MICA. The eMICA is summarised in Table 1.

Table 1. The extended model of Internet Commerce Adoption (eMICA) (Doolin et al. 2002, adapted from Burgess and Cooper (2000).

EMICA	Examples of functionality
Stage 1: promotion	
Layer 1: basic information	Company name, physical address and contact details, area of business
Layer 2: rich information	Annual report, email contact, information on company activities
Stage 2: provision	
Layer 1: low interactivity	Basic product catalogue, hyperlinks to further information, online enquiry form
Layer 2: medium interactivity	Higher-level product catalogues, customer support (e.g., FAQs, sitemaps), industry-specific value added features
Layer 3: high interactivity	Chat room, discussion forum, multimedia, newsletters or updates by email
Stage 3: processing	Secure online transactions, order status and tracking, interaction with corporate servers

Law and Hsu's (2005) study supports eMICA model because they found that the second and third most valued website dimensions for online bookers were the facilities information and contact information, respectively. The highest rated indicators for facilities information were hotel location maps (mean 6.0855; scale from 1=very unimportant to 7=very important), hotel features (5.851), and for contact information they were telephone number (6.3059) and address (6.2072) as identified also in the basic information level in the eMICA. However, according to Law and Hsu (2005), the reservation information is the most important dimension driving online purchases. This information is called rich information in the eMICA. The room rates (mean 6.5428) and check rates and availability (mean 6.4013) were the highest rated attributes indicating reservation information in Law and Hsu's (2005) study. The features used in eMICA are quite similar to features used in other studies assessing website design in hospitality (Hashim et al., 2007). The only dimension absent in eMICA is trust, but information and process, value added, relationships, and design and usability are included in some measure.

3 Method and Data

In this study, the level of Internet commerce adoption in accommodation companies is determined through website content analysis according to eMICA model. As presented in Table 1, the eMICA consists of five layers in three stages. In this study, following functionalities were used to measure the adoption of Internet commerce: In Layer 1 of Stage 1, company name, physical address, phone number and area of business are all important basic features on a website. In this study, all these features are combined into single factor: basic information. A company must have all the information mentioned in the eMICA model in their websites in order to be counted as having basic information. In eMICA Layer 2 of Stage 1 consists of annual report, email contact and information on company activities, that is rich information content. For this study, following features were chosen to represent high information content: e-mail address, description of the company activities, accommodation prices or special offers, a map guiding travellers to the company (Lexhagen, 2005) location and information on the area surrounding the company. Layer 1 of Stage 2 is low interactivity. In this study it includes basic product catalogue, i.e. description of the company facilities and rooms, including pictures. Also hyperlinks to further information and to other sites and online enquiry form, which can be used to contact the personnel in the accommodation company, are included in this layer. In Layer 2 of Stage 2 the level of interactivity develops further. These features that enable interactivity are called as the higher-level product catalogues in eMICA. These can include panorama pictures, video, and flash-animation. Customer support is also important at this stage. In this study, customer support is counted if there is a single customer support feature on the site. Onsite search engine, FAQ, and chat service are used to represent customer support. This layer also includes industry-specific value added features. Only one such feature was included in this study: the use of recommendation sites such as Tripadvisor (www.tripadvisor.com). These recommendation sites provide the user the possibility to e.g. compare prices that is very important value-adding feature on travel websites (Lexhagen 2005). In the third and final layer of Stage 2 there is high interactivity such as chat room, discussion forum, multimedia, and newsletters. For this study three features were measured: use of multimedia, possibility to subscribe a newsletter, and whether there exists a guestbook, forum or any kind of social media interface (e.g. Facebook, Twitter) on the website. Multimedia included among other things sounds, video, web cam or panoramas and flash-animation not included in higher-level product catalogues. The last, third stage in the eMICA is processing. The processing stage was divided into two features, online booking or reservation and online transaction. According to eMICA, this is the final stage of the Internet commerce adoption.

Focus in this study was on independent and often smaller Finnish accommodation companies and their European counterparts. Thus, the hotel chains were excluded from the study. Choosing the websites for this study proved to be difficult. On one hand there is no list for independent accommodation providers in Finland. On the other hand, the websites included in this study should be important for those who use Internet to plan and book their holidays. Therefore, the websites were chosen for this study based on their ranking at Trivago (www.trivago.com).

Trivago is a European online-service for travellers seeking advice regarding their travel destination and hotel selection. At the moment, 7 million people visit Trivago a month. The service has over 15 million hotel reviews and 7 million photos for 300 000 destinations. (Trivago Hotelier 2009 [Sep 12, 2009]). Users also can rate the hotels and in this study user-generated ranking was chosen as the selection criteria for accommodation companies, as companies for high ranking are assumed to be more interesting for travellers than companies with low ranking. Trivago collects user

56

reviews from multiple sources, including TripAdvisor, and therefore should provide good listing of accommodation companies.

The list for independent accommodation companies was collected in August 2009 during a four day period. The rankings were used to find the most popular independent accommodation companies in Europe and in Finland. Accommodation providers in Finland and in Europe were listed by their rankings at Trivago.com and the first 25 independent accommodation providers were chosen. Content analysis was conducted on these 50 web pages. Each site was examined in details and the properties and different features on the site were identified. This study was only interested in the level of eMICA, and only measures used were ordinal, meaning the website either has the feature or does not have the feature. The data was then analysed by using cross tabulations with Fischer's exact test to find out if the Finnish and the European websites differ from each other statistically in their use of different features. Finnish and European websites are also compared in their number of features measured in this study by using ANOVA. ANOVA is used to test the hypothesis that means are equal between the number of Finnish and European website features.

4   Results

Results of this study are depicted in Figure 1 and Figure 2. In Figure 1, the levels of the eMICA can be found from the top of the Figure. As noted previously, the three stages are divided into six layers. In the Figure 1, the level of adoption grows from left to right. Different website properties and the number of Finnish and European accommodation companies having those properties on their websites are on the vertical axis.

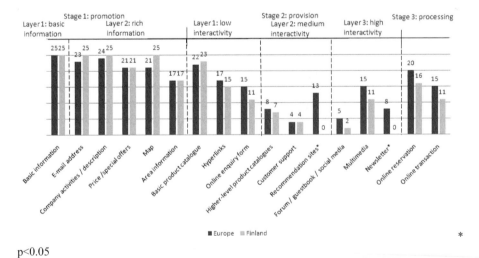

p<0.05

Fig. 1. Level of Internet Commerce Adoption in the websites of independent European and Finnish accommodation companies

All companies in this study, both Finnish and European, have the basic information about their company on their website. Differences between company websites begin arising when the second layer of the first stage is examined. All the Finnish companies have e-mail address, description of company or its activities and a map on their websites. The same is not true for European travel websites, as there are some websites that lack these features. There are also some Finnish and European websites that do not have price information or information on surrounding area on their websites. Still, majority of the websites have at least some of these features, i.e. rich information.

As stage 2 progresses, the level of interactivity intensifies. Majority of the companies have basic product catalogue and hyperlinks on their websites. European companies have more often online enquiry form on their websites than Finnish companies, but the difference is not statistically significant. The number of websites having medium interactivity features is much lower than in Layer 1 of Stage 2. Especially in Finnish websites the use of recommendation sites in non-existent, whereas more than half of the European websites utilize some form of recommendation site features. This difference is statistically significant (χ^2=17.6, p<0.001). The number of high interactivity features in Layer 3 of Stage 2 is also quite low, except for the use of multimedia. Some websites provide guestbook for their visitors, but there is not a website in this study that has some kind of forum for its users or that utilizes social media elements in their websites, not including the use of recommendation sites. There is a possibility of subscribing a newsletter on eight European websites, whereas no Finnish website in this study offered newsletter subscription. The difference is also statistically significant (χ^2=9.5, p=0.004). Last stage of the eMICA, i.e. processing, includes online reservations and online transactions. The companies having possibility of online transaction also had the reservation option. Almost all the European accommodation companies had some kind of reservation option on their websites. Of these sites, 15 had the possibility of online transactions. Many Finnish companies had also invested in this third stage, as over half had the possibility of online reservation and 11 companies provided online transactions.

Number of measured features was also examined between the Finnish and the European companies. In Figure 2 the accommodation companies' websites have been organized according to the number of features they have on their websites from the website with the lowest number of features to the website with the highest number. As can be seen from Figure 2, European websites have more features than Finnish websites. The difference is statistically significant (F=5.658 / p=0.021). Only the Finnish websites with the lowest number of features can compete with their European counterparts; otherwise European websites have more features.

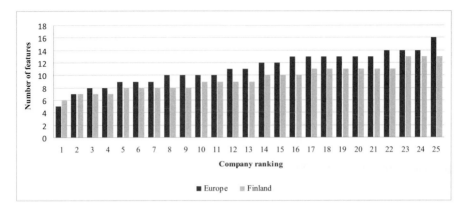

Fig. 2. Number of features on a website: comparison by ranking

5 Discussion

Burgess and Cooper's (2000) eMICA supposed that more mature websites have more functions and features because the expertise of the use of Internet technologies increases. We did not study the age of the websites but the results indicate clearly that eMICA does not progress linearly from simple to more sophisticated features with time. As shown in Figure 1, the level of eMICA is very high at the Stage 1, but gradually gets lower until the second and the third layer of stage 2, in which it is very low, particularly among the Finnish websites. In Stage 3 there is a high increase when comparing to previous layers. Many accommodation companies in this study offer their customer either the chance to reserve a hotel room and about half of the companies offer their customers a chance to pay their purchase online. This finding was not congruent with Schmidt et al.'s (2008) notice about the gap between customer expectations to book online and hotels' policies to encourage internet users to do business with the traditional distributers.

The companies in this study prefer to provide their customers a brochure and booking services at the same time, mostly neglecting interactivity. The high proportion of the companies using multimedia, thus investing in high interactivity, can be explained by incorporation of Flash-animation in their websites. Flash-animations are used in many ways, and one company used only Flash in its website. If the use of Flash-animation would be part of the basic or higher-level product catalogue, the use of high interactivity features would be almost non-existent, especially in Finnish websites.

The only statistically significant differences between Finnish and European websites exist in the second and third layer of Stage 2, medium and high interactivity. It seems that even though interactivity is not of the highest importance in European websites, the accommodation companies have invested in it more than in Finland. Especially in the Finnish websites the lack of use of recommendation websites could be observed. The Finnish accommodation companies chosen for this study had top rankings in recommendation websites and could use these rankings as a marketing tool as their European counterparts do. Also, the use of newsletter as a marketing channel is far more advanced in European accommodation companies than in Finnish companies. Newsletters are a good way to collect customer information, in this case their e-mail addresses and to post marketing material for customers.

The results suggest that, if measured by eMICA model, the independent Finnish accommodation companies are lagging behind in their Internet marketing efforts compared to European independent accommodation companies. This can be seen from Figure 2. Figure 1 indicates that when it comes to promotion, Finnish websites are equal or even better than European websites, but in stages two and three European websites take the lead.

6   Conclusions, limitations and further research

The eMICA is a useful but not foolproof model to examine the important properties of websites. It is especially useful as a benchmarking tool. By using eMICA, it was possible to systematically identify the features the independent accommodation companies have and do not have on their websites. This provides opportunity for companies to gain competitive advantage by investing on value adding features that their competitors do not have. It is relatively easy to see industry standards, that is the features that customer expects, and also the features that are not common and produce additional value for customer (Lexhagen, 2005). In the context of the websites in this study, competitive advantage could be gained by investing in interactivity and social media. It seems that in current industry standards company must have basic and rich information on their websites, and even a low level of interactivity. Especially the Finnish websites lack features that encourage customers to interact. The use of recommendation sites or newsletter subscription would be easy and inexpensive tools to stand out from the other accommodation providers.

The eMICA suggests that companies with processing features are at the highest level of the Internet commerce adoption. The results of this study suggest otherwise, particularly in the context of independent accommodation companies. Most of the companies had at least some kind of processing features in their websites, even though Stage 2 features could not be found. This means that companies with only basic promotion features on their websites can also provide a possibility for online reservation or even for transaction. The reason for this could be found from the resources of companies in question. The study was taken among independent and thus in many cases quite small companies. We did not compare the financial or human resources of the companies. The criteria to choose the companies into the study were their rating in Trivago.com. Because the website design is dependent on the amount of resources used, according to this study it seems that the companies with limited amount of resources have decided to invest them straight away into the processing stage.

Again, the results show that although the independent accommodation providers do not have some features identified in eMICA model (e.g. higher-level product catalogues, customer support, and recommendation sites), they are valued by customers in recommendation services. Interestingly, the Finnish companies were rated high even though they did not use any of the recommendation features on their own website. This could indicate that Finnish accommodation companies are lagging behind their customers in the use of Internet as a medium.

The results clearly demonstrated that eMICA could not be used as the model to measure the level of Internet commerce adoption for the independent accommodation companies. Websites of independent accommodation companies do not follow the eMICA model, but prefer to skip layers and stages in order to emphasize on processing features. That is why the websites could not be distinguished as clearly being at a certain stage of website development. The strength of eMICA, however, is that it does not require subjective judgment compared to measures used in other studies (e.g. Musante et al., 2009). In eMICA the feature is either present or it is not, meaning that results from different studies can be compared.

During the decade since MICA and eMICA were introduced, a lot has changed. We can see that by comparing recent studies to the studies made by Burgess and Cooper (2000, Burgess et al. (2001), Doolin et al. (2002), Burgess et al. (2003) as well as Pracy and Cooper (2000). The results of this study and the study by Lemmetyinen and Suomi (2006) show that nowadays level of Internet adoption cannot be categorized into levels or stages as eMICA suggests because websites emphasize different things. Earlier studies conducted in the early 2000s could clearly categorize websites into different stages based on their eCommerce adoption.

There are several limitations for this study, but they are also very interesting topics for future research. The number of websites included in this study is relatively low and includes only websites from the lists of a recommendation service. It is a challenge to obtain scientifically sound list of hotel websites, but this study presents one option for it. In further research more accommodation websites from several regions or destination should be included. The accommodation companies of this study also have to compete with hotel chains. Thus, further research should take hotel chain websites into comparison.

Also, the features included here are only small part of features present at different accommodation websites. There could be hundreds of features on a single website and this study included only some of those. The features chosen for this study are important for many hotel websites (Zafiropoulos & Vrana, 2006) and are based on the eMICA model and the studies of Lexhagen (2005) and Burgess and Cooper (2002) as well as Hashim et al. (2007). In the future it could be useful to include some measures of trust, such as date of the last update or privacy statements, when comparing websites.

It was assumed in this study that Internet marketing and website design is important for all accommodation companies. In reality it might not be the case as different companies have different marketing strategies. Some companies can emphasize on traditional brochures to reach their target markets whereas some use radio or other media as a marketing channel. Different marketing strategies can also affect website design, some segments can for example use Internet only to find information and then book their holidays through travel agency. This is the reason why eCommerce adoption cannot be measured by only using website design. Interviews or questionnaires to accompany website evaluation would probably provide better results, even though answers can be difficult to obtain.

This study used Internet recommendation service Trivago.com to choose accommodation companies and their websites to be analyzed. Recommendation sites are very useful in finding out who the competitors are among those markets that use these sites to choose their holiday destination or accommodation company. Especially those companies that rent high proportion of their rooms online should pay attention to Internet recommendation services.

It would be important to develop the eMICA to be better suitable for comparing hotel websites. The results should not encourage practitioners to add all features to their websites, but only those that are expected and those that produce additional value for customers and users.

References

Burgess, L. & Cooper J. (1998). The Status of Internet Commerce in the Manufacturing Industry in Australia: A Survey of Metal Fabrication Industries. *CollECTeR '98 Conference Proceedings, September 1998, Sydney, Australia.*URL: *http://www.collecter.org/archives/1998_September/06.pdf.*

Burgess, L. & Cooper J. (2000). Extending the viability of MICA (Model of Internet Commerce Adoption) as a metric for explaining the process of business adoption of Internet commerce. *Paper presented at the International Conference on Telecommunication and Electronic Commerce*, Dallas, November.

Burgess, L. Cooper, J. Alcock, C. McNamee, K. & Doolin, B. (2003) Use of the web for destination marketing by regional tourism organisations in the Asia-Pacific region. In Andersen, K. Elliot, S. Swatman, P. Trauth E. & Bjorn-Andersen, N. (Eds.) *Seeking success in ebusiness*. USA: Springer.

Chaffey, D. Ellis-Chadwick, F. Johnston, K. & Mayer, R. (2006). *Internet Marketing. Strategy, Implementation and Practice*. England: Pearson Education Ltd.

Doolin, B. Burgess, L. & Cooper, J. (2002). Evaluating the use of the Web for tourism marketing: a case study from New Zealand. Research note. *Tourism Management*, 23(5): 557-561.

von Dran, G.M. Zhang, P. & Small, R. (1999). Quality websites: An application of the Kano Model to website design. *Proceedings of the Fifth Americas Conference on Information Systems,*August 13-15.

Hashim, N. Murphy, J. & Law, R. (2007). A Review of Hospitality Website Design Frameworks. In Sigala, M. Mich, L. & Murphy, J. (Eds.) *Information and Communivation Technologies in Tourism 2007*. Austria: Springer.

Jeong, M. Oh, H. & Gregoire, M. (2003). Conceptualizing website quality and its consequences in the lodging industry. *Hospitality Management, 22(2): 161-175.*

Law, R. & Hsu, C. (2005). Customers' perceptions on the importance of hotel website dimensions and attributes. *International Journal of Contemporary Hospitality Management, 17(6): 493-503.*

Lemmetyinen, A. & Suomi, R. (2006). Cooperation of small enterprises in a web-based tourism network – case of the Old Mail Road in finland, Åland and Sweden. In Keller, P. & Bieger, T. (Eds.) *Marketing Efficiency in Tourism: Coping with Volatile Demand.* Berlin: Erich Schmidt Verlag GmbH & Co.

Lexhagen, M. (2005). The importance of value-added services to support the customer search and purchase process on travel websites. *Information Technology & Tourism,* 7(1): 119-135.

Musante, M. Bojanic D. & Zhang, J. (2009). An evaluation of hotel website attribute utilization and effectiveness by hotel class. *Journal of Vacation Marketing,* 15(3): 203-216.

Nysveen, H. Methlie, L.. & Pedersen, P. (2003). Tourism websites and value-added services: The gap between customer preferences and website offerings. *Information Technology & Tourism,* 5: 165-174.

Pracy, D. & Cooper, J. (2000). Internet Commerce Adoption by Small and Medium Sized Enterprises in the Illawarra. *CollECTeR 2000 Conference Proceedings, Decenber 2000, Brisbane, Australia.* URL: *http://www.collecter.org/archives/2000_December/01.PDF.*

Schmidt, S. Serra Cantallops, A. & Pizzutti dos Santos, C. (2008). The characteristics of hotel websites and their implications for website effectiveness. *International Journal of Hospitality Management,* 27(4): 504-516.

Starkov, M. & Price, J. (2006). Hotelier's 2008 Top Ten Internet Marketing Resolutions. URL: *http://www.hospitalityebusiness.com.* Jul 25, 2009.

Statistics Finland (2009). Changes in Internet usage: Results from the 2008 survey on ICT usage. URL: *http://www.stat.fi/til/sutivi/2008/sutivi_2008_2009-04-27_tie_002_en.html.* Aug 2, 2009.

Teo, T. & Pian, Y. (2003). A contingency perspective on Internet adoption and competitive advantage. *European Journal of Information Systems,* 12(2): 78-92.

Timmers, P. (1998). Business Models for Electornic Markets. *Electornic Markets,* 8(2): 3-8.

Trivago Hotelier (2009). Trivago is Europe's biggest hotel search. URL: *http://www.hotelier.trivago.com/hotelgateway.php?&pagetype=faq_aboutus.* Sep 12, 2009.

Zafiropoulos, C. & Vrana, V. (2006). A framework for the evaluation of hotel websites: the case of Greece. *Information Technology & Tourism,* 8(3-4): 239-254.

Use of Internet Applications & Tools by Health Tourism Agents in Malaysia: An Exploratory Study

Sudipta K. Sarkar[a],
Pradip K. Sarkar[b]

[a]Berjaya University College of Hospitality, Malaysia
sudipta@berjaya.edu.my

[b] School of Business Information Technology
RMIT University, Australia
pradipta.sarkar@rmit.edu.au

Abstract

Medical tourism is a rapidly growing industry stimulated by the rise in demand for relatively cheaper yet high quality medical services amongst citizens in wealthy nations. The phenomenon has been driven by affordable air travel and the proliferation of online tools and applications and a global electronic business network. In these host nations, companies have been established that act as intermediaries between the healthcare recipients and medical institutions, referred to as Health Tourism Agents (HTAs). Malaysia has joined the list of countries promoting its medical infrastructure to healthcare customers from other countries. This paper describes an investigation into the use of conventional web-enabled tools, such as websites, blogs, and forums, in the dissemination of information, maintaining relations with customers and business partners, and evaluation of the quality of services by customers, by examining five such HTAs in Malaysia.

Keywords: Medical tourism, eServices, online Healthcare services, Malaysia

1   Introduction

Medical Tourism is experiencing enormous growth in the present era with relatively rich citizens of developed countries visiting developing countries for affordable medical treatments, due to which the developing world fast becoming a hub of medical or health tourism (Bookman, 2008). According to the Dubai seminar on Health Tourism Development held in October (2008), medical tourism is growing at a rate of 20-30% every year in terms of medical tourist visits to destinations across the world and the industry is worth. The medical tourism industry, currently worth US$56 billion, is a direct result of the globalization of the Healthcare industry (Jagyasi, 2008). According to Cetron et al. (2006), medical tourism is expected to generate approximately $2.3 billion for each of the incumbent countries by 2012. The rapid development of medical tourism can be attributed to a number of national and global factors, including high cost of healthcare in industrialized nations, the ease and affordability of international travel, the rise in electronic business and Internet-enabled communication, currency exchange rates that favour citizens from wealthier countries, and the emergence of a higher quality of healthcare services in developing countries (Panda & Awadzi, 2006, Harowitz and Rosensweig, 2007).

Indeed, some developing countries have been able to take advantage of medical tourism, owing to their growing level of technological sophistication, healthcare infrastructure, advanced medicine and pharmaceuticals, low prices of surgical and other medical procedures, and shorter waiting periods (Edelheit, 2008). Therefore, a distinct tourism niche has gradually emerged that is aimed at meeting the needs of a growing number of people from affluent societies (Connell, 2006). In 2007, more than 750,000 US citizens travelled overseas to receive less expensive medical treatments (Albert, 2008). According to the Deloitte Center for Health Solutions Research, that number is expected to grow to 6 million by 2010, having the potential to decrease US health care expenditures by billions of dollars. Outbound US medical tourism figures indicate $2.1 billion spent by Americans for healthcare overseas (Albert, 2008).

Asia is one of the most promising medical tourism markets in the world, with a revenue of US$ 3.4 Billion in 2007, accounting for nearly 12.7% of the global market (Bharat Book Bureau, 2008; Siddiqi, 2006). More than 2.9 million patients visited Thailand, India, Singapore, Malaysia and the Philippines in 2007. Singapore is targeting to attract one million foreign patients annually and push the GDP contribution from this sector to over US$1.6 billion, while Malaysia expects medical tourism receipts to be in the region of US$590 million by 2011. Malaysia, the latest entrant to the list of countries providing medical alternatives, is focused on providing a good value for the patient who comes prepared to take advantage of the high quality and reasonable price of health care (O'Reilly & Lamb, 2006). The number of foreigners seeking healthcare services in Malaysia has grown from 75,210 patients in 2001 to 296,687 patients in 2006. The large volume of patients in 2006 brought approximately US59 million or RM203.66 million in revenue (Tourism Malaysia, 2008). The number of foreigners visiting the country for medical tourism has more than tripled since 2003 to hit a total of 341,288 in 2007. For the first nine months of 2008, over 282,000 foreigners came to Malaysia for medical treatment, generating revenue of about US $63 million – a 16% increase from the year before (Ang, 2009). Malaysia has actively sought to encourage doctors to return from overseas, firstly, to be involved in medical tourism and, secondly, to provide more equitable health care (Chong et al.., 2005).

Growth in medical tourism has been facilitated by the rise of the Internet, and the emergence of healthcare intermediaries or *Health Tourism Agents* (HTAs) between international patients and hospital networks (Connell, 2006; Steele, 2007). This paper presents a study into how the Internet, via company and 3rd party websites as well as blogs and forums, is being harnessed by Malaysian HTAs in promoting their services and in their interactions with potential and current customers.

2 Literature Review

2.1 Medical Tourism and the Role of the Healthcare Intermediary

With the advent of the Internet and affordable air travel, the healthcare market has transitioned over the years from a patient –centered to a consumer-centered industry (Albert, 2008). Medical Tourism could be defined as "a set of activities in which a person travels across national boundaries, to avail medical services with direct or indirect engagement in leisure, business or other purposes" (Jagyasi, 2008). Some researchers call medical tourism as a kind of niche tourism where people travel often long distances to obtain medical, dental and surgical care, while simultaneously being holidaymakers (Connell, 2006). Medical tourists can be potentially anyone; patients and their families; participants in academic medical conferences and conventions; business-to-business meetings between product and service vendors, and any mix of the above (Albert, 2008). On the other hand, some health professionals argue against referring to international patients as tourists, though certain touristic activities, such as engaging in cultural and culinary activities in the host nation may be undertaken (Jagyasi, 2008). Recreational travel is rarely included as part of the overseas health treatment (Harowitz and Rosensweig, 2007).

Owing to the differences in medical tourism and leisure or business travel, the services of a medical care arranger or facilitator are imperative in the provision of travel solutions or in the identification of travel agents with expertise in organizing travel plans for visitors seeking medical care (Roger, 2008). These service providers are *one-stop facilitators* that arrange and coordinate overseas medical treatments for traveling patients and their companions, including planning for the trips, flight reservations, transportation, appointments with doctors, hospitals and booking procedures (Lagiewski & Myers, 2008; Schutte,2008). Medical Tourism companies come in different sizes and shapes, and not all the service providers offer ancillary services, such as flight and accommodation bookings and leisure activities. The core of medical tourism constitutes high quality medical treatment with the added advantage of tourism (Jagyasi, 2009). Constituents for a successful inbound medical tourism practice include "patient-centred" concierge services, high quality of medical care, and affiliations (long-term relationships) with clinics and institutions abroad (Moreno, 2009). In countries of origin of the medical tourists, new companies, such as Gorgeous Getaways (Australia), specialising in cosmetic surgery taking place in Thailand and Malaysia, have emerged (Connell, 2006). These medical care arrangers or facilitators essentially act as intermediaries, thus our reference to them as Health Tourism Agents (HTAs).

2.2 Role of the Internet in Medical Tourism

The use of information and communications technologies in providing medical advice and supporting general healthcare when patients and medical personnel are separated by physical distance is referred to as *telemedicine* (George & Henthrone, 2009). Technological developments in Information and Communication (ICT) technologies drive medical tourism (Baron, 2007; Jagyasi, 2008; Steele, 2007). ICT in health or e-

Health is considered to be an essential aspect of medical tourism (Constantinides, 2009). Ann Séror (2009) and Talh & Salim (2005) emphasize the role of information and communication technologies (ICT) in enabling cross-border consumer mobility to obtain health care products or services. For most medical travelers, the first point of contact with a hospital or clinic is usually through the web site of the Health Tourism Agent (HTA) (Treatmentabroad, 2009). Healthcare services can be promoted and facilitated effectively through an online medium. Such services constitute payments, access and transfer of medical records and test results, referrals, enrollment and actual medical appointments (David, 2009). Internet tools and applications can assist HTAs in managing medical resources, compliance with clinical best practices, thereby yielding great benefits to the quality of services offered to patients (Talh & Salim, 2005). Furthermore, health tourism agents use websites with features such as search engines, booking systems, online chat and personalization tools to interact with patients (Hansen 2008, Zhao & Dholakia, 2009).

However, the suitability of the Internet for promoting and offering services to consumers depends largely on the characteristics of the services being offered (Phau & Poon 2000). Based on their development of a taxanomy of eServices, Lee & Park (2008) discussed the notion of *professional* services as being purchased with the outmost discretion by extremely discerning customers. Healthcare is considered to be an archetypical professional service (Wilson, 1994). Thus, the strategies relevant to any provider of online professional services can be applied in online medical service provision. Medical services tend to be expensive as they require a high level of expertise from service providers and a costly labour force. Their delivery is customized according to the needs of the respective customers. The frequency and duration of customer-provider interactions are greater and the actual medical treatment takes place offline rather than online. According to Riley Dall'Olmo et al. (2009), the intangible nature of professional services can reduce the suitability of the Internet as a distribution channel. Indeed, the more customized and personalized a service is, the less likely that consumers intend to acquire it online. Medical services are "high-contact, customized, personal services" that require face-to-face interactions between patients and service providers and the issue of trust is crucial (Åhlström & Nordin, 2006; Ellram et al., 2004; Lee & Park, 2008). Bendoly et al. (2005) and Riley Dall'Olmo et al. (2009) stress the importance of online/offline integration of services (i.e., face-to-face interactions in tandem with online activity).

Nevertheless, online consultations before the commencement of the medical trip can facilitate in generating more realistic expectations in patients (George and Henthrone, 2009). Likewise, online follow-ups with patients following the medical trip can be instrumental in minimizing cognitive dissonance, redressing patient complaints, and boosting service loyalty. Customer Relationship Management (CRM) via a loyalty and membership system is considered to be a worthwhile pursuit for providers of online professional services. It is also deemed highly important for online service providers to ensure the usefulness, ease-of-use, and pleasure factors of their websites (Lankton & Wilson, 2007).

Medical service providers and HTAs can also stress the quality of their services and their reputation by referring the customers to eminent third party websites. Studies have revealed that potential customers, in their decision-making process regarding the quality of a medical package or the reputation of a provider, participated in 3rd party forums, blogs, and chatrooms, to seek alternate sources of information and possibly in-depth personal accounts by former patients (Misra et al., 2008). Some of these interactions led to actual decisions in selection of a suitable HTA. Indeed, consumers seek information from online sources for a number of reasons – probing into new information, confirming information, or seeking information to solve problems or address concerns (Case et al., 2005; Montoya-Weiss et al., 2003; Lankton & Wilson, 2007).

Thus, it is of prime importance for online service providers to ensure that the information needs of consumers regarding the company and the services it offers are satisfied (Piccoli et al., 2004, Stafford, 2003; Tanriverdi, 2006). (George& Henthorne, 2009). However, in the Malaysian context, the healthcare industry has been affected by slow ICT adoption (http://www.nst.com.my/techNu, 2009). Moreover, some medical tourism websites, including those hosted by the tourism authorities, have amounted to not more than basic front ends that promote travel arrangements, but fail to provide adequate information to patients (Barron, 2007; Shah, 2008). Challenges faced in the Malaysian healthcare tourism sector have been attributed to insufficient allocation of funds for research and development in the ICT, thereby slowing down the penetration rate of the Internet. In view of this, our paper is aimed at conducting an exploratory investigation into the use of Internet tools and applications by medical tourism providers in Malaysia in promoting healthcare services and in interacting with potential and existing customers.

3   Research Methodology

Owing to the lack of prior research on how Internet tools and technologies are being utilized by HTAs in promotions and interactions with customers, especially in the Malaysian context, an exploratory study was conducted by interviewing the CEOs of six major companies in the industry. A positivist approach was deemed unsuitable owing to the lack of the existence of "a priori fixed relationships within phenomena which are typically investigated with structured approaches" (Orlikowski & Baroudi 1991). In line with the objectives of the study, a qualitative approach was adopted (Strauss & Corbin 1990, Walsham 1993b, Klein & Myers 1999).

The interviews with the CEOs of the five medical tourism providers lasted approximately one hour and were audio-taped with the permission of the interviewees. Interview data was later analysed through various iterations of coding by looking for themes concerning issues associated with the role of Internet tools and websites in customer interactions. The initial codes were based on the themes set by the interview questions. As a courtesy to the interviewees and following research ethics practice, the names and organisations of the interviewees were kept anonymous in this paper.

The five companies were selected on the basis of their prominence in the medical tourism industry in Malaysia. All of them offered exclusive medical services to customers from overseas. The interview with the CEO in the 5th organization did not reveal any new issues, thereby ensuring the sufficiency of the number of cases for the exploratory study (Glaser & Straus 1967, Miles & Huberman 2002).

4 Discussion of Findings

From the analysis of the interviews, a number of issues emerged with regards to the role of Internet tools and technologies in the services offered by HTAs in Malaysia. The interviews with CEOs revealed four issues, namely the use of online infrastructure to meet information needs of potential customers, maintaining relationships with existing customers, providing supporting services, and finally looks at the roles of relevant 3rd party websites, blogs, and forums. The findings have been summarized in Table 1.

4.1 Meeting information needs

In all the five cases, the company website was the first point of contact between the prospective customers and the medical tourism providers. All the five websites provided interactive online forms that could be filled in and sent electronically to the providers. In addition, basic email facilities were also offered. This initial point of contact with often followed by further emails and telephone calls. Some of the websites offered video and audio clips, and online chat forums. All the five companies stressed the importance of their websites as "initial points of contact" and in satisfying the information needs of prospective and existing customers. HTA-A, HTA-B, and HTA-E offered a one-stop shop facility through their websites, which included both medical and other relevant information. HTA-A claimed to facilitate direct online communications between affiliated doctors and prospective customers via email. Both HTA-B and HTA-E shared their analyses of customer information with affiliated medical institutions in order to propagate a continual service improvement program. HTA-B posted case studies and testimonials from past customers on its websites aimed at meeting the information needs of prospective customers. HTA-E offered a limited set of case studies and testimonials, owing to the specific nature of its services, concerned with privacy and confidentiality issues. It was also keen on an online chat feature on its website but cited time differences and the difficulty in putting together a round-the-clock helpdesk team as obstacles. The websites of HTA-C and HTA-D were entirely focused on the dissemination of medical information and did not contain any of the comprehensive features embedded by the other three companies. Both of these companies believed that their role was strictly that of an intermediary between the patients and the medical institutions, but did not consider it important to provide travel and general tourism information. HTA-D, however, admitted to their urgent need in getting its website up to-date with necessary information, in addition to improving the quality of its web content. All five companies held the view that their online presence was important in ensuring that the information needs of their customers were met.

According to the CEO of HTA-C:

"The website itself does not bring in too many clients to us – they are referred to us by our network of affiliated doctors in the clients' countries of origin. But - yes - it (the website) is definitely the first point of contact between a client and us, following the referral."

4.2 Maintaining relationships with Customers and Affiliated Medical Institutions

HTA-A, HTA-B, and HTA-E were also using online tools to elicit customer feedback and provide post-treatment consultations. The feedback obtained from customers through an online form led to the content in the testimonials sections. It is to be noted that participation in the testimonials by customers was voluntary. These companies also offered a personalization feature for existing customers once they were logged into the website.In HTA-D, the online feedback feature remains in its latency due to supposed inactivity from customers. HTA-C indicated that its customers preferred to share their views and receive follow-up consultations via a telephone call. HTA-E was in the process of enhancing its feedback and testimonials section at the time of the interview, possibly anticipating a rise in online participation by customers.

Moreover, HTAs -A, -B, and -E have in place a web-enabled Business-to-Business (B2B) link to a network of affiliated medical institutions, through which market research activities were intended to be undertaken. HTA-C, despite expressing no interest in eliciting feedback and publishing testimonials online, had a similar link to its medical affiliates.

"We do engage in some level of interactions with our affiliated hospitals via the Internet"

4.3 Providing supporting services

The same web-enabled B2B links to logistics providers and to sections of the tourism industry also allowed HTAs -A, -B, and -E, to arrange airport transfers, accommodation and in some cases, leisure activities, to their customers, even though it was only HTA- A that had joined the Worldspan and Galileo network with air travel booking agents, owing to its relatively advanced ICT infrastructure. Despite non-participation in a B2B network, HTAs -C, and -D also organized logistics and accommodation, but the choices afforded to customers were restricted to a few fully-serviced apartments with 'adequate' amenities. None of the companies were overtly concerned with leisure tourism though HTAs-A, -B, and -E were able to organize such activities due to the B2B link.

According to the CEO of one of the HTAs:

"Normally we don't advise our patients to do tours but some do go to local trips like KL tour but trips that involve overnight stays are not advised by us nor the doctors."

Also, another CEO quoted:

"Generally, patients do not go for trips. This is due to cost and medical reasons and medical procedural complications. "

4.4 Presence in relevant 3rd party websites, blogs, and forums

All the companies were interested in reviews of their services in relevant blogs, forums, and 3rd party websites, as they considered the significance of these channels as sources of independent information to prospective customers. The exception was HTA-C, whose CEO was not convinced of the usefulness of web 2.0 tools as venues of information dissemination, and did not regard the company's online presence as an important source of competitive advantage. It offered the most specialized treatments and relied more heavily on telephone and email exchanges and directed major efforts to the actual delivery of the medical package, which also included convenient transportation and lodging facilitates for customers.

CEO of HTA-C:

"We don't consider blogs and forums as appropriate venues to discuss serious issues like health."

5 Conclusion and Directions for Future Research

All the five companies were primarily using their websites to fulfill the information seeking needs of prospective customers. HTA-C maintained a basic level of web infrastructure as ICT was not at the core of its strategic planning. At the other end of the spectrum, HTA-A had implemented the most advanced online infrastructure in line with its inclusion of ICT in its strategic initiatives. Interestingly, the companies that offered a broader range of services from dental surgery to optical treatments highlighted the importance of Internet tools and technologies in their interactions with customers and network of affiliates. HTAs -A, -B, and -E belonged to this category. They were also the larger of the five HTAs. In contrast, HTAs -C and -D offered a narrower yet highly specialized set of services, which demanded a greater level of privacy and confidentiality commitment from these providers. Such services included arrangements for cosmetic surgery and fat reduction treatments. This is why they were not particularly keen on online testimonials. They offered exclusive services and directed large efforts on the actual delivery of medical and supporting services to the customer.

However, the disinterest in blogs and forums was only found in the case of HTA-C whose CEO was not an earnest advocate of web tools in general. HTA-D, on the other hand, was aware of the importance of blogs and forums in creating awareness of its services to prospective customers worldwide. Companies maintaining a wider portfolio of medical services were also aiming at a wider and larger customer base, thus necessitating their consideration of a more in-depth use of online tools and technologies to operate efficiently. Thus, the level of ICT sophistication can vary within the same industry in accordance with the portfolio and nature of medical services provided.

This study also confirms the notion of *professional services*, stipulated by Lee & Park (2008), which asserts the greater importance of actual offline interactions in service delivery, while highlighting the importance of online tools in information dissemination and promotion of services. All five medical tourism providers directed their core efforts towards organizing the actual delivery of the medical tourism, while maintaining varying levels of online sophistication. HTAs deal with serious issues of healthcare and therefore needs to depend on relationship marketing for pre- visit and especially post-visit communication with customers. Relationship marketing has a long term orientation. Both traditional direct marketing forms and digital direct marketing technologies need to be adopted. (Kotler, et al., 2006). It can also be induced that the step towards more integrated web applications by HTAs -A, -B, and -D was in line with the notion of Customer Relationship Management (O'Leary et al.., 2004) and e-marketing (Chaffey et al.., 2003) adopted by larger organizations. This essentially attributes the organizational size and scale of operations to the level of sophistication of the IT infrastructure. Interestingly, the study also hints at the *Perceived Usefulness* factor in the Technology Acceptance Model (TAM) (Davis, 1989). This is clearly demonstrated in the case of HTA-C, whose CEO expressed a lack of optimism with regards to the usefulness of web technologies to the company's growth in its customer base, though it was not the intention of this paper to quantitatively validate the fact.

Future research will be directed at investigating the online information seeking activities of offshore healthcare customers and the influence of online media, such as websites and blogs, on their decsion-making process, with implications for continued research on Business-to-Consumer (B2C) trust and redress. Indeed, HTAs and healthcare providers will not be able to ignore user-generated content, such as blogs containing accounts of experiences by former healthcare customers. Online communities have widened the marketing scope and can influence prospective customers' decision-making process when it comes to assessing the quality of services and reputation of companies (McCabe 2009, Wang et al. 2002). In that regard, peer-to-peer communications hold the same credibility as word-of mouth information.

Table 1. Summary of Findings

	Meeting information needs	Maintaining relationships	Providing supporting services	Presence in relevant 3rd party websites, blogs, and forums.
HTA-A	- First point of contact - One-stop shop for medical and other relevant information - Linking customers directly with doctors	- Feedback and follow-up consultations - Personalization - Information sharing with medical institutions	- Organizing logistics and accommodation - Air ticket booking facility - Providing information about leisure activities	- Listed in Tourism Malaysia website - Affiliation with Medical Tourism Association (MTA) - Write-ups in travel blogs
HTA-B	- First point of contact - One-stop shop for medical and other relevant information - Offers case studies and testimonials	- Feedback and follow-up consultations - Personalization - Information sharing with medical institutions	- Organizing logistics and accommodation - Providing information about leisure activities	- Listed in reputed websites dedicated to offshore healthcare services - Applying to get listed on the MTA portal
HTA-C	- First point of contact - No-frills website with entire focus on medical information	- Not reliant on web tools for feedback and follow-up consultations - Information sharing with medical institutions	- Organizing logistics and accommodation - No information about leisure activities	- Not keen on write-ups in blogs and forums
HTA-D	- First point of contact - Working on improving web content - Information needs updating	- Feedback area inactive	- Organizing logistics and accommodation - Brief information about leisure activities	- Write-ups in travel blogs
HTA-E	- First point of contact - One-stop shop for medical and other relevant information - Unable to offer online chat owing to time differences - Offers limited case studies and testimonials - Information sharing with medical institutions	- Feedback and follow-up consultations - Working on getting the testimonials section going - Personalization - Information sharing with medical institutions	- Organizing logistics and accommodation - No information about leisure activities	- Write-ups in healthcare forums

References

Albert, D. (2008), Medical Tourism; Progress and Prospects, *Medical Tourism Magazine* Oct, 30, 2008, www.medicaltourismmag.com (Accessed June 12, 2009).

Åhlström, P., & Nordin, F. (2006) Problems of establishing service supply relationships: Evidence from a high-tech manufacturing company. *Journal of Purchasing and Supply Management*, 12(2), pp 75–89.

Bendoly, E., Blocher, J.D., Bretthauer, K.M., Krishnan, S. & Venkataramanan, M. A. (2005) Online/in-store integration and customer retention. *Journal of Service Research*, 7 pp 313-27.

Case, D. O., Andrews, J. E., Johnson, J. D. & Allard, S. L. (2005) Avoiding versus seeking: The relationship of information seeking to avoidance, blunting, coping, dissonance, and related concepts. *Journal of Medical Library Association*, 93(3), pp 353–362.

Cetron, M. J., Demicco; F. J. & Davies, O. (2006) *Hospitality 2010: The future of hospitality and travel.*, New York: Prentice-Hall.

Dall'olmo Riley, F., Scarpi, D. AND Manaresi, A. (2005) Drivers and barriers to online shopping: the interaction of product, consumer, and retailer factors. In CLARKE, I. & FLAHERTY, T. E. (Eds.) Advances in Electronic Marketing. Hershey, PA., Idea Group Publishing.

Davis, F. D. (1989). Perceived usefulness, perceived ease of use, and user acceptance of information technology. *MIS Quarterly*, 13(3), 319-339.

Ellram, L. M., Tate, W. L., & Billington, C. (2004) Understanding and managing the services supply chain. *Journal of Supply Chain Management*, 40(4), pp 17-32.

George, B. P. & Henthorne, T. L. (2009) The Incorporation of Telemedicine With Medical Tourism: A Study of Consequences.

Grover, V., Teng, J. T. C. & Fiedler, K. D. (2002) Investigating the role of information technology in building buyer–supplier relationships. *Journal of the Association for Information Systems,* 3(7), pp 217–245.

Hansen, F. (2008) A Revolution in Healthcare; Medicine meets the marketplace, The Review.

Harowtiz, M. D., & Rosenweig, J.A. (2007) Medical Tourism – Healthcare in the Global Economy, The Physician Executive, November.December, 2007.

Kotler, P., Bowen, J. & Makens, J. (2006), Marketing for hospitality and tourism, Pearson Education,USA

Lankton, N. K. & Wilson, V. (2007) Antecedents and Dimensions of Online Service Expectations. *IEEE Transactions on Engineering Management*, 54(4), pp 776-788.

Lee, S. & Park, Y. (2008) The classification and strategic management of services in e-commerce: Development of service taxonomy based on customer perception. Expert Systems with Applications, 36 pp.

McCabe, S. (2009) Martketing Communications in Tourism & Hospitality: Concepts, Strategies and Cases, Butterworths-Heinemenn, UK.

Misra, R., Mukherjee, A. & Peterson, R. A., Balasubramanian, S. & Bronnenberg, B. J. (2008) Value Creation in Virtual Communities: The Case of a Healthcare Website. International *Journal of Pharmaceutical Healthcare Marketing*, 2(4), pp 321-337.

Montoya-Weiss, M. M., Voss, G. B. & Grewal, D. (2003) Determinants of online channel use and overall satisfaction with a relational, multichannel service provide. J. Acad. Market. Sci, 31,(4), pp 448–458,.

O'Leary, C., Rao, S., & Perry, C. (2004) Improving Customer Relationship Through database/ Internet marketing: A theory building action–research project, *European Journal of Marketing*, 38(3/4), pp 338-354.

Peterson, R. A., Balasubramanian, S., & Bronnenberg, B.J. (1997) Exploring the implications of the Internet for consumer marketing. *Journal of the Academy of Marketing Science*, 25(4), pp 329-346.

74

Phau, I. & Poon, S. M. (2000) Factors influencing the types of products and services purchased over the Internet. Internet Research: Electronic Networking Applications and Policy, 10(2), pp. 102-113.

Piccoli, G., Brohman, M. K., Watson, R. T. & Parasuraman, A. (2004) Net-based customer service systems: Evolution and revolution in web site functionalities. Decision Sciences, 35(3), pp 423–455.

Riley, F. D. O., Scarpi, D. & Manaresi, A. (2009) Purchasing services online: a two-country generalization of possible influences. *Journal of Services Marketing*, 23(2), pp 93-103.

Shah, B. J. (2008) An Insight into Malaysia's Medical Tourism Industry from a New Entrant Perspective, MBA thesis, Tanaka Business School, Imperial College London, United Kingdom

Stafford, T. F. (2003) Differentiating between adopter categories in the uses and gratifications for Internet services. *IEEE Trans. Eng. Management*, 50(4), pp 427–435.

Wilson, A. (1994) Emancipating the Professions, Chichester, Wiley and Sons.

Hong Kong Residents' Perception of Travel Websites

Shanshan Qi [a]
Rosanna Leung [a]
Rob Law [a], and
Dimitrios Buhalis [b]

[a] School of Hotel and Tourism Management
The Hong Kong Polytechnic University, Hong Kong
{shan.qi, rosanna.leung, hmroblaw}@polyu.edu.hk

[b] School of Services Management
Bournemouth University, United Kingdom
dbuhalis@bournemouth.ac.uk

Abstract

At present, Internet applications have been well adopted in the tourism industry. In terms of online marketing, consumers online purchase intention is always recognized as one of the most popular topics in both academia and industry. This research makes an attempt to investigate the perception of residents in Hong Kong, grouped in experienced and inexperienced travelers, of online and offline perceptions. Empirical findings indicated that both groups of travelers considered price and online payment security were equally important, and website reputation was more important to inexperienced travelers. Respondents did not shop online mainly because online transactions are too complicated and insecure. They preferred face-to-face interactions. Drawing on the findings, recommendation and suggestions to the industry were provided.

Keywords: experienced traveler, inexperienced traveler, online purchase intension, online channels

1 Introduction

Information & Communication Technologies (ICTs) in general and the Internet in particular, have been developed as one of the most effective tools to travel and hospitality marketing (Marussen, 1997; Hanna and Millar, 1997; Buhalis, 1999). The Internet has revolutionized the operation of tourism and hospitality industries, and changed customers' information search and purchase behaviours (Chung and Law, 2003). In terms of Internet users, the global population has increased 225% from 2000 to 2007 (Internet World Stats, 2007). The Internet provides consumers with a new platform to shop. Some examples of the benefits of online purchasing include time saving, price comparison, social interaction, and information gathering (Ahuja, Gupta and Raman 2003; Rohm & Swaminathan, 2004).

Marcussen (1997) stated that online activities between suppliers and customers will become more interactive, and online bookings and payment of services within the travel and hospitality settings will be more prevalent. However, Curtis (2000) argued that despite the large online population increase in recent years, consumers are more likely to browse on the Internet for information search rather than to purchase online. In order to better develop and promote travel related products, tourism suppliers should understand the determinants of consumer intentions to purchase online (Lin, 2007). Prior studies have investigated consumer online buying behaviors (Lin, and Lu, 2000; Shih, 2004; Chu, 2001; Karayanni, 2003). Prior studies have shown that the factors affecting online purchase intention include payment security, price, website reputation, website usability (design or ease of use), and website functionality (content) (Kim and Kim, 2004; Koo, 2006; Law and Hsu, 2006; Ho and Lee, 2007).

Although prior studies have investigated consumers' purchase intentions on travel websites, these studies rarely compare and contrast the perceptions of the experienced and inexperienced travelers and identifying the reason of why the travelers do not purchase online. Additionally, this study selects Hong Kong consumers as target respondents. This is because Hong Kong is a well developed region in tourism. In 2008, Hong Kong was ranked second in the Euromonitor International's Top City Destinations Ranking. Song, Wong and Chon (2003) stated that Hong Kong is a very popular and unique travel destination which represents western life style with Chinese traditions. It presents a diverse, cultural and sophisticated metropolis (HKTB Around the world, 2007). Additionally, Hong Kong is one of the leading outbound tourist generators in the Asia-Pacific region (Zhang, Qu and Tang, 2007).

This study makes an initial attempt to determine online and offline perceptions of travelers in Hong Kong based on their travel experience (in terms of experienced and inexperienced travelers). The objectives of the study are:

- to compare and contrast the perceptions between experienced and inexperienced online buyers on the factors affecting online purchase intention;
- to identify the differences between experienced and inexperienced online buyers on travel related website selections; and
- to summarize and classify the reasons for why consumers do not make online purchase.

2 Literature review

The primary reasons of consumers to shop online are convenience, time saving, better prices, availability, and customer service (Ahuja, Gupta and Raman, 2003; Rohm & Swaminathan, 2004). In the context of tourism, online sources provide a highly effective medium to travelers. However, it remains largely unknown on what factors affect consumers' decision making on online purchase. Prior studies strived to investigate this topic. For instance, Beldona, Morrison, and O'Leary (2005) summarized nine reasons for consumer purchasing on travel related websites. Buhalis and Law (2008) designated that online privacy is the main reason for many travelers to use the Internet for information search and subsequently making purchase offline. Additionally, Kim and Kim (2004) found that convenience, price, and safety are the three significant reasons for both online and offline customers. Similarly, Wolfe, Hsu, and Kang (2004) argued that the lack of personal service, security issues, lack of experience, and time consuming are the four major reasons for consumers not buying travel products online. Weber and Roehl (1999) further suggested that website designers in the hospitality industry should understand the differences and characteristics between online and offline customers for setting website and marketing strategies.

In general, the first step for selling online is to attract consumers. This requires a qualified website performance measurement such as website design and visual appeal (Kim and Steol, 2003). Bai, Law, and Wen (2008) also indicated that website quality has an indirect impact on customers' online purchase intentions. The perceived website usefulness can thus be a scale to reflect the website's ability to attract existing customers (Shankar, Smith, & Rangaswamy, 2000). In terms of consumers' online search behavior, they are more likely to search on the basis of brand names (Andrews and Currim, 2004). Beatty and Ferrell (1998) also found that the familiarity can increase trust, thus, the possibility of purchasing online may be affected by consumers' familiarity with a particular brand. Moreover, Koo (2006) argued that during the purchase stage, purchase-related services such as information quality, security, and product assortment seem more important to consumers. Additionally, the payment security and privacy concerns were the major concerns to many consumers while shopping online (Ahuja, Gupta and Raman, 2003). Price has been found as a major reason to consumers who make online purchasing (Starkov and Price, 2003), because online promotions always provide lower prices than offline (Degeratu, Rangaswamy and Wu, 2000).

Despite the existence of many prior studies on examining online consumers' purchase intentions, these prior studies have largely failed to investigate the views of consumers on their ways of choosing travel websites. To fill this research gap, this study makes an attempt to identify the specific reasons for why offline travelers did not make online purchase, identifying the differences on choosing travel websites between experienced and inexperienced travelers, and finding out online buyers' perceptions in different factors that may affect their decision making on online purchase. These factors consisted of payment security that refers to the perceived trustfulness of online transaction, price that is the price of online travel related products, and website's reputation which relates to the determination of how well or bad of an online brand may affect on consumers' online opinion. The other two other factors were also examined in this study were website's usability that refers to the website design and easy of use and website functionality for showing the website content. A contribution of this research is the comparison of differences between experienced and inexperienced travelers on their views. In other words, this research not only identifies the perceptions of online and offline respondents but also compares the difference between these two groups on their perceptions.

3 Methodology

A questionnaire was designed to examine the perception of experienced and inexperienced travelers on travel websites. The questionnaire included two main sections. A qualifying question at the beginning of the questionnaire asked whether a respondent had purchased any travel related products/services from the Internet in the past 24 months. If not, they were requested to specify the reason. The first section asked the respondents to indicate where they had purchased their online travel products, and asked them to indicate three most important factors among the five factors of payment security, price, website's reputation, website's usability, and website's functionality, which may affect consumers' online purchase decision making. The second section collected the respondents' demographic data in terms of gender, age group, education level, self-determined travel experience, and average monthly household income.

The data were collected by telephone interviews in March 2009 in Hong Kong. All telephone numbers of the samples were generated by a random-digit dialing sample method. Each sampled respondent were contacted three times until this survey could be successfully completed or could not be further answered. A total of 17,837 numbers had been dialed and the contact rate was 82.55%. At the end, 1,478 telephone interviews were completed successfully and the response rate was 10.0%.

4 Findings

Among the 1,478 respondents, 189 had purchased from travel related websites in the past 2 years, 70 of them were self-identified as experienced travelers, and 119 were self-identified as inexperienced travelers, representing 37.1 and 62.9 percent of the qualified sample in Table 1.

The numbers of male and female respondents were about the same. A majority of online buyers in Hong Kong were aged from 26 to 45, completed college/university diploma degree, with high monthly family income. The experienced travelers were generally aged 36 to 45, completed college/university diploma degree and with more than HK$70,000 monthly family income. In contrast, the inexperienced travelers were younger, aged 26 to 35, completed college/university diploma degree, with HK$20,000 to HK$39,999 monthly family income. The findings indicated that the experienced travelers were more mature with higher education qualification and monthly family income, and for this reason, they have more disposable income to travel than the younger respondents

Table 1. Demographic Profile for Respondent who has Online Purchase Experience

Variable	Experienced Traveler (N=70)		Inexperienced Traveler (N=119)	
Gender (N=185)	**Number**	**%**	**Number**	**%**
Male	29	35.4%	53	64.6%
Female	41	38.3%	66	61.7%
Age (N=189)				
25 or less	5	20.0%	20	80.0%
26-35	13	22.8%	44	77.2%
36-45	27	44.3%	34	55.7%
46-55	17	56.7%	13	43.3%
56-65	6	60.0%	4	40.0%
66 or above	2	100.0%	0	0.0%
Education (N=189)				
Less than secondary/high school	5	24.0%	16	76.0%
Completed secondary/high school	9	25.0%	27	75.0%
(Attended) Some college or university	3	25.0%	9	75.0%
Completed college/university diploma degree	40	40.0%	60	60.0%
Completed postgraduate degree	13	65.0%	7	35.0%
Income (HK$) (N=158)				
Less than 9,999	4	80.0%	1	20.0%
10,000 –19,999	5	25.0%	15	75.0%
20,000 – 29,999	6	20.0%	24	80.0%
30,000 – 39,999	8	25.0%	24	75.0%
40,000 – 49,999	7	30.4%	16	69.6%
50,000 – 59,999	9	56.3%	7	43.8%
60,000 – 69,999	3	42.9%	4	57.1%
70,000 or above	14	53.8%	12	46.2%

Note: i.* Significant at $p<0.05$

ii. Some respondents did not provide information for certain variables, leading to unequal number of respondents in the variables.

Respondents were asked to indicate the online channels which they purchased their travel products in the past two years. The results were divided into two groups of experienced and inexperienced travelers. The terms "supplier" and "travel agent" refer to the websites that are owned by suppliers (e.g. hotels or airlines) and travel agents. The term "others" was used to describe and categorize, based on respondents' input, as online travel insurances, online fund transfer, and online ticket purchasing. It is possible that some respondents purchased via multiple channels, and different combinations are exhibited in Fig. 1.

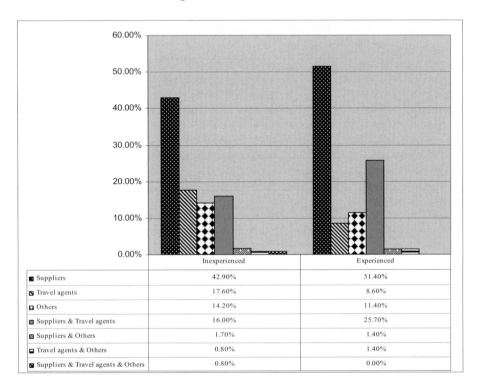

	Inexperienced	Experienced
Suppliers	42.90%	51.40%
Travel agents	17.60%	8.60%
Others	14.20%	11.40%
Suppliers & Travel agents	16.00%	25.70%
Suppliers & Others	1.70%	1.40%
Travel agents & Others	0.80%	1.40%
Suppliers & Travel agents & Others	0.80%	0.00%

Fig. 1. Online Channels Selection

According to the empirical, both inexperienced and experienced travelers were more likely to purchase directly from the websites of suppliers. Moreover, many respondents purchase the travel products by combining both supplier and travel agent websites. Additionally, experienced travelers were more likely to purchase on supplier websites (51.4%) or used both supplier and travel agent websites (25.7%). A few of them also purchased from other kinds of websites (11.4%) or travel agent websites (8.6%). In contrast, among the inexperienced travelers, 42.9% of them purchased from supplier websites, and only a few made purchase from travel agent websites (17.6%), others (14.2%), and supplier and travel agent websites (16.0%).

This study also investigates the perceptions of the factors which may influence consumers' online purchase decision-making. In the survey, online travel product buyers were asked to indicate the top three important factors among the five factors, and the ranked results are showed in Table 2.

Apparently, payment security was the most important factor to both experienced and inexperience travelers. Price and websites' reputation were indicated as the second and third most important factors. To experienced travelers, payment security and price were equally important. However, payment security was considered as more important than price by inexperienced travelers This shows that inexperienced travelers are unfamiliar with online purchasing process, and thus, payment security was considered as more important than price. Furthermore, website's reputation was more important to inexperienced travelers as compared with experienced travelers. Such a result is likely attributed to inexperienced travelers' limited travel and online purchase experience, and for this reason, a website with a good creditability appears more important. As well, website usability is less important to experienced travelers. However, it was more important to inexperience travelers. Experienced travelers generally have plenty of travel and online purchase experience which may take them less time to learn on how to make an order from a travel website. Hence, the factor of website functionality was considered as relatively more important.

Table 2. Perceived Importance of Different Factors

Variable	Experienced (n=70)		Inexperienced (n=119)	
Perceived Important Factors	**Number**	**%**	**Number**	**%**
Payment security	58	82.9%	104	87.4%
Price	58	82.9%	100	84.0%
Website's reputation	45	64.3%	87	73.1%
Website's usability (Design or ease of use)	18	25.7%	28	23.5%
Website's functionality (Content)	21	30.0%	23	19.3%

The research also invited the respondents who had not purchased any travel products online in past two years to specify the reason why they did not make any online purchase. In total, 478 respondents (37.08%) answered this question. Table 3 grouped these reasons into five main categories.

Respondents mainly pointed out that they prefer to buy travel products from traditional travel agents in order to get "person-to-person contact". The benefits of personal service are easy to communicate, get interactions during purchase, get immediate response when asking questions, and receive a formal receipt after payment. Many people also indicated that they "do not use online shopping" which is caused by many reasons such as they do not know how to purchase online, cannot find suitable travel plans or products, perceive online purchase procedures as complicated and not easy to get refund, and rather ask for help from friends or family members. Some respondents also considered "price" and "security" are the major two barriers which block their decision on online purchase. They thought that the price offered on a website is unstable or unreal. To these respondents, the Internet is not a secure and reliable source to expose their personal information and credit card details.

Moreover, many respondents merely used the Internet as an information center for information gathering but not purchasing.

Table 3. The Reasons for not Purchasing Online

Classified Reasons	Reasons from the Respondents
1 .Lack of person-to-person contact	Prefer going to travel agents in-person Travel agents' office location are already convenient Need formal receipts No human interactions/want to have human interactions during purchase Not easy to communicate online Can't make immediate enquires online
2. Do not want to use online shopping	Online procedures are too complicated and not easy to get refund Online services and products provide little details/do not have enough choices and information No travel plans No suitable products Do not like shopping online Ask help from family members/friends instead of the Internet Do not know how to shop online Not necessary
3. Price	Price may not be the lowest
4. Insecure	Not feeling reliable to purchase online Not feeling secure to provide personal information online No confidence Feel unreal
5. Internet information is for reference only	Surfing online for reference only For reference only, not intent to buy online

Table 4 presents the percentages of the five reasons listed in Table 3, categorized by experienced and inexperienced travelers. Apparently, the primary reason for consumers not to purchase online was "do not want to use online shopping" as indicated in Table 3. There were eight sub-reasons within "Do not want to use online shopping" which indicated why people do not choose online channel to purchase. In general, the consumers consider online information is limited or not detailed enough, they like to ask suggestions and help from friends, and online procedures are too complicated which is not easy to them to get refund. The second reason was "insecure". There were four sub-reasons within "insecure" which indicated that consumers feel online environment is unreliable and they do not have the confidence on providing personal information online. The "Lack of person-to-person contact" was the third reason. There are small group of consumers (10.8%) require for person to person contact during their purchasing. The "Price" and "Internet information is for reference only" were the fourth and fifth reason. In general, experienced and inexperienced respondents had similar results. The only difference was that inexperienced users were more likely to use the Internet for reference and to search for travel information.

Table 4. Reasons for Experienced and Inexperienced Travelers not purchase online

Reasons of not purchase online	Experienced (n=83)		Inexperienced (n=395)	
	Number	%	Number	%
1. Do not want to use online shopping	47	56.6%	172	43.5%
2. Insecure	24	28.9%	143	36.2%
3. Lack of person-to-person contact	9	10.8%	62	15.7%
4. Price	3	3.7%	9	2.3%
5. Internet information is for reference only	0	0.0%	9	2.3%

5 Discussion and Conclusions

This study has compared the differences between inexperienced and experienced travelers on their online and offline purchasing intention. In general, Hong Kong online buyers were young and highly educated with fairly high monthly family income. This result matches with Kim and Kim (2004)'s study, which indicated that consumers who search or purchase online were relatively young, highly educated and with high incomes. Additionally, the results showed that compared with their inexperienced counterparts, experienced travelers were older, had higher education background, and with higher monthly family income. They were also likely to make purchase solely from supplier websites or shopping by combining both supplier and travel agent websites. These findings showed that experienced travelers are more affordable on online purchase and skilful in making travel orders online. They could easily make their own travel plans and got lower price than inexperienced travelers. In contrast, inexperienced travelers were more likely to make their online purchase separately. This is because they have less travel experience and it is not easy for them to make an independent travel arrangement. Therefore, practitioners should be aware of the differences between these two groups of consumers. For instance, travel agents should list their special promotions at a visible place on their website as a remarkable sign to experienced travelers. Online suppliers could also try to provide a comprehensive product list in order to attract the attention from inexperienced travelers.

In this research, the perceived most important factors to Hong Kong online buyers were *payment security, price,* and *website's reputation.* As previously mentioned, payment security was the major barrier for online purchase and price was recognized as an important factor to consumers to shop online (Starkov and Price, 2003; Buhalis and Law, 2008). However, both experienced and inexperienced travelers have different perceptions on these three factors. Payment security was considered as a more important factor to the inexperienced travelers. As discussed, inexperienced travelers have less online travel purchase experience. As such, they have more concerns when making online payment. Thus, practitioners should provide more background information about their online payment system in order to increase the purchase intension of inexperienced travelers. Furthermore, although website usability and functionality were not indicated as important factors to online buyers, these are still the fundamental factors for website development. Prior studies have shown the website usefulness performance could affect the attractiveness to online consumers (Law and Hsu, 2006; Bai, Law and Wen, 2008).

The major contribution of this research is to identify the reason why offline consumers do not make online purchase. Empirical findings revealed that the major factor affecting inexperienced travelers was "Do not use online purchase". Based on the sub-reasons of "Do not use online purchase", practitioners should consider providing comprehensive information with a simple website structure and signing a clear statement on how to refund online. To provide an online forum for consumers to communicate and share experiences is also very important on attracting consumers to visit and purchase. The consumers also indicated that they feel insecure to pay online and prefer to have face-to-face interactions. Practitioners ought to improve the website credibility in order to increase the online visit and booking rate. Another reason that showed offline respondents seldom use the Internet as an information resource was attributed to their unawareness of the benefits for going online. According to the reasons which appear that website usefulness is very important on attracting offline consumers especially on the development of website structure, credibility and payment functions. Additionally, Marcussen (1997) found that the younger generation has more computer and online experience than the older generation. In other words, they are more likely to use the Internet than their parents. Although many travelers still refused to use the Internet to make their travel arrangement, managers of the hospitality industry still need to make efforts on advertising the benefits of online purchasing as young people can spread the information to, and possibly influence, their parents for make online purchases.

6   Limitations and Future Study

This study has two limitations. Firstly, this research only focused on respondents with online purchase experience and the perceptions of offline travelers were not analyzed. The second limitation relates to the ranking method. Respondents were asked to select three most important factors out of a list without providing any ranking or rating. Therefore, the result can only present the total occurrence of different factors but not ranking the importance of these factors. Future studies can, and should, extend the survey in order to gather the ranking of the importance factors. Future studies can also investigate more thoroughly the effects of travel experience on online purchase and identify the attributes that may affect travelers' behaviors. Lastly, it would be beneficial for future research to focus on exploring the perceptions of experienced and inexperienced travelers on one single online channel such as a specific hotel website.

References

Ahuja, M., Gupta, B., & Raman, P. (2003). Empirical Investigation of Online Consumer Purchasing Behavior. *Communications of the ACM,* 46(12), 145-151.

Andrews, R. L., & Currim, I. S. (2004). Behavioral differences between consumers attracted to shopping online versus traditional supermarkets: Implications for enterprise design and marketing strategy. *International Journal of Internet Marketing and Advertising,* 1(1), 38-61.

Bai, B., Law, R, & Wen, I. (2008). The impact of website quality on customer satisfaction and purchase intentions: Evidence from Chinese online visitors. *International Journal of Hospitality Management,* 27(3), 391–402.

Beatty, S. E., & Ferrell, M. E. (1998). Impulse buying: Modeling its precursors. *Journal of Retailing,* 74(2), 169–191.

Beldona, S., Morrison, A. M., & O'Leary, J. (2005). Online shopping motivations and pleasure travel products: a correspondence analysis. *Tourism Management,* 26(4), 561–570.

Buhalis, D. (1999). Marketing the competitive destination of the future. *Tourism Management,* 21(1), 97-116.

Buhalis, D., & Law, R. (2008). Progress in information technology and tourism management: 20 years on and 10 years after the Internet - The state of eTourism research. *Tourism Management,* 29(4), 609–623.

Chu, R. (2001). What do online Hong Kong travelers look for on airline/travel websites? *International Journal of Hospitality Management,* 24(4), 475-492.

Chung, T. & Law, R. (2003). Developing performance indicator for hotel websites. *International Journal of Hospitality Management,* 22(1), 119-125.

Curtis, J. (2000). Cars set for online sales boom. *Marketing,* 10(1), 22-23.

Degeratu, A. M., Rangaswamy, A., & Wu, J. (2000). Consumer choice behavior in online and traditional supermarkets: The effects of brand name, price and other search attributes. *International Journal of Research in Marketing,* 17(1), 55–78.

Euromonitor International's Top City Destinations Ranking (2009). http://www.euromonitor.com/_Euromonitor_Internationals_Top_City_Destinations_ Ranking (accessed date: 28/10/2009).

HKTB Around the world (2007). http://www.discoverhongkong.com/eng/about-hktb/images/2006-2007-06.pdf (accessed date: 28/10/2009).

Hanna, J. R. P., & Millar, R. J. (1997). Promoting tourism on the Internet. *Tourism Management,* 18(7), 469-470.

Ho, C. I. & Lee, Y. L. (2007). The development of an e-travel service quality scale. *Tourism Management,* 28(6), 1434-1449.

Internet World Stats. (2007). Retrieved online from http://www.Internetworldstats.com/stats.htm (accessed date: 13/08/2009).

Karayanni, D. A. (2003). Web shoppers and non-shoppers: compatibility relative advantage and demographic. *European Business Review,* 15(3), 141-152.

Kim, W, G., & Kim, D, J. (2004). Factors affecting online hotel reservation intention between online and offline customers. *International Journal of Hospitality Management,* 23(4), 381–395.

Kim, S., & Steol, L. (2004). Apparel Retailers: Website quality dimensions and satisfaction. *Journal of Retailing and Consumer Services*, 11(2), 109–117.

Koo, D-M. (2006). The fundamental reasons of e-consumers' loyalty to an online store. *Electronic Commerce Research and Applications,* 5(2), 117–130.

Law, R. & Hsu, C. H. C. (2006). Importance of hotel website Dimensions and Attributes: Perceptions of online Browsers and online Purchasers. *Journal of Hospitality & Tourism Research,* 30(3), 295-311.

Lin, H-F. (2007). Predicting consumer intentions to shop online: An empirical test of competing theories. *Electronic Commerce Research and Applications,* 6(4), 433–442.

Lin, J, C-C & Lu, H. (2000). Towards an understanding of the behavioural intention to use a web site. *International Journal of Information Management,* 20(3), 197–208.

Marcussen, C. H. (1997). Marketing European Tourism Products via Internet/WWW. *Journal of Travel & Tourism Marketing,* 6(3), 23-34.

Rohm, A. J., & Swaminathan V. (2004). A typology of online shoppers based on shopping motivations. Journal of Business *Research,* 57(7), 748-757.

Shankar, V., Smith, R., & Rangaswamy, A. (2000). *Customer satisfaction and loyalty in online and offline environments.* Working Paper, Center for Electronic Commerce Research, Smeal College of Business, Pennsylvania State University. Retrieved online from www.ebrc.psu.edu/whatsNew/ (accessed date: 13/08/2009).

Shih, H-P. (2004). An empirical study on predicting user acceptance of e-shopping on the Web. *Information & Management,* 41(3), 351–368.

Starkov, M., & Price, J. (2003). Online travelers prefer booking directly on the hotel website. *WiredHotelier.com.* Retrieved online from http://www.wiredhotelier.com/news/4015607.html (accessed date: 13/08/2009).

Song, H., Wong, K., & Chon, K. (2003). Modeling and forecasting the demand for Hong Kong tourism. *Hospitality Management,* 22 (4), 435-451.

Weber, K. & Roehl, W. S. (1999). Profiling people searching for and purchasing travel products on the World Wide Web. *Journal of Travel Research,* 37(3), 291-298.

Wolfe, K., Hsu, C. H. C., & Kang, S. K. (2004). Buyer characteristics among users of various travel intermediaries. *Journal of Travel & Tourism Marketing,* 17(2/3), 51–62.

Zhang, H,Q., Qu, H & Tang, V,M,Y. (2004). A case study of Hong Kong residents' outbound leisure travel. *Tourism management.* 25(2). 267-273

E-Success: An Instrument for Measuring Website Success

Marcel Grüter [a],
Olivier Blattmann,
Simone von Burg, and
Thomas Myrach

[a] Institute of Information Systems, Information Management
University of Bern, Switzerland
thomas.myrach@iwi.unibe.ch

Abstract

The following study describes the development of e-Success, an instrument for assessing the success of websites from a business perspective. E-Success is based on a model derived from theory and incorporates a measurement and evaluation process, as well as an extensive catalog of objectives. By evaluating objectives according to their importance for a company, e-Success may be used to assess the success of websites of the most diverse businesses, regardless of size or sector. This enables improvement measures to be derived and provides the foundation for a successful Internet presence. Furthermore, empirical use of the instrument among Swiss hoteliers and Valais winemakers indicates specific strengths and weaknesses of e-Success.

Keywords: successful websites; success measurement; measurement instrument; objectives; monitoring of objectives.

1   Introduction

Nowadays virtually every business, from the global corporation to the smallest enterprise, has its own website. According to the Federal Office of Statistics (2007), in 2005 over 80% of all Swiss companies have their own website. An Internet site may take many different forms, from the simple, electronic calling card to highly complex portals with numerous functions. The characteristic of the website is occasionally associated with the degree of maturity of a company's internet use (e.g. Chaffey, Mayer, Johnston, & Ellis-Chadwick, 2001). In this case, however, it is argued that the specific characteristic of a website is not necessarily determined according to such a pattern, but rather by its orientation toward specific objectives that a company intends to achieve with the website. Only by means of a targeted website, which is tailored to the company, can the potential of the internet be used to optimum effect (Merx & Wierl, 2001). The literature already contains a range of approaches for assessing web presences (Müller-Lankenau, Kipp, Steenpass, & Kallan, 2005). These are frequently based on theories and models that have been discussed in other areas of IS research and trans-ferred to internet applications (e.g. adoption theory, satisfaction research, quality measurement). These models are often focused on specific aspects of the quality of internet sites such as – for example – online shopping (e.g. Barnes & Vidgen, 2002). Online sales, however, is not equally important for all businesses. Therefore not every model is equally suitable for all business and sectors. DeLone &

McLean (2004) introduce a model which deals not with the quality, but with the success of a website along the lines of IS Success by DeLone & McLean (1992; 2003). However, an ope-rationalization – which should ideally be independent of business and sector – has not yet been carried out. The measurement instrument presented in this study is intended to solve this problem. In this paper, e-Success is presented as a literature-supported instrument for determin-ing the commercial success of websites. In business administration, success is typical-ly measured in connection with a previously defined objective (Hutzschenreuter, 2007). Thus a result is only evaluated as being successful if the defined objective has been reached or exceeded. Based on this perspective, e-Success records the success of an internet presence according to a company's defined objectives. Strengths and weaknesses of a website can be localized with reference to the defined objectives, and this forms the basis upon which to look for improvement measures. Moreover, e-Success may be used for all types of business irrespective of size and sector. In this paper the development of e-Success is demonstrated and empirically supported by an implementation among selected Swiss hoteliers and winemakers. The results show strengths and weaknesses of e-Success and form the basis for empirical/quantitative testing of the model. In the following section, the basic theoretical models on which e-Success is based are presented, and the e-Success model is derived from these. In a further section the literature-supported development of e-Success is demonstrated. Subsequently the implementation of an empirical preliminary test among Swiss hoteliers and winemak-ers is described. Finally, in the last section, the results of the preliminary test are dis-cussed, limitations of the instrument are established, and implications are drawn for its practical application and for further research into e-Success.

2 The e-Success model

2.1 Theoretical Foundations

The basic principles of the e-Success model are featured in the works of DeLone & McLean (1992; 2003; 2004) and Riemer & Müller-Lankenau (2005). Firstly, the popular "IS Success Model" presents a reference framework for determining the benefit of an information system which is illustrated by means of various interconnected effectiveness categories (DeLone & McLean, 1992; 2003). Secondly, the "e-Commerce Objectives System" presents a model for deriving objectives which businesses can define and pursue by using their internet presence (Riemer & Müller-Lankenau, 2005). The e-Success model, which is illustrated in Figure 1, was developed as a synthesis between the E-Commerce Objectives System and the Updated IS Success Model. The synthesis of the two approaches is based on the fact that the IS Success Model incorporates only categories for the success of an information system. However, these are not objectives as such but merely describe cause-effect relationships and influences. The E-Commerce Objectives System, on the other hand, formulates specific objectives which businesses can pursue by using their websites. Firstly, it offers the possibility of reformulating the effectiveness categories of IS Success into objectives. Secondly, the incorporation of the E-Commerce

Objectives System enhances the reference to the application of the model in the context of Internet sites, since the IS Success Model was originally developed in the context of information systems. The synthesis of the two models thus produces a framework for formulating objectives that businesses may pursue with their websites.

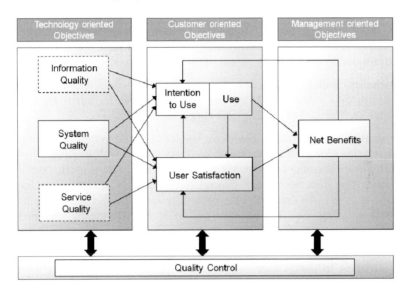

Fig. 1. The e-Success model

In the e-Success model, the six categories of information, system and service quality, use/intention to use, user satisfaction and net benefits are taken from the IS Success Model and the three types of technological, customer and management-oriented objectives are assigned from the E-Commerce Objectives System. Quality control is added as a further category. It's importance for tourism management is particularly emphasized by Müller (2004). In difference to the other categories the quality control is not part of the causal logic of the model. Interdependencies are indicated in the various objectives: the achievment of technology-oriented objectives is the basis for customer-oriented objectives which in turn influence positively the management-oriented objectives (Riemer & Müller-Lankenau, 2005). Of course, these general dependencies do not exclude that there may be trade-offs between particular objectives in a different type. In a ressource-based view, e.g., the management objective of cost reduction may somewhat contra-dict a customer oriented objective of high user satisfaction. In our operationalization, however, we have defined management objectives with respect to the use of a web site in comparison to other contact channels.

2.2 Categories

The definitions of the seven categories from the IS Success Model in e-Success have been adapted for the purposes of the E-Commerce Objectives System, so that they can be used for the context of internet sites. Following DeLone & McLean (2004) the meaning of these seven categories is explained briefly below.

Information quality. In this category, all information provided on the website is assessed. This includes content provided directly on the site as well as any material offered for downloading, such as – for example – brochures, documents, etc. The category of information quality includes both technological and customer-oriented aspects and therefore cannot be clearly assigned to one of these objective dimensions. This is illustrated in the model by means of the dashed boxes.

System quality. With system quality, the actual technical conditions and performance of the information processing system are assessed. These include – for example – components such as ease of use, response times, etc.

Service quality. Service quality covers all services offered to the user by a provider via their website. One such service might be direct contact with an employee, such as – for example – answering inquiries via a contact form. It also evaluates services that are not provided directly but are generated individually according to individual customers, such as – for example – the personalization of a website or handling of a user's personal data. Service quality likewise cannot be clearly assigned to an objective dimension since, like information quality, it includes technological and customer-oriented contents.

Usage (intention to use). Usage indicates the type, extent and intensity of use of a website by a user, whereby the user can decide whether and to what extent they use the site. This is in contrast, for example, to information systems which an employee must inevitably use frequently because this is all that is available in the company. Intention to use, on the other hand, indicates the intention of a consumer actually to use the website. This may be negative, for example if one of the three previous categories is not fulfilled, i.e. if the site cannot be loaded (system quality), the information requested from the site is not available (information quality), or the contact facility for obtaining the necessary information is missing (service quality).

User satisfaction. This category assesses satisfaction according to the usage of a website. This may, for example, be manifest in that the customer visits the site again, leaves positive feedback or activates more transactions. This category is thus dependent upon usage since only if the site has already been used can it be used again. However, if the customer's requirements are satisfied, then this may again lead to usage or intention to use. These two categories therefore interact.

Net benefits. This category summarizes all positive and negative effects of a website for the company that provides the site, in a trade-off. This may be, for example, the marketing effects of a site, such as increased awareness, or economic effects such as increased sales. The net benefit for the supplier results from the customer-oriented figures, but also itself influences the usage (intention to use) or user satisfaction. Depending on whether the net benefit is positive or negative, more or fewer resources may be made available for meeting the customer-oriented objectives.

Quality control. E-Success pursues the objective of enabling the implementation of the corporate objectives on the website to be measured. Use of the website counts as successful only if the established potential for improvement is also developed and implemented with appropriate measures (Douglas & Judge, 2001). To guarantee this outcome it is necessary to review the implementation of the improvement measures (Deming, 2000). Only then can the defined objectives be achieved and the improvement process followed to its conclusion. Quality control should, on the one hand, be used to check whether the website actually corresponds to the capabilities of the business, so that implementation of the potential for improvement may also be realistically assessed. On the other hand, problem areas can be analyzed and improvement options formulated, possibly by means of web evaluation.

3 Developing e-Success

3.1 Objectives

E-Success is intended to be used as an instrument for determining the success of a website. For this purpose a catalog of objectives has been formulated for each of the seven categories of the e-Success model, which businesses may pursue with the use of their website. 42 objectives were identified as part of a comprehensive literature analysis. Table 1 provides an overview of the catalog of objectives for e-Success. In addition to the objectives, important sources are also shown in the table. The well-cited studies of 1) DeLone & McLean (2003), 2) Barnes & Vidgen (2002), 3) Parasuraman, Zeithaml & Berry (1985), 4) Müller (2004), 5) Wang & Strong (1996) and 6) Parasuraman, Zeithaml & Malhotra (2005) were also considered for this purpose. When the objectives were being formulated, care was taken to ensure that this was done in a comprehensible and sector-independent way.

3.2 Measurement

In order to determine the success of a website, the individual objectives are each evaluated according to their effectiveness (Martilla & James, 1977). This weighting enables objectives that are less important for a business to be ignored and important objectives taken into account accordingly. An iterative process is carried out in the application of e-Success:

1. The importance of each objective is evaluated for the company in question, with the following questions being asked: "How important is this objective to you with reference to your company's website?" The answer is supplied on a Likert scale of 1 to 5, with 1 being "The objective is not important at all" and 5 being "The objective is very important".
2. The question is also asked as to whether the objective is monitored in the company: "Is this objective measured in the company?" If the answer is "Yes", the monitoring instrument is requested.
3. Next, the degree to which the objective is achieved, i.e. the actual or estimated performance of the website with reference to a specific objective, is requested. The following question is asked for each objective: "To what extent has this objective been achieved?" The answer is again given on a Likert scale of 1 to 5, in which 1 is "The objective has not been achieved at all" and 5 is "The objective has

been completely achieved". If no systematic measurement is carried out (cf. step 2) then the company is asked to estimate the level of achievement intuitively.

4. The performance difference is calculated for each objective. This is calculated as the difference between the degree of achievement and the specified importance of the objective (performance difference = degree of achievement of objective – effectiveness).

Table 1. E-Success Objectives

No.	Objectives	Sources
	Information quality	
1	Information is up-to-date	2,5
2	Information is complete	1,5
3	Information is relevant for customers	1,2,5
4	Information is comprehensible	1,2,5
5	Information is clearly structured	5,6
6	Information is credible	1,2,3,5,6
7	Information is accurate	2,4,5,6
8	The range of information is appropriate	2,5
9	The appropriate format has been selected for displaying the information	2,4
10	Information meets customer expectations	1,3
	System quality	
11	The website is easy to use	1,2,6
12	The website is easy to navigate	1,2,6
13	Secure data transfer is guaranteed	2,3,4,5,6
14	The website has a personalization function	1
15	The website is easy to maintain	1,5
16	The internet pages load quickly	1,6
17	All applications on the website run reliably	1,3,6
18	The website can always be called up	1,3,4,5,6
	Service quality	
19	The website has an attractive design	2,5
20	Contact options are easily visible to customers	2,3
21	Employees have the necessary knowledge and expertise to respond to customer inquiries and requests	1,3,4
22	Inquiries are answered efficiently	1,3,4
23	Inquiries are answered effectively, i.e. in an appropriate manner	1,3
24	The service meets the customer's individual expectations	1,2,3,4
25	The service exceeds the customer's expectations	4
26	Security in handling personal data is guaranteed	2,6
	Usage (intention to use)	
27	The website has a high number of visitors	1
28	Many transactions are carried out via the website	1
29	The website invites users to linger, awakens new expectations, and is stimulating, surprising and entertaining	1
	User satisfaction	
30	Visitors return to the website	1
31	Visitor feedback on the website is positive	1
32	The website creates a positive experience for visitors	2
33	Customers use the website repeatedly for transactions	1
34	The website creates a community feeling	2
	Net benefits	

35	Increased transactions are noted as a result of use of the website	1,5
36	Use of the website enables the awareness level to be increased	1
37	Use of the website leads to time savings	1
38	Use of the website leads to cost savings	1
39	The website communicates the desired picture/image of the company	1
Quality control		
40	The website corresponds to the staffing, technical and financial capabilities of the company	3
41	Errors that occur are recognized and treated as opportunities for improvement	4
42	Improvements are carried out and their success monitored	4

3.3 Analysis

Finally, the results are analyzed. To be able to measure the success of a company's Internet presence, the instrument must – on the one hand – be formulated generally so that the measurement is sufficiently reliable and can also be compared with other measurements. On the other hand, it should also be specifically adaptable to the extent that it enables individual statements to be tailored to the company, thus generating maximum possible usage for the individual company. These two mutually competing claims are implemented in e-Success by the application of an analysis scheme following the Importance Performance Analysis according to Martilla & James (1997). The objectives and the items summarized according to categories are organized into a portfolio, with the axes being importance of objective and degree of achievement of objective. An Importance-Performance portfolio such as this is shown in Figure 2. The performance difference diagonal is marked between the two axes. All points on these straight line have a performance difference of zero in each case, i.e. importance is equal to degree of achievement. This indicates optimum usage of available resources in order to achieve the objectives according to their importance. If the point lies to the left of the diagonal, then the performance difference is negative and the objective is not fulfilled. If the point is to the right of the diagonal then the performance difference is positive and the objective is thus exceeded.

In order to improve the optical readability of the data, further diagonal reference lines are drawn parallel to the middle diagonal. These indicate the distance from the optimum in each case. This means that the performance difference on the first reference line to the left and right of the middle diagonal is -1 and 1 respectively, etc. The further away the lines are from the optimum, the worse the performance difference. This is clarified further by the shading from white to dark grey. In the white area, convergence toward the optimum is desirable but not essential. The further into the light and dark grey an objective is situated, the more urgently it must be addressed. The axis for achievement of objective is also used for visually clarifying objectives with high and low importance. Objectives above the achievement axis should be treated as having priority over those below it. This is achieved in that, if a large number of objectives are unachieved, those that are ranked as particularly important are dealt with first.

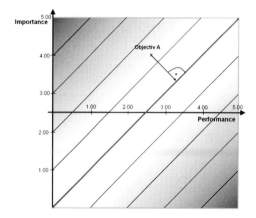

Fig. 2. E-Success Importance-Performance Portfolio

4 Applying e-Success

The application of e-Success in practice is used as a preliminary test for the e-Success model, for the applicability of the catalog of objectives and for the evaluation of the measurement and evaluation process. In order to demonstrate the flexibility of the instrument, e-Success was applied in two different industries. In a first preliminary test three Swiss hoteliers were questioned about their websites, and eight Valais winemakers were interviewed in a second preliminary test. This survey consisted of a 30-minute telephone interview with the person responsible for the Internet presence in each company. The interviews were then evaluated. After the first part of the survey was completed, the testers were additionally asked in an open section whether they were aware of monitoring instruments and measures for improving this situation, and whether they used these.

4.1 E-Success and hoteliers

Managers or website administrators of three hotel operations from a major tourist location in the Bernese Oberland were selected for the first installation of the measurement instrument. The star classification was used as the selection criterion. One hotel each was selected from the four-star, three-star and two-star category. There are negative performance differences for 26 out of 30 objectives covered in this survey (86%). The objectives are therefore below the required level. Two objectives (7%) have a performance difference of 0 and are thus fulfilled. Two further objectives (7%) show a positive performance difference and have therefore been exceeded. On the basis of the findings on the use of the instrument in this first preliminary test the catalog of objectives was revised, resulting in the catalog of objectives shown in Table 1. In the first line of this certain objectives were worded more clearly and the catalog was extended from 30 to 42 lines. In addition, the Importance-Performance portfolio of Martilla & James (1997) was revised and the scheme shown in Figure 2 was developed. The first version of e-Success and the modifications on the basis of the first preliminary test are documented in Blattmann, von Burg, & Grüter, (2008) and von Burg, Blattmann, & Grüter (2009).

4.2 E-Success and Winemakers

The eight winemakers interviewed reflect the typical structure of the wine-growing sector in Valais. The individual winemakers have a production volume of approximately 30,000 to 800,000 liters of wine per year and therefore constitute small and medium-sized enterprises such as are typical for Swiss wine production overall. The results of the survey are shown in the evaluation portfolio in Figure 3. In addition to the distribution of average performance differences of the individual objectives, the average performance differences of the seven categories from the e-Success were also marked in the portfolio. As the diagram shows, the achievement levels are below the corresponding effectiveness level for 41 of the 42 objectives (97.6%) across all the businesses. Subsequently, if viewed across all businesses (with reference to the eight winemakers interviewed), a consistently negative balance in performance differences can be recorded across all the businesses. The required objectives could only be achieved to an unsatisfactory level. Furthermore, it can be seen that 25 out of 42 objectives (59.5%) have a performance difference lower than minus one. However, the performance difference is not lower than minus three for any of the objectives considered.

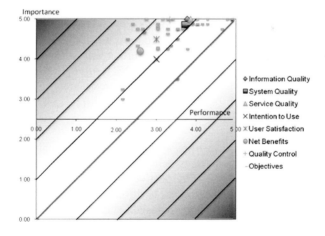

Fig. 3. Winemakers' Importance-Performance portfolio

As may be seen in Figure 3, all seven categories have a negative performance difference. The portfolio thus indicates a need for improvement in every category. The largest differences in performance are to be seen in usage (intention to use) (-1.96) and in net benefits (-1.53), followed by user satisfaction (-1.31), quality control (-1.17) and information quality (-1.15). The smallest differences in performance, with values not going below minus one, may be seen in the categories of service quality (-0.89) and system quality (-0.97).

5 Concluding Remarks

5.1 Discussion of e-Success

The implementation of e-Success among three Swiss hoteliers and eight Valais wine-makers enabled the instrument's strengths and weaknesses to be identified. In general, the application of the instrument in two different sectors confirmed the sector-independence of e-Success. Evaluation of the objectives depending on their importance also proved useful. Thus the instrument may be used flexibly and comparisons may be made with reference to the success of different websites. The logic of the e-Success model could be confirmed for the most part. Up to the usage (intention to use) value, the performance differences in the categories reflect the causal relationships of the e-Success model. This means that information quality, system quality and service quality have the smallest performance differences, which are increasingly larger in the subsequent categories. After all, if the three quality categories have shortcomings, then logically the subsequent categories are likewise not fulfilled. If these also have shortcomings in terms of achievement of objectives, then the cumulative performance difference must be even more profound. Only the net benefits category, as the "final" category, does not have the lowest value as modeled, but the category of usage (intention to use) does. This could indicate that the net benefits depend not only on usage (intention to use) and on user satisfaction, but also on further influencing factors. Due to the non-representative nature of the sample, however, this irregularity will not be discussed further here since there is currently not enough data for reliable interpretation, and since this result may also have been due to a chance variation or distortion as a result of unanswered items.

5.2 Practical Implications

E-Success offers businesses an instrument enabling them to analyze the success of their website. By recording the levels of achievement of objectives according to their importance, e-Success can be used irrespective of the company size and sector. It promises optimum distribution of resources to different objectives in accordance with their importance. In addition, it supports managers with structured quality control and in-house success analysis. E-Success can therefore be used to carry out a fundamental assessment in order to derive quality assurance and improvement measures. It permits analysis, in quite specific terms, of where the problem areas are and where the improvement measures need to be applied. In addition, the success of any improvement measures implemented may be reviewed in a subsequent stage. However, even though this may enable meaningful results to be determined, businesses should look carefully at the evaluation of the individual objectives as well as their relative importance. This is the only way in which benefit may also be derived from the analysis.

5.3 Limitations and Future Research

The long catalog of objectives appears to be a disadvantage. There is therefore a risk that the questions will be answered in an arbitrary rather than a deliberate manner. All objectives were assessed as relatively important and therefore there was little differentiation between them. This inflation of importance may have been due, among other things, to the brief reflection time during the telephone interviews and the length of the questionnaire. Furthermore, during the preliminary test minor ambiguities were found with regard to the exact meaning of individual terms. For example, in the section on information quality a few respondents failed to understand the meaning of the terms "personalization function" or "community feeling". In addition, feedback indicated that certain objectives are difficult to estimate and that such estimation should actually be carried out by the Internet users themselves. A further disadvantage may sometimes be the fact that scarcely all objectives can be measured, since otherwise a disproportionally large outlay would be incurred depend-ing on the company. Thus an intuitive estimation of achievement levels is necessa-rywhich is subject to possible distortions such as social desirability, and subsequently, to a tendency to overestimate the achievement of objectives (Diekmann, 2004). To date, e-Success has been empirically tested only by means of a minor random sample. Even though this process permits initial conclusions to be drawn regarding the quality and reliability of the instrument, it does not, however, offer a foundation for statistical analysis of the postulated relationships in the model. In a subsequent stage, therefore, the items, categories and the entire model in the larger context should be quantitatively tested by means of a written online survey. A quantitative survey could also stem the inflation of importance to some degree. Since the respondents needed to reply relatively quickly during the telephone interview, the assessments of the importance of the individual objectives turned out all to be similarly high. In a written survey the respondents have more time to consider the evaluation of the dif-ferent objectives more accurately. This would enable the importance evaluation to be carried out with a greater degree of differentiation. It would be possible, in a subsequent stage, to derive benchmarks on the basis of a quantitative study. These could be used to derive recommendations in the individual categories and objectives. Thus, for example, the analysis of general problem areas provide indicators for the development and implementation of improvement options. It would also be conceivable for different instruments for monitoring to be compiled or developed in order to measure objectives that have not yet been systematically monitored. Such further developments, which are suitable for practical application, would increase the value of e-Success still further.

References

Barnes, S. J., & Vidgen, R. T. (2002). An Integrative Approach to the Assessment of E-Commerce Quality. *Journal of Electronic Commerce Research*, 3(3), 114-127.

Blattmann, O., von Burg, S., & Grüter, M. (2008). Erfolgreicher Interneteinsatz – e-Success: Ein Instrument zur Bestimmung des Erfolgs von Internetauftritten. Getestet bei Schweizer Hotelleriebetrieben. *Working Paper Nr. 20, Institut of Information Systems, University of Bern.* Bern.

98

Chaffey, D., Mayer, R., Johnston, K., & Ellis-Chadwick, F. (2001). *Internet Marketing*. München: Pearson Studium.

DeLone, W. H., & McLean, E. R. (1992). Information Systems Success: The Quest for the Dependent Variable. *Information Systems Research*, 3(1), 60-95.

DeLone, W. H., & McLean, E. R. (2003). The DeLone and McLean Model of Information Systems Success: A Ten-Year Update. *Journal of Management Information Systems*, 19(4), 9-30.

DeLone, W. H., & McLean, E. R. (2004). Measuring e-Commerce Success: Applying the DeLone & McLean Information Systems Success Model. *International Journal of Electronic Commerce*, 9(1), 31-47.

Deming, E. (2000). *Out of the Crisis*. Cambridge: The MIT Press.

Diekmann, A. (2004). *Empirische Sozialforschung: Grundlagen, Methoden, Anwendungen*. Hamburg: Rowohlt Taschenbuch Verlag.

Douglas, T. J., & Judge, W. Q. (2001). Total Quality Management Implementation and Competitive Advantage: The Role of Structural Control and Exploration. *Academy of Management Journal*, 44(1), 158-169.

Federal Office of Statistics (2007). *IKT-Infrastruktur in den Unternehmen*. Retrieved from http://www.bfs.admin.ch/bfs/portal/de/index/themen/16/04/key/approche_globale.indicator.30201.302.html.

Hutzschenreuter, T. (2007). *Allgemeine Betriebswirtschaftslehre: Grundlagen mit zahlreichen Praxisbeispielen*. Wiesbaden: Gabler.

Martilla, J. A., & James, J. C. (1977). Importance-Performance Analysis. *Journal of Marketing*, 41(1), 77-79.

Merx, O., & Wierl, M. (2001). Qualität und Qualitätskriterien im E-Commerce. In A. Hermans and M. Sauter (Eds.), *Management-Handbuch Electronic Commerce* (88-100). München: Verlag Franz Vahlen.

Müller, H. R. (2004). *Qualitätsorientiertes Tourismus-Management*. Bern: Haupt.

Müller-Lankenau, C., Kipp, A., Steenpass, J., & Kallan, S. (2005). Web-Evaluation: Erhebung und Klassifikation von Evaluationsmethoden. *Working Paper Nr. 22, Kompetenzcenter für Internetökonomie und Hybridität, Universität Münster*. Münster.

Parasuraman, A., Zeithaml, V. A., & Berry, L. (1988). SERVQUAL: A Multiple-Item Scale for Measuring Consumer Perceptions of Service Quality. *Journal of Retailing*, 64(1), 12-40.

Parasuraman, A., Zeithaml, V. A., & Malhotra, A. (2005). E-S-QUAL: A Multiple-Item Scale for Assessing Electronic Service Quality. *Journal of Service Research*, 7(3), 213–233.

Riemer, K., & Müller-Lankenau, C. (2005). Web-Evaluation: Einführung in das Internet-Qualitätsmanagement. *Working Paper Nr. 21, Kompetenzcenter für Internetökonomie und Hybridität, Universität Münster*. Münster.

Von Burg, S., Blattmann, O., & Grüter, M. (2009). Weiterentwicklung von eSuccess - Ein Instrument zur Bestimmung des Erfolgs von Internetauftritten. *Working Paper Nr. 223, Institut of Information Systems, University of Bern*. Bern.

Wang, R. Y., & Strong, D. M. (1996). Beyond Accuracy: What Data Quality Means to Data Consumers. *Journal of Management Systems*, 12(4), 5-34.

Presenting UsERA: User Experience Risk Assessment Model

Alessandro Inversini[a]
Lorenzo Cantoni[a], and
Davide Bolchini[b]

Webatelier.net
[a]School of Communication Sciences
University of Lugano, Switzerland
(alessandro.inversini, lorenzo.cantoni)@usi.ch

[b]Human-Computer Interaction Program
School of Informatics, Indianapolis
Indiana University, U.S.A.
dbolchin@iupui.edu

Abstract

Ensuring usability is an extremely important issue for DMO websites which act as information hubs for all destinations' stakeholders. This work presents an approach to integrate *usability* evaluation and analysis of *usages* for DMO websites in an innovative and holistic framework, called UsERA (user experience risk assessment model), based on the notion of risk analysis. The approach is exemplified through its application to the usability and usage data an Italian DMO website. The results from this case study illustrate a close relationship between usability evaluation and usages analysis and show how this relationship can be studied to enhance managers' critical thinking about website improvements.

Keywords: user experience; risk; vulnerability; resilience; usability analysis; destination management organization.

1 Originality

While Destination Management Organizations (DMO) are realizing the importance of online communication for the accomplishment of their mission, they still need a general framework to analyze their actual performances and systematically inform their improvement. Both usability analyses and usages analyses (also known as log file analysis, or web analytics) are extensively applied to address these issues, providing interesting results and suggestions. Nonetheless, a more *systemic* approach is needed, able to detect problems (coming from different data sources about the users and the design) and to prioritize them, so that DMO website managers could take better informed decisions, and better invest their money and resources, ensuring that these efforts are aligned with their business goals. In this paper, a combination of both approaches - usability and web analytics - is proposed, showing how they can complement each other, and how – once combined – they can provide website managers with much more than just the sum of each individual analysis. The combined approach proposed in this paper yields to the UsERA (User Experience Risk Assessment) Model. The UsERA Model describes the interplay between usability and usages analysis formalizing the interaction between the two approaches and leading to more structured information for website destinations' managers.

2 Review of Background

According to Garrett (2003), "user experience is not about how a product works on the inside (although that sometimes has a lot of influence), but it is about how it works on the outside, where a person comes into contact with it and has to work with it". The same author describes the website as a "self service product", where no instruction manual or seminar is provided: users face the website alone, only with their experience guiding them (Garrett, 2003). Furthermore, Kuniavsky (2003) investigated the concept of user experience identifying three main factors that positively affect user experience, namely (i) functionality, which considers the website usefulness with regard to the users, (ii) efficiency, which considers the time needed by the users to accomplish specific tasks, and finally (iii) desirability, which considers the users' feelings of surprise and satisfaction with regards to the web application. ISO (International Organization for Standardization) defines usability (ISO 9241) as "the effectiveness, efficiency and satisfaction with which specified users achieve specified goals in particular environments". The various aspects of this definition are also supported by Cantoni and Tardini (2006) which define usability according to the Website Communication Model (in short WCM) as "the adequacy of contents/functionalities (pillar I [of the Website Communication Model - WCM]) and accessibility tools (pillar II), between themselves and with respect to the users (pillar IV) and the relevant context (world). Moreover, this adequacy has to be measured by taking into consideration the goals of people who commission, design, develop, promote and run the website (pillar III)" (Cantoni and Tardini, 2006: 129-130). Usage analysis (or log files analysis) is, in general, one of the most interesting activities to perform on a website if there is no possibility of involving users during usability testing (Atterer et al., 2006). In general terms, log files are the traces left by the user while visiting the web site; this specific group of files reside on the server that record users' activities while they are visiting the website. The study of the log files is not an engineering activity as such: log files analysis can give interesting information at a communicative level (Cantoni and Ceriani, 2007) such as the study of the users' paths along the website (Pitkow, 1997), by which it is possible to optimize the communication flow of the application. As one of the main purposes of a DMO website is to attract and increase visits to the destination (Shanshan et al., 2007), the quality of its online communication should be very high; otherwise, as explained by some empirical studies, a huge amount of users might leave the website because of usability problems (e.g. Souze et al., 2000). Moreover, as stated by the World Tourism Organization, DMO websites can promote destination products (WTOBC, 2000), and act as a bridge in promoting services and products and communicate with the market (Pike, 2005). A system, which hosts other services or products (or in other words, gives visibility to third party websites), should be well-designed and have great performances in order to satisfy both investors and end-users. Good website usability normally leads to a good website performance; therefore usability performance is a key success factor for a website (Douglas and Mills, 2004; Nielsen, 2003).

Several different researches have focused on the comparative evaluation of destinations' websites in terms of features, functions, lay-out and information presentation (e.g. Getz et al., 1998; Buhalis and Spada, 2000; Wang and Fesenmaier, 2006). Few of them focus on pure usability (e.g. Au Yeung and Law, 2003; Zhou and DeSantis, 2005), and even fewer are related to DMO website usability (e.g. Shanshan et al., 2008).

3 Theoretical Framework

The theoretical and methodological foundations developed by the community of scholars and design professionals in many fields (human-computer interaction design, usability, interaction design, marketing, software engineering) to tackle various aspects of the user experience have remained very isolated and self-contained. The consequence of such conceptual fragmentation has been a proliferation of methods and techniques that lacks a comprehensive, holistic perspective on the issues at stake. In particular, there are two areas which have seldom dialogued with one another: the study of *usability* and the study of *usages*. On the one hand, usability studies have typically focused on the empirical evaluation of the efficiency and effectiveness of the website to support user goals and tasks, with the aim of improving the quality of the design (Au Yeung and Law, 2003; Brinck, 2002; Nielsen, 1994). On the other hand, the study of *usages* has mainly addressed the analysis of website traffic, aggregated user's paths and ecological factors (referrals, in coming and out coming websites), with the purpose of informing marketing actions and visibility (Atterer, 2006). The common, unifying factor among these two areas of concerns is the study of the user as a *person exposed* to a complex, articulate – and oftentimes unpredictable – communication artifact. Interestingly, this type of situation is not at all exclusive or uniquely distinctive of electronic communication. The study of analyzing, evaluating and predicting the consequence of a person's exposition to potentially adverse events is common to many other disciplines, including – just to name a few – public health, security engineering, emergency management, and finance (Adams, 1995; Blaikie, 1994). In their theoretical frameworks, these disciplines have always leveraged a basic construct: the notion of *risk*. The relevant components, and formulae, defining *risk* vary from discipline to discipline, given the different type of problems to solve and analyze. We therefore do not review all the possible combinations and variants of conceptual constructs defining risk in the abovementioned disciplines. For the sake of our theoretical elaboration, however, we have identified some important, common factors determining risk which are readily applicable to the study of the user experience in interactive communication. The design and deployment of a destination website can be considered an enterprise which is subject to some degree of risk: actual users are often unknown (although possibly predicted during design), the actual behaviors of the users on the site is often unknown from the outset, and the actual effect or outcome of the experience with the site on the user is difficult to predict. Most importantly, the complexity of the design features of large web applications (and their *emergent properties* due to their interconnectedness) poses additional levels of unpredictability to such factors, augmenting the *risk of negative user experiences*. A proper analysis of the user experience risk would inform project managers, communication and web designers in making decisions concerning questions such as: what parts of the application require immediate attention for re-design or improvement? Are my users exposed to potentially negative experiences? How can I optimize the good experiences on my site? Our innovative contribution is the elaboration of few, basic constructs to analyze and characterize such hurdle of *risk* issues by *holistically* leveraging current approaches to *usability* analysis and *usage studies*. Overall, the risk of negative user experiences with the site is determined by 3 basic factors: threats, vulnerability and resilience (see Fig. 1), which are explained in detail in the following paragraphs.

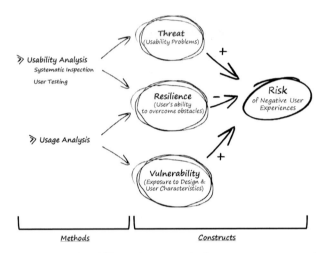

Fig. 1. The synergy of usability and usage analysis to capture user experience risk.

3.1 "Threats" as Usability Problems Inherent to the Design

The design complexity of large destination websites is often prone to usability problems. Although there are many definitions of usability problems, for the purpose of our framework, we define a usability problem as a design defect that is a potential *threat* to an optimal user experience. A long standing tradition of web usability analysis and web engineering acknowledges that usability problems of varying severity are typically inherent to how the application has been designed and, therefore, eventually lie at one or more of the following design dimensions (Triacca, et al. 2005): (i)*Content*: the core information messages of the websites, from text, to multimedia. An example of potential threat, or usability problem, at this level is the presence of non obsolete content, or the absence of contact information. (ii) *Information architecture*: the overall organization of the content in chunks and sections. An example of potential threat at this level is the classification of the content using a limited set of criteria (e.g. only by geographical location) which do not correspond to the user's natural reasoning in exploring information (e.g. I want to go skiing, no matter the specific location). (iii) *Navigation and interaction*: the strategies by which users can use and move around the information architecture through links and interact with content. An example of threat at this level is the lack of intuitive mechanisms to use an interactive map, to navigate to in-depth information from it and to print the desired information. (iv) *Services & transactions*: the strategies by which specific operations and services are organized, structured and made accomplishable by the user. (v) *Search functionality:* the way an internal search engines supports accurate and efficient retrieval of information. (vi) *Labeling and interface semiotics*: the way in which all the above mentioned aspects are conveyed at the interface level through naming conventions, layout strategies, metaphors and labels. This analytical modeling of the threats reveals critical areas of the site that do not necessarily determine a risk of negative experiences, but need to be carefully and jointly considered with respect to the vulnerability that our users may manifest.

3.2 "Vulnerability" as Exposure to Usability Problems

An area of the site (a list of hotels) with severe usability problems (out-of-date or missing contact information) may not be considered a too dangerous threat if, for instance, no user ever bumped into it (because it was completely buried in the site architecture). The fact that the list of hotels is very difficult to find mitigates the potentially destructive effect of the threat because the actual exposure of our users to it can be considered very low or null. This simple example shows that user's *vulnerability* to a threat can be defined as the exposure of the users to it, identified in terms of actual traffic or potentially accessible pathways. Of course, the fact that few users access the list of hotels has to be carefully analyzed: is that in line with overall website goals or that should be the most important website area? Are there usability problems (most probably in the navigation layer) that prevent users from reaching it? Are promotional activities bringing the most appropriate publics to the website? Etc. In addition, vulnerability also depends on the specific characteristics of our users, which may be more or less sensitive to a threat. For example, web-savvy users may find no problem in downloading an additional Flash player to enjoy a video. Senior citizens new to web technology, on the contrary, may have a hard time in figuring out what to do in this situation. The consideration of these elements determines important factors that influence the degree of vulnerability of our users.

3.3 "Resilience" as the User's Ability to Overcome Usability Problems

Whereas vulnerability identifies the danger of a potential or actual exposure to a threat, risk can be highly mitigated by considering how and whether users actually overcome – or "survive" to (in virtual sense) – a threat. Let's assume that users often visit the section to subscribe to the newsletters, and they go through a cumbersome set of poorly organized pages to create an account, necessary to subscribe to the newsletter. The fact that 90% of the people accessing the newsletter section are eventually able to complete the task is a clear sign of high *resilience*, which is the capability of the users to overcome obstacles posed by existing threats. And this mitigates the overall risk of negative user experiences. As the user population changes, however, this resilience may radically and suddenly vary, causing a high level of risk.

3.4 The Synergy between Usability Analysis and Usage Studies

In this perspective, the existing methods and approaches to usability analysis and usage analysis can work in concert to address the key issues outlined by our user experience risk framework. Usability analysis can unearth the threats for the user experience. The main outcome of usability analysis is, in fact, an organized set of usability problems inherent to the design. Besides, usage analysis perfectly works as a complementary analytical toolkit to determine vulnerability in terms of intensity of traffic to poorly designed areas. Moreover, the study of usages can be applied to reveal episodes of resilience, as the analysis of the full paths of the user and their conversion rate is taken into consideration. Usage analysis gives only inferential indications about users behavior on the website (Cantoni and Ceriani, 2007). In sum, UsERA Model maps usability shortcomings inherent to design (threats), the actual usages of the website or the exposure to usability problems (vulnerability) and the ability of the users in overcoming the usability problems (resilience). The model emphasizes the relationship among usability and usages, to give indications to website's managers. UsERA Model results should be compared with the objectives and goals of the website managers (as it is stated in the usability definition by Cantoni and Tardini, 2006), to formulate appropriate design interventions. For example, consider that a given section of the website (e.g. accommodation) might be strategic for the DMO. Usability analysis indicates that it has a poor usability (high risk) and usage analysis indicates that it has high access (high vulnerability), and that most users do not complete a reservation (low resilience). With these data at hand, properly framed according to the proposed model, website's managers might think to plan an intervention of some kind. On the contrary, if the section is not strategic, website's managers acknowledge that there are some problems which are not so important to solve immediately. Within the whole model, log files analysis is a tool to enhance and where possible confirm the need of redesign interventions. The following sections articulate the application of our approach to the evaluation of the user experience risk analysis of an Italian destination website, opportunistically chosen (i.e. www.turismo.ravenna.it). The purpose is to show how this conceptual framework can translate into an analytical instrumentation which can be organically used to inform new discoveries in the study of the user experience and to enable better designs.

4 Research Design

To validate the above presented model, two different activities were performed on the Ravenna DMO website. Firstly an expert review following Mile+ guidelines (Milano Lugano Evaluation Method – Triacca et al., 2005) was performed. MiLE+ is a structured usability inspection protocol for large content-intensive websites which has been empirically validated on hundreds of web applications since 2002 and successfully applied to various website domains, from cultural heritage, to ecommerce, to bioinformatics. The evaluation was based on an elaborated version of the Destination Usability Kit (i.e. presented by Inversini and Cantoni, 2009) which counted 8 user profiles (i.e. description of possible users of the application), 10 goals (i.e. high level objectives of the possible users), 72 tasks (i.e. atomic actions which the user can perform on the application) and 40 evaluation heuristics (i.e. evaluation metrics). Usability issues were isolated and described in order to assess website threats. Secondly, a log files analysis over one year timeframe was conducted in order to assess vulnerability and resilience of the real users on the website. Log files were analyzed using the popular free software Funnel Web Analyzer (www.quest.com) filtering robots, crawler, internal access (i.e. Ravenna municipality) and reserved areas. Usability results and log files results were then displayed on a website map obtained with a reverse engineering exercise; different colors highlighted different website sections where risks of negative user experience could be founded.

5   Results

5.1 Usability

Ravenna DMO website presented several usability issues (n=35) which might affect the user experience while navigating it. In the next paragraphs four general (i.e. common in the whole website) and relevant (i.e. affecting most of the tasks) usability issues are presented. The first usability issue is related to the *accuracy of the information*: 6 tasks (T2.1, T2.8, T2.13, T4.1, T4.6, T8.2) out of 72 are affected by this major problem: in general terms it is possible to argue that information is often not precise, and poorly structured. Hyperlinks pointing to external resources are sometimes broken. Second level menus *position consistency* also affects different tasks (3 out of 72- T1.1, T2.1, T3.1): the navigation menu is often placed above the text and it is not visible by users using screens with a resolution less than 1324x768. In this issue two different usability problems can be highlighted: *(i) layout conventions*: it very uncommon to have second level navigation menus positioned above the the main content. Existing patterns in web page design follow different convention. *(ii) orientation*: the awkward position of the menu affects the sense of overall orientation in the navigation architecture (Where am I and Where I can go).

Fig. 2. Navigation position consistency - *T1.1- Find the city overview*

Ravenna DMO website has also some problems related to the *segmentation of the information*: the number of tasks affected by this problem is 5 out of 72 (T1.1, T1.2, T1.4, T3.8, T6.1). Information segmentation refers to editorial decision of the website designers and content managers to actually segment the information within different pages. Information should be well divided and organized in the whole website in order to let the user easily access each piece of information. Finally, the accommodation section and particularly the booking system is affected by a different number of usability issues. This issue represents a critical threat (Inversini and Cantoni, 2009) for third party stakeholders (e.g. hotels and attractions managers). The booking system seems to be a major problem which affects all the scenarios in which a booking activity is foreseen (e.g. T4.1 Find a hotel for less than x Euros per night – Figure 3).

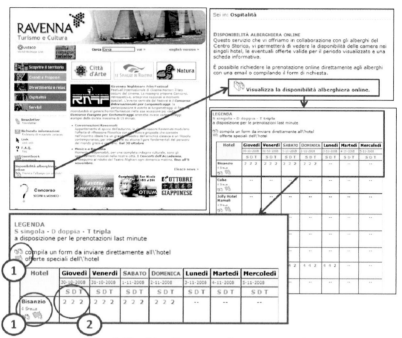

Fig. 3. Booking System turismo.ravenna.it

Usability issues are in this case related with: (i) *depth anticipation*: the user is not aware of the path and steps s/he is supposed to do inside the application to accomplish the task s/he has in mind; the user should click several times before arriving to the dedicated hotel page – choosing an hotel according to the availability – and discover that s/he need to ask (trough hotel website or as in most of the cases via email) the room availability. (ii) *icons predictability*: icons (number 1 in figure 3) are explained above the table of the hotel availability, but the is no clue about the meaning of the number and the letter in the cells (number 2 in figure 3). (iii) *labeling consistency*: two labels identify accommodation sections: "ospitalità" (i.e. ospitality) and "disponibilità alberghiere" (i.e. accommodation availability); information is not consistent and these two different buttons lead to different pages/sections (e.g. the first lead the user to the single hotel liking her/him to the hotel website, while the second label lead the user to a table of availability in figure 3 the user reaches the enquiry form where s/he could see only the availability but not directly book the hotel). The above mentioned usability issues may represent a threat within the website. On one side, the general usability issues above described generated a set of redesign recommendations that may be checked only with the involvement of real users (i.e.

user testing); but on the other side, the accommodation section was suitable for a vulnerability and resilience study. Next paragraphs describe the end users traffic on the website outlining the most viewed sections in the website and analytically describing the accommodation sections.

5.2 Usages

The log file analysis was carried out over one year period (1st of October 2007 – 1st of October 2008); Ravenna DMO websites (main website and sub domains) received 29,637,297 hits in 461,980 visitor sessions, for a total number of 289,714 unique visitors. The most visited page was the home page, which collected 69.1% (354,925 hits) of the total hits. Then different pages about the Ravenna events and initiatives such as: "notted'oro" (34,283 hits) and "mare d'inverno" (9,834 hits) were quite popular among users. Recurrent users' paths were mostly related with events: "notte d'oro" (16,169 sessions) and "mare d'inverno" (2,538 sessions). One unexpected popular sessions also regarded the bus and cycling paths download (4,099 sessions). Most of the single sessions were just initiate and terminate in the home page (116,193 sessions).

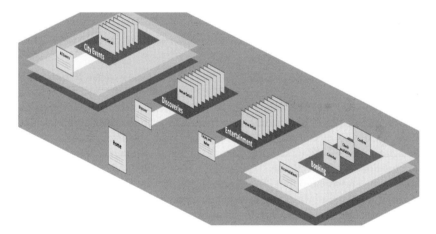

Fig. 4. Risk map of Turismo Ravenna: areas at risk are characterized by threat, vulnerability and resilience layers. The darker the resulting top layer is, the higher is the resulting risk.

As usability evaluated threats (i.e. usability problems inherent to the design), log files will help in evaluating resilience as users' ability to overcome the obstacle (i.e. accomplish tasks) and vulnerability as the degree of exposure to design (i.e. general visits). Figure 4, shows the usages with the website as explained in the previous paragraph. In general terms, it is possible to claim that events section was the most popular section within the website (1,331,800 hits and 334,683 user sessions); users can find and download online guides, maps and brochures. Accommodation section presented few accesses and was further investigated: total hits count for the whole accommodation section over the given period (the analyzed year) is 901 (i.e. 0,003%). Among these, 297 hits were on the home page of the accommodation section (32% of

901) but only few user sessions stopped on the accommodation home page (0.002%): anyway due to the website structure it was not possible to follow all the user paths inside the accommodation section because some part of it have been hosted on a different web server (different server log files were not available for analysis). Log file data showed two important results: on one hand, most of the users of Ravenna DMO website overcome usability issues (i.e. threats) to reach the given piece of content (e.g. news/events) demonstrating a high resilience in a high visited section (high vulnerability); risk is not high and usability problems seem not to strongly influence the user experience. On the other hand, threats (i.e. usability problems) within the accommodation section are quite high; resilience is high because few paths stopped into the accommodation home page (i.e. 0.002%) so that users overcome the obstacle; risk is low, mainly due to the low users' exposure. Before going for a complete website redesign based on usability report, Ravenna Tourism managers might acknowledge that users overcome some usability issues (e.g. the general ones) leading to the high visits of news and events sections. On the contrary, they should reflect on usability issues related to accommodation sections (for example labeling consistency): the two different access structures used to access accommodation sections (which might be seen as great effort to draw traffic on this specific section) turned in poor results in terms of usability and usages.

6   Conclusions and Future Work

UsERA model analysis suggested that Ravenna DMO visitors have a high resilience (i.e. users ability to overcome the obstacles) when dealing with specific information (such as events). On the other hand considering the accommodation section, although the risk represented by this section is low (mainly due to the poor number visits) the decisions about the redesign should be balanced with the managerial and strategic vision behind this specific website section: creating, managing and promoting an accommodation section could be strategic for a destination and managers can put lots of efforts (time and money) in it. The poor number of visits suggest to revise it both in technical terms (i.e. usability) and in strategic terms (i.e. relevance of the section and its promotion). Unfortunately, due to its intrinsic characteristics and due to the fact that for the considered case study they were incomplete, log files analysis could give only inferential indications at communication level (Cantoni and Ceriani, 2007). Nevertheless these indications could be really useful for destination managers to prioritize website interventions (as for example working on access structure of the accommodation section and on its promotion). Finally, Ravenna destination managers recently decided to implement a new booking system on the website informally demonstrating the importance of the accommodation section for the DMO. This new reservation system could lead to a better user experience within the booking process itself, but as the website general structure remained as it was before, it would be difficult for users to overcome usability problems (threats), leading to a poor use of the system. Usability and log files are only one of the possible measurement techniques to assess these quality problems. Results might be discussed with website's managers and should be confronted with the overall goals of the online communication. UsERA Model, gives relevant information on the studied website, highlighting the possibility of a poor user experience. Results must be confronted with online communication managers' objectives to decide interventions. Destinations' managers could find in UsERA Model a possible way to associate different quality assessment tools for their online communication in order to tackle quality issues and take more informed decisions about their websites strategy. Online tourism websites represent a ideal field for usability and usages studies due to the different type of activities that can be performed by users on websites; future work will concentrate in deeply validate the model presented through cases to be analyzed in the field of tourism but also in other fields.

References

Adams, J. (1995) *Risk*, University College London Press, London, pp 228.

Atterer,R., Wnuk, M., & Schmidt, A. (2006). Knowing the user's every move: user activity tracking for website usability evaluation and implicit interaction. *Proceedings of the 15th international conference on World Wide Web*, Edinburgh, Scotland

Au Yeung, T., &Law, R. (2003). Usability Evaluation of Hong Kong Hotel Websites. *Information and Communication Technology in Tourism*, eds. City

Blaikie, P., Cannon, T., Davis, I., & Wisner, B. (1994) *At Risk: Natural Hazards, People's Vulnerability, and Disasters*. Routledge, London, 333–352.

Bolchini, D., & Garzotto, F. (2008). Value-Driven Design for "Infosuasive" web applications. *Proceedings of the ACMInternational World Wide Web Conference*, Beijing, China.

Bolchini, D., & Paolini, P. (2006). Interactive Dialogue Model: a Design Technique for Multi-Channel Applications, *IEEE Transactions on Multimedia*, 8 (3), 529-541.

Brinck, T., Gergle, D., & Wood, S.D. (2002). Usability for the web. Morgan Kaufmann

Buhalis, D. (2003). *eTourism: Information technology for strategic tourism management*. Prentice Hall, Harlow.

Buhalis, D., & Spada, A. (2000). Destination Management Systems: criteria for success – an exploratory research. *Information and Technology in Tourism*. 3:41-58

Cantoni L., & Ceriani L. (2007). Fare comunicazione online, analisi dell'attività di un sito internet attraverso i file di log. Comunicazione Italiana, Roma.

Cantoni, L., & Tardini, S. (2006). *Internet*. Routledge, London – New York.

Carroll, J. (2002). *Making Use – Scenario-based design of Human-Computer Interactions*. MIT Press.

Douglas, A., & Mills, J.E. (2004). Staying Afloat in the Tropics: Allying a Structural Equation Model Approach to Evaluating National Tourism Organization Websites in the Caribbean. In Law, R. and Mills, J.E., *Handbook of Consumer Behavior, Tourism and the Internet*, 269-293

Garrett, J.,J. (2003). *The elements of users experience*. AIGAl, NY.

Getz, D., Anderson, D., & Sheehan, LA. (1998). Roles, issues, and strategies for convention and visitors' bureaux in destination planning and product development: a survey of Canadian Bureaux. *Tourism Management*,19: 331-340.

Green, TRG., & Benyon, DR.(1996).The skull beneath the skin; Entity-relationship modeling of information artifacts. *International Journal of Human-Computer Studies*, 44(6), 801-828.

Inversini, A., Botturi, L., & Triacca, L. (2006). Evaluating LMS Usability for Enhanced eLearning Experience. *Proceedings of EDMEDIA 2006*, Orlando, USA, 595-601.

Inversini, A., & Cantoni, L. (2009) Cultural Destination Usability: The Case of Visit Bath. In W. Hopken, U. Gretzel & R. Law (Eds.), *Information and Communication Technologies in Tourism 2009* – Proceedings of the International Conference in Amsterdam, Netherland (pp. 319-331). Wien: Springer.

Kuniavsky, M. (2003). *Observing the User Experience: A Practitioner's Guide to User Research*. San Francisco: Morgan Kaufmann.

Matera, M., Costable MF., Garzotto F., & Paolini P. (1996). SUE Inspection: An Effective Method for Systematic Usability Evaluation of Hypermedia, *IEEE Transaction*, Vol.32, No. 1.

McKercher B., & du Cros, H. (2002). *Cultural Tourism: The Partnership between Tourism and Cultural Heritage Management.* Paperback.

Nick Brooks, Vulnerability, risk and adaptation: A conceptual framework, Tyndall Centre for Climate Change Research

Nielsen, J. (1999). *Designing web Usability*, New Riders.

Nielsen, J., & Mack, R. (1994). *Usability Inspection Methods*, Wiley.

Pike, S. (2005). *Destination Marketing Organizations*. Elsevier. Oxford

Pitkow, J. (1997). In search of reliable usage data on the WWW. In *Sixth International World Wide Web Conference*, pages 451–463, Santa Clara, CA, 1997.

Shanshan,QI., Buhalis, D., & Law, R. (2007). Evaluation of the Usability of Chinese Destination Management Organization Website. *Information and Communication Technologies in Tourism 2007.* Wien: Springer.

Speroni, M., Paolini, P., & Bolchini, D. (2006). Museum Website Interface Elements: Do Users Understand Them? In *Proceedings of Museum and the Web Conference*, Albuquerque, New Mexico, USA.

Triacca, L., Bolchini, D., Botturi, L., & Inversini, A. (2004). MiLE: Systematic Usability Evaluation for E-learning Web Applications. *Proceedings of EDMEDIA 2004*, Lugano, Switzerland, 4398-4405.

Triacca, L., Bolchini, D., Botturi, L., & Inversini, A., MiLE: Systematic Usability Evaluation for E-learning Web Applications, in in L. Cantoni & C. McLoughlin (Eds). *Proc. ED-MEDIA 2004 World Conference on Educational Multimedia, Hypermedia & Telecommunications*, Lugano, Switzerland, June 2004, 4398-4405.

Triacca, L., Inversini, A., & Bolchini, D. (2005). Evaluating Web Usability with MiLE+. Web Site Evolution IEEE Symposium, Budapest: Hungary.

Triacca, L., Inversini, A., & Bolchini, D. (2005). Evaluating Web Usability with MiLE+, in *Proc. Seventh International Symposium on Web Site Evolution (WSE 2005)*, Budapest, September 2005, 22-29.

Wang, Y., & Fesenmaier, DR. (2006). Identifying the success factors of web-based marketing strategy: an investigationof convention and visitors bureaus in the United States. *Journal of Travel Research*.44:239-249

Werthner H., & Klein S. (1999). *Information Technology and Tourism – A Challenging Relationship*. Wien - New York, Springer Verlag.

Whiteside J., Bennet J., & Holtzblatt K. (1988). Usability engineering: Our experience and evolution, in *Handbook of Human-Computer Interaction*, M. Helander, Ed. Amsterdam, The Netherlands, North-Holland, pp.791-817

WOTBC (2001). E-business for Tourist, Practical Guidelines for destination and business. Published by the World Tourism Orgnaization.

Zhou, Q., & DeSantis, R. (2005). Usability Issues in City Tourism Website Design: a Conceptual Analysis. *IEEE, International Professional Communication Conference*.

The Pro's and Contra's of an Interactive Location Based Service Using UMTS Transmission

Martin Goossen[a],
Ron van Lammeren[b], and
Arend Ligtenberg[b]

[a]Wageningen University and Research Centre
Landscape Centre, The Netherlands
Martin.goossen@wur.nl

[b]Wageningen University and Research Centre
Centre for Geo-Information, The Netherlands
Ron.vanlammeren@wur.nl
Arend.ligtenberg@wur.nl

Abstract

This research presents the Digital Dowsing Rod (DIWI[1]) a framework of a Interactive Location Based Service (iLBS) to explore the cultural heritage of a region. The DIWI consists of a service oriented architecture (SOA), a web-client, a content management system and a mobile client based on smart phones and windows mobile technology. Users can generate their own POIs (called Parlance Points) at a location and share them immediately with other users reaching these locations. An extended user test was carried out in the "Grebbelinie" area, the Netherlands. The testers hiked and biked via different routes through that area using the application. Despite a number of technical shortcomings of the UMTS transmission in a rural area, the DIWI was positively valued by the testers, but the added value of the information of the Parlance Point was limited. But for personal use the PP does have an additional value.

Keywords: Interactive Location Based Services, Web Map Services, Service Oriented Architecture, Cultural-historic information, User Generated Content, UMTS transmission

1 Introduction

Location-Based Services (LBS) are a booming topic in business (Raper et al, 2007) and science (Raper et al, 2007 (2)). They are defined as "geographically-oriented data and information services to users across mobile telecommunications networks" (Jiang, B. & X. Yao, 2006). Contemporary devices combined with software developments based on Web 2.0 extend LBS into the direction of interactive Location-Based Service (iLBS). With iLBS, the user of a mobile smart-phone is no longer simply the consumer of location and of context dependent information via push and pull interfaces, but also becomes a participant in collecting data and reviewing information. Interactive LBS constitutes the next stage – locative media (Tuters, M.& K. Varnelis, 2006) – in the use of mobile phone technology. The current generation

---

[1] DIWI refers to the Dutch translation of Digital Dowsing Rod: "DIgitale WIchelroede"

mobile phones provide many functions to acquire location-based data (via GPS) by text files, digital pictures, sound files and video streams. These data can be gained at will and can be stored and shared via wireless internet. Therefore, we define iLBS as "geographically-oriented data and information services to support user communities across mobile telecommunications networks". Most current LBS applications deliver one-way access to information (D'Roza and Bilchev, 2003). Interesting information is pushed to the user based on the location. They do not allow users to add and share own information and experiences. Some users have a lot of knowledge about heritage and nature at the spot which they want to share with others. iLBS give them the opportunity to do this directly, without going back home first to add information on a website. And other users can react directly on this added information when they reach the spot. They can read the review of today's dinner of a certain restaurant for example. This kind of application is rather new.

This research presents the Digital Dowsing Rod (DIWI) a framework of a iLBS to explore the cultural heritage of a region. The DIWI is one of the first applications with a two-way access to information through the use of UMTS transmission. It would be interesting to know if this type of interactivity would give an added value to existing LBS approaches (Espinoza et al., 2001). Until now there is not very much known about the users acceptance of iLBS and mobile multimedia services which aims at the enhancement of access to specific information about landscape, nature, cultural heritage and other tourist amenities, and as such provide additional ways to explore and learn about the landscape, with the exception of some studies (Schmidt-Belz et al., 2003, Margherita, 2004). To clarify the value of applying iLBS in recreational context as sketched above explicit insight is needed in its acceptance. The Technology Acceptance Model (TAM) is still the predominant model for examining factors involved in the acceptance of new technology by users (Davis, 1993, Sharp, 2007). Its basic concepts are the use, usefulness and enjoyment.

With DIWI the users can explore the cultural history of a region based on their own preferences. Additionally users can capture, add and share information based on their location. The goal of this research is to develop a generic architecture together with an accompanying software framework that supports an efficient realization of an interactive location based service targeted to providing cultural-historical information to visitors of landscapes. The hypotheses is that the DIWI will give an added value to an outdoor experience.

2   The concept of the Digital Dowsing Rod

In the "Digital Dowsing Rod" (Ligtenberg et al, 2008) project, a consortium developed and tested an interactive location-based service. This service provides cultural-historic landscape information in two ways: from narratives and from facts and figures. The Digital Dowsing Rod (DIWI) is location-based and service-oriented. It can be used to reveal the hidden history of a landscape to visitors and provide them with cultural-historical information that is detectable in the surrounding landscape, using broadly available devices. The HTC P3600 was selected as mobile device. This smart phone (PDA) has GPS, UMTS/HSDPA for data transmission, and audio-video record and display functions. With the pilot application, a "thin" mobile client, users are served by a tailor-made user interface. The user interface resembles information based on different data types. This information consists of maps, walking and biking routes and point-of-interest (POI) locations that are all indicated on these maps, multimedia presentations of cultural-historic information and personal experiences in text, photo, audio and video formats linked to the POIs. By using the smart phone, visitors can explore a landscape and its cultural history using various levels of freedom. This freedom is important because modern tourists are capable of defining their own needs and preferences. They are not always satisfied with the "travel agent's standard offer". Modern tourists want to have it all, but not at the same time and not at the same spot. Diversity has become a new keyword in tourism planning (Goossen et al, 2009). For that reason a DIWI-user can choose from different modes: (a) a predefined trail with historical accounts (b) a personalized route based on personal preferences including related personal historical accounts and (c) a forage through the landscape that takes for granted whatever historical information will be encountered. Furthermore the DIWI application provides the opportunity to record, store and upload personal location based experiences via text processing, voice recording or photo/video camera. Users can generate their own POIs and share them immediately with other users reaching these locations.

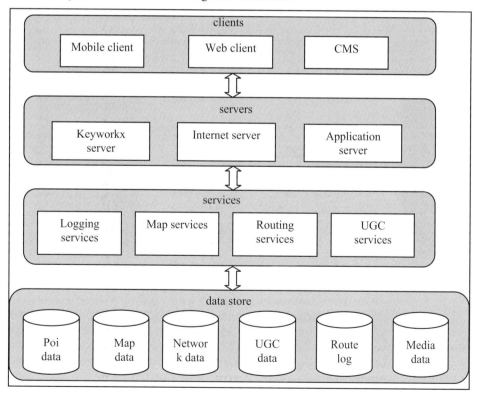

Fig. 1. Four-tier architecture of the Digital Dowsing Rod

Figure 1 shows the outline of the Service Oriented Architecture (SOA) of the Digital Dowsing Rod. This four-tier architecture consists of three clients: (a) web client, (b) mobile client and (c) content management system client (CMS). A web client allows users that have logged in to explore predefined routes, create their own routes, and view routes they have followed before as well as their user-generated POIs. A CMS allows administrators and managers to add and manage predefined POIs, including multi-media files, and to moderate and manage the user-generated content (personal POIs). Through the mobile client, the user can view a map, a route, points-of-interest, and the position of the device. In fact, it promotes interactivity in LBS because it allows users to generate, store and upload their personal text, sound, photo and video files to the data stores.

2.1. Web client

Besides exploring the predefined routes users can login into a personal part of the website to construct personalized routes and review the trips they have done. Figure 2 shows the web interface that allows users to generate a personal route. In the current version of generating personalized routes a user can choose a starting point, walking or cycling trip and its preferred distance. Moreover two landscape preferences can be selected out of six (closed agricultural landscape, half-open agricultural, forest, heath and dunes, natural grasslands/swamp/reed, stream/rivers/pond/lakes). Based on these preferences the system tries to fit a route as close as possible to the users' wishes. This generated route is available on the mobile client after login.

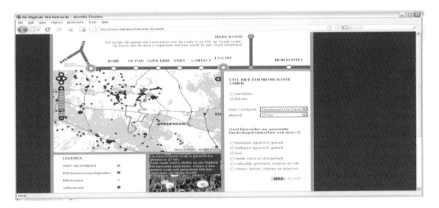

Fig. 2. Web interface for generating personal routes.

Figure 3 shows a user track and the location a user added some own user generated content ("diamond"). By clicking one of listed routes on the right side a crumb-trail will be generated showing the followed route. User generated POI is shown on the map as small red diamond shaped icons. Clicking on the "diamond" shows the content of the user generated POI.

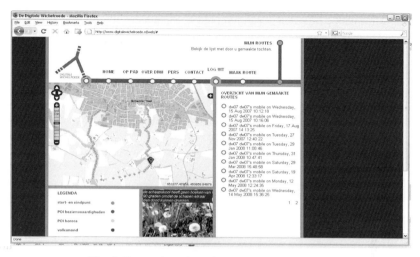

Fig. 3. Logged track and user generated content

2.2. Mobile Client

A custom mobile client has been build based on the .net 2 compact framework on Window mobile 5. The application is implemented as thin client fully depending on GPS and minimal a UMTS connection. On logon the client connects to the server, and the predefined and personal generated routed are fetched from the server. After login of a user he or she can choose to walk a route (including personal route) or just start to roam around. Using Web Mapping Services route information is combined with a reference base map (currently a detailed topographical map). There is no active navigation system build in. This means a user just tracks himself on the map checking if he or she is still on the route. If a POI is within a certain distance to the user, he or she will be signaled and is given the opportunity to read, watch or listen to the information. By activating the add photo button the build in camera of the Smartphone will be activated. After making the movie shot or photo the results will automatically be uploaded and added to the DIWI database. The DIWI-mobile client also is equipped with a "go-home" button. This option triggers the system to calculate the shortest path to the starting point. For this service and the personalized route service a dedicated network data set consisting of cycling and walking paths was created.

2.3. Content Management

A content management system (CMS) allows for the management of POI's and user content (only accessible for administrators, content providers, and moderators). Via the POI management screen (Figure 4) POI's could be added by clicking a location on the map or entering coordinates. Besides a description and classification of the POI, media can be linked to the POI by selecting from a media library. Existing POI's can be selected by clicking on the map. All poi's within a user defined range will be highlighted and listed by their name. From that list the POI to be edited may be selected. The change of a POI location could be established by dragging the selected POI-object to another location. User generated content might be reviewed and deleted if necessary .

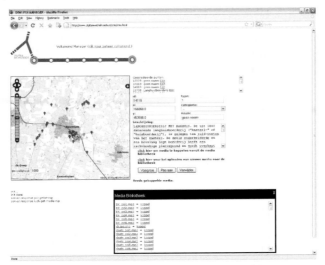

Fig. 4. content management system DIWI: POI edit screen

2.4. Data Store

As Figure 1 shows, all data is stored in various databases (data store tier). For the storage of maps, routes (predefined routes) and networks we used a native data model (Oracle spatial). Data has been implemented as an Open GeoSpatial Consortium (OGC, 2008) compliant Web Mapping Services (WMS) using ArcIMS. All user generated content is stored in the user generated content database (UGC data). The automatically-generated user tracks, from the client-docked GPS whose signals are caught every 15 seconds, are stored in the Trip Logs. All media related either to predefined POIs or user-generated POIs will be stored in the media data. Instead of the term user-generated POIs, from now on we will use the term Parlance Points (PP), as parlance refers to fact, figures and anecdotes that are conventional wisdom.

2.5. Digital Dowsing Rod Case Study

The DIWI application was tested in the "Grebbelinie" area (Figure 5) in The Netherlands. This rural area, originally reserved as a military defense area, exposes fortifications and areas that were inundated in the past. Its use for military purposes lasted from the mid-18th century until World War II. This 60-km long line of defense was demilitarized in 1940, after just five days of war. Many remnants of old battlements are still present today, and some have been reconstructed. Because of the history of heroic actions and battles throughout the centuries, anecdotes are plentiful. Moreover, one also finds beautiful scenery and high biodiversity in the Grebbelinie area.

By means of a media offensive by regional broadcast stations, newspapers, and websites (of newspapers and of cultural-historical organizations), people were informed about the objectives of the project, the landscape history to be studied, and invited to register as test persons. In total, 387 persons applied through the Internet and filled in an on-line questionnaire about their interests and background, to find out to which social and demographic group (Dekker et al, 2003) they belonged, and their level of experience with mobile phone and GPS technology. By the web client they were given the opportunity to select and view routes to prepare a walking or biking trip through the Grebbelinie area. Twenty predefined routes were provided by three sites to start a round trip: Grebbeberg, Renswoude and Scherpenzeel. Eventually, 150 persons tested the DIWI application in the Grebbelinie during five weekends (Friday to Sunday) in March and April 2008. On whichever weekend day they preferred, the volunteers walked (77%) or biked (20%) a previously-selected route within a time-slot of three hours maximum. At the beginning of their walk or bike trip, they were instructed on how to use the client interface and the options there were to generate their own content. During the instruction session, we stated very clearly that they would be able to record experiences and accounts from their own cultural-historical knowledge of the area.

All trips were GPS-tracked. We even registered all of the people's interactions with the device when creating Parlance Points during the trip. At the end, the testing group filled in an extensive exit questionnaire about the usability of the application, according to the combined Technological Acceptance Model (e.g., (Davis, 1993, Sharp, 2007)) in combination with the Hedonic Information systems approach (van der Heijden, 2004). In the end, 150 persons produced valid datasets, which could be used for analysis (Goossen et al, 2008). The Parlance Points (PPs) that were generated by the user, such as recorded texts, pictures and videos, were geo-coded by latitude and longitude. These PPs represented the personally-experienced cultural history of the landscape.

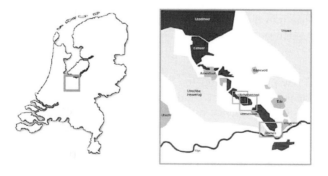

Fig. 5. The "Grebbelinie" in the Netherlands and starting points

3   Results

The average age of the users was 48. About 67% was male and 33% female. Most of the testers followed a higher education. The general opinion about the usefulness was measured using a seven point Likert-scale where 1 represents "disagree very much", 4 "neutral" and 7 "agree very much". About 66% of the testers is positive about the usefulness. The average judgment is 4.7. The general opinion is that the mobile client is easy to use. The overall perceived use is on average also an 4.7. Nearly 76% of the testers is rather positive about the perceived enjoyment. The average score is 5. In general 70% of the testers score the DIWI application with an average score of 4.8 (at a 7-point scale with 7 as highest). About 86% of all testers agrees that the mobile client is "special". Almost 75% selects that the client is an aid to explore a region and 60% thinks it is beneficial to the experience of the landscape. The most often mentioned (table 1) added values to the use of DIWI are: the possibility to retrieve information on the spot, never loose the way, and uploading of personal content (PP).

Table 1. General overview for the general acceptance of the DIWI (n=150)

Reason	# times mentioned
Information	43
Information on the spot	27
Don't loose track/GPS	20
Interactive	13
Replacement of maps	13
Exiting / fun	11
Types of media	11
Made environment more interesting	7

Many testers considered the DIWI as a better alternative for paper maps, guides and information panels. 88% of the testers will, once upgraded to a proper product, recommend the DIWI to others. 21% will use it themselves while 61% postpone use due to the costs of the needed data connection (however, currently the average cost of a fast UMTS/HSDPA connection is dropping in the Netherlands). About 11% does not know if to use it in the future and 6% certainly will not use the DIWI. Often the latter is due to extended technical problems faced during use of the DIWI by these respondents.

Figure 6 shows the general rating for the perceived additional value of the DIWI compared to not using the DIWI. Additionally the testers were asked to value the various types of media offered by DIWI. From Table 2 it appears that testers especially like the diversity in media types but tend to aim for sound and less for text. The readability, in this case related to the screen reflection and contrast under day light conditions, of the mobile client is seen as the most problematic. No significant differences have been observed between experienced PDA or smart phone users and non-experienced testers indicating that the general design of the application is well accessible.

About 90% of the testers reported problems using the DIWI, ranging from poor visibility of the screen in sunlight to complete failure of the application. To value the usefulness an inventory of problems encountered by the testers was made. Table 3 shows the distribution for the signaled problems for each of the starting locations and in total. Based on Table 3 one may conclude that the stability of this mobile client and its screen quality need to be improved. Like other LBS examples battery life is a serious problem. During the DIWI-test on average a battery ran for two hours (by continuous use of back light, gps, data transmission and regular recordings). Interesting enough all testers had an external battery that easily could be connected when the local battery run out of power, but from the results it curiously turns out that 30% of the test group didn't use that option.

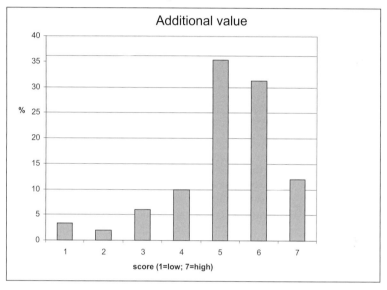

Fig. 6. additional value of the DIWI

Table 2. Distribution of the preferences for various types of media in % of N (N = 150)

Type media	%
Text	17
Photo	2
Video	5
Sound	37
Diversity	31
No-pref.	5
Unknown	3

Table 3. Type and distribution of encountered technical problems of the mobile client per starting point in % of the test group (Ntotal=150)

Problem type	Grebbeberg	Renswoude	Scherpenzeel	Ntotal
Need to restart	66,0	51,9	51,7	60,5
Poor visibility of the screen due to sunlight	38,5	55,5	55,2	44,7
GPS went down	45,0	33,3	31,0	40,1
Battery empty	28,6	44,4	34,5	32,7
Long waiting times (downloads)	33,0	25,9	31,0	31,3
Application "freezed"	18,7	29,6	6,9	18,4
Did not receive information about the poi's	17,6	11,1	6,9	14,3
Went lost	5,5	11,1	10,3	7,5
No topographical map	5,5	11,1	6,9	6,8
No sound	3,3	-	3,4	2,7
Problem in typing text	1,1	-	-	0,7
Other	**33,0**	**40,7**	**34,5**	**34,0**

3.1. Parlance Point (PP)

One of the innovative features of the DIWI platform is the ability to add and share personal information by uploading location based content (movie clips, photo's and text). About 54% of the testers added personal content. The testers who did not add content had various reasons: 29% just did not feel the need to add content, 17% experienced it as too complicated and 7% blames the (bad) weather conditions. Of all the testers, 74% appreciated the idea of adding information themselves. We did not limit the selection of the originally stored 345 PP beforehand, and accepted that all PPs show evident historic features. In general, every person stored on average three PPs during his or her trip. Of the total number of PPs, 28% were text, 6% video and 67% photographs especially of the landscape scenery, objects along the route, and family snap shots. Approximately 38% of the PPs were dedicated to the cultural history of the landscape. This means that the user in this study recorded many other topics as well.

The additional value of these personal content for the general community is rather limited. Most of it can be classified as too private (not only the family snap-shots but also route notes and corrections). 62% of the testers switched on the PP on the mobile client to see what others "left behind". Because many of the PP was of a too private or specific nature the evaluation of the content turns out negatively. The testers do not agree with the proposition that user generated content is interesting and as such an added value to exploring and learning about the region (see Table 4). However for purely personal use (for example reviewing the trip on the website) the PP does have an additional value, because it offers a personalized location based digital album.

Table 4. Average rating of the user generated content (PP) on a 7 point scale with 7 as highest

	Avg. rating
Nice	3,6
Interesting	3,2
Text of other is superfluous	4,3
Photo's of others are superfluous	4,5
Movie clips of others are superfluous	4,5
Provided additional information	3,2

4   The pro's and contra's of iLBS

4.1. Regarding the architecture

The system presented in this paper has been designed to deliver a complete framework for a full interactive location based system application. The approach of using a distributed architecture has an important advantage. It supports an easy on-line and real-time connection of new data sources (personalized routes and personal POI's) without the need of transferring all information to a central system. As such it keeps the maintenance, update and extent of content (PP, DIWI POI's, maps, routes, etc) effectively and realizable by the source owners and the user community. During the user test, the application based on the framework turns out to function quite well. Besides these benefits many, well-known, problems have been run into related to the stability of different servers, the mobile network, and battery life. A crash-test has not been performed during the project but considering the reported failures it is a major point of concern. The test area is known for its variable coverage of UMTS/HSDPA. For one start location the data connection often "degraded" to GPRS connection which appeared to be only sufficient for sending the GPS coordinates to the server and serving the periodic map updates. For downloading of POI media (with the exception of text) GPRS appeared to be insufficient. A (temporal) solution was implemented enabling the client to grab POI media data belonging to a location from a storage-card when the bandwidth was insufficient for timely delivery of media. This option, however, hampers the maintainability of the DIWI because of the PP updates. The conclusion is that in certain rural areas the stability of UMTS is often problematic.

4.2. Regarding the content

Calculating interesting and reliable routes, requires a comprehensive network based on the description of available cycle tracks and footpaths. Such a network is not yet available, at least not for the whole of the Netherlands. For the test a network was digitized based on routes offered by tourists' offices by maps, topological data and selected and validated gps-tracks. Additionally creating and compiling POI's, movie, and sound clips requires lot of work. In the DIWI cases professional story writers and voice over's have been contracted to create attractive and understandable content.

In the DIWI-project, the users were asked how many PPs they downloaded during their trip and how they assessed the quality of these PPs. Of the testers, 62% downloaded user-generated content to see what others had "left behind". Because 47% of the user-generated content appeared to be of a personal nature (events and objects), the assessment was not very positive. The testers did not agree with the proposition that user-generated content is interesting and as such, an added value to explore and learn more about the region. The idea of communities forming around similar experiences of landscapes appeared not to be fulfilling a need of users. In contrast, the assessment showed that for personal use (e.g., reviewing their own trip on the website) the user-generated content (especially events and objects) have an additional value. From additional analysis it appeared that the user generated content could be divided into private data and location based cultural-historic data. The first is not of much value for sharing while the second will be.

For general use, it would be recommendable to serve the user generated content according various classes, allowing users to only pick those information interesting to them, like reviewing today's menu of a restaurant or information about specific flora and fauna. A community based editor could support such classification. It should be stressed upon that the results of this test is based on a very specific group of testers with a dominance of relatively high educated testers.

References

Davis, F. D. (1993) User acceptance of information technology: system characteristics, user perceptions and behavioral impacts. *International Journal of Man-Machine Studies, 38*, 475-487.

Dekker, P., Lampert, M., & Spangenberg, F. (2003). Political disaffection: The Netherlands in 2002. Paper presented at the *Annual WAPOR Conference in Prague*, September 2003.

D'Roza, T. & Bilchev, G. (2003) An Overview of Location-Based Services. *BT Technology Journal, 21*, 20-27.

Espinoza, F., Persson, P., Sandin, A., Nyström, H., Cacciatore, E. & Bylund, M. (2001) GeoNotes : Social and Navigational Aspects of Location-Based Information Systems. *Ubicomp 2001: Ubiquitous Computing.*

Goossen, M., van Lammeren, R., & Ligtenberg, A. (2008) A. *De Digitale Wichelroede en haar gebruikers. Interactieve Location Based Services voor cultuur-historische landschapsbeleving.* CGI-report 2008-04/Alterra report 1759, Wageningen University and Research: Wageningen, The Netherlands 2008.

Goossen, M., Meeuwsen, H., Franke, J. & Kuyper, M. (2009) My ideal tourism destination: Personalized destination recommendation system combining individual preferences and GIS data. *Journal of ITT* Volume 11, no. 1 pp. 17-30.

Jiang, B., & Yao, X. (2006) Location based services and GIS in perspective. Comput. Environ. Urban Syst. 2006, 30, 712–725.

Ligtenberg, A., van Lammeren, R., Goossen, M., & Bulens, J. (2008) Enhancing the experience of the landscape: The digital dowsing rod. In *Location Based Services and TeleCartography II: From Sensor Fusion to Context Models, Lecture Notes in Geoinformation and Cartography*, Gartner, G., Rehrl, K., Eds., Springer: Berlin, Germany, 2008, pp. 239–261

Margherita, P. (2004) Determinants of adoption of third generation mobile multimedia services. *Journal of Interactive Marketing, 18*, 46-59.

Open Geospatial Consortium, Inc.® (OGC) Homepage. http://www.opengeospatial.org/ (accessed February 2008).

Raper, J., Gartner, G., Karimi, H., & Rizos, C. (2007) Applications of location-based services: A selected review. J. Location Based Serv. 2007, 1, 89–111.

Raper, J., Gartner, G., Karimi, H., & Rizos, C. (2007(1)) A critical evaluation of location based services and their potential. J. Location Based Serv. 2007, 1, 5–45.

Schmidt-Belz, B., Laamanen, H., Poslad, S. & Zipf, A. (2003) Location-based mobile tourist services-first user experiences. *Information and Communication Technologies in Tourism*, 115–123.

Sharp, J. H. (2007) Development, extension, and application: a review of the technology acceptance model. *Information Systems Education Journal,* 5, 1-11.

Tuters, M., & Varnelis, K. (2006) Beyond locative media: Giving shape to the internet things. *Leonardo 2006*, 39, 357–363.

Van de Heijden, H. (2004). User acceptance of hedonic information systems. *MIS Q. 28*, 695–704.

Acknowledgements

The authors like to express their gratitude to all staff of the Digital Dowsing Rod project members, Alterra, DS Landschapsarchitects, Galileo Communication Projects, Municipality of Utrecht, KPN, Dutch Cadastre, Province of Utrecht, Foundation "Vernieuwing Gelderse Vallei", Waag Society and Wageningen University, for their participation in, dedication to and support of the DIWI- project. The project has been partly funded by the Dutch National Research program committee on Geo-Information (RGI), the Province of Utrecht and the Dutch Ministry of Agriculture, Nature and Food quality.

Usability Guidelines for WAP-based Travel Planning Tools

Sabine Schneider[a,b],
Francesco Ricci[b],
Adriano Venturini[a], and
Elena Not[a,c]

[a] eCTRL Solutions
Italy
venturini@ectrlsolutions.com

[b] Faculty of Computer Science
Free University of Bozen-Bolzano, Italy
fricci@unibz.it
sabine.schneider@stud-inf.unibz.it

[c] Center for Information Technology
Fondazione Bruno Kessler, Italy
not@fbk.eu

Abstract

Designing effective and efficient user interfaces for supporting complex tasks on mobile devices remains an intriguing problem. The rapidly evolving hardware and software mobile environments are complicating the design of elaborated applications like travel planning. Allowing mobile users to review their travel-plan information while travelling has been addressed by a recent R&D project. In order to improve usability and derive good design guidelines, two alternative WAP-based solutions were experimented: one based on providing explicit guidance and information, and another focussed on brevity and iconic metaphors. These two designs enabled to investigate mobile users' preferences and behaviour and the effects on usability and effectiveness. A user study was conducted and users' behaviour on both variants was logged. Using objective measures and users' subjective perceptions, the effects of design options, users' age and proficiency with WAP applications were tested. This study allowed deriving some guidelines by analysing which graphical components better support mobile usability, and which solutions should be avoided.

Keywords: Travel Planning; Usability; Mobile Internet; WAP, Web Portal.

1 Introduction

Nowadays cell phones are so popular and ubiquitous that most of us couldn't imagine living without them. More and more people use these communication and information access tools, and the functionalities and the challenges provided by these devices are growing (Turban et al., 2008) (Bertelè & Rangone, 2007) (Nielsen, 2009).

After the initial difficulties of the first WAP version in the late '90s, most people wouldn't have imagined that Mobile Internet would have ever gained a remarkable market share. But a recent survey in Germany (www.heise.de [May 08, 2009]) revealed that more than a third of Germans use their cell phones (at least sometimes) to navigate or read emails and another third intends to surf with their cellular phone (or at least to try it) within this year. According to GSM Association, more than 4 billion mobile connections were active already by year-end 2008, while the number of PC users is expected to hit 1 billion only in 2010. This growing availability and convenience of wireless communication technology as well as the wide diffusion of free Wi-Fi connectivity are the main drivers for the development of mobile services and mobile-friendly web pages.

Thus, information providers that want to address this challenging and emerging market have to go mobile, but the keyword is not to *miniaturise* existing Web-based services to run on mobile devices, but to *mobilise* them (www.littlespringdesign.com [June 04, 2009]). In fact, depending on the usage context, only some of the functionalities provided by an existing application or web page are of interest for the mobile user. For example, as in our case study, a traveller who used the PC to plan his holidays may not be anymore interested in flight suggestions while he is visiting the selected destination; or someone travelling in a northern Finnish province will not be likely to look for the weather conditions in southern Finland. Here the work of mobile designers begins: not by dropping some functionalities and by letting the rest to run on small screens with limited computational power, but by rethinking and redesigning a completely new mobile context-aware user friendly system (Jones & Marsden, 2005) (Cena et al., 2006).

The project "Country Portal for Finnish Tourism" was aimed at developing a newer advanced tourism portal for the Finnish country - VisitFinland.com. One of the main objectives of this project was to enable the user to obtain personalised travel recommendations and help while searching for accommodations or sightseeing. This recommendation service is supported by Trip@dvice, a recommendation technology already integrated successfully in various other country portals (Venturini & Ricci, 2006). Trip@dvice exploits case-based reasoning to support conversational interaction, intelligent ranking and data mediation. It helps the travellers to find the most appropriate travel destination, and recommends them which sightseeing attractions and events that would best fit their needs and expectations by looking at previous users' tastes and ratings.

Indeed, recommendation technologies have proved to effectively help users to face the problem of information and choice overload (Fesenmaier et al. 2006) (Adomavicius & Tuzhilin, 2005). However, when we consider the issue of accessing the same type of information, or to perform similar decision making tasks, through mobile devices, the information overload problem gets even harder, and the additional limitations of the mobile devices make it difficult to design an effective solution (Ricci & Nguyen, 2007). In fact, in principle, mobility makes it possible to deliver context-aware information services to mobile users wherever they are and whenever they need, but, system designers have to deal with the consequences of mobility and device limitations on human computer interaction. The approaches that were successful on PCs cannot be directly applied to mobile devices mainly due to their limitations in screen size and computational power, but also because of the impact of the external environment and the behavioural characteristics of mobile users.

The practical motivation that initiated our study was the design and development of a mobile service (a mobile travel-planning agent) for VisitFinland.com, so that the largest number of cellular phones users, irrespectively of the phone characteristics, but just supporting WAP 2.0 access (Shiller, 2003) could be effectively assisted in reviewing travel plans created on the PC-based web interface. Mobile-friendliness is the core aspect that we concentrated on. The mobile travel planner is not providing the same functionalities as the online PC-based system, but only a customised subset of them, realised in a different way, due to the mentioned limitations of wireless communication technologies and mobile devices interfaces. Moreover, to assure the best usability, and to identify design guidelines of general applicability, we built two alternative WAP-based systems, both offering the same logical functionalities, but with some notable differences in the user interface. In this way, alternative approaches to common design problems were compared. For instance, the usage of radio buttons in comparison to links for option selection, or the provisioning of extensive information and instructions vs. a faster navigation, or a different usage of colours and icons. These two running versions were compared, with respect to effectiveness, efficiency and usability, in a user study described later in this paper. That study enabled us to test a number of research hypotheses. The practical outcome of this research work is the improved usability of the VisitFinland.com WAP-system. In addition, we believe that the emerged results have a more general applicability and the derived guidelines can be taken, together with the results of other similar and complementary projects (Buhalis & Pistidda, 2009) (Haid et al., 2008) (Kramer et al., 2007) (Lee et al., 2007), as a basis for improving the user acceptance of WAP-based mobile designs.

2 Travel Planning Functions and GUI

As we mentioned in the Introduction, one of the main use case was to provide ubiquitous access to the travel plans built previously by the users (using the PC-based version of the portal). In addition, we were required to make available this functionality to the largest number of mobile devices (users). For this reason we opted for WAP 2.0 xhtml, as the vast majority of current mobile phones support WAP browsing and we discarded other appealing options, such as J2ME or Android. It is worth noting that nowadays, as an effect of the newly introduced, more effective, mobile Web browsers, as that included in the iPhone, Web browsing (WAP xhtml) is becoming more and more popular.

In addition, specific design guidelines for the whole portal were defined during the GUI analysis phase. In particular, the guidelines stated that the usage of mobile services should be as simple as possible on every kind of device, even in presence of a very limited screen size. For this reason, most graphical elements were oriented in a

128

list-based fashion, such that with minimal scrolling users could find the information they need, and tables should be avoided if possible. The required travel planning system functionality is summarised in Fig.1. The user enters the mobile application through a main menu of the mobile portal. On this main (or home) page there are links to all the major functions, such as the mobile travel plan inspection system, but also other features like map browsing, or the function allowing the user to write and share notes, and many others. Here we focus on travel plan browsing since the other functions are not relevant to the research hypotheses discussed in this paper.

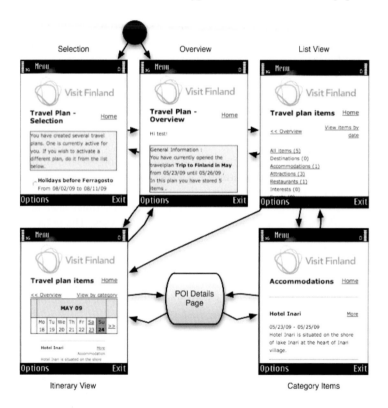

Fig. 1. First version of the user interface and system page-flow (V1)

From this main menu, the user can access the mobile travel planner, and inspect the travel plans that he created with the PC-interface of the web portal. After having selected one of these plans, the system shows an overview page, containing some general information regarding the selected travel, i.e. the time duration of the travel plan and the number items (points of interest) that the user booked or planned to visit (included in the plan). From this page, the user can also go back and select another travel plan (if available), or proceed and browse the single items – either in a list ordered by category, or grouped by day, i.e. in a calendar.

In the list view all the available product categories (e.g. accommodations, events, attractions, restaurants,..), are listed, and for each category the number of items present in the selected travel plan is displayed. By clicking on one of these category links, the user is forwarded to a corresponding page listing the planned items belonging to the selected category. Each of these items has a "details page", which is accessible by clicking on a link, and a short description shown below the item title. If the user chooses to activate the itinerary view, he is presented with a small horizontal calendar, containing the days of the 'active' week. The current date is preselected if it belongs to the planned travel. Otherwise, when the planned holiday is in the past or in the future, the nearest day to the current date is preselected. The user is able to browse the items planned for another day by clicking on its date, and can switch week or month, by clicking on the provided side arrows. The items planned for the selected day are always shown below the calendar in a list containing the item titles, some short descriptions and a link to a details page.

3   Research Hypothesis

In addition to the system version illustrated in the previous section (V1), we designed a variant system (V2), providing the same required functions, but with some differences in the graphical user interface and in the logical system interaction. The page-flow of the second version is depicted in Fig.2. These changes are motivated by some recent studies on WAP usability (Buchanan et al., 2001) (Jones and Marsden, 2005) (Forum Nokia, 2008) (Nielsen, 2009) (http://patterns.littlespringsdesign.com/ [October 29, 2009]). We will now motivate individually the changes made in the second version with corresponding hypotheses linking these differences in mobile web design to an expected effect on the user. These hypotheses should be interpreted as conjectures that V2 improves V1 because of the mentioned difference.

H1: Radio-button list (V1) vs. list with links (V2): Radio-button lists are often used to present to the user alternative options to choose: the user can choose an item, read the others, and - if necessary - choose another item. Then, the user is forwarded to the next page by clicking on a button below the list. On the other hand, by using a list of links, the user selects one and the page opens immediately after clicking. We conjectured that links (V2) are more usable than radio-buttons (V1) when choosing among a set of similar products to inspect (as in the case of alternative travel plans to inspect, see Fig.1 and Fig. 2, "Selection" screen), i.e., there is an impact on the time, the perceived effort, and on the number of clicks, for solving the planning task.

H2: Detailed instructions (V1) vs. faster navigation (V2): Generally, very detailed information and instructions lead to slower navigation on a mobile device because of the small screen size. In V1, to improve information provision, there are very detailed instructions for the user (see for example Fig. 1, "Overview" screen). In V2 some of this information is missing, leaving some more space for other information to be displayed earlier on in the navigation process, e.g. combining the overview page with the list of categories (see Fig. 2, "Overview" screen). We conjectured that mobile users will not read many instructions (V1), and thus will prefer a more compact but faster navigation (V2), in order to get the information needed as soon as possible.

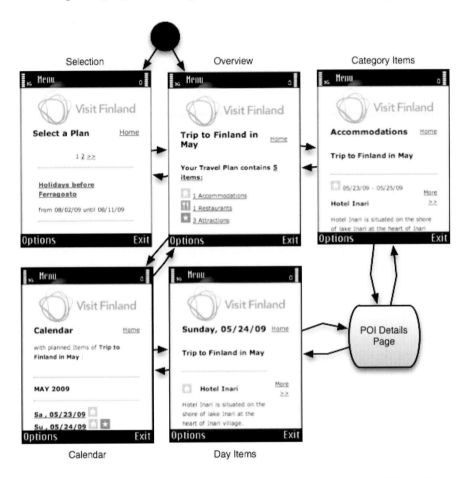

Fig. 2. Modified work-flow and interface to (possibly) improve usability (V2)

H3: More extensive information (V1) vs. short descriptions with icons (V2): In many cases the system designer can decide whether to show some information using textual descriptions, which require less system memory (faster download), or icons, which need less space, but are slower to download. In V1 the information is very detailed, whereas in V2 small icons replace some of these descriptions (e.g. names of the categories). We conjectured that icons are easier to see and to interpret; thus they will positively influence perceptions of ease, efficiency and effectiveness.

H4: Horizontally oriented calendar (V1) vs. list of days (V2), and forward-/backward- links (V1) vs. scrolling (V2): There are very different approaches to visualise calendars. In general it is possible to show a calendar in a horizontally oriented table, representing weeks or even months in a very evocative way. In this case, to change the current selected week (or month) the user clicks on a link. Or it is possible to represent a calendar in a vertical list of days where the user can navigate by scrolling up and down. In V1 the calendar is represented with a horizontal table, showing one week of the travel in each screen. In V2 instead a list of days, linking to the details of each specific day, is used. We conjectured that the list of days is easier to use (as scrolling is very simple), and gives a better overview of the travel; thus the second will be preferred by the majority.

Some other general hypotheses regarding the system evaluation were defined:

H5: Age influences time: Younger participants will be faster in completing the tasks.

H6: Habit influences time: Participants who have been using internet on a mobile device (a cellular phone or a PDA) will be faster in completing the scenario than people who have never tried this technology before.

H7: Habit influences clicking: Testers that already used Mobile Internet before will also use the system in a more efficient way, i.e. with fewer clicks.

H8: Neither age nor habit influence the participant preference for one version: There might be some differences in the personal preferences of the participants; but neither their age, nor their knowledge or use of mobile internet will influence these preferences.

4 Evaluation Strategy

For mobile systems evaluation it is important to use a concrete mobile device when performing a usability analysis, as emulators on a PC might impact on the perceptions about ease of navigation (Jones & Marsden, 2005). For these reasons we initially tested the two mentioned versions on a range of devices with different characteristics to assure portability and robustness of the system, as well as a smooth rendering of the graphical interface. Then we finally performed a focussed user test where one single device was adopted since we could not control the variability of the devices in a rather small group of testers (25). We adopted a within-group model, where four user tasks were created: two tasks to be completed with one system variant, and two slightly different tasks with the other version. The first set of tasks included: a) "In which hotels have you slept during 'Carnival 2008'?", and a) "What have you planned for the 10th August 2009 in the 'holidays before Ferragosto' plan?". The second set of tasks included: a') "Which attractions will you see in your 'early summer holidays' plan?", and b') "Where have you been on 31st December 2008 in the 'Christmas holidays'? plan". Hence, in each task the participants were asked to find some information (specific to the given task) and to use the different views as well as the menu. The two sets of tasks were randomly swapped, such that their (possibly different) easiness would not influence the results, i.e. half of the testers performed tasks a) and b) on the first system version and tasks a') and b') on the second one, and the other half vice-versa. During the task completion the beginning (login) and the end (logout) were logged (timestamp), such that the time a participant took for the completion could be computed afterwards. Also the numbers of clicks were logged, in order to obtain some information about the (objective) effort a user took to complete the scenario.

A questionnaire was developed to measure the (subjective) usability reusing the NASA task load index (humansystems.arc.nasa.gov/groups/TLX/ [May 06, 2009]) and IBM's Computer System Usability Questionnaire (Lewis, 1995). It was slightly adapted to the special needs of the study. It asks for some general/personal information (required for the statistical analysis), and contains twelve statements to evaluate the user interface, the information provided, the usage learning, some overall perceptions, the perceived performance. The statements were evaluated on a scale ranging from -2 (strongly disagree) to +2 (strongly agree): after having tested each system variant the users where asked to evaluate the statements Q1-Q12 (Table 1). In the end, after testing the second version (either V1 or V2 according to the randomly selected order), the user was asked to provide some free comments about the two system versions and to explicitly compare the two systems, namely to mention the preferred one along different aspects: overall impression, interface, information presentation and the main functionalities (Q13-Q19 in Table 1).

Table 1: Usability Questionnaire

User Interface	Q1	It was simple to use this system
	Q2	I can effectively complete my task using this system
	Q3	The interface of this system is pleasant
Information	Q4	The organization of the information provided by the system is clear
	Q5	It was easy to find the information I needed
	Q6	The information is effective in helping me complete the scenario
Learning	Q7	It was easy to learn to use this system
Overall	Q8	Overall, I am satisfied with this system
	Q9	I like using this system
Work Load	Q10	The task was not mentally demanding
	Q11	I didn't have to work hard to accomplish my level of performance
	Q12	I was not insecure, discouraged, irritaded, stressed and annoyed
Comments	Q13	Most positive aspects (if any)...
	Q14	Most negative aspects (if any)...
Conclusions	Q15	Which system do you prefer?
	Q16	Which system has the better interface?
	Q17	Which system is more useful and informative?
	Q18	Which category view do you prefer?
	Q19	Which calendar do you prefer?

The analysis was performed by 25 participants, aged from 12 to 60; 12 test participants were experts in computer science (students or professors). The remaining 13 testers were some of our acquaintances; they have a medium/low computer usage experience: 7 were using the computer at home or in the office, and 6 of them were barely capable to use the computer. The different ages and background knowledge were distributed equally between the two test-groups. Moreover, no one was told which one was the original or the "improved" version. All the tests were performed in a similar context, i.e. a silent room with not much people in it; the same cell phone; everyone got the experiment explained before, and got questions answered during the test.

5 Results

5.1 Usability Evaluation

Looking at the differences in the evaluation according to the 12 statements in Table 2, it is clear that for all the statements the evaluation of V1 is lower then V2. Especially with respect to the simplicity (Q1) the users evaluated better V2. The lowest results (for both versions) are for statement Q9 ("I like using this system"). Hence suggesting that both GUIs could be further improved. It is possible to conjecture that links were easier to use, looking at the answers to statements Q1 ("It was simple to use the system"), Q2, ("I can effectively complete my task using this system"), and Q3, ("The interface of this system is pleasant"). This conclusion is further supported by looking at the users' comments, stating that links are preferred. Thus the first hypothesis H1, that links are preferred over radio buttons, is supported in the analysis. In general, V1 is based on the idea of providing to the user extensive information, while V2 tries to keep the instructions and information short, and to replace some information with icons. Since V2 was rated higher than V1 – on average for each single statement – one could derive that users prefer short information and small icons when using a mobile device. We found also many positive comments for the usage of icons. Thus, hypothesis H3 is supported by the results obtained from the usability test.

Table 2: Average answer to usability statements for the two system versions

	Q1	Q2	Q3	Q4	Q5	Q6	Q7	Q8	Q9	Q10	Q11	Q12	Average
V1	0,88	0,92	0,76	0,80	0,64	0,96	1,16	0,84	0,52	1,04	1,04	1,04	0,88
V2	1,60	1,44	1,28	1,44	1,44	1,24	1,52	1,40	0,80	1,28	1,32	1,52	1,36
p	0,00	0,02	0,02	0,00	0,00	0,07	0,01	0,00	0,05	0,06	0,09	0,03	0,00

Calculating the t test (two-tailed, paired) for the 12 statements, we found that in 9 cases there is more than 95% confidence that these differences are significant. Only on three statements (Q6, Q10 and Q9), regarding perceived performance and information presentation, the two systems are not *significantly* different, but for all the other statements they are.

5.2 Performance of the users in the different systems

By comparing the average task execution time and the number of clicks, it results that the users needed about *42% more time* to complete the scenario with V1, and on average they needed *7 clicks more* to complete the tasks on V1 (on V2 the average number of clicks was 10.8). Both differences are significant and therefore V2 can be confidently considered as simpler to use.

5.3 Final comparison between the two versions

The users' overall preferences were even clearer than the answers to the statements: 23 out of 25 participants preferred V2, one did not express any preference and another one preferred V1. The different implementations of the overview and the categories list provide good examples supporting hypothesis H2: detailed navigation in the overview page on one side, and faster navigation in the second version on the other side. The fact that 17 testers voted for the category page of V2, while only four preferred V1 (and – again – the additional comments expressed by the participants further support this) leads us to conclude that hypothesis H2 is supported, namely that users prefer faster navigation to more detailed information. Hypothesis H4 compares the two versions of the calendars: V1 implements a horizontal calendar, which is recognised as a traditional calendar by most of the people and therefore the users should be familiar with it. V2 contains a completely different calendar, presented as a list of days, that was (possibly) easier to use, but perhaps less common. The resulting data shows that 17 test participants preferred the V2 calendar, while only five preferred the horizontal one. Thus, hypothesis H4 is supported. Using a χ^2 test on the questions about the users' final preferences we could derive that these answers are significantly different (at least for 98.05%) from those that would be obtained by an equal probability for the replies (i.e. which system is preferred). Therefore the results are relevant for the study and the hypotheses are validated.

5.4 Influences and correlations within the results

Calculating correlation we discovered that the frequency of Internet usage does not have any significant influence, neither on the participants' preferences, nor on the required time or numbers of clicks. Similarly for the past usage of WAP: it does not have any influence on the testers' preferences, neither on the time needed for task completion. The only correlation that is significant enough to be mentioned is the positive correlation between WAP knowledge and the number of clicks employed in the first version. Therefore, hypothesis H6 (that habit influences time employed) is not confirmed, as well as hypothesis H7 (that habit influences the number of clicks). Even more: H7 is partially rejected as the correlation is positive and not – as assumed before – negative. The second part of hypothesis H8 is supported: knowledge of Internet or WAP is not significantly correlated with the users' preferences. Hypothesis H5 – age is correlated with the time required to complete the task – is supported: As the (positive) correlation is not caused by chance – with a certainty of 98% (V1) or even by nearly 100% (V2). This means, on average, that younger people took less time to complete the scenario. Thus, H5 is supported. We finally observe that regarding the impact of age on system preference (H8), the results did not show any significant difference.

6 Conclusions

Mobile usage is still a major challenge for many websites. In a recent mobile study performed by J. Nielsen (http://www.useit.com/alertbox/mobile-usability.html [July 20, 2009]) the average success rate (in performing typical tasks) was only 59%. That is substantially lower than the 80% success rate that they obtained when testing websites on a regular PC. In order to detect usability problems of a mobile travel planning web site (version 1) we designed and developed a second version that we thought would be more specifically suited for mobile devices (version 2). 25 people tested both versions using just one type of smartphone (Nokia N95) with a mid-sized screen and with a standard phone keypad. The success rate of our mobile travel planning web site was very high; all but one tester completed their assigned tasks. On a 1-5 scale the first version got a 3.88 average rate and the second 4.36. So we can conclude that in our travel planning mobile web sites we did not find major usability issues when the application was running on a phone of that class. Moreover, the second version was considered as better than the first one for some reasons that we collected and we propose here as useful design guidelines for future WAP applications:

G1: Lists with links are preferred over radio buttons.
G2: Faster navigation is preferred over detailed descriptions.
G3: Short descriptions with icons are preferred over extensive information.
G4: Scrolling is preferred over forward/backward links.
G5: Age positively influences time, younger people need lees time.
G6: Habit does not influence time, i.e., more experienced people may not use less time or clicks.

Beside this useful outcome, it's important to note that some users stated that the design could be improved (for both V1 and V2), so some further efforts should be made to enhance the GUI experience. Hence some future work could be focussed to either improving the usability of the current functions or to mobilise additional features, such as the mobile recommendation service for alternative contextual conditions (e.g. in case of rain or for a change in the itinerary). Another option would be to design still another version for touch-screen phones (such as the iPhone or the new Google Android devices). The Web experience on these phones is so superior that even applications that appear poor on standard feature phones or smartphones looks much better on these devices. All these aspects could further attract more users to use the system. In conclusion, we believe that the outcome of this study shows that mobilized Web sites, when browsed on reasonable featured phones as those we used in our test, can be as effective as Web sites on regular PC. Moreover, the guidelines that we derived can be used as an additional set of recommendations that, together with the still growing outcome of similar studies (http://www.forum.nokia.com/ [September 28, 2009]), can help to incrementally improve the future mobile web/WAP applications in tourism. We know that the underestimation of the importance of the user interface design factors can jeopardise the acceptance of a mobile service and can lead to the failure of the service, even though the functionalities are interesting for the user. Hence, the outcome of this work should be considered as a small but concrete contribution to the knowledge on WAP usability and the diffusion of mobile services for tourists.

References

Adomavicius, G., & Tuzhilin, A. (2005). Toward the next generation of recommender systems: A survey of the state-of-the-art and possible extensions. *IEEE Transactions on Knowledge and Data Engineering*, 17(6), 734-749.

Bertelè, U., & Rangone, A. (2008). Rapporto mobile and wireless business. Politecnico di Milano.

Buchanan, G., Farrant, S., Jones, M., Thimbleby, H., Marsden, G., & Pazzani, M. (2001). Improving mobile internet usability. In Proceedings of the 10th international Conference on World Wide Web (Hong Kong, Hong Kong, May 01 - 05, 2001). WWW '01. ACM, New York, NY, 673-680.

Buhalis, D., & Pistidda, L. (2009). Wireless Applications in Destinations. Information and Communication Technologies in Tourism 2009, 161-171.

Cena, F., Console, L., Gena, C., Goy, A., Levi, G., Modeo, S., & Torre, I. (2006). Integrating heterogeneous adaptation techniques to build a flexible and usable mobile tourist guide. *AI Communications* 19(4), 369–384.

Fesenmaier, D. R.,Werthner, H., & Woeber, K. (2006). Destination Recommendation Systems: Behavioural Foundations and Applications. CABI Publishing.

Forum Nokia. (2008). Getting Started with Mobile Design. Version 1.0; June 5, 2008. http://www.forum.nokia.com/

Haid, E., Kiechle, G., Göll, N., & Soutshek, M. (2008). Evaluation of a Web-based and Mobile Ski Touring Application for GPS-enabled Smartphones. Information and Communication Technologies in Tourism 2008, 313-323.

Jones, M., & Marsden, G. (2005). Mobile Interaction Design. John Wiley and Sons.

Kramer, R., Modsching, M., & ten Hagen, K. (2007). Behavioural Impacts of Mobile Tour Guides. Information and Communication Technologies in Tourism 2007, 109-118.

Lee, J., & Mills, J. E. Exploring Tourist Satisfaction with Mobile Technology. Information and Communication Technologies in Tourism 2007, 141-152.

Lewis, J. R. (1995). IBM Computer Usability Satisfaction Questionnaires: Psychometric Evaluation and Instructions for Use. ACM - International Journal of Human-Computer Interaction. oldwww.acm.org/perlman/question.cgi?form=CSUQ (May 07, 2009).

Nielsen, J. (2009). Mobile Usability Test Findings. http://www.useit.com/alertbox/mobile-usability.html

Ricci, F., & Nguyen, Q.N. (2007). Acquiring and revising preferences in a critique-based mobile recommender system. *IEEE Intelligent Systems* 22(3), 22–29.

Shiller, J.H. (2003). Mobile Communications. Addison-Wesley.

Turban, E., Lee, J.K., King, D., McKay, J., & Marshall, P. (2008). *Electronic Commerce*. Prentice Hall.

Venturini, A. & Ricci, F. (2006). Applying trip@dvice recommendation technology to www.visiteurope.com. In Proceedings of the 17th European Conference on Artificial Intelligence, Riva del Garda, Italy, Aug 28th - Sept 1st, 607-611.

Acknowledgements

We gratefully acknowledge the fruitful collaboration with the partners of VisitFinland (MEK – the Finnish Tourist Board, EC3 Networks, Siemens, Asio, Lixto) for the support provided during the design and the final integration of the mobile travel planner service in the country portal for Finnish tourism.

Application of QR Codes in Online Travel Distribution

Michael Canadi[a],
Wolfram Höpken[a/b] and
Matthias Fuchs [b/c]

[a]Business Informatics Group,
University of Applied Sciences Ravensburg-Weingarten, Germany
michael.canadi@hs-weingarten.de, wolfram.hoepken@hs-weingarten.de

[b]eTourism Competence Center Austria (ECCA)
University of Innsbruck, Austria
wolfram.hoepken@ecca.at, matthias.fuchs@ecca.at

[c]The European Research Institute (ETOUR),
Mid-Sweden University, Sweden
matthias.fuchs@etour.se

Abstract

Mobile services support various situations in everyday life and with the spread of mobile internet and better equipped mobile devices mobile services are becoming increasingly important, especially in tourism. Mobile tagging, based on QR codes or similar approaches, offers a technique to increase the accessibility of mobile services. In this paper potential applications of QR Codes in tourism, and specifically within a cultural institution (the Mercedes-Benz Museum), are identified and prototypically implemented. In a second step, these application scenarios are evaluated within a test user study. Results show that both, usability and intention to use the services are potentially high and QR codes are able to provide additional comfort in accessing mobile content and services.

Keywords: location-based services, mobile tagging, cultural tourism, QR codes

1 Introduction

Through a spread of mobile Internet and mobile devices with a wide range of additional functionalities, mobile services are becoming increasingly important (Henseler, 2009). As main reason for the evolution from online to mobile applications can be mentioned ubiquity and the increased usability (BVDW & J&S, 2008). The acceptance of mobile services significantly increased with the availability of powerful mobile devices of the latest generation (Nielsen, 2009). However, a still strong barrier for a more widespread use of mobile services is a fast and comfortable access to the services. *Mobile tagging* offers the opportunity of such an easy access by linking mobile services to physical objects, using 2D codes, here mobile codes. The *QR code* as a specific form of mobile code offers a solution for connecting physical and virtual content to provide users with additional information or enable access to mobile services. The paper at hand investigates application scenarios for mobile tagging and

QR codes in the tourism domain and more specifically in the context of museums. Based on existing information services of a museum, like brochures, information boards or online services, potential applications of mobile tagging with QR codes are identified and prototypically implemented. An evaluation with a test user group gains first insights into user acceptance and potential benefits of such application scenarios within the museum context. The paper is structured as follows. Section 2 gives a brief overview of the technical background of QR Codes and a short introduction into the technique of mobile tagging. Section 3 discusses existing approaches and related projects. Section 4 introduces the developed application scenarios at the Mercedes-Benz Museum and shows their prototypical implementations. Section 5 describes the evaluation of the scenarios within a test user study. The final section gives a conclusion and outlook on possible future work.

2 QR codes and mobile tagging

With the intention of developing symbols with enlarged capacity and reduced size two-dimensional codes were invented as an advancement of common one-dimensional barcodes. Different approaches can be classified into *composite codes*, *stacked codes*, *dot codes* and *matrix codes*. QR codes are a variation of matrix codes. Further advancements are *3D codes* with the additional dimension *colour-depth* (Lenk, 2003) and *4D codes* with multi-sequential display (Langlotz & Bimber, 2007). Choosing a particular code type depends on the requirements of the application scenario. This paper will focus on QR codes, due to their technical advantages (i.e. combining positive characteristics of several code types) and degree of standardization.

Developed 1994 by Denso Wave Incorporated (Denso, 2000) the QR code was initially used for tagging and tracking parts in automotive production. The QR code is standardized in several international bodies, i.e. AIM International, JIS and JAMA, ISO, Chinese and Korea National Standard, Vietnam National Standard and further utilized in several application standards, i.e. ISO and IEC. The specification defines the QR code regarding symbol size, information type and volume, data conversion and error correction functionality. Depending on the type of use data the capacity varies between 2,531 characters (8 bit binary data) and 7,098 characters (numeric data). The QR code structure (see Fig. 1.) consists of reserved areas for position detection, alignment, timing, version and format as well as the use data area.

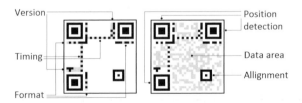

Fig. 1. QR code structure

Specific features of QR codes are 360° readability, resistance to nonlinear view (e.g. due to uneven surface (Soon, 2008) and error checking and correction (ECC). A complex Reed-Solomon-Code (ten Hompel, 2008) is implemented to identify and recover unusable data blocks, in case of partial damage or contamination (Lenk, 2002). QR codes can be generated with standardized code generators and decoded with handheld scanners, fix-placed charge couple device (CCD) terminals or mobile devices, offering a camera for optical recognition and decoding software for interpreting the contained information. The Physical World Connection (PWC) describes the idea of creating an automated connection between physical reality and content within the Internet. Main target is the creation of a medial convergence where the user isn't just provided with information but rather forced to act interactively. *Mobile tagging* defines the technique of creating such a connection by using two-dimensional codes, in this context typically called *mobile codes*, in combination with common mobile devices for their recognition. The QR code either contains data directly or connects to online data. After scanning the code, contained information, e.g. predefined SMS or E-mails, contact information, phone number or hyperlink to online data can be used on the mobile device.

3   Existing approaches and related work

Mainly in Japan, but also in Europe, a number of projects already identified opportunities of mobile tagging in tourism. Encoding data directly into QR codes is typically used in the following application areas:

- *Physical objects* and *places* can be digitally enhanced by simple messages or descriptions
- Encoding a phone number or predefined E-mail or SMS lowers the barriers of getting in contact to an organization or person
- For *transferring contact information* the QR code supports a standardised VCard format (electronic business card), e.g. used by Sims Kultur Online (Sims, 2009)
- The QR code's *special appearance* can have a positive effect on the attractiveness of marketing material, e.g. used in the project Code Unique Hotel (S&P, 2009)

Encoding hyperlinks into QR codes is used in the following application scenarios:

- Linking additional information to an object can be relevant for product information and marketing. Providing user-relevant information is normally restricted by product design and size. In Japan, QR codes are attached to fruits or vegetables, providing information on cultivation, used pesticides, crop and packing date (http://www.japanfs.org/en/pages/025772.html [Oct. 9, 2009]).
- QR codes can generate interlinkage between media of different types. Welt Kompakt (Welt Kompakt, 2007), for example, integrates QR codes to combine the content of a newspaper and highly actual multimedia mobile information. The Sun (The Sun, 2007) connects online content with mobile content to promote mobile services and support the portability of provided information.
- Based on the idea of adding content to physical places, a connection to mobile internet content can extend static information to real *location-based services*. Tag

City (The Thing, 2006) and Tag Your City (m-otion, 2007) implemented this concept by attaching 2D codes with encoded tourist information to relevant historical and cultural places in Frankfurt and Vienna. Following the concept of opening code creation to the public, the community platform for cultural locations Swiss Kaywa designed a mobile location guide called DocoDare (Kaywa, 2009).

- The National Theatre Darmstadt (Staatstheater Darmstadt, 2009) and Centre of Art and Media Technology Karlsruhe (ZKM) (ZKM, 2009) use QR codes to enable fast and easy access to their *mobile platform*.

- *Mobile couponing* (Ivancsits, 2006) describes the distribution of coupons via mobile phones. In this context a coupon is understood as information which offers owners discounted or even free purchase of goods or access to services. ZKM (ZKM, 2009) offered access to its archive as a gift for visitors, by linking a QR code to a hidden video. Sony Australia gave away playstations to the first ten customers who scanned a QR code successfully and answered the given task (Broughall, 2009). In Japan, Coca-Cola promoted a new line of tea products (Coca-Cola, 2009) by embedding QR codes to the back of the label. Customers could get a product for free by verifying the QR code at vending machines with integrated CCD-scanners.

- In *mobile ticketing* (Ivancsits, 2006) the QR code is used to transfer authorisation information in a secure way and offers a paperless alternative to print-out tickets. Examples for mobile ticketing with 2D codes are Deutsche Bahn (DB, 2009) Lufthansa (Deutsche Lufthansa, 2009) and Deutsche Post (DP, 2009).

4 Development of application scenarios

This paper presents four typical application scenarios of QR codes in cultural tourism, derived from existing best practice applications and prototypically implemented at the Mercedes-Benz Museum in Stuttgart:

- Enriching products by attaching mobile content, exemplarily implemented at the souvenir shop
- Support of advertising activities within the concept of event promotion
- Realisation of location-based services at places with historical relevance
- Ticket distribution and access control with a mobile ticketing service

Before describing the above concepts in more detail, the following section discusses the integration of QR codes into the overall architectural environment.

4.1 Architectural integration of QR codes

QR codes can be integrated into the overall system architecture in various ways depending on the service to be realised. The role of the QR code is either to provide additional information by tagging real-life objects and marketing material or to serve as a mean for identification and authorization (see also Fig. 2).

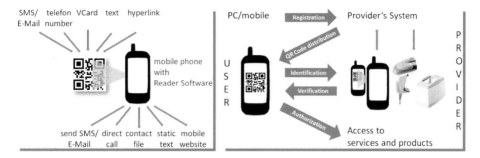

Fig. 2. Integration of QR codes into the architectural environment

Providing additional information via QR codes can be realised in different ways:

- Static text directly encoded into the QR code and accessible without a mobile internet connection.
- Link to download information in various formats like PDF, img, video, etc. A mobile internet connection is needed only once, but a special viewer application is required on the mobile device.
- Link to a mobile website. A wide range of information can be provided and retrieved over a mobile Internet connection or alternatively by saving the website offline as a bookmark.
- VCard (electronic contact format) to generate a standardized contact in the mobile phone's contact list, including name, address, different phone-numbers, E-mail and website information. The QR code can contain the VCard directly or link to an internet address for download. Directly integrating high quantity information can enlarge the QR code and influence its readability.

Providing QR Codes to the user as a mean of identification and authorization can be realised by the following techniques:

- Transferring the QR code as an image over *MMS* (Multimedia Message Service). This technique requires the user to enter his personal mobile phone number and MMS-services are not commonly available on an international level. There is no need for a mobile internet connection but service costs can appear.
- *Downloading* the QR Code as an *image* from a *personal mobile website*. Accessing the QR code requires a mobile internet connection. For further access, the mobile websites can be stored as a bookmark and in this way the QR code can be made available offline.

Table 1 gives an overview on the different techniques of QR code usage and links them to the application scenarios they are used in.

Table 1. Techniques of QR code usage

Providing information	Encoding static text	Souvenir product	Tourist information on	
	Link to a PDF document	Tourist information		
	Link to a mobile website	Souvenir cross-selling	Tourist information	Event information
	Encoding a VCard	Tourist information		
Identification and authorisation	QR Code distribution via MMS	Mobile ticketing national		
	QR Code as download within a personal mobile website	Mobile ticketing international		

4.2 Souvenir Shop

As a standard part of every museum the souvenir shop of the Mercedes-Benz Museum offers different products with historical background, e.g. model cars, but also items of the brand's classic collection, like accessories or fashion. Using QR codes, added to the product label, offers an additional benefit to customers by connecting physical objects with digital information and services. The following two concrete application scenarios have been developed and prototypically implemented.

Cross-selling. The QR code contains a direct hyperlink to recommended offers related to the purchased product. In general, the QR code links to products belonging to the standard portfolio of the shop. In case of a special promotion, the QR code links to a restricted product area which is not reachable from the common platform (following the concept of mobile couponing). For security purpose the concept ensures a single access based on a unique transaction number and product code.

Background information. Especially for products with historical relevance, background information can be accessed by including a QR code into product labels, e.g. of model cars. Additionally to static offline information, the application scenario provides online data by linking to a mobile website, offering additional information e.g. on the history of the particular model car. Compared to common print information costs can be reduced and the hedonistic attractiveness is increased.

4.3 Event information

To promote special events, offered by the museum, different media types, e.g. print and online promotion, are used in parallel. The combination of such different media types can be achieved by QR codes, placed within print media, as a connection between physical and online content. In this application scenario QR codes are used to reach two different objectives, on the one hand to support actuality of information and on the other hand to provide access to a wide range of additional mobile services.

Actuality. During the soccer world championship 2010, the museum will offer public viewing events. Typical for such events is the primary need for simple, but highly up-to-date information, rather than a wide range of additional services. In this context a print campaign with flyers and billboards promotes the event in general. Detailed information for each particular game, e.g. kick-off or actual score, are available by accessing the mobile website. By embedding a QR code into the design of print media, containing a fix hyperlink to the mobile website, additional data with high actuality can be provided.

Mobile services. Another application scenario is the open air cinema in line with the Festival "Museumssommer 2009". In contrast to the pervious purpose, actuality is less important because event information is rarely or never changing. Instead, the focus is to supply interested persons with basic information and additional mobile services. Therefore the mobile website provides event information, e.g. time, location and event description, as well as services for ticket booking and a preview function for the offered movie program. The implementation of the QR Code is based on encoding a hyperlink to lead to the mobile website.

4.4 Tourist information

In addition to the local exhibition the museum offers historical places and tours to relevant milestones in the automotive history, e.g. the birthplace of Gottlieb Daimler or the garage where the first car was invented. Information on those places and tours is also available on the museum's website to support visitors during trip planning.

At home. While planning a tour at home users get relevant visitor information via the museum's website, including contact and address, opening times and fees. With an integrated QR code this data is linked to corresponding mobile services for further use during the journey. Optionally and for evaluation purpose, a pdf-file download is offered as an alternative mode of information distribution. The comparison allows conclusions about user's preferences and usability (see section evaluation). In addition, contact data is offered to be saved on the mobile device in form of a VCard. Technically the QR code links to a mobile service for downloading, as a common syntax for encoding contact information directly into QR codes is not available, yet.

On location. At the historical places the QR code is used to provide additional location-dependent services. By tagging physical historical objects, information on the historic background can be displayed offline (directly encoded within the QR code) or online with multimedia items, i.e. sound and video over a mobile internet connection. Compared to classic information-boards the QR code needs less space and information is updateable.

4.5 Ticketing

For the distribution of tickets the museum offers different booking services. The visitor is able to buy entrance cards at the local point of sale or make the reservation by phone or internet. At the moment the number of visitors reaches 2,000 each day, half booking locally at the point of sale and the other half in nearly equal parts through telephone and internet. The existing online ticketing process offers ticket reservation, online payment and ticket distribution, either as print-out or picked-up at the local office. The print-out includes a 1D barcode and allows direct access via the museum's CCD-terminals.

The main goal of mobile ticketing is to create an autonomous booking process without a dependency of a PC or additional hardware. All actions including reservation and payment, ticket distribution and access via the CCD terminal are handled with the visitor's mobile device. The ticket data, similar to the 1D barcode for printed tickets, is encoded into a QR code and provided to the visitor via a restricted area within the mobile website. The website displays personal information of the visitor and an image of the QR code. For validation at the CCD-terminals the unique transaction number in combination with personal information allows a comparison with the registered ticket within the ticket management system. Additionally, the paperless distribution of tickets can be used as an extension of the existing online ticketing service. The mobile ticket distribution, described above, is offered as an additional option to the existing online ticketing process. As no mobile internet connection can be assumed in this case, the QR code is provided via MMS.

5 Evaluation

According to the technology acceptance model (TAM) (Davis, 2003), basic factors determining the users' intention to use an innovative technology or service is the perceived benefit (i.e. usefulness) on one hand and the ease of use (i.e. usability) of the service on the other. The following evaluation intends to tentatively estimate the visitor's propensity to use the services described above. By collecting both quantitative and qualitative data of a small group of test persons, conclusions are drawn about usefulness and usability of the services. The aim of the evaluation is twofold: To evaluate the concrete implementation of the QR code as well as to evaluate the application model behind, since the functionality of the tagging solution is directly connected to the perceived quality of the provided service.

5.1 Experimental setup

The evaluation was supported by an online test setting (Kuckartz, 2009). The test persons received a short introduction into the handling of QR codes and the necessary hardware. In order to ensure evaluation, the various concepts have been thoroughly explained and prototypically displayed to give the test persons a realistic impression of the service. The design of open and standardized questions followed a controlled scheme (Diekmann, 2007) with the focal points benefit (i.e. usefulness), usability (i.e.

ease of use) and relevance. The test sample consists of different persons, regarding age, gender, and skill-level. Also the equipment varies over different mobile devices and reader-applications. Moreover the prototypes include different variations of the way the QR code is implemented into the application scenario, with the goal of provoking reactions in regard to display rules and arguments.

5.2 Results

A totality of 17 test persons (i.e. 4 female and 13 male) have participated to the evaluation lasting for seven days. The participants are working in the Internet division of Mercedes-Benz and show rather balanced skill-levels. The sample can be arranged in three age-groups, twenties (41 per cent), thirties (51 per cent) and forties (6 per cent). The used mobile devices were mainly smart phones and PDAs but also a number of conventional mobile phones. Interestingly enough, the type of mobile device had no influence on evaluation results. Naturally, navigating within mobile content and displaying complex content is more difficult on older devices. But concerning the usage of QR codes itself, improved cameras or larger displays had no significant influence on user acceptance. Table 2 displays the aggregate evaluation. Usability, usefulness and relevance were scaled from 1 ('worst') to 4 ('best'). The question for a planned 'future use' recorded the decision opportunities 'yes' or 'no'. In order to compare the answers obtained from the test persons, both value domains are converted into percentages of the maximal score values.

Table 2. Summary of results

	Usability	Usefulness	Relevance	Future use
Souvenir shop	87.50	75.00	73.21	64.29
Event information	88.33	85.00	80.00	86.67
Tourist information	81.67	81.67	78.33	66.67
Mobile Ticketing	85.00	83.33	80.00	86.67

In summary, the majority of the test persons perceived the QR code as a relief to accessing mobile services and table 2 clearly displays that the evaluation result was generally positive. More precisely, with respect to usability, the rather simple concepts, namely event and souvenir information via QR codes, reached the relatively highest value. By contrast, tourist information and mobile ticketing as the obviously more complex application scenarios seem to be harder to handle. Interestingly, with regard to the usefulness dimension, the 17 test persons voted the latter application prototype as second best after event information. In general, the obtained evaluation results show a clear preference for scenarios with a relatively wider range of services that are typical for mobile use. For instance, the opportunity for ordering and validating tickets via a mobile service and, similarly, the offerings of extended information and services for events have been judged as most interesting and innovative scenarios (Table 2).

Main problems occurred in handling the reader software and finding the optimal distance between the mobile camera and the QR code. For this reason two test persons even wished to stop the test. In general, not more than one QR code should be placed in the same context to avoid confusing the user. Considering code specific rules, like minimum printing size, resolution and required margins assured readability within the test environment. Additional easements, such as explaining text helped to further increase usability. As high connection costs are still an important obstacle for mobile services, it has to be mentioned that at the time of the evaluation a majority of test users used a flat rate cost model with an unlimited internet connection time.

Souvenir shop. The connection between physical products and subsidiary product-information in form of a direct link to information within a mobile service created an additional benefit for the test users. The concept of additional product offerings opens the opportunity of shopping independently from opening hours of the (e.g. souvenir) shop. However a definite preference for one of the applications' *cross-selling* or *background information* couldn't be observed.

Event information. An identified benefit of this scenario is the achieved individuality and flexibility in designing the advertising medium, thereby eliminating the problem of relatively limited space for placing event information. In particular the QR code proofed to raise awareness through its unusual appearance. Using the QR Code as a direct link to the expected information minimizes the need for searching and navigating in mobile content. The majority of the participating test persons clearly preferred a wide spectrum of mobile services with several functions to retrieve information regarding the event.

Tourist information. Interlinking information from PC to the mobile device proofed to effectively assist users in planning a personalized tour. Compared to offer techniques for data synchronisation between a PC and a mobile device, the easy scalability of QR codes increased the usability of this interface. Another clear benefit dimension (i.e. usefulness) is the opportunity to further handle the information in other applications of the mobile device such as navigation software or a contact list. However, in this special case a provision of information in PDF or similar formats decreased usability for most test persons since only few mobile devices supported such formats. Most users without an unlimited mobile internet connection judged the optional saving function for mobile content as bookmarks as an important functionality, since it gives users the opportunity to avoid costs from a permanent Internet connection. When finally used for tagging of locations, QR codes increase flexibility as an alternative to guides and information boards. Information can be placed more flexible at the objects and kept up-to-date by changing mobile content.

Mobile Ticketing. The opportunity of an autonomous process for reservation and booking was clearly accepted as an innovative benefit by the test users. One of the most important benefits is the exclusion of additional hardware and the opportunity of an independent access at the entrance of the museum. Thus the provision of mobile solutions for complex scenarios puts emphasis on reduced system requirements and a comprehensible design. Interestingly, security aspects (e.g. prohibiting falsification or duplication of tickets) have not been judged as relevant by the test persons. As a whole the test user' evaluation clearly proofed the ability of QR codes to provide additional comfort (i.e. usability) and benefit (i.e. usefulness) in accessing mobile content and services. Put differently, mobile services gain new possibilities in supporting mobility and flexibility by closely interlinking physical objects and mobile services. To sum up, by the use of QR codes the physical environment can be enhanced by additional information and services in a powerful and flexible way.

6   Conclusion and future work

The paper presented application scenarios for QR codes in online travel distribution, especially in the sub-domain of museums, based on the technique of mobile tagging. By using QR codes the Mercedes-Benz Museum increases the range of product information and cross-selling potentials within the souvenir shop, provides tourist information and services for visitors, e.g. of historical places, as well as event information and services for exhibitions and festivals. Additionally, the museum enhanced the existing online ticketing with a mobile ticketing process, using QR codes as authorization technique. Generally, linking physical objects to additional information, especially via mobile services, enables several beneficial application scenarios. The executed evaluation clearly proved the benefits of mobile tagging via QR codes in a museum environment. Most users could easily handle the technique of scanning QR codes and the ease of accessing mobile services by QR codes was judged as potential boost of mobile services. However, user acceptance depends on a careful implementation of QR codes, following certain rules as identified in this paper. At present the largest barrier for mobile tagging is its limited publicity. Users as well as service providers mainly still don't know about the opportunities of QR codes and how they can be handled on mobile devices. Wide spread availability of efficient and user friendly software for creating and reading QR codes is necessary. The success of QR codes in the context of mobile tagging is of course strongly linked to the diffusion of mobile services in general. With more powerful mobile devices and an increasing acceptance of mobile services, mobile tagging based on QR codes will become more and more important.

References

BVDW & J&S (2008). Jahrbuch Deutscher Multimedia Award: *Interaktive Trends 2006/2007*. Bundesverband Digitale Wirtschaft and J&S Dialog Medien GmbH, Düsseldorf-Hamburg, Germany, pp. 26-30.

Broughall, N. (2009). *Sony's First QR Code is A Giz AU Competition to win 10 Playstation 3s*. Allure Media, Sydney, Australia, http://www.gizmodo.com.au/2008/07/sonys_first_qr_code_is_a_giz_au_competition_to_win_10_playstation_3s/ [Oct. 17, 2006].

Coca-Cola   (2009).   Coca-Cola   Central   Japan   Co.   Ltd.,   Yokohama,   Japan, http://c.cocacola.co.jp/haishin/ccnews/090511/html/index.html [Aug. 24, 2009].

Davis, C. K. (2003). *Technologies and methodologies for evaluationg information technology in business*. IRM Press, Hershey, PA, USA.

DENSO (2000). *QR Code.com*. Denso Wave Inc., http://www.qrcode.com [Sept. 24, 2009].

Deutsche Bahn (2009). Deutsche Bahn AG, Germany, http://www.bahn.de/p/ view/buchung/ mobil/handy_ticket.shtml [July 19, 2009].

Deutsche Lufthansa (2009). Info & Service: *The Mobile Boarding Card*. Deutsche Lufthansa AG, Frankfurt, http://www.lufthansa.com/online/portal/lh/de/info_and_services/checkin?nodeid =2141196&l=de&cid=18002 [Sept. 2, 2009].

Deutsche Post (2009). http://www.deutschepost.de/intnernetmarke [Sept. 17, 2009].

Diekmann, A. (2007). *Empirische Sozialforschung: Grundlagen, Methoden, Anwendungen*. Rohwolt Taschenbuch-Verlag, Hamburg, pp. 410-414.

Henseler, W. (2009). Interfacing Media Future – The Future of Automotive Web. Cooperative Workshop at the Daimler AG Stuttgart, Germany.

Ivancsits, R. G. (2006). *Mobile Couponing und Mobile Ticketing – Instrument des Customer Relationship Management im Mobile Marketing*. Dr. Müller, Saarbrücken, pp.7-109.

Kaywa (2009). DocoDare: *All about mobile Life*. Kaywa AG, Zurich, Switzerland, http://mobile.kaywa.com/files/dokodare2009.ppt [June 23, 2009].

Kuckartz, U. (2009). *Evaluation online: Internetgestützte Befragung in der Praxis*. VS Verlag für Sozialwissenschaften, GWV Fachverlage GmbH, Wiesbaden, pp. 33-67.

Langlotz, T. & Bimber O. (2007). Unsynchronized 4D Barcodes: *Coding and Decoding Time-Multiplexed 2D Colorcodes*. Bauhaus University, Weimar, Germany.

Lenk, B. (2002). Handbuch der automatischen Identifikation: *2D Codes, Matrixcodes, Stapelcodes, Composite Codes, Dotcodes*. Vol. 2, Monika-Lenk Fachbuchverlag, Kirchheim unter Teck.

Lenk, B. (2003). Handbuch der automatischen Identifikation: *ID-Techniken, 1D Codes, 2D Codes, 3D Codes*. Vol. 1, Monika-Lenk Fachbuchverlag, Kirchheim unter Teck.

m-otion (2007). *Tag Your City*. m-otion communications GmbH, Vienna, http://www.tagyourcity.at/img/TYC_Folder_A5_Web.pdf [26.aug.2009].

Nielsen (2009). *Mobile Media View Q1 2009*. The Nielsen Company, Hamburg London.

Pixelpark (2007). White paper: *Mobile Tagging mit 2D Code*. Pixelpark Agentur, Hamburg.

S&P Architects (2009). Code Unique Infosheet – Studio City Hotel. Söhne and Partners, Vienna, http://www.soehnepartner.com/projekte/hotel/studio-city-hotel/28-178.htm [Sept. 17, 2009].

Sims (2009). Die Kultur-Sozial-Community, http://www.simskultur.net/baden-wuerttemberg/karlsruhe/zkm-zentrum-fuer-kunst-und-medientechnologie-karlsruhe [Aug. 25, 2009].

Soon, T. J. (2008). *The Synthesis Journal:* Section three – the QR Code. iTSC Information Thechnology Standard Comitee, Singapore, pp. 59-78.

Staatstheater Darmstadt (2009). Darmstadt, Germany, http://www.staatstheater-darmstadt.de/mobile [Oct. 6, 2007]; http://www.staatstheater-darmstadt.de/presse/presse/dein-handy-ein-star.html [Sept. 24, 2009].

Ten Hompel, M., Büchter, H. & Franzke, U. (2008). *Identifikationssysteme und Automatisierung*. Springer-Verlag, Berlin, Germany, pp. 85-89.

The Sun (2007). How to crack QR smart codes. News Group Newspapers Ltd., London, http://www.thesun.co.uk/sol/homepage/news/article543361.ece [Sept. 23, 2009].

The Thing (2006). *Tag City Project*. The Thing, http://www.tag-city.net [Sept. 13, 2009].

Welt Kompakt (2007). *Welt Kompakt führt den 2D-Code ein*. Springer-Verlag, Berlin, Germany, http://www.welt.de/webwelt/article1344905/WELT_KOMPAKT_fuehrt_den_2D_Code_ein.html [Sept. 30, 2009].

ZKM (2009). *ZKM mobile tagging*. Zentrum für Kunst und Medientechnologie, Karlsruhe, Germany, http://2009.zkm.de/2009 [Sept. 29, 2009].

Acknowledgements

The authors would like to thank Igor Druzović and Henning Neef from Mercedes-Benz Internet Applications for the collaboration in developing prototypes and the Mercedes-Benz Museum Stuttgart, Germany, especially Heidrun Jopp and Thilo Wessel, for supporting the project and offering the experimental environment.

Evaluation of the Concept of Early Acceptance Tests for Touristic Mobile Applications

Manfred Bortenschlager[a],
Elisabeth Häusler[a],
Wolfgang Schwaiger[b]
Roman Egger[c], and
Mario Jooss[c]

[a,b] Salzburg Research Forschungsgesellschaft, Austria
Mobile and Web-based Information Systems
[a] elisabeth.haeusler, manfred.bortenschlager@salzburgresearch.at
[b] wolfgang.schwaiger@gmail.com

[c] Fachhochschule Salzburg, Austria
roman.egger, mario.jooss@fh-salzburg.ac.at

Abstract

Mobile applications are finding increased acceptance in tourism, particularly tourist services like city, sport or museum guides. The potential of mobile services is difficult to estimate a priori because hardly any user acceptance tests can be carried out before having a concrete implementation of that service. In this work we present a methodology and a through evaluation that allows a rapid development of high-fidelity prototypes of mobile applications. Goal of the empiric part of the investigations was the development of a mobile prototype with the "NetBeans Mobility Pack" software in the shortest possible time and to subsequently test it as to suitability for practical use in the real context.

Keywords: early acceptance test, rapid prototyping, simulation framework, NetBeans, mobile application

1 Introduction

Technologically mobile devices are getting more and more advanced and mobile services increasingly penetrate the relevant markets. The topic currently is highly up-to-date and many companies and research institutes are engaged with it. Especially, developments such as the iPhone App Store, Android Market Place, etc. or the upcoming programming language JavaFX reflect the importance of mobile services in our market. It shows that the future of mobile services with about four billion mobile phones worldwide has an ongoing big potential (Göll, Lassnig, Rehrl, 2009). According to research studies, a majority of tourists is already using an Internet connection to access tourist information. Moreover, 91.7% of the respondents can imagine using a mobile device to gather information before or during their vacation. Furthermore, an average of 84.97% is open minded in buying tickets, accepting restaurant recommendations, or in getting a selection of objects of interest using a mobile device (Egger et al., 2005).

Too short is the debate about the development of mobile services. Under the slogan "Rapid Prototyping" subsumed, there are a number of interesting opportunities to develop mobile applications. However, as the target group is analogously high, the acceptance of a mobile service on the market is difficult to estimate a priori. Does the user like the service? Is the service useful? Does it cover all needs? etc. Currently, most acceptance tests are carried out – if they are carried out at all – with an already implemented and finished service. Due to this fact, enterprises risk potentially high false investments because of the wrong decision to develop a mobile application which does not get accepted on the market.

The remainder of this paper is organised as follows: Section 2 gives a short introduction to the topic of experience prototyping. Furthermore, Section 3 introduces a framework for fast building high-fidelity prototypes of mobile applications (NetBeans Mobility Pack). The methodology and results of the evaluation undertaken in this research are presented in Section 4. Section 5 summarises this work, and outlines key findings and key aspects for further research.

2 Theoretical Background – Agile Software Development

According to the facts mentioned in the beginning of this work, the special challenge lies in a correct estimation, whether a service is useful in real use. New services often do not generate the estimated turnover expected by the service providers. Additionally, mobile software has a short time-to-market period that is limited to a few months (Bortenschlager and Kiechle, 2006). So, it is recommended that the limited time period is used as efficiently as possible in terms of client- and market orientation of an intended (mobile) application.

To address the problem of fast product life cycles in dynamic markets, the method of Agile Software Development is strongly recommended. Agile Development describes a way of *experience prototyping*. Generally a prototype is an approximation of a system that exhibits the essential features of the final version of that system. (Adamopoulos 2009) Experience Prototyping is a technique which was first established by the manufacturing and design industry. Manufacturing processes often require a fast development of prototypes, for example the production of a new car series or the construction of new computer cases etc. Prototypes do not implement or contain the full functionality or the finest possible form of the product. The purpose of this process is to get a presentable form of the subsequent developed product. In the context of software development the definition of experience prototyping by the manufacturing industry can be assumed in any way. (Schwaiger, 2007) It allows developers, users and clients to get an impression of the developed products already in early stages of the design process. Ideas and modifications from responsible actors can be easily taken into account. (Bortenschlager et al., 2007). Software frameworks for rapid prototyping that allow the automatic generation of early prototypes are a possible way to support this process. Further more rapid prototyping technology has an advantage of its low overall cost due to the building materials and the processing principle. (Yu et al. 2003)

Software prototypes offer a minimum set of functionality, but provide a first impression of the future look and feel, and the behaviour of an intended application. The functionality (e.g. network communication, position determination, etc.) is simulated to a large extent. Basic functionality is thus demonstrated to the potential users. Thus more valuable statements about the acceptance based on their feedback can be met. Such software frameworks are therefore particularly suited for early acceptance tests of mobile applications. Furthermore, the results of user tests provide valuable statements whether the development and implementation of the tested service shall be continued or not. Companies benefit by using software prototypes because unprofitable investments and wrong decision makings can be identified early enough to avoid false investments. (Bortenschlager et al., 2007). Therefore, experience prototyping techniques such as rapid prototyping have a high potential to reduce costs of product development which is also stated in related literature (e.g. Lan, 2009, Rupp et al., 2003).

3 NetBeans MobilityPack

A great number of various solutions for Rapid Prototyping available on the market: CCC Cybelius Maestro™ (http://www.cybelius.com), d.tools (http://hci.stanford.edu/dtools), Flash Lite (http://www.adobe.com/products/flashlite), NetBeans Mobility Pack (http://www.netbeans.org/products/mobility), Niccimon platform (http://www.niccimon.de) are the most important products.

In recent research work (Bortenschlager et al., 2007) we already evaluated different software frameworks concerning the rapid prototyping of mobile services according to following criteria:

- Generation of mobile application for the Java 2 Micro Edition Platform (J2ME)
- Simulation of context factors (location, time, etc.)
- Network communication (GSM, GPRS, UMTS, Bluetooth, etc.)
- Representation of workflows (modulation of states and state transitions)
- Support of dialogues and graphical user interfaces
- Drag & Drop editor
- Involvement of multimedia content (pictures, videos)
- Presentation of digital maps
- Remote control (while testing)
- Documentation (recording of user's actions)

The result of the evaluation shows that the NetBeans Mobility Pack (http://www.netbeans.org/kb/55/mobility.html) in combination with the NetBeans Integrated Development Environment (http://www.netbeans.org) most appropriately addresses the needs for a rapid prototyping framework for mobile applications. Thus, we also used this software for the presented study in this paper.

Fig. 1 shows a screenshot of the development environment of the NetBeans MobilityPack Software. On the left hand side the structure of the software project is shown. In the middle of the screen there is a drag & drop editor which allows a rapid modelling of a mobile service. Users are provided numerous ready-to-use modules from the right hand side (e.g. different screen, command buttons, etc.).

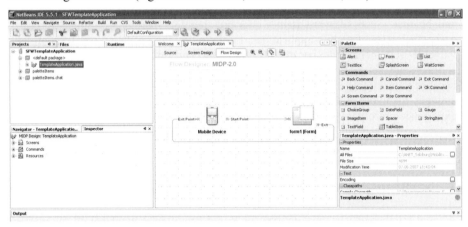

Fig. 1. NetBeans MobilityPack - Development Environment

After designing the mobile application within the editor it can easily be run on a mobile device emulator on the PC. Furthermore, it can directly be transferred to a mobile phone via Bluetooth or USB cable to test the application in real environment.

4 Methodology and Evaluation

The evaluation for the rapid prototyping using NetBeans was performed on two levels. The goal of a first step was to develop a scenario that had been previously defined in as short a time as possible using the "NetBeans Mobility Pack". The issue here was to measure the work time required for implementation of the scenario and to evaluate the "feasibility" for this in the course of the development work. The parameters and measurement criteria were thus set to the time that would be required for the implementation and the scenario-specific programming in respect to the functional range of the prototype. The scenario description comprised an order to this effect for the implementation of a navigation function, a search function and a ticketing function. The navigation aimed at bringing the user from a point of interest (POI) A to POI B. The POI should moreover be provided with a text description of the sight plus an appropriate photograph to go with it. Navigation should be intuitive and self-explanatory and ultimately move over into a ticketing function. It was defined that an entry ticket for a museum be bought using the mobile terminal. The search function had to be implemented for finding a suitable restaurant in the framework of research. The tourist should be offered a multiple choice of food & beverages such as for example "country-style food, gourmet food, quick snacks, good value and good tasting" etc.

In addition to the prototype programming task assignments, the technical competences required also needed to be checked to ensure that the prototype programming could actually be implemented as required. The check was performed by a test group (6 persons) consisting of three programmers plus a control group of three non-developers. Both groups had to develop and create the prototype according to the specified tourism scenario within a maximum time span of 40 hours. According to other research studies in the usability field range six to twelve test subjects in order to arrive at usable insights (Dumas/ Redish 1999). Each test person received a template in addition to the brief project information/introduction, so as to be able to document the separate implementation steps (the logical cycle) with NetBeans. The test persons not only received this template, but were given a qualitative questionnaire to fill in as a means of documenting all their assessments, experiences and problems encountered in a structured manner.

Furthermore a user experience test was carried out using the Morae software. The advantage of the method employed is the precise analysis of the user's behaviour: his/her interaction with the system is recorded by a camera, while the statements made by the test person are documented by the thinking-aloud method, and all the text entered, mouse clicks, mouse movements, etc. are recorded. These recordings were subsequently evaluated and interpreted.

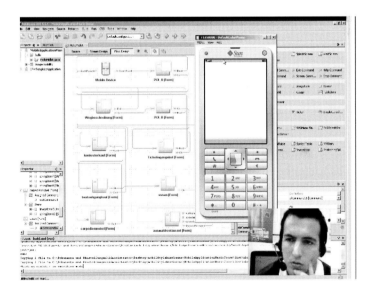

Fig. 2. User experience test with Morae

An evaluation of the prototype in a real context followed in a second step. In the course of this, 16 persons in the age group 18 to 30 were interviewed about their impressions about a prototype developed by the control group. According to Lamnek (2005), the random sample size is adequate for samples of the kind and plays a minor role in qualitative social research in general. The interview takes on an important position in empirical research because the unrivalled density of the data obtained from the practical user knowledge of the interviewees is the most important of the practical research advantages of this kind of survey. (comp. Bogner/Menz 2005) The interviews followed a discussion guideline that was based on theoretical findings and also developed from personal specialist knowledge of the subject. This is also recommended by Döring und Bortz (2005) as a means of making the results from the interviews comparable. The evaluation of the interviews was oriented to a significant extent along the qualitative content analysis technique developed by Mayring (2002). Suggestions from Bogner/Menz (2005); Meuser/Nagel (2005) and Diekmann (2005) were also brought in for the application of the methodology.

In order to achieve a realistic assessment of the practical suitability of the prototype developed using NetBeans, answers to the following questions were needed. "How realistic is the prototype created with the aid of the NetBeans Mobility Pack? Can the prototype be compared with a real application? Would you use the prototype?

It should be remarked here that this was not a matter of evaluating a starting point scenario (or how someone gets from POI A to POI B), but it was rather about how realistic the effect of the prototype was. The test persons were given a Nokia 6110 Navigator as a mobile terminal. The task assignment was explained to the test persons in a one-to-one discussion before the test. Following on from this, the test persons carried out the tests independently. The results were kept in a written record and evaluated.

4.1 Results of the prototype development

A total of six persons carried out the development tests in the scope of the first prototype development investigation level. Even those test persons unfamiliar with the technicalities of programming were able to implement the scenario relatively well. Difficulties arose in particular in using some specific elements that were not cited in the Help function. In addition, NetBeans required graphic capabilities; in other words, the test persons had to be able to work with other programs (e.g. Photoshop) in order to achieve the desired results. Figure 4 shows the network plan of the scenario realised to specification within some 5 hours (4h 55min.) together with examples for buying a ticket.

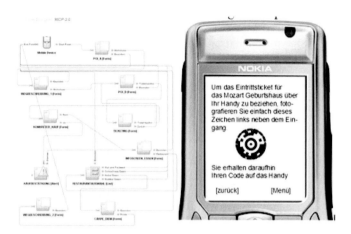

Fig. 3. Flow charts of the scenario realisation / presentation for buying a ticket

For those test persons who had no programming knowledge, the NetBeans Mobility Pack represented a powerful programming tool with a very complex structured "Help" function (F1) that could not answer all the questions put. As a result, system messages occurring in specific situations could not be correctly interpreted with the result that the problems that cropped up could not be resolved satisfactorily. The available time of 40 hours was by a long way not required by any of these 3 test persons. One test person needed XX hours, the 2ⁿᵈ test person had the prototype ready in eight hours, the 3ʳᵈ test person, however, threw in the towel after 14 hours of the test run since no progress was in sight. In order to ensure efficient implementation by a non-developer, the system would need to improve the Help function and offer a brief virtual introduction containing plenty of information at the very beginning when the program starts up. The statements made by the test persons on the suitability of NetBeans for non-developers were clear: *"Not suitable for people without programming knowledge". "The tool in the current version is only suitable for successful rapid prototyping when this is done by a programmer."*

Those test persons with programming knowledge, however, had no problems in implementing the scenarios. They needed from 150 to 240 minutes for the creation of the scenarios. The view expressed by this test group was that NetBeans is a very simple and intuitive tool. The screens and elements can basically be implemented without any previous knowledge or specialisation for the technology they are based on. Problems arose only in saving the project. Qualitative statements in this area were: *"In principle the tool is suitable for rapid prototyping, since a complex mobile application of substantial content can be developed in a very short time". "Should not actually be a problem. Implementation is done without writing or looking at a single line of code."*

156

Figure 4 shows a comparison of the development time required by all of the test persons. What can be clearly seen here is that four of the six test persons very quickly completed the prototype creation. Three to five hours were the average for the creation work.

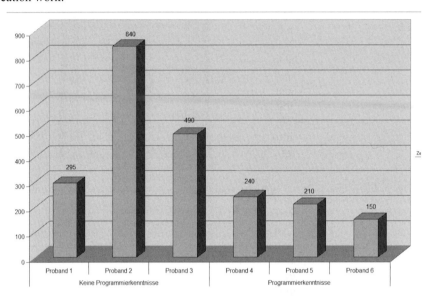

Fig. 4. The length of time needed for prototype creation in minutes

It can therefore be said in conclusion that NetBeans can be regarded as a suitable tool for rapid prototyping if the user has a basic technical background.

4.2 Results of the prototype evaluation in a real context

A total of 16 test persons were presented with a "non-developer" implemented prototype. The interviews with the test persons brought a clear result to light, because they all assessed the prototype as being very realistic and comparable with a "real" application. The realistic presentation of the maps and the text information were emphasised as particularly positive features. 15 of the 16 interviewees said they would be ready to use the prototype because of the logical traceability it offers. The fact that numerous test persons would have liked to have seen more pictorial material on the sights and less text information, that they wanted to see zoom functions in the map presentations etc. is knowledge relevant for an actual implementation, but not of significance for the objectives of the study. At this point it would also have been possible to compare the acceptance of the prototypes with the Technology Acceptance Model (TAM) or one of the further developed models derived from it. In the present study, however, the issue was above all the achievement of qualitative results in the form of assessments from the test persons.

5 Discussion and Conclusion

The rapid prototyping project was implemented in a period of some 12 months and the results can be regarded as thoroughly fruitful. The creation of the prototype was implemented satisfactorily by five out of six participating test persons. Of the three non-developers, two test persons were able to create the prototype with the NetBeans Mobility Pack in a relatively short time (295 minutes and 490 minutes respectively). By comparison, the experienced programmer group needed 200 minutes each on average. This shows that rapid prototyping with the NetBeans Mobility Pack is also suitable for persons without extensive programming knowledge. Improvement potential – and here all six test persons were in agreement – is in the tutorials, which were either incomplete or too complex (above all for persons without programming knowledge). The use of additional guidelines and templates would be very helpful at this point. The cost savings for the development of mobile prototypes with the NetBeans Mobility Pack are essential.

In addition, the requirement of short time to market that is essential for mobile technologies is met by the rapid implementation. Numerous content providers in the tourism area are currently squaring up to the challenge of dealing with mobile applications, potential services and the likely opportunities they will bring on the market. In the NetBeans Mobility Pack, a professional tool for rapid prototyping is available for the fast, inexpensive and relatively simple advance analysis and evaluation of those developments that promise potential for the future. Rapid prototyping is a very good method for the rapid production of prototypes based on a few core data. Moreover, with rapid prototyping shortens the development time of new products, the costs of development and by improving the quality of the products.

References

Adamopoulos, D., Haramisb, G., & Papandreouc, C (1998). Rapid prototyping of new telecommunications services: a procedural approach. *Computer Communications* 21, 211-219.

Bogner, A., & Menz, W. (2005): Das theoriegenerierende Experteninterview. Erkenntnisse, Wissensformen, Interaktion. In: Bogner, A., Littig, B., & Menz, W. (Hrsg), *Das Experteninterview. Theorie, Methode, Anwendung.* 2nd edition. Wiesbaden: VS publishers, 33-70.

Bortz, J., & Döring N. (2005): *Forschungsmethoden und Evaluation für Human- und Sozialwissenschaftler.* 3rd revised edition. Heidelberg. Springer publishing house.

Bortenschlager, M., Haid, E., & Schwaiger, W. (2007): A rapid Prototyping Software Framework for Early Acceptance Testing of Mobile Applications. In Frew, A. (Eds.): Proceedings of EyeForTravel 07. London.

Bortenschlager, M., & Kiechle, G. (2006): Eine Testmethodik für mobile Anwendungen. *Tourismusjournal*, 3 (8), 371-375.

Dumas, J., & Redish, J. (1999). *A practical guide to usability testing.* Exeter: Intellect Books.

Göll, N., Lassnig, M., & Rehrl, K. (2009): Location-Based Services im mTourismus – Quo Vadis? In Egger, R. & Jooss, M. (Eds.), *mTourism: mobile Dienste im Tourismus.* Urstein: LIT publishers (in print).

158

Egger, R. et al. (2005): Akzeptanz und Nutzung des Internet und mobiler Endgeräte durch potenzielle Österreich-Urlauber. Forschung Urstein GmbH, Zentrum für Zukunftsstudien.

Lamnek, S. (2005): Qualitative Sozialforschung. In: König, E. & Zedler, P. (Hrsg.): Qualitative Sozialforschung. 4.Auflage. Weinheim, Basel: Beltz publishers.

Lan, H. (2009): Web-based rapid prototyping and manufacturing systems: A review. *Computers in Industry* in press.

Mayring, P. (2002): Einführung in die Qualitative Sozialforschung. Weinheim; Basel: Beltz publishers.

Rupp, M, Burg, A., & Beck, E. (2003): rapid prototyping for wireless designs: the five-ones approach, *Signal Processing*, 83(7), 1427 - 1444.

Schwaiger, W. (2007): Software Framework for rapid Prototyping and Early Acceptance Testing of Mobile Applications. Salzburg: Diploma Thesis.

Yu, G., Ding, Y., Li, D., & Tang, Y. (2003): A low cost cutter-based paper lamination rapid prototyping system. *International Journal of Machine Tools & Manufacture* 43; 1079–1086.

Advanced Visitor Tracking Analysis in Practice: Explorations in the PortAventura Theme Park and Insights for a Future Research Agenda

Antonio P. Russo[a]
Salvador Anton Clave[a]
Noam Shoval[b]

[a] Department of Geography, University Rovira i Virgili, Tarragona, Spain
antonio.russo@urv.cat, salvador.anton@urv.cat

[b] Department of Geography, Hebrew University of Jerusalem, Israel
noamshoval@mscc.huji.ac.il

Abstract

In this article we discuss the strategic use of visitor tracking data in the good management of visitor attractions and tourist destinations, also highlighting the challenges that could be presented by tracking visitors in different attraction types and sites. Based on the practice and results from a tracking experiment in the PortAventura theme park, an enclosed and controlled environment, we then illustrate the actual and potential uses that attraction managers can do of this information, proposing a number of logistic and technical solutions to enhance the use of tracking data in this specific type of attractions. Finally, the paper present a future research agenda into visitor spatial behaviour using tracking technologies in semi-open and open environments other than theme parks and leisure attractions.

Keywords: attraction management, spatial behaviour, GPS, tracking, research agenda

1 Advanced visitor tracking research

There is today a large body of research regarding tourism in attractions sites and destinations, but a distinctive lack of detailed data on the spatial behaviour of visitors, which diminishes its practical relevance for policy and management (Dietvorst 1995; Thornton et al. 1997; Shaw et al. 2000). The few existing studies that do address this subject are generally descriptive and at case-study level and do not attempt to deal with the factors which form the basis of spatial activity. Certain studies have focused on specific perspectives and their impact on spatial activity, for example religion (Shachar and Shoval 1999), spatial preferences and types of recreational activities (Anton Clavé, Nel.lo and Orellana, 2007) the purpose of the visit (Montanari and Muscara 1995), gender (Carr 1999), the number of visits to the city (Oppermann 1997), or the type of organization - as an individual or a group (Chadefaud 1981). However, even in sites where visitor surveys are undertaken regularly, the detailed geographical aspects of the visit are usually neglected, being assumed impossible to gather through direct empirical research (Meng et al. 2005).

Yet, these detail matter Thornton et al. (1997: 1849) note that understanding the spatial and temporal behaviour of tourists in destinations could enhance the management of transportation or attractions, and contribute to extend the geographical distribution of visitors and visitor expenditure within regions; in addition, it could improve marketing strategies (p. 1850) and several other aspects. More specifically, destinations and attractions are often conjuncts consisting of various – and often a great deal of – micro-segments and environments, like the trails in a natural park, the attractions and services in a theme park, the heritage elements in a historical city, or the public spaces and commercial alleys within a large tourist city. Knowing exactly, respectively, which trails have been hiked, for how long, and with what effort, which rides or shows have been attended (and how much they've been enjoyed), which monuments visited or photographed, and which type of shops and squares have attracted the attention of visitors, could lead to a radical improvement in the performance of such destinations, from many points of view (as will be illustrated in this note), through accurately designed solutions regarding elements such as like signposting, opening times, licensing, pricing, public transport engineering, etcetera.

While we may obtain general knowledge on the activity of visitors through traditional or "low-tech" methods like surveying, the main factor that hampers the availability of detailed spatial data is the complexity of the environment: the unfamiliar morphology of the site or attraction makes it hard for the tourists to navigate their way in it, and consequently to recall it in a survey at the end of the visit. Other methods, like following and recording the time-activity of visitors, personally or through the analysis of CCTV cameras (Hartmann 1988; Gali-Espelt and Donaire-Benito 2006), faces relevant problems of privacy infringement, and is hardly considered cost-effective for the limited size of sampling that it allows or the impossibility of segmenting track data according to the actual characteristics of the visitor tracked.

This picture changes with the development of new technology-enhanced methods, which are detailed in various papers (Shoval and Isaacson 2006, 2007; Shoval 2008; Spek 2008) and in recently published books (Schaick and Spek, 2008; Shoval and Isaacson 2010). In the last decade, the use of Geographic Information System (GIS) and related technologies in the analysis of territory and human spatial behaviour has become widespread. However, the potential of tracking technologies such as Global Positioning System (GPS) for tracking pedestrians has remained virtually untapped. To date, most research based on material gathered by advanced technologies has been limited to transport studies tracking the spatial paths of motorised vehicles.

One possible explanation is that gathering data from pedestrians through GPS is far more complicated than doing so from motorised vehicles. Whereas the tracking system for a car is just a device that after being installed easily would not affect the nature of the data collected, with pedestrians the tracking system has to be both small and "passive" so as not to disrupt or affect the subject's normal behaviour; requirements often difficult to meet. The methodological body based on the joint use of this new generation of tracking technologies (TT) for the collection of spatial data on visitors, possibly to be integrated by surveying activities, and the use of GIS for the elaboration and representation of visitor spatial behaviour is defined in this note as Advanced Visitor Tracking Analysis (AVITA). The specific TT can be divided into two groups: technologies that rely on the satellite based Global Positioning System (GPS); and technologies that are reliant on land-based antennas, of which Cellular Cell Identification, Time Difference of Arrival (TDOA) and Angle of Arrival (AOA) are the main examples (see further detail on tracking technologies in Shoval and Isaacson, 2006). In this paper we especially focus on the practicalities and potential impacts of GPS-based AVITA.

2 Expected impacts of AVITA in the management of visitor attractions and tourist destinations

TT allow the collection of detailed spatial data from a sample of visitors, who accept to take part in the experiment and to carry with them a GPS device for the duration of visit to a site. The moment of the delivery of the device is an opportunity both to validate the acceptance of visitors to participate in the experiment, eventually having them signing documents that allow privacy-protected information to be used (according to national regulations), and to collect basic socio-demographic information on the participants that would be used to segment the collected tracking data.

Once these data are obtained, they can be elaborated through the statistical and GIS-based techniques that form part of AVITA. This allows the obtainment of the following information and their use in standard attraction and site management:

- The identification of general patterns of spatial behaviour of visitors, segmented by socio-demographic characteristics
- The analysis of the influence of the duration of visits (time-budgets) on the spatial behaviour of visitors
- The sequence and selection of visits to distinct attractions or landscape elements, segmented by time-budgets
- The analysis of the use of transport means (pedestrian, private transport, collective transport, public transport)
- The analysis of congestion in different locations
- The daily "life cycle" of attractions
- The generation of "clusters" of mobility across different groups

A critical element of AVITA is represented by the method of data collection, and specifically on the method of delivery of GPS devices. The cost-effectiveness of the tracking experiments greatly depends on the practical possibility of getting in touch with large masses of visitors to be sampled on entrance to the site, and on exit (thus the risk that costly GPS devices are not given back is minimised). This possibility is of course highest in the case of enclosed attractions and conjuncts, with a small number of gateways: theme parks, natural parks, archaeological compounds, etc. In all these cases, the moment of the purchase of an entry ticket (or authorisation in the case of protected natural environment functioning with quota systems) allows a prior screening of the potential participants to the tracking experiment, enabling a more effective sampling according to groups and socio-demographic characteristics. In other circumstances, getting in touch with participants, sampling them accurately, and getting the devices back can be tricky; these situations – and possibly methods to be deployed in those cases – are analysed later.

It was stated before that GPS-based data collection can be integrated by qualitative information which could be collected at the moment of the restitution of the device, like satisfaction and motivation data, or even quantitative, like expenditure at different locations. In fact, often – and especially for attractions that already have some general knowledge of the spatial activity of visitor but cannot relate it to individuals – this information is the most precious outcome of AVITA, as will be argued later in the case of PortAventura.

The power of the two collection methods – spatial data collected via GPS and additional information collected through direct interviews – is enhanced through their integration: by tracking visitors to a specific location during their visit, more precise questions can be done regarding their behaviour ('when you were in site X at 16.15 hours, how did you like it? Who in your group chose to stop here? How much money did you spend in this place?' etc.); this information, as argued above, is very hard to collect through non-technological surveying methods because usually visitors do not recall with sufficient precision what they did during their visit and where, but prompted with information on their actual behaviour, or shown a printed track of their activity, this information will easily surface. Secondly, by stratifying spatial data according to behavioural data, more exact knowledge on the relation between space-time behaviour and subjective information – like satisfaction and expenditure – can be retrieved. Thus, additional AVITA output that uses survey data regard:

- The analysis of spatial decisions (choice of a particular track, member of the party who selects the track, satisfaction levels)
- Tourist expenditure by area
- The time-space analysis of tourist consumption and expenditure

The collection of such integrative information poses additional challenges regarding the conduction of the experiment. Specifically, surveys have to be based on tracking data, in order to select the most meaningful questions to ask the sampled participants using the only opportunity of contact that is feasible and cost-effective to arrange, that of the moment of the restitution of the GPS device. This means that track data have to be immediately downloaded and charted in an easily readable format or else that they should prompt the construction of an on-purpose questionnaire. To this end, specific software may have to be developed.

3   Lessons from the PortAventura pilot visitor tracking

As a practical example of the value of AVITA, of its potential impacts for site management, and of the difficulties encountered in the development of the tracking experiment, we will now illustrate the activity of a research group within an applied research project commissioned by PortAventura, the largest theme park in Spain, in the year 2008, having been authorised to use this information by the PortAventura theme park management. With about 3.5 million visitors per year, the PortAventura theme park is a one of the key attractions of the Costa Daurada tourist area, in the south of Catalonia (at 1 hr. drive from the city of Barcelona). It is also one of the top European theme parks (Anton Clavé, 2007). It was designed as a round-the-world trip visiting exotic places organising this central theme through a carefully planned selection of four exotic places (Mexico, Polynesia, China and the Far West) from a point of departure themed as a small Mediterranean fishing port. Moreover, since 1998 PortAventura is enjoying a phase of expansion heading in the direction of transforming the original theme park into a tourist and recreation complex that currently includes four 500-room hotels, a water park, a Beach Club located on the seafront, three golf courses and a convention centre.

The management of PortAventura had expressed its interest for a better knowledge of spatial patterns in the visits to its installations and in its whereabouts, as well as of the determinants of spatial decisions according to groups. The ultimate stated objective of the park was to improve their knowledge of the consuming behaviour of visitors based on their spatial activity: whether specific groups displayed different visiting and purchasing behaviour at different times of the day, the process of making decisions regarding consumption, and the reaction to queues, congestion and atmospheric incidences in terms of the use of the theme park facilities, attractions, services and shops. Some of this information was already available at the level of a single shop or attraction, but could hardly be related to specific groups and to their spatial activity. By this knowledge, the park management is hoping to improve the park processes (opening times and programming; location of complementary services; signposting). In perspective, once spatial activity analysis would be structurally integrated in the park's control operations, they were also interested to gather information that could improve the planning of new services and attractions, as well as the management of visitors outside of the park's precinct.

A pilot study was then commissioned to a joint Israeli-Spanish research team in 2008-2009, including researchers who pioneered the application of advanced methods for visitor tracking and spatial data analysis (N. Shoval and his associates), experts in the treatment of track data in a GIS environment (A. Ben-Nun and M. Isaacson), theme park experts (S. Anton Clavé), and site management experts (A. Russo). The pilot study was carried out in two periods of one week, at the beginning of April and at the beginning of July 2008, the former when the park observed "low season" opening times (10-19 or 20 during the weekend) and the second with "high season" opening times (10-23). In total, 288 GPS tracks were recorded, and 254 interviews to sampled participants in the tracking experiments were executed by PortAventura's staff.

The "pilot" nature of this experiment was due to the intention not only to obtain some results – only preliminary in nature, due to the limited size of the sample (still satisfactory, as specific sampling groups were selected) – but especially to test the "procedure", amending possible mistakes and improving "on the field" the mechanisms of visitor sampling, the delivery and recovery of GPS devices, the surveying of participants, and the representation and analysis of results. The idea was to define and transfer a standard procedure for visitor tracking and analysis that could be replicated in the future by the park management without the need of an active assistance of researchers.

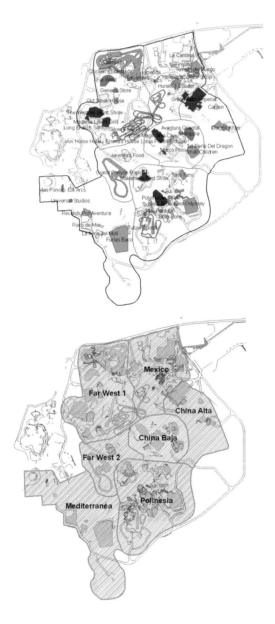

Fig. 1. The cartography of PortAventura theme park prepared for the pilot project

Adapting the general method applied in previous occasions by the Israeli researchers (Shoval 2008), a similar experiment was designed. The park surface was subdivided into seven areas (See Figure 1), within which narrower polygons were identifying the various instalments (in five categories: shows, rides, restaurants, shops and games) and their immediate proximity, so as to track the passage and time spent by each participant in each of them. A further layer of cartographic definition would subdivide the whole park surface in 20×20 meters cells.

The experiment was limited to the track of three specific groups, so as to keep the significance of the small sample as high as possible, that is Spanish, British and French family groups with children. At the gates of the park, surveyors collecting information on visitors (demographic data and ways of visiting the park) screened potential subjects with those characteristics, and asked if they were available to take part in the tracking experiment. The acceptation rate has been very high, with more than a half of the contacts resulting in an agreement to take part in the experiment, even with no foreseeable payback (a small souvenir was eventually handed over to participants when they returned the device). As the number of GPS devices available was limited to 20 daily, which were to be busy all day, in the first hour after the park opened all the devices were generally given away. Approximate times of return were recorded and a telephone contact number of the participant, so that an appointment could be done for the restitution of the devices.

At the end of the second round of tracking, 288 tracks were recorded; 11 have been eliminated from the analysis because they encountered some anomaly in the functioning or in the restitution procedure. Participants were also asked to answer some questions at the end of the visit, and 254 agreed to be interviewed.

A team of researchers kept track of the devices, and, on restitution, could download and chart the data using a special software package prepared on purpose (PARTAS: The PortAventura Real Time Analysis Software). Based on the charting of the participants' spatial activity, questions with close answers were asked regarding:

- the reasons for visiting a particular attraction or restaurant, or the reasons for not visiting them once time had been spent in its proximity ("control questions" were asked as to whether a visit to a particular attraction, resulting from the chart of spatial activity, had actually been paid, and in this way test the exactness of the tracking; this test resulted in a very high significance, with only a few "visits" having been misjudged);
- the behaviour at shops (reasons for not entering / not buying / buying, and in the latter case, the recipients of the souvenir, the member of the group who made the decision to buy, and having or not planned the purchase in advance).

These questions obviously did not cover the whole range of qualitative information that could be obtained by visitors. A choice had been made to keep the survey as short as possible in order to test and enhance the procedure on the spot. The procedure for the delivery of the questionnaire was perfected in progress: while during the first wave of tracking printed questionnaire were used and questions regarding specific attractions were selected on the base of what surveyors could read in the chart regarding the spatial activity of participants (which required some "rule of thumb" in the choice of questions and a subsequent activity of data inputting to record the data), in the second PDAs were used containing the full list of questions, which could be selected automatically based on the chart reading and immediately transferred to the data base. This improvement abated the possibilities of faults by surveyors and increased the speed of the elaboration of data, which could in principle be effected during the experiment.

To sum up, the research could use information coming from the integration and elaboration of three blocks of data sources:

- *Basic demographic data* (nationality, n. of children in the group and age of children) on the participants, collected through PortAventura's standard procedures of daily visitor surveying.
- *Tracking data* obtained from the delivery of GPS devices to 277 sampled participants.
- *Additional qualitative information* from 254 interviews conducted at the moment of the restitution of the GPS devices.

This pilot study highlighted what are the main insights that may be obtained from Advanced Visitor Tracking Analysis in an enclosed attraction site like a theme park:

- The analysis of visitor activity in the site and the way they allocate their time between different types of activities, distinguishing by visitor types or groups;
- A better understanding of the visitors' choice process once in the site;
- Forecasts of the changes in visitors' activity due to unforeseeable alterations in the site conditions (closed attractions, weather conditions, opening hours, etc.)
- The detection of congestion areas and "hot spots".

This information can be a key input to important decisions regarding the planning, management, marketing of a site:

- Improve programming according to busy times and areas
- Improve routing of visitors
- Plan for more efficient park operations (closing times, pricing, etc.)
- Improve efficiency of park services
- Cater more effectively for visitors with special needs or atypical profiles
- Renovate attractions and services, plan for new ones (type, location, opening hours, etc.)
- Develop a marketing strategy according to the behaviour of different types of visitors
- Offer services to specific type of visitors according to their preferences/demands

More sophisticated data collection and analysis techniques may be performed in the future to respond to the further demand of detailed knowledge on the spatial activity and purchasing behaviour of visitors coming from the tourist sector and site managers. In the future, it also might be interesting to integrate sequence alignment analysis (already used by the HUJ team in other projects) and other advanced statistical analysis to get better information on the sequential behaviour of visitors.

We also obtained process information allowing the future refinement of the procedures of data collection and analysis of the spatial activity of visitors. Regarding this, the pilot study has been judged satisfactory, with very high response rates, which has in an important impact on the cost-effectiveness of the tracking activity (a minimum number of surveyors could be used throughout the experiment), no loss or malfunctioning of the machinery used, and extremely user-friendly equipment for the retrieval and charting of data. These good results prompted the park management to ask for an extension of the pilot research, with the final goal to be empowered and trained to conduct not only the tracking activity, but also the data analysis, *in house*. To this aim, critical aspects have been identified in the production of questionnaires based on the charts, which as mentioned above has been partly automatised during the pilot study (but not completely), and the possibility to automatise also the production of weekly or monthly reports including a number of standard analytic information by the elaboration of the three data sources mentioned above. Both enhancements are currently been worked out.

4   An AVITA research agenda for the next decade

Applied research on the methodology, technical requirements, and exploitation of advanced visitor tracking analysis is already published in tourism and geography journals. However, an important breakthrough is still to be achieved: the conduction of AVITA research in partially enclosed or altogether "open" environments. While the issue of the use of exact geographic data about the time-space behaviour of visitors, mobility patterns, flows and congestion, and the attraction power of landmarks is clearly demonstrated by literature on tourism management in sites and cities (Jansen-Verbeke and Lievois, 2004), there is no consolidated experience of tracking the movement of visitors in "open" destination areas.

The conduction of the PortAventura pilot tracking allowed the research team to recognise what key issues should be addressed in order to a move to a different and less controlled research environment: semi-open (but gated) and open tourist areas, like archaeological areas, natural parks, heritage cities, large cities, coastal areas, and whole destination regions, provided. Clearly, the main challenge presented by tracking research in these areas is the possible absence of exclusive entry and exit points which allow a screening of visitors and facilitate the delivery and retrieval of GPS devices; the extension of the areas and the possibility of transiting areas where the satellite signal could be lost; and the length of the visits which may complicate the analysis of the spatial behaviour of visitors. To deal with this additional difficulties, it could be necessary to adapt the existing technology to a context of multi-day visits (extending the duration of batteries of GPS devices distributed at airports, HST stations of tourist offices, or even changing the type of GPS device, which may require using different kinds of GPS, or even a switch from GPS-based tracking to mobile telephony-based tracking), or, alternatively, to experiment a new "logistic" of the experiment, like sampling made at hotels with hotel staff in charge of collecting devices and charging them every night. In any case, the method of delivery and recollection of the devices has to be accurately designed and it might present an implicit "risk cost" for no-returns. Obviously, in such "open" environments also the range of research objectives could extend well over those that have been identified for a theme park, involving issues of transport and transit management, mobility infrastructure development, road pricing and visitor taxation, urban and attraction planning, and so forth.

This framework of analysis could also be extended to other tracking techniques, such as cellular phones. There is a growing literature on the implementation of these methods for tourism research (see for example: Ahas et al. 2007; Ahas et al. 2008; Ratti et al 2006; Reades et al. 2007) and in other contexts as well such as commuter mobility (González et al., 2008). The use of this technology raises an important issue of dealing with privacy infringement in the access to telephone data, which is discussed in Reades (2008). This literature, and privacy concerns, also suggests that mobile tracking lends itself to the analysis of the mobility of large masses of visitors, rather than individuals or small groups, so that the two techniques should be seen as complementary rather than alternative, and possibly implemented simultaneously. In this framework, studying aggregate tourist mobility as "differential mobility" from residents' and other city users' mobility could open new opportunities for mobility planning and risk management at a regional or even national level, providing important inputs for risk management, event management, transit pricing policies, and the management of collective tourism transport; whereas the GPS-based tracking analysis could focus on the study of visitor behaviour within each group. Finally, it should be noted how the integration of interactive multimedia guides, personalised information systems, secure e-commerce, content production and GPS technology could be a natural follow up to AVITA research; for instance, allowing the production and delivery of tailored content based on the spatial activity of visitors. However, the exploration of the potential uses and formats is still in its infancy.

5 Conclusions

This paper presented the authors' experience in the design and conduction of a pilot study based on the tracking of visitor spatial activity through the integration of GPS-based data transmission and a GIS-based analytic platform, following a model denominated AVITA (Advanced Visitor Tracking Analysis), which uses both quantitative data collected through GPS tracking and qualitative information collected by questionnaires based on the spatial activity of visitors as charted and "translated" from the tracking format through a purposely built software package.

The present work did not focus on the results from the pilot tracking activity in PortAventura, which are limited by the small size of the experiment and the "learning by doing" framework in which the experiment was developed. Rather, it focuses on the importance of such analysis for management, as expressed by the representatives of one of the most important European leisure attractions, and on the process of gathering and analysing the right data to satisfy this demand. It also suggests which further steps and issues should be taken into consideration to extend the range and nature of attractions and destination areas to be studied in relation to visitor spatial behaviour. As a final remark based on these results, authors are convinced not only that the potential for advanced visitor tracking in the enhancement of the performance of attraction and destinations is enormous, but that the possible articulations of this research field and its integration with other groundbreaking areas of IT-based tourism management are very promising.

References

Ahas, R., Aasa, A., Mark, U., Pae, T., & Kull, A. (2007) Seasonal tourism spaces in Estonia: Case study with mobile positioning data. *Tourism Management* 28(3): 898-910.
Ahas, R., Aasa, A., Roose, A., Mark, U., & Silm, S. (2008) Evaluating passive mobile positioning data for tourism surveys: An Estonian case study. *Tourism Management* 29(3): 469-86.
Anton Clavé, S. (2007) *The global theme park industry*. Wallingford, CABI.
Anton Clavé, S., Nel.lo, M., & Orellana, A. (2007) Coastal Tourism in Natural Parks. An analysis of demand profiles and recreational uses in protected natural areas. *Journal of Tourism and Development*, 7, 67-79.
Carr, N. (1999) A study of gender differences: young tourist behaviour in a UK coastal resort. *Tourism Management*, Vol. 20, 2: 223-228.
Chadefaud, M. (1981) *Lourdes: un pèlerinage, une ville*. Aix-en-Provence: Edisud.
Dietvorst, A. G. J. (1995) Tourist Behaviour and the Importance of Time-Space Analysis, in G. J. Ashworth & A. G. J. Dietvorst (eds.) Tourism and Spatial Transformations. Wallingford: CAB International.
Gali-Espelt, N. & Donaire-Benito, J.A. (2006) Visitors' behavior in heritage cities: The case of Girona. *Journal of Travel Research* 44(4): 442-48.
González, Marta C., Hidalgo, César A., & Barabási, Albert-László (2008), Understanding individual human mobility patterns. *Nature*, Vol. 453: 779-782.
Hartmann, R. (1988) Combining field methods in tourism research. *Annals of Tourism Research* 15: 88-105.
Jansen-Verbeke, M. & Lievois, E. (2004) Urban tourismscapes: research-based destination management. in Smith, K.A. & Schott, C. eds., *Proceedings of the New Zealand Tourism and Hospitality Research Conference 2004*. Wellington, 8-10 December. pp. 170-179.
Meng, L., Zipf, A., & Reichenbacher, T. (eds.) (2004) *Map-based mobile services: Theories, methods and implementations*. Ber
Montanari, A. and C. Muscarà (1995) Evaluating Tourist Flows in Historic Cities: The Case of Venice, *Tijdschrift voor Economische en Sociale Geographie*, Vol. 86, 1: 80-87.
Oppermann, M. (1997) First-time and repeat visitors to New Zealand, *Tourism Management*, vol. 18, 3: 177-181.
Ratti, C., Pulselli, R.M., Williams, S., & Frenchman, D. (2006) Mobile landscapes: Using location data from cell-phones for urban analysis. *Environment and Planning B* 33(3): 727-48.
Reades, J. (2008) People, places & privacy, International Workshop Social Positioning Method (SPM) 2008. Tartu, Estonia, 10-14 March, 2008. (Can be accessed at: http://www.reades.com/ privacy/).
Reades, J., Calabrese, F., Sevstuk, A., & Ratti, C. (2007) Cellular census: Explorations in urban data collection. *Pervasive Computing* 6(3): 30-8.
Schaick, J., & van der Spek, S. (Eds) (2008). *Urbanism on Track*. Delft University Press.
Shachar, A. and N. Shoval (1999) Tourism in Jerusalem: A Place to Pray, in D. Judd & S.S. Fainstein (eds.) *The Tourist City*. New Haven: Yale University Press.
Shaw, G., Agarwal, S. & Bull, P. (2000) Tourism consumption and tourist behaviour: a British perspective, *Tourism Geographies*, 2 (3): 264-289.
Shoval, N. (2008) Tracking Technologies and Urban Analysis. *Cities* 25(1): 21-28.

Shoval, N., & Isaacson, M. (2006) The application of tracking technologies to the study of pedestrian spatial behaviour, *The Professional Geographer* 58(2): 172-183.

Shoval, N., & Isaacson, M. (2007) Tracking Tourist in the Digital Age. *Annals of Tourism Research* 34(2): 141-159.

Shoval, N., & Isaacson, M. (2010) *Tourist Mobility and Advanced Tracking Technologies.* London and New York: Routledge. In press.

Spek, S. van der (2008) Spatial Metro: Tracking Pedestrians in Historic City Centres. *In* J. van Schaick & S. van der Spek (eds) *Urbanism on Track: Application of Tracking Technologies in Urbanism.* Amsterdam: IOS Press. 79-102.

Thornton, P.R., Williams, A.M. & G. Shaw (1997) Revisiting time-space diaries: an exploratory case study of tourist behaviour in Cornwall, England, *Environment and Planning A*, 29 (10), 1847-1867.

Monitoring and Managing Visitors Flows in Destinations using Aggregative GPS Data

Noam Shoval

Department of Geography
The Hebrew University of Jerusalem, Israel
noamshoval@huji.ac.il

Abstract

Recent technological developments have produced a range of sophisticated and readily available digital tracking technologies, of which the best known is the Global Positioning System [GPS]. Yet, despite this remarkable surge in technology, researchers in the field of tourist studies have failed to take full advantage of what these relatively new systems have to offer. Tracking technologies are able to provide high-resolution spatial and temporal data that could potentially, aid, augment, and advance research in various areas in the field of tourist studies. This article present the possibility to use aggregative data obtained from GPS receivers in order to better understand the impact of visitors on destinations. The data presented in this paper were collected in four different locations: PortAventura amusement park and the Mini Israel theme park (two enclosed outdoor environments) the Old City of Akko in Israel (a small historic city) and Hong Kong a truly World City.

Keywords: Historical Cities, Theme Parks, Pedestrians, Tracking, GPS.

1   Introduction

Tourism in general, and in cities in particular, is a growing sector. Much urban tourism, researchers find, is concentrated in well-defined areas within the city. Leisure and cultural tourists are spending more of their time in the CTD (central tourist district), an area that usually includes a historic city center as well. Business travelers spend more of their time in the CBD (central business district) and in conference centers. Due to the increasing numbers of tourists, the spatial activities of tourists throughout different parts of urban centers are some of the forces that shape city centers as we know them today.

Tracking technologies present a great opportunity for the study of the impact that tourism has on urban centers and urban systems, as a result there is growing literature that documents the implementation of those technologies in tourism research (Ten Hagen et al., 2005; Shoval and Isaacson, 2007; Shoval, 2008; Spek, 2008; Shoval and Isaacson, 2010). Data collected using these technologies are more exact and can be gathered with greater ease and on larger scales in comparison with the time-space data that have been available until now. One approach when looking at the data collected is to put the tourist in the center of the discussion and present the ways in which the analysis of time-space data collected using advanced tracking technologies can contribute to understanding the tourist's spatial activity throughout his or her visit to a destination. However, in this paper we use another approach. We look at time-space data collected using advanced tracking technologies but place the destination at the center of the discussion, enabling a greater understanding of how spatial activities of visitors generate different space throughout the location at different times and how visitors consume the destination itself. The data presented in this paper are aggregated figures that present the combined activity of many visitors in time-space throughout a destination. Such analysis can facilitate decisions such as where to set up new attractions and where to promote private-sector tourist services. This different angle opens many new points of view and questions that can now be addressed using high-resolution spatial data; these were virtually unobtainable using the traditional methods of data-collection on spatial activity.

New possibilities that arise include estimating the physical carrying capacity of attractions throughout the destination and of the destination itself; locating areas that remain out of the scope of the tourists' routes and that have unrealized potential that can be developed; and determining the effect that the time of day, weather, days of the week, and the seasons of the year have on the spatial consumption of the tourist destination. Tourism, especially activities located within urban areas, which comprise a large percentage of the tourism industry, could greatly benefit from the kind of digital tracking methods that are able to trace pedestrian routes over long periods of time and, additionally, can do so both accurately and consistently. This is because the business, commercial, and leisure activities of most cities are largely concentrated in the city center, which is thus distinguished by high levels of pedestrian movement. This is true even in more developed urban economies, which have seen a move of business activity to the periphery in recent years; the town center in these remains at the heart of the town's social, cultural, and administrative life (Haklay et al. 2001, 343). The cases discussed in this paper use GPS technology. The data is collected by distributing GPS devices to visitors at a destination. This data can be downloaded from the devices when they are returned at the end of the visit and can also stream into the system in real time using cellular communications to transfer the data.

2 Aggregative Data Obtained from GPS Devices

Below we present some results from studies that were carried out using GPS receivers in three different locations: PortAventura amusement park and the Mini Israel theme park (two enclosed outdoor environments) and the Old City of Akko (a small historic city).

2.1 PortAventura

An example of an exploration of aggregative time-space activities of visitors within a destination is a study that was conducted in the PortAventura amusement park. The project was a joint venture of the Universitat Rovira i Virgili School of Tourism and Leisure, the Hebrew University of Jerusalem, and the theme park itself.

PortAventura theme park is located in Catalonia, Spain, next to the holiday resort of Salou, approximately one hour's ride south from Barcelona. Though identified with Universal Studios, the park is owned and operated by the Caixa banking group, which bought Universal Studios' shares in the park in 2004. Adjacent to the park are four hotels operated by the park and many others that are privately owned. In recent years, the park has exceeded four million visitors annually.

Park Structure. PortAventura is divided into five thematic areas. Each area represents a different geographic region and is designed according to the landscape and cultural characteristics that distinguish that location. The thematic areas are: the Mediterranean, Polynesia, China, Mexico, and the Far West. The Mediterranean area is located at the park entrance, while the other four areas are arranged in a circle. This means that a visitor who arrives at the park has to cross the Mediterranean section and then decide whether to circle the park from the right, starting from Polynesia, or from the left, starting from the Far West (see figure 1).

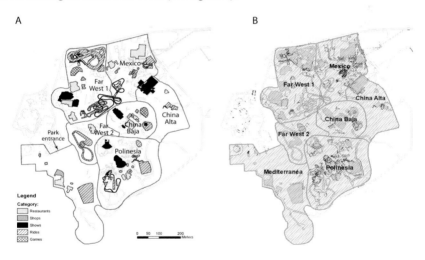

Fig. 1. Map of PortAventura theme park

Fieldwork and Sampling. The fieldwork for the PortAventura study was conducted in two phases of one consecutive week each. The first phase took place during the spring of 2008 and the second phase during the summer of 2008. The sample was restricted to families with young children. Of the 288 families who took part in the study, 277 families were included in the final analysis (96 percent). Three different types of data were collected for each family using three different data-collection methods: 1) Visitors' socio-demographic and personal data were collected by park employees at the park entrance using a conventional questionnaire; 2) Time-space data were obtained from the GPS devices, which were set to sample the location of the visitors every ten seconds; and, 3) Data regarding the visitors' decision-making were collected using designated software. When visitors returned from the day at the park, GPS data were automatically processed, and a table specifying the park sites visited by the families was produced. This table allowed the interviewers to question the visitors as to their motivations and decision-making processes during their visits.

The sample of visitors who were asked to participate in the research was restricted to families with young children. This choice was motivated by the fact that a small group was needed to make the sampling statistically significant, and that this group was of interest to the park management. There were a total fourteen days of sampling in two rounds of one week each, in April and July 2008. Twenty GPS loggers were used. A total of 288 GPS tracks were recorded and 254 interviews were conducted by the park's staff. The missing interviews were primarily due to the fact that the park did not have staff available to interview all of the participants in a timely fashion. Before the study began, the park's management hoped to interview approximately one quarter of the participants; the results far exceeded everyone's expectations. Information collected from eleven participants was excluded for the following reasons: four participants carried devices that turned off during their visits; six participants had devices that did not function properly and thus the spatial data were incomplete; and one participant who participated was mistakenly included (he did not meet the inclusion criteria). The size of the final sample used for analysis included 277 participants, or 96 percent of the total sample.

The external conditions within the park differed between the two phases of research. The park was open for nine hours a day in April (10:00 a.m.–7:00 p.m.) and for thirteen hours a day in July (10:00 a.m.–11:00 p.m.). In April there were low temperatures with light showers from time to time and in July there were high temperatures with one day of extreme weather conditions that included heavy rain in the afternoon and evening.

Time Distribution. Figure 2 details the average amount of time the participants spent in various parts of the park. The first thing that the reader notices when looking at the diagram is the striking imbalance in the integrated amount of time spent in each zone and the relation between the time spent in the different areas. The subjects spent the most time during the first pilot, in the Far West section of the park (Far West2). The extra time that the visitors had in the second phase due to the longer opening times was mostly spent in Polynesia. This is a very interesting finding. One would think that the time that was added to the visitor's time budget as a result of longer hours of operation would either be divided evenly over space or divided over space in proportion to the popularity of the zone. Knowing that most of the additional time allocated to visitors is spent in one zone has great importance for the park's management, which must allocate employees throughout the park and needs an understanding of how to deploy its staff in the most efficient way. These findings are very useful when considering the operation costs incurred as a result of the longer operation hours. If a city were studied in a similar manner, the results obtained by analyzing the way in which space is consumed could help the city's tourist authorities formulate a more reasonable tourist planning policy: a policy aimed at managing tourist flows in a more rational manner, a policy deliberately designed to relieve the burden from the town's more congested areas, both at set times and in general, by, among other things, encouraging tourists to explore other, less crowded sites. The result of such a policy would be a more equally distributed pattern of tourist temporal and spatial activity, one that could benefit both tourists and the town as a whole.

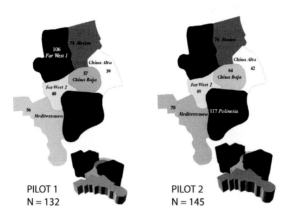

PILOT 1
N = 132

PILOT 2
N = 145

Fig. 2. Average length of stay (min.) of all visitors in the park's thematic areas

Temporal Cycles of a Destination. Figure 3 shows where the participants spent their time throughout the cycle of a day at the PortAventura theme park in each of the two phases of the study. The longer opening hours in the second phase can be seen on the x-axis. These graphs were created using the map of attractions produced by the park's management. The map contains five different types of attractions: rides, shops, shows, restaurants, and games. Each attraction was represented using a polygon shaped to include the waiting line for the attraction and the area of the attraction itself. This is important because many of the rides are very fast and locating the participant riding on a roller coaster can be difficult if the participant does not spend time waiting on line.

The total volume of activity was at its highest shortly after the park opened and all of the GPS devices were distributed. As the day progressed, the total volume of activity diminished as people slowly left the park. Both figures show a similar pattern: people enter the park and rush to get on rides, resulting in a peak in the ride graph. As the day progresses, people spend less and less time on the rides. The restaurant graph shows a clear peak at lunchtime during both phases and another much smaller increase at dinnertime during the second phase when the park was open until midnight and people ate their dinner there. Peaks in the show graph can be explained by the schedule that most of the shows follow (some shows are open the entire time and people walk in and out as they please). Both games and rides display very low volumes of activity. This may have nothing to do with the actual spatial activity of the participants; it may be linked more with the limitations of the GPS technology, which had difficulty locating participants within the very small store and game polygons. In addition, the stores were mostly located within built structures, making for a more challenging environment for the GPS.

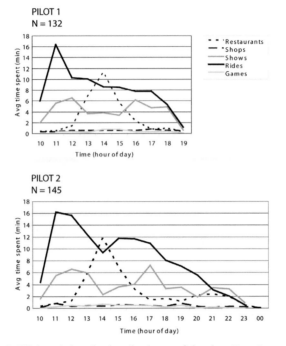

Fig. 3. Visitors' time budget by hour of the day, PortAventura

2.2 Mini Israel Miniature Park

Mini Israel is a park located in Israel, midway between the capital, Jerusalem, and the economic center, Tel Aviv. The park hosts hundreds of miniature models of key locations in Israel. The layout of the models in the park does not reflect the physical structure of the country; rather, the park is shaped like a Star of David. A study of the time-space activity of visitors to the park was carried out in the summer of 2006. During the study, visitors to the park were approached and asked to carry GPS units with them throughout their visit. The park is outdoors and has very few buildings; it is therefore an ideal location for using GPS technology.

The data obtained in the study were used to create a typology of the use of the parks by visitors. Four categories of the areas in the park were created based on how those areas were used by visitors. This analysis is presented as a demonstration of a practical tool for understanding the spatial activity within a destination and managing the way visitors flow through an attraction. To carry out this analysis, the area of the park was divided onto a raster (a grid); each cell was sized at 2 x 2 meters. The number of visitors that passed through each cell in the grid was counted. The cells in the grid were then classified into two categories: high-traffic cells and low-traffic cells (Figure 4A; high-traffic areas are dark and low-traffic areas are light). At the same time, another raster was calculated. In this raster, the average length of a visit was calculated for each cell. As with the first raster, the results were divided into two categories, cells with long average stays and cells with shorter average stays (Figure

4B; cells with high average stays are dark and cells with low average stays areas are light).

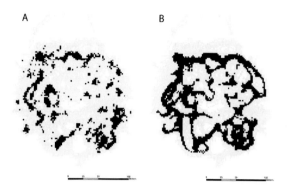

Fig. 4. (A): Classification of cells into high-traffic and low-traffic cells according to the amount of people that passed through each cell; (B): Classification of cells into high average and low average according to length of stay

Combining both categories using the criteria presented in the table below resulted in a grid with four categories. The categories are displayed in Figure 5. Each category explains the way that the visitors to the park used its space. Some areas in the park are used as corridors through which people pass but do not spend time; other areas serve as basins that channel the flow of people into them.

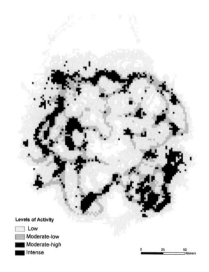

Fig. 5. Classification reflecting usage of the space throughout the Mini Israel park

Table 1. Cell classification, defining activity in each cell

	Low-traffic Area	High-traffic Area
Short Average Stay in Cell	Low activity, low traffic, and short stays.	Moderate–low levels of activity, high traffic, short stays.
Long Average Stay in Cell	Moderate–high levels of activity, low traffic, long stays.	Intense activity, high traffic, and long stays.

2.3 The Old City of Akko

Akko is one of the world's oldest continuously inhabited towns in the world. In 2002, UNESCO added Akko's Old City to its list of World Heritage sites, bringing it to the attention of the international tourist market and prompting Israel to devote more resources to the town's development.

Visitors' Impact and Management Implications. The GPS devices carried by the experiment's subjects throughout their entire tour of Akko's Old City were used to collect data on the subjects' locations. They did so by registering the precise location and exact time each location was logged. This spatial-temporal information was recorded at an extremely high level of intensity: one location per second. This meant that if, for one reason or another, the GPS satellite signal was blocked, as is often the case in dense urban environments, it was possible to reestablish a connection, and thus obtain a reading, the moment the device acquired a direct line of sight to the satellite system; this in turn meant that any breaks in the track sequences were reduced to an absolute minimum.

The aggregate analysis analytical approach looks at the subjects' effect on the city or how the city is "consumed." Based upon aggregate data rather than single observations or clusters of observations, such a city-centered analysis can be used to indicate which are the more popular sites and neighborhoods in a town and which tend to be neglected; or, alternatively, which of the town's routes are well worn and which remain virtually unused. The data obtained using the GPS devices were analyzed in aggregate. Such an analysis, which ignores the individual visitor, serves to reveal how the urban space is exploited or "consumed" by all tourists. In our case, the high-resolution data provided by GPS were used to create a "pixilated" map of Akko, which highlighted just how the town's urban space was consumed. The spatial consumption was measured by percentage of time spent in the different locales plus the intensity of activity per cell of a size of 10 meters x 10 meters, which is two times above the average accuracy of the 5 meter accuracy of the GPS units used in this study (see Figure 6).

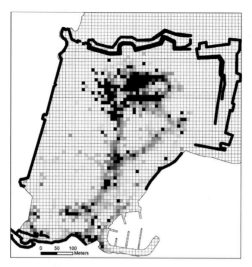

Fig. 6. Tourist activity in Old Akko—two-dimensional

Pixelating the Town. Another means of examining temporal and spatial behavior in aggregate, one which similarly exploits the advantages of the GPS system in terms of providing accurate and high-resolution data, consists of dividing the town's urban space into squares and counting the total number of signals picked up by the GPS receivers per square. Obviously, the size of the grid's squares depends on the size of the urban space studied, with larger-scale studies requiring larger squares and smaller ones smaller squares. Before it is possible to begin the discussion on three-dimensional visualization, it is important to note that in this chapter the three-dimensional visualizations are actually pseudo-three-dimensional figures. The figures are rendered in a way that gives the illusion of a third dimension but, since they were created on a computer screen and printed on paper, this remains an illusion only.

Adding a third dimension opens new possibilities for plotting time-space data (Figure 7). The third dimension, along with the color that was used in the two-dimensional figures, can help the researcher to understand the different amounts of time that each unit represents. Adding a horizontal dimension helps the researcher to understand the difference between the different quantities; this is made possible due to the fact that height is a scalable dimension while color scales are much more difficult and less exact for the human eye to interpret. This technique of plotting is very effective in studying the general impact that spatial behavior has on the location being studied.

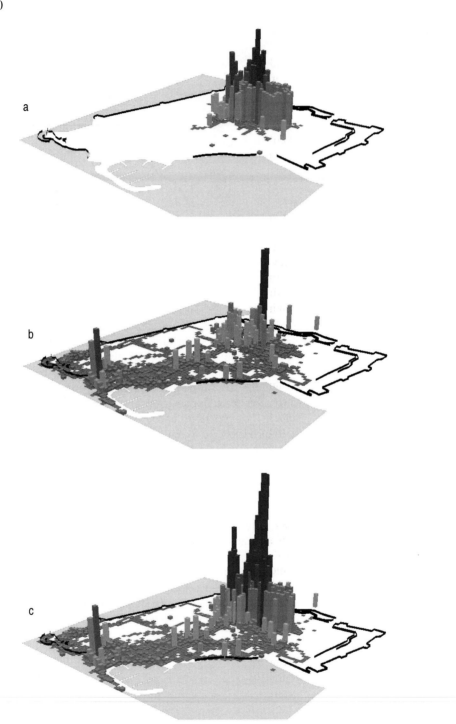

Fig. 7. Tourist activity in Old Akko—three-dimensional

This technique allows the researcher to distinguish between "Hot Spots," locations that are well-exposed to the visitor; "Not Spots," locations that do not exist for the visitor and are not visited at all; and transition areas through which the visitor passes but does not stop to spend time. This technique analyzes all of the time spent in the city and therefore is useful for learning about the city; however, it is not effective as a tool for shedding light on individual tourists. Figures 6 and 7 depict which areas in town boast high levels of concentrated tourist activity and which plainly suffer from a dearth of tourists, darker colors mean more intensive levels of activity. Indeed, viewed as whole, the map exposes a marked spatial imbalance between the town's sites, an imbalance rooted in the way Akko's tourist industry developed over the years. Of all the columns in figure 7c, the most prominent column is located in the area containing the visitors' center, the underground Crusaders' Halls, and the Turkish Bath House. The figure also reveals which of the possible routes linking Akko's various centers of activity are the most commonly used. Apparently, most visitors to Akko tend to move in a southerly direction: setting off from the visitors' center and ending up, by way of the local market, at the Templars' Tunnel and the restaurants alongside the marina. Once the subjects who only visited the Crusaders' Halls are weeded out from those who explored the town's other sites as well, the resulting diagrams' topography, not surprisingly, changed. Thus, figure 7a, based solely on the sequences of those subjects who limited their visit to a tour of the visitors' center, Crusaders' Halls, and Turkish Bath House complex, contains a single concentration of fairly tall columns; while the topography of figure 7b, based on the remaining sequences, is, predictably, much more diffuse. Tourist flows in Akko's Old City are dispersed unevenly throughout the town's various locales, with a great many visitors venturing no further than the visitors' center, the Crusaders' Halls, the Turkish Bath House complex, and the Templars Tunnel—all sites run by the Old Acre Development Company. These findings, it should be noted, match those obtained by other similar studies, which also analyzed the spatial activity of tourists in small historical areas.

2.4 Hong Kong

An example of a preliminary analysis of aggregative use of space in a large scale multifunctional world city of about seven million inhabitants can be seen in a small sample of a study in Hong Kong. The data presented belong to a two-year project (2008–2010) that, at the time of writing, had recently begun. The study is being conducted as a partnership between Robert (Bob) McKercher of the School of Hotel and Tourism Management at the Hong Kong Polytechnic University and Noam Shoval of the Department of Geography at the Hebrew University of Jerusalem. The two parts of figure 8 presents the aggregate activity of first-time visitors to Hong Kong (n=77) and of the repeat visitors (n=40) who were tracked with a GPS device in Hong Kong and its adjacent territories and islands. The tourists were sampled at the lobby of the Harbour Metropolis Hotel in Kowloon and were requested to carry a GPS device for the day. The central part of Hong Kong (including Kowloon and Hong Kong Island) was divided into a raster of 200 meters by 200 meters. The accumulative time spent by all the tourists in each pixel is represented in the figure in a three-dimensional view.

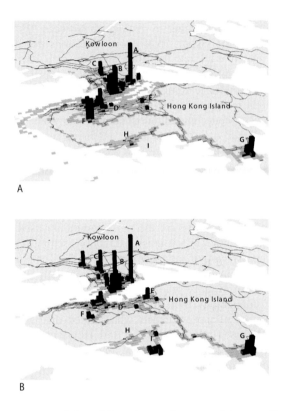

Fig. 8. Aggregate activity of first-time and repeat visitors to Hong Kong

When looking at the two figures, it is clear that the highest peak in the figure is the Harbor Metropolis Hotel (A) where the tourists were sampled. This is a result of tourists waiting for the shuttle bus or returning to the hotel to rest in the middle of the day. Extensive time was spent in the shopping district in south Kowloon (B) around Nathan road. However we can see that first-time visitors tend to be less represented in the various markets around Mongkok (C) in Kowloon. On Hong Kong Island it is interesting that the tourists did not spend significant time in any of the built areas in the northern part of the island (D) aside in the area of the ferries landings, but this may be a bias based on the place of sampling that is located in Kowloon. This hypothesis will, we hope, be validated in the future, as the plan is to conduct some of the sampling in hotels on Hong Kong Island. Some repeat visitors did, however, explore the district of Causeway Bay (E). As expected, there is a significant concentration of activity of first-time visitors in the Victoria Peak area (F) and less of repeat visitors. Both groups visited Stanley (G), but it is somehow surprising that none of them visited the area of Aberdeen (H) though repeat visitors did visit the Ocean Park theme park that is located nearby (I).

3   Conclusion

The study of visitors' time-space activity in the various destinations presented in this chapter added to our knowledge of spatial and temporal behavior of visitors. This knowledge can and should be exploited to better regulate tourist flows throughout the destinations studied. Thanks to the GPS- or cellular-derived information, tourists may now be encouraged to visit previously deserted parts of a destination, from the scale of a miniature park to the national scale. Tourists can be prompted to visit popular attractions at specific times in order to reduce congestion and to allow them to fully benefit from their time in the city. Such information can also facilitate decisions as to where to set up new attractions and where to promote private-sector tourist services. In each and every case, the result of research will be the reduction of congestion in hitherto overcrowded, over-exploited areas and the general enhancement of the physical and social carrying capacity. Lew and McKercher (2004; 2006) have suggested that urban tourist flows clearly have a tendency to spread themselves unevenly, both spatially and temporally. As a consequence, while the more popular sites and access routes in a destination often suffer from over-crowding and severe congestion, others are severely under-exploited, a state of affairs that points to a grossly inefficient use of economic and social resources and one which is ultimately unsustainable as well. There is clearly an urgent need for tourist management schemes designed to maneuver visitors around destinations in a more rational way. Such schemes would doubtless benefit from tracking-technology-based studies that are a remarkably efficient means of collecting a mass of high-resolution data on the spatial and temporal behavior of tourists.

References

Haklay, M., O'sullivan, D., & Thurstain-Goodwin, M (2001) "So go downtown":Simulating pedestrian movement in town centres, *Environment and Planning B*, 28(3): 343-59.

Lew, A.A. & McKercher, B. (2004) Travel geometry: macro and micro scales considerations. Paper presented at the Pre-Congress Meeting of the International Geographic Union's Commission on Tourism, Leisure and Global Change. Loch Lomond, Scotland, 13th-15th August, 2004.

Lew, A.A. & McKercher, B. (2006) Modeling tourist movements: A local destination analysis, *Annals of Tourism Research*, 33(2): 402-23.

Shoval, N. (2008) Tracking technologies and urban analysis, *Cities*, 25(1): 21-8.

Shoval, N. and Isaacson, M. (2007) Tracking tourist in the digital age, *Annals of Tourism Research*, 34(2): 141-59.

Shoval, N. & Isaacson, M. (2010) *Tourist Mobility and Advanced Tracking Technologies*. London and New York: Routledge.

Spek, S. van der (2008) Spatial Metro: Tracking Pedestrians in Historic City Centres, in J. van Schaick & S. van der Spek (eds) *Urbanism on Track: Application of Tracking Technologies in Urbanism*, Amsterdam: IOS Press. 79-102.

Ten Hagen, K., Modsching, M., & Kramer, R. (2005) A Location Aware Mobile Tourist Guide Selecting and Interpreting Sights and Services by Context Matching. Paper presented at the 2nd Annual International Conference on Mobile and Ubiquitous Systems: Networking and Services, 17-21 July, San Diego, CA.

Tracking Tourists in Historic City Centres

Stefan van der Spek[a],

[a] Department of Urbanism / Chair of Urban Design
Delft University of Technology, the Netherlands
s.c.vanderspek@tudelft.nl

Abstract

According to the initiators of the 'Spatial Metro project' the first impression when visiting a city centre is the most important one (Hoeven, Smit & Spek, 2008). Unfortunately, mostly cities are chaotic and confusing places. The Spatial Metro project addresses the topic of improving city centres for pedestrians, especially for shoppers and tourists. The question HOW and with what MEANS can only be answered if the cities have insight in the ISSUES, the VARIABLES or optional INTERVENTIONS and influence of specific SOLUTIONS. Questionnaires or street-interviews can provide information about the expectations and experience of visitors. But, more important is the information on *spatial behaviour of visitors* (Shoval & Isaacson, 2007), indicating *destinations*, *routes* and *duration* and thus also *not-visited locations* (Schaick & Spek, 2008). TU Delft developed a tool to collect spatio-temporal data and applied this tool in three cities: Norwich, Rouen and Koblenz (Hoeven, Smit & Spek, 2008). *This chapter will focus on a method for tracking tourists in city centres.*

Keywords: GPS-tracking; tourists; city centre; space-time; mapping; urban design.

1 Introduction

"Cities can be chaotic and confusing places at the best of times - even for local people! Visitors are neither helped nor encouraged by unattractive surroundings when they reach main arrival points such as airports, bus and railway stations, and car parks. Once in the city they can be further frustrated by a lack of helpful signs and by unwelcoming public spaces. Spatial Metro aims to make city visits more enjoyable for pedestrians by making them easier to navigate, easier to walk around, and easier to understand and appreciate." (www.spatialmetro.org, [Sept. 24, 2007])

'Discovering the City on Foot' is the theme of Spatial Metro – a European project co-funded by the Interreg IIIb initiative. The publication of the project called 'Street-Level Desires' (Hoeven, Smit & Spek, 2008) describes that the project is about *'developing network of thematic pedestrian routes and reinforcing the identity of these routes with special paving, lighting and public art consisting of visual devices'*. According to Van der Spek (in: Hoeven, Smit & Spek, 2008) important outcomes will be *'the design of metro-style maps, information gateways or welcome points where relevant information is easily available about the city, and the design of key locations or 'stations' along the routes as places to enjoy and discover more about the city'*.

In the Spatial Metro project (2005-2008) a group of five cities co-operate in order to *'improve their historic city centres for pedestrians'*: Norwich (UK), Bristol (UK), Rouen (F), Koblenz (D) and Biel/Bienne (CH). All these cities have a preserved historic city centre with a mediaeval street pattern. Especially, this kind of urban structure is difficult to navigate and difficult to change by physical, spatial interventions. The cities are confronted with large-scale out-of-town retail development. The challenge is to preserve the historic, medieval city centre as an attractive destination for shopping, living and tourism: a vital city core.

The cities invest in different ways to improve the quality for visitors. In Norwich -the lead partner- focus is on the design of so-called stations: the main nodes in the pedestrian network, the urban tissue. As a result, two public spaces will be redeveloped. Key issue in Bristol is the introduction of a new type of information system. Rouen focuses on a light master plan for guidance and safety at night. Koblenz upgrades the pedestrian network based on a design competition and introduces a Bluetooth based information network. Finally, in Biel/Bienne the principals of *'Shared Space'* (http://en.wikipedia.org/wiki/Shared_space [Sept.30, 2009]) have been applied to the redevelopment of the central square. (Spek, 2007)

The motivation to invest in their historic city centres is explained by Van der Hoeven (in: Hoeven, Smit & Spek, 2008): *'Visitors who plan a day trip to a city will stay in town for an average four to four-and-half hours and spend about $100. If the welcome they receive is inhospitable, the destination is confusing and demands are no met, the same visitor will tend to leave after only two hours and spend less than $50. If their arrival is welcoming, the destination is safe, clean, relaxed and intelligible ad if visitors are able to navigate their way around and their original expectations are fulfilled or surpassed, they will stay for six to seven hours and spend in excess of $150.'* This statement clearly describes the opportunity and challenge for the cities to attract and keep visitors.

A relevant question is how efficient the investments in the different fields are: do visitors stay longer, do they visit other (unexpected) locations, do they spend more money and do they return another time? Here, TU Delft was introduced to develop a method to measure the effects of the investments (Schaick & Spek, 2008). The task for TU Delft in this project was to *get insight in behaviour, expectations* and *experience* of visitors. Herefore, TU Delft developed a method using street-interviews. These interviews were related to *experience* of the visitors and linked with *spatial behaviour* and *urban design* issues.

In this chapter we will elaborate the development and application of methods used by TU Delft to collect information about *expectations, experience* and *actual spatial behaviour* of visitors of the city centre. The information is based on two publications: 'Street-Level Desires' and 'Urbanism on Track'.

2 Theory / Issues

Shoval & Isaacson (2007) state based on the experience of Fennell in his study on spatial behaviour of tourists that *'in the future the observation of behaviour of tourists in time and space would be best accomplished with tracking technologies, as traditional methods most commonly are deficient in the level of accuracy and/or the validity of the data collected'*. For TU Delft, a method for observing visitors behaviour was essential to measure the difference in behaviour before and after investments.

Counting pedestrians (Gehl, 2004) is a known method in the participating cities, but this only delivers intensities of people, no background information and no information about route, destinations and duration. Direct-observation or shadowing as described by Millonig et al (2009) and Shoval & Isaacson (2007) implies several issues: labour-intensive, time-consuming, lack of additional, non-visual data, and it poses ethical questions. Shoval & Isaacson (2007) experimented with several new methods for tracking tourists based on new technologies: Global Positioning System (GPS), Mobile Phone (Cellular Triangulation & Time Difference of Arrival (TDOA)) and Hybrid Assisted-GPS. They concluded that Cellular Phone has some advantages (compare with Ratti et al., 2006), especially in an urban environment, but GPS is far more accurate on the micro-level (Shoval & Isaacson, 2007).

GPS is a Position Determination Technology (PDT) using Global Navigation Satellite System (GNSS). GPS can be used for tracking: real-time or offline collection of trajectories of movement. A trajectory contains the spatio-temporal information and is based on a recorded geoposition at a specific time interval (Raper et al, 2007; Spek et al., 2009; Millonig et al, 2009).

In 2005 and 2006 TU Delft tested several GPS devices (GARMIN etrex legend, map60), e.g. in Norwich (June and September 2005) and in Delft (February 2006). At that time, GPS was NOT capable of collecting *accurately* and *reliable* spatio-temporal data in historic city centres (see field research report, HOD-509). Since then, GPS devices have improved, e.g. by the introduction of high sensitive receivers using Sirfstar III, MTK and MTK-II chipsets, such as Garmin MAP60Cx and Qstarz BT-Q1000P/X. Still, GPS tracking in city centres encounters some issues due to multipath effects, blocked signals and limited indoor reception (Raper et al, 2007; Millonig et al, 2009). Nevertheless, according to the 'Urbanism on Track' workshop held in Delft in January 2007, GPS-tracking potentially offers an essential instrument for collecting spatio-temporal data (http://bk.tudelft.nl/uot [Sept. 30, 2009]) and (Schaick & Spek, 2008).

In 2007 TU Delft developed and applied a method using GPS technology for tracking visitors. This method will be explained in Paragraph 3. The results will be discussed in Paragraph 4. The conclusions can be found in Paragraph 5: Outcomes & Outlook.

3 Research method

The collection of spatio-temporal data using GPS technology is divided in two parts: (1) data collection and (2) data handling. The first part focuses on the fieldwork, deploying GPS devices and retrieving data. The second parts focuses on working with the data. (Spek et al., 2009)

Part 1: collection of data: preparation & field work

[a] Preparation of the experiment: setting up the project, defining goals, method, way of working, contacting potential participants or locations.

[b] Deploying devices: fieldwork, contacting participants.

[c] Using device: participants walk or travel around.

[d] Returning device: collecting the information and linked questionnaire.

Part 2: data handling: processing, visualisation & results

[a] Retrieval & validation: validity check of data (errors, mismatches).

[b] Processing & conversion: work with GPX software to correct errors, and clean/filter the information, finally convert data to GIS and database environment(s).

[c] Analysis: application of static and dynamic analysis tools, such as density, direction, space-time diagrams, change/move. Use the database to select trajectories by theme. Statistical analysis of background and trip data.

[d] Visualisation & interpretation: The last part consists of imaging and concluding based on the images. This part is essential to address urban design issues in relation to movement.

4   Results

In 2005 TU Delft carried out two street-interview sessions: one in Norwich (Heritage Open Days, September 2005[1]) and one in Rouen (Christmas shopping, December 2005[2]). The street-interviews deliver two sets of data: social-geographical background data of the participant and specific data on the experience of the visit. Hence, spatial information was collected by questioning 'good & bad practices' of: (1) shopping, (2) leisure and (3) culture.

The GPS-tracking was carried out in only three cities of the Spatial Metro project: Norwich, Rouen and Koblenz. For one whole week, people entering the city centre from two specific parking facilities were asked to participate in the research by carrying a GPS device during their visit. The parking facilities offered easy access to potential participants and ensured the return of the GPS device. The collection of spatio-temporal data was accompanied by a questionnaire collecting personal and trip related information (more information on the procedures can be found in: Hoeven, Smit & Spek, 2008). Using the questionnaire, TU Delft was able to filter the data by theme and subtheme, e.g. duration, purpose, familiarity, origin, age, gender, group. The subthemes were used for analysis and visualisation: density drawings were made for every (sub)theme and compared (a) within a (sub)theme, (b) between locations and (c) between cities. In this chapter, the density drawings based on purpose, subthemes leisure and shopping are used. The data was collected with an interval of 5 seconds.

In Norwich the research was carried out from Wednesday June 20 until Tuesday June 26, 2007. The access points were St. Andrews (1000P) on the north side and Chapelfield Mall (1000P) on the south side. In total 640 people participated in Norwich. The results are described in Paragraph 4.1.

In Rouen the research was carried out from Monday, October 1 until Saturday, October 6. The parking facilities used for distribution and collection of the devices

---

[1] see HOD Field Research report (HOD509), TU Delft / City of Norwich, 2006
[2] see ROUEN Field Research report (ROUEN512), TU Delft / City of Rouen, 2006

were Vieux Marché (400P) on the west side and Haut Vieille Tour (425P) on the south side. Here, 420 people participated. The results are described in Paragraph 4.2.

Finally, in Koblenz the research was carried out from Monday, October 8 until Saturday, October 13. The access points were Löhr-Center (1400P), a huge shopping mall on the west side of the city and from Görresplatz (390P), an underground parking on the east side of the historic city centre. In Koblenz 300 people participated. The results are described in Paragraph 4.3.

4.1 Norwich

Norwich is situated in East Anglia, UK. Although the city has around one hundred thirty thousand inhabitants, the city has a large retail centre including two shopping malls, due to the central role the city plays in the region. Its well-preserved medieval centre with over thirty churches characterizes the city centre. New developments are Forum (2002) – information centre, central library and BBC building, Riverside Entertainment Centre and Chapelfield Mall (2005). Other places of interest are the famous central Market, St. Peter Mancroft Church, the Castle, Dragon Hall, Elm Hill, Tombland, the Cow Tower and the Norwich Cathedral on the Eastside. The Roman Catholic Cathedral is located on the Westside. Norwich is a vibrant city: yearly many festivals are organised, e.g. the Heritage Open Days. (Hoeven, Smit & Spek, 2008)

4.1.1   Norwich St. Andrews

The tracking of tourist who access the city from St. Andrews results in a clear and logical shape. The main tourist attractions can be recognized: Castle, Castle Mall, Tombland Square, London street, Elm Hill, Norwich Cathedral, St. Mary Coslany and The Forum. Surprisingly, the walking radius for tourism is unexpectedly less than the radius of shoppers or local people departing from St. Andrews: the radius of tourist is around 600m, but shoppers and locals easily walk up to 800 meters (see Fig. 2).

190

Fig. 1. St. Andrews: Point Density (time-corrected).
Left: Tourism; Right: Shopping (c) 2009 TU Delft

4.1.2 Norwich Chapelfield

Chapelfield parking is as expected less popular for tourists visiting Norwich. St. Andrews counts 12% and Chapelfield 8% of tourist trips. Based on this research, tourists mostly walk via Chapelstreet towards the Forum and beyond and to the pedestrian zone, Castle street and some to the Castle. Compared to St. Andrews tourist from Chapelfield avoid attractions like 'Elmstreet' and the 'Norwich Cathedral'. Concluding: Chapelfield Mall is located at the southern edge of the city centre and mostly facilitates the core. People who park here only visit nearby tourist attractions. People who park at St. Andrews seem to use a wider range of the city, not only using attractions in the core, but also in different directions (see Fig. 2). (Hoeven, Smit & Spek, 2008)

Fig. 2. Norwich, Chapelfield: Point Density(time-corrected).
Left: Tourism; Right: Shopping (c) 2009 TU Delft

4.2 Rouen

Rouen (F) is situated along the River Seine and is the capital of Normandy, France. The city counts around one hundred thousand inhabitants. Like Norwich, much of the historic city centre has been preserved. Rouen is, like Norwich as well, a vibrant city offering year-round cultural events and a popular tourist destination. Main tourist destinations are the Gross-Horloge (a giant medieval clock), the late-gothic 13th century Cathedral (Notre Dame) and many monumental buildings, e.g. Palais de Justice, St. Maclou Church and St. Ouen Abbey (see Fig. 2). (Hoeven, Smit & Spek, 2008)

4.2.1   Rouen Vieux Marché

About 18% of the visitors who park at Vieux Marché are there for tourism purposes. This group mainly consists of regular visitors (40%). Thus, remarkably tourism is also a visiting purpose for those who are common with Rouen. Starting from Vieux Marché tourists don't go much further than the Notre Dame Cathedral and their route is mainly limited to the Rue de Gross Horloge. Incidentally, people continue walking to other attractions, such as Hotel de Ville and Eglise de St. Maclou (up to 800m). Some people take another route back to Vieux Marché resulting in a round trip, i.e. by walking via alternative shopping street on the northern side. Place Verdrel is hardly visited, but this might be explained by the street-interview held two years earlier indicating this square as an unsafe place (see Fig. 3).

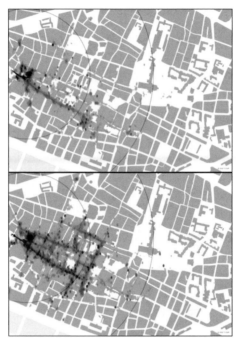

Fig. 3. Rouen, Vieux Marché: Point Density(time-corrected).
Left: Tourism; Right: Shopping (c) 2009 TU Delft

4.2.2 Rouen Vieux Haut Vieille Tour

About 21% of the visitors who park at Haute Vieille Tour are there for tourism reasons. The tourists at Haute Vieille Tour have almost the same pattern of use compared to Vieux Marché: The main line can be recognised starting at Eglise St. Maclou reaching until Vieux Marche. Some tourists also visit till far up Rue de Jeanne d'Arc. In contrast to the shoppers departing from Haute Vieille Tour, Vieux Marché is a destination for tourists departing from Haute Vieille Tour. The tourists departing from Vieux Marché are much more directed to the Cathedral through the Rue de Gross Horloge whereas the visitors from Haute Vieille tour don't have such a clear path. This is probably due to the visual relation between Vieux Marché and the Cathedral, but which is less apparent in the other direction (see Fig. 4).

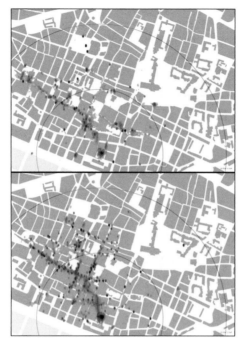

Fig. 4. Rouen, Haut Vieille Tour: Point Density(time-corrected).
Left: Tourism; Right: Shopping (c) 2009 TU Delft

4.3 Koblenz

Koblenz is situated on the corner of Rhine and Mosel. The German Corner (Deutsche Ecke) marks the place where Rhine and Mosel merge. The city count around one hundred thousand inhabitants, comparable to Rouen and Norwich. Due to several wars, the small historic city centre is enclosed by a grid structure with buildings from newer ages. The shopping area is mainly located outside the historic, medieval core. The core itself is characterised by several public squares. Main attractions are the German Corner, Florins Church and square, Görresplatz, Am Plan and Löhr-Center. Tourist arrive in Koblenz by coach, train and by boat! This makes the Peter-Altmeier quay an important access point for the city! (Hoeven, Smit & Spek, 2008)

4.3.1   Koblenz Löhr-Center

The tourists parking in the Löhr-Center are as expected usually not locals or not very familiar with the city centre. In average they spent more than two hours in the city. A part of this group visited the Altmeier Ufer (Mosel quays) towards the 'Deutsche Ecke'. The major part of the tourists spends its time in the Löhrstrasse, Am plan, the Firmungstrasse and have the Jesuitenplatz as a destination. It is remarkable that these tourists hardy visit the Konrad-Adenauer Ufer (Rhine quays), the Palace (Schloss) or even Görresplatz (see Fig. 5).

194

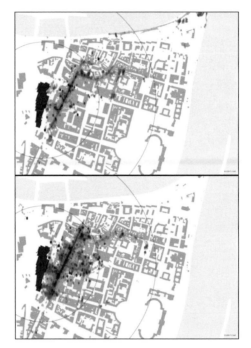

Fig. 5. Koblenz, Löhr-Center: Point Density(time-corrected).
Left: Tourism; Right: Shopping (c) 2009 TU Delft

4.3.2   Koblenz Görresplatz

The tourists who parked in Görresplatz mainly have a regional or national background. Görresplatz attracts a higher amount of tourists. This group is not characterised by a specific duration, but for familiarity it is clear that a larger part of this group visits Koblenz for the first time. Just like Löhr-Center, the statistical data for tourists from Görresplatz shows two different types of visitors: some strolling along the main shopping streets (like Firmungstrasse, Am Plan and Löhrstrasse) -this activity is probably characterized by walking, watching and maybe drink something in a café- and the other type represents the people sightseeing along the Rhein, the famous 'Deutsche Ecke' and the Mosel quays where the boat trips start (see Fig. 6).

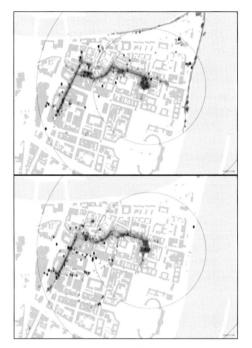

Fig. 6. Koblenz, Görresplatz: Point Density(time-corrected).
Left: Tourism; Right: Shopping (c) 2009 TU Delft

5 Conclusion & Outlook

The method used by TU Delft is mainly based on aggregated data, such as density analysis. This reduces the data to main shapes based on collective behaviour. A strong aspect of this way of working is that privacy of aggregated data is not an issue. But, (automatic) analysis of individual trajectories, showing destinations, and duration for individuals and for groups could offer new insights. New drawing techniques are essential, e.g. space –time diagrams for individuals and accumulated space-time diagrams for groups. This would add the behaviour in time, as introduced in the field of human geography by Hägerstrand (1970) and also used by Shoval & Isaacson (2006). It could be useful to expand the method with other types of questions, not only profiling the participant and outlining the trip, but also involving aspect of motivation, choices, satisfiers and dissatisfiers. This would encourage the discussion on quality of public space and could relate the studies easier to urban design aspects.

As stated shortly in the introduction, several methods for collecting spatio-temporal data are available. In the case of Spatial Metro TU Delft choose for GPS. GPS is accurate, but the method requires distribution and collection of devices. If ethical issues can be limited and if a mobile phone would be capable of long-time tracking (more than today's 2-4 hour battery life), mobile phones have two advantages: (1) assisted GPS working indoor as well and (2) real-time tracking. A system to collect and link the attached interview data is required.

Finally, the method uses a combination of questionnaire and tracking technology. Limited feedback is only collected at the end of the trip. The street-interviews are not valid resources for collecting spatio-temporal data, but could be used after GPS tracking to collect information on unexpected results, e.g. hardly used public space. In this case questions raised by the outcomes of the spatio-temporal data can be answered using street-interviews after the processing and analysis of the data. This would improve the method by introducing an induction phase. This way, the method would consist of three phases: (1) induction (street-interviews and urban analysis: hypothesis), (2) spatio-temporal data collection (processing, analysis, conclusions) and (3) feedback based on results using a second round of street-interviews.

References

Hägerstrand, T. (1970). What about people in regional science? *Papers of the Regional Science Association*. 24: 07-21.
Hoeven, F.D. van der, Smit, M.G.J. & Spek, S.C. van der (2008). *Street-Level Desires*. Charleston, SC: Booksurge Publishing.
Gehl, J. & Gemzoe, L. (2004), *Public Space – Public Life – Copenhagen*, Danish Arch. Press, Copenhagen
Millonig, A., Brändle, N., Ray, M. & Spek, S.C. van der (2009). Pedestrian Behaviour Monitoring: Methods and Experiences. In B. Gottfried (Eds), *Ambient Assisted Living*. Bremen, Germany, IOS-press.
Raper, J., Gartner, G., Karimi, H. & Rizos, M.C. (2007). A Critical Evaluation of Location Bases Services and their potential. *Journal of Location Based Services* 1(1): 05-45.
Ratti, C., Pulselli, R.M., Williams, S. & Frenchman, D. (2006). Mobile Landscapes: using location data from cell phones for urban analysis. *Environ. Plan. B-Plan. Design* 33: 727-748.
Schaick J. van & Spek, S.C. van der (2008). *Urbanism on Track*. Amsterdam, NL: IOS-press.
Shoval, N. & Isaacson, M. (2007a). Tracking Tourists in the Digital Age. *Annals of Tourism Research* 34 (1): 141-159.
Shoval, N. & Isaacson, M. (2007b), Sequence Alignment as a Method for Human Activity Analysis in Space and Time, *Annals of the Association of American Geographers* 97-2, 281–296.
Spek, S.C. van der (2008). Mapping Pedestrian Movement – Using Tracking Technologies in Koblenz. In G. Gartner & K. Rehlr, *Location Based Services and Telecartography II*. Heidelberg: Springer-Verlag.
Spek, S.C. van der, Schaick, J. van, Bois P.G. de & Haan, A.R. de (2009). Sensing Human Activity: GPS tracking. *Sensors* 9: 01-22.
Spek, S.C. van der, (2007). Spatial Metro: Strategies to Improve City Centres for Pedestrians. *Proceedings Walk21 conference*, Walk21, Toronto, 2007.

Acknowledgements

The GPS-tracking research was developed and carried out within the Spatial Metro project. This project was co-funded by the European Union Interreg IIIb initiative. Special thanks goes to the Cities of Norwich, Rouen, and Koblenz for cooperating and making the research possible. The research team consisted of <names hidden>. The images with time-correction have been produced by <name hidden> in Spring 2009.

Looking Does not Automatically Lead to Booking: Analysis of Clickstreams on a Chinese Travel Agency Website

Jun Shao[a] and Ulrike Gretzel[b]

[a]Center for Recreation and Tourism Research
Peking University,China
shaojun_bj@hotmail.com

[b]Laboratory for Intelligent Systems in Tourism
Texas A&M University, USA & University of Wollongong, Australia
ugretzel@tamu.edu

Abstract

Chinese small and medium travel agencies are increasingly focusing on online business, and understanding the transactional patterns of their Website visitors is very important to them. Clickstream sequence analysis can provide the needed insights into booking processes. This study applied an adaptable algorithm to explore how Chinese online travel agency visitors book hotel products. The findings reveal that a high percentage of abandonment occurs after searching for a hotel room and before submitting the final order confirmation. Recommendations are proposed for identified key events in the online hotel booking process.

Keywords: clickstream analysis; adaptable web process analysis; online booking; online travel agency.

1   Introduction

eCommerce has been increasingly adopted by the travel and tourism industry in China, especially by small or medium enterprises (SMEs) (ASOCIO, 2008). However, recent research indicates that Chinese travel agencies still lag behind in their adoption of Internet technologies (Li & Suomi, 2008). Unlike the big online travel agency companies, such as ctrip.com and elong.com, who own technical systems and teams, SMEs among the Chinese travel agencies usually outsource their website design and maintenance. Yet, given the rather high competition in their market, increasing online transactions by improving the web design is critical for them.

Analysis of clickstream data can discover a visitor's usage pattern of a website, since the clickstream data recorded in the web server's log files contains the click information of each visitor, such as timestamps, IP address, URL, status, and transportation bytes (Lee et al., 2001). Assuming that there is an ideal path that leads to booking, this paper employs clickstream analysis to identify problematic events in the clickstream of the users of a Chinese travel agency Website.

2 Background

Reasons for not making a booking when using a travel agency Website are manifold. First, not all searching is goal-directed and travel Website consumers often enter the sites with exploratory search motives (Park & Chung, 2009). Second, there might be structural or cultural barriers to online booking. Li and Buhalis (2005) identified lack of self-efficacy and perceptions of the Internet as not fitting one's lifestyle as important e-Commerce barriers for Chinese online consumers. Li and Suomi (2008) suggest that perceived security risks and lack of trust are the main barriers to e-Tourism in China. Indeed, e-Commerce levels are generally very low in China, with the number of online searchers greatly outnumbering the number of online shoppers (CNNIC, 2009). Third, the market structure might provide incentives to search online but shop offline (e.g. additional services provided when booking occurs offline). Finally, usability issues of the Websites can prevent Website users from booking online. Lu, Lu and Zhang (2002) found general dissatisfaction with the quality of tourism Websites in China.

2.1 Online shopping cart abandonment

The loss of e-Commerce potential is the greatest when consumers actually start the booking process but then fail to complete it. About 75% of online consumers abandon their carts before making a final purchase (eShopability.com, 2009). Cart abandonment analysis is considered an important way to increase e-Commerce revenues (eMarketer.com, 2009a). Since tourism products (such as airline tickets, hotel rooms and car rentals) have no delivery-related issues, abandonment reasons in the context of tourism industry are somewhat different from consumer product contexts. Among the reasons for abandonment reported by MediaPost (2001) and Shenton (2002), the reasons relevant for tourism products include: 1. Meeting a malfunction as payment is being processed; 2. Not getting an acknowledgement after an order has been placed; 3. Changing mind and discarding cart contents; 4. Comparison shopping or browsing; 5. Checkout process is too long; 6. Unavailability of products at checkout time; 7. Checkout requires too much personal information; 8. Poor site navigation and long download time; 9. Lack of contact information; 10. Checkout process is confusing; 11. Site requires registration before purchase; and, 12. No gift certificates.

Research studies regarding shopping cart abandonment have looked at the issue from various perspectives. From the perceived performance risk perspective, uncertainty or perceived risks in the context of consumer decision making include financial, social, psychological, performance, procedural, and privacy risks (Hogarth, Michaud & Mery,1980; Rogers,1995) . Moore and Mathews (2006) found that the evaluation of the brand, the price of the product, web design, and the e-retailer's site reputation play an important role in perceiving performance risk. Other studies have focused on the characteristics of the online buyers. Factors identified include attitude toward online shopping (Milgram, Sroloff & Rosenbaum, 1988), "uncertain need" for a product and past experience (Ram, 1987), value consciousness (Sproles & Kendall, 1986), high quality consciousness and being confused by overchoice (Sproles & Sproles, 1990). Cho, Kang and Cheon (2006) summarized the reasons for shopping cart abandonment in four categories—perceived uncertainty, medium/channel innovation, contextual, and consumer characteristics, and found that delay reasons related to perceived uncertainty explain shopping cart abandonment better than overall hesitation and final payment hesitation, while medium/channel innovation factors predict better for hesitation in payment than for shopping cart abandonment and overall hesitation. Consumer characteristics are more closely related to overall hesitation than to payment hesitation and cart abandonment. Most recently, Close and Kukar-Kinne (2009) proposed a model to predict the factors which influence the frequency of online shopping cart use including the following: current purchase intent, price promotions, entertainment purpose, organizational intent, and research and information search. They uncovered that a considerable number of shoppers uses online shopping carts as a shopping organization tool to store and organize their consideration set for a possible future purchase — either at that site, a competitor's site, or using a traditional retail channel.

2.2 Web site design and shopping cart abandonment

Problems of web site design become barriers to shopping cart abandonment. According to eMarketer.com (2009b), web site design or usability issues and pricing are tied for the second common reason with 13% of respondents. To discourage shopping cart abandonment, the following measures have been suggested to website designers: streamlining the checkout processes, putting reviews and price comparisons on the product page, reminding consumers about earlier searches (O'Donnell, 2007), increasing session timeouts (Kohavi & Parekh, 2003), as well as applying Single-Screen Checkout applications which allow consumers to keep product pages on their screens and see how their totals change as they add or delete items from their shopping carts (Greene, 2005). Also, commercial software has emerged to help e-commerce sites reduce shopping cart abandonment, such as eBSure suite (Callaghan, 2000). By measuring how much time a transaction takes and the reason for any excessive delay, the software can report a user's experiences leading up to a transaction abandonment. Customer-care technologies can be used to improve the usability of web site, such as voice over IP, dynamic and searchable lists of frequently asked questions (FAQ) and online chatting to allow customers get the answers they need to buy goods right away (Schwartz, 2001).

As recent research revealed that Web page design has significant impacts on online consumers' attitudes and behaviours (Chatterjee, 2008), it is important to gain insights into the differences between consumers' actual online booking behaviour and the web design of particular booking processes.

2.3 Clickstream analysis applied in tourism research

There exists a very rich literature on clickstream analysis applied in the marketing context including web usage and navigation, internet advertisements, and online shopping and e-commerce, as reviewed by Bucklin and Sismeiro (2009). Similarly, given the importance of understanding users' clickstream, there is increasing research available applying clickstream analysis to the tourism industry. Active research fields within tourism include tourism recommendation systems (TRS), online travel information search, and visitor behaviour on tourism related websites (including destination websites and hotel websites).

To evaluate tourism recommendation systems, Zanker et al. (2008) applied clickstream sequence analysis to explore empirically the friction provoking users to exit the TRS. When measuring clickstream's complexity, they followed the indictors of clickstream compactness and stratum used by Senecal (2005) and initially proposed by McEneaney (2001). To explore how consumers find and browse hotel websites, Schegg et al. (2005) used a commercial web log analysis tool named WebTrends to analyze the log files of a hotel website, combining with manual evaluation to the content and information construct of the website. Following Schegg et al. (2005), Leung and Law (2008) analyzed the information retrieved by visitors and their access paths. Regarding the research field of visitor behaviour on tourism destination websites, Anuar, Xiang and Gretzel (2009) studied eBrochure usage patterns on a convention and visitors bureau in the United States by analyzing the web log files. They also emphasized the importance of data mining on web clickstream data in terms of browsing pattern discovery, which could not be provided by general page view analysis. However, overall, there is no research applying clickstream analysis to discover why consumers abandon online hotel booking processes.

2.4 Process sequence matching with a designed web process sequence

The online shopping process is a typical web process sequence (WPS) which has a pre-determined start state and an expected termination state. A designed Web process sequence (DWPS) is a transaction-oriented sequence of steps necessary to complete a specific goal on a Website (Wang & Wang, 2009). As user clickstream sequences recorded by web servers are non-numerical (the click events are represented by characters rather than numerical data), popular pattern discovering methods (e.g. time series analysis (TSA), associate distance measure (ADM) method, sequence alignment method (SAM), high frequency patterns (HFP) methods) and commercial sequence data analysis software programs (e.g., IBM DB2 Intelligent Miner, 2009) are not suitable for analyzing DWPS. TSA is inadequate to analyze the non-numerical clickstream, the ADM and SAM methods do not explicitly describe the time measure of a sequence, and HFP methods are not suitable to discover the patterns of DWPS where the frequency is not important. Therefore, Wang and Wang (2009) proposed an adaptable web process sequence analysis algorithm to match users' actual online processes with desired DWPS for improving e-commerce transactions.

Different from the exact process sequence matching methods in that heuristics relevant to DWPS must be applied, Wang and Wang (2009) called their process sequence matching method "adaptable", because the method considers both the uncertain local loops in the process sequences and uncertain interruptions of the process sequences. The local loops refer to instances such as a customer repeatedly putting items into the shopping cart, and the uncertain interruptions refer instances where someone might leave during the online shopping process and may or may not return. The adaptable matching method regards local loops as repeated events and sets an interval threshold to determine whether a process is terminated. According to Wang & Wang (2009), their algorithm consists of three main steps. First, assemble designed web process sequences based on Web log records for each of the process actors(online consumers), named Θ. Each sequence contains three items, i.e. process actor, event of the process (clicking a page designed for the process), and time of the event of the Web process. Second, generate the norm designed Web process sequences based on examining the website, named Ψ. The norm DWPS consists of ideal events of clicking a series of web pages. For instance, an ideal online hotel booking DWPS may include searching a hotel, searching for a room in this hotel, reserving the hotel room, and making a payment. Third, matching these two sequence datasets, and obtaining an output table which represents the events and local loops, e.g., repeated hotel room searches, specified by norm designed web process sequences, the number of the processes that has reached the corresponding event (or local loop), and the average interval time between the corresponding event (or local loop) and the next event (or local loop).

To measure the dissimilarity between all Θ and Ψ, Wang and Wang (2009) use process sequence matching. "The first event e_{Norm-1} of Ψ is used to search Θ. If e_{Norm-1} is found in Θ, then record the time t1, and the process continues to the second event e_{Norm-2}. This process proceeds until e_{Norm-T} is reached, or Θ is ill-terminated. If the event in Ψ is a local loop, E_{Norm-i}, which could be a set of events, is used to search Θ repeatedly until the loop is ended in Θ."(Wang & Wang, 2009: 108). Since deviation from the typical DWPS can contribute to understanding shopping cart abandonment, we applied the web process sequence analysis algorithm proposed by Wang and Wang (2009) to the hotel booking process on an online Chinese travel agency Website.

3 Methodology

3.1 Data Source

The clickstream data from a Chinese travel agency website was analysed. The website provides hotel booking, car rental, meeting reception, tour consulting, and discount flight tickets especially for Hainan Island, a popular vacation destination in South China. Among its various online booking businesses, online hotel booking is the most important. Typically, the peak season of Hainan spans from October to May. The first week in October is a Golden Week of Chinese National Holiday, which means that from September 1 onward, increased traffic volume is recorded on the site during this time period.

One week (from 0:00am September 1, 2009 to 0:00am September 8, 2009) worth of data was extracted from the overall data set. To identify a hotel booking process, two selecting rules are implemented to assemble the DPWS dataset. First, only the click records whose URL information includes "/hotel/" are regarded. In total, 2,613 click records or 1,351 click sequences were assembled, meaning that these click sequences reached hotel-related pages. Second, to identify a click sequence which has reached a process of searching or booking rather than just browsing and then exiting, only those click sequences including "/hotel/show.asp" are selected. Finally, we got 819 click sequences which involved hotel searching or booking processes.

3.2 Data Analysis

To investigate whether visitors search and book the hotels according to the DPWS designed into the Website, this study implemented an algorithm in a Java program called "Analyser" following the methodology proposed by Wang & Wang (2009). The authors chose java language due to its cross-platform capacity.

The input of "Analyser" is as follows:

1. The web log database contains 819 click sequences which have reached hotel searching or booking processes.
2. A norm designed web process event sequence from searching hotel information to booking hotel was identified. By investigating the Chinese travel agency website, we derived the designed online hotel booking progress as shown in the second column of Table 1. It should be noted that there are 5 entry or starting points including the homepage of the web site, the page of hotel booking in the main menu of this web site, and travel information search engines such as qunar.com, all of which will lead to the hotel booking process. The ideal sequence represented by URLs is "hotel/show.asp"-"hotel/room.asp" - "hotel/order.asp" -"hotel/save.asp" -"hotel/pay.asp";
3. A threshold for interruption intervals of the web process was set to 30 minutes. It is assumed that if an online user left the Web site and did not return to the hotel booking process within a half hour, the process ended in adequately.

4 Results and Discussion

4.1 Sequence Matching Results for Online Hotel Booking Processes

After running the java program named "Analyser", we obtained results in terms of the events included in the actual clickstreams of the Website users and compared them to the events in the DWPS (Table 1). As shown in Table 1, our analysis of sequences reveals that in the week under investigation, there are 819 processes that reached the page of "hotel/show.asp", suggesting that these users were browsing hotel information. Among these browsing sequences, there are only 102 processes showing interest in more detailed information at the hotel room level, and 67 processes involved submitting booking requests. However, all of them were abandoned before an online confirmation was made. But this does not necessarily mean that there were no transactions at all. Because a floating window featuring an image of online service staff linking to an online chat feature and the toll-free service number are put in a very conspicuous position on the page of "hotel/order.asp", when inputting the order information on this page, a user might click the floating window to talk with the online service staff or call the service line instead of confirming the order by clicking the "Order it" button on the bottom of this web page. While this step might reduce perceived performance risks for the customer, it certainly leads to less efficiency in the process for the online travel agency.

To further compare the actual behaviours to the ideal process, we use the abandonment percentage. By identifying the last clicked URL in the online hotel booking sequence, we can determine the abandonment point. For instance, if a click sequence ends at "hotel/show.asp", we can learn that the user abandoned the online booking progress and left after searching hotel information. There were three abandonment points after searching for hotel information and before the ideal exit point (i.e. payment): "hotel/show.asp", "hotel/room.asp", and "hotel/order.asp".

Table 1. Sequence Matching Results for Online Hotel Booking Processes

Events(e_i)	Web Pages	Local loop	Number of processes that reached e_i	Average interval time between e_i and e_{i+1}(Seconds)
Access the homepage of the website	Homepage of the website	Y	276	131.021
Access the page of the hotel product	hotel/	Y	168	90.505
Searching hotels by city name, area, and checking in/out date	hotel/hotel. asp	Y	192	121.181
Browsing hotels by star rating	hotel/star.as p	Y	3	35.667
Browsing the general hotel information and room rates matching the search	hotel/show. asp	Y	819	186.321
Displaying the room rate after choosing a room type	hotel/room. asp	Y	102	106.372
Inputting personal information after clicking "I want to book the room"	hotel/order. asp	Y	67	181.117
Confirm a hotel order	hotel/save.a sp	-	0	-
Making Payment	hotel/pay.as p	-	0	-

By dividing the amount of the click sequences which have not reached the ideal exit page "hotel/pay.asp" by those that reached the page of "hotel/show.asp", we can get corresponding percentages of online ordering abandonment. For instance, as shown in line 5 and line 6 in Table 1, among the 819 processes which reached the page of "hotel/show.asp", there are only 102 processes reaching the ideal next page of "hotel/room.asp", indicating the other 717 (the result of 819 minus 102) sequences ended at the abandonment point of "hotel/show.asp", meaning the users just browsed hotel information with room rates of all the room types which matched their searching criteria and then left the website. Accordingly, the abandonment percentage at this point is 87.55% (717 divided by 819), meaning 87.55% of the users left the web site after browsing the hotel information. The findings and our comments are summarized in Table 2.

4.2 Potential Reasons for Abandonment and Comments for Web Design

Table 2. Interpretation and Comments for Online Hotel Booking Processes

Abandonment point	Percentage	Potential Reasons	Comments for Web Design
1.Left after browsing hotel information	87.55% (717/819)	-Room rate might not be competitive -A user might cannot find the "Order it" button -A user might use the online floating window to chat or call by phone	-Put the "Book it" button in an attention-getting position -Record the online chatting clickstream for further tracking.
2.Left after choosing a room in a hotel and before clicking "I want to book the room"	34.31% (35/102)	-Unsatisfied with information of room facilities and amenities -A user might use the online floating window to chat or call by phone to confirm	-Record the online chatting clickstream for further tracking. -Optimize the online chatting design -Add a "Continue booking" link
3.Left after clicking "I want to book the room" and before confirming	100% (67/67)	-A user might use the online floating window to chat or call by phone to confirm -A user might be uncertain about how to order or how to pay	-Provide payment information -Provide more alternative options for online payment. -Add a "Continue booking" link

Following the identification of the high abandonment points, the investigation of the actual Websites reveals that in Abandonment point 1, where the pages show information about the hotels and provide very detailed descriptions about the location, star rating, brand as well as the facilities and amenities of the room, the "Book it" button can not be easily found without dragging down the side bar. As such, this could make a potential tourist leave easily. In addition, room rates might not be competitive enough to lead the user to book a hotel and users might not have found what they needed. The website has already taken advantage of a few marketing tools that can reduce negative perceptions of price, such as putting price comparisons (the inflated regular price and a discount price) on the hotel product page (O'Donnell,

2007), and the room rates can be searched through popular tourism search engines in China (e.g., qunar.com). Thus, the abandonment is likely due to usability issues, which is in line with the survey results of eMarketer.com (2009b).

As for the abandonment occurring both before requesting a hotel room booking order (Abandonment point 1 and 2) and before confirming the order (Abandonment point 3), the prominent display of the online chat and the phone number have to be considered. Since the room rate is very time–sensitive, through these two ways of communication one can get an instant response whether the room and the price are available. Thus, a visitor might prefer chatting or calling rather than completing the order form online and then wait for the service staff to reach them. However, there are no measures taken to track if a user calls to make the purchase. Although the web site designers have realized the importance of using customer-friendly methods such as online chatting (Schwartz,2001), unfortunately this Chinese travel agency has outsourced the floating window application, the main web site application and the tracking of clicktreams to different software vendors. Thus, the use of the floating window is currently not tracked and, therefore, cannot be analyzed. Much insight could be gained if such data was actually available and, therefore, we recommend that the travel agency should demand tracking of the feature. Another suggestion to the website is to add a "Continue booking" link to the pages of FAQ and payment process introduction.

5 Conclusions

Overall, our application of the adaptable matching algorithm proposed by Wang and Wang (2009) to the clickstream data of a travel agency website succeeded in discovering the transaction sequence patterns against a desired process. The findings show that the actual sequences deviate greatly from the ideal process. High abandonment was found throughout the process, suggesting that usability issues might exist. An actual analysis of the pages confirms potential usability issues.

There are some limitations to the study. One is the volume of data, as we only had the permission to use a 1-week time-frame of data. Tracking data for a longer timeframe, especially for the entire month of September would provide more reliable insights. Another limitation is the lack of payment clickstream. SME travel agencies in China typically separate the booking and the payment process to confirm the customer's order with the hotel first. The results also show the limitations of behavioural clickstream data in that the "why" cannot be answered unless additional analyses (in our case an observation of the actual page) are undertaken.

References

Anuar, F., Xiang, Z., & U. Gretzel, (2009). Effectiveness of eBrochures: An analysis of use patterns. In W. Höpken, U. Gretzel, & R. Law (Eds.), *Information and Communication Technologies in Tourism 2009* (pp. 333-342). Vienna, Austria: Springer Verlag.

ASOCIO (2008). E-Commerce set to Rise 45% Among China SMBs in 2008. Accessed online (October 11, 2009) at: http://www.asocio.org/newsdetail2.php?newsid=107.

Bucklin, R. E. & C. Sismeiro (2009). Click Here for Internet Insight: Advances in Clickstream Data Analysis in Marketing. *Journal of Interactive Marketing.* 23(1): 35-48.

Callaghan, D. (2000). Keeping e-carts moving. *eWeek* .17(20):44

Chatterjee, P. (2008).Are unclicked ads wasted? Enduring effects of banner and pop-up ad exposure on brand memory and attitudes. *Journal of Electronic Commerce Research,*.9(1):51-61.

Cho, C., Kang, J. & H. J., Cheon (2006). Online Shopping Hesitation. CyberPsychology & Behavior. 9(3): 261-274.

Close, A. G. & M. Kukar-Kinne (2009) .Beyond buying: Motivations behind consumers' online shopping cart use. *Journal of Business Research* (In Press).

CNNIC (2009). CNNIC publishes 24th Statistical Report on Internet Development in China. Accessed online (October 11, 2009) at:
http://www.cnnic.net.cn/html/Dir/2009/07/28/5644.htm

eMarketer.com(2009a). What's the Best Way to Improve Conversions? Accessed online (November 2, 2009) at: http://www.emarketer.com/Article.aspx?R=1007354.

eMarketer.com(2009b). Keys to E-Commerce Success. Accessed online (November 2, 2009) at: http://www.emarketer.com/Article.aspx?R=1007358.

eShopability.com (2009). eShopability:The Facts. Accessed online (October 7, 2009) at: http://www.eshopability.com/.

Green, M.V. (2005). It's All About the Carts. *Stores*.87(1), p. 100, 102

IBM.(2009). DB2 Intelligent Miner.Accessed online (April 22, 2009) at: http://www.ibm.com.

Hogarth, R.M., Michaud, C., & Mery, J. (1980). Decision behavior in urban development: a methodological approach and substantive considerations. *Acta Psychologica* 45:95–117.

Kohavi, R & R Parekh.(2003).Ten supplementary analyses to improve e-commerce web sites. *Proceedings of the Fifth WEBKDD workshop: Webmining as a premise to effective and intelligent Web Applications, ACM SIGKDD, Washington, DC, USA.* 29-36

Lee, J., Podlaseck, M., Schonberg, E. & H. Robert, (2001).Visualization and Analysis of Clickstream Data of Online Stores for Understanding Web Merchandising, *Data Mining and Knowledge Discovery.* 5, 59–84.

Leung, R. & R. Law, (2008). Analyzing a Hotel Website's Access Paths. In O'Connor, P. Höpken, W. & Gretzel, U. (Eds.), *Information and Communication Technologies in Tourism 2008.* pp. 255-266. New York: Springer-Verlag, Wien.

Li, H. & Suomi, R. (2008). Internet Adoption in Tourism Industry in China. In Oya, M., Uda, R., Yasunobu, C., (Eds.), *IFIP International Federation for Information Processing*, volume 286: Towards Sustainable Society on Ubiquitous Networks, pp. 197-208. Boston, MA: Springer.

Li, L. & Buhalis, D. (2005). Predicting Internet Usage for Travel Bookings in China. In A. Frew (Ed.), *Information and Communication Technologies in Tourism 2005*, 429-439. Vienna, Austria: Springer Verlag.

Lu, Z., Lu, J., & Zhang, C. (2002). Website Development and Evaluation in the Chinese Tourism Industry. *Networks and Communication Studies*, 16(3-4), 191-208.

MediaPost. (2001). Online shoppers drop carts. Accessed online (September 22, 2009) at: http://www.mediapost.com/publications/?fa=Articles.showArticle&art_aid=81467.

McEneaney, J. E. (2001). Graphic and numerical methods to assess navigation in hypertext. *International Journal of Human-Computer Studies*.55 (5),761-786.

Milgram, N.A., Sroloff, B., & Rosenbaum, M. (1988). The procrastination of everyday life. *Journal of Research in Personality.* 22:197–212.

Moore, S. & S., Mathews (2006). An Exploration of Online Shopping Cart Abandonment Syndrome--A Matter of Risk and Reputation. *Journal of Website Promotion.* 2(1/2):71-88.

O'Donnell,J.(2007). Buying online gets even easier. USA Today. 11/16/2007. Section: Money, Pg. 03b

Park, J. & Chung, H. (2009). Consumers' travel website transferring behavior: analysis using clickstream data-time, frequency, and spending. *The Service Industries Journal*, 29(10), 1451-1463.

Ram, S. (1987). A model of innovation resistance. *Advances in Consumer Research* 14:208–212.

Rogers, E.M. (1995). *Diffusion of Innovations,* 4th ed.New York: The Free Press.

Schegg, R., Steiner, T., Gherissi-Labben, T., & Murphy, J. (2005). Using Log File Analysis and Website Assessment to Improve Hospitality Websites. *In A.J. Frew (Eds),Information and communication Technologies in Tourism 2005*, pp. 566-576. NewYork: Springer-Verlag, Wien.

Schwartz, M. (2001). The Care and Keeping of Online Customers. *Computerworld.* 35(2) Section: Technology.

Senecal, S., Kalczynski, P. J. & Nantel, J. (2005). Consumers' decision-making process and their online shopping behaviour: A Clickstream analysis, *Journal of Business Research*.58(11):1599-1608.

Shenton, J.(2002) Shopping cart abandonment, Global Millennia Marketing. Accessed online (September 22, 2009) at: http://www.globalmillenniamarketing.com/shopping%20_cart_abandonment_survey.htm.

Sproles, E.K., & Sproles, G.B. (1990). Consumer decision-making styles as a function of individual learning styles. *Journal of Consumer Affairs*.24: 134–147

Sproles, G.B., & Kendall, E.L. (1986). A methodology for profiling consumer's decision-making styles. *Journal of Consumer Affairs.* 20:267–279.

Wang, H.,& S. Wang (2009). Adaptable Algorithm for Designed Web Process Sequence Data Analysis. *Journal of Electronic Commerce Research*,10(2),104-113.

Zanker, M., Fuchs, M., Höpken, W., Tuta, M. & N. Müller. (2008). Evaluating Recommender Systems in Tourism - A Case Study from Austria. In O'Connor, P. Höpken, W. Gretzel, U.(Eds.), *Information and Communication Technologies in Tourism 2008.* pp. 24-34. New York: Springer-Verlag, Wien

Acknowledgements

The implementation of the adaptable web process algorithm was supported by Mr. Huadong Zhong. The data access authorization was coordinated by Mr. Xiaolong Lu.

Why Some Internet Users Don't Buy Air Tickets Online

Enrique Bigné,
Silvia Sanz,
Carla Ruiz and
Joaquín Aldás

Department of Marketing
University of Valencia, Spain
{Enrique.bigne; silvia.sanz; carla.ruiz; Joaquin.aldas}@uv.es

Abstract

This work attempts to identify the determinant variables that make some Internet users not to buy airline tickets online. The Technology Acceptance Model (TAM) and the Theory of Planned Behaviour (TPB) have been used as the conceptual reference framework, with the addition of the influence of perceived risk and trust. The results of the empirical study of Internet users who never have purchased an airline ticket online suggest that both subjective norm and attitude have a direct influence on airline ticket purchase intention. Ease of use has also proved to be a significant variable, because it has an indirect influence on behaviour through perceived usefulness, trust and risk. Risk, trust and perceived behavioural control were found to influence purchase intention through attitude. The results also show that risk is a multidimensional variable and that the dimensions do not all exercise the same influence on airline ticket purchase intention. Managerial implications are provided.

Keywords: online purchase; airline ticket; Technology Acceptance Model; Theory of Planned Behaviour; trust; risk.

1 Introduction

The benefits (time and cost savings, easy to compare offers, price reductions, etc.) that Internet offers consumers make it an ideal medium for delivering tourism services. With regard to the airline industry, the Internet enables customers worldwide to book air tickets rapidly and conveniently and with substantial price savings (Kim et al., 2006). In Spain, as in the US and Europe, the products most commonly sold online are travel-related (Forrester Research, 2007, 2009; Red.es, 2009). Travel tickets in Spain concentrate 62.6% of total electronic commerce, followed by hotel reservations (43%) and show tickets (41%). In Spain, as in other countries, growing Internet use to find information about travel services has not been accompanied by a similar growth in the number of online shoppers. According to the study "Internet 2008" (BBVA, 2008), despite the fact that 68.3 per cent of Internet users based their travel services purchase decisions in brick-and-mortar agencies on information they had obtained from the Internet, only 13.5 per cent of Internet users purchased online travel services in 2008. The purchase confirmation process is therefore one of the aspects of greatest concern for airline companies and online travel agencies.

Internet users are not a homogeneous group (Chen et al., 2001; Chen et al., 2004; Yven and Lavin, 2003). Although dramatic differences were discovered between Internet users, there is very limited research on how and why certain groups of Internet users shop online tourism products while others are reluctant to accept e-shopping (Kamarulzaman, 2007). It is crucial for companies to understand non-purchasing Internet users' attitudes, perceptions and their online browsing patterns, in order to develop effective strategies to convert them to e-shopping (Rohm and Swaminathan, 2004; Vrechopoulos et al., 2001). Furthermore, the group of Internet users interested in future purchases online is capable of acting as a leader of opinion in relation to other consumers (Vrechopoulos et al., 2001).

Given the importance of Internet shopping as a source of income for airline companies and high user demand, in-depth research is required. In the last twenty years, different lines of research have focused on identifying certain factors influencing acceptance of Information Systems and have provided models and theoretical proposals. In particular, the Technology Acceptance Model (TAM) introduced by Davis (Davis, 1989, Davis et al., 1989) and the Theory of Planned Behaviour (TPB) (Ajzen, 1991; Taylor and Todd, 1995) have received considerable attention from the scientific community and its use has extended to the study of tourism services (Kamarulzaman, 2007; Lee et al., 2006). Although TAM and TPB have successfully explained behavioural intentions, previous research pointed out that TAM (Moon and Kim, 2001) and TPB's (Liao et al., 1999) fundamental constructs do not reflect the specific influences of usage-context factors that may alter users' acceptance. Therefore, we believe that the original TAM and TPB should be considered with more belief-related variables (trust and risk) to properly explain the intention to use online tourism services. Previous research has found trust issues and risk perception to be crucial drivers of Internet tourism services adoption (Chen 2006; Kamarulzaman, 2007). Thus, in virtual environments it is fundamental to increase consumer trust, as the risk associated to possible losses from the online transaction is greater than in traditional environments. This work attempts to identify the determinant variables that make some Internet users not to buy airline tickets online despite of being one of the most popular products sold online. The Technology Acceptance Model (TAM) and the Theory of Planned Behaviour (TPB) have been used as the conceptual framework, incorporating variables concerning consumer characteristics (perceived risk and trust), to provide an improved model for consumers' acceptance of Internet to purchase airline travel tickets.

2 Literature Review

2.1 Technology Acceptance Model

The Technology Acceptance Model (TAM) was developed by Davis (1989) to explain acceptance of information technology for different tasks. He showed that the intention to use a system is determined by what an individual believes about that system. Davis et al. (1989) identified perceived usefulness and perceived ease of use as the basic determining factors in information system acceptance. Both the perceived usefulness and the perceived ease of use influence individual attitudes towards a technology. The relation between perceived usefulness and attitude is justified by "expectation-value" models (Ajzen and Fishbein, 1980). Perceived ease of use affects attitudes in two ways: self-efficiency and instrumentality (Davis et al., 1989) so that the simpler the interaction with a system, the greater the individual's sensation of efficiency and control (Bandura, 1982). In addition, perceived ease of use influences perceived usefulness, since a system's simplicity can improve the result (Davis, 1989; Davis et al., 1989), and a technology is perceived as being more useful if it is easier to use (Venkatesh and Davis, 2000). As Kim et al. (2008) pointed out, if the airline website is easy of understand or learn to operate, the Internet user will be more likely to perceive convenience, usefulness and develop positive attitude. We, therefore, posit that:

H1. The perceived ease of use of Internet for airline ticket purchase positively influences Internet non-purchasers attitude towards buying airline tickets online.
H2. The perceived usefulness of Internet for airline ticket purchase positively influences Internet non-purchasers attitude towards buying airline tickets online.
H3. The perceived ease of use of Internet for airline ticket purchase positively influences the Internet non-purchasers perceived usefulness of Internet for airline ticket purchase.

Attitude and perceived usefulness, in turn, predict the individual's behaviour intention. Thus, according to Davis et al. (1989), perceived usefulness is the cognitive determinant of intention whereas attitude represents the affective component. Previous research focused on tourism services (Kim et al., 2008) has evidenced the influence of perceived usefulness in online purchase intention. Therefore, we hypothesize that,

H4. The Internet non-purchasers perceived usefulness of Internet for airline ticket purchase positively influences the future airline ticket online purchase intention.

Attitude becomes a positive mediator between beliefs (perceived usefulness and perceived ease of use) and intentions/behaviour (Bajaj and Nidumolu, 1998). In the context of airline tickets purchase, previous research (Kim et al., 2007) shows that favourable attitudes influence positively the use of Internet as a purchase channel for tourist services. We, therefore, posit that, if a Internet user perceives high usefulness in airline websites, their attitude towards purchasing airline travel tickets will improve.

H5. Internet non-purchasers attitude towards using Internet for airline ticket purchase positively influences airline ticket online purchase intention.

2.2 Theory of Planned Behaviour

The Theory of Planned Behaviour (TPB) is also an extension of the Theory of Reasoned Action. It adds the construct perceived control to subjective norm and attitude as an additional antecedent to intention and behaviour (Ajzen, 1991) with the aim of contemplating situations where individuals do not have full control over their behaviours (Taylor and Todd, 1995). The Theory of Planned Behaviour considers behaviour intention as the best indicator of behaviour, as it expresses the effort which individuals are prepared to make to carry out a given action (Ajzen, 1991). Behaviour intention is a function of attitude, subjective norm and perceived behavioural control (Ajzen, 1991; Taylor and Todd, 1995). The influence of subjective norm and perceived behavioural control on purchase intention has also been evidenced in later research (Cho and Hwang, 2001; Keen et al, 2004; Kanning et al., 2008). We posit the following hypotheses in relation to the TPB model:

H6. Subjective norm positively influences Internet non-purchasers airline ticket online purchase intention.

H7: Perceived control positively influences Internet non-purchasers airline ticket online purchase intention.

2.3 Perceived Shopping Risk

In the context of virtual environments we can define perceived purchase risk as the Internet user's expectations of losing in a given electronic transaction (Forsythe and Shi, 2003). Several studies have considered perceived risk as a multidimensional construct which subdivides into several losses, which together, explain the overall risk associated with the purchase of a product or service. In the sphere of electronic transactions, the identified risk dimensions are: performance, psychological, time, social and privacy (Cunningham et al., 2005; Forsythe and Shi, 2003):

- Performance: fear that the product or service acquired will not meet consumer expectations, in our particular case, that the ticket purchased is not received, does not allow the flight to be taken, etc..
- Psychological: fear of loss of self-esteem due to the wrong choice of product/service, that is, a ticket which does not finally provide the experience of the desired flight, generates anxiety and stress in the consumer.
- Time: the sensation of wasting time associated with the purchase. In particular, the time which the consumer perceives he or she has unnecessarily spent in looking for and finding a ticket on the Internet or in making the online purchase.
- Social: the consumer's fear that the people around him or her may consider the choice inappropriate. In particular, when the consumer perceives that the people whose opinion he or she values think that the decision to purchase an airline ticket online is imprudent or mistaken.
- Privacy: loss of control over personal information. For example, if the consumer perceived that the airline company had violated his or her privacy by using personal information to send unwanted e-mails.

The online purchase of airline tickets has high levels of perceived risk, due both to the shopping channel being used (Internet) (Cunningham et al., 2005) and the intangible nature of the service (Boksberger et al., 2007). The study by Cunningham et al. (2005) evidences that the perception of possible losses associated to the reservation and purchase of airline tickets online is greater than the perceived risk of purchase through traditional channels.

Perceived risk plays an important role in shopping behaviour because it influences other consumer perceptions (perceived ease of use and perceived usefulness). According to the Electronic Commerce Acceptance Model (Lee et al., 2001), the perceived usefulness of the technological platform, Internet in our case, is determined by the perceived purchase risk. The combination of uncertainty (likelihood of loss) and danger (cost of the loss), which are components of perceived risk, reduce perceived usefulness and adoption. This relation has also been found by Cheng et al. (2006) and Seyal and Rahman (2007), so that the greater the perceived risk, the lower the perceived value of use of the system to acquire the product. Previous studies have found that ease of use reduces the uncertainty and risk of system use (Featherman and Pavlou, 2003). Thus, electronic services which are perceived as being complex are considered problematic in terms of performance and generate much uncertainty for the consumer (Moore and Benbasar, 1991). Similarly, if consumers see electronic services as easy to use, they will think that the services will perform well, evaluating them more favourably and being more willing to adopt them. Thus,

H8. Perceived purchase risk has a negative influence on the Internet non-purchasers perceived usefulness of Internet to purchase airline tickets.
H9: Perceived ease of use of Internet to purchase airline tickets has a negative influence on Internet non-purchasers perceived purchase risk.

2.4 Trust

Trust occurs when: "one party has confidence in a exchange partner's reliability and integrity" (Morgan and Hunt, 1994). Many researchers have conceptualized trust as a set of specific beliefs dealing with the honesty, benevolence and competence (Donney and Canon, 1997) of a particular e-service vendor. Nowadays, many companies largely base trust on the competences their customers perceive, especially in high perceived risk environments like Internet. Focusing on the relation between TAM model perceptions and trust, previous studies have reported the influence of ease of use as an antecedent of trust (Kamarulzaman, 2007; Koufaris and Hampton-Sousa, 2002; Wu and Chen, 2005). Perceived ease of use has a positive influence on trust as it promotes a favourable impression towards the online seller in the initial adoption of the service. Research by Wu and Chen and Koufaris and Hampton-Sousa (2002), also evidences the role of trust as a consequence of perceived ease of use. Hence the following research hypothesis:

H10. Perceived ease of use has a positive influence on Internet non-purchasers trust in online airline travel tickets.

In the sphere of online tourist services, Chen's (2006) study shows that perceived risk negatively influences trust in a given website. Other studies (Flavián and Guinaliu, 2006) also show that reducing perceived safety and privacy risks are determinants in creating consumer trust in Internet. Therefore, trust and perceived purchase risk are inversely related (Mayer et al., 1995), so that the smaller the perceived purchase risk, the greater the trust in the seller or channel. Therefore, we posit that,

214

H11. Perceived purchase risk negatively influences Internet non-purchasers online trust.

Prior research has shown that perceived risk in e-commerce has a negative effect on attitude towards the behaviour (Shih, 2004; Van der Heijden et al., 2003). Similarly, empirical evidence has underlined the direct, positive influence of trust on shopping attitude (George, 2002; McKnight et al., 1998; Pavlou and Fygenson, 2006; Wu and Chen, 2005). Research by George, (2002) and Wu and Chen (2005) have all suggested that trust impacts intention through positive attitude. Pavlou and Fygenson, (2006) suggested that trust is an antecedent of attitude due to confident expectations. McKnight et al. (1998) also posits that trust is a belief that affects attitude, which in turn results in the intention to engage in trust related behaviour with a specific e-service supplier. Therefore, we hypothesize that,

H12. Perceived risk has a negative influence on Internet non-purchasers attitude towards airline tickets online shopping.
H13. Online trust in an airline website has a positive influence on Internet non-purchasers attitude towards airline tickets online shopping.

Figure 1 presents the research model for the study.

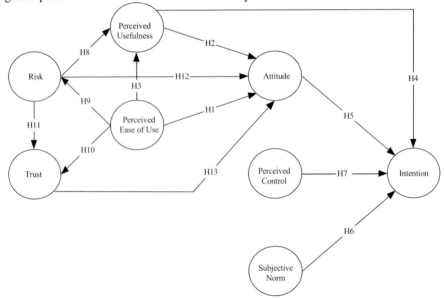

Fig. 1. Research model

3   Method

The sample included 309 non-purchasing Internet users. Sampling was by gender and age quotas based on Internet user characteristics periodically examined by the Spanish E-Commerce Association in the study "Surfers on the Net" (AIMC, 2007) which is a important directory of Internet users in Spain. Out of the total sample, 65% were men and 35% women. A large percentage of the interviewees belong to the age segment between 16 and 34 (67%) and are also medium educated (50.5%) with an above average level of income (55.7%). The questionnaire design was based on scales adapted from previous studies and measured by multiple item 7-point Likert-type scales. The scale items for perceived ease-of-use and perceived usefulness were taken from the study of Davis (1989), Davis et al. (1989) and Lee et al. (2006). Subjective norm, perceived control and attitude were measured following the studies by Taylor and Todd (1995) and Bhattacherjee (2002). Online purchase intention was measured following the studies of Taylor and Todd (1995) and Gefen and Straub (2000). The scale items for trust (Doney and Canon, 1997; Flavián and Guinaliu, 2006) and perceived risk dimensions (Jarvenpaa and Todd, 1997; Featherman and Pavlou, 2003) were also measured using adapted scales validated in previous research on E-commerce. In the present paper, a formative operationalization has been chosen for risk construct. To make sure this part of the model is identified; three reflective indicators measuring global risk perception were added to the formative risk construct configuring an identified MIMIC model (Diamantopoulos and Winklhofer, 2001).

4 Results

The measurement instrument was validated in two stages following Ulaga and Eggert's (2005) recommendation. Because trust and risk are second order factors, in the validation process, firstly confirmatory factor analyses were done on the six latent variables of the risk construct and on the three variables of the trust construct using robust maximum likelihood verification (Satorra and Bentler, 1988). After that, summated scales converted the dimensions of each concept into first order indicators of the trust and risk constructs and were incorporated in this way to the final measurement model, which is reflective in the case of trust and formative in the case of risk. To assess measurement reliability and validity of the final measurement model, a confirmatory factor analysis (CFA) containing all the multi-item constructs in our framework was estimated, again, with EQS 6.1 (Bentler, 1995) using the maximum likelihood method. The criteria for analysing this measurement model's reliability and validity were the same as those applied in the previous validation process. The final measurement model showed no problems of convergent and discriminant validity, as it can be seen in tables 1 and 2. After that, we tested the proposed conceptual model (Figure 1) using structural equation modelling. The initial estimation did not offer a reasonable fit (S-B X2 =740.6; df=309; p=0.000; BBNFI=.819; BBNNFI=.858; CFI=.884; IFI=.886; RMSEA=.067). The initial model was re-specified according to the suggestions of the Lagrange multipliers test for which a theoretical basis was found. In particular, two new relations were added to the model. 1) Subjective norm-Risk and 2) Perceived control-Attitude. The theoretical logic of these additional relations shall be dealt with later in the discussion of the results. After including the above relations the final model was obtained which shows a much more appropriate fit (BBNFI=.860; BBNNFI=.881; CFI=.904; IFI=.905; RMSEA=.064) (see Table 3).

Table 1. Reliability and convergent validity of the final measurement model.

Dimens.	Indicator	Load	Robust t	Aver. loads	Cronbach α	Compos. Reliab.	AVE
Trust	Hon.	0.72**	10.71				.64
	Benev.	0.85**	14.07	.80	.84	.84	
	Comp.	0.83**	12.97				
Usefuln ess	V41	0.81**	13.19				.75
	V42	0.91**	12.52	.87	.90	.90	
	V43	0.88**	13.62				
Ease	V45	0.80**	15.83				.73
	V46	0.87**	15.98	.85	.91	.92	
	V47	0.89**	15.79				
	V48	0.86**	15.83				
Attitude	V37	0.89**	18.12				.75
	V38	0.92**	17.87	.86	.92	.92	
	V39	0.93**	16.97				
	V40	0.71**	12.51				
Control	V49	0.75**	10.06				.64
	V50	0.81**	15.57	.80	.84	.84	
	V51	0.84**	14.24				
Norm	V52	0.76**	15.20				.55
	V53	0.58**	9.54	.73	.78	.78	
	V55	0.86**	17.52				

S-B χ2 (df = 155) =358.53 (p<0,00); NFI=.867; NNFI=.900; CFI=.918; IFI=.920; RMSEA=.065 **p<.01; *p<.05

Table 2. Discriminant validity of the final measurement model.

	1	2	3	4	5	6
1. Trust	**.64**	.20	.22	.23	.12	.22
2. Usefulness	[.32;.58]	**.75**	.53	.45	.25	.26
3. Ease	[.33;.61]	[.63;.82]	**.73**	.32	.32	.15
4. Attitude	[.35;.61]	[.57;.78]	[.44;.69]	**.75**	.33	.37
5. Control	[.19;.51]	[.36;.63]	[.43;.69]	[.45;.71]	**.64**	.48
6. Norm	[.35;.59]	[.39;.63]	[.25;.51]	[.49;.74]	[.59;.80]	**.55**

The diagonal represents the average variance extracted AVE. Above the diagonal is the variance shared by each pair of factors (squared correlation). Below the diagonal the 95% confidence interval for the inter-factor correlation.

The results emphasise that the risk perceived by non-purchasing Internet users is almost equally economic-functional (B=.240; t=5.50), psychological (B=.267; t=3.65) and privacy (B=.232; t=5.32), that is, non shoppers are basically afraid the ticket will be of no use or that there will be a fraudulent use of the payment method used, which is normally a credit card. There are also fears over transaction privacy, i.e., that the information might be used to send commercial offers or spam. Both things probably explain the equivalent weight of the psychological risk of the transaction: inconvenience, anxiety or unnecessary tension. In contrast, the Internet user does not see the online purchase of airline tickets as negative social pressure (B=-.003; t=-0.05) in his/her immediate environment (friends, relations), nor does he/she consider that a system such as the Internet is going to be less efficient in terms of time (B=.076; t=1.26) than a traditional transaction. In accordance with the hypothesis, risk reduces the perception of Internet's usefulness as a format for acquiring tickets (B=.104; t=2.09) but, above all, it reduces trust in the channel (B=.559; t=5.15). The combined effect of both facts is less willingness to use Internet for this purpose as shown by the negative influence of risk on shopping attitude (B=.116; t=2.02). The results also show that several instruments help to reduce the perception of risk in the online purchase of airline tickets. We find that the subjective norm (B=.282; t=4.64) and perceived ease of use (B=.079; t=1.96) play an important role in this task. The easier the non-purchasing Internet user perceives the use of an airline's website to be, the greater the trust in the website's honesty, competence and benevolence (B=.315; t=3.95). Further, the user perceives greater usefulness of the medium (B=.701; t=10.27), which is one of the main determinants of a favourable attitude towards the online purchase of tickets (B=.375; t=3.81) which in turn is the main antecedent to future use intention of the medium to acquire airline tickets online (B=.390; t=4.08).

Table 3. Hypotheses testing

Hypothesis	Sign	Relation	Standardised coefficient	Robust t value
H1	+	Ease of use-Attitude	$-.006^{ns}$	-0.05
H2	+	Usefulness-Attitude	$.375^{**}$	3.81
H3	+	Ease of use-Usefulness	$.701^{**}$	10.27
H4	+	Usefulness-Intention	$-.099^{ns}$	-1.19
H5	+	Attitude-Intention	$.390^{**}$	4.08
H6	+	Subjective norm-Intention	$.296^{**}$	3.40
H7	+	Perceived control-Intention	$-.017^{ns}$	-0.16
H8	–	Risk-Usefulness	$-.104^{*}$	-2.09
H9	–	Ease of use-Risk	$-.079^{*}$	-1.96
H10	+	Ease of use-Trust	$.315^{**}$	3.95
H11	–	Risk-Trust	$-.559^{**}$	-5.15
H12	–	Risk-Attitude	$-.116^{*}$	-2.02
H13	+	Trust-Attitude	$.164^{*}$	2.23
Not hyp		Control-Attitude	$.329^{**}$	3.73
Not hyp		Norm-Perceived risk	$-.282^{**}$	-4.64
Construct		Econom-Functional risk	$.240^{**}$	5.50
Formative risk		Social risk	$-.003^{ns}$	-0.05
		Time risk	$.076^{ns}$	1.26
		Psychological risk	$.267^{**}$	3.65
		Privacy risk	$.232^{**}$	5.32
S-B X^2 (df = 307) = 696.49 (p<0,00); NFI=.860; NNFI=.881; CFI=.904; IFI=.905; RMSEA=.064				

**p<.01; *p<.05; ns not significant

Trust also has a significant influence on a favourable attitude towards use of the medium (B=.164; t=2.23). Thus, the more certainty there is that virtual shops are trustworthy because they know how to do their work (competence), take into account the impact of their actions on customers (benevolence) and are honest (honesty), the more favourable the attitude towards them. Furthermore, there was no hypothesis on the significant influence of perceived control on attitude towards the medium, which is also very important (B=.329; t=3.73). This result highlights the important mediator role of attitude in forming intention, as seeing oneself as having the skills and capabilities to purchase a ticket online does not significantly influence intention (B=.-.017; t=-0.016), but previously modifies attitudes. Something similar happens with perceived usefulness which does not have a direct influence on intention either (B=-.099; t=-1.19) rather it previously modifies attitude. Unlike control, subjective norm does not require previous modification of attitudes to have a positive influence on purchase intention which once again emphasises the influence that a favourable environment of opinion leaders has on confirming the future behaviour of potential online shoppers.

5 Conclusions

Technological development in recent years has meant a radical change in the tourist industry which has significantly affected relations between channel members. Consumers' shopping behaviour has also undergone profound change, in particular in their relationship with airlines due to the interactive nature of the shopping process and the fact that the geographical barriers of time and space have been overcome. This research makes two main contributions. From the theoretical point of view, TAM and TPB models have been integrated jointly with the constructs perceived risk and trust to explain the determining factors in online travel services acceptance for non-purchasing Internet users. The proposed model helps to complete previous research on e-tourism services that partially analyse these relationships and integrates different theoretical frameworks. The formative conception of risk is also a methodological contribution. Most studies choose a reflective approach to the concept assuming that there is a common cause for the different risk dimensions. The formative conception of risk developed in this study, allows us to evaluate the relative impact of each risk dimension instead of treating it as a whole. Therefore, managers should focus their efforts on attacking the risk dimensions attending to their level of importance instead of wasting resources on the irrelevant ones.

The importance of the influence of attitude on purchase intention means that airline managers need to analyze continuously and systematically the factors in the use of airline websites which improve consumer attitude (website user-friendliness, range of flights, cost savings, etc…). For their part, web sites must not only be designed to be easy to use and provide utilitarian benefits, but shopping must also be fun. Furthermore, it is important to decrease the perceived risk in web sites which can only be achieved by allowing the user to access easy to use pages and full information (thereby helping to reduce psychological risk and performance risk), but also by offering the possibility to contact the airline, providing users with information on their consumer rights and personal data protection and on the web site's security systems (thereby helping to reduce privacy risk and performance risk). Consumers are reluctant to share personal information. Therefore, we recommend airlines avoiding customers forcing to fill out forms as a prerequisite for obtaining information on the airline web site, letting the consumers decide how they would like to receive information. Product performance risk should be faced by airlines providing detailed and updated information regarding the characteristics of the flights offered online. The influence of trust in attitude towards online shopping involves companies in the sector carrying out a series of actions. Therefore, we firstly recommend airlines practice sincerity and transparency in terms of being able to fulfil the commitments and promises made. Secondly, the airline's communication policy must be to transmit a message which promotes achievement of objectives which are complementary to those of the consumer and which provide him or her with a greater sense of well-being. Thirdly, considerable investment is needed to provide the resources necessary to improve performance of the tasks and ensure that consumers perceive greater competence and skill in the organisation they are interacting with. The importance of subjective norm led us to suggest that advertisements should try to stimulate individual perceptions of what others think about the use of Internet to purchase airline travel tickets. A strategy could be to use the opinion leaders and famous people with whom users can identify to suggest the use of Internet to purchase airline travel tickets.

In terms of the limitations of this research, firstly it should be highlighted that the study is restricted to the use of a specific service (airline tickets). Therefore, it is proposed to contrast the model with a sample of users of another type of online travel service and compare the results. The sample of our study was limited to non-purchasing Internet users. A possible future line of research would be to contrast the proposed model with a sample of Internet users who have purchased an airline ticket online in order to analyse whether the results remain valid. Given the growing importance of the low cost airlines business model, another possible line of research would be to apply the proposed model to a sample of users and non users of this travel service and compare the results obtained. Another interesting future research line could be to analyze the interaction among domain specific variables as quality of service of a given airline website, consumer compatibility with online services and post-purchase experience and the variables included in the conceptual model proposed.

References

AIMC (2007). *Navegantes en la Red*. Available in http://www.aimc.es, 03-09-2008.
Ajzen, I. & Fishbein, M. (1980). *Understanding attitudes and predicting social behaviour.* Englewood Cliffs, Nueva Jersey, Prentice Hall.
Ajzen, I. (1991). The theory of Planned Behavior. *Organizational Behavior and Human Decision Processes* 50: 179-211.
Bajaj, A. & Nidumolu, S.R. (1998). A feedback model to understand information system usage. *Information & Management* 33: 213–224.
Bandura, A. (1982). Self efficacy mechanism in human agency. *American Psychologist* 37: 122-147.

220

BBVA (2008). Internet en España. Fundación BBVA. Available in http: http://www.scribd.com/doc/2913831/Estudio-Internet-2008-Fundacion-BBVA

Bhattacherjee, A. (2002). Individual trust in online firm: scale development initial test. *Journal of Management Information Systems* 19 (1): 211-241.

Boksberger, P.E., Bieger, T. & Laesser, C. (2007). Multidimensional analysis of perceived risk in commercial air travel. *Journal of Air Transport Management* 13 (2): 90-96.

Chen, C. (2006). Identifying significant factors influencing consumer trust in an online travel site. *Information Technology & Tourism* 8 (2): 197–214.

Chen, K., Tarn, J.M., Han, B. (2004), "Internet dependency: its impact on online behavioral patterns in e-commerce", *Human Systems Management*, 23 (1): 49-58.

Cheng, J.M-S., Sheen, G.L. & Lou, G.C. (2006). Consumer acceptance of the Internet as a channel fuction perspective. *Technovation* 26: 856-864.

Cho, D.-W. & Hwang, K.-Y. (2001). Determinants of Internet banking usage behavior: applying theory of planned behaviour. *Korean Management Review*, 30 (4): 1225-1249.

Cunningham, L.F., Gerlach, J.H., Harper, M.D. & Young, C.E. (2005). Perceived risk and the consumer buying process: Internet airline reservations. *International Journal of Service Industry Management* 16 (4): 357-372.

Davis, F.D (1989). Perceived usefulness, perceived ease of use, and user acceptance of information technology. *MIS Quarterly* 13 (3): 319-340.

Davis, F.D., Bagozzi, R.P. & Warshaw, P.R. (1989). User acceptance of computer technology: a comparison of two theoretical models. *Management Science*, 35: 8.

Diamantopoulos, A. & Winklhofer, H.M. (2001). Index construction with formative indicators: an alternative to scale development. *Journal of Marketing Research* 38 (2): 269-277.

Doney, P.M. & Cannon, J.P. (1997). An examination of the nature of trust in buyer-seller relationships. *Journal of Marketing* 61 (April): 35-51.

Featherman, M.S. & Pavlou, P.A. (2003). Predicting E-services Adoption: A Perceived Risk Facets Perspective. *International Journal of Human-Computer Studies* 59: 451-474.

Flavián, C. & Guinaliu, M. (2006). Consumer trust, perceived security, and privacy policy: three basic elements of loyalty to a web site. *Industrial Management & Data Systems* 106 (5/6): 601-620.

Forrester Research (2007). *Trends 2007: travel eCommerce.* Available in http://www.forrester.com/reasearch/document/excerpt/0,7211,40799,00.html, 19-10-2009.

Forrester Research (2009). US eCommerce Forecast, 2008 To 2013. Available in http://www.forrester.com/Research/Document/Excerpt/0,7211,53345,00.html, 19-10-2009.

Forsythe, S. & Shi, B. (2003). Consumer patronage and risk perceptions in Internet shopping. *Journal of Business Research* 56 (11): 867-875.

Gefen, D. & Straub, D.W. (2000). The relative importance of perceived ease of use in IS adoption: a study of e-commerce adoption. *Journal of the Association for Information Systems* 1 (October): 1-15.

George, M.Z. (2002). Promoting services via the Internet: new opportunities and challenges. *Journal of Services Marketing* 16 (5): 412-423.

Jarvenpaa, S.L. & Todd, P.A. (1997). Is There a Future for Retailing on the Internet. In R.A. Peterson (Eds.), *Electronic Marketing and the Consumer.* Thousand Oaks, Sage Publications.

Kamarulzaman, Y. (2007). Adoption of travel e-shopping in the UK International. *Journal of Retail & Distribution Management* 35 (9): 703-719.

Kanning, U.P., Vogler, S., Bernhold, T., Gellenbeck, K. & Schlockermann, B. (2008). Determinants of the implementation of facility management in German communes. *Facilities*, 26 (9/10): 418-425.

Keen, C., Wetzels, M., De Ruyter, K. & Feinberg, R. (2004). E-tailers versus retailers. Which factors determine consumer preferences. *Journal of Business Research* 57 (7): 685-695.

Kim, D.Y., Lehto X.Y. & Morrison, A. M. (2007). Gender Differences in Online Travel Information Search: Implications for Marketing Communications on the Internet. *Tourism Management* 28 (2): 423-433.

Kim, H.; Kim, T. & Shin, S. (2009). Modeling roles of subjective norms and eTrust in customers' acceptance of airline B2C eCommerce websites. *Tourism Management* 30(2): 266-277.

Kim, W.G., Ma, X. & Kim, D.J. (2006). Determinants of Chinese hotel customers' e-satisfaction and purchase intentions. *Tourism Management* 27 (5): 890-900.

Koufaris, M. & Hampton-Sousa, W. (2002). Customer trust online. Examining the role of the experience with the web site. *CIS Working Papers Series*, available in http://cisnet.baruch.cuny.edu/papers/cis200205.htm, 23/08/2008.

Lee, D., Park, J. & Ahn, B.S. (2001). On the explanation of factors affecting: E-commerce adoption. *Proceeding of the 22nd International Conference on Information Systems* (ICIS). New Orleands, Louisiana, USA.

Lee, H.-H., Fiore, A.M. & Kim, J. (2006). The role of the technology acceptance model in explaining effects of image interactivity technology on consumer responses. *International Journal of Retail & Distribution Management* 34 (8): 621-644.

Liao, S., Shao, Y.P., Wang, H. & Chen, A. (1999). The adoption of virtual banking: an empirical study. *International Journal of Information Management* 19: 63-74.

Mayer, R., Davis, J. & Shoorman, F. (1995). An integrative model of organizational trust. *Academy of Management Review* 20 (3): 709-734.

Mcknight, D.H., Cummings, L.L. & Chervany, N.L. (1998). Initial trust formation in new organizational relationships. *Academy of Management Review* 23 (3): 473-490.

Moon, J. & Kim, Y. (2001). Extending the TAM for a world-wide-web context. *Information and Management* 38: 217-230.

Moore, G. & Benbasar, I. (1991). Development of an instrument to measure the perceptions of adopting an information technology innovation. *Information Systems Research* 2 (3): 192-222.

Morgan, R. & Hunt, S. (1994). The commitment trust theory of relationship marketing. *Journal of Marketing* 58 (July): 20-38.

Pavlou, P.A. & Fygenson, M. (2006). Understanding and predicting electronic commerce adoption: An extension of the theory of planned behaviour. *MIS Quarterly* 30 (1): 115–143.

Red.es (2009). La sociedad en red: informe anual de la sociedad de la información en España 2008. Ministerio de Industria, Comercio y Turismo.

Rohm, A. & Swaminathan, V. (2004). A typology of online shoppers based on shopping motivations. *Journal of Business Research*, 57(12): 748-757.

Seyal, A.H. & Rahman, N.A. (2007). The influence of external variables on the executive use of the Internet. *Business Process Management* 13 (2): 263-278.

Taylor, S. & Todd, P. (1995). Understanding information technology usage: a test of competing models. *Information Systems Research* 6 (2): 144-176.

Ulaga, W. & Eggert, A. (2005) Relationship value in business markets: the construct and its dimensions, *Journal of Business-to-Business Marketing*, 12 (1): 73-99.

Venkatesh, V. & Davis, F.D. (2000). A theoretical extension of the technology acceptance model: Four longitudinal field studies. *Management Science* 46 (2): 186–204.

Vrechopoulos, A., Siomkos, G. & Doukidis, G. (2001). Internet shopping adoption by Greek consumers. *European Journal of Innovation Management*, 4(3):142-152.

Wu, I.L. & Chen, J-L. (2005). An extension of trust and TAM model with TPB in the initial adoption of on-line tax: an empirical study. *International Journal Human-Computer Studies* 62: 784-808.

Yuen, C.N. & Lavin, M.J. (2003). Internet dependence in the collegiate population: the role of shyness. *CyberPsychology & Behavior*, 7(4): 379-383.

Extracting Room Prices from Web Tables - an Ontology-Aware Approach

Christina Buttinger[a],
Christina Feilmayr[a],
Michael Guttenbrunner[a],
Stefan Parzer[a], and Birgit Pröll[a]

[a]Institute for Application-Oriented Knowledge Processing,
Johannes Kepler University Linz, Altenbergerstr. 69, 4040 Linz, Austria
{cbuttinger, cfeilmayr, mguttenbrunner, sparzer, bproell}@faw.jku.at

Abstract

The growing amount of semi-structured and unstructured data on tourism Web sites with heterogeneous designs requires information extraction (IE) mechanisms, to create, for instance, tourism portals. In order to build semantic eTourism environments, the acquisition of room prices is of particular interest. Room prices and related information often appear in tabular structures, which still challenge Web information extraction techniques. In this paper, we begin by identifying various price table patterns which are characterized by the position of a number of features that determine a room price. We then describe an extended ontology model for tourism prices. Finally, we present TAINEX, a plug-in for functional and structural analysis and data interpretation of price tables, which extends the existing prototype TourIE, a rule-/ontology-based information extraction system for Web sites with heterogeneous designs.

Keywords: Ontology-based Information Extraction, Table Information Extraction, Price Table Pattern, Tourism Price Ontology, Ontology-aware Price Annotation

1   Introduction

Since the beginning of the World Wide Web, the tourism industry, i.e., airlines, car rental companies, and accommodation providers, has taken advantage of this medium to bring its products into the living rooms of the prospective customers. Although a large number of accommodation providers decide to subscribe to a Web portal and thus present their products in a more structured and easily comparable way, a considerable number of *accommodation Web sites* are *maintained individually*. This enables accommodation providers to stand out from their competitors by, for example, presenting more information and choosing more appealing and trendy presentation techniques, which results in heterogeneous presentations.

The growing amount of semi-structured and unstructured data on tourism Web sites with heterogeneous design requires information extraction (IE) techniques for the semi-automatic acquisition of structured data in order to create, for instance, tourism Web portals or tourism recommender systems. However, for the time being, IE systems applied to real-world Web sites still have to cope with basic deficiencies, e.g., tables used for layout purposes.

224

Extraction of table data is not trivial but necessary because a large part of price-related information is presented in tabular form. According to [10][16], tables are usually designed for better human readability and incorporate many semantic hints which machines cannot interpret. [6] pointed out that tables contain visual cues such as background color and font metadata to help human readers to distinguish individual building blocks or logical cells of the contained relational information. These heterogeneous tables are designed to the taste of the accommodation provider or the Web page designer. Moreover, HTML tables are often misused for design purposes and, thus, do not adhere to HTML validity demands. The resulting challenge is highlighted in Figure 1. As shown, the following price features help users to assess the costs of an overnight stay: *room type* (e.g., standard, superior), *time period* (often representing a tourist *season*), information about the included meals (e.g., half-, full-board), and some additional information such as the name of the room (e.g., "Zirbenzimmer", "Fritzerkogel") or a price domain (price per room, price per person). In the depicted case, the room type and time period appear in the column heading. Rooms and their associated price descriptions are listed in several rows of the table. Appropriate data items have to be brought into relation.

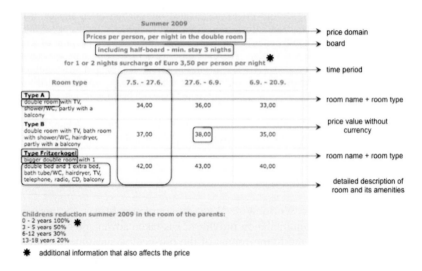

Fig. 1. Example of a Price Table on Tourism Web Sites

There are a couple of applications for the information extraction of tourism contents that include prices. For example, *CERNO* [12], a lightweight application for extracting tourism information from advertisements, is based on an accommodation advertisement schema that describes information of interest which is to be extracted. This schema tends to be rather general and therefore only allows a rough classification of tourism information. Concentrating on extracting information from tourism advertisements, it provides only text analysis with annotation of sentences. Tables and lists containing detailed information about rooms and prices are not considered.

The research project *SEMAMO* [17], which is based on LIXTO1, is targeted at analyzing and monitoring price trends and product development and changes. The focus of this project is a simple price extraction and the detection of changes in these semi-automatically extracted elements.

In this work, we concentrate on extracting detailed semantic tourism information from tables in Web pages. The task of table processing in the field of information extraction from Web pages involves various challenges and therefore needs specialized solutions. Our contributions to the subject of (price) table information extraction in the tourism domain are (a) an *analysis of price table patterns and their various features*, (b) the creation of an ontology to *permit ontology-aware price information* and therewith a semantic description, (c) the presentation of an *approach to price table processing* focusing on functional and structural analysis and data interpretation that extends the existing prototype TourIE, a rule-/ontology-based information extraction system for heterogeneous Web sites with heterogeneous design.

2 Price Table Patterns in Tourism Web Sites

Price patterns are a main point of interest in the information extraction of tourism Web sites. Representing prices in as much detail as possible is a task necessary for creating precise and comprehensive systems for tourism data extraction. A set of 30 Web pages was used to analyze the features of tourism price patterns for bookable rooms. Besides the well-known standard pattern of value and currency, a couple of additional features were identified that have an effect on prices and therefore help to define price patterns in more detail. Section 3 discusses the structures of these features and the price label in detail.

26 Web pages of the set contained room prices stored in tables. For this reason, the presented work concentrates on extracting and combining information from price tables. Data tables generally consist of data and header cells. If we consider price tables in tourism Web sites as specialized data tables, then cells containing the prices correspond to data cells, while features that affect room prices (i.e., room type, room description, time period, price domain, and board) are header types, which can be vertical or horizontal. In this work, we identified types of price table pattern realized by combining the previously mentioned cell type features, structural elements, and table contents. These patterns form the basis for identifying table data and their relations. In the next section, a selection of price table patterns is presented.

Price table pattern #1 "Time period/Room Type and Board"

In price pattern #1, the time period is contained in the vertical header, while room type and board can be found in the horizontal header. A missing board information in the header information indicates that board is not offered for a special room type.

---

1 http://www.lixto.com

Table 1. Price Table Pattern #1 "Time Period/Room Type and Board"

	Room type & Board	Room type & Board	Room type
Time period (from-to)	<Price>	<Price>	<Price>
Time period (from-to)	<Price>	<Price>	<Price>
Time period (from-to)	<Price>	<Price>	<Price>
Time period (from-to)	<Price>	<Price>	<Price>

Price table pattern #2 "Room type and Board/Time period"

In this pattern, board is presented in the second column and price cells in the third column contain a price domain (e.g., price per room) below the price value. This shows that additional features can be included in price cells, which makes them "impure" data cells.

Table 2. Price Table Pattern #2 "Room Type and Board/Time Period"

		Time period (from-to)	Time period (from-to)	Time period (from-to)
Room type	Board	<Price> price domain	<Price> price domain	<Price> price domain
	Board	<Price> price domain	<Price> price domain	<Price> price domain
Room type	Board	<Price> price domain	<Price> price domain	<Price> price domain
	Board	<Price> price domain	<Price> price domain	<Price> price domain
Room type	Board	<Price> price domain	<Price> price domain	<Price> price domain
	Board	<Price> price domain	<Price> price domain	<Price> price domain

Price table pattern #3 "Time period"

Only information about time period and price is displayed in the table. Further important information, such as room type or description, is provided in a text segment below the table.

Table 3. Price Table Pattern #3 "Time Period"

Time period (from-to)	<Price>
Time period (from-to)	<Price>
Time period (from-to)	<Price>
Time period (from-to)	<Price>

Additional information, room type

Price table pattern #4 "Room type/Time period and Board"

This table pattern is far more complex than those mentioned above. It is characterized by more than one time period per cell and different room prices for the same room type. Therefore, room types are listed more than once, while on other Web pages, room types are used as main headers (cf. Table 1). Moreover, prices differ according to board type, and therefore a second horizontal header is needed.

Table 4. Price Table Pattern #4 "Room Type/Time Period and Board"

	Time period (from-to)		Time period (from-to)		Time period (from-to)	
	Board	Board	Board	Board	Board	Board
Room type	<Price>	<Price>	<Price>	<Price>	<Price>	<Price>
Room type	<Price>	<Price>	<Price>	<Price>	<Price>	<Price>
Room type	<Price>	<Price>	<Price>	<Price>	<Price>	<Price>

Price table pattern #5 "Price features split over two tables"

In order to obtain the entire price-relevant information, these "simple" tables have to be joined according to the room names to other tables containing, for instance, the room type.

Table 5. Price Table Pattern #5 "Price Features split into two Tables"

Room Name	Description	<Price>
Room Name	Description	<Price>
Room Name	Description	<Price>
Room Name	Description	<Price>

Room Name	Room type
Room Name	Room type
Room Name	Room type
Room Name	Room type

In the course of our analysis of room price table patterns, we identified two more patterns which are described in [14].

3 Tourism Price Ontology

Ontologies provide a formal conceptualization of a particular domain that is shared with a group of persons and used for offering semantic description. The semantics of representing (room) prices alone requires complex statements. Above all, describing a price requires relating between the value of a price itself and its validity. In the field of table processing, ontologies can be employed to understand tables. Therefore, they are especially suited for information extraction applications that handle tables. On the one hand, ontologies exist that represent the semantic coherence between concepts extracted from tables. On the other hand, ontologies can be used for defining both input and output descriptions of table knowledge [13]. In the field of Web information extraction, *extraction ontologies* help to identify text terms by (a) matching wordings with concepts of the ontology, (b) giving text phrases semantic background and (c) linking different parts of text in terms of understanding [4]. Ontologies can help to find header candidates and check possible connections between cell contents, which makes table information extractions robust and fast.

The price features of Section 2 establish the basis for defining the key ontology concepts and their relations in order to model an ontology, which is needed for ontology-aware annotation of room prices. An ontology for room prices must provide information about:

Room. A room is a static, dependent indoor space located in an accommodation building (e.g., a hotel, motel, bed & breakfast) and is offered for booking.

Room Type. The room type is denoted by various terms in tourism Web sites. Even though single room, double room, twin room, shared room and apartment are perhaps the best-known, there are many more terms for defining rooms.

Room name. There is also the possibility of named rooms, which requires a complex form of named entity recognition.

Description. A detailed description provides additional information on a room. This description is usually provided in the form of free text and is not covered within the scope of this work.

Time Period. The time period confining the duration of validity of a particular price is usually given by declaring start and end date, by stating the season, or by combining these.

Season. A season is always related to a time period. Tourism regions often define tourism-related seasons, such as high season, low season or public holidays. In different tourism regions a season can have different time periods.

Price Domain. The price domain is a scale for quantitative values. The two common ways for pricing are room price per night and room price per person.

Board. Information about board includes, for example, breakfast, half board, full board, and self-catering. Although the number of feature characteristics is small, there are different variants of wording.

Room Price. A room price indicates the costs of booking a room for a defined time period and is valid for a specific type of measurement (price domain). A price consists of structured numbers – the value – mostly headed or followed by some sort of currency symbol.

There are several ontologies (e.g., the accommodation ontology[2] within the ebSemantics project, Harmonise[3], QALL-ME[4]) providing concepts and/or relations for representing room prices of accommodations. In our work, we tried to reuse, refine and extend existing ontologies to attain a complex price model. The ebSemantics ontology was an appropriate starting point because it relates its concept accommodation and its subclass room to the concept ProductOrService of the eCommerce ontology GoodRelation5. Referencing a tourism domain to the domain of eCommerce established new perspectives for modeling room prices in an ontology. Ontologies commonly applied for eCommerce are, for instance, eClassOWL6, unspcOWL7, and the GoodRelation ontology [8], which is based on the well-known price-modeling schema of Kelkar, Leukel, and Schmitz [11]. While state-of-the-art hotel and tourism domain ontologies are inadequate to tackle complex price description, eCommerce ontologies, and in particular the GoodRelation ontology, better fit our purpose. To fulfill the requirements of ontological price description, we take the GoodRelation ontology as a starting point and reuse a subset thereof.

The GoodRelation ontology covers key concepts of typical business scenarios for commodity products and services at a high level of detail and complexity. Figure 2 depicts an attempt to formulate the room prices with concepts borrowed from the GoodRelation ontology. The orange boxes depict concepts of GoodRelation (identified by using the namespace gr:). For specified object and data type properties, a link to the GoodRelation properties is set. The red boxes and arrows signify open issues that constitute a possible extension of the GoodRelation ontology.

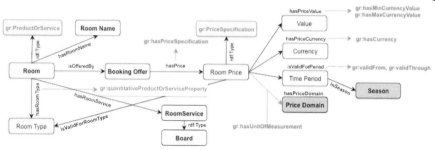

Fig. 2. Using the GoodRelation Ontology for Price Description

In our application scenario, the room concept can be assigned to the abstract gr:ProductOrService concept describing product or service types. The room price is a

2 http://www.ebsemantics.net/doc/
3 http://www.harmo.ten.info
4 http://qallme.itc.it
5 http://www.heppnetz.de/projects/goodrelations/downloads/
6 http://www.heppnetz.de/projects/eclassowl/
7 http://www.cs.vu.nl/~mcaklein/unspsc/

price specification which is defined as the price of a booking offer. A booking offer may be linked to multiple price specifications (gr:hasPriceSpecification) that depend on different sets of conditions. A room price is primarily characterized by the

- monetary amount; which can be specified by a lower (gr:hasMinCurrencyValue) and an upper (gr:hasMaxCurrencyValue) bound of money for a price range.
- currency for the given room prices; using the ISO 4217 standard (gr:hasCurrency).
- time period; the beginning (gr:validFrom) and the end (gr:validThrough) of the validity of a booking offer and additionally a relation to seasonal information (inSeason).

Price calculation requires an extension of „Unit-of-Measurements". A measurement provides information about the board, the price domain (e.g., price per person or per night), and the room type. In the GoodRelation ontology, a unit of measurement is a point of reference and the scale for quantitative values, which can refer, for example, to a technical/physical unit (e.g., price/kg). For tourism-related prices, such a data type property (gr:hasUnitOfMeasurement) is not adequate because it works with standardized units of measurement, namely the UN/CEFACT [15]. Furthermore, an object property is needed to enable a relation between a specific room price and instances of a board and a price domain. The room type belongs to the description of the room itself. The GoodRelation ontology offers an object property (gr:quantitativeProduct-OrServiceProperty), a super-property of all quantitative properties for product and services which specifies quantitative characteristics. That is, the data type property hasRoomType would be a sub-property of the GoodRelation property. Nevertheless, there is another shortcoming. The property which describes the quantitative values of a product cannot be related to the price specification. For this reason, an object property (isValidForRoomType) for the description of further conditions of a room price is needed.

4 Price Table Analyses and Interpretation in TourIE

The TourIE prototype developed by FAW [5] focuses on accommodation Web sites and aims to extract some of the information most commonly specified in a tourist's search for accommodation [3]: accommodation name, available facilities, room price, location, swimming, accommodation category, images, etc. To improve the extraction results of price information, the current TourIE version is extended by a price table information extraction plug-in named TAINEX. Table processing can generally be broken down into (a) table locating, (b) table recognition, (c) functional and structural analysis, and (d) data interpretation [9]. TAINEX focuses on functional and structural analysis and data interpretation rather than locating tables, which is covered by [6][7][10]. As propagated by [10], an approach based on finding headers was chosen in this work. This approach, which defines table cells either as header cells or data cells, was extended by the identification of semantic concepts of the price ontology (cf. section 3) contained in these cells.

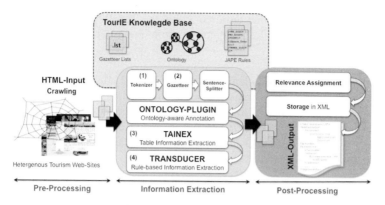

Fig. 3. Price Table Extraction in TourIE

Figure 3 shows TAINEX as part of the overall TourIE architecture. TourIE comprises three main phases: pre-processing, information extraction, and post-processing. In the pre-processing phase, a crawler collects Web pages of an accommodation provider's Web site and determines Web pages which contain room prices by using a support vector machine (SVM)-based Web page classification. The second phase covers the core extraction process. It is based on the text engineering framework GATE8, which allows for the application of existing text processing resources and for the integration of new resources in a pipeline and provides the rule language Jape. In the course of extraction, a Web page is passed from one resource to the next (cf. middle column of Figure 3): First, a tokenizer identifies individual tokens from a Web page (1). These tokens may then be annotated using the vocabulary in the TourIE knowledge base. A gazetteer resource annotates tokens with keywords from gazetteer lists (2) (e.g., the keyword "season", which may indicate a time period in the adjacent cell), whereas the ontology plug-in annotates tokens with according label names and property values of the room price ontology (cf. Section 3). Using these annotations, TAINEX (3) is able to interpret the information within the cells and, supported by a transducer resource (4), relates the price value to the corresponding price features. In the post-processing phase, the result is stored in a specified XML format that corresponds to the room price ontology.

TAINEX - TAble INformation EXtraction

A prior version of TourIE did not contain a table extraction component. Price extraction was realized by simply skipping the tabular structure and treating the tokens within the cells as continuous text. The detection of prices followed a bottom-up approach that assembles a price annotation from small price fragments found by regular expressions. With this approach it was possible to extract prices from continuous text. The extraction quality for prices in tables was low because most of the information contained in table headers was incorrectly related to extracted prices.

---

8 http://www.gate.ac.uk

232

As shown in Figure 3, TAINEX is one resource within the TourIE pipeline, which is used to analyze and interpret tables containing room prices and comprises the following four steps:

(1) Reading and storage of HTML elements. Reading of HTML elements is based on JDOM9, the well-known open source Java library for reading, manipulating, and writing XML data. JTidy10 is applied in a preceding step to better cope with invalid HTML. After reading the HTML-Code, the HTML elements as delivered by JDOM are stored according to [20] by their name and position in the text to allow direct random access to the XML-elements.

(2) Detecting merged cells. Cells that span several columns or rows have to be detected. Spanning cells are usually header cells containing information that is significant for all spanned columns or rows (cf. table pattern #2). As suggested in [20], these cells are divided into individual cells corresponding to the former count of spanned cells. For instance, a cell which spans two columns is divided into two individual cells, each containing the same information as the original cell. An alternative approach for splitting cells is to provide a pointer to the shared header cell in each data cell.

While steps (1) and (2) are domain-independent, steps (3) and (4) make use of tourism-specific knowledge, e.g., the vocabulary modeled in the room price ontology.

(3) Determining data and header cells. Tourism-related price-table cells containing the price value (cf. section 3) are defined as *data cells*, whereas cells containing, for instance, room names, time periods, or seasons are defined as *header cells*. A data cell can be determined by applying, e.g., the following Jape rule:

["Ontology->Room Price->Currency Symbol"]? [\d]{1,3}([\.,][\d]{1,3})*

The determination of header cells, as well as the identification of the contained price feature (e.g., season) is realized by Jape rules, that match the terms in the cells against keywords in a gazetteer list or entries of the room price ontology respectively, e.g., half-board of concept board (cf. Figure 3). As pointed out in Section 2, a header cell can contain more than one feature type.

(4) Relating data and header cells. Relations are created between data cells and header cells according to the following algorithm: Beginning with the top left cell of the table at position (0,0), the algorithm iterates over the table cells. When locating the first data cell at position (x,y), the cells at position (0..x-1,0..y-1) are identified to be the determining header cells. Successively, the corresponding headers for each data cell are determined. Thereafter, the results are stored in the specified XML file.

---

9 http://www.jdom.org/
10 http://jtidy.sourceforge.net/

TAINEX currently supports most of the price table patterns introduced in Section 2. Implementation work to recognize, for instance, pattern #3 is still in progress. A preliminary evaluation of TAINEX's IE quality, performed on a test set of Web pages that contain only supported price table patterns, showed satisfactory results with respect to F-measure. However, a comprehensive evaluation covering Web pages with (a) all known price patterns and (b) unknown price patterns is planned as future work.

5   Lessons Learned and Future Work

In this paper, we discussed the task of extracting room prices and various price features from HTML tables as they appear in individually maintained and thus heterogeneous accommodation Web sites. In the course of specifying room prices, we identified a number of price table patterns. These formed a basis for reusing, refining, and extending existing ontologies to create a complex ontological description of a room price model. Thus, we established the basis for precise and comprehensive ontology-aware room price extraction. Finally, we presented the extension of TourIE by TAINEX, the tabular price extraction plug-in. Below, we list some challenging issues that emerged in the course of our work and are partly subject of future work:

Improper use of HTML. Although HTML tables were originally designed as containers of plain data, they are frequently used to design the layout and look-and-feel of HTML [10].

Standards for naming room features. Even if standards, for instance, for the room type exist (single, double etc.), there is a number of other terms used on individually maintained accommodation Web sites.

Individual room names. The existence of named rooms (e.g., "Stifterzimmer", "Schwalbennest-Suite") gives rise to a complex Named Entity Recognition (NER) task, which we plan to deal with in future work.

More room-price-related features. There are even more features that affect a room price than discussed here. As part of future work, we consider the challenging tasks of integrating, for example, reductions for children according to the child's age and price variations related to length of stay.

Combining table data with free text descriptions. We identified a considerable amount of accommodation Web sites where price features are not entirely contained inside a table, but can also be found in full text paragraphs before or after a table. For new TAINEX versions, we will have to cope with this kind of combined data structure.

Dependency of extraction performance on quality of ontology. In the current version of TourIE, the identification and extraction of price features is based on gazetteer lists and ontological concepts, relations, and instances. Thus, the correctness and completeness of the domain-specific ontology is critical to the extraction performance. In order to ensure maximum correctness and completeness of the ontology, techniques such as quality assurance and ontology population must be considered.

References

Appelt, D., & Israel, D. (1999). Introduction to Information Extraction Technology. A Tutorial Prepared for IJCAI-99, SRI International

Cohen, W.W., Hurst, M., & Jensen, L.S. (2002). A Flexible Learning System for Wrapping Tables and Lists in HTML Documents. In 11th Int. World Wide Web Conference, Honolulu

Dolnicar, S., & Otter, T. (2001). Marktforschung für die Österreichische Hotelklassifizierung (Market Research for the Austrian Hotel Classification Schema; in German). Vienna, Austrian Chamber of Commerce

Embley, D. W., & Tao, C. (2005). Liddle, S.W.: Automating the Extraction of Data from HTML Tables with Unknown Structure. *Data Knowledge Engineering* 54(1): 3-28

Feilmayr, C., Parzer, S., & Pröll, B. (2009). Ontology-based Information Extraction from Tourism Web sites, accepted for publication in JITT (Journal of Information Technology and Tourism) Workshop on Tourism, Search and the Internet

Gatterbauer, W., & Bohunsky, (2006). P.: Table Extraction Using Spatial Reasoning on the CSS2 Visual Box Model. In: Proceedings of the 21st National Conference on Artificial Intelligence (AAAI 2006), July 2006, MIT Press, Cambridge

Gatterbauer, W., & Bohunsky, P. (2007). Herzog, M., Krüpl, B., Pollak, B.: Towards Domain-Independent Information Extraction from Web Tables, Proceedings of the 16th international Conference on World Wide Web, May 08-12, 2007, Banff, Alberta, Canada

Hepp, M. (2008). GoodRelations An Ontology for Describing Products and Services Offers on the Web. In: Gangemi, A. & Euzenat, J.: *Knowledge Engineering: Practice and Patterns*. 16th International Conference, EKAW 2008, Acitrezza, Sicily, Italy September 29 - October 3, 2008, Proceedings. Berlin - Heidelberg - New York: Springer, 329 - 346

Hurst, M. (2001). Layout and Language. Challenges for Table Understanding on the Web. In Proc. WDA at ICDA'01, 27--30. IEEE

Jung, S., & Kwon, H. (2006). A Scalable Hybrid Approach for Extracting Head Components from Web Tables. /IEEE Trans. on Knowledge and Data Engineering/ 18, 2 Feb.

Kelkar, O., Leukel, J., & Schmitz, V. (2002). Price Modeling in Standards for Electronic Product Catalogs Based on XML. In: Proceedings of the 11th International World Wide Web Conference (WWW 2002), Honolulu, Hawaii, USA, May 7-11

Kiyavitskaya, N., Zeni, N., Mich, L., Cordy, J. R., & Mylopoulos, J. (2007). Annotating Accommodation Advertisements Using CERNO. ENTER 2007: 389-400

Lopresti, D., Embley, D.W., Hurst, M., & Nagy, G. (2006). Table Processing Paradigms: A Research Survey, *International Journal of Document Analysis and Recognition*, 8 (2-3), 66-86, Springer, June

Scharrer M. (2009). TAINEX - Ein Tool für Table Information Extraction, Technical Report, Johannes Kepler University Linz

United Nations Economic Commission for Europe (UN/CEFACT), Rec. No. 20 (2006). Codes for Units of Measure Used in International Trade, CEFACT/ICG/2006/IC001

W3C, Tableless Layout, http://www.w3.org/2002/03/csslayout-howto, last visit: 8.Sept.09

Walchhofer, N., Pöttler, M., & Werthner, H. (2008). Semantic Market Monitoring in Tourism, *Journal of Information Technology* & Tourism Workshop Series, Oktober, Vienna

Wang, Y., & Hu, J. (2002). Detecting Tables in HTML Documents. In Fifth IAPR International Workshop on Document Analysis Systems, Princeton, New Jersey, August

Wang, H. L., Wu, S. H., Wang, I. C., Sung, C. L., Hsu, W. L., & Shih, W. K. (2000). Semantic Search on Internet Tabular Information Extraction for Answering Queries. In Proc. of the 9th Int. Conference on Information and Knowledge Management, CIKM '00. ACM

Yang, Y., & Luk, W. (2002). A Framework for Web Table Mining, Workshop On Web Information And Data Management Archive, Proceedings of the 4th International Workshop on Web Information and Data Management, pp.36-42, Virginia, USA

DMOs, e-Democracy and Collaborative Destination Management: An Implementation Framework

Marianna Sigala [a]
Dimosthenis Marinidis [a]

[a] Department of Business Administration
University of the Aegean, Greece
[m.sigala; dmarinidis]@aegean.gr

Abstract

Destination management is a collaborative process requiring DMOs to reconcile the diverging interests of various stakeholders and actively involve them in decision and policy making processes. Web 2.0 tools and e-democracy applications empower DMOs to further enhance the role and participation of tourism stakeholders in such collaborative processes, but the literature has paid limited attention to such issues. This paper synthesizes literature from stakeholder theory, collaborative decision making and e-democracy to develop a framework showing how DMOs can exploit Web 2.0 for developing collaborative decision-making processes. The theoretical and practical implications of this framework are discussed.

Keywords: web 2.0, collaboration, destination management, decision-making and policy making, e-democracy

1 Introduction

Destination management is a 'collective effort that requires various organizations and businesses in a geographically limited area to harmoniously work together to achieve a common goal' (Grangsjo, 2003; Vernon et al. 2005). Hence, in order to preserve a lead position for the destination (Wang, 2008a; Rodriguez-Diaz & Rodriguez, 2008), the development and maintenance of collaborative relations amongst tourism stakeholders is a challenging necessity for destination management organizations (DMOs). However, destination collaboration usually brings together various types of organizations and firms possessing different ideologies and values (Sigala, 2009), which if not reconciled during the collaboration process, they may in turn upset the equilibrium of the collaborative effort (Wang, 2008b). Thus, in order to be successful, DMOs should: first identify and understand the various stakeholders (i.e. their profile, aims and interests), analyse their capacities, knowledge and willingness to engage in collaborative destination management practices; and then, identify ways and tools for engaging stakeholders and supporting their participation in collaborative activities. Nowadays, due to their social communication and coordinated capabilities, Web 2.0 tools are increasingly being used for developing and enforcing numerous e-democracy applications (Fuchs, 2006). Such e-democracy applications aiming to foster e-participation also offer numerous e-opportunities to DMOs for involving the various tourism stakeholders and engaging them in collaborative decision-making and policy development processes related to destination management.

This study aims to analyse and propose a framework showing how DMOs can exploit Web 2.0 for developing and supporting applications that aim to involve and enhance the participation of the various tourism stakeholders in decision-making processes related to collaborative destination management. To achieve this, the paper first conducts a thorough literature review of three related fields (stakeholder theory, collaboration/collaborative decision-making and e-democracy) demonstrating how these fields are related and applicable to collaborative destination management that DMOs are responsible to foster. In synthesising this literature, the paper concludes by developing a framework that analyses the ways in which DMOs can use web 2.0 tools for supporting collaborative decision making and destination management activities.

2 Web 2.0, DMOs and destination management

Advances in web 2.0 support the creation of the Travel 2.0 context (Merritt, 2006), which defines a new level of tourists' and businesses' empowerment, participation and functionality/role. Indeed, the two major features of Web 2.0 namely, user-generated content (UGC) and social networking capabilities, are transforming both tourism demand and supply, since they change the way people search, read, evaluate, disseminate, write and use information. Several papers examine the impact of UGC and social maps on trip planning processes, travelers' behaviour and decision-making processes (e.g. Breslow and Sardone, 2007; Cox et al. 2008; Kopera 2009; Saranow, 2004). So far, fewer studies have focused in investigating the ways in which web 2.0 transform business operations such as, eCRM or new product development (e.g. Sigala, 2008), while less studies have examined the exploitation of web 2.0 by DMOs (e.g. Linaza et al. 2008; Hamill et al. 2009). Although DMOs have been reluctant to integrate social networking functions in their strategies (Gretzel, 2006; Hamill et al. 2009), some have recently begun to incorporate web 2.0 functionality in their websites (Cox et al. 2008; Beirne, 2007). However, research has mainly focused on investigating the DMOs' use of Web 2.0 for marketing purposes ignoring the affordance of Web 2.0 to support e-democracy projects, which aim to engage and enhance the participation of tourism stakeholders in collaborative decision-making processes for destination management.

3 Stakeholder theory

3.1 Stakeholder theory in tourism and destination management

Although the stakeholder theory has its roots and is well established in the business management and public administration literature (Clarkson 1995; Donaldson & Preston 1995; Jones 1995; Stoney & Winstanley, 2001; Berman et al. 1999; Savage et al. 1991; Frooman, 1999; Freeman and Reed, 1983), there is still research implying that the concept of stakeholder remains blur and unclear (Brummer, 1991) due to its vagueness, broadness or narrowness of its definition (Alkhafaji, 1989; Thompson et al., 1991). However, the following stakeholder definition provided by Freeman (1984, p. 25) is widely recognised and so, this is adopted also here for identifying the stakeholders of DMOs:*"any group or individual who can affect, or is affected by the achievement of a corporation's purpose"*. From a stakeholder perspective, the destination can be seen as an open system of numerous and varied stakeholders that are interdependent on each other because: they share limited community amenities and resources; there is a potential negative impact of economic tourism development on the socio-cultural and natural environment which can negatively affect both firms and public bodies; and despite the fragmentation of the tourism industry, the tourism product has a systemic nature because it is perceived as "all-in-one experience" even if it encompasses services provided by different firms. The "destination" is also the most appropriate unit of study in tourism, since destinations include and are comprised of all the interactions developed among the several tourism stakeholders, i.e. the tourists (demand), the industry (suppliers), and the hosts (including residents and environment). The destinations also *"generally comprise different types of complementary and competing organizations, multiple sectors, infrastructure and an array of public/private linkages that create diverse and highly fragmented supply structure"* (Pavlovich, 2003, p.203). The literature (Sautter & Leisen, 1999; Hardy & Beeton, 2001; WTO, 2007) provides a wide consensus regarding the various destination stakeholders that include: local businesses, residents, employees, activist groups, government/regulators, educational institutions, competitors, business chains and associations, tourists. Thus, the destination environment is complex, dynamic and fragmented by several firms and organisations, which although have numerous linkages and interdependencies (Rodriguez & Rodriguez, 2008), none of them is able to control the destination. Destinations are also consisted of multiple stakeholders that often hold diverse and divergent views, interests and values (Wang, 2008b). These stakeholders' characteristics coupled with the pace of change create a *turbulent environment* that make destination management a complex and uncertain process (Jamal & Stronza, 2009). Moreover, as tourism stakeholders are important key players influencing the success or failure of tourism in a region, their participation and involvement in destination management, planning and development is a must (Yoon, 2002). Consequently, stakeholder theory is considered as appropriate for investigating issues related to common good and destination management.

Consequently, the literature does not only argue the applicability of stakeholder theory in tourism, but it also positively acknowledge its positive influence for effective (collaborative) destination management. Analytically, stakeholder theory can (Moscardo, 2008): aid public-private sector interactions; coordinate tourism planning; and enhance the community involvement to represent the real public interest. Numerous tourism and planning studies also advocate the need to actively involve stakeholders in decision-making and planning in tourism endeavours (e.g. Jamal & Getz, 1995; Jamal et al., 2002) and support the development of collaboration processes (Araujo & Bramwell, 2002; Innes & Booher, 1999; Timothy, 1999) amongst stakeholders. The trends of the "new tourism" era also demand a more balanced approach in the decision-making processes taking place *"between those with the funds and those who have to live with the outcome and are expected to provide the hospitality"* (Wheeler, 1993: 355). Community based tourism (CBT) and stakeholder involvement is also proposed as a corrective style to destination management, because it can significantly contribute to the equal and publicly fair distribution and dissemination of tourism benefits amongst various stakeholders and different dimensions (e.g. economic, social, cultural, environmental), which in turn can lead to a more sustainable destination development (Timothy, 1999; Sautter & Leisen, 1999). CBT and the new tourism era also require the engagement and exploitation of the intelligence of all stakeholders for building up a community capacity that is required if stakeholders are supposed to get involved in the evaluation and selection of potential tourism development projects (Moscardo, 2008). The concept of community capacity currently receives an increasing interest in assisting the coordination and active involvement of stakeholders in destination management, because it basically represents the readiness (or capacity) of the community stakeholders' to participate in decision-making activities. Deriving from the concept of social capital, the existence and the building of community capacity is a necessary precondition of collaborative destination management activities (Woodhouse, 2006), because community capacity refers to: a) the community's awareness of and education in tourism development issues; b) the collective knowledge and ability within the community itself; and c) the existence and ability of the community stakeholders to use this knowledge for defining problems and identifying/evaluating potential solutions - options.

3.2 Stakeholders' collaboration, DMOs and destination management

DMOs are becoming prominent "destination developers" by: a) acting as catalysts and facilitators for the realization of tourism developments (Dore & Crouch, 2003); and b) offering a supporting role and infrastructure to their stakeholders to facilitate them to improve their competitiveness and to ensure the sustainability of tourism resources (Molteni & Sainaghi, 1997; Flagestaad & Hope, 2001). However, as destination management is a collective effort requiring various organizations and firms in a geographically limited area to harmoniously work together to achieve a common goal (Grangsjo 2003; Vernon et al., 2005), DMOs should play a key role in addressing the varied (and conflicting) needs of the different tourism stakeholders (Howie, 2003). To that end, DMOs should act as a "hub firm" in the tourism system, which brings together different stakeholders' interests, coordinate activities, provide leadership in expanding the beneficial community impacts of tourism in the destination and pool resources towards developing an integrated system (Semercioz et al., 2008). The main role of DMOs is to improve the development and management of tourism by enhancing coordination and collaboration between the (competing) stakeholders (Dwyer & Kim, 2003). Divergent stakeholders' interests require DMOs to be able to respond in a poly-inclusive manner (Fenema & Go, 2003) by developing an agile organization that supports DMOs' relationships with stakeholders and fosters the stakeholders' participation in destination management processes. Thus, although the fragmented nature of destination products has often acted as a barrier to the recognition, acceptance, and adoption of collaborative destination practices, stakeholder theory advocates that DMOs need to act as catalysts aiming to synthesise the divergent views and interests into a common destination voice and policy by fostering and supporting collaboration processes amongst tourism stakeholders.

However, although several studies investigate collaboration and inter-organizational relations in tourism (Fridgen, 1986; Selin & Beason, 1991; Munoz & Garcia, 2002), there are very few studies discussing destination stakeholders and their relations with

DMOs. Sheehan & Ritchie (2004) made valuable contributions to the understanding of tourism from an inter-organizational perspective by investigating the connection between stakeholder approach and DMOs. When applying Friedman & Miles' (2002) model for understanding the relationships between the DMOs and the different stakeholders, D'Angella found that firms perceived information sharing as risky, and so she argued that DMOs should play a fundamental role in knowledge management processes within destinations. Sigala (2009) also found that tourism stakeholders were reluctant in releasing and sharing performance information within a DMS implementation context, and she argued that it is the role of DMOs to lead a knowledge management strategy at a destination level by creating and supporting a centralised mechanism for information collection, sharing and analysis. The same study (Sigala, 2009) has also shown that different stakeholders held conflicting perceptions and expectations regarding the role and the collaborative functions that DMOs and DMSs should perform. Overall, studies (Ladkin & Martinez- Bertramini, 2002; Sigala, 2009; Katsouli, 2007; Wang, 2008a and 2008b) have found that the following factors of public and private tourism stakeholders constrain the development of collaboration amongst them. The public sector is characterised by the following factors hindering the possibility of undertaking joint decision-making processes: cultural barriers; lack of shared vision of tourism development; centralisation, bureaucracic inertia, not flexible decision-making mechanisms, corruption and power; lack of trained and competent staff; limited budget of regional and local public institutions; and lack of clearly defined roles, due to the presence of multiple public agencies involved with tourism issues that have overlapping duties and responsibilities. On the other hand, the private sector is characterised by: an absence of a long-term strategy towards joint decision-making, collaborative practices and common good; short-term individualist objectives; lack of trust to public organisations and their resources' management; poor awareness about public tourism policies; slow decision-making processes and implementation of decisions; and lack of an organisation that can lead and articulate collaborative planning efforts.

Overall, the review of this field has shown that due to the complexity and fragmented nature of the tourism industry, individual actions are not anymore sufficient (Getz & Jamal, 1995) and so, effective destination management requires DMOs to foster a more active and collaborative participation of the various tourism stakeholders in decision making processes (Hardy & Beeton, 2001; Selin, 1999). As it is also shown that community capacity building is a precondition of an effective stakeholder participation, it becomes evident that the first stage of any DMO's initiative to use Web 2.0 for collaborative destination management should involve the building and continuous enhancement of the community capacity of stakeholders. Indeed, the social intelligence and the networking capabilities of Web 2.0 can significantly assist in stakeholders' networking, coordination and community capacity building. In addition, Web 2.0 tools and applications can also help the (traditionally public) DMOs to overcome their inelastic and bureaucratic machineries inhibiting them to coordinate public and private tourism stakeholders (Lickorish et al. 1991; Sigala, 2009) and to undertake collaborative activities. The process for developing collaborative actions is analysed below.

4 Collaboration, collaborative tourism planning and management

Initially studied in the field of environmental planning and management, collaboration is defined as the "pooling of appreciations and/or tangible resources (information, money, labour etc.) by two or more stakeholders to solve a set of problems which neither can solve individually" (Gray 1985: 912). Collaboration is also "…a process of shared decision making among key stakeholders of a problem domain about the future of that domain" (Gray 1985: 913) whereby power is shared, and stakeholders take collective responsibility for their actions and subsequent outcomes from those actions (Jamal & Getz, 1995; Selin & Chavez, 1995). In a similar vein, collaborative planning is defined as a collective decision making process for resolving conflicts and advancing shared visions involving a set of diverse stakeholders. Many studies (e.g. Gray, 1985, 1989; Caffyn, 2000; Selin & Chavez, 1995) examined collaboration formation processes in different disciplines and for solving problems in every sector of society (i.e. business, government, labor, environment), while several studies have also demonstrated the applicability of interorganisational collaboration on CBT (Jones, 2005; Jamal & Getz, 1995) and destination management (Vernon et al. 2005).

Analytically, Jamal & Getz (1995: 188) defined and advocated collaborative planning in tourism as "a process of joint decision-making among autonomous, key stakeholders of an inter-organisational community tourism domain to resolve planning problems of the domain and/or to manage issues related to the planning and development". In tourism, collaboration was found to occur when a group of autonomous stakeholders engage in an interactive process, using shared rules, norms, and structures to act or decide on issues related to a particular problem domain (Wood & Gray 1991) through a process of exchange of ideas and expertise and pooling of financial and human resources (Vernon et al., 2005). Bramwell & Lane (2000) also argued that by combining knowledge, expertise, and capital resources, collaborative strategy can produce consensus and synergy amongst tourism stakeholders, leading to new opportunities, innovative solutions, and a greater level of effectiveness that would not have been achieved by stakeholders acting alone. Collaboration is also advocated to reflect a distinctive form of participation in tourism policy making, as it involves a face-to-face dialogue that implies both mutual learning and shared decision-making (Bramwell & Lane, 2000; Bramwell & Sharman, 1999). Researchers also highlight the need for an integrated tourism planning defined as an interactive or collaborative approach which requires the participation and interaction between the various levels and types of stakeholders and governance units within the planning process (Hall & McArthur, 1998). In policy making, tourism stakeholders may participate in two types of decision making coordination processes (Spann, 1979): a) developing an implementation strategy for achieving pre-agreed aims/policies (administration coordination), and b) negotiating for reaching consensus over the policies and their aims (policy coordination). Overall, it is widely accepted that collaboration and the coordination of the tourism stakeholders' interests are a must offering many opportunities and benefits for effectively managing destinations.

The collaboration process (as it is also applied in tourism) follows a widely accepted three stage process (Jamal & Getz, 1995; Vernon et al. 2005): problem setting (identifying key stakeholders and issues); direction setting (identifying and sharing future collaborative interpretations; appreciating a sense of common purpose); and implementation (institutionalising the shared meanings and actions that emerge). Recently, Moscardo (2008) added the need of first building community capacity in the collaboration process if stakeholders' participation is to become more effective. Collaboration processes require several other pre-conditions including (Gray, 1989; Jamal & Getz, 1995): shared vision; mutual understanding of the interdependence of partners and the benefits to derive; solutions emerging from a constructive dealing of differences; joint ownership and collective responsibility for decisions and the future of the domain; power and legitimacy of the collaboration process. Other authors (e.g. Bramwell & Sharman, 1999) have examined the factors affecting the success of collaboration which are related to: the scope of collaboration (e.g. representation and types of stakeholders, support of the project); the intensity of collaboration (e.g. the nature and frequency of involvement, information flow, mutual understanding, learning and respect); and the degree of consensus amongst stakeholders emerging over the form, the implementation and the assessment of policies.

5   e-Democracy for destination management: proposed framework

Over the last two decades, the need to involve citizens into democracy's sphere has been increased rapidly, while nowadays ICT and Internet advances have expanded and boosted this citizens' engagement. e-Democracy is viewed as one of the four e-government actions (Carrizales, 2008) representing Internet-driven innovations aiming to improve citizen access to government information and services, and ultimately equitable participation in government. The concept of citizen may refer to any type of stakeholder including people, organizations, NGOs, firms, public organisations etc. e-Democracy is defined as the electronic representation of the democratic processes which aims to enhance the quality of democratic processes by breadthing and deepening the citizens' participation into the democratic processes (Stephen et al., 2006) and by assisting the application of direct democracy on a large scale. Breadthing and deepening refers to the increased and effective participation of citizens' in all stages of public decision making (referring to: problem identification, setting and understanding; development of policies, directions and solutions; implementation of decisions; and evaluation of decisions) with increased power, interactive communication, collaborative decision making and with possibilities to set and negotiate the agendas of decision making processes. e-Democracy can be applied to a variety of democratic processes including: administration, service delivery, decision making and policy making processes (Lehtonen, 2007). In this vein, e-democracy can lead to: better quality of decision making processes and outcomes for all stakeholders-citizens involved; transparency and openness; better informed-citizenry; increased accountability and less corruption (Carrizales, 2008).

Similar to collaborative decision making processes and CBT (e.g. Jones, 1995), the existence of social capital is also found as a critical pre-condition for the success of e-democracy initiatives (e.g. Komito, 2005). Hence, in order to effectively implement e-democracy, the support and the enhancement of the knowledge capital of citizens is widely recognised as a pre-requisite initial information stage of any e-democracy project. For example, Macintosh (2004) identified the following levels of citizens' participation in e-democracy: e-information referring to a one-way channel that informs citizens about a variety of resources available; e-consultation which is a limited two-way channel aiming to gather feedback from citizens, but without governments being obliged to use and incorporate this feedback into their decision making processes; and active e-participation which is a more enhanced two-way channel where citizens have more power over policy formulation and decision making processes. Other authors have identified the following dimensions of e-democracy that also represent these different stages and levels of citizens' participation (Bekkers, 2004; von Lucke 2004): e-information (information acquisition & formation of an opinion), e-participation (direct or indirect participation in decision making processes) and e-voting (empower to final decision outcome).

Table 1. Collaborative destination management: a type of e-democracy for DMOs

	e-democracy	Collaborative destination management
Scope	Create bottom-up approaches, empower all citizens to breadthen and deepen their participation in democratic processes	Destination management requires CBT approaches aiming to increase stakeholders' participation in decision making and support bottom-up approaches to destination management, planning and development
Pre-condition	Social capital that ensures citizens' capability (e.g. information, awareness, opinion formation etc) and willingness (trust, social cohesion and responsibility) to participate in e-democracy processes	Community capacity (a social capital constructs) enables stakeholders to participate in tourism management and planning by: being aware, being able to propose and select appropriate policies and solutions; taking up tourism business and other opportunities for benefiting from tourism development policies; managing tourism impacts and finding solutions to eliminate unavoidable problems.
Process	Engage citizens in all stages of democratic decision making processes through the use of ICT and web 2.0	Engage stakeholders in all stages of the collaborative decision making process

It is evident that e-democracy aims to exploit ICT for empowering people to actively participate in bottom-up decision making processes, to (collaboratively) make informed decisions, and to develop social and political responsibility for both the formulation and implementation of public policies. Thus, e-democracy represents an appropriate theoretical underpinning and it provides several practical examples on how DMOs can exploit Web 2.0 for implementing collaborative destination management and policy decision making processes. Overall, the literature review provides several arguments and similarities (Table 1) demonstrating that collaborative destination management supported by Web 2.0 can be considered as a type of e-democracy that DMOs can and should pursue. Finally, by summarising the literature, Table 2 presents the framework showing how the web 2.0 tools can be used by the DMOs for engaging stakeholders in all the stages (from information to policy formulation, evaluation and re-improvement) of the collaborative decision making process within a destination management context.

Table 2. Web 2.0 and collaborative decision-making for destination management

Decision making process	Scope and role of the Web 2.0 tools	Web 2.0 tools & examples of e-democracy applications
Information provision	To represent, structure, disseminate, share and manage the information to all tourism stakeholders	RSS for stakeholders' alerts and information provision; publication and analysis of policies, their aims and implementation rules on a G2C blog; use of tags (folksonomies) for categorising and searching policies and information (e.g. statistical data); representation of a destination in a virtual word (SecondLife) for informing stakeholders on public issues *EXAMPLES: www.regulations.gov (online directory for finding, reading and commenting on all regulations, RSS feeds alerts), www.whatdotheyknow.com (request of public services/information)*
Building of community capacity	To support individuals coming together to form communities, to progress shared agendas and to shape and empower such communities	Development of digital communities on social networking websites for creating stakeholders' cohesion and community building. *EXAMPLES: www.moveon.org, www.groupsnearyou.com, www.london.gov.uk/young-london (tools for forming citizens' online communities for collaborative practices)*
Problem - setting **&** **Formulation, evaluation and selection of solution**	To collect stakeholders' feedback, opinion and information in order to identify and prioritise problems and issues	e-Consultation: forums, blogs, wikis that allow stakeholders to contribute their opinion, either privately or publicly, on specific issues, e.g. use a wiki whereby stakeholders can share their expertise and collaborate on the formulation of a legislation, policy or destination marketing budget formulation and allocation *EXAMPLES: www.ili.gr (contest for policy formulation for the redevelopment of an area), http://dialogues.listeninigtothecity.org*
	To facilitate dialogue amongst stakeholders and exchange of expertise and information	e-Campaigning: stakeholders using web 2.0 tools (e.g. blogs, groups in social networks) for lobbying, petitioning and other forms of collective action. For example, ecologists starting up a group on Facebook running a petition to protect a region from tourism development *EXAMPLES: www.standagainstpoverty.org* e-Deliberation or e-discussions: chat, forums, virtual words that support virtual, small and large-group discussions, allowing reflection and consideration of issues. For example, using SecondLife for conducting an open dialogue with several stakeholders *EXAMPLES: www.hearfromyourmp.com, www.writetothem.com, http://www.number10.gov.uk/news/webchats*
	To provide a medium for conducting elections, polls or petitions so the	e-Mediation: web-based discussions aiming to resolve disputes or conflicts *EXAMPLES:*

	necessary information (or public power) is gathered for setting agendas, selecting or putting policies in force	*http://ec.europa.eu/yourvoice/consultations, www.democracyforum.org.uk* e-Spatial planning. using geocollaborative portals for urban planning and environmental tourism impact assessment. e.g. stakeholders can include geotags on a collaborative map for showing regions affected by tourism activity and sharing expertise on what should be done e-Polling. asking stakeholders to vote or evaluate specific policies or solutions for measuring public opinion and sentiment (stakeholders' opinion is not policy binding) *EXAMPLES: www.euoparl.europe.eu , www.tellparliament.net, www.askbristol.com* e-Voting: for elections, referenda or local plebiscites (stakeholders' opinion is policy binding) *EXAMPLE: www.howtheyvote.ca*
Implementation & Evaluation and Monitoring	To provide stakeholders the tools to enforce and push the appropriate implementation of policies and collaborative actions by creating transparency and awareness of policy implementation or non implementation To monitor and evaluate the results of policies and collaborative actions	Use of web 2.0 tools (e.g. blogs, forums, social networks etc.) so that stakeholders: pressure government to implement policies accurately: e.g. stakeholders showing on a publicly available map regions whereby DMOs need to take action, e.g. clean a beach support each other in issues related to government policies: e.g. tourism entrepreneurs providing information to others on how to submit a bid, a permit application etc report offenders to government: submit online offenders expose offenders of government regulation: e.g. publish material and evidence on websites showing which and how firms do not obey in policies *EXAMPLES: www.soundcopyright.eu/blog (for enforcing the implementation of regulations on copy right), www.fixmystreet.com (for reporting and monitoring the implementation of projects), www.safeline.gr (for reporting the infringement of laws), www.pledgebank.com*

The framework provides a useful guideline to DMOs for developing e-democracy projects, because it highlights the need to first identify and select the stage and the level of participation in which DMOs wish to involve stakeholders in decision making processes (how deep and how wide stakeholder participation to allow). The framework also provides the following practical guidelines to DMOs wishing to exploit web 2.0 tools for supporting collaborative decision making and stakeholder involvement in destination management:

- every e-democracy project should first aim to built and develop the community capacity of their stakeholders and develop mechanisms (e.g. trust mechanisms) that maintain this social capital; for example, never ask stakeholders' opinion in a poll or expect stakeholders to effectively contribute to policy writing without first informing them about the related issue and its relevant constraints

- e-democracy projects should involve the *appropriate* number and type of stakeholders and so, issues related to the accessibility and digital divide that may inhibit the relevant stakeholders to take part in such initiatives need to be addressed. To achieve that, the following guidelines are provided to DMOs: identify the different stakeholders' needs and wants; provide the mechanisms for involving all the appropriate stakeholders in decision making processes; and use methods for collecting, consolidating and synthesising different perspectives into a common destination voice

- develop e-democracy projects that do not only require the stakeholders' consultation and opinion, but they also empower stakeholders in decision making. Stakeholders' active participation in decision making increase transparency and stakeholders' responsibility/accountability for implementing the policy. To that end, DMOs should provide mechanisms that enable and empower stakeholders to: a) take active participation in both administration and policy coordination decision making policies; and b) engage in the various stages of the decision making processes, e.g. Agenda Setting, Analysis, Policy Creation, Implementation, Monitoring.

The framework also provides a good model for future studies aiming to further explore the DMOs' use of web 2.0 for e-democracy. So for example, the framework provides the following research suggestions for directing future studies: whether the types of DMOs (public or private) affect the level of stakeholders' e-participation in e-democracy projects; whether the type of destination management decision (e.g. budget allocation, regional planning, marketing activities etc.) affect the type of e-democracy project and/or the level of stakeholders' e-participation. Future studies should also aim at investigating how DMOs can overcome the different factors inhibiting e-democracy success such as: digital divide, stakeholders' representation and DMOs adoption of e-democracy; organisational and institutional changes required for implementing e-democracy; the impact of e-democracy on the quality of both the process and outcomes of collaborative destination management processes.

6   Conclusions and Implications

This paper highlights the need that DMOs should start adopting e-democracy applications into the functionality of their DMS in order to take benefit of the information revolution and to engage more effectively tourism stakeholders into collaborative destination management and policy planning processes. The literature has shown that the sustainability and the quality of destination management can be greatly enhanced by adopting collaborative processes amongst tourism stakeholders, and that the web 2.0 provides DMOs with several tools to achieve this. To that end, DMOs should undertake major organisational and technological changes in order to become more stakeholder-centred in their operations and mechanisms. In general, collaborative destination management was approached as a type of an e-democracy project that can be implemented by DMOs. This paper presented a framework based on which DMOs can design and implement e-democracy projects. Since the topic is new and not yet adopted by any DMO, the framework also offers several examples of e-democracy projects exploiting web 2.0 tools that DMOs can also adapt to their own needs for supporting collaborative destination management practices. The framework also provides several practical implications and directions for future research.

Reference

(for a full reference list please ask the authors for a copy)

Bramwell, B., & Lane, B. (2000). *Tourism Collaboration and Partnerships: Politics, Practice and Sustainability*. Clevedon: Channel View Publications.

Cox, C., Burgess, S., Sellitto, C., & Buultjens, J (2008). *Consumer-generated web-based tourism marketing*. Australia: CRC for Sustainable Tourism Pty Ltd.

Freeman, E. (1984). *Strategic Management: A Stakeholder Approach*. London: Pitman.

Grangsjo, Y. (2003). Destination Networking: Co-opetition in Peripheral Surroundings. *International Journal of Physical Distribution & Logistics Management* 33(5): 427-48.

Gray, B. (1985). Conditions Facilitating Interorganizational Relations. *Human Relations* 38(10): 911-36.

Gretzel, U. (2006). Consumer generated content: trends and implications for branding. *e-Review of Tourism Research* 4(3): 9-11.

Hamill, J., Attard, D., & Stevenson, A. (2009). National DMOs & web 2.0. Mercati e competitività

Hara, N. (2008). Internet use for political mobilization: Voices of participants. *First Monday Journal*, 13(7)

Hardy, A.L. & Beeton, R.J.S. (2001). Maintainable versus sustainable tourism: defining the nexus. *Journals of Sustainable Tourism* 9(3): 168-192.

Jamal, T., & Getz, D. (1995). Collaboration theory and community tourism planning. *Annals of Tourism Research* 22:186-204.

Jones, T. (1995). Instrumental stakeholder theory: a synthesis of ethics and economics. *Academy of Management Review* 20(2): 404–437.

Moscardo, G. (2008). *Building community capacity for tourism development.* CABI International, Oxfordshire, UK

Sautter, E.T. & Leisen, B. (1999). Managing Stakeholders: A Tourism Planning Model. *Annals of Tourism Research* 26(2): 312-328.

Scholz, T. (2008). Market ideology and the myths of web 2.0. First *Monday Journal*, 13(3)

Selin, S., & Chavez, D. (1995). Developing an Evolutionary Tourism Partnership Model. *Annals of Tourism Research* 22(4): 844-56.

Semercioz, F., Donmez, D., & Dursun, M. (2008). Relationships between DMOs and destination stakeholders: a research in regions of marmara, aegean and mediterranean in Turkey. J*ournal of Commerce & Tourism Education Faculty* 1.

Sigala, M. (2009). Destination Management Systems: a reality check in the Greek tourism industry. In Gretzel, U. et al. (Eds.) *Information and Communication Technologies in Tourism*, ENTER 2009, Springer-Verlag, Vienna, pp. 481-492

Timothy, D.J. (1999). Participatory planning: a view of tourism in Indonesia. *Annals of Tourism Research* 26(2): 371-391

Vernon, J., Essex, S., Pinder, D., & Curry, K. (2005). Collaborative policymaking: local sustainable projects. *Annals of Tourism Research* 32(2): 325-45.

Wang, Y. (2008a). Collaborative destination marketing: Roles and strategies of convention and visitors bureaus. *Journal of Vacation Marketing* 14: 191.

Wang, Y. (2008b). Collaborative Destination Marketing: understanding the dynamic process. *Journal of Travel Research*, 47(2):51 - 166

eLearning Offers by Destination Management Organizations

Lorenzo Cantoni
Nadzeya Kalbaska

webatelier.net
Università della Svizzera italiana, Switzerland
{lorenzo.cantoni;nadzeya.kalbaska}@usi.chb

Abstract

Tourism has been and is being deeply affected at all levels by Information and Communication Technologies in general, and the Internet in particular. In this paper the peculiar case of digital technologies being used by national Destination Management Organizations (DMOs) to offer learning experiences – eLearning – to Travel Agents and Tour Operators is presented and analyzed. Among all United Nations countries, 37 offer an eLearning program to better equip travel professionals in performing their consulting and selling activities. All those courses have been attended online and analyzed, in order to outline their main characteristics and their advantages, as reported by the course providers themselves. The researched field has proved to be very interesting and promising, thus future research lines are suggested and outlined.

Keywords: eLearning, eTourism, tourism training, s trainings, DMO.

1 Introduction

The role and importance of Destination Management Organizations (DMOs) for the tourism industry, and the success of a country as a whole, as well as for regions and cities in particular has been and is being widely recognized, even more after the Internet revolution, which has offered them the chance to reach global audience. On one side DMOs can act directly in contact with tourists themselves, on the other side, they are enabled by Information and Communication Technologies (ICTs) to better support and prepare travel professionals – Travel Agents and Tour Operators around the globe, offering them more extensive and current information. Moreover, they can leverage on the digital technologies in order to offer a full learning experience (eLearning) about the destination and its attractions, so that professionals can better serve their clients/potential tourists when presenting a given destination. eLearning has then entered the DMOs' toolbox, offering them an additional channel to impact the market, as well as offering to travel professionals a further support to their selling activities.

In this paper, national DMOs websites are studied in order to assess how many of them provide an eLearning practice for the Travel Agents. Their global distribution will be presented as well as their main characteristics and declared advantages for DMOs and Travel professionals will be subsequently analyzed. Further research lines are then suggested and outlined.

2 Theory

ICT and the Internet are tremendously important for Hospitality and Tourism industry in general and for DMOs in particular. According to Frew and O'Connor (1999) as well as to Marcussen (2008) this happens due to the fact that the Internet has become a preferred channel for destinations to market themselves and their products on a global level: particularly, Destination Management Systems (DMS) are crucially important for the Small and Medium Size Tourism Enterprises (SMTEs), which lack the capital and expertise to undertake a comprehensive marketing strategy and rely on destination authorities and/or intermediaries for the promotion and coordination of the tourist products. As reported by World Tourism Organization (2008), much is going on the tourism technology arena today that is influencing the way consumers decide, buy and exchange the information. Demand patterns are also changing as contemporary, sophisticated travelers seek new experiences, often based on information. Gretzel, Yu-Lan and Fesenmaier (2000), as well as Buhalis (2003) indicate that nowadays tourists request a wide variety of information on areas, facilities, attractions and activities at destinations both before departure (while looking for accommodation options, flights, weather, maps and attractions); upon arrival and after their travel experience (while writing comments/reviews, uploading pictures and videos about the trip). For instance, figures by WTO demonstrate that in 2008 41% of all tourists that arrived in Spain booked their trip through the Internet, or that in 2007 in the United States of America, for the first time ever, the number of trips bought online exceeded those purchased offline. This shows that the Internet and new technologies have become a key competitive factor for both destinations and tourism enterprises. All of the abovementioned changes are impacting the way destinations and travel companies manage and market themselves.

Recently, Wang (2008) stressed the importance of DMSs for DMOs marketing strategies. In his review of relevant works in the field he pointed out four key areas that should be considered while marketing the destination trough the Internet:

- the website should serve the needs and interests of major target groups (Angehrn, 1997; Sigala, 2003);
- the development of the website should be coupled with strategic promotional plan targeted at the site's audience to gather and attract large amount of visitors (Wang and Fesenmaier, 2004);
- website performance and quality should be assessed by DMO in order to understand at what extent the website is working (Sweeney, 2000; Inversini and Cantoni, 2009);
- online marketing should have a positive impact on the DMO, such as cost reduction through savings on printed materials and on the use of a call centre (Chathoth, 2007).

Nowadays it is becoming quite evident that if DMOs use new technologies properly, while spreading clear, up-to-date, appropriate and catchy messages to potential tourists, they will have higher chances to be selected among the competitors, while generating a tremendous value for the country, region or city they promote.

DMOs use new technologies not just to spread marketing message but also to coordinate all the partners and industries involved in the production and delivery of the tourist activity/product. In fact, according to Carey, Gountas and Gilbert (1997) as well as to Baloglu and Mangaloglu (2001) tour operators/travel agents that sell the destinations' packages are one of the major powerful and influential bodies for the nature of the tourism demand. They are also instrumental in determining market trends and may affect the demand levels for the destinations. In some cases the level of influence on the demand is far greater from the mass tour operators than from the destination's own marketing, as the travel agents are still significant opinion makers for the clients worldwide. Images, perception and knowledge of the Travel Agents about destinations can have a significant impact on potential travelers' vacation decision-making process (Baloglu & Mangaloglu, 2001).

According to WTO (2008), there are several inter-mediators that serve as sales channels for DMOs, and as a result should be taken into consideration: tour operators which offer tours to and within the destination; retail travel agents; conference and meeting organizers; incentive travel organizers; exhibition organizers; online distribution channels. The relationship process between Destination Management Organizations, Travel agents and Consumers can be explained with the next figure (Fig.1.), showing tour operators and travel agents being and serving as inter-mediators in the relationship between DMOs and future tourists – consumers of the DMO's product.

| DMOs | *(B2B)* → | *(B2C)* → | | Tourists |
| | | Tour Operators / Travel Agents | *(B2C)* → | |

Fig. 1. Relationship between Destination Management Organizations, Travel Agents and Consumers

As Baloglu and Mangaloglu (2001) confirmed: marketers of the destinations, particularly National Tourism Offices, should take necessary action in order to improve their weak or negative images and promote their strengths in targeting travel intermediaries. Moreover, WTO stated that online sales support for tour operators and agents can leverage significant additional business. To be effective, support materials and information are needed to be adapted to each major market and segment. There are several ways of this support: website, e/newsletters and online trainings: "destination specialist" programs. Some of the advices for the E-marketing campaign of the DMOs, created collaboratively by the World Tourism organization and European Travel Commission (WTO, 2008) are structured in this way:

> "DMO can give vital information and sales back-up online to travel companies that actively sell the destination in source markets, including the home market. Such companies are usually, though not always, based in the source market(s), or have a dedicated sales activity there. They may operate online and/or offline.

The primary tool for providing support to them are special areas of the DMO's website, e-newsletters and online trainings – all of them can help and encourage travel agents/operators to sell the destination rather than a competitors one.

There are some DMOs that offer training and accreditation online to retail travel agents to become 'destination specialists'. This service is delivered online, either direct by the DMO or in conjunction with a specialist company:

- Directly, an example is www.pv-pro.com, the training site of the Puerto Vallarta Tourism Board, Mexico;
- With a commercial company, which may attract a wider range of agents, such as www.tauniv.com.", (p.197-199)

The eLearning community has also been investigated, but no research has been found here on the tourism subject; for instance, the database of articles and papers managed by the Association for the Advancement of Computers in Education (AACE), which lists 20,303 items, list only two relevant articles in the tourism field (AACE, 2009). The mentioning of the "destination specialist" training by WTO (2008) was the only one we were able to tackle in the dedicated literature. As a result it could be important to admit that up to now, the tourism researchers didn't pay much attention to the concept of eLearning practices run by DMOs. Consequently, a map of existing online courses offered by DMOs to travel agents and tour operators has not yet become available, nor a consistent analysis of its contents. In the article of Cantoni, Kalbaska and Inversini (forth.) a first classification of existing online courses in the field of hospitality and tourism has been undertaken. According to it, four different categories of providers have been modeled: Academic, Corporate, Destination Management Organization and Independent. Moreover two different models of the course delivery were applied to the classification: Business to Client (B2C) and Business to Business Model (B2B). According to the abovementioned research Online Academic Courses as well as Online Independent Courses represent the Business to Client model of teaching, while Online Corporate Courses and Online Destination Management Organization courses represent a clear Business to Business Model of the training delivery (see **Fig. 2**). In the case of online training courses offered by Destination Management Organization, the sender of the message as well as the addressee are clearly defined. They are: Destination Management Organizations and Travel Agents accordingly.

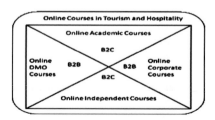

Fig. 2. Classification of online courses in Tourism and Hospitality domain

This article proposes the first map of current online training programs provided by Destination Management Organizations, while analyzing them as well as finding their main common characteristics. At the same time, several related issues will be identified, and proposed for future research.

3 Research Design

3.1 Purpose of this study

The general purpose of this study is to map and analyze, according to formal criteria of knowledge map classification (Eppler, 2008) existing online training courses for travel agents and tour operators offered by Destination Management Organizations directly or through a third service-provider, in order to understand main characteristics of those courses, their settings, key providers, as well as major benefits of creating online training courses and participating in them for DMOs and travel agents accordingly. Consequently, main research objectives are:

- to identify presence of eLearning practices created by DMOs with the main goal of training travel agents and/or tour operators;
- to identify the providers and core characteristics of these training courses;
- to understand the main benefits for DMO and travel agents of those courses, as stated by those courses' providers themselves.

3.2 Methodology

In order to fulfill the abovementioned goals, as well as to evaluate the viability of the eLearning training programs for travel agents, the investigation used a multiple case study research approach. According to Collins (2002), the multiple case study research method is appropriate for a research that involves an in-depth evaluation of novel instructional solutions within a real-life context. Looking for existing eLearning practices for travel agents that are being currently run by Destination Management Organizations, the study concentrated on National DMOs. All 192 officially recognized UN member states (United Nations Memberstates, 2006) were taken into consideration within the research. Then, authorized websites of the National Tourist Offices/National Tourism Boards/Ministries of Tourism were tracked through the most popular search engine www.google.com (Comescore, 2008). Once identified the official country tourism board' websites worldwide, all the eLearning practices for travel agents/tour operators were extracted from them. Each available eLearning course was attended and analyzed in a four day period in May, 2009, from Lugano (Switzerland). Finally, a matrix for the analysis has been created in order to be used as an instrument for the content analysis (Riffe, Lacy & Fico, 1998) of present online trainings courses. The codebook created for the content analysys of online trainings proposed by DMOs was composed of four sections, developed based on the eLearning training courses analysis triangular model (Cantoni & Tardini, 2006; Cantoni, Botturi, Succi & New MinE Lab, 2007) presented below:

People

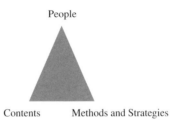

Contents   Methods and Strategies

Fig. 3. eLearning training courses analysis triangular model

While analyzing the "People" section, the next points were taken into consideration: users of the eLearning courses; providers of the service. By evaluating "Methods and Strategies", the following items were tracked: learning settings; offered assistance; teaching tools; language of the course; number of modules; evaluation process; awarded title/certificate for the course completion. Through the "Contents" analysis, presented topics within the courses were investigated. In addition to the abovementioned sections, "General information" data were tracked down, such as: name of the country; title of the course; official name of the Destination Management Organization; presence/absence of the official logo of the DMO on the course' website; cost; timing; date of the last access to the course.

4   Results of the research

4.1 Triangular model

General information. The map below (Figure 4) represents in dark grey existing online training courses that are run by National Destination Management Organizations. The white color shows the absence of the online course on the website of this particular destination. 37 countries out of 192 official members of United Nations present a Destination training course for Travel Agents. This number accounts for 19.3% of the total number of world countries.

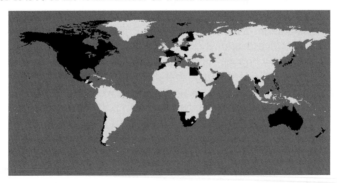

Fig. 4. Geographical distribution of available DMO courses (dark shading)

As for the regional distribution, European and American Destination Management organizations are leading with 11 and 10 courses respectively, while Africa and Asia + Middle East regions present 7 courses each, whereas Australia and Pacific have just 2 courses each to train travel agents. Table 1 shows regional distribution of the courses as wells as their title:

Table 1. Regional distribution of the DMO courses and their titles

Region	Country	Title of the course
Europe	Austria	Austria Expert Program
	Finland	Visit Finland Specialist
	France	Destination France
	Iceland	Iceland Informer
	Italy	Ciao Italia
	Lithuania	Lithuania Training Course
	Malta	Maltawiz
	Montenegro	Montenegro E-learning
	Norway	Norway Knowledge
	Poland	Visit Poland
	Portugal	Portugal Specialists
Americas	Antigua and Barbuda	A-Z Antigua and Barbuda
	Chile	Chile Destination Specialist Program
	Bahamas	Bahamas Specialist Program
	Canada	Canada Specialist Programme
	El Salvador	El Salvador Specialist Graduate
	Honduras	Honduras Specialist
	Jamaica	Jamaica Training Program
	Mexico	Magic of Mexico
	Trinidad and Tobago	Trinidad and Tobago - the true
	United States	Visit USA Training
Africa	Egypt	Egypt Specialist Program
	Kenya	Jambo Kenya
	Mauritius	Mauritius Training Course
	Morocco	Morocco Champions Program
	Namibia	Namibia Know It All
	South Africa	South Africa's Destination Specialist
	Tunisia	Teach me Tunisia
Asia + Middle East	Japan	Essential Japan
	Jordan	Jordan Ambassador
	Oman	Oman Academy
	Philippines	Philippines Specialist Program
	Sri Lanka	Sri Lanka Specialists
	South Korea	Stopover Seoul
	Thailand	Thailand Golden Agents
Australia and Pacific	Australia	The Aussie Specialist Program
	New Zealand	Explore New Zealand Program

In fact, three other courses have been identified, but at the time of the research they were not accessible online: Brazil Specialist Travel Agent Programme, Tourism

Malaysia e-training and Switzerland Travel Academy. The time needed to fulfill each single training course varied significantly – from 40 minutes to accomplish the Mauritius Training Course up to 25-30 hours to be able to finish the Explore New Zealand Program. On average 4-5 hours were enough for a course completion. Due to the fact that for the Destination Management Organizations a training course can generate significant financial revenues, all of the courses were free of charge for travel agents in order to attract a higher number of training participants.

People. The main public of the DMOs online training courses are Travel Agents and Tour Operators. In fact, while registering for the course in 33 cases out of 37 the official registration number of a Travel Agent was asked. Nevertheless it was possible to register even without having an official travel agent number, just "pretending to have one", while creating a travel agent registration number. In the remaining four cases, other publics could also enter the course, as the Travel Agent Number was not asked. Unfortunately, there is no officially open data on the number of training agents that follow the courses. There is just one declaration of the number of students that are attending the Tourism Australia course - Aussie Specialist. On the official website of the Tourism Australia was indicated that in May 2009 there were over 11.000 fully qualified Aussie Specialist agents around the world, and thousands more in training. Below there are some snapshot of the number of qualified Aussie Specialists within some of Tourism Australia's key markets: UK – 2025; Germany – 1577; China – 1554; USA – 1080; New Zealand – 820; India – 407, etc. (Tourism Australia, June 2009). These numbers show that well structured and thoughtfully promoted courses can generate significant additional revenues for the destination, while promoting and selling the country through travel agents. Apart from four Destination Management Organizations that are directly managing their courses, there are five main companies-providers of these eLearning services: TravelUNI (16 courses), Travel Agent Academy (8), Destination Ventures (3), The Travel Institute (3), Online Travel Training (3). All the providers are registered either in UK or in USA, targeting accordingly those markets of travel agents. The same fact may explain that English language is the only offered language by all courses providers.

Methods and Strategies. The "Travel Agent Academy" pointed out on their website that destination trainings are the most advanced, interactive and effective travel agent training and educational platform available today. Using reach media, flash, video, interactive maps, high-impact image formats and navigation, every program is unique, reflecting the singular characteristics of each destination or supplier. In fact several training tools are used within the training programs: representation of the content with text (all the courses), with videos (13 courses), glossary (4 courses), suggested websites in order to get more profound information on most interesting topics (13 courses), possibility to get required information through an interactive map (12). In 8 cases travel agents have an option to print the content of the training course in order to study offline and then get back to the training module and fulfill the final test. In five cases the user have a possibility to interact with other travel agents through a forum or chat.

None of the courses provide a video conference possibility or tutor assistance option, except for the Virtual Travel Professor, a tool created within the Egypt Specialist Program. This instrument gives the opportunity to the users to ask questions and receive answers directly from the sponsoring supplier or a destination. Still the users of most of the courses (35) get the possibility to send an e-mail to the indicated e-mail address and get technical or content support. There was just one training course – Visit USA Training, which proposes two levels of difficulty of training texts and tests. Just in one case the storytelling principle is personified: by penguins Joe & Sally within the Austria Expert Program.

As for the evaluation, all of the courses use objective tests (e.g. multiple choice questions, True/False questions), which can be directly managed by an automatic system, while none of them provide a subjective test option (e.g. short essay or paper), which should be checked by external reader/reviewer. In 17 cases the timing within the evaluation process was integrated in order to bring "stressful" and "close to reality" atmosphere of the travel agency, where the clients is asking direct questions to the travel agents and needs an immediate response. Anyway, in all cases, the Travel Agent have an option to come back to the proposed materials and revise missing information. In four cases travel agents at the end of the course were asked to give their feedback to the course creator in order those could understand all of the advantages and disadvantages of the course performance. In each training course an official logo of the DMO is present, showing strong ties between the training website and the official country tourism portal. Moreover in most of the cases, within the training course the official country portal was mentioned several times to redirect travel agents to the main source of information where they can get regularly updated data. At the end of 17 courses, the user gets the possibility to receive a certificate (**Fig. 5**), which attest to represent the ability of the user to fulfill the course and get an official recognition. The certificate can be downloaded and printed (e.g. **5.1.** and **5.2.**) from the course. In some cases (e.g. **5.3.**) the recognition certificate is mailed to the users by land post. Some examples of certificates can be seen below: Certification of Successful Completion of Mauritius Training Course, the Philippines Specialist Program, the Aussie Specialist certificate.

Fig. 5. Examples of DMOs training courses certificates: Mauritius Training Course; Philippines Specialist; Program Aussie Specialist.

Contents. As for the Topics presented within the Training courses, the structure in most cases was rather similar: all the courses present the information about the Destination (Geographical position, Demographics, Languages Spoken, etc.); while 36 courses had dedicated training modules to History, Culture and Traditions of the Destination; 35 courses gived general information about Accommodation and Transportation system within the destination, whereas 33 indicated the Formalities Issues. 26 courses out of 37 presented Selling tips to travel agents such as the resorts of the destination that are appropriate for family holidays, or honeymoon options, etc. Just 13 courses offered help to travel agents in the Itinerary Planning (e.g. presenting pre-defined packages for winter tourism or for eco tourism).

5   Declared Benefits

Reasons to take part in a training course for travel agents as well as to create a new course for the DMOs were mapped within the official descriptions on the courses' websites, as a result they were classified as the declared benefits for the destinations and for travel agents (sales, marketing and personal).

5.1 Benefits for the destination

Destination Ventures, one of the courses' provider, indicates on its website that tourism suppliers and destinations need to treat their agents like any business would treat their own sales team. That means providing education, insights, and tools that not only create true product expertise, but also provide the sales team of a destination with reusable client outreach resources. According to the service providers (Destination Ventures and Travel Agent Academy), the Destination Specialist courses can empower their sales forces on a global basis, while allowing travel agents to learn at their own place (from home or office), earn "Specialist" status, and post their sales in a "Loyalty points" program. Training courses will make learners active participants as they can expand their understanding and confidence in selling the destination or resort. The training course can increase the travel agents learning results, and will decrease the training costs for the DMO.

5.2 Benefits for travel agents

The programs are designed mainly to provide travel agents and distributors with the knowledge and skills to sell the destination effectively. Main mentioned benefits are the next: access to structured information, flexibility and asynchronous nature of the educational activities. All the benefits of fulfilling the course by travel agents, as stated on the analyzed websites, can be divided into three main groups: Sales, Marketing and Personal benefits (Recognition).

Sales benefits

- participation in the course will help the business of travel agents grow, by the maximization of sales through the access to special offers from other suppliers;

- travel agents that successfully finish the course will become a part of an officially registered travel agents-list (base) on the destination website;
- attending of the course will add value in selling the destination, as the news and developments in the country will be sent to the travel agents through a dedicated mailing list to keep them updated.

Marketing benefits

- specialist logo that is sent to travel agents via email can be used afterwards in all marketing materials, including business cards, letterheads and travel agent' websites;
- travel agents will be able to take advantage of the country national communication campaigns through the access to national promotional portals and materials (e.g. online brochures).

Personal benefits

- travel agents will get a chance to receive the knowledge that is needed to sell the destination with confidence. Increased itinerary planning skills and knowledge means better customer satisfaction level for the future clients of this travel agency, and as a result, higher revenues in the future;
- possibility to download the certificate or get it by land post. Certificate of participation that can be displayed in the store can serve as a key competitive advantage of being a recognized specialist;
- chance to participate in an educational/familiarization trip, the trip that is organized by the National Tourist Boards. Main aim is to take professionals to visit the country/destination and experience it firsthand.
- the top sellers of the destination will be able to get special bonuses, as well as will get an access to specially prepared gifts (pens, maps, travel kits, T-shirts, etc.).

6   Discussion and Future Research

In this paper, the world of online courses offered by DMOs to travel agents and tour operators has been introduced and explored, measuring its dimensions and offering a first outline of it. This analysis has shown a live and promising field, which complements other information and communication activities run by DMO in order to communicate themselves to tourism professionals, and – trough them – to their prospective tourists. This research should be complemented by further analyses, aimed in particular at assessing and evaluating the effectiveness and efficiency of the studied eLearning programs. Following the evaluation model proposed by Kirkpatrick (1994), future research lines should assess

- the reaction to those eLearning courses on the side of learners: *are they comfortable/happy with them? What are the main drivers for a travel agent to start this learning experience?*
- their actual knowledge: how *much and what did they learn about the destination?*

- how much of the learned information could be *transferred* to the everyday professional life of people attending the courses: *have they become better sellers of the concerned destinations?*
- the global impact of the offered training onto the actual selling of the destination: *were those courses able to increase the overall selling of the destination?*

All the above sketched research lines require a direct involvement of both DMOs and learners, and are to be conducted adopting different research methodologies. In addition, a further research line could study the instructional design of the concerned courses, looking at its soundness and offering insights on how to make it better, providing enhanced learning experiences that will become more satisfying and effective at the same time.

References

AACE. (2009, January). Association for the Advancement of Computing in Education. Retrieved from: http://www.editlib.org/

Angehrn, A. (1997). Designing mature Internet business strategies: the ICDT model. *European Management Journal*, 15(4), 361-369.

Baloglu, S., & Mangaloglu, M. (2001). Tourism destination images of Turkey, Egypt, Greece, and Italy as percieved by US-based tour operators and travel agents. *Tourism Management*, 22 (1), 1-9.

Buhalis, D. (2003). eTourism: information technologies for strategic tourism management. Essex: Pearson Education.

Cantoni, L., Botturi, L., Succi, C., & New MinE Lab. (2007). E-learning. Capire, progettare, comunicare, Milano: Franco Angeli.

Cantoni, L., Kalbaska N. & Inversini, A. (Forthcoming). eLearning in Tourism and Hospitality: a Map. Accepted by *Journal of Hospitality, Leisure, Sport and Tourism Education*.

Cantoni, L. & Tardini, S. (2006). Internet, London (UK) – New York (NY): Routledge

Carey, S., Gountas, Y., & Gilbert, D. (1997). Tour operators and destination sustainability. *Tourism Management*, 18 (7), 425-431.

Chathoth, P.K. (2007). The impact of information technology on hotel operations, service management and transaction costs: a conceptual framework for full-service hotel firms. International *Journal of Hospitality Management*, 26, 395-408

Collins, G. R. (2002). A Satellite-based Internet Learning System for the Hospitality Industry. *Online Journal of Distance Learning Administration*, 5 (4), 1-10.

Comescore. (2008, March), comScore Releases December U.S. Search Engine Rankings. Retrieved from http://www.comscore.com/press/release.asp?press=2016

Eppler, M. (2008). A process-based classification of knowledge maps and application examples. *Knowledge & Process Management*, 15 (1), 59-72.

Frew, A., & O'Connor, P. (1999). Destination marketing system strategies: Refining and extending an assessment framework. In D. Buhalis (Ed.), Information and Communication Technologies in Tourism (pp. 398-407). Berlin: Springer Verlag.

Gretzel, U., Yu-Lan, Y., & Fesenmaier, D. (2000). Preparing for the New Economy: Advertising Strategies and Change in Destination Marketing Organizations. *Journal of Travel Research*, 39(2), 146-156.

Inversini, A., Cantoni, L. (2009). Cultural Destination Usability: The Case of Visit Bath. In W. Hopken, U. Gretzel & R. Law (Eds.), Information and Communication Technologies in Tourism 2009 - Proceedings of the International Conference in Amsterdam, Netherland (pp. 319-331). Wien: Springer.

Kirkpatrick, D.L. (1994). Evaluating Training Programs: The Four Levels. San Francisco: Berrett-Koehler.

Marcussen, C. (2008, January). Trends in European Internet Distribution – of Travel and Tourism Services. Retrieved from www.crt.dk/uk/staff/chm/trends.htm

Riffe, D., Lacy, S., & Fico, F. (1998). Analyzing media messages: Quantitative content analysis. New Jersey: Lawrence Erlbaum Associates, Inc.

Sigala, M. (2003). Developing and benchmarking Internet marketing strategies in the hotel sector in Greece. *Journal of Hospitality & Tourism Research*, 27(4), 375-401.

Sweeney, S. (2000). Internet Marketing for Your Tourism Business. Gulf Breeze, FL: Maximum Press.

Tourism Australia (2009, June). Tourism Australia Online Marketing. Retrieved from http://www.tourism.australia.com/Marketing.asp?sub=0399

United Nations Memberstates. (2006, July). Uited Nations (UN). Retrieved from: http://www.un.org/en/members/index.shtml

Wang, Y. (2008). Web-based destination marketing systems: Assessing the critical factors for management and implementation. International Journal of Tourism Research, 10(1), 55-70.

Wang, Y., & Fesenmaier, D. R. (2004). Towards understanding members' general participation in and active contribution to an online travel community. *Tourism Management*, 25(6), 709-722.

WTO (2008). Handbook on E-marketing for Tourism Destination. Madrid: World Tourism Orginization & European Travel Commision.

Online Destination Marketing: Do Local DMOs Consider International Guidelines for Their Website Design?

Julia Hofbauer,
Brigitte Stangl, and
Karin Teichmann

Institute for Tourism and Leisure Studies
Vienna University of Economics and Business, Austria
juliahofbauer@gmx.net, (brigitte.stangl, karin.teichmann)@wu.ac.at

Abstract

Websites of destination management organisations (DMOs) have to meet certain criteria in order to guarantee high quality of tourism-related information. The World Tourism Organisation (UNWTO) and the International Federation for IT and Travel & Tourism (IFITT) developed guidelines for DMOs to improve the quality and effectiveness of their presentation on the Internet. This study applies a content analysis to evaluate 80 local DMO-websites in Austria concerning the implementation of the guidelines from UNWTO/IFITT. Furthermore, due to the growing importance of Web 2.0 applications, it is assessesed if Web 2.0 features are implemented on websites of local DMOs. The study reveals gaps between the recommendations for the design of DMO-websites and their actual implementation. Results show that the guidelines compiled by UNWTO/IFITT receive limited or no attention for the design of DMO-websites. Moreover, it is detected that Web 2.0 applications are entirely absent on all of the 80 investigated local DMO-websites.

Keywords: DMO-website evaluation, online marketing, guidelines for website development, website design, Web 2.0.

1 Introduction

Without doubt, more and more travellers use the Internet as a source of information (Euromonitor International, 2008). In doing so, users demand websites that provide interfaces to translate features and operations in a clear and intuitive way. Therefore, a successful website needs to react to information inquiries in an effective and useful way (De Marsico & Levialdi, 2004).

A survey of U.S. online travellers conducted by Buhalis (2003) showed that travellers mainly use five different types of websites either for trip planning or for booking purposes. According to the study, websites of suppliers are mostly used for travel planning (77 %) and travel booking (77 %). Destination websites are ranked second, i.e. 68 % of online travellers from the U.S. use websites of destination management organisations (DMOs) to plan their vacation and nearly one third uses DMO sites to book travel-related products. Due to the importance of DMO-websites as a source of information, a consistent presentation has to be ensured (UNWTO, 1988). In order to meet the demands of users on DMO-websites best, experts developed and published guidelines and instructions for designing websites (e.g. 6A concept, Internet Marketing Star). In 2004 and 2005, the UNWTO/IFITT finalized an international scheme named "Destination Web Watch" (Destination Web Watch, 2009).

The present study first compares five different guidelines for website design with each other. Then, it examines if and how the guidelines developed by the UNWTO/IFITT are considered for the design of local DMO-websites. Furthermore, due to the ever increasing importance of Web 2.0 the study evaluates the availability of Web 2.0 applications on local DMO-websites by using a checklist. Based on the guidelines and this checklist, the quality and range of tourism-related information published on official websites of Austrian reporting municipalities (i.e. municipalities with more than 1,000 overnight stays) are assessed. Each reporting municipality represents a tourism destination in Austria. The study concludes with managerial and theoretical implications.

2 Theoretical Foundations

In general, websites should be developed for relevant target groups and must provide information about products and services offered. Furthermore, it needs to be guaranteed that the website loads quickly (UNWTO, 2005) and that individual inquiries are executed properly. Moreover, contact details are essential (UNWTO, 2004). Also, the opportunity to order or download brochures must be provided and security standards have to be taken into account. To make the website more attractive, emotive pictures as well as logos can be used on the website (Sweeney, 2000). Most importantly, a well prepared, faultless content is obligatory (Baggio, 2003). This especially applies for websites which are available in different languages (Sweeney, 2000).

Next to general suggestions, several recommendations tailored to tourism-related websites exist. Firstly, the content of a DMO-website needs to provide information about a destination as well as about the products and services it offers. Secondly, up to date information is as important as presenting information relevant to the target group (Sweeney, 2000).

According to a survey conducted by Choi, Lehto & Oleary (2007), US and Canadian tourists have different expectations concerning the content and functionalities of DMO-websites at different levels (country, state/province and city). The results of the study show that on country level, information about accommodation (66.3 %), maps (48.3 %), and culture (40.9 %) are requested. On state level, information about accommodation (75.4 %), maps (58.1 %), and tourist attractions & sights (49.2 %) should be provided. Details about accommodation (79.6 %), maps (55.1 %), and events (51.6 %) are highly demanded on city level, too.

Different frameworks and suggestions for designing an optimal DMO-website can be found in literature. According to the 6A concept, six key aspects (namely attractions, amenities, activities, accessibility, ancillary services and available packages) have to be considered for the development of the website's content (Buhalis, 2003). The success of a website can be increased by well combined aspects, such as giving information about attractions enriched with ancillary services. An example is to offer maps where relevant attractions are marked.

Another framework refers to the Internet Marketing Star. According to Benkendorff and Black (2000), the Internet Marketing Star consists of four categories: site planning characteristics (goals and strategy of the online marketing activities), site management characteristics (managerial issues), site design characteristic (website interactivity, navigation and functionality), and site content characteristics. Site content characteristics refer to the key areas readability, integrity (credibility, relevance and accuracy of the information), value-added features (for example virtual postcards) and the marketing mix (Benkendorff & Black, 2000).

The Institute for Futures Studies and Technology Assessment and the German Economic Institute for Tourism Research at the Munich University adopted the AIDA (i.e. attention, interest, desire, action) concept to evaluate Internet activities of European DMOs (ITZ, 2003). In doing so, attention deals with the framework of the website content. Interest applies to the information of the relevant destination and desire refers to details about accommodation facilities. Action stands for booking, reservation and interaction possibilities.

Another model, called 2QCV3Q Meta Model, has been used to evaluate the quality of websites of regional tourist boards in the Alps (Mich, Franch, Cilione & Marzani, 2003). "Qvis?" considers the elements of the website identity and the image of the organisation whereas "Qvid?" refers to the content. C stands for "Cvr?" and deals with the functions offered by the DMO-website. "Vbi" includes factors that contribute to the ease of access of a website. Furthermore, the maintenance of the website ("Quando?"), the usability ("Quomodo?") and the feasibility ("Quibus Auxiliis?") are considered in the model.

The World Tourism Organisation (UNWTO) and the International Federation for IT and Travel & Tourism (IFITT) developed a further scheme for DMOs to assess the quality of their web activities. This framework is called the UNWTO/IFITT Destination Web Watch. 150 items were identified jointly by experts from the UNWTO as well as IFITT. The items can be classified into seven categories (UNWTO, 2005): (1) accessibility and readability, (2) identity and trust, (3) customization and interactivity, (4) navigation, (5) findability and search engine optimization, (6) technical performance, and finally (7) the service concept (i.e. the quality of website services).

As Table 1 shows, all these models have similarities. The content and features, which are in common to at least three methods, are italicized in Table 1. The recommendations of the 6A concept designed to publish details about gastronomy, events, sports and recreation facilities are similar to the guidelines developed by the UNWTO/IFITT. According to the approaches of the Internet Marketing Star and the UNWTO/IFITT, contact details and the possibility to print information in an adequate form must be provided. The concepts of the Internet Marketing Star, the AIDA model and of the UNWTO/IFITT recommend DMOs to inform about accommodation facilities, sights, natural resources and cultural offers on their websites.

Table 1. Comparison of guidelines for content and features on DMO-websites (own illustration)

Content and features on DMO-websites	1*	2*	3*	4*	5*
Details about gastronomy, events, sport and recreation facilities, shopping facilities, special offers of travel agencies and other suppliers of the service industry	X				X
Selection of language, consistent structure of the website, contact details, feedback form, guestbook, e-cards and forums, printable and storable version of the website		X			X
Information about public transport			X		X
Actuality of information		X		X	X
Natural resources, cultural offer, sights, details about accommodation facilities	X		X		X
Complete, relevant, readable and coherent content, booking and reservation facilities, possibilities to download and order brochures		X	X		X
Multimedia applications	X	X	X		X
Maps and descriptions of landscape/cityscape and surroundings	X	X	X		X
Consistent design and navigation		X	X	X	X

*Note: (1) 6A concept, (2) Internet Marketing Star, (3) AIDA model, (4) 2QCV3Q, (5) UNWTO/IFITT Destination Web Watch guidelines.

However, despite the growing importance of Web 2.0 for the service industry, recommendations to use Web 2.0 applications on DMO-websites are not yet included in the guidelines and models discussed above. Web 2.0 describes the second generation of web services which enables the communication and an exchange of information between users (Lee & Gretzel, 2006). Particularly for travel-related websites, the involvement of users and the implementation of Web 2.0 applications gain in importance. According to the UNWTO and the European Travel Commission (ETC), online communities, wikis, blogs and tags are opportunities for DMO-websites to attract potential visitors. For instance, in online communities, a DMO can act as a host and can inspire visitors to interact with others. Discussions and posts allow a DMO to publicly respond to suggestions and representations while increasing its trustworthiness. Blogs can not only be used to "listen" what tourists have to say about a destination but also to communicate news and late-breaking information (such as short-term difficulties in public transport) (ETC/UNWTO, 2008).

3   Hypotheses and Method

Due to the fact that the UNWTO/IFITT Destination Web Watch comprises all recommendations of the other four guidelines and models discussed, the present study evaluates websites based on the UNWTO/IFITT recommendations. Furthermore, due to the particular importance of Web 2.0 applications, these applications and their usage on DMO sites are examined based on different criteria. Before the websites are evaluated, however, general information about the type of the website, the owner of the website and links to other DMOs (i.e. if a local tourist office has an own website or if all tourism information is provided by the municipality) need to be verified. This is a prerequisite since websites of a reporting municipality are differently designed compared to websites of regional tourist boards. Thus, this check makes sure that only similar types of websites (i.e. websites of municipalities) are compared. In this study, websites of regional tourist boards are excluded from the analysis. The type of the website is determined by a clear statement on the website, by an indication of the municipality as owner of the website or by a special URL. In Austria, websites refer to an official website of a municipality if the URL includes the letters "RIS" (RiS-Kommunal 3.0, 2008).

The present study applies a content analysis to reveal the strengths and weaknesses of official websites of reporting municipalities in Austria. Reporting municipalities are local DMOs with more than 1,000 overnight stays per year. These municipalities need to report their number of overnight stays by law. In 2007, Austria recorded around 1,600 reporting municipalities which generated approximately 120 million overnight stays in the tourism year 2007 (TourMIS, 2009/10/01). Each municipality represents a tourism destination in Austria. To compare municipalities with the highest number of overnight stays with municipalities with a low record of overnight stays, in this study, only websites of municipalities of the provinces of Tyrol (41.5 million overnight stays) and Burgenland (2.7 million overnight stays) are analyzed. In 2007, Tyrol consisted of 279 and Burgenland of 71 reporting municipalities (Statistics Austria, 2008). To evaluate which and how many reporting municipalities own a website, the name of each municipality has been entered into the search engine Google. Out of 279 and 71 reporting municipalities respectively, in Tyrol 239 (86 %) had an official website and in Burgenland, 43 (61 %).

In Austria, suppliers of the service industry have to render financial contributions to the municipalities by means of local taxes and public dues. In return, the municipality supports the businesses in their marketing activities by means of publishing vital tourism information on the official website of the municipality. Hence, municipalities, which comprise a larger number of suppliers, should have a more comprehensive knowledge about existing guidelines and should put a stronger focus on website design. Therefore, depending on the importance of tourism, the following is proposed:

H1: There is a significant, positive relation between overnight stays and the amount of tourism information published on the official website of a municipality.

As mentioned in the section on theoretical foundations, to provide a selection of languages is especially important for the tourism industry. In 2007, 94 % of people visiting Burgenland came from Austria and Germany. Compared to that, in Tyrol, 60 % of overnight stays were assigned to tourists coming from Austria and Germany (TourMIS, 2009/03/27). Due to the higher importance of non-German speaking markets for Tyrol, the following hypothesis is proposed:

H2: The official websites of reporting municipalities of Tyrol offer more foreign languages to select compared to official websites of reporting municipalities of Burgenland.

Users expect from DMO-websites that they present current and multimedia-based information (eTourism Foundation Dialog, 2009). Thus, tourism websites should not only provide information recommended by the UNWTO/IFITT guidelines but they should additionally offer Web 2.0 applications. Web 2.0 applications allow DMOs to improve information presentation and to interact with travellers. Due to the importance of local DMO-websites as a source of information as well as a booking platform the following is proposed:

H3: The amount of Web 2.0 applications is positively related with the overnight stays recorded by the municipalities.

In this study, 80 websites (30 websites of municipalities of Burgenland and 50 websites of Tyrolean municipalities) are analyzed based on the UNWTO/IFITT guidelines. The municipalities have been selected at random based on a list of Statistics Austria including all Austrian reporting municipalities (Statistics Austria, 2008) In addition to that, the municipalities are evaluated if Web 2.0 features are implemented on their websites.

Based on the guidelines suggested by the UNWTO/IFITT complemented by Web 2.0 applications, a list of different criteria is developed. According to this, the results of the proposed hypotheses are based on the following information, which is gathered from 80 websites (30 websites of municipalities of Burgenland and 50 websites of Tyrolean municipalities):

(1) *Accessibility and readability*: According to the guidelines, visual, hearing, speech, cognitive, physical and neurological limitations of users must be taken into account for the development of a website.

(2) *Findability and search engine optimization:* An easily findable website is the base for successful online marketing activities. When searching online by means of search engines, the website must appear on the first page of the result list.

(3) *Service concept:* Information services supply users with all elements published on the website. Recommended services are contact services (i.e. how to get in contact with the DMO or with other users), transaction services (such as payment services, booking services or other services), entertainment services (i.e. applications and functions which provide an experience to the users), and relationship services (for example newsletters and price reductions).

(4) *Web 2.0 applications:* The second generation of web services facilitates communication with users as well as between users (e-cards, blogs, tags, tag-clouds, wikis, online communities).

4 Results

When entering the name of the reporting municipality in the search engine "Google" (www.google.at, 2009), each of the official websites of the municipalities is among the first ten search results presented in Google. With regard to the content management systems used, differences specific to the province are identified. 72 % of the Tyrolean websites use the content management system "RiS-Kommunal" (software specially adapted to needs of public authorities). In Burgenland, almost no municipality uses this software for the management of its website. In general, the websites of both provinces (i.e. Tyrol and Burgenland) use similar design elements. For instance 97 % of the analyzed websites use a logo (in most cases the respective emblem of the municipality) which is published on every web page.

Concerning general information about tourist offices, 46 % of the municipalities of Burgenland do not have an own regional or a local tourist office. 27 % are members of a local tourist office and 10 % of a regional tourist office. Only regional tourist offices have own websites in Burgenland. If there is only a local tourist office it shares the website with the respective municipality. In Tyrol, only 4 % of the analyzed reporting municipalities do neither belong to a local nor to a regional tourist office. 88 % are represented by a regional tourist office and 2 % are represented by a local as well as a regional tourist office. All related regional tourist offices in Tyrol have an own website and approximately 87 % of the municipalities link from their own website to the website of the regional tourist office.

In terms of the website's accessibility and readability, about 96 % of the analyzed websites are exclusively published in German language (*H2 rejected*). Only the websites of three reporting municipalities from Burgenland (namely the websites from Rust, Pinkafeld and Wieden) provide the possibility to select other languages than German. Only on 7 % of the websites from Burgenland and on 58 % of the websites of Tyrolean municipalities the font size and the contrast of the website can be changed.

Considering information services, 67 % of the websites of municipalities of Burgenland provide details about cultural and natural attractions as well as information about accommodation and activities. The other websites (33 %) do not provide sufficient information about tourism offers. 92 % of the websites of Tyrolean municipalities do not give detailed information about the whole tourism offers such as attractions, activities, and accommodation facilities. Only on 8 % of the websites these details are published. In general, it can be observed that the websites of municipalities of Burgenland provide detailed information. Compared to that, Tyrolean municipalities mostly publish insufficient information on their websites *(H1 rejected)*.

When investigating transaction services, three (Rust, Güssing and Oggau) out of 80 municipalities provide online booking possibilities. However, no single website of the analyzed websites enables visitors to book tickets for public transport or for events. Brochures can be downloaded on the websites of eight municipalities from Burgenland. Ten municipalities indicate on their websites, that brochures can be ordered on request. In Tyrol no single website allows the user to download brochures. In addition, no information is given on how to order brochures.

With regard to the availability of Web 2.0 applications, unexpected results are found. Surprisingly, not a single website out of the 80 analyzed websites of the reporting municipalities allows sending e-cards. Furthermore, blogs, tagging possibilities, tag clouds, wikis or online-communities are not implemented on any of the websites of reporting municipalities of Burgenland and Tyrol *(H3 rejected)*.

5 Discussion

There is evidence that information provided on the Internet supports travellers in their decision-making process (Buhalis, 2003; Choi, Lehto & Oleary, 2007). Moreover, fact is that experts have established various kinds of recommendations how to design websites in order to cater user's needs (Benkendorff & Black, 2000; ITZ, 2003; Mich, Franch, Cilione & Marzani, 2003). However, the results of this study show that the guidelines developed by the UNWTO and IFITT receive limited or no attention for designing websites of local DMOs. In particular, destinations, which attract many visitors per year, could take advantage out of their online presence while providing tourism-relevant information at the same time.

Official websites of the Austrian reporting municipalities are top-ranked when entering the name of the municipality, i.e. the destination in the search engine Google (www.google.at, 2009). Hence, as revealed by Buhalis (2003) DMO websites are an important source of information. This in turn calls for professionally designed websites providing travellers with relevant information as suggested by various guidelines. Tourism-related details should even be published on a local level, i.e. on official websites of the Austrian reporting municipalities. Based on the results of the present study, it is strongly recommended to improve the information quality as well as the presentation of content of the websites analyzed. This is not only true for municipalities with high numbers of overnight stays but also for all municipalities independent from the number of overnight stays. It is not sufficient to provide a link to websites, which offer information that is more comprehensive. In doing so, a competing municipality could attract potential tourists who visit a website of a regional tourism office – competitors are just one click away.

Web 2.0 applications may facilitate a more diversified information presentation (text, video, audio), content combination as well as interaction. However, despite the growing importance of Web 2.0 applications, no single website of the analyzed municipalities provides applications of this kind on its official website. This might be missed opportunities from a DMO's point of view. Interaction of users with the website, with the DMO as well as with other users can strengthen the trustworthiness of a destination and potentially increase the intention to visit a destination. Furthermore, it could offer opportunities to "listen" what consumers have to say and what they really expect. Hence, user generated content might provide opportunities to respond to negative word of mouth, because users are saying what they want anyway. If they do not tell it on "my website" they will say it somewhere else. Moreover, DMOs would have the chance to recognize certain trends, or consumers could even get involved in product development.

When talking about recommendations for the industry, municipalities should not entirely put the responsibility for destination marketing activities on the national, regional or local tourist offices. Every municipality needs to improve and evaluate the information relevant for travellers. Therefore, municipalities should provide details about their services offered on their official websites as well as guarantee easy access to this information. This is particularly relevant for reporting municipalities (i.e. municipalities with more than 1,000 overnight stays per year) which are not member of a local tourist office. Websites can easily be adapted appropriately with marginal efforts. An informative and well-designed website does not require huge financial investments but attracts potential tourists while delivering additional revenues for a municipality.

Concerning theoretical implications, the results of the present study highlight the need for international guidelines to consider technical developments and requirements. Furthermore, it demonstrates the necessity of guidelines for globally evaluating DMO websites. However, there is a need for updating guidelines more recently. Web 2.0 applications are already common practice and therefore must be taken into account in guidelines. If guidelines are not updated more frequently, although technology is changing rapidly, their value is questionable.

The results of the study clearly show that the insufficient information on tourism-related issues as well as the lack of quality of the websites may be due to fact that municipalities fully rely on the online marketing activities of tourist offices. In addition, lack of quality of tourism related information on the websites may also be a consequence of lack of funding, lack of manpower or lack of importance attached to tourism by the municipalities. To assess these implications more into detail, however, representatives of the municipalities must be interviewed. Knowledge about the strategic orientation, about the importance of the tourism industry and about financing issues is vital in order to learn more about the reasons why international guidelines have only received limited attention. Furthermore, in order to justify international guidelines, such as those developed by the UNWTO/IFITT, it might be worth analyzing if DMOs are aware of existing guidelines.

References

Baggio R. (2003). A Website Analysis of European Tourism Organizations; Vol. 14, No. 2, pp 93-106; Bocconi University; Mailand-Italien

Benckendorff P.J. & Black N.L. (2000). Destination marketing on the Internet: A case study of Australian Regional Tourism Authorities; Journal of Tourism Studies; Vol. 11, No. 1; pp 11-21

Buhalis D. (2003). eTourism: information technologies for strategic tourism management; Issue 1; Harlow-England; Pearson Education Limited

Choi S, Lehto X.Y. & O'Leary J.T. (2007). What Does the Consumer Want from a DMO Website? A Study of US and Canadian Tourists' Perspectives; International Journal of Tourism Research; No. 9; pp 59-72

De Marsico M. & Levialdi S. (2004). Evaluating web sites: exploiting user's expectations; International Journal of Human-Computer Studies 60; pp. 381–416

Destination Web Watch; http://www.destinationwebwatch.org/about-web-watch-page.html; (retrieved on 2009/09/08)

ETC/UNWTO (2008). Handbook on E-marketing for Tourism Destinations; World Tourism Organization, European Travel Commission; Madrid-Spanien

eTourism Foundation Dialog 2009: „eQualität" als Destinationsstrategie?; http://www.tourismuspresse.at/presseaussendung.php?schluessel=TPT_20090327_TPT 0001&ch=tourismuswirtschaft; Egger R. (retrieved on 2009/03/29)

Euromonitor International (2008). http://www.portal.euromonitor.com/passport/ResultsList.aspx; (retrieved on 2008/11/06)

Google; www.google.at; Websiteanalyse; (retrieved on 2009/02-03)

IZT– Institut für Zukunftsstudien und Technologiebewertung/dwif – Deutsches Wirtschaftswissenschaftliches Institut für Fremdenverkehr e. V. (2003). Neue IuK-Technologien und ihre Relevanz für die Wettbewerbsfähigkeit touristischer Destinationen Trends, Daten und Fakten im internationalen Vergleich; Britta Oertel, Thomas Feil, Sie Liong Thio unter der Mitarbeit von Jens-Ake Güldner; Werkstatt-Bericht Nr. 56; March

Lee K.S. & Gretzel U. (2006). Consumer Generated Media (CGM); Laboratory for Intelligent Systems in Tourism; Texas; A&M University; *in* Linaza M.T., Lölhöffel F., Garcia A., Lamsfus C., Alzua-Sorzabal A. & Lazkano A.; Mash-up for Small Destination Management Organizations Websites; Information and Communication Technologies in Tourism; pp 130-140; Springer Wien – New York; 2008

Mich L., Franch M., Cilione G. & Marzani P. (2003). Tourist Destinations and the Quality of Web sites: A Study of Regional Tourist Boards in the Alps. ENTER 2003, Helsinki, January 28-31

RiS-Kommunal 3.0 Leistungsbeschreibung (2008). RiS GmbH; Ing. Kaplangasse 1, 4400 Steyr, Austria

Statistics Austria - Meldestatistik Tourismus in Österreich (2008). Bundesanstalt Statistik Österreich; 1110 Wien, Guglgasse 13; christa.schischeg@statistik.gv.at

Sweeney S. (2000). Internet Marketing for Your Tourism Business: Proven Techniques for Promoting Tourist-based Businesses Over the Internet; Gulf Breeze-Kalifornien; Maximum Press

TourMIS - Meldestatistik der Statistik Österreich (Jahresdaten), Alle Unterkunftsarten, Reiseziel Österreich, Periode Tourismusjahr 2007; http://tourmis.wu-wien.ac.at; (retrieved on 2009/10/01)

TourMIS - Meldestatistik der Statistik Österreich (Jahresdaten), Alle Unterkunftsarten, Reiseziel Burgenland/Tirol, Periode Tourismusjahr 2007; http://tourmis.wu-wien.ac.at/cgi-bin/tmintro.pl; (retrieved on 2009/03/27)

UNWTO (1988). Guidelines for the Transfer of New Technologies in the Field of Tourism; World Tourism Organisation, Madrid; *in* Buhalis D.; Strategic use of information technologies in the tourism industry; Tourism Management; Vol. 19; pp 409-421; 1998

UNWTO (2004). Survey of Destination Management Organisations; Report; World Tourism Organisation; Madrid-Spanien

UNWTO (2005). Evaluating and Improving Websites – The Tourism Destination Web Watch; World Tourism Organization; Madrid-Spanien

How Communication Modes Determine Website Satisfaction

Brigitte Stangl[a],
Astrid Dickinger[b]

[a] Institute for Tourism and Leisure Studies
Vienna University of Economics and Business, Austria
Brigitte.stangl@wu.ac.at

[b] Department of Tourism and Hospitality Management
MODUL University Vienna, Austria
astrid.dickinger@modul.ac.at

Abstract

With the growing importance of the Internet as an information source and increased competition online, website designers have to take into account a variety of aspects to meet the target groups' preferences. The study at hand focuses on the influence of users' preferred communication modes to get an understanding of drivers of website satisfaction. The research model extends known theories from the technology acceptance literature and tests the influence of communication mode through the evaluation of a website. The model is tested employing structural equation modelling. Multiple group analysis exhibits differences between people who prefer text over visual based communication modes. The results reveal major differences between the two preferred communication modes. The main driver for verbalizers is content while the main driver of satisfaction for visualizers is design. These results indicate that website designers need to take the preferred mode of communication into account to facilitate online information search.

Keywords: communication mode, online search, website design, website satisfaction

1 Introduction

With travellers increasingly searching for information online, the importance of the Internet as an information source is well established (Beldona 2005; Xiang and Gretzel 2009). Accordingly, the Internet has been the subject of research with regards to acceptance, usage and satisfaction for years. Some streams of research focus on website evaluation, i.e. the satisfaction with a website (Barnes and Vidgen 2002; Parasuraman, Zeithaml and Malhotra 2005), information system success (DeLone and McLean 1992), persuasiveness of a website (Kim and Fesenmaier 2009) and acceptance of a website (Davis, Bagozzi and R. 1989; Venkatesh, Morris, Davis and Davis 2003; Wixom and Todd 2005). All of these projects have the aim to understand what makes people use information technology.

When it comes to further investigating the user, literature review reveals that users' characteristics also become relevant. Some studies focus on demographic characteristics such as age and gender (Venkatesh, Morris et al. 2003), others on past Internet experience, domain specific innovativeness (Agarwal and Prasad 1998), intrinsic motivation (Venkatesh 2000), voluntariness of use (Venkatesh, Morris et al. 2003), knowledge about the topic (Marchionini 1995), or cultural differences (Chau, Cole, Massey, Montoya-Weiss and O'Keefe 2002).

There are streams of research that try to understand how people learn and search for information. Usually searching and browsing is differentiated. Searching is more analytical and planned while browsing is stimulus driven (Hoffman and Novak 1996; Janiszewski 1998). Different ways of interacting with websites, e.g. through highly pictorial elements or text based navigation metaphors, lead to different ways of cognitive processing (Guttormsen Schär and Krueger 2000). This navigation behaviour connected to cognitive processes is closely linked to learning (Guttormsen Schär and Krueger 2000). Therefore, a well designed website organizes information in a way that users can easily learn more about the relationships of the content (Holtze 2000).

Research on learning styles is primarily conducted by scientists from the field of cognitive and educational psychology and by researchers from business schools but has not been investigated from an interdisciplinary perspective (Coffield, Moseley, Hall and Ecclestone 2004). The domains of e-learning and distance learning have shown more interest in understanding how people acquire knowledge through websites. There is an abundance of literature on cognitive style/learning style which has emerged in the last decade (Cassidy 2004). The present study focuses on the user to explain satisfaction – we include both traditional website evaluation constructs as well as the users' preferred mode of communication which in turn is one part of what experts call learning style. Since the field of learning styles is vast, we focus on communication mode which is more appropriate in our context.

We investigate what has been neglected so far from an interdisciplinary point of view, i.e. we take into account users preferred communication mode. Thus, this research contributes to literature in various ways: i) we attempt to fill the void in understanding the relationship between communication modes and antecedents to website satisfaction ii) we provide insights into website design taking into account users' preferred mode of communication and iii) we shed light on the unexplored field of differences between visualizer and verbalizer in the context of tourism.

The remainder of the article is organized as follows: in section two we present the theoretical background. We provide a rather comprehensive review of learning theory. Literature concerning information systems and well known concepts used for hypotheses development are briefly presented. Then we explain the research method, data collection, analyses, and the results of the study. The paper closes with a discussion and implications.

2 Theoretical Background

There is no common notion or conceptual framework for learning styles. The overview by Coffield et al. (2004) provides insights into the complexity of the field and the number of individual models. Some provide behaviouristic theories as well as objectivistic and constructive philosophies. Cognitive theories focus on problem solving, or new cognitive learning models are based on information processing. Learning style theories examine how people perceive information, come to a decision, and interact with their environment (Cassidy 2004). However, website design literature has hardly included factors such as learning styles, users' preferences and perceptions on system interaction types (Holtze 2000; Sabry and Baldwin 2003), although related issues are highly relevant for designing interfaces successfully. For instance, based on the field Dependence/Independence Model there is evidence that the individual's ability to distinguish relevant from irrelevant content in a whole bunch of information differs (Witkin, Moore, Goodenough and Cox 1977). According to the learning Perceptual Preference Model, styles are influenced by the preferred sensory stimuli. Most people use a mixture of four available styles, i.e. auditory, visual, tactile, and kinaesthetic (Wooldridge 1995). A paper by Holtze (2000) discusses the application of learning styles to web page design; however, it only stresses the relevance of considering those. The research at hand goes a step further by empirically investigating the affect of styles on the perceptions of a website in a tourism context.

In order to account for different learning styles, four dimensions have to be addressed (Felder and Silverman 1988): sensing (concrete, fact oriented) or intuitive (abstract, theory oriented), visual (pictures, diagrams) or verbal (written, spoken), active (learning by doing) or reflective (learning by thinking things through), and sequential (incremental steps) or global (holistic process). Quite a number of learning style measures have been developed, e.g. the Learning Style Index (Felder and Soloman 1991), the Learning Style Inventory (Kolb 1976), the Attributional Style Questionnaire (Peterson, Semmel, von Baeyer, Abramson, Metalesky and Seligman 1982), or the Learning Style Questionnaire (Allinson and Hayes 1988). Another inventory to understand how users process information is provided by Fleming and Baume (2006) through VARK. VARK is the acronym for visual, aural, read/write and kinesthetik which has been used for years to test for preferences regarding e.g. symbolic information (maps, diagrams, charts) and written words (Fleming and Baume 2006). Customers exhibit strong preferences in how they make choices so it seems worthwhile to investigate the preferences with regards to how they acquire information (Fleming and Mills 1992).

Web designers commonly differentiate representations of text, voice, audio, picture, and moving pictures. With regards to learning styles, a majority of people learn text based as opposed to audio. Even though voice is the most natural communication mode this does not hold true in a computer mediated environment (Guttormsen Schär, Kaiser and Krueger 1999). Voice is more context dependent and more suitable to just extend the information content of pictures (Guttormsen Schär and Krueger 2000). Research found that the usage of text and voice have a negative learning effect, pictures in combination with voice a positive learning effect, and all three at the same time a negative learning effect (Guttormsen Schär, Kaiser et al. 1999). On the Internet, visual stimuli are predominant while sounds are, yet, more sparsely used. This is also considered in this research through a focus on text based information provision.

Selection of communication modes corresponding to learning styles aims at presenting information in order to match a person's perceptual and cognitive system (Guttormsen Schär and Krueger 2000). Hence, knowledge about the preferred communication modes would allow marketers to better tailor information to improve their online communication strategies. Media should match the aspects of the information they want to convey. Guttormsen, Schär and Krueger (2000) propose text based information to present basic abstract characteristics and logic conditions while pictures should preferably be used to present information about an object and its functions. Furthermore, using moving pictures can make information even more realistic. It is not yet explored how these principles from selected communication modes would apply in designing a tourism website.

3 Hypotheses Development

The adoption of innovations has been investigated for years resulting in different theories, i.e. the diffusion of innovation (Rogers 1995), the Technology Acceptance Model (Davis 1989), the Social Cognitive Theory (Compeau, Higgins et al. 1999), the Task-Technology Fit model (Goodhue and Thompson 1995) and most recently Unified Theory of Acceptance and Use of Technology (Venkatesh, Morris et al. 2003). In the field of marketing, quite a lot of researchers focus on the influence of perceived website performance (e.g. usefulness, enjoyment, content quality) on the satisfaction with web pages (DeLone and McLean 1992; Wolfinbarger and Gilly 2001; Barnes and Vidgen 2002; Parasuraman, Zeithaml et al. 2005). This is especially important since satisfaction leads to loyal users and consequently to a successful website. All these streams of research are relevant for the hypotheses development of the present study. Since the focus of the study is not the test of established hypotheses, these are all explained in brevity. The focus is on the moderation of these relationships due to the learning types (verbalizer vs. visualizer) as explained at the end of this section.

Usefulness and Ease of Use. According to the Technology Acceptance Model by Davis (1989), a system has to be both easy to use as well as useful, i.e. it also has to help users' to perform better. Hence, perceived ease of use as well as usefulness are important. Both concepts influence users' satisfaction with a system (Davis, Bagozzi et al. 1989).
H1: Perceived usefulness has a direct positive effect on satisfaction.
H2: Perceived ease of use has a direct positive effect on satisfaction.

Enjoyment. Recently, ICT-adoption research includes emotional aspects too (Venkatesh 2000), and there is already evidence that hedonic and enjoyment oriented use drives the adoption and the intention to revisit a site (Venkatesh and Brown 2001). People who perceive a usage scenario as playful (based on the flow theory by Csikszentmihalyi (1975)) are motivated to e.g. browse a site or shop online due to the pleasure they experience (Moon and Kim 2001). Surfing the Internet becomes an end in itself. Thus, we propose:
H3: Enjoyment has a direct positive effect on satisfaction.

Website Design. According to Norman (2002), users' satisfaction increases if the site architecture matches the users' mental model, i.e. the better users' requirements are fulfilled the more satisfied people will be (Sullivan 1997).
H4: Website design has a direct positive effect on satisfaction.

Content Quality. In order to satisfy user, information needs to be relevant, easy to understand and read, and it should be offered in an appropriate format (Barnes and Vidgen 2000).

H5: Content quality has a direct positive effect on satisfaction.

Satisfaction and Loyalty. According to Rust and Oliver (1994), a service needs to be able to arouse positive emotions to satisfy consumers. Satisfaction literature postulates a direct link from satisfaction to outcome measures, e.g. repurchase intentions and customer loyalty (Cronin, Brady and Hult 2000; Fornell 1992; Fornell, Johnson, Anderson, Cha and Bryant 1996; Oliver 1997). In an online context, loyalty is defined as the intention of users to revisit a website or to tell others about the site and to recommend it (Oliver 1997, 392).
H6: Satisfaction has a direct positive effect on loyalty.

Mode of communication. People absorb information differently. However, there are several researchers who strongly support the duality of human information processing (HIP), this approach has also been applied in the field of learning (Bloom 1956; Krathwohl, Bloom and Masia 1964). According to Bloom et al. (1956; 1964), there are two categories: Cognitive people have analytic and systematic skills while affective types prefer intuitive and unsystematic processes. Jung (1971) suggests a continuum including two extreme forms called "sensors" and "intuitors". Sensors want to learn by doing, i.e. they do not look at the website as a whole, but they will make a quick decision and start clicking. Sensors perceive it as frustrating if information cannot be gathered intuitively but rather involves reading a lot of instructions. Intuitors are looking for patterns, they prefer websites with information organized by concept (Holtze 2000). The dual approach has been conceptualized using many different terms. Other terms used are verbalizer or verbal (comparable to intuitors who are great conceptual thinkers and cognitive) and visualizer or imagery (similar to sensors and affective learners) (Paivio 1971; Richardson 1977). Major differences concerning information processing/learning, i.e. precisely their preferred mode of communication between the analytic type and the intuitive type is what all these models have in common. This is also in line with the split-brain research stipulating that left-brain dominant learners tend to have characteristics of sequential learners while right-brain dominant people learn more globally (Ornstein 1977; Sperry 1961).

Since verbalizer (i.e. people preferring text based communication modes) and visualizer (i.e. people preferring more visual communication modes) are particularly important in an online context (Drago and Wagner 2004), these two styles are included in the present study. People favoring visual communication modes (in the following called visualizer) prefer presentations, they can easily remember faces but tend to forget names, and their interest is attracted by movement or action but not by noise. People favoring text based modes (in the following called verbalizer) can remember things best if they take notes, listen to lectures, and they are interested in hands-on tasks (Drago and Wagner 2004; Fleming and Mills 1992).
Due to the differences between visualizer and verbalizer concerning their preferred communication mode the following hypotheses are proposed:

H7: Compared to visualizer, for verbalizer, the relationship between:
a) usefulness and satisfaction is strengthened.

b) ease and satisfaction is strengthened.
c) enjoyment and satisfaction is attenuated.
d) website design and satisfaction is attenuated.
e) content quality and satisfaction is strengthened.

Figure 1 presents the proposed research model reflecting the hypotheses developed earlier. Apart from testing the overall model, the difference between the two groups of preferred communication modes (i.e. verbalizer and visualizer) is analyzed. Thus, multiple group analysis will provide insights into the differences of path estimates between the two modes.

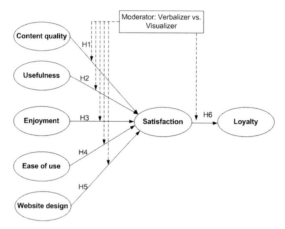

Fig. 1. Research Model

4 Method

An online survey was carried out for two weeks among Austrian Internet users. Respondents were recruited via e-mail providing them with the background of the study and a link to the website we used for the evaluation. Respondents were asked to search the website for some specific information to simulate the situation of actual information search. This approach is used in various studies on information search and website evaluation. Respondents were invited to participate in the study and asked to forward the e-mail to friends to also fill out the questionnaire; thus, a snowball sampling approach was used. Participants were faced with a specific search task for travel information. Based on that task they assessed the website. The specific site was developed in the course of a research project and provides traditional keyword search as well as unique graphic search support in the form of tag clouds and ontologies.

Following the hypotheses, seven constructs are included in the study. The questionnaire consists of previously developed and tested multiple item Likert-type scales. Ease of use and usefulness are measured by four items each adapted from Davis (1989) and Davis and Bagozzi (1989). Three items from van der Heijden (2003) are adapted for enjoyment. Five items from Barnes and Vidgen (2000) are the basis for content quality, and the four measures for website design are adapted from Lee et al. (2002). Satisfaction and loyalty are measured by five and three items respectively. Those are adapted from Cronin and Brady (2000), Oliver et al. (1997) and Moon and Kim (2001). The communication mode is measured using six items. Three are adapted from the VARK questionnaire (Fleming and Mills 1992) and three are adapted from the Learning Style index by Felder and Soloman (1991). A pre-test among 35 students scrutinized the measurement instrument and provided the clarity and readability of the questionnaire.

5 Analyses

To identify the different communication modes, the Typology Representing Network (TRN-32) toolkit, using the neural gas algorithm (Martinetz and Schulten 1991), was used to perform a cluster analysis (Mazanec 2001). As expected the clustering procedure favoured two segments, i.e. verbalizer (32 %) and visualizer (68 %). The test statistics support a two segment solution as the weighted simple structure index (wSSI) arrives at .61 and the uncertainty reduction yields 99 %. The individual's segment membership is used as the grouping variable in a second step. As such we follow Baron and Kenny's (1986) approach to test moderator effects through multiple group analysis when the group membership is known.

The Structural Equation Model (SEM) is estimated using Mplus, a second generation SEM software tool (Muthén and Muthén 2007). Mplus offers estimators which are robust against non-normal distributed data. Moreover, the tool provides a multiple group analysis function which allows the estimation of hypothesized differences between verbalizer and visualizer. After assessing the measurement model the structural model is estimated (Anderson and Gerbing 1988). Only items loading in excess of .5 are included in the measurement model. Local fit measures concerning reliability are in accordance with the levels recommended by Fornell and Larcker (1981). Table 1 shows that the average variance extracted (AVE) and composite reliability (CR) are well above the suggested thresholds of .5 and .7 respectively.

Table 1. Measurement Model

	Content quality	Usefulness	Enjoyment	Ease of use	Website Design	Satisfaction	Loyalty
AVE	0.632	0.730	0.661	0.592	0.514	0.709	0.734
CR	0.896	0.915	0.854	0.852	0.808	0.924	0.892

6 Results

6.1 Sample Profile

After data cleaning, the final sample consists of 238 fully completed questionnaires. Gender is nearly equally distributed with 43.7 % female and 56.3 % male respondents. The average age of the sample is 28.3 years. Concerning profession, 43.5 % are white collar workers, 40 % are students, 7.3 % are self employed, and the rest comprises housewives, unemployed persons, blue collar workers and retired persons. The respondents can be considered as experienced regarding Internet usage with 83 % using it constantly or several times a day. 9 % use the Internet once a day and the rest less frequently. Regarding usage of the Internet, 39 % indicate to have used it for more than 10 years, 48 % between 5 and 10 years, and the remaining 13 % have used the Internet for up to five years.

6.2 Overall Model

Investigation of the fit indicators shows that data fit the model well. Muthén and Muthén (2007) recommend the Tucker-Lewis index (TLI) and the comparative fit index (CFI) when the MLR estimator is employed. The TLI should be above the level of .9 (Hu and Bentler 1995) which is achieved by .920. Now the CFI is consulted and is above the required cut-off value with .929. The Root Mean Square Error of Approximation (RMSEA) is at a satisfying level of .060, and the Standardized Root Mean Square Residual is at .056. The results of the SEM indicate that design has the strongest effect on satisfaction (H5; β=0.381), followed by content quality (H1; β=0.352) and usefulness (H5; β=0.327). The other antecedents of satisfaction (ease of use and enjoyment) do not show significant effects. The effect of satisfaction on loyalty is strong and positive with β=0.820. Since this path coefficient is rather high, we investigated discriminant validity of loyalty and satisfaction. A comparison of the average variance extracted and the shared variance shows that the concepts discriminate rather well.

6.3 Multiple Group Path Analysis

In order to reveal assumed heterogeneity between different communication modes, i.e. between verbalizer and visualizer, a multiple group path analysis is carried out. Three models were estimated to secure that a change of the coefficients is not due to measurement error but due to a change in the hypothesized effects (Steenkamp and Baumgartner 1998). The path coefficients for the overall models and the two groups are presented in Table 2 (figures in brackets are not significant).

Table 2. Path estimates for the overall model and the multiple group model

	Overall model	Verbalizer	Visualizer	p-values
H7a) Usefulness -> Satisfaction	0.327	0.365	0.305	< 0.0001
H7b) Ease of use -> Satisfaction	(0.029)	(0.125)	(-0.018)	-
H7c) Enjoyment -> Satisfaction	(-0.079)	(0.040)	(-0.114)	-
H7d) Website design -> Satisfaction	0.381	(0.147)	0.497	< 0.0001
H7e) Content quality -> Satisfaction	0.352	0.391	0.319	< 0.0006

In order to reveal differences between the two groups a t-test is conducted. The p-values indicate that there are significant differences between people who prefer text based communication modes and those who prefer visual ones. The main driver for verbalizers is content quality (H7e: β=0.391) followed by usefulness (H7a: β=0.365). Interestingly the effect of design is not just attenuated it is actually not significant any more for the verbalizer group. For visualizer, however, website design is by far the main driver of satisfaction (H7d: β=0.497). This is followed by content quality (H7e: β=0.319) and usefulness (H7a: β=0.305). There are no differences between the two groups concerning the effect of satisfaction on loyalty (p < .3118). This is intuitive since the effect of satisfaction on loyalty is not moderated by the preferred communication mode of people but the effect should be present for all groups.

7 Discussion and Limitations

The research investigates the moderating effect of communication mode on the relationship between antecedents and satisfaction. A survey among 238 Internet users gives insights into this phenomenon. The results reveal that there is a significant difference regarding the importance of antecedents on satisfaction based on the individual's preferred mode of communication. Thus, this information should be taken into account when websites are created.

The satisfaction of people who prefer text based communication modes (i.e. verbalizer) is driven by the content followed by the usefulness of a website. While for people favoring visual modes (i.e. visualizer) satisfaction is mainly driven by the design of a website. The inclusion of the effect of satisfaction on loyalty reveals that there are certain concepts which have the same effect for all individuals. An explanation might be that if people are satisfied they tend to become loyal in general, i.e. if they are satisfied they tend to revisit a website irrespective of their preferred mode of communication.

According to previous literature, website designers need to take their target group into account (De Marsico and Levialdi 2004; Sullivan 1997). However, based on the results of this study, a website needs to be designed also considering the preferred mode of communication of the target group. Due to the complexity of a journey, especially in tourism, different online searching types are prevalent. Some travelers may search analytically or holistic as well as goal oriented or exploratory. It might increase satisfaction as well as loyalty if the design of websites aims at matching traveler's perceptual and cognitive systems.

Although this study provides new insights into satisfaction with websites based on preferred mode of communications, there are still various research avenues to pursue. A first limitation lies within the data available to us. Our data contain intention measures rather than behavioral measures. While many website evaluation studies apply such an approach, follow up studies should consider using actual behavioral data. A second limitation is the fact that the study is based on a convenience sample. Also the sub-samples become rather small for the multiple group analysis. Additionally, the results are based on the evaluation of only one website. Therefore, future research should further investigate the influence of the preferred mode of communication across various types of websites.

The study at hand focused on verbalizer and visualizer; however, there might be groups who are a mixture of both or who prefer audio and kinesthetic cues. For those types an investigation of how watching and clicking as well as animations with sound work would be worthwhile. Future research should further differentiate between the search metaphors such as maps, tag clouds and ontologies to provide further insights into how searchers can be supported in their respective search tasks. As Fleming and Baume indicate (2006), communication mode preferences are only stable in the medium term and not fixed. Thus, a longitudinal study would merit investigation.

282

References

Agarwal, R. & Prasad, A. (1998). A Conceptual and Operational Definition of Personal Innovativeness in the Domain of Information Technology. *Information Systems Research*, 9(2), 204-215.

Allinson, C. W. & Hayes, J. (1988). The Learning Style Questionnaire: An Alterntive to Kolb's Inventory? . *Journal of Management Studies,* 25(3), 269-281.

Anderson, J. C. & Gerbing, D. W. (1988). Structural Equation Modeling in Practice: A Review and Recommended Two-Step Approach. *Psychological Bulletin*, 103, 411-423.

Barnes, S. & Vidgen, R. 2000. Webqual: An Exploration of Web Site Quality. Proceedings of the Eighth European Conference on Information Systems, Vienna.

Barnes, S. J. & Vidgen, R. T. (2002). An Integrative Approach to the Assessment of E-Commerce Quality. *Journal of Electronic Commerce Research,* 3(3).

Baron, R. M. & Kenny, D. A. (1986). The Moderator-Mediator Variable Distinction in Social Psychological Research: Conceptual, Strategic, and Statistical Considerations. *Journal of Personality and Social Psychology*, 51(2), 1173-1182.

Beldona, S. (2005). Cohort Analysis of Online Travel Information Search Behavior: 1995-2000. *Journal of Travel Research*, 44(November), 135-142.

Bloom, B. S. (1956). *Taxonomy of Educational Objectives*. New York: David McKay.

Cassidy, S. (2004). Learning Styles: An Overview of Theories, Models, and Measures. *Educational Psychology*, 24(4), 419-444.

Chau, P., Cole, M., Massey, A. P., Montoya-Weiss, M. & O'Keefe, R. M. (2002). Cultural Differences in the Online Behavior of Consumers. *Communication of the ACM,* 45(10), 138-143.

Coffield, F., Moseley, D., Hall, E. & Ecclestone, K. (2004). Should We Be Using Learning Styles? What Research Has to Say to Practice. London: Learning and Skills Research Centre.

Cronin, J. J. J., Brady, M. K. & Hult, G. T. M. (2000). Assessing the Effects of Quality, Value, and Customer Satisfaction on Consumer Behavioral Intentions in Service Environments. *Journal of Retailing*, 76(2), 193-218.

Csikszentmihalyi, M. (1975). Beyond Boredom and Anxiety. San Francisco, CA: Jossey-Bass.

Davis, F. D. (1989). Perceived Usefulness, Perceived Ease of Use, and User Acceptance of Information Technology. *Management Information Systems Quarterly*, 13(3), 319-340.

Davis, F. D., Bagozzi, R. P. & R., W. P. (1989). User Acceptance of Computer Technology: A Comparison of Two Theoretical Models. *Management Science,* 35(8), 982-1003.

De Marsico, M. & Levialdi, S. (2004). Evaluating Web Sites: Exploiting User's Expectations. *International Journal of Human-Computer Studies*, 60, 381-416.

DeLone, W. H. & McLean, E. R. (1992). Information Systems Success: The Quest for the Dependent Variable. *Information Systems Research*, 3(1), 60-95.

Drago, W. A. & Wagner, R. J. (2004). Vark Preferred Learning Styles and Online Education. *Management Research News*, 27(7).

Felder, R. M. & Silverman, L. K. (1988). Learning and Teaching Styles in Engineering Education. *Engineering Education,* 78(7), 674-681.

Felder, R. M. & Soloman, B. A. (1991). Index of Learning Styles. 09/14, from http://www.ncsu.edu/felder-public/ILSpage.htm.

Fleming, N. & Baume, D. (2006). Learning Styles Again: Varking up the Right Tree! *Educational Developments, SEDA Ltd,* 7(4), 4-7.

Fleming, N., D. & Mills, C. (1992). Not Another Inventory, Rather a Catalyst for Reflection. *To Improve the Academy*, 11, 137-147.

Fornell, C. (1992). A National Customer Satisfaction Barometer: The Swedisch Experience. *Journal of Marketing*, 56(1), 6-21.

Fornell, C., Johnson, M. D., Anderson, E. W., Cha, J. & Bryant, B. E. (1996). The American Customer Satisfaction Indes: Nature, Prupose, and Findings. *Journal of Marketing*, 60(10), 7-18.

Fornell, C. & Larcker, D. F. (1981). Evaluating Structural Equation Models with Unobservable Variables and Measurement Error. *Journal of Marketing Research*, 18(1), 39-50.

Guttormsen Schär, S., Kaiser, J. & Krueger, H. 1999. Multimedia: The Effect of Picture, Voice, and Text for the Learning of Concepts and Principles. HCI International 99, Mahwa, N.J., Lawrence Erlbaum.

Guttormsen Schär, S. & Krueger, H. (2000). Using New Learning Technologies with Multimedia. *IEEE Multimedia,* 7(3), 40-51.

Hoffman, D. L. & Novak, T. P. (1996). Marketing in Hypermedia Computer-Mediated Environments: Conceptual Foundations. *Journal of Marketing*, 60(July), 50-68.

Holtze, T. L. (2000). Applying Learning Style Theory to Web Page Design. *Internet Reference Services Quaterly*, 5(2), 71-80.

Hu, L.-T. & Bentler, P. M. (1995). Evaluating Model Fit. In R. H. Hoyle, *Structural Equation Modeling: Concepts, Issues and Applications.* Thousand Oaks: Sage Publications.

Janiszewski, C. (1998). The Influence of Display Characteristics on Visual Exploratory Search Behavior. *Journal of Consumer Research*, 25, 290-301.

Jung, C. G. (1971). The Collected Works of C. G. Jung. Princeton, NJ: Princeton University Press (originally published 1921).

Kim, H. & Fesenmaier, D. R. (2009). Persuasive Design of Destination Web Sites: An Analysis of First Impression. *Journal of Travel Research*, 47(1), 3-13.

Kolb, D. A. (1976). Learning Style Inventory: Technical Manual. Boston: McBer & Company.

Krathwohl, D. R., Bloom, B. S. & Masia, B. B. (1964). Taxonomy of Educational Objectives. New York: David McKay.

Lee, Y. W., Strong, D. M., Kahn, B. K. & Wang, R. Y. (2002). Aimq: A Methodology for Information Quality Assessment. *Information & Management*, 40, 133–146.

Marchionini, G. (1995). *Information Seeking in Electronic Environments.* Cambridge, New York: Cambridge University Press.

Martinetz, T. M. & Schulten, K. J. (1991). A "Neural-Gas" Network Learns Topologies. In T. Kohonen, K. Mäkisara, O. Simula and J. Kangas, *Artificial Neural Networks.* Amsterdam: North-Holland.

Mazanec, J. A. (2001). Neural Market Structure Analysis: Novel Topology-Sensitive Methodology. *European Journal of Marketing,* 35(7-8), 894-916.

Moon, J.-W. & Kim, Y.-G. (2001). Extending the Tam for a World-Wide-Web Context. *Information & Management*, 38, 217-230.

Muthén, L. & Muthén, B. (2007). *Mplus User's Guide. Statistical Analysis with Latent Variables.* Los Angeles: Muthén & Muthén.

Norman, D. A. (2002). *The Design of Everyday Things.* New York: Basic Books.

Oliver, R. L. (1997). *Satisfaction: A Behavioral Perspective on the Consumer.* New York: McGrawHill.

Oliver, R. L., Rust, R. T. & Varki, S. (1997). Customer Delight: Foundations, Findings, & Managerial Insight. *Journal of Retailing*, 73(3), 311-336.

Ornstein, R. E. (1977). *The Pyschology of Consciousness.* New York: Harcourt Brace Jovanovich.

Paivio, A. (1971). *Imagery and Verbal Processes.* New York: Holt.

Parasuraman, A., Zeithaml, V. A. & Malhotra, A. (2005). E-S-Qual a Multiple-Item Scale for Assessing Electronic Service Quality. *Journal of Service Research*, 7(3), 213-233.

Peterson, C. R., Semmel, A., von Baeyer, C., Abramson, L. Y., Metalesky, G. I. & Seligman, M. E. (1982). The Attributional Style Questionnaire. *Cognitive Therapy and Research,* 6, 287-300.

Richardson, A. (1977). Verbalizer-Visualizer. A Cognitive Style Dimension. *Journal of Mental Imagery*, 1, 109-126.

Rust, R. T. & Oliver, R. L. (1994). Service Quality: Insights and Managerial Implications from the Frontier. In R. L. O. Roland T. Rust, *Service Quality: New Directions in Theory and Practice.* New York: Sage Publications Inc.

Sabry, K. & Baldwin, L. (2003). Web-Based Learning Interaction and Learning Styles. British *Journal of Educational Technology*, 34(4), 443-454.

Sperry, R. W. (1961). Celebral Organization and Behavior. *Science*, 133(3466), 1749-1757.

Steenkamp, J.-B. & Baumgartner, H. (1998). Assessing Measurement Invariance in Cross-National Consumer Research. *Journal of Consumer Research*, 25(1), 78-90.

Sullivan, T. (1997). *All Things Web: The Value of Usability.*

Van der Heijden, H. (2003). Factors Influencing the Usage of Websites: The Case of a Generic Portal in the Netherlands. *Information & Management,* 40, 541-549.

Venkatesh, V. (2000). Determinants of Perceived Ease of Use: Integrating Control, Intrinisc Motivation; and Emotion into Technology Acceptance Model. *Information Systems Research*, 11(4), 342-365.

Venkatesh, V. & Brown, S. (2001). A Longitudinal Investigation of Personal Computers in Homes: Adoption Determinants and Emerging Challenges. *MIS Quarterly*, 25(1), 71-102.

Venkatesh, V., Morris, M. G., Davis, G. B. & Davis, F. D. (2003). User Acceptance of Information Technology: Toward a Unified View. *MIS Quarterly*, 27(3), 425-478.

Witkin, H. A., Moore, C. A., Goodenough, D. R. & Cox, P. W. (1977). Field-Dependent and Field-Independent Cognitive Styles and Their Educational Implications. *Review of Educational Research*, 47(1), 1-64.

Wixom, B. H. & Todd, P. A. (2005). A Theoretical Integration of User Satisfaction and Technology Acceptance. *Information Systems Research*, 16(1), 85-102.

Wooldridge, B. (1995). *Increasing the Effectiveness of University/College Instruction: Integrating the Results of Learning Style Research into Course Design and Delivery.* Westport, CT: Greenwood Press.

Xiang, Z. & Gretzel, U. (2009). Role of Social Media in Online Travel Information Search. *Tourism Management,* Forthcoming.

The Impact of Culture on eComplaints: Evidence from Chinese Consumers in Hospitality Organisations

Norman Au[a]
Rob Law[a], and
Dimitrios Buhalis[b]

[a]School of Hotel and Tourism Management,
The Hong Kong Polytechnic University, Hong Kong
{hmnorman, hmroblaw}@polyu.edu.hk

[b] ICTHR School of Management,
Bournemouth University, UK
DBuhalis@bournemouth.ac.uk

Abstract

Culture plays an important role in determining how product/service consumption is evaluated and the resulting complaining behaviour when dissatisfaction occurs. At present, the rapid advancement of web 2.0 technologies enabled hotel customers to use them easily for reporting negative experiences on the Internet. The purpose of this study is to investigate the cultural impacts on e-complaint by Mainland Chinese and non-Chinese hotel customers. Through content analysis of 964 individual complaint cases reported on TripAdvisor and Ctrip travel review websites for Hong Kong hotels, nine e-complaint categories were identified and compared. Mainland Chinese customers were found having far less complaint items in almost all complaint categories comparing to the non-Chinese customers. A two-way contingency table analysis further revealed that a significant relationship is found between e-complaint categories and room rates in the case of Mainland Chinese customers. The implications of the findings are discussed and future cultural e-complaint research for the hospitality industry is suggested.

Keywords: culture, complaints, e-complaints, Mainland Chinese, Hong Kong, hotels.

1 Introduction

In order to be successful in today's highly competitive business environment, it is important for hotels to ensure that guest satisfaction is achieved. As hotels provide products and services that are perceived in different ways by different people, different customers will have varied levels of satisfaction or dissatisfaction in responding to the same or similar service and product consumption. Negative word-of-month and complaint are the two common post-dissatisfaction behaviours adopted (Singh, 1990). Consumer complaint behaviour has attracted considerable attention in the marketing literature in the past (Singh, 1988). This is not surprising as Kelly and Davis (1994) showed that the strong relationship between satisfaction with complaint handling and customer trust and commitment with an organization. Previous studies have also indicated that although demographic characteristics such as age, gender and education level do influence complaint behaviour (Han et al., 1995), customers with different cultural background are also likely to have different types of complaint behaviour and intentions (Liu and McClure, 2001; Huang et al., 1996), as well as the resulting level of satisfaction (Hoare and Butcher, 2008).

China is a fast growing tourism market to international destinations in recent years (China Tourism Statistics Bulletin, 2007). Despite the recent outbreak of the financial crisis, the fundamentals still remains healthy for the growth of Chinese economy (BBC News, 2009). As such, business travel is likely to be supported by increasing domestic consumption investments and leisure travel will also increase with the increasing level of disposable income. With a long history of unique Chinese culture, to gain an understanding and insights on how Mainland Chinese tourists respond or interpret service failure events can help firms to develop more effective service recovery strategies to capture this market in the future.

The rapid growth of the Internet and the proliferation of review sites have enabled customers to bring their complaints online and to make them transparent to the entire world (Buhalis and Law,2008). Weblogs for example are a very important information source for international travellers for obtaining tourism advice and suggestions at specific destinations (Litvin et al., 2008). In particular, Web 2.0 serves as a channel for disseminating service experiences, being that positive or negative, becomes popular at present due to the fast development and applications of technologies. This rapid development, together with the result of word-of-moth communications on experienced services and goods, lead to the emergence of many online feedback/review forums. In the context of China, Internet use has increased substantially since 1997. To demonstrate, online population in China has skyrocketed from 630,000 in early 1997 to almost 300 million in 2009 (CNNIC, 2009). In spite of the importance of online forums, to date, the issue of online complaint management has received limited attention from both researchers and practitioners (Zaugg, 2006). In particular, only a few studies have focused on cultural differences in complaint behaviour in hotel industry (Ngai et al., 2007). To the best knowledge of the authors, no prior studies have ever looked at cultural impacts on complaint behaviour in the hotel industry, using online channels. Building on previous study by Au et al. (2009) regarding complaints on the online environment, this paper extends the study to compare how complaint behaviour differs between Mainland Chinese travellers and other travellers. Using content analysis of secondary data collected on two popular travel review websites (TripAdvisor and Ctrip), this research analyzes the types of complaints on e-channels by these two groups of e-consumers. The study uses the hotels in Hong Kong, a primary travel destination in Asia with many world-class hotel properties, as a case. The study also examines the relationship between the types of e-complaints and room rates.

2 Literature Review

2.1 Culture and Complaints

Hofstede (1980, p. 260) defined culture as the "collective programming of the mind which distinguishes one group of people from another." National cultures mainly differ along four dimensions of power distance, individualism versus collectiveness (I/C), masculinity versus femininity, and uncertainty avoidance. The I/C dimension particularly has resulted in fundamental differences in consumer behaviour between Eastern and Western cultures (Patterson and Smith, 2003). Many past studies are confined to American and European samples and failed to appreciate how culture can powerfully shape consumer behaviour (Chiu et al., 2001). Indeed cultural difference is a critical component in affecting how the product/service consumption is evaluated and what response actions will be taken when dissatisfaction occurs. In addition, previous studies have shown that customers with different cultural backgrounds may have different preferences on what is important, how service should be delivered, and whether complaints were to be raised if the expected standard has not been achieved (DeFranco et al. 2005). For example, it is important to meet the safety concerns of Japanese guests and managers must emphasize the aspect of psychological safety when designing hotel products offering. Japanese guests also demand more constant attention and care than American tourists (Ahmed and Krohn, 1992). Similarly, Mattila (1999) suggested that Western consumers might be more prone than Asian consumers to turn to the physical environment for evidence of a service's quality. Asians may expect more personalized service as their cultural backgrounds reflect large power distance. Westerners, however, have core values and tend to include fun and enjoyment whilst regarding the hedonic dimension of consumption as more important than Asians do. Such cultural-based differences in the evaluation process may also depend on customers' purchase-related goals (Mattila, 1999). In the event of service failure, Ngai et al. (2007) discovered that Asian guests are less likely to complain to the hotel for fear of "losing face" and are less familiar with the channels for complaining than non-Asian guests. Asians are more likely to take private action, such as making negative word-of-mouth comments to friends and others.

Moreover, Gu and Ryan (2008) were among the few researchers who investigated Mainland Chinese preferences of hotel attributes in China. Their study found the main determinants of satisfaction are external environment, reputation, and cleanliness of bedrooms. To examine the cultural characteristics of the Mainland Chinese, Hofstede's (1980) characterization of cultural dimension showed the China group as having high power distance, low individualism, and moderate uncertainty avoidance (Tsaur et al., 2005). China's significantly higher power distance as compared to other countries in East Asia and the world average is indicative of a high level of inequality of power and wealth within the society (www.geert-hofstede.com/hofstede_china.shtml [September 1, 2009]). On the other hand, the low individualism ranking may be attributed, in part, to the high level of emphasis on a collectivist society by the communist rule. It is manifested in a close and committed member 'group', be that a family, extended family, or extended relationships. Loyalty in a collectivist culture is paramount. The society also fosters strong relationships where everyone takes responsibility for fellow members of their group.

The unique cultural values of Mainland Chinese thus help to identify the factors contributing to their perceptions of service or product quality, as well as satisfaction and the propensity to complaint. It also specifies which behaviour is important and which should be avoided within a culture. Perhaps, due to the high power distance characteristics, Ho (1980) found that Chinese attach great importance to the face issue. A study from Chiu et al. (2001) also discovered that because of the salience of face concerns in Chinese culture, people are less likely to complain on a channel which involves direct personal confrontation with the responsible party in a redress seeking situation. Heung and Lam (2003) also suggested that the Chinese tend to adopt an unassertive style of communication approach which often leads to avoidance or silence even if they are dissatisfied. However, it is not clear whether that online channels would become an alternative channel which Chinese are motivated to express their dissatisfaction in avoiding the issue of direct contacts. Or else, leaving the underlying conflicts unsolved in order to assure that the dyadic relationship is not upset.

2.2 Web 2.0 Technologies and Complaint

In an early study, Albrecht and Zemke (1996) found only 5% of dissatisfied customers have voiced their complaints. This low percentage is likely to change now as the fast development of Web 2.0 technologies facilitates a fast and easy e-platform for people to express their complaints without any geographical and time constraints. Even entire web sites have been developed to highlight the problems of organisations, such as http://www.untied.com/ Additionally, electronic word-of-mouth influences more people and can be accessed easier than the traditional channels. Web 2.0 refers to a second generation of web-based communities and hosted services available on the World Wide Web that lets people collaborate and share information online (Hsu & Hsu, 2008). Examples of the major applications of Web 2.0 technologies in the tourism and hospitality industries include RSS (Really Simple Syndication), Blogs (Weblogs), Wikis, Podcasting, and MMORPG (Massively Multiplayer Online Role Playing Game) (Sigala, 2009). The content and information generated by users of Web 2.0 technologies are having a tremendous impact not only on decision making behaviour of Internet users, but also on e-business model that the tourism business need to develop to adapt (Sigala, 2009). Many new types of tourism cyber-intermediaries have been established that have a great impact on tourism demand and supply. Examples of web review sites for the tourism industry include tripadvisor.com, ctrip.com, and gazetters.com. These sites are becoming a very important source for international travellers to get travel advice and suggestions. This does inspire or discourage the willingness to travel and visit a particular destination or supplier, to an extent that these people can even collaborate with others online and organize simultaneously a trip with their friends (Sigala, 2009). Marriott, for example, has created its own weblog on its website to take advantage of such an e-marketing opportunity.

In the existing hospitality literature, there is a limited number of published articles on complaint behaviour on e-channels. In their study, Lee and Hu (2004) analyzed the content of 222 hotel customers' record on an e-complaint forum (Complaints.com). Empirical findings showed that 75% of the failure cases fell into five categories of: service provided not agreed upon, service declined in quality, rude customer service representatives, service never provided, and overcharged. These categories were all related to service delivery failure. In another recently conducted study, Vermeulen and Seegers (2008) examined the effects of online hotel reviews on consumer choice. Empirical findings showed positive online reviews have a significant impact on travellers' decision making, in general and in particular, for lesser-known hotels. Lastly, Au et al. (2009) analyzed 453 cases of individual hotel complaints, as recorded on TripAdvisor, and found the complaints generally fell into nine categories.

3 Research Method

In this research, the dataset for hotel reviews posted by the Mainland Chinese travellers was collected from Ctip.com in the period January to June 2009; whereas for hotel reviews posted by non-Chinese travellers were collected from TripAdvisor.com in the period February to July, 2008. Ctrip.com is a leading travel service provider of hotel accommodation, airline tickets and packaged tours in China. The website has experienced substantial growth and is one of the best known and leading travel brands in China in hotel room and air ticket reservation business. In 2006, Ctrip had an astonishing figure of 5.45 million hotel stay days booked, while the next highest site named eLong had just 2.53 million days booked (Zhang and Zhang, 2008). Unlike TripAdvisor, reviews posted on the Ctrip site are from Mainland Chinese travellers for two reasons. First, almost all complaints were written in simplified Chinese. Second, only members with a local (China) area mobile phone number are allowed to post reviews on the site. In contrast, TripAdvisor was setup in early 2000 by the same company operating Expedia. Tripadvisor.com was chosen in this research because of its large scale of coverage on travel destinations and accommodation reviews (Law, 2006). In each year, more than 15 million of potential hotel consumers use review sites prior to making their decisions on hotel selection (Tripadvisor, 2009). TripAdvisor has a primary goal of providing unbiased recommendations to users for travel-related information. The website indexes hotels from cities in most cities worldwide, together with reviews posted by travellers.

As stated, hotels in Hong Kong, a special administrative region of China, were selected in this research. The hotels as retrieved on both websites can be listed according to popularity, price, or class. During the data collection, the reviews were sorted in ascending order on the basis of members' rating. To ensure the sufficiency of data for analysis and to maintain the operational efficiency, a maximum of 10 reviews (with complaints) in each hotel were extracted for further analysis. In total, 511 individual reviews (complaints) on 86 different Hong Kong hotels were collected and analyzed from the Ctrip; whereas the corresponding number for TripAdvisor is 453. This study adopted content analysis for the collected data. On the basis of the complaints reported from customers on both websites using the grounded theory approach and keyword analysis, the complaints were classified into nine different categories, including: space, bedding, décor, cleanliness, utilities/amenities, provision of amenities, service, price, and miscellaneous (others). Additionally, information regarding room rate or class of a hotel was collected for further analysis with a two-way contingency table analysis.

4 Findings and Discussion

4.1 e-Complaint Categories between Mainland Chinese and non-Chinese

The number of complaint cases on Hong Kong hotels under the nine different categories is presented in Table 1. These nine categories are service, space, cleanliness, utilities,, bedding, price, provision of amenities, décor, and miscellaneous. The total percentage of complaint cases made by Mainland Chinese travellers (i.e. on Ctrip) are considerably lower than non-Chinese in all complaint categories, except "Decor". Such a phenomenon seems consistent with the findings from Lee and Sparks' (2007) study which suggested that interpersonal harmony is highly valued in the Chinese Confucian culture. Hence, Chinese customers are more willing to compromise or not demand a better solution after a service failure, as a gesture of "giving face" to others. This is in contrary to culture in many other western countries. Becker (2000), for example, discovered that Americans actually enjoy complaining about unsatisfactory products and services. They strongly believed that such acts will lead to product/service quality improvement in the future. Nevertheless, the three highest reported complaint categories, namely service, miscellaneous, and space, are the same for both the Mainland Chinese and non-Chinese. These categories, however, differ in terms of their absolute percentages. In the case of the Mainland Chinese, the percentages are 38% (service), 40% (Miscellaneous) and 39% (Space); whereas for non-Chinese, the percentages are 54% (service), 52% (Miscellaneous) and 47% (Space) respectively. This indicates these three areas require particular management attention from hotels in order to seek for possible improvements. For service category, the common examples of failures include slow services, language incompetence, and poor attitude of staff in response to guest requests. The Mainland Chinese customers, however, felt that their services received was worse than Western guests, such as hotels ignored their requests for non-smoking rooms. Their complaint percentages were significantly lower on staff competency (6 % vs 13%) and personal interaction (6% vs 9%) comparing with non-Chinese customers. Chinese customers who live in a collectivist society may have low service expectations, and thus put less emphasis on interaction quality as suggested by Hoare and Butcher (2008).

There are other miscellaneous complaints that were raised by Mainland Chinese only. Examples of these complaints include lack of sea view from the room, the building looks very old, and lots of noise from the street can be heard in the room. Apparently, Mainland Chinese have high expectations on the surroundings of hotels in Hong Kong with the price they pay in comparison with the room rate that is charged by similar hotels in Mainland. This is also consistent with findings from Gu and Ryan (2008) that the external environment of a hotel is one of the main determinants for satisfaction of Mainland Chinese customers. Complaints regarding small space of guestrooms, bathrooms or hotels in general (e.g. guest lifts and corridors) are another category of major complaints as reported by both Mainland Chinese and non-Chinese (39% vs 47%), though for some reasons the percentages are much smaller specifically for bathroom space in Mainland Chinese cases (1% vs 6%). Such a finding is largely due to the high price of land in Hong Kong, and thus the maximization of space in local hotels in Hong Kong.

Table 1. Cases of E-Complaints on Ctrip and Tripadvisor by Complaint Categories

Complaint Category	Sub-category	Ctip-HK		Tripadvisor-HK		
		Cases	% of Total (n=511)	Cases	% of Total (n=453)	Difference % of Total
Service	General service	49	9.6	50	11	-1.4
	Courtesy	43	8.4	34	7.5	+0.9
	Responsiveness	33	6.5	35	7.7	-1.2
	Competency	26	5.1	60	13.2	-8.1
	Personal interaction	30	5.9	41	9.1	-3.2
	Others	11	2.2	25	5.5	-3.3
Total		192	37.6	245	54.1	-16.5
Miscellaneous	Others	23	4.5	65	14.3	-9.8
	Location	53	10.4	39	8.6	+1.8
	Noise	55	10.8	38	8.4	+2.4
	Smell	25	4.9	45	9.9	-5.0
	Food	19	3.7	19	4.2	-0.5
	Pest	7	1.4	29	6.4	-5.0
	View	21	4.1	n.a.	n.a.	n.a.
Total		203	39.7	235	51.9	-12.2
Space	Space in general	35	6.8	50	11	-4.2
	Guest room	155	30.3	135	29.8	+0.5
	Bathroom	8	1.6	28	6.2	-4.6
Total		198	38.7	213	47	-8.3
Cleanliness	General cleanliness	5	1	43	9.5	-8.5
	Guest room	12	2.3	60	13.2	-10.9
	Public areas	3	0.6	11	2.4	-1.8
	Toilet	4	0.8	22	4.9	-4.1
	Others	0	0	17	3.8	-3.8
Total		24	4.7	153	33.8	-29.1
Utilities		96	18.8	149	32.9	-14.1
Bedding		44	8.6	114	25.2	-16.6
Price		42	8.2	110	24.3	-16.1
Provision of Amenities		67	13.1	108	23.8	-10.7
Decor		96	18.8	73	16.1	+2.2

The two complaint categories that featured the largest gap between Mainland Chinese and non-Chinese are cleanliness (8% vs 34%) and bedding (9% vs 25%), both related to the physical comfort of the environment. It can be expected that the general living standard in developing countries such as China is relatively lower than developed countries. In addition, prior exposure to other hotel accommodation in different travel destinations is likely to be less in the case of Mainland Chinese. This may offer some possible explanations of Mainland Chinese who tend to be more "tolerable" and less demanding in these two aspects. Price is the next complaint category where Mainland Chinese have reported significantly less cases comparing to non-Chinese (8% vs 24%). When examining this in conjunction with the other category – decor, which is the only category where Chinese have a higher complaint percentage than non-Chinese (19% vs 16%), reveal some characteristics of traditional Chinese cultural behaviour particularly for those who stayed in a high-class luxury hotel. Chinese place great importance on the "face" issue. When travelling with friends or family, they would try their best to ensure that they are perceived as a "generous host", who can afford and willingly to spend on something which all can be proud of. The outlook, décor, and the view of the room are the attributes that are associated with such an impression. This may explain why the Mainland Chinese is non-sensitive to price but sensitive to decor and outlook of the premise. The remaining two reported complaint categories are functionality and provision of utilities in rooms. Examples of these complaints include toilet flush and the Internet connection are not functioning properly, lack of LCD TV in room, poor quality of shampoo, and tooth brush not provided. Again, the relatively low complaint percentages of Mainland Chinese as compared to non-Chinese may indicate that the former group is less demanding on such provision particular for those who stayed in the budget hotels.

4.2 Significant Relationships between Categories of E-Complaint and Room Rates

A two-way contingency table analysis was conducted using SPSS software (v. 17.0) to evaluate whether different categories of e-complaints are related to hotel room rates. The findings indicated the existence of significant relationships between them but only in the case of Mainland Chinese travellers. This implies that different room rates charged by hotels are prone to specific types of complaints. The results are depicted in Table 2, where a total of four categories, namely: space, bedding, décor, and miscellaneous were found to have significant associations. Based on the results of significance tests, the Chi-square values for space, bedding, décor, and miscellaneous were 43.152 ($p = .000$, N = 512), 15.437 ($p = .004$, N = 512), 23.537 ($p = .000$, N = 512) and 44.476 ($p = .025$, N = 512), respectively.

For space, it appears that the two hotel groups charging the lowest room rates (HK\$200-\$499 and HK\$500-\$799) and the group charging the highest rates (>\$1,400) have received a higher percentage of complaints. The fact that high land price of Hong Kong implies most budget hoteliers may have to make a compromise decision of convenient location at the expense of room size to ensure higher occupancy rates. Those who are paying a lot more to stay in a higher-class hotel are likely to have higher expectations for spacious rooms, so are their chances of getting disappointment in reality. The issue of small room size in budget hotels may also be associated with and partly explains more complaints on bedding in this category. Examples of complaints include beds are too short or small, the mattress are too hard or soft, and blankets are worn-out. Though complaints related to bedding are relatively few (8.6% for Chinese), a comfortable bed with decent quality blanket is often regarded as the core product provided by a hotel. Serious attention is still needed from hotel managers to rectify the issue. For higher class hotels, normally there is a guideline on the standard of bedding and linen to achieve, as reflected in very few complaints found in these hotel categories (3-5%).

Table 2. Relationships between Hotel Room Rates and Tendency to Complain across Different Complaint Categories

	Reported Cases by Complaint Categories				Total
Room Rates (HK$)	Space (Not Complained)	Bedding (Not Complained)	Decor (Not Complained)	Miscell-aneous	Complained (Not Complained)
$200 - $499	83 (91)	15 (159)	30 (144)	64 (110)	192 (504)
$500 - $799	80 (95)	25 (150)	23 (152)	78 (97)	206 (494)
$800 - $1,099	20 (60)	2 (78)	15 (65)	29 (51)	66 (254)
$1,100 - $1,399	3 (42)	2 (43)	20 (25)	13 (32)	38 (142)
$1,400 or higher	12 (25)	0 (37)	8 (29)	19 (18)	39 (109)
Total Cases	511	511	511	511	2044
Chi-Square	43.152	15.437	23.537	44.476	
p-value	.000*	.004*	.000*	.025*	
df	12	4	4	28	

In relation to complaints on decor, the results show that there is a higher tendency for Mainland Chinese to complain in the top two highest rated hotel categories (20 cases out of a total of 45, and 8 cases out of a total of 37) than others. This seems to be in agreement with the observations described previously where Chinese travellers are characterized by high power distance culture. The higher the class of a hotel, the more they would regard as "losing face" and dissatisfied if the outlook appearance does not convey such luxurious standard in front of their companions. Lastly, for complaints on miscellaneous items, over 50% (19 cases out from a total of 37) of Mainland Chinese who stayed in the highest hotel room rates category have made a complaint. Such high percentage of complaints is likely due to their high expectation of quality standard that should be delivered from these hotels.

5 Conclusions

This study has offered better understanding and useful insights of the impact of culture on e-complaints based on a study about Hong Kong hotels. Apparently, culture plays an important role in determining how customers expect services to be delivered as well as their complaint behaviour. Today's service managers in the hotel industry should be aware of the cost of ignoring cultural norms. The classification of e-complaints into nine categories should provide more detailed information on what causes customer dissatisfaction and make customers to subsequently express their negative comments online. One important observation from this study is that on average Mainland Chinese customers have far less complaint items in each reported case across in almost all complaint categories (except decor) in comparison with non-Chinese hotel customers. Lee and Sparks (2007) discovered that in the Chinese culture, a person's own aggressive behaviour in public may result in him or her losing face and even his/her group members losing face. As such, they tend not to complain in public to avoid taking such risks. Yet there is evidence from the study to suggest that such practice even applies also to the online environment despite there is no physical confrontation with other people. So the culture norm of the Mainland Chinese to seek harmonious relationship in hospitality service encounter contexts and not demanding a better solution after a service failure, could be perceived as an act of giving face. The ease of access to the Internet and usage in China are other factors affecting the ability to report dissatisfied experiences online. Therefore it is crucial for hotel managers be aware that when dealing with Mainland Chinese customers, no complaints received does not necessarily mean they are satisfied. The high percentage of complaints on service failure by both Mainland Chinese and non-Chinese customers suggested that provision of good training on service skills as well as on cultural differences for hotel employees are urgently needed.

Understanding which hotel class is more prone to specific types of complaints has implications on the formulation of appropriate hotel marketing strategies, as well as the pricing and product mix for specific market segments. For budget hotels in particular, management needs to ensure that there is a right match between what can be realistically offered by the hotel and what standard is expected by different target customer groups. While some items such as small room size may not be easily rectified, management should seek improvement, where appropriate, both externally like exterior decor and design and internally through the provision of decent bedding. In addition, management should provide adequate information to manage customer expectations to be at a realistic level.

This research has the limitations of conducting research on the basis of analyzing secondary data collected from the Internet. One important limitation is that the respondents are likely to be associated with higher education and higher income level/s, and with more knowledge of Internet usage. As such, it is possible that complaints from certain groups of customers are excluded. Also, it is difficult to ensure the accuracy and reliability of the complaints. Furthermore, in this study, only complaints as reported by non-Chinese users on Tripadvisor.com and those reported by Mainland Chinese users on Ctrip.com for Hong Kong hotels were analyzed. Future research can be extended to other travel websites and other nationalities with different cultures. More complex models could then be developed to identify patterns on e-complaint behaviour by different hotel customers in varied cultural backgrounds. This will certainly benefit hotel managers to better formulating specific policies in responding to e-complaints by different customer groups online.

References

Albrecht, K. & Zemke, R. (1996). *Service America! Doing Business in the New Economy.* Homewood, IL: Dow Joes-Irwin.

Ahmed, Z. U. & Krohn, F. B. (1992). Understanding the Unique Consumer Behavior of Japanese Tourists. *Journal of Travel and Tourism Marketing* 1(3): 73-86.

Au, N., Buhalis, D. & Law, R. (2009). "*Complaints on the Online Environment – The Case of Hong Kong Hotels*". In Hopken, W., Gretzel, U. and Law, R. (Eds.), Information and Communication technologies in Tourism 2009. Springer-Verlag Wien-New York 73-85.

BBC News (2009). China Economic Growth Accelerates. *http://news.bbc.co.uk/2/hi/business/8319706.stm.* [Retrieved on 28.10.2009]

Becker, C. (2000). Service Recovery Strategies: The Impact of Cultural Differences. *Journal of Hospitality and Tourism Research* 24(10): 526-38.

Buhalis, D., and Law, R., (2008). Progress in Tourism Management: Twenty years on and 10 Years after the Internet: The state of eTourism Research, Tourism Management, 29(4), 609–623.

Chiu, C. Y., Tsang, S. C. & Yang, C. F. (2001). The Role of Face Situation Attitudinal Antecedents in Chinese Consumer Complaint Behavior. *The Journal of Social Psychology* 128(2): 173-180.

China Internet Network Information Centre (CNNIC). (2009). *Internet Fundamental Data.* www.cnnic.net.cn [Retrieved on 02.09.2009]

China Tourism Statistics (2007). China Tourism Statistics Bulletin 2007 Report. National Tourism Administration of the PRC. *http://en.cnta.gov.cn/html/2008-11/2008-11-9-21-35-50326.html.*[Retrieved on 28.10.2009]

Defranco, A., Wortman, J., Lam, T. & Countryman, C. (2005). A Cross-cultural Comparison of Customer Complaint Behavior in Restaurants in Hotels. *Asia Pacific Journal of Tourism Research* 10(2): 173-190.

Gu, G. & Ryan, C. (2008). Chinese Clientele at Chinese Hotels – preferences and Satisfaction. *International Journal of Hospitality Management* 27: 337-345.

Han, S., Keng, K. A. & Richmond, D. (1995). Determinants of Consumer Complaint Behavior: A Study of Singapore Consumers. *Journal of International Consumer Marketing* 8(2): 59-76.

Heung, C. S. & Lam, T. (2003). Customer Complaint Behavior towards Hotel Restaurant Services. *International Journal of Contemporary Hospitality Management* 15(5): 283-289.

Ho, D. Y. F. (1980). Face and Stereotyped Notions about Chinese Face Behavior. *Philippine Journal of Psychology* 13:20-33.

Hoare, R. J. & Butcher, K. (2008). Do Chinese Cultural Values Affect Customer Satisfaction / Loyalty? *International Journal of Contemporary Hospitality Management* 20(2): 156-171.

Hofstede, G. H. (1980). *Culture's Consequences: International Differences in Work-related Values.* Sage Publications, Beverly Hills, CA.

Hsu, C. J. & Hsu, C. M. (2008). The Relationships Between Service Quality and Customer Satisfaction in a Leading Chinese Web 2.0 Company. *The Business Review* 11(1): 84-89.

296

Huang, J. H., Huang, C. T. & Wu, S. (1996). National Character and Response to Unsatisfactory Hotel Service. *International Journal of Hospitality Management* 15(3): 229-243.

Kelley, S. W. & Davis, M. A. (1994). Antecedents to Customer Expectations for Service Recovery. *Journal of the Academy of Marketing Science* 22(1): 52-61.

Law, R. (2006). Internet and Tourism – Part XXI: Trip Advisor. *Journal of Travel & Tourism Marketing* 20(1): 75-77.

Lee, C. C. & Hu, C. (2004). Analyzing Hotel Customers' E-Complaints from an Internet Complaint Forum. *Journal of Travel & Tourism Marketing* 17(2/3): 167-181.

Lee, Y. L. & Sparks, B. (2007). Appraising Tourism and Hospitality Service Failure Events: A Chinese Perspective. *Journal of Hospitality & Tourism Research* 31(4): 504-529.

Litvin, S. W., Goldsmith, R. E. & Pan, B. (2008). Electronic Word-or-mouth in Hospitality and Tourism Management. *Tourism Management* 29(3): 458-468.

Liu, R. R. & MuClure, P. (2001). Recognizing Cross-Cultural Differences in Consumer Complaint Behavior and Intentions: An Empirical Examination. *Journal of Consumer Marketing* 18(1): 54-74.

Mattila, A.S. (1999). The Role of Culture and Purchase Motivation in Service Encounter Evaluations. *Journal of Services Marketing* 13(4/5): 376-389.

Ngai, W. T., Heung, C. S., Wong, Y. H. & Chan, K. Y. (2007). Consumer Complaint Behavior of Asians and Non-Asians about Hotel Services: An Empirical Analysis. *European Journal of Marketing* 41(11/12): 1375-1391.

Patterson, P. G. & Smith, T. (2003). A Cross-cultural Study of Switching Barriers and Propensity to Stay with Service Providers. *Journal of Retailing* 79: 107-120.

Sigala, M. (2009). *WEB 2.0 in the tourism industry: A new tourism generation and new e-business models.*http://www.traveldailynews.com/pages/show_page/20554, [Retrieved on 30.08.2009].

Singh, J. (1988). Consumer Complaint Intentions & Behavior: Definitional and Taxonomical Issues. *Journal of Marketing* 52(1): 93-107.

Singh, J. (1990). A Typology of Consumer Dissatisfaction Response Styles. *Journal of Retailing* 66(1): 57-99.

Tripadvisor (2009). www.tripadvisor.com [Retrieved on 03.09.2009]

Tsaur, S. H., Lin, C. T. & Wu, C. S. (2005). Cultural Differences of Service Quality and Behavioral Intention in Tourist Hotels. *Journal of Hospitality & Leisure Marketing* 13(1): 41-63.

Vermeulen, I. E. & Seegers, D. (2008). Tired and Tested: The Impact of Online Hotel Reviews on Consumer Consideration. *Tourism Management* doi:10.1016/j.tourman.2008.04.008.

Zaugg, A. D. (2006). *Online Complaint Management @Swisscom – A Case Study.* Working Paper No. 183. Instituts fur Wirtschaftsinformatik der Universitat Bern, Bern.

Zhang, L. & Zhang, M. (2008). Market Structure of China's Network Industry. *Journal of Chinese Economic and Foreign Trade Studies* 1(1): 75-87.

Acknowledgements

This research was supported in part by the Hong Kong Polytechnic University [Grant number: 1-ZV3U].

Do Negative Experiences Always Lead to Dissatisfaction? – Testing Attribution Theory in the Context of Online Travel Reviews

Jingxian Jiang[a],
Ulrike Gretzel[a], and
Rob Law[b]

[a]Laboratory for Intelligent Systems in Tourism
Texas A&M University, USA
{kellyjiang;ugretzel}@tamu.edu

[b] School of Hotel and Tourism Management
Hong Kong Polytechnic University, Kowloon, Hong Kong
hmroblaw@polyu.edu.hk

Abstract

The literature generally suggests that negative experiences should lead to dissatisfaction. However, attribution theory has been proposed to explain why this is not always the case. Using a sample of online hotel reviews, this paper tests how attribution and reference to eWOM mediate the influence of negative experiences on satisfaction. The results support only one of the hypotheses and generally only a small portion of the variance of satisfaction can be explained with the proposed model. Theoretical and practical implications are discussed.

Key words: negative experience; satisfaction; attribution; reference to WOM; online reviews

1 Introduction

The specific characteristics of the services provided by hotel establishments and the nature of the hotel industry (e.g. high labour turnover) make it very difficult to con-sistently deliver high quality experiences. Moreover, tourist experiences are coopera-tively produced by hotels, attractions, restaurants and many other players at the desti-nation, including local residents. This can make quality control very difficult. In other words, it is likely that tourists encounter various negative experiences during a hotel stay, some of which are caused by mismanagement in the hotel and others by external factors. Extant literature supports that negative experiences produce a dissatisfying outcome (Bougie, Pieters, & Zeelenberg, 2003; Reichel, Lowengart, & Milman, 2000; Swan & Combs, 1976). However, little existing work discusses the alternative possi-bility. That is, tourists reporting satisfaction despite encountering unexpected or adverse occurrences.

Guest satisfaction is significant because it determines whether a tourism product or service can survive the market (Gursory, McCleary & Lepsito 2003, 2007) by influ-enceing the future choice and consumption of tourism products and services (Kozak & Rimmington 2000) and the spread of word-of-mouth (Litvin, Goldsmith & Pan, 2008). Despite the growing literature on satisfaction in the tourism and hospitality field, little is known about if and how specific negative experiences influence satisfaction. In order to shed light on this issue, this paper will examine the content of online hotel reviews and the respective satisfaction ratings.

2 Background

2.1 Service Failure/Negative Experience

Service failures are critical incidents in guest experiences (e.g., Chuang & Hoffman, 1998). Consumer reactions to their negative experiences due to service failure can be categorized as attitudinal and behavioural. Attitudinal reactions refer to disappoint-ment, anger, satisfaction/dissatisfaction etc., and behavioural reactions refer to com-plaining, leaving, switching, loyalty/disloyalty and other responses. Service failure has been a great concern to researchers and practitioners because it can damage future patronage and generate negative word-of-mouth. In the tourism/hospitality context, Some of the studies related to service failure compared the effects of service failure and/or recovery strategies in tourism sectors between the U.S. and other countries (e.g., Bejou, Edvardsson & Rakowski, 1996; Mueller Palmer, Mack & McMullan, 2003), others focused on specific complaint behaviours of the consumers (e.g., Huang Huang & Wu, 1996; Park, Lehto & Park, 2008; Yuksel Kilinc & Yuksel, 2006).

2.2 Satisfaction/Dissatisfaction

Dissatisfaction is one of the reactions to service failure. It is an attitudinal consequence of service failure that can influence behaviour. For example, guests often complain about service failure to express their dissatisfaction with service providers (Huang et al., 1996; Bateson and Hoffman, 1999) and might subsequently switch to other service providers (Ross, 1999). Guests' dissatisfaction is likely to be intensified when they encounter service failures repeatedly and do not witness the service providers making sufficient recovery efforts (Weiner, 2000).

Guest satisfaction can be understood by different models. One of the most popular models is the expectancy-disconfirmation model, which summarizes satisfaction as the discrepancy between guests' prior expectations and perceived service performance (Parasuraman, Zeithaml & Berry, 1985; Oliver, 1980; Oliver, 1997). Similarly, other models, such as Adams' (1965) equity theory and Kano's (1984) three-factor theory (basic factors/dissatisfiers, excitement factors/satisfiers, and performance factors/one-dimensional factors) consider guest satisfaction as a cognitive construct. In tourism and hospitality, cognitive measurement of guest satisfaction and the relationship be-tween service quality and guest satisfaction have been widely analyzed (e.g., Bowen & Clarke, 2002; Kozak, 2001; Mey, Akbar & Fie, 2006Ryan & Cessford, 2003). Be-sides the cognitive perspective of satisfaction, the role of affect in consumption is attracting increasing attention (e.g., Oliver 1993; Oliver 1997; Oliver, Rust & Varki 1997; Westbrook 1987; Yu & Dean 2001). Tourism and hospitality scholars echo this trend in acknowledging the cognitive-affective dimensions of guest satisfaction (Rodriguez del Bosque & San Martin, 2008; Wirtz, Mattila & Tan 2000).

2.3 Accounting for Negative Experience

Negative experiences regarding service failures do not necessarily lead to dissatisfaction because on one hand, companies and their employees will apply recovery strategies such as acknowledging the problem and apologizing, and compen-sating for service failure (Clemmer & Schneider, 1996), inducing a state of satisfac-tion in the guest. On the other hand, whether guests will be satisfied or dissatisfied after exposure to negative experiences is also determined by factors outside of the control of service providers. One of these factors is whether guests attribute the cause of the negative experience to the service provider or not.

Attribution theory is a framework to explain the causal effect between two incidents (Folkes, 1988), assuming that people tend to uncover and evaluate the causes of their satisfaction/dissatisfaction. Attribution theory emphasizes the interaction between the attributions one makes about one's own and others' performance as well as its effect on one's subsequent choices and actions (Weiner, 1985). There are two major attribu-tion paradigms. One is Kelley's model (Kelley, 1967, 1971a, 1971b); the other is introduced by Weiner et al. (1971). Kelley's model, known as Kelley's cube, not only points out possible causes for an event, namely, person, stimulus and/or situation, it also delineates which type of informational process (consensus, consistency and dis-tinctiveness) is needed to make an inference in terms of the three classes of causation. The other model proposed by Weiner et al. (1971) and further modified by multiple researchers (Abramson, Seligman & Teasdale, 1978) mainly focuses on the behavi-oural and motivational consequences of attributions rather than the process used for attribution. In particular, the degree to which a person perceives an occurrence is caused by the person's self or external environment (internal/external locus) (Weiner et al., 1971), whether or not the cause of the outcome changes over time (stabil-ity/instability) (Weiner, 1979; Weiner et al., 1971), and the degree to which the cause of the outcome is generalizable across situations (globality/specificity) (Abramson et al., 1978) are proposed to account for a specific outcome. In order to integrate the ob-server view of Kelley's model and self-attribution view of Weiner's model, Martinko and Thomson (1998) proposed a compressive attribution framework pairing Kelley's informational characteristics with Weiner's attribution dimensions. In general, attribu-tion theory has been widely discussed in the literature (Heider, 1985; Kelley, 1973; Weiner, 1985; Martinko & Thomson, 1998; Oliver, 1993; Laczniak, DeCarlo, & Ramaswami, 2001) and has also been studied in the context of e-Commerce (Harris, Mohr, & Bernhardt, 2006).

2.4 The Role of Reliance on eWOM

Electronic word of mouth (eWOM) is typically defined as positive or negative statements made by potential, actual, or former guests about a product or company available to the public via the Internet (Hennig-Thurau Gwinner,Walsh & Gremler, 2004). Online consumer reviews are the most accessible and prevalent form of eWOM (Chatterjee, 2001). Some forms of online reviews, such as opinion-platforms have established themselves as important venues for eWOM (Hennig-Thurau et al., 2004). It can be assumed that attitudes/expectations formed based on eWOM are particularly strong as it is perceived as particularly credible (Yoo & Gretzel, 2009) and constitutes a form of social validation (Shavitt & Brock, 1994). Online reviews are critical especially in the context of tourism, where personal sources are particu-larly influential (Litvin et al., 2008). Indeed, online reviews are heavily used by tou-rism consumers and have been found to have great impacts on trip decisions (Yoo & Gretzel, 2008a).

2.5 Conceptual Model

Attribution theory provides a venue to explore dimensions that lead to different levels of satisfaction. Thus, attribution theory is an important framework to account for neg-ative experiences in the tourism and hospitality field, where the quality of experiences is often out of the control of service providers. In this paper, a conceptual framework based on Martinko and Thomson (1998)'s comprehensive attribution model and the role of reliance on eWOM when forming initial opinions (Figure 1) is proposed in the context of online hotel reviews in an attempt to understand the mechanism of negative experiences resulting in satisfaction rather than dissatisfaction. The model assumes that whether negative experiences have an influence on the overall satisfaction expressed in the online review depends on whether the expectations were formed based on eWOM and how the cause of the negative experience is attributed.

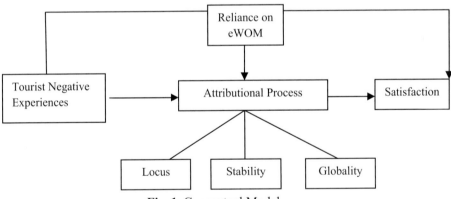

Fig. 1. Conceptual Model

Reference to eWOM means whether guests obtained information about the hotel via eWOM. The impact of eWOM reference on satisfaction can be explained by expectancy-disconfirmation mechanisms. eWOM influences consumers' purchase decision making (e.g., Senecal & Nantel, 2004) by strongly affecting consumers' product judgements (e.g., Varadarajan & Yadav, 2002). To that respect, good eWOM will create stronger positive expectations, because messages from eWOM are seen as more trustworthy than marketer information (Yoo and Gretzel, 2009). Stronger attitudes are harder to change, which means that negative experiences will likely be discredited, minimizing service quality gaps. At the same time, eWOM could lead to the discrediting of perceived negative performance based on social influence mechanisms (Shavitt & Brock, 1994). Asch's (1955) infamous conformity experiment demonstrated that individuals change their opinions if they are inconsistent with the opinions of others. Travellers might also be inclined to change their perceptions to avoid cognitive dissonance if they had very strong positive opinions established through eWOM.

Based on the literature, three dimensions of attribution, locus, stability and globality were adopted in this paper. The locus dimension refers to whether the cause of a negative occurrence can be attributed to the service provider (internal) or other parties/factors (external). The locus dimension establishes that external attribution is likely to decrease the level of dissatisfaction caused by negative experiences. For instance, if the negative experience was caused by bad weather and was not under the control of the service provider, dissatisfaction with the tourism service is less likely to occur. This process might also be influenced by refrence to eWOM in that if a strong positive opinion was formed through eWOM, attribution to external factors is more likely to happen. The stability dimension measures whether the occurrence is attributed to a one-time only incidence (accident) or something that will occur again (chronic problem). Unstable attribution will have a smaller influence on satisfaction than stable attribution. Travellers with positive eWOM in mind are more likely to think that negative events are temporary situations as those who wrote the positive eWOM did not experience them. Globality denotes whether the negative experience is attributed to a very specific, isolated factor or to the overall incapacity of the service provider. Global attribution is of course assumed to lower overall satisfaction more. We further propose that travellers who had been persuaded through eWOM are less likely to engage in global attribution.

The hypotheses can be summarized as follows:

H1: Tourists are more satisfied with the overall hotel experiences if they attribute the negative experience more to external factors than internal factors.

H2: Tourists are more satisfied with the overall hotel experiences if they attribute the negative experience more to unstable factors than stable factors.

H3: Tourists are more satisfied with the overall hotel experiences if they attribute the negative experience more to specific factors than global factors.

H4: Tourists that were influenced by positive eWOM will show greater satisfaction.

H5: Tourists that were influenced by positive eWOM tend to attribute the negative experience to external, unstable and specific factors, and thus are more satisfied with the overall hotel experience.

3 Methodology

3.1 Data Collection

In this study, online hotel reviews serve as the data source to test the proposed relationships. Online consumer reviews and ratings are an independent information resource in the context of travel (Yoo & Gretzel, 2008a). As a type of consumer-generated content (Yoo & Gretzel, 2009), they are more credible than information provided by marketers (Smith, Menon & Sivakumar, 2005) and perceived as particularly influential (Bickart & Schindler, 2001). In tourism, hotel reviews are the most prominent review category and are viewed to have the greatest impact on travel decisions (Gretzel, Yoo & Purifoy, 2007). 1037 online hotel reviews concerning hotel experiences in mainland China posted between 2004 and 2008 written by US travellers were obtained from Tripadvisor.com, which is one of the primary hotel product comment platforms (Yoo & Gretzel, 2008a). Specifically, review contents as well as the overall satisfaction ratings on Tripadvisor given by the reviewer were collected.

3.2 Data Coding

The reviews were manually coded to derive indications of attribution and reliance on eWOM as well as positive and negative sentiment of the review. The coding process involved two stages. In the first stage, locus, stability, globality, reliance on eWOM and satisfaction were coded. In particular, locus was identified as being internal when the reviewers blamed the service provider and as external if other factors (weather, other travellers, etc.) were blamed. In terms of stability, deficiencies of the hotel's room design, (in-room) amenities, facilities, business equipment, health equipment, location, transportation, and characteristics of the destination were categorized as stable as they cannot be easily changed and other items (food, service, price) as unstable. Globality was coded based on whether the negative experiences can be generalized to all possible encounters with the hotel. Dummy coding was used for the three attribution dimensions because reviews could contain mixed comments, thus leading to six variables. eWOM influence was encoded as being present if the reviewer referred to choosing the hotel based on recommendations found on Tripadvisor or other online eWOM sources. Satisfaction was captured through three variables: positive sentiment of the review, negative sentiment and the overall satisfaction rating (on a scale from 1 to 5) given by the reviewers. Positive and negative sentiment coding involved using General Inquirer, a computer assisted tool for content analysis (Stone et al., 1966) to count positive and negative words as an indicator of positive sentiment. For the sake of accuracy, all reviews were rechecked manually and the word counts which contained positive words but in fact expressed disapproval were excluded (e.g., in the sentence "The staff do their job well but are not friendly.", the word "friendly" will be not be treated as a positive count since it signifies a negative opinion). Positive and negative sentiment were expressed as the ratio of positive/negative word counts to the total number of words of the review.

During the second stage of coding, the seven dummy variables representing internal/external locus, stableness/unstableness, globality/specificity and eWOM were coded by another coder adhering to the above rules. The results were than compared to the initial coding. Intercoder-reliability was high across the variables. In those cases where differences occurred, the two coders engaged in discussions to reach agreement.

3.3 Data Analysis

To address the research question, only those reviews expressing negative experiences were included in the analysis. A total of 407 cases were retained for analysis. In this way, negative experience became a predetermined condition for the relationships between attribution dimensions, reliance on eWOM and satisfaction expressed in online hotel reviews. Separate general linear models (GLMs) were run for each of the three satisfaction variables.

4 Results

The mean of the overall satisfaction scores is 3.478 with a standard deviation of 1.228, indicating that although tourists encountered various negative events during their stay in the hotels, they tend to be satisfied with their experiences. Descriptive statistics for attributional dimensions and reliance on eWOM are presented in Table 1. Of all the 407 reviews, 141 cases (34.6%) stated they had been influenced by eWOM. In general, the negative experiences were more likely to be attributed to internal factors, but were perceived as unstable and as specific.

Table 1. Descriptive statistics

eWOM	Locus		Stability		Globality		Total
	Internal	External	Stable	Unstable	Global	Specific	
Reference to eWOM	32.4%	6.6%	23.3%	26.0%	2.5%	34.6%	34.6%
No reference to eWOM	60.2%	12.8%	41.1%	47.2%	6.1%	64.6%	65.4%
Total	92.6%	19.4%	64.4%	65.8%	8.6%	99.2%	100%

Regression analyses between positive/negative sentiment and overall satisfaction were conducted to establish whether the three variables should be treated separately. Table 2 shows that the relationship between positive/negative sentiment and satisfaction are both significant (t_1=9.131, p<.05; t_2=-10.830, p<.05). However, positive sentiment only explains 16.9% of the variation in satisfaction ratings and the Beta coefficient is not very high. Similarly, negative sentiment accounts only for 22.3% of the variation in satisfaction ratings. This further confirms a disconnect between the description of the experience and the actual overall satisfaction rating giving. Therefore, three separate models were run.

Table 2. Relationship between positive sentiment and overall satisfaction

Model	Beta	t	Sig.
1. Positive Sentiment	.156	9.131	.000
2. Negative Sentiment	-.228	-10.830	.000

Dependent variable: satisfaction
Adjusted R Squared of Model 1= .169
Adjusted R Squared of Model 2= .223

Table 3. GLM Results

Independent variables	Beta Values		
	Model with Satisfaction	Model with Positive sentiment	Model with Negative sentiment
internal locus =0	1.593	-1.400	-2.990
external locus=0	-.128	.873	-3.476*
stablity =0	.535	-1.815	-.927
unstablity=0	.505	1.379	-3.173*
globality =0	1.366*	2.367	-4.624*
specificity=0	.021	2.517	-1.693
reliance on eWOM	.062	-.450	-.079
global=0 * external=0	-.417	-1.039	3.759*
global=0 * stable=0	-.067	2.000	.628
global=0 * unstable=0	.007	.057	2.247
specific=0 * external=0	.128	-1.873	2.976
internal=0 * stable=0	-1.269	1.755	1.736
internal=0 * unstable=0	-.996	1.151	3.030
external=0 * stable=0	.426	.775	-.431
external=0 * unstable=0	.976	-.735	1.956
Intercept	1.979*	2.483*	7.693*
Adjusted R Squared	.256	.052	.109

$*p<.05$

The results of the GLM analyses are presented in Table 3. H3 regarding the influence of global attribution was supported, but only for two of the models that included satisfaction and negative sentiment as the dependent variable. That is, other conditions being equal, when guests do not attribute negative experiences to the overall incapability of hotels in providing quality services, their satisfaction with the entire experience will be higher and the negative sentiment will be lower. Interestingly, but not surprisingly, no significant influences were found for the positive sentiment model.

With respect to locus and stability significant effects were found only for the model with negative sentiment as the dependent variable. When no external attributions were present, negative sentiment was lower. Similarly, if no unstable factors were mentioned, negative sentiment was lower. This is somewhat unexpected but makes sense in that these factors probably caused a lot of negative expressions if they were present. The important result is that they did not influence satisfaction. It is also noteworthy that in the model with negative sentiment as the dependent variable, there is a significant interaction effect between global and external attributions; however, the interpretation of the relationship is difficult.

5 Conclusions

Lack of attribution of a negative experience to global factors was found to significantly increase satisfaction. However, no other significant influences on satisfaction were found. Also, while some factors my lead to less negative sentiment, the same factors do not lead to increased satisfaction. Further, there were only weak correlations between positive sentiment and satisfaction and negative sentiment and satisfaction. These findings challenge our general understandings of what should drive satisfaction ratings and question the usefulness of the ratings. This has of course enormous practical implications for hoteliers who increasingly rely on the satisfaction ratings on review platforms as performance measures. Also, satisfaction was rather high across all reviews. The fact that these reviews, although they explicitly included comments about negative experiences, were generally connected to rather positive ratings, is surprising and warrants further exploration. Conformity pressures when submitting the review if a majority of others had evaluated the experience as positive as well as self selection biases (Yoo and Gretzel, 2008b, report that online travel review writers differ significantly from non-writers) could play a role.

One limitation of the study is of course the coding of factors as either present or absent, not accounting for the extent to which they were present or absent and not encoding how many different issues were mentioned in the review. There could be thresholds for attribution theory. Also, for some issues mentioned, attribution might have been unclear. For instance, noise from the street was encoded as an external factor but could also be seen as a problem due to the hotel windows not being soundproof if no details were mentioned in the review. Another issue is that only reviews of Chinese hotels were used. Because of the 2008 Olympics and the general view of China as a developing country strongly promoted through the media, hotel guests could have been more forgiving. Thus, there is clearly a great need to shed further light on the issues addressed in this study through future research using different data.

References

Abramson, L, Y, Seligman, M, E. P., & Teasdale, J, D. (1978). Learned helplessness in humans: Critique and reformulation. *Journal of Abnormal Psychology, 87,* 49-74,

Adams, J. S. (1965). Inequity in social exchange. In L. Berkowitz (Ed.), *Advances in Experimental Social Psychology* (Vol. 2, pp. 267-299). New York: Academic Press.

Asch, S. E. (1955). Opinions and social pressure. *Scientific American, 193,* 31-35.

Bateson, J.E.G. & Hoffman, D.K. (1999) *Managing Services Marketing.* Fort Worth, Texas: Dryden Press.

Bejou, D., Edvardsson, B. & Rakowski, J.P. (1996). A critical incident approach to examining the effects of service failures on guest relationships: the case of Swedish and US airlines. *Journal of Travel Research,* 35 (1), 35-40.

Bowen, D. & Clarke, J. (2002). Reflections on tourist satisfaction research: past, present and future. *Journal of Vacation Marketing,* 8, 297–308.

Bougie, R., Pieters, R., & Zeelenberg, M. (2003). Angry guests don't come back, they get back: The experience and behavioral implications of anger and dissatisfaction in services. *Journal of the Academy of Marketing Science,* 31(4), 377-393.

Chatterjee, P. (2001). Online reviews-Do consumers use them? In M. C. Gilly, & J. Myers-Levy, (Eds.), *ACR2001 Proceedings* (pp. 129-134). Provo, UT: Association for Consumer Research.

Clemmer, E. C., & Schneider, B. (1996). Fair service. In Swartz T. A., Bowen D. E., & Brown S. W. (Eds.), *Advances in services marketing and management*, 5, pp. 213–229. Greenwich, CT: JAI Press.

Folkes, V. S. (1988). Recent attribution research in consumer behavior: A review and new directions. *Journal of Consumer Research*, 14(4), 548-565.

Gretzel, U., Yoo, K. H. & M. Purifoy (2007). Online Travel Reviews Study. College Station, TX: Laboratory for Intelligent Systems in Tourism.

Gursoy, D., McCleary K. W., & Lepsito L. R. (2007). Propensity to Complain: Affects of Personality and Behavioral Factors. *Journal of Hospitality & Tourism Research*, 31 (3), 358-386.

Gursoy, D., McCleary K. W., & Lepsito L. R. (2003). Segmenting Dissatisfied Restaurant Guests Based on Their Complaining Response Styles. *Journal of Food Service Business Research*, 6 (1), 25-44.

Harris, K. E., Mohr, L. A., & Bernhardt, K. L. (2006). Online service failure, consumer attributions and expectations. *Journal of Services Marketing*, 20(7), 453-458.

Heider, F. (1958). *The Psychology of Interpersonal Relations*. New York: Wiley.

Hennig-Thurau T.,Gwinner, K.P.,Walsh,G., & Gremler, D.D.(2004). Electronic word-of-mouth via consumer-opinion platform:what motivates consumers to articulate themselves on the internet? *Journal of Interactive Marketing*, 18(1), 38-52.

Huang, J.H., Huang, C.T. & Wu, S. (1996). National character and response to unsatisfactory hotel service. *International Journal of Hospitality Management*, 15(3), 229-243.

Kano, N., 1984. Attractive quality and must-be quality. *Hinshitsu: The Journal of the Japanese Society for Quality Control*, 14 (2), 39–48.

Kelley, H. H. (1967). Attribution theory in social psychology. In D. Levine (Ed.), *Nebraska   Symposium on Motivation* (pp. 192–238). Lincoln: University of Nebraska Press.

Kelley, H. H. (1971a). Attribution in social interaction In E Jones, D. Kanouse, H Kelley, R. Nisbett, S. Valins, &B.Weiner (Eds.). *Attribution. Percewmg the cause of behavior (^ip 1-26)* Morristown, NJ General Learning Press.

Kelley, H. H. (1971b). Attribution in social mteraction. In E. Jones, D. Kanouse, H. Kelley, R. Nisbett, S. Valins, & B. Weiner (Eds), *Atiribution: Perceiving the cause of behavior* (pp 151-174). Momstown. NJGeneral Learning Press.

Kelley, H. H. (1973). The processes of causal attribution. *American Psychologist*, 28(2), 107-128.

Kozak, M., & Rimmington M. (2000). Tourist Satisfaction with Mallorca, Spain as an Off-Season Holiday Destination. *Journal of Travel Research*, 38 (3), 260-269.

Kozak, M. (2001). A critical review of approaches to measure satisfaction with tourist destinations. In A. G. Woodside, J. A. Mazanec, J. R. Brent Ritchie, I. Geoffrey, & G. I. Crouch (Eds.), *A critical review of approaches to measure satisfaction with tourist destinations,* Vol. 2 (pp. 303–320). New York: CABI Publishing.

Laczniak, R. N., DeCarlo, T. E., & Ramaswami, S. N. (2001). Consumers' responses to negative word-of mouth communication: An attribution theory perspective. *Journal of Consumer Psychology,* 11(1), 57-73.

Litvin, S., Goldsmith, R.E., & Pan, B. (2008). Electronic word-of-mouth in hospitality and tourism management. *Tourism Management*, 29(3): 458-468.

Martinko, M. J, & Thomson, N. F. (1998). A synthesis and extension of the Weiner and Kelley attribution models. *Basic and Applied Social Psychology*, 20(4), 271-284.

McConnell, B., & Huba, J. (2007). *Citizen marketers: When people are the message.* Chicago: Kaplan.

Mey L. P., Akbar A. K., & Fie D. Y. G. (2006). Measuring service quality and guest satisfaction of the hotels in Malaysia: Malaysian, Asian and non-Asian hotel guests. *Journal of Hospitality and Tourism Management,* 13, (2), 144-160.

Mueller, R.D., Palmer, A., Mack, R. & McMullan, R.(2003). Service in the restaurant industry: an American and Irish comparison of service failures and recovery strategies. *International Journal of Hospitality Management*, 22, 395-418.

Oliver, R. L. (1980). A cognitive model of the antecedents and consequences of satisfaction decisions. *Journal of Marketing Research*, 17(4), 460-469.

Oliver, R. L. (1993). Cognitive, affective, and attribute bases of the satisfaction response. *Journal of Consumer Research*, 20: 418–430.

Oliver, R. L. (1997). *Satisfaction: A Behavioral Perspective on the Consumer*. New York: McGraw- Hill.

Oliver, R. L,. Rust, T., & Varki, S. (1997). Guest Delight: Foundations, Findings, and Managerial Insight. *Journal of Retailing*, 73 (3), 311-36.

Parasuraman, A., Zeithaml, V. A., & Berry, L.L. (1985). A conceptual model of service quality and its implications for future research. *Journal of Marketing*, 49(Fall), 41-50.

Reichel, A, Lowengart, O, & Milman, A. (2000). Rural tourism in Israel: service quality and orientation. *Tourism Management*, 21(5), 451-459.

Rodriguez del B., I., & San Martin, H. (2008). Tourist satisfaction: A cognitive-affective model. *Annals of Tourism Research*, 35(2), 551-573.

Ross, I. (1999). Switching processes in guest relationship. *Journal of Service Research*, 1 (August), 68-85.

Ryan, C., & Cessford, G. (2003). Developing a visitor satisfaction monitoring methodology: quality gaps, crowding and some results. *Current Issues in Tourism*, 6, 457–507.

Senecal, S. & Nantel, J. (2004). The influence of online product recommendations on consumers' online choices. *Journal of Retailing*, 80(2), 159-69.

Shavitt, S. & Brock, T. C. (1994). *Persuasion: Psychological Insights and Perspectives*. Englewood Cliffs, NJ: Prentice Hall.

Smith, D., Menon, S., & Sivakumar, K. (2005). Online Peer and Editorial Recommendations, Trust, and Choice in Virtual Markets. *Journal of Interactive Marketing*, 19(3): 15-37.

Swan, J. E., and Combs, L. J. (1976). Product performance and consumer satisfaction: A new concept. *Journal of Marketing*, 40(2), 25-33.

Stone, P.J., Dunphy, D. C., Smith, M.S., & Ogilvie, D. G. (1966). *The General Inquirer: A Computer Approach to Content Analysis*. Cambridge, MA: MIT Press.

Varadarajan, P.R. & Yadav, M.S. (2002). Marketing strategy and the internet: an organizing framework. *Journal of the Academy of Marketing Science*, 30(4), 296–312.

Weiner, B., Frieze, I , Kukla, A., Reed, L. Rest, S., & Rosenbaum, R. M(1971). *Perceiving the causes of success and failure*. Morristown, NJ General Learning Press.

Weiner, B. (1979). A theory of motivation for some classroom expenences. *Journal of Educational Psychology, 71,* 3-25.

Weiner, B. (1985). An attributional theory of achievement motivation and emotion. *Psychological Review, 92*(4), 548-573.

Weiner, B. (2000). Attributional thoughts about consumer behavior. *Journal of Consumer Research*, 27(December), 382-387.

Westbrook, R.A. (1987). Product/consumption-based affective responses and postpurchase processes. *Journal of Marketing Research*, 24 (August), 258-270.

Wirtz, J., Mattila, A. & Tan R. (2000). The moderating role of target-arousal on the impact of affect in satisfaction – an examination in the context of service experiences. *Journal of Retailing*, 76, 347–365.

Yu, Y.-T. & Dean, A. (2001). The contribution of emotional satisfaction to consumer loyalty, *International Journal of Service Industry Management*, 12 (3), 234-250.

Yoo, K. H. & Gretzel, U. (2008a). Use and Impact of Online Travel Reviews. In O'Connor, P., Höpken, W. & Gretzel, U. (Eds.). *Information and Communication Technologies in Tourism 2008*, 35-46. Vienna, Austria: Springer.

Yoo, K. H. & Gretzel, U. (2008b). Understanding Differences Between Online Travel Review Writers and Non-Writers. In Hara, T. (Ed.), *Proceedings of the 13th Annual Graduate Education and Student Research Conference in Hospitality and Tourism*, Orlando, FL, January 3-5, 2008, pp. 21-29.

Yoo, K. H. & Gretzel. U. (2009). Comparison of Deceptive and Truthful Travel Reviews. In Höpken, W. Gretzel, U. & Law, R. (Eds.). *Information and Communication Technologies in Tourism 2009*, 37-48. Vienna, Austria: Springer.

Yoo, K.-H., Lee, Y.-J., Gretzel, U. & Fesenmaier, D. R. (2009). Trust in Travel-Related Consumer Generated Media. In W. Höpken, U. Gretzel & R. Law (Eds.), *Information and Communication Technologies in Tourism 2009*, pp. 49-60. Vienna, Austria: Springer Verlag.

Yuksel, A., Kilinc, U.K. & Yuksel, F. (2006). Crossnational analysis of hotel guests' attitudes toward complaining and their complaining behaviors. *Tourism Management*, 27(1), 11-24.

Quantifying Brand Values Perception in Destination Websites: a Design Requirements Perspective

Tao Yang
Davide Bolchini

School of Informatics – Indianapolis / Human-Computer Interaction
Indiana University, USA
[taoyang, dbolchin]@iupui.edu

Abstract

This paper presents a framework for systematically evaluating the short-term brand values perception of content-intensive destination websites. The approach leverages state-of-the-art research methods in value-driven design and brand experience evaluation, and offers ready-to-use techniques to test the degree in which brand values are actually perceived by the target users. Finally, the proposed framework provides a way to quantify brand values perception and transform these results into readable indicators to inform requirements for site redesign.

Keywords: user experience, destination website, requirements, brand values, user profiles.

1 Introduction

According to Mich et al. (2005), a tourist destination is a "well-defined geographic area" that offers "attractions and services" serving tourists on location, and the operators there should help visitors to "take advantage of the full offering." In particular, designing a website for a tourist destination, as shown in the related research (Han & Mills, 2006; Mich et al., 2005; Morrison et al., 2005; Park & Gretzel, 2007), is a complex task that requires the consideration of many factors. The major aim of all these factors is to help promote the tourism experience introduced on the website (Park & Gretzel, 2007) and attract users to eventually visit the destination physically. In this view, besides designing a usable website, it is important to let the users know why the destination is so valuable that worth their time, energy, and money to visit. The effective communication of the destination's brand values (as related to the tourism experience) is therefore a crucial concern that informs the overall design effort (Corigliano & Baggio, 2006; Mich et al., 2005; Zach et al., 2007).

Our former research in value-based design (Bolchini et al., 2008; Bolchini et al., 2009), embraces the notion of "brand value" as the moral, ethical, social, or cultural beliefs which an entity is committed to. Unlike generic human values, such as human welfare, privacy, and trust (Friedman & Kahn, 2003), brand values tend to be entity-specific, and because of this specificity the users could memorize or build certain emotional relation with the entity. From the perspective of the managers of a destination, the capability of their website in conveying the intended brand values is the most important indicator of the quality of their online communication. Effective brand values communication is a way to attract and establish long-term relationship with the users, which could bring much benefit to them.

Although many instruments have been developed for evaluating the quality of destination websites, most of them investigate the effect of each service or function provided by the website, or devise general criteria for evaluating a website's marketing or promotional effectiveness. Not enough attention has been paid to the design of systematic approaches that can be used specifically for assessing a website's effectiveness in communicating *intended brand values*.

One approach to tackle this problem is investigating whether and how much the users could perceive the brand values. Readable yet accurate indicators are needed to quantify users' brand values perception. Evaluators can benefit from a systematic evaluation of the website brand values perception as they could judge whether the websites' communication impact has met their expectation or not, and then improve the website accordingly.

2 Related Work

According to a survey which was done by Han and Mills (2006), almost 50 different instruments have been developed for evaluating tourism websites. To generalize, there are about five trends. First, considering website as a "marketing tool," designers judge a tourism website by whether it contains the features that are necessary for online marketing, such as contact information, directions, ticket reservation, and introduction to exhibits etc. (Murphy, et al. 1996). Second, benchmarking approaches are used to set benchmarks that should be taken into account when designing or evaluating tourism websites. For instance, Schegg et al. (2002) set a five-dimension benchmark for hotel websites, which are "service processes, customer relationships, value-added services, creating trust, and cyber marketing." Third, goal-oriented evaluation approaches. The most well-known approach in this trend is the Balanced Scorecard (BSC), which provides guidelines for generating specialized evaluation criteria, which directly target to a tourism organization's business goals (Morrison et al., 2005). Fourth, some of the features are not necessities for tourism websites, such as search engine, online community, and personalization, but they could "add value" to the tourism organization if properly used. Studies were also carried out to assess the effect of these features (Nysveen et al., 2003). Last, being aware of the amount of evaluation instruments, which caused inconvenience for people to choose from them, researchers tried to condense them into one (Han & Mills, 2006; Mich et al., 2005). For example, using the grounded theory, Han and Mills integrate all the evaluation instruments into a three-dimension benchmark: "aesthetics features, informative features, and interactive features" (Han & Mills, 2006). However, none of these approaches seeks to evaluate a tourism website's communication impact.

The research on evaluating web communication impact has been for long intertwined with online branding. According to Knemeyer (2004), "brand represents the intellectual and emotional associations that people make with a company, product, or person." In the online environment, this association is usually established through using the website. However, most of the users do not bother to open web pages of mission statement or introduction to read the brand values of an entity. By contrast, their experience with the brand is just based on a short-term interaction with the website sections that they are interested in. Therefore, value-based design approaches have been proposed to integrate the intended brand values into the design elements of a website, and make sure that users have the opportunity to perceive them during the interactive experience. For example, by considering human values in the design process, Value Sensitive Design (VSD) approach helps generate design concepts that will minimize the chance to cause moral or ethical concerns (Friedman & Kahn 2003; Friedman, et al. 2006). Then, from a more structured perspective, Value Centered Design (VCD) recommends principles and the procedure to use brand values as the major driver to analyze requirements, design, and evaluate products (Cockton, 2005).

To evaluate the effectiveness of online branded communication, Ha and Perks (2005) proposed to judge the quality of online brand experience by calculating the amount of users' "positive navigations," such as subscribing to a newsletter or using the online communities, intended as an indicator which shows how much they get involved in the website. Realizing that "trust" toward a brand is a key component of online brand experience, Tsygankov (2004) suggests to check whether a website contains the design elements which can be considered as necessary for building brand trust. Müller (2006) went a step further. He used a 7 point scale from "not at all representative" to "very representative" for users to judge how much the website could represent the brand.

Although each of these evaluation approaches touches an important aspect of a website's ability to communicate a brand, none of them takes into account the brand values that a specific website intends to communicate. Moreover, it is necessary to also consider the relevance of a brand value to a certain user type. For example, the prospective employees of a tourist destination would care more about the brand values that are relevant to the workforce, such as "offering a work environment in which people can maximize their potential," but the visitors of the destination would pay little attention to this. To tackle this challenge, we leverage our former work in Value Driven Design (VDD) (Bolchini et al., 2008) to develop a new approach to systematically evaluate brand values perception (Bolchini et al., 2009).

Leveraging these results from our recent research, we propose here the following key methodological advances which can be particularly useful to the professionals' and scholarly community of web design and management in the tourism domain. First, we have framed the theoretical background of value-based design and evaluation in the relevant body of knowledge on tourism website design and evaluation. Secondly, we have remodeled and simplified the key methodological concepts to make the adoption of the technique easier and its deployment more feasible in real world web projects. In this perspective, to be of more practical support for professionals, we have extended our methodology by including user recruitment strategies, user task design, and reusable evaluation instruments. Finally, we introduce here readable visual indicators to communicate and display the brand evaluation results at the proper level of granularity for web managers and decisions makers.

3 Requirements-Driven Evaluation Framework

In a nutshell, the main contribution of our evaluation approach can be summarized as follows:

1 Providing a method for eliciting and analyzing the intended brand values of an existing website and create user evaluation instruments.

2 Providing an analytical approach to quantify brand values perception. In particular, we establish a simple formula to appraise whether a user's attitude toward a brand value is positive or negative.

3 Taking into account the relevance of a brand value to a certain user group. Recruit the most suitable users to test their perception of the brand values which are important to them.

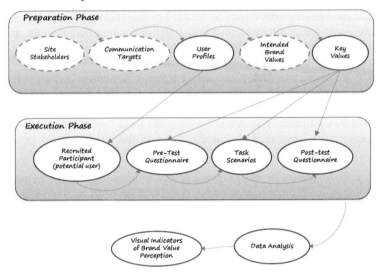

Fig. 1. A Framework for Evaluating Brand Values Perception

Our framework has two phases: a preparatory phase and an execution phase. In the preparatory phase, a model of the website's brand values communication and the related evaluation instruments (scenario-based tasks, pre-test and post-test questionnaires) are created. Then, the instruments and the model will be used for carrying out the actual user test.

After the user test, leveraging the data analysis algorithm we devised, the designers will obtain a measurement of brand value perception that takes into account the characteristics of a particular user group, the communication goal, and users' attitude. More than just a "grade" indicating good or bad, this measurement could be easily targeted back to certain design elements of the website for conducting corresponding design improvements.

From next section, we will demonstrate our evaluation approach in detail by using it to evaluate an existing cultural destination website.

4 The National Gallery of Canada Website

We will apply our evaluation approach on the National Gallery of Canada (www.gallery.ca). The National Gallery of Canada was built in 1880, one of the oldest Canadian cultural destinations. It is a "cultural" destination because it offers culture-oriented attractions and services, such as paintings and ancient sculptures. The reason we choose this specific website is that it is content-intensive: it contains nearly

70 types of content pages which are used to offer instructions for visitors to plan their visit, demonstrate key exhibits, and introduce main services. Therefore, unlike the marketing websites, for example, vehicle and fashion websites, which use large amount of videos and animations of their product, but not much written content, to attract audiences, this website integrates a considerable number of brand values in its informational and functional content, which is worth to be evaluated.

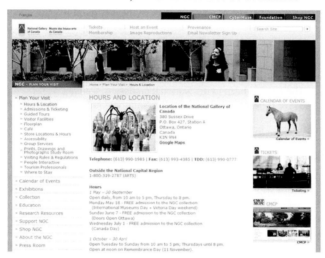

Fig. 2. The National Gallery of Canada.

Although we illustrate a specific example of application of the method, our framework applies to any cultural destination websites or, more in general, to any brand and content intensive tourism website.

5   Preparation Phase: Targets and User Profiles

As mentioned in the related work, each brand value has different relevance for different user groups. So the first step of our approach is to clearly define a user profile for the evaluation. The rule of thumb for defining a user profile is first to look at the stakeholders of the website (For the National Gallery of Canada, they could be the director of the gallery, the website designer, and the marketing representative etc.). Then, from these stakeholders we could identify their *communication targets*, which are the people to whom the brand values communication is directed (Bolchini et al., 2008). For the National Gallery of Canada, they could be first-time visitors, returning visitors, members of the gallery, schools, or even the prospective employees etc.

Second, the users' prior knowledge about the entity and the website should also be considered. The communication impact is measured by the amount of brand values that the users newly perceived during the evaluation process. However, people have different prior knowledge. The communication impact could be quite low for a person who is very familiar with the entity or its website, but relatively high for those who know nothing about them. In this case the evaluation results will not be comparable among different users. Even though, theoretically, we can recruit people with same prior knowledge, many studies have shown that prior knowledge is very difficult and time-consuming to assess (Baird & Phau, 2008; Romaniuk & Nicholls 2006). Moreover, to test the short-term communication impact, we do not want it to be influenced too much by prior knowledge. Therefore, we suggest recruiting people who have zero prior knowledge ("zero acquaintance," Han & Mills, 2006), then, the communication impact we will obtain would be purely caused by the website. Hence, a user profile named *first-time visitors* was defined for the National Gallery of Canada:

Table 1. User Profile Defined for Evaluation

First-time Visitors to the National Gallery of Canada
• Have never been to the National Gallery of Canada
• Have little knowledge about the National Gallery of Canada
• Have never used the National Gallery of Canada website
• Use the Internet more than 5 hours a week

Then, we created a *pre-test questionnaire* by transforming above criteria into questions. For example, "Have you ever been to the National Gallery of Canada?" By administering the questionnaire, ten participants were recruited for the evaluation.

6 Preparation Phase: Modeling the Brand Values Communication

To evaluate a website's capability to communicate the intended brand values, we need to know in which way these brand values are integrated into each part of the website. However, the brand values are usually not directly conveyed to the users except the web pages for mission statement or introduction. Most of the time, they are communicated implicitly in the website to the users through its services and functions. Therefore, we need to do following analysis to build a model of the brand values communication to help us fully understand the website's communication requirements.

6.1 Elicit the Communication Intentions

A cultural destination usually puts its most prominent brand values on the home page of its website by virtue of slogans or banner ads. Besides this, there is always a "mission statement" or "introduction" section that used to list and introduce its intended brand values. Therefore, from these two sources, we can elicit the brand values that are relevant to our user profile. We found from the mission statement page of the National Gallery of Canada website eight brand values it wants to communicate. However, some of them, such as "The Gallery values its workforce," have nothing to do with first-time visitors. Therefore, we selected three from them which are highly relevant. They are: Accessible, Excellence of Collections, and Engaging.

6.2 Modeling the Communication Strategy

Next, we need to further understand what strategies the current website adopts to communicate these brand values in other sections of the site, which are more prone to be used by the users. The technique we use is *key value inspection*, in which we could build a relation between brand values communication and website content units (pages or areas) by inspecting the website. For example, we found that, to support the communication of the brand value "accessible," the National Gallery of Canada website first provided a lot of guidance on the website for the users to make a comprehensive plan to visit the gallery; second, on the website, the services for disabled people are introduced; third, the gallery has a travelling exhibition program, which gives all Canadians an opportunity to see the exhibitions of the gallery without coming to Ottawa; fourth, special education programs are offered for people with special needs. These strategies are used to communicate more concrete messages to substantiate the claim of a brand value, so we call them *key values*. After the key value inspection, a brand values communication model was built (see Table 2).

Table 2. Brand Values Communication Model for the Gallery Website

Intended Brand value	Key Values with Their Location
Accessible	Plenty of guides • Plan Your Visit> Guided Tours • Plan Your Visit> Visitor Facilities
	Accessible for people with special needs • Plan Your Visit> Accessibility
	Accessible for all Canadians • Exhibitions> Touring Exhibitions
	Specified education programs for people with special needs • Education
Excellence of Collections	Reveal the past, celebrate the present, and probe the future • Exhibitions
	International • NGC Collection
	A sense of identity • NGC Collection> Canadian Art
Engaging	Planning visit to the National Gallery of Canada is a pleasure • Plan Your Visit
	Interactive • Plan Your Visit> Floor Plan
	Specified education programs for different age group • Education

This model demonstrates how and where each brand value is communicated in the website, according to which, we will create tasks and questionnaire for the evaluation.

7 Evaluation Phase: Task Scenarios & Brand Values Assessment

Two types of evaluation instruments are needed. The first one is a set of tasks. These tasks are created by writing a scenario, which is a story of using the website that naturally touches all the content units listed on the second column of Table 2. Then, the scenario is transformed into tasks. By doing them, users have the opportunity to perceive the brand values communicated. The scenario we wrote is about a visitor who wants to go for a trip in Canada, so he/she browses the website of the National

Gallery of Canada to see if it is a place worth visiting. The tasks include choose the exhibits they like and look for ticket price, parking instruction, and services provided.

Another instrument is a *post-test questionnaire* for capturing what brand values that the users have learned. It consists of two sections. The first section is used to test users' perception of each key value. The questions in this section are set by translating each key value into a meaningful statement. Users could choose from a 5-point scale from strongly disagree to strongly agree based on their attitude toward the key value. For example, the key value "international" is translated into the following statement:

| **The collections of the National Gallery of Canada are very international.** |
| Strongly Disagree   Disagree   Neutral   Agree   Strongly agree |

Then, after the users have been exposed to all these key values, we want to know whether they are strong enough to support the communication of the corresponding brand values. Hence, in the second section of the questionnaire, we incorporate each brand value into a question "Are you confident to say...?" to find out if the communication strategies that the website adopts are successful. For example, the brand value "accessible" is put into the following question:

| **Are you confident to say the National Gallery of Canada is very accessible?** |
| Not at all confident   Not very confident   Somewhat confident   Very confident   Extremely confident |

With these two instruments well prepared, we are ready to carry out the actual user test. The main steps are: firstly, explain to the users the purpose and the procedure for the evaluation; secondly, let the users carry out the scenario-based tasks (think aloud during the whole process); finally, ask them to fill out the post-test questionnaire.

8 Data Analysis: Quantifying the Brand Values Perception

8.1 Adjusting Brand Values through Reliability Analysis

After the evaluation, we firstly scored the post-test questionnaires collected from the users based on the rating scale shown in Table 3.

Table 3. Rating Scale   **Table 4.** Reliability Analysis

Section I	Section II
Strongly disagree=0	Not at all confident=.2
Disagree=1	Not very confident=.4
Neutral=2	Somewhat
Agree=3	confident=.6
Strongly agree=4	Very confident=.8
	Extremely confident=1

Brand Value	Alpha
Accessible	0.749
Excellence of Collections	0.851
Engaging	0.693

Then, before calculating the brand values perception, we need to run a reliability analysis with the key values under each brand value. This analysis is necessary in that we built the brand values communication model based on the key value inspection, supposing that these key values could collectively support the communication of the brand values. However, we need means to justify this. After the reliability analysis (see Table 4), we found that all key values work well except *interactive*, which is used to support the communication of the brand value *engaging*. It is not well correlated with the other four key values ($r = 0.071$), which means interactivity may not give visitors an engaging feeling. Therefore, we removed "interactive" from the scale and the Cronbach's Alpha is improved to 0.776. This analysis ensures the accuracy when calculating the communication impact of the brand values.

8.2 Formula of Brand Values Perception

The formula of brand values perception is developed by modeling the process how a user perceives a brand value. First, by doing the scenario-based tasks, users are directed to the content units where the key values are communicated. The percentage of how much the brand value's corresponding key values are perceived can be calculated by the total score of these key values divided by the highest possible value of this total score, which stands for an ideal condition in which users *strongly agree* with each key value. This can be represented by the following formula:

$$P(X) = \frac{SUM\,(KV_i)}{SUM\,(KV_i)_{Max}} \tag{1}$$

In the above formula, P(X) stands for the percentage of the perception of brand value X. $SUM(KV_i)$ is the total score of the corresponding key values (KV) of X, while $SUM(KV_i)_{Max}$ is the highest possible value of this total score. In addition to this, even if all the key values are completely perceived by the users (P(X) = 100%), we are not sure whether these key values are competent enough to support the communication of the brand value. Therefore, we multiply formula (1) by user's confidence level ($Conf_X$) and come up with the formula of brand values perception:

$$CI(X) = \frac{SUM\,(KV_i)}{SUM\,(KV_i)_{Max}} * Conf_X \tag{2}$$

On the left side of the formula, CI(X) stands for the communication impact of the brand value X. If the users both completely perceived all the corresponding key values and are one hundred percent confident about the messages delivered by the brand value, the communication impact is 100%. If the users are *neutral* (=2) to each key value and are only *somewhat confident* (=60%) about the brand value, the communication impact is 30%. Because both *neutral* and *somewhat confident* are on the *edge* of positive and negative attitude, we can use 30% as an *edge criterion* to judge whether the communication impact is positive or negative.

The evaluation results indicate that all the intended brand values conveyed by the National Gallery of Canada website to its *first-time visitors* have positive communication impact (> 30%) (see Fig. 3). On average, *accessible* has a communication impact of 59%, *excellence of collections* 48%, while *engaging* 66%.

9 Discussion and Design Implications

Based on the evaluation results, at least from the communication viewpoint, we could say that the National Gallery of Canada website is well designed, because all of its brand values are positively communicated to the users. However, the edge criterion 30% is only a division of positive or negative attitude. We cannot say the design is

318

good enough if the communication impact is only slightly above 30%. The stakeholders of an entity can set their own standard that they expect to achieve. If the evaluation result does not meet their expectation, they could further analyze the results for possible improvement strategies. For example, if we set our expected communication impact of each brand value as 60% (see Fig. 3), two of the brand values, *accessible* and *excellence of collections*, cannot meet this standard.

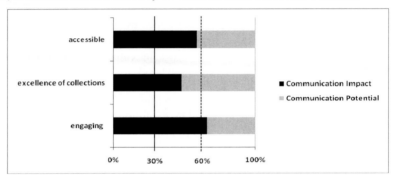

Fig. 3. Communication Impact of Each Brand Value

Firstly, we could analyze how these two brand values are communicated in the website by looking up their corresponding key values. As analyzed before, four key values are used to support the communication of *accessible*. However, the key value *accessible for all Canadians* only has an average score of 2.6 (an acceptable score should be above 3.0, which is *agree* in the Likert scale). As for *excellence of collections*, it is supported by three key values. First, besides introducing some of the key exhibitions, which are currently exhibited in the gallery, all of the former exhibitions (which could be traced back to the year 1880) and their future exhibitions are also included in the website to show that the works of art *reveal the past, celebrate the present, and probe the future*. Second, by presenting some of their foreign art works, the gallery wants to show that their collections are quite *international*. Third, the Canadian arts are introduced in more detail to try to provide Canadians with *a sense of identity* with Canada's rich visual-arts heritage. However, the last two strategies are not so effective. The key values *international* and *a sense of identity*, only have an average score of 2.4 and 2.6 respectively.

Secondly, find out the reasons why those key values are not well communicated. The key value *accessible for all Canadians* is communicated by introducing the touring exhibitions of the gallery. However, what art works will be actually exhibited in the touring exhibitions can only be found in a PDF brochure. Although the brochure is well designed, most of the users do not want to open it because it takes time to download. As for *international*, several users commented that the collections of the National Gallery of Canada were not very international because most of the collections listed on the website were Canadian arts, which is to say that the foreign exhibits listed on the website are not enough to give users an international impression. Last, most of the users encountered difficulty when trying to choose the exhibitions they like, because many of the titles of the exhibitions are very vague and the images of some of the exhibitions are missed. They cannot see why these exhibitions are so valuable that could give all Canadians *a sense of identity*.

Finally, based on the above analysis, strategies for improving the communication of these key values could be proposed accordingly. For the touring exhibitions, more details, such as the art works that are going to be exhibited and the "on-tour educational programs," which are introduced in the brochure, should be presented on the website. To enhance the international character of the gallery, the existing collections coming from all over the world should be emphasized in the design. To give Canadians a sense of identity, the strategies to present the art works on the website should be rethought. More explanatory titles, anticipatory content, photos, or even video could be used to show the special identity of the Canadian arts.

10 Conclusions, Limits and Future Work

The value-driven evaluation approach proposed in this paper provides a systematic technique to model the intended brand values of a destination website and evaluate how each brand value is effectively conveyed during a user's session with a website. The simple formulae provided to quantify brand values perception offer designers a powerful tool to judge the quality of the brand values communication and devise strategies to improve the communication of the weakly communicated brand values. Among the limits of the current study, first, we should note the limited sample size of the testing approach. We adopted a "usability-test" evaluation approach to demonstrate the data analysis and the overall method. However, as larger data samples are available, the proposed evaluation technique can be applied as well to treat these data. Having said that, we acknowledge that recruiting small sample of participants is an approach often used by usability professionals to efficiently get quick and insightful results to iteratively inform redesigns in short round of revisions.

A second limit concerns the consideration of users with zero acquaintance with the site and with the brand. We acknowledge that, in reality, users always approach a website with some kind of expectation (precise or ill-defined), which may concern the venue, the experience, the brand, the website, or all three elements combined. A refinement of the evaluation technique, which is under investigation, is the integration of pre- and post- brand perception data in the calculation of the brand perception.

Finally, we acknowledge that there at least three viable methods to characterize "user profiles" and user tasks: (1) asking stakeholders – leveraging their domain knowledge – about intended users/tasks and actual users/tasks; (2) inferring intended user profiles and intended tasks from website content; and (3) surveying actual visitors of the site. Although our approach does not prescribe the use of one specific data gathering technique, in our study we focused on the consideration of the communication "intentions" as can be efficiently inferred or hypothesized from the actual content and services offered by the website, and therefore we considered the intended user profiles and tasks. In this perspective, we used method n.2 to demonstrate some key characteristics of the target users and tasks. To capture actual users and actual tasks performed on the site (which may not correspond to the intentions of the stakeholders), interviews to site stakeholders and surveying actual visitors of the site would be ideal to triangulate the results on user profiles and tasks.

References

Baird, M. & Phau, I. (2008). A Conceptual Analysis of the Effects of Product Prototypicality on Brand Resonance in Brand Extensions. Proceedings from Australian and New Zealand Marketing Academy Conference. 1-7.

Bolchini, D., Garzotto, F. & Paolini, P. (2008). Value-Driven Design for "Infosuasive" Web Applications. Proceedings from the WWW08 Conference, Beijing, China. 745-754.

Bolchini, D., Yang, T & Garzotto, F. (2009). Evaluating the Communication Design of Branded Websites – A Value-Based Framework. Proceedings from the 27th ACM International Conference on Design of Communication (SIGDOC), Bloomington, IN. 73-80.

Cockton, G. (2005). A Development Framework for Value-Centered Design. Proceedings from CHI 2005. 1292-1295.

Corigliano, M. A. & Baggio. R. (2006). On the Significance of Tourism Website Evaluations. Proceedings from ENTER 2006: International Conference in Lausanne, Switzerland. 320-331.

Friedman, B. & Kahn, P. H. (2003). Human Values, Ethics, and Design. In J. A. Jacko and A. Sears (Eds.). The Human Computer Interaction Handbook. Lawrence Erlbaum Associates. 1177-1201.

Friedman, B., Kahn, P. & Borning, A. (2006). Value Sensitive Design and Information Systems. In Zhang, P & Galletta, D (eds.). Human-Computer Interaction and Management Information Systems: Foundations. New York. 348-372.

Ha, H. & Perks, H. (2005). Effects of Consumer Perceptions of Brand Experience on the Web: Brand Familiarity, Satisfaction and Brand Trust. Journal of Consumer Behavior. 4 (6), 438-452.

Han, J. H. & Mills, J. E. (2006). Zero Acquaintance Benchmarking at Travel Destination Websites: What is the First impression that National Tourism Organizations Try to Make? International Journal of Tourism Research. 8, 405-430.

Knemeyer, D. (2004). Brand Experience and the Web. Digital Web Magazine. Retrieved from http://www.digital-web.com/articles/brand_experience_and_the_web.

Mich, L., Franch, M. & Martini, U. (2005). A Modular Approach to Quality Evaluation of Tourist Destination Web Sites: The Quality Model Factory. Proceedings from ENTER 2005: the International Conference in Innsbruck, Austria. 555-565.

Morrison, A. M., Taylor, J. S. & Douglas, A. (2005). Website Evaluation in Tourism and Hospitality: The Art is Not Yet Stated. Journal of Travel & Tourism Marketing. 17 (2), 233-251.

Müller, B. (2006). Navigation Experience on a Brand's Website and the Consequences on Brand Image. In The Thought Leaders International Conference on Brand Management.

Murphy, J., Forrest, E., Wotring, C. & Brymer, R. (1996). Hotel Management and Marketing on the Internet. Cornell Hotel and Restaurant Administration Quarterly. 37 (3), 70-82.

Nysveen, H., Methlie, L. B. & Pedersen, P. E. (2003). Tourism Web Sites and Value-Added Services: The Gap between Customer Preferences and Web Sites' Offerings. Information Technology & Tourism. 5, 165-174.

Park, Y. A. & Gretzel, U. (2007). Success Factors for Destination Marketing Web Site: A Qualitative Meta-Analysis. Journal of Travel Research. 46 (1), 46-63.

Romaniuk, J. & Nicholls, E. (2006). Evaluating Advertising Effects on Brand Perceptions: Incorporating Prior Knowledge. Int. Journal of Market Research. 48 (2), 179-192.

Schegg, R., Steiner, T., Frey, S. & Murphy, J. (2002). Benchmarks of Web Site Design and Marketing by Swiss Hotels. Information Technology & Tourism. 5, 73-89.

Tsygankov, V. A. (2004). Evaluation of Website Trustworthiness from Customer Perspective, a Framework. Proceedings from the 6th international conference on Electronic commerce.

Zach, F., Xiang, Z. & Fesenmaier, D. R. (2007). An Assessment of Innovation in Web Marketing: Investigating American Convention and Visitors Bureaus. Proceedings from ENTER 2007: the International Conference in Ljubljana, Slovenia. 365-376.

Applying a Conceptual Framework to Analyze Online Reputation of Tourism Destinations

Alessandro Inversini[a],
Elena Marchiori[a],
Christian Dedekind[a], and
Lorenzo Cantoni[a]

[a]webatelier.net
Faculty of Communication Sciences
University of Lugano, Switzerland
(name.surname)@usi.ch

Abstract

Destination managers are investing considerable efforts (time and money) in order to market their destination online without considering that unofficial information competitors (e.g. blogs, wiki, media sharing website etc) are gaining more and more popularity among internet users. This research uses online reputation as a metric to make sense out of the huge amount of user generated contents available online applying a conceptual framework to the reputation analysis: Destination Online Reputation (DORM). The model, derived from the popular models used in corporate reputation analysis has been tested within the tourism online domain accessible trough search engine of a popular English destination: London. Results demonstrate the validity of the model in understanding and managing destination online reputation.

Keywords: web reputation, destination information competitors, web2.0, destination online reputation.

1 Introduction

Tourism has been always recognized as an information intensive domain (Gretzel et al., 2000; Buhalis, 2003). Actually, in few other business areas generation, gathering, processing, application and communication of information are as important for day-to-day operations as for the travel and tourism industry (Poon, 1993). Furthermore, the continuous development of ICT during the last decades has had profound implications for the whole tourism industry (Buhalis, 2000). Tourism can be generally understood as an experience, which needs to be communicated (Inversini and Cantoni, 2009): social media, and in general terms the so called web2.0 are enabling tourists to share information on the internet in the so called "read and write web", where the end user has become both information consumer, player (Nicholas, et al., 2007) and provider. Internet has become the primary way used by Destination Management Organizations (DMO) to communicate with prospective tourists (Buhalis, 2003); different strategies can be highlighted within the tourism domain (Choi et al., 2007), and different content providers (Inversini and Buhalis, 2009) are nowadays populating the online tourism domain (Xiang et al., 2009). Destinations such as visitlondon.com and http://us. holland.com are reacting to this proliferation of contents created by the users (UGC = user generated contents) and are incorporating UGC as part of their websites (Inversini and Buhalis, 2009). DMO and tourism managers in general, understand that ICT, if managed properly, can generate a tremendous positive value for their organizations (Lee, 2001).

On one side, destinations are providing information to prospective travellers in a factual (informative) way (Inversini et.al., forthcoming); on the other side, UGC are going more and more visibility among search engine results (Gretzel, 2006). This research was developed as a first step into a structured analysis of destination online reputation and was based on the Reputation Quotient and the RepTrak models developed by the Reputation Institute (www.reputationinstitute.com). These models are used in several studies to measure the reputation of firms and other types of organizations – e.g. countries (Passow et al., 2005).

2 Related Work

Recently Xiang, Wöber and Fesenmaier (2008) and Xiang and Gretzle (2009) described the Online Tourism Domain accessible trough search engines; within this online tourism domain (Xiang et al., 2009), it is actually possible to find official destination and attraction websites (e.g. cultural heritage attraction websites) as well as unofficial sources of information (Xiang and Gretzel, 2009) such as blogs (Thevenot, 2007), online communities, social networks, personal websites etc. Information has become available both from official and unofficial sources (Anderson, 2006). Unofficial websites are competing to reach end users presenting almost the same information as the official websites do (Inversini & Buhalis, 2009). This ever-increasing web2.0 phenomenon (O'Reilly, 2005), which enables individual users to produce so called User Generated Contents (UGC), is contributing significantly to the massive growth of information on the web.

Observing the World Wide Web, it is possible to identify two types of websites: (i) web1.0 websites: web pages of services, business etc. presenting their business, selling a product or integrating business processes (Cantoni and Di Blas, 2002), and (ii) web2.0 websites, which are defined as social websites and primarily contain UGC published by end users (Boulos and Wheelert, 2007). Web2.0 sites (also called "social media"), can be generally understood as internet-based applications that encompass "media impressions created by consumers, typically informed by relevant experience, and archived or shared online for easier access by other impressionable consumers" (Blackshaw, 2006). Social media are important as they help spread within the web the electronic Word of Mouth (Litvin, Goldsmith, & Pan, 2008) which represents "a mixture of facts and opinions, impressions and sentiments, founded and unfounded tidbits, experiences, and even rumors" (Blackshaw & Nazzaro, 2006).

Marketing managers and researchers are exploiting new ways to use social media within the online promotion activities in order to take advantage of this "electronic word-of-mouth" (Litvin, Goldsmith, & Pan, 2008). Schmallegger & Carson (2008) suggested that the strategy of using blogs as an information channel encompasses communication, promotion, product distribution, management, and research.

Other authors propose to view UGC websites as an aggregation of online feedback mechanisms, which use internet bidirectional communication to share opinions about a wide range of topics such as: products, services and events (Dellarocas, 2003), creating a network of digitized word-of-mouth (Henning-Thurau et al., 2004). The aggregation of the entire range of online representations creates the web reputation of organizations (Dellarocas, 2001 and 2005; Bolton et al., 2004). Managing the increasingly diverse range of sites and contents that build the web reputation, requires a cross-disciplinary approach, which incorporates ideas from marketing, social psychology, economics and decision making science (Malaga, 2001). Thus it is possible to argue that the construct "online reputation" can be formed within the so called Web 2.0, and can be managed by destinations (Inversini, 2009) holistically to attract more tourists.

Reputation actually is considered to be a major asset for individuals, firms, organizations and countries. The term has been defined by the Webster's Revised Unabridged Dictionary (1913) as "the estimation in which one is held; character in public opinion; the character to attribute to a person, thing or action [...]". One of the most complete definitions of reputation was presented by Solove (2007): the author explained it as a core component of the identity, defining reputation as the opinion of the public, which is formed upon the behavior and character of an individual, firm or country.

According to Fombrun, Gardberg, and Sever (1999), corporate reputation is "a collective assessment of a company's ability to provide valued outcomes to a representative group of stakeholders".Dowling (2001) complemented this definition by arguing that the sum of all the activities performed by a firm contributes to the creation of its reputation.. This information, which might come from different sources (e.g. press releases, word-of-mouth, advertisement, etc.), is the result of all behaviors, actions or activities performed by a firm. From this information each individual then, creates its own personal perception or reputation. This situation limits the ability of organizations to manage their own reputation, due to the fact that it is not possible to restrict people from making judgments (Solove, 2007).

The tourism industry, as any other service industry sells intangible products characterized mainly by being inseparable (production and consumption occurring at the same time), perishable (services cannot be stored and consumed at a later point in time) and heterogeneous (substantial differences in the services due to the human factors as production inputs) (Sirakayaa & Woodsideb, 2005). Dowling (2001) argued that firms in the services or experience industry, and tourism is one of them, should invest more in developing their image and reputation. Furthermore, the author explained that due to the inseparability and heterogeneity nature of the tourism products, customers are keener to select tourism service providers upon their reputation. So that studying tourism related online word of mouths (and more in general social media) and connecting them to the concept of reputation is a starting point to make sense out of the huge amount of contents generated online by the users working on a specific construct (i.e. online reputation).

3 Research Design

3.1 Destination Online Reputation Model

This research presents and describes the application of a conceptual framework, DORM (Destination Online Reputation Model), to analyse the User Generated Contents (UGC) around a tourism destination. Destination online reputation was recently investigated by Inversini, Cantoni and Buhalis (Forthcoming) and Inversini and Cantoni (2009) thanks to content analysis on destination related search engines results.

Within this study, researchers have set the following research objective: to test DORM framework, analyzing and measuring how the core dimensions and the reputation drivers are relate to the user generated contents of a tourism destination. DORM considers the specific characteristics of a tourism destination as a unique and complex organizational unit of the tourism industry. Researchers used the Reputation Quotient and the adapted version RepTrak (2006) presented by the Reputation Institute (RI) which are based on 23 drivers that work as predictors of reputation (Vidaver-Cohen, 2007). The drivers are grouped in 7 core dimensions: Organizational Leadership, Product & Services quality, Workplace environment, Performance, Citizenship activities, Innovation initiatives and Governance procedures.

Using these two models (RQ and RepTrak) as a base, authors were able to adapt the core dimensions and reputation drivers to the reputation of a tourist destinations considering its peculiar characteristic of the tourism industry. The framework was created and adapted thanks to an extensive literature review and it was validated through semi structured interviews with domain experts (i.e. new media, economics of tourism, brand reputation and practitioners) in order to collect the interviewees' perception on how the elements of the proposed model relate and influence the perception of reputation in regards of a tourism destination (Marchiori et al. forthcoming).

During the semi structured interviews, domain experts were asked to rank the importance of each of the 7 core dimensions featured by the model and to add any additional element perceived as having an influence upon the overall reputation of a destination and which was not previously considered. Results confirmed the 7 core dimensions and 22 reputation drivers presented in Table 1:

Table 1. DORM core dimensions, drivers and related literature

Core Dimensions	id	Drivers	Literature
Products and Services	[d1]	[D] offers quality tourism products and services	Caruana, 1997; Augustyn, 1998; Sönmez, 1998; Sproles, 1999; Vidaver-Cohen, 2007; Sönmez & Graefe, 1998; D'Amore and Anuza, 1986; European Commission, 2003.
	[d2]	[D] offers a pleasant environment.	
	[d3]	[D] features adequate infrastructure for tourists.	
	[d4]	[D] offers a safe environment	
	[d5]	[D] offers products and services that are good value for the money	
Leadership	[d17]	[D] presents accurate information of their tourism products and services.	Jamal & Getz, 1995; Heath & Wall, 1992 Getz, et al., 1998; Gretzel, et al., 2006; Pike, 2008; Ritchie & Crouch, 2003; Heath & Wall, 1992; Presenza, Sheehan, & Ritchie, 2005.
	[d18]	[D] presents an accurate image as a tourism destination.	
	[d19]	[D] uses their resources and infrastructure adequately.	
Innovation	[d6]	[D] continuously improves their tourism products and services	De Jong et al.,2003; Hjalager1997 and 2002 Jacob et al., 2003; Rindova, 2005; Radu & Vasile, 2007; Lopez et al., 2003; Rindova, 2005.
	[d7]	[D] presents innovative tourism products and services	
Performance	[d16]	[D] is a sustainable tourism destination.	Lancaster, 1966; Divisekera, 2003; Liljander & Strandvik, 1997; Oliver, 1993; Yu, et al., 2007; Yu & Dean, 2001; Bigné & Andreu, 2004.
	[d20]	[D] outperforms other competitor tourism destinations.	
	[d21]	[D] meets my expectations as a tourism destination.	
	[d22]	[D] offers a satisfying tourism experience.	
Society	[d8]	[D] encourages responsible behavior between their visitors / residents.	Tosum, 2002; Crick, 2003; Ryan, 1995 Allen et al., 2005; Carey et al., 1997; Fuchs and Weiermain, 2004; Pizam et.al., 2000; Brunt & Courtney, 1999; Russo & VanDer
	[d9]	[D] offers interesting local culture and traditions.	
	[d10]	[D] has hospitable residents.	
Environment	[d14]	[D] is responsible in the use of their environment.	Blanco, 2008; Keller, 2008; Nicolau, 2008; Tearfund, 2002; Tilt, 1997; Dodds & Joppe, 2000.
	[d15]	[D] supports ecological initiatives.	
Governance	[d11]	[D] tourism industry and organizations cooperates and interacts between them	Palmer, 1998; Manning, 1998; Beritelli, et.al 2007; Gnoth, 1997.
	[d12]	[D] tourism industry and organizations behave ethically in confront of their visitors and residents.	
	[d13]	[D] delivers tourism products and services that match their offering.	

This model was used to analyse DMOonline reputation in order to capture and analyse what actually is said in the online dialogues around a given destination.

3.2 DORM conceptual framework application

This preliminary test of DOMR was conducted thanks to an online case study; the presence of reputation drivers was assessed thanks to a content analysis. London was chosen for this preliminary research.

The online case study consisted of three main steps: (i) query selection and search activities, (ii) results classification and (iii) content analysis. Google was used as search engine for the study is the most used search engine, also in the travel sector (Hopkins, 2007; Bertolucci, 2007).

1. Query selection: 10 keywords were selected in order to perform the search on Google. Relevant tourism keywords were selected thanks to two web services given by Yahoo and Google (seggestqueries.googole.com and ff.search.yahoo.com), which suggest related user search for a given term (in this case the input term was "London"). Among 15 keywords suggested by the services, only 10 tourism related keywords have been selected for in order to perform the study: (i) london times, (ii) london weather, (iii) london eye, (iv) london underground, (v) london fog, (vi) london England, (vii) london map, (viii) london hotels, (ix) london transport, (x) london zoo. The 10 keywords were used to perform 10 different search activities on google.com (international results only) considering the first three results pages as relevant for the end user (Comescore, 2008).

2. Results classification: unique results (Table 2) obtained from Google, were firstly classified according to Inversini, Cantoni and Buhalis (forthcoming) in: (i) BMOW – "Brick and mortar" organizations' websites, including all players that are doing business also in the offline world. Most of these organizations were doing business long before the internet was developed. (ii) MOOWAI – Mere online organizations' websites and individual websites, including all individual websites – mainly blogs – and those organizations doing business (almost) exclusively online. These providers couldn't be even conceivable without the info-structure provided by the internet. (iii) not working websites. This classification elaborates the one given by Anderson (2006) and Inversini and Buhalis (2009) because of the extreme complexity of the tourism domain, where the simply difference among official and unofficial sources is not enough.

Table 2. Unique results classification

	Unique results	BMOW	NW	MOOWAY	
Google.com	463	106	0	357	
				UGC	
					95

Among the results obtained considering both organic and sponsored websites (total results: 463), the websites belonging to the MOOWAY (357 results) which contained user generated contents (UGC) were 95 (approximately 20,51%). This first result suggested that social media represented a substantial part of the online tourism domain and play an important role in shaping it (Greztel and Xiang, 2009).

3. Content analysis: The 95 websites hosting user generated contents (UGC) identified were used for a content analysis based on a reputation codebook (Inversini et al., forthcoming) and on the DORM framework. Content analysis moved from

previous studies in the field (e.g. Inversini et al., forthcoming; Inversini and Cantoni, 2009; Xiang and Gretzel, 2009). Firstly the coder was asked to classify the 95 UGC websites to the following types (Xiang and Gretzel, 2009) in order to describe the information market around the online tourism domain:

- Virtual Community (e.g. Lonely Planet, IgoUgo.com, Yahoo Travel);
- Consumer Review (e.g. Tripadvisor.com);
- Blogs and blog aggregators (e.g. personal blog, blogspot);
- Social Networks (e.g. Facebook, Myspace);
- Media Sharing (Photo/Video sharing – e.g. Flickr, YouTube);
- Other (e.g. Wikipedia, Wikitravel).

Secondly, the pages identified as UGC were examined using specific guidelines (Inversini et al., forthcoming) in order to associate the topics contained within the page to the DORM drivers.

4 Results

User Generated Contents (UGC) information market around London online tourism domain have been represented in Figure 1. Among the categories selected for the analysis, the majority of websites were classified under the category "Other", which counted 34.7% of the total results and it was represented mainly by Wikipedia pages. The rest of the UGC websites were balanced between: Consumer Review (19.7%), Media Sharing (19.7%), Blogs and blog aggregators (17.3%). Few websites were Virtual Community (8.7%) and no mentions for Social Networks and Web1.0 websites.

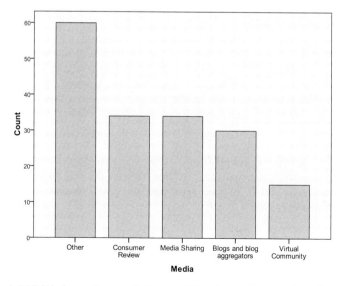

Fig. 1. UGC information market around London online tourism domain

Once the UGC websites were identified, contents from each single landing page was analyzed and associated to specific drivers. Where more than one driver was presented on the same landing page, coder was asked to classify them using (where needed) more than one driver (e.g. a blog can have a post which talk about Products and Services and a comment about Society, in that case the coder will count two items).

From 95 UGCs, the coder was not able to associate 22 search results to any drivers (approximately 12.7% of the total results). A further qualitative analysis showed that the content of these 22 search results was mainly not relevant for the tourism field (i.e. contents about people, journals, advertisements, news, websites guidelines which have London as part of the title name). Keywords which mainly gave applicable websites were: *Transport, Map, Hotels* in fact they were tourism related keywords. On the contrary, keywords as *Fog, Times* and *Underground* were the ones which mainly gave the not-applicable urls in fact they were partially tourism related keywords.

Thus from 73 remaining urls, coder found 151 drivers (approximately 2.06 drivers per landing page). Coder was also asked to define the value of the judgments expressed within the following metric:

- The item does not express any value judgment
- The item expresses a value judgment:
    - o   The item expresses positive value judgments
    - o   The item expresses positive value judgments as well as negative judgments
    - o   The item expresses more negative value judgments rather than positive ones
    - o   The item expresses negative value judgments

Table 3 below shows that the online word-of-mouth perceived London with the following reputation dimensions frequencies and argument values:

1) Products and Services dimension counted for 63.6% of the total results with an overall of positive values expressed. Nevertheless a negative mention was d3: *[D] features adequate infrastructure for tourists.* Comparing this result against the distribution of the drivers on the media, shows that this core dimension is mainly presented on Consumer Review websites, Other and Media Sharing websites.

2) Innovation dimension counted for 12.6%. The vast majority of comments were positive, nevertheless negatives mentions were for d6: *[D] continuously improves their tourism products and services*; and d7: *[D] presents innovative tourism products and services.*

3) Society dimension counted for 11.9% with both negative mentions (d8: *[D] encourages responsible behaviour between their visitors /residents*), as well as positive value judgments.

4) Leadership dimension counted for 5.3% with few positive presences. Nevertheless a negative mention was for the driver d17: *[D] presents accurate information of their tourism products and services.*

5) Environment dimension counted for 3.3% with few positive mentions as well as items without any judgment expressed.

6) Performance dimension counted for 2% with only 3 presences: two were positive and one negative for the driver d22: *[D] offers a satisfying tourism experience.*

7) Governance dimension counted for 1.3% with one positive presence.

The negative mentions counted for 10.3% of the total arguments value results and they were mainly presented on Media Sharing websites (e.g. YouTube.com), Blogs and Consumer Review websites as for example, Tripadvisor.com.

No value judgments expressed counted for 51% of the total results and they were mainly in "Other" media. Out of 77 no-value results 14 were Wikipedia pages which usually presents item description rather than judgments.

The not mentioned drivers were part of the reputation dimensions which obtained few mentioned: Environment with the missing driver d15: *[D] supports ecological initiatives*; and Governance with the missing drivers d12: *[D] tourism industry and organizations behave ethically in confront of their visitors and residents;* d13: *[D] delivers tourism products and services that match their offering.*

5 Discussions and Conclusions

DORM framework was applied to the analysis of the user generated content around London. Within this particular case, out of the 7 core dimensions analyzed within the UGC information market, only four of them can be considered as predictors of reputation: (i) Products and Services, (ii) Innovation, (iii) Society, and (iv) Leadership dimensions. In addition, the online dialogues for the given keywords about London have been observed mostly in websites which share contents (namely in Other media, Media Sharing, Consumer Reviews and Blogs), than websites which are more related (or present) user profiling characteristics such as virtual communities or social networks.

In the presented case study, DORM is able to capture and map the online dialogues (the ones which express values judgments) using only its first 4 dimensions (out of seven). The arguments which express values judgements count approximately 93% of the results. Actually, online reputation investigation with DORM can be carried out only with the first ten drivers (out of 22). Furthermore, within the "not applicable user generated contents" (the ones not relevant for the tourism domain) no suggestions to complete/increase the core dimensions and driver were found. The lacking of some drivers (and the limited item presence for Environment, Performance, and

Governance dimensions), allows to hypothesize some future works: (i) to run the research for other different destinations in order to test DORM and verify if other dimensions are missing; (ii) to use in future research a list of tourism keywords (to query search engines) in order to understand if the limited presence of some drivers are related to the query inquire or to the actual online reputation market around a destination; and (iii) to investigate the official websites in order to have a comparison between the online dialogues and the contents provided by institutional websites or by destination management organization's websites in terms of online reputation. Finally, this kind of study has some limitations. It is (i) time consuming: coder has been extensively trained to analyse and codify each landing page and to catalogue it; (ii) it is related only to one popular destination (London). Nevertheless, destinations managers who are investing time and efforts in online promotion activities, should find in DORM a structured approach to monitor the reputation dimensions of a destination.

Table 3. DORM drivers table with presence and argument values results

Core Dimensions	Drivers	UGC total items	Don't express a value	Express a value
Products and Services 96 items = 63.6%	[d1]: [D] offers quality tourism products and services	29	14	15
	[d2]: [D] offers a pleasant environment	26	17	9
	[d3]: [D] features adequate infrastructure for tourists	13	4	9
	[d4]: [D] offers a safe environment	9	6	3
	[d5]: [D] offers products and services that are good value for the money	19	12	7
Innovation 19 items = 12.6%	[d6]: [D] continuously improves their tourism products and services	3	0	3
	[d7]: [D] presents innovative tourism products and services	16	8	8
Society 18 items = 11.9%	[d8]: [D] encourages responsible behaviour between their visitors / residents	10	1	9
	[d9]: [D] offers interesting local culture and traditions	4	2	2
	[d10]: [D] has hospitable residents	4	3	1
Leadership 8 items = 5.3%	[d17]: [D] presents accurate information of their tourism products and services	1	0	1
	[d18]: [D] presents an accurate image as a tourism destination	1	1	0
	[d19]: [D] uses their resources and infrastructure adequately	6	4	2
Environment 5 items = 3.3%	[d14]: [D] is responsible in the use of their environment	2	2	0
	[d15]: [D] supports ecological initiatives	0	0	0
	[d16]: [D] is a sustainable tourism destination	3	2	1
Performance 3 items = 2%	[d20]: [D] outperforms other competitor tourism destinations	1	0	1
	[d21]: [D] meets my expectations as a tourism destination	1	0	1
	[d22]: [D] offers a satisfying tourism experience	1	0	1
Governance 2 items = 1.3%	[d11]: [D] tourism industry and organizations cooperates and interacts between them	2	1	1
	[d12]: [D] tourism industry and organizations behave ethically in confront of their visitors and residents	0	0	0
	[d13]: [D] delivers tourism products and services that match their offering	0	0	0
Total 100%		151	77	74

References

Anderson, C. (2006). *The Long Tail: Why the Future of Business is Selling Less of More.* Hyperion, NY.

Bertolucci, J. (2007). Search engine shoot-out. PC World, 25(6), 86-96.

Blackshaw, P. (2006). The consumer-generated surveillance culture. Retrieved October 13, 2008, from http://www.clickz.com/showPage.html?page=3576076.

Blackshaw, P., & Nazzaro, M. (2006). Consumer-generated media (cgm) 101: Word-of-mouth in the age of the web-fortified consumer.

Bolton,G.E., Katok,E., & Ockenfels, A. (2004). How Effective Are Electronic Reputation Mechanisms? An Experimental Investigation. *Management Science*, 50(11), 1587-1602

Boulos MN, & Wheeler S. (2007) The emerging Web 2.0 social software: an enabling suite of sociable

Buhalis, D. (2000). Marketing the competitive destination of the future, *Tourism Management.* Vol.21(1), pp.97-116.

Buhalis, D. (2003). eTourism: Information technology for strategic tourism management. Prentice Hall, Harlow.

Cantoni, L. & DiBlas, N. (2002) Teorie e Pratiche della Comunicazione, Apogeo, Milano.

Cantoni, L. & Tardini, S. (2006). Internet (Routledge Introductions to Media and Communications). Routledge, London – New York.

Choi,S., Lehto, XY., & Oleary, JT. (2007). What does the consumer want from a DMO website? A study of US and Canadian tourists perspectives. *International Journal of Tourism Research.* 9, 59-72

Comescore, (2008), comScore Releases December U.S. Search Engine Rankings, Retrieved March 2008, http://www.comscore.com/press/release.asp?press=2016

Dellarocas, C., (2005). Reputation Mechanism Design in Online Trading Environments with Pure Moral Hazard. *Information Systems Research,*16(2)

Dellarocas,C. (2003). The Digitization of Word-of-Mouth: Promise and Challenges of Online Reputation Mechanisms, *Management Science*, 49 (10), 1407-1424

Dowling, G. (2001). Creating Corporate Reputations. Identity, Image, and Performance. Oxford: Oxford University Press.

Dowling, G. (2008). Creating better corporate reputations: an Australian perpective. In Melewar, T. C. (2008) Facets of Corporate Identity, Communication and Reputation (pp. 178-196). London: Routledge.

European Commission (2003) Enterprise DG Publication: A Manual for Evaluating the Quality Performance of Tourist Destinations and Services. Luxembourg: European Commission.

Fombrun, C. J., Gardberg, N. A., & Sever, J. M. (1999). The Reputation Quotient sm: A multi-stakeholder measure of corporate reputation. *The Journal of Brand Management*, 7 (4), 241-255.

Gretzel, U. (2006). Consumer generated content - trends and implications for branding. *e-Review of Tourism Research,* 4(3), 9-11.

Gretzel, U., Fesenmaier, D., Formica, S., & O'leary, J. T. (2006). Searching for the Future: Challenges Faced by Destination Marketing Organizations. *Journal of Travel Research* . 45: 116-126.

Gretzel, U., & Yoo, K. H. (2008). Use and Impact of Online Travel Reviews, Information and Communication Technologies in Tourism 2008, Innsbruck, Springer Vienna.

Gretzel, U., Hwang, Y. H. & Fesenmaier, D. R. (2006). "A Behavioural Framework for Destination Recommendation Systems Design." In Destination Recommendation Systems: Behavioural Foundations and Applications, edited by D. R. Fesenmaier, K. Wöber, and H. Werthner. Wallingford, UK: CABI.

Gretzel, U., Yuan, Y., & Fesenmaier, D. (2000). Preparing for the New Economy: Advertising Strategies and Change in Destination Marketing Organizations. *Journal of Travel Research,* Vol. 39, No. 2, 146-156

Henning-Thurau, T., Gwinner, K.P., Walsh, G., & Gremler, D. (2004) Electronic Word of Mouth via consumer opinion platforms: what motivates consumer to articulate themselves on the Internet? *Journal of Vacation Marketing*, 18 (1), 38-52

Hjalager, A.M. (1997) Innovation Patterns in Sustainable Tourism: An analytical typology. *Tourism Management*. 18(1): 35-41.

Hopkins, H. (2008) Hitwise US travel trends: how consumer search behaviour is changing. Available from: http://www.hitwise.com/registration-page/hitwise-report-travel-trends.php

Inversini, A., & Buhalis, D. (2009) *Information Convergence in the Long Tail. The Case of Tourism Destination Information*In. In W. Hopken, U. Gretzel & R. Law (Eds.), Information and Communication Technologies in Tourism 2009 - Proceedings of the International Conference in Amsterdam, Netherland (pp. 381-392). Wien: Springer.

Inversini, A., & Cantoni, L. (2009) Cultural Destination Usability: The Case of Visit Bath. In W. Hopken, U. Gretzel & R. Law (Eds.), Information and Communication Technologies in Tourism 2009 – Proceedings of the International Conference in Amsterdam, Netherland (pp. 319-331). Wien: Springer.iProspect,

Inversini,A., Cantoni,L., & Buhalis,D. (forthcoming) Destinations Information Competition and Web Reputation. To be published in the International Journal of IT in Travel and Touirsm

Keller, P. (2002) Management of cultural change in tourism regions and communities. United Nations, UNPAN, New York.

Lee, S. (2001). Modeling the business value of information technology. *Information and Management*, 39 (3), 191-210

Litvin, S. W., Goldsmith, R. E., & Pan, B. (2008). Electronic word-of-mouth in hospitality and tourism management. *Tourism Management*, 29, 458-468.

Malaga, R. A. (2001) Web-based reputation management systems: Problems and suggested solutions. Electronic Commerce Research, 1(4).

Marchiori, E., Inversini, A., Cantoni, L., & Dedekink, C. (forthcoming). Managing Tourism Destinations Online Reputation. Submitted to 6th Thought Leaders International Conference in Brand Management.

Nicholas, D., Huntington, P., Jamali, H.J. & Dobrowolski, T. (2007) Characterizing and evaluating information seeking behavior in digital environment: spotlight on the bouncer. *Information processing and Management*, 43(4), pp 1085-1102.

O'Reilly, T. (2005) What Is Web 2.0. http://www.oreillynet.com/pub/a/oreilly/tim/news/2005/09/30/ what-is-web-20.html

Passow,T., Fehlmann,R., & Grahlow, H. (2005) Country reputation from measurement to management: The case of Liechtenstein. Corporate Reputation Review.

Poon, A. (1993) Tourism, Technology and Competitive Strategies. Wallingford, CT: CAB International, Oxford.

Presenza, A., Sheehan, L., & Ritchie, B. J. (2005) Towards A Model of the Roles and Activities of Destination Management Organizations. Journal of Hospitality, Tourism and Leisure Science.

Schmallegger, D., & Carson, D. (2008) Blogs in tourism: Changing approaches to information exchange. *Journal of Vacation Marketing,* 14(2), 99-110.

Solove, D. J. (2007) *The future of Reputation. Gossip, rumor, and privacy on the internet.* London: Yale University Press.

Thevenot, G. (2007) Blogging as Social Media. *Tourism and Hospitality Research*, Vol 7, 3 /4, pp 282-289

Vidaver-Cohen, D. (2007) Reputation Beyond the Rankings: A conceptual framework for Business School Research. *Corporate Business Review.* 10(4): 278-304.

Xiang, Z. & Gretzel, U. (Forthcoming). Role of Social Media in Online Travel Information Search. Submitted to Tourism Management.

Xiang, Z., Wöber, K., & Fesenmaier, D. R. (2008) The representation of the tourism domain in search engines. *Journal of Travel Research.* 47: 137-150

An Analysis of the Impact of Tourism Journals on Google Scholar

Rob Law

School of Hotel & Tourism Management
Hong Kong Polytechnic University
hmroblaw@polyu.edu.hk

Abstract

In spite of the increasing emphasis on the quality of publications in academia, there exists no standard list of ranked journals that is accepted by all universities and researchers. Such an absence of ranked journals is particularly true in the context of tourism, an emerging academic discipline. This study introduced a novel approach that evaluates the impact of tourism journals, which is operationalized as the average number of citations for each published article in the included tourism journals that are found by Google Scholar [GS]. Utilized the data collected from GS in three different time periods, findings showed the mostly cited journals generally matched prior studies. In particular, Tourism Management [TM] ranked first in 2009 among all included journals. In addition, the Journal of Information Technology & Tourism [JITT], which ranked fifth among all included journals, appears as the specialized journal that received the largest average citations.

Keywords: Google Scholar, Tourism Journals, Citation Counts

1 Introduction

Other than teaching and service, it is generally agreed that university faculty members need to participate in scholarly activities, in general and in particular in publications. At a time when academic research was at an early stage, publications in any refereed channels served to meet the requirements of research well, but that was then. At present, publications in quality research journals are generally required for tenure, promotion, and other major judgmental assessments (Cobanoglu & Moreo, 2004; McKercher, Law, & Lam, 2006; Sheldon and Collison, 1990). In a recently conducted global survey, Law and Chon (2007) found university program heads in tourism and hospitality perceived publications in first-tier research journals the most important among all items in a list of 31-item research-related activities. Yet, the existing tourism literature has no published articles that clearly indicate the tiers or categories of existing research journals.

In view of the importance of publication in research journals, prior studies have largely investigated quality of journals in tourism and hospitality (Ferreira, DeFranco, & Rappole, 1998; McKercher et al. 2006), as well as in main stream business disciplines (Barman, Tersine, & Buckley, 1991; Linton & Thongpapanl, 2004). These prior studies made attempts to evaluate (or rank) research journals in specific disciplines according to different evaluation criteria, and with a similar aim of gauging comparative (or relative) quality of the available journals in a comprehensible way.

Generally speaking, prior studies on journal evaluation fall into two major categories of peer assessment and numeric counting (Law & van der Veen, 2008). While studies in each of these categories both have merits and limitations, there does not seem to have a commonly agreeable approach for journal evaluation. Scholars do, however, agree with the importance that journal publications should have an impact on knowledge development (Schmidgall, Woods, & Hardigree, 2007; Xiao & Smith, 2008). Taking this into consideration, this research presents a study that used GS, a free online searching tool for scholarly publications, to find the impact of tourism and hospitality journals. In this paper, the impact of a journal is operationalized as the average number of citations for each published article based on the results of GS search. Findings of this novel approach would be of interest to academic researchers and funding authorities to determine the influence (or impact) of different tourism and hospitality journals. Different researchers have argued that the impact of a journal, and thus its published articles, is directly related to the quality of the journal (Murphy & Law, 2008; Schmidgall et al., 2007).

2 Literature Review

As previously stated, the increasing demand for academic research and publications necessitate the need to evaluate the quality of research journals. As such, researchers have conducted different studies in two broad categories of peer assessment and objective numeric counting.

In a peer assessment evaluation, the quality of research journals is usually measured by questionnaires with Likert-point scales. Examples of some recently conducted surveys included tourism journals (Frechtling, 2004) and accounting journals (Herron & Hall, 2005). Although peer assessment methods have the advantages of collective opinion, the approach suffers from limited sample size and personal bias. In another study, McKercher et al. (2006) carried out a global survey on quality of 70 journals in tourism and hospitality. Findings were then listed according to the composite score which was computed by perceived quality and percentage of awareness. Apparently, McKercher et al.'s (2006) study was the largest in terms of sample size. Ranking journals based on awareness benefits generic journals that have a wide audience but penalize specialized journals which have a focused scope. It is, therefore, necessary to develop more objective methods of evaluation.

Using some numeric numbers as the proxy for journal quality, objective numeric counting is another main stream of journal evaluations. Ryan (2005) stated that journals can be ranked by measuring the number of online hits or downloads. However, downloading an article does not necessarily mean the downloaded article is read. More importantly, an article can virtually be downloaded for numerous times in an automated way. In another study, Polonsky, Jones, and Kearsley (1999) used university library holdings to rank marketing journals. The method, albeit unique, is strongly biased against those journals with a high price tag.

Another proxy for quality of a journal relates to the number of citations its published articles received. Researchers have advocated that higher quality articles are cited more frequently than lower quality ones (Schmidgall et al., 2007; Vastag & Montabon, 2002). Jamel, Smith, and Watson (2008), however, cautioned that the number of citations may have little, if any, evidence of a publication's scholarly value. Still, citations are widely used at present as a measurement for journal quality. The world's most widely used Thomson Scientific ISI Impact Factor (IF) is basically the ratio of the number of citations received and the number of citable articles in a specific period of time. The major limitation for using IF to evaluate tourism journals is that only a small percentage of the existing tourism journals is ISI listed.

As a freely available online search tool for scholarly publications, GS has attracted the interest of researchers for its wide coverage of publications in various formats and from different types of repositories (Neuhaus, Neuhaus, & Asher, 2088; Meier & Conkling; 2008; Xiao & Smith, 2008). In particular, Neuhaus et al. (2008) stated that GS has been used by most university libraries. Meier and Conkling (2008) further found nearly 90% of publications in the engineering literature can be retrieved by GS in 2007. In any study, Walters (2007) claimed that GS indexes the greatest number of articles (93%) and the most uniform publisher and data coverage among eight selected databases. Findings from these prior studies strongly hint the advantage for using GS as an online tool for searching scholarly publications.

A database search showed two published articles have used GS to rate tourism and hospitality journals in the existing literature. Specifically, Law and van der Veen (2008) examined the citation counts of eight hospitality journals. A major limitation of that study was primarily the exclusion of tourism journals. In another study, Murphy and Law (2008) presented the GS visibility, which was measured as the total number of citations, for 50 tourism journals. Although this study included more journals than Law and van der Veen's (2008) work, ranking journals based on total number of citations is favorable to the older journals and those journals that published many papers. This is in accordance to what Joseph and Hoey (1999) had argued. As such, a more objective counting using GS would be desirable.

3   Methodology

In this study, the total number of articles in each of the included tourism and hospitality journals that were published since 2000 till the data collection period, together with the total number of citations in the same time period, were retrieved using GS. The year 2000 was chosen as the benchmark owning to the rapid growth of the worldwide tourism and hospitality industries. The impact of a journal was then computed as the average number of citations per published article in that time period. Although the computational complexity may not be sophisticated, the approach is novel and more objective than prior studies in the field.

While it is good to include all tourism and hospitality journals in the analysis, there does not exist a list of all existing journals in tourism and hospitality. Apparently, the list of 59 journals in tourism and hospitality provided by Arendt, Ravichandran, and Brown (2007) appeared as the most comprehensive and updated one. This study thus used all but three of these 59 journals. Three journals were excluded in this study. In particular, Tourism in Marine Environments and Journal of Leisure Research were excluded because they are not directly related to tourism and hospitality. In addition, European Journal of Tourism Research was not included due to its short history (the first issue was published in 2008). Data collection was conducted using Google Scholar (http://scholar.google.com) in three time periods in May 2008, June 2009, and August 2009.

4 Findings and Discussion

Tables 1, 2, and 3 present the findings of the organized data in three data collection periods. In each of these tables, the third column shows the total number of citations for a journal, the fourth column is for the total number of papers found on GS, and the last column is the average number of citations per paper which is numerically derived from the corresponding numbers in the previous two columns.

According to findings derived from the data collected in May 2008 (i.e. Table 1), Annals of Tourism Research [ATR] ranked first, followed by TM, and Journal of Travel Research [JTR]. This matches findings of prior studies in which these three journals were often rated/ranked on top of tourism journals (McKercher et al., 2006, Murphy & Law, 2008). Interesting enough, Tourist Studies [TS], which ranked 43rd in Murphy and Law's (2008) study and 23rd in McKercher et al.'s (2006) study, appears as the fourth one in Table 1. Moreover, JITT, a specialized journal, which was at the 47th position in Murphy and Law's (2008) study and at the 19th position in McKercher et al. (2006) study, ranks eighth in this study.

Table 1. Citation Ranking of Tourism and Hospitality Journals - May 2008

Journal	C	P	CpP
Annals of Tourism Research	5378	651	8.26
Tourism Management	5889	799	7.37
Journal of Travel Research	2731	419	6.52
Tourist Studies	510	102	5.00
Cornell Hotel & Restaurant Administration Quarterly	1692	353	4.79
Journal of Vacation Marketing	1056	257	4.11
Journal of Sustainable Tourism	1084	278	3.90
Information Technology & Tourism	427	112	3.81
Event Management	309	91	3.40
Journal of Hospitality, Leisure, Sport & Tourism Education	112	33	3.39

Journal of Travel & Tourism Research	19	6	3.17
International Journal of Hospitality Management	1118	362	3.09
Tourism Geographies	700	239	2.93
Current Issues in Tourism	537	191	2.81
International Journal of Contemporary Hospitality Management	1199	430	2.79
Tourism Economics	675	259	2.61
Tourism Recreation Research	399	159	2.51
Tourism Today	15	6	2.50
Journal of Hospitality & Tourism Research	529	236	2.24
International Journal of Tourism Research	817	380	2.15
Information Technology in Hospitality	2	1	2.00
Journal of Ecotourism	186	94	1.98
Journal of Hospitality & Tourism Management	84	46	1.83
Tourism & Hospitality Research	326	179	1.82
UNLV Gaming Research & Review Journal	50	29	1.72
Tourism Review	69	42	1.64
Journal of Travel & Tourism Marketing	473	293	1.61
Tourism Analysis	348	216	1.61
Tourism in Marine Environments	8	5	1.60
Journal of Sport Tourism	63	42	1.50
Journal of Hospitality Financial Management	3	2	1.50
Journal of Hospitality & Tourism Education	118	82	1.44
Tourism Culture & Communication	98	69	1.42
Journal of Hospitality & Leisure Marketing	258	190	1.36
Scandinavian Journal of Hospitality & Tourism	164	122	1.34
Journal of Tourism & Cultural Change	67	54	1.24
International Journal of Hospitality & Tourism Administration	122	117	1.04
China Tourism Research	1	1	1.00
FIU Hospitality Review	25	28	0.89
Anatolia: An Int. J. of Tourism and Hospitality Research	80	107	0.75
Asia Pacific Journal of Tourism Research	148	211	0.70
Tourism & Hospitality: Planning and Development	46	67	0.69
Journal of Quality Assurance in Hospitality & Tourism	53	83	0.64
Tourism Review International	71	121	0.59
ASEAN Journal on Hospitality & Tourism	16	37	0.43
Journal of Teaching in Travel & Tourism	59	141	0.42
Journal of Foodservice Business Research	54	166	0.33
Journal of Human Resources in Hospitality & Tourism	20	80	0.25

Journal of Convention & Event Tourism	11	48	0.23
Acta Turistica	7	36	0.19
Journal of Foodservice	9	54	0.17
Journal of Heritage Tourism	3	19	0.16
Tourism: An International Interdisciplinary Journal	1	9	0.11
International Travel Law Journal	0	105	0.00
Journal of Hospitality, Tourism, Leisure Science	0	0	0.00
Consortium Journal of Hospitality & Tourism Management	0	0	0.00

Remarks: **C** = No. of Citations, **P** = No. of Papers, **CpP** = No. of Citations per Paper

Table 2 shows the findings based on the data collected in June 2009. In general, most journals had attained a higher level of citations per published article as compared to the findings in Table 1. However, the first three journals have changed their positions in the order of TM, JTR, and ATR. While there is no change in the fourth ranked journal, JITT is at the fifth position in Table 2. In addition, when the data collection was repeated in August 2009, findings are presented in Table 3, which broadly follow that in Table 2.

Table 2. Citation Ranking of Tourism and Hospitality Journals - June 2009

Journal	C	P	CpP
Tourism Management	14573	1287	11.32
Journal of Travel Research	6648	633	10.50
Annals of Tourism Research	11375	1143	9.95
Tourist Studies	1059	145	7.30
Information Technology & Tourism	989	139	7.12
Journal of Sustainable Tourism	2841	405	7.01
Journal of Vacation Marketing	2228	323	6.90
Cornell Hotel & Restaurant Administration Quarterly	3120	507	6.15
Event Management	806	151	5.34
Tourism Geographies	1592	299	5.32
Current Issues in Tourism	1544	301	5.13
International Journal of Contemporary Hospitality Management	1918	388	4.94
UNLV Gaming Research & Review Journal	151	31	4.87
International Journal of Hospitality Management	2445	534	4.58
Journal of Hospitality, Leisure, Sport & Tourism Education	259	57	4.54
Journal of Hospitality & Tourism Research	1221	274	4.46
Journal of Travel & Tourism Research	29	7	4.14
International Journal of Tourism Research	2383	580	4.11

Tourism Economics	1548	386	4.01
Journal of Ecotourism	560	140	4.00
Tourism Today	34	10	3.40
Journal of Travel & Tourism Marketing	1934	588	3.29
Tourism Culture & Communication	44	14	3.14
Tourism Recreation Research	813	265	3.07
Scandinavian Journal of Hospitality & Tourism	460	152	3.03
Journal of Foodservice Management & Education	9	3	3.00
Journal of Hospitality & Tourism Management	259	91	2.85
Tourism and Hospitality Research	691	258	2.68
Journal of Hospitality Financial Management	7	3	2.33
Journal of Hospitality & Leisure Marketing	112	50	2.24
International Journal of Hospitality & Tourism Administration	467	209	2.23
ASEAN Journal on Hospitality & Tourism	15	7	2.14
Anatolia: An Int. J. of Tourism and Hospitality Research	48	23	2.09
Tourism & Hospitality: Planning and Development	182	89	2.04
Tourism Analysis	609	312	1.95
Journal of Hospitality & Tourism Education	210	114	1.84
Journal of Tourism & Cultural Change	150	82	1.83
Tourism: An International Interdisciplinary Journal	28	18	1.56
Tourism Review International	221	179	1.23
Journal of Quality Assurance in Hospitality & Tourism	222	181	1.23
Tourism Review	257	236	1.09
Journal of Convention & Event Tourism	87	88	0.99
Asia Pacific Journal of Tourism Research	265	274	0.97
Journal of Foodservice	91	107	0.85
FIU Hospitality Review	67	79	0.85
Journal of Teaching in Travel & Tourism	156	205	0.76
Journal of Heritage Tourism	46	61	0.75
Journal of Foodservice Business Research	151	208	0.73
Journal of Human Resources in Hospitality and Tourism	73	127	0.57
Information Technology in Hospitality	13	24	0.54
China Tourism Research	22	42	0.52
Journal of Sport Tourism	15	29	0.52
Acta Turistica	27	80	0.34
International Travel Law Journal	2	116	0.02
Consortium Journal of Hospitality & Tourism Management	0	0	0.00
Journal of Hospitality, Tourism, Leisure Science	0	0	0

Table 3. Citation Ranking of Tourism and Hospitality Journals - August 2009

Journal	C	P	CpP
Tourism Management	15272	1337	11.42
Journal of Travel Research	6830	632	10.81
Annals of Tourism Research	12502	1191	10.50
Tourist Studies	1090	146	7.47
Information Technology & Tourism	1028	139	7.40
Journal of Sustainable Tourism	2962	406	7.30
Journal of Vacation Marketing	2281	325	7.02
Cornell Hotel & Restaurant Administration Quarterly	3341	508	6.58
Tourism Geographies	1836	307	5.98
Event Management	831	151	5.50
Current Issues in Tourism	1594	308	5.18
International Journal of Contemporary Hospitality Management	1998	394	5.07
UNLV Gaming Research & Review Journal	155	31	5.00
Journal of Hospitality, Leisure, Sport & Tourism Education	273	55	4.96
International Journal of Hospitality Management	2537	539	4.71
Journal of Hospitality & Tourism Research	1289	284	4.54
International Journal of Tourism Research	2448	581	4.21
Journal of Ecotourism	582	140	4.16
Tourism Economics	1570	386	4.07
Journal of Travel & Tourism Research	31	8	3.88
Tourism Culture & Communication	63	17	3.71
Journal of Travel & Tourism Marketing	2075	591	3.51
Tourism Recreation Research	890	257	3.46
Tourism Today	34	10	3.40
Journal of Hospitality & Leisure Marketing	104	31	3.35
Scandinavian Journal of Hospitality & Tourism	473	152	3.11
Journal of Foodservice Management & Education	9	3	3.00
Journal of Hospitality & Tourism Management	264	91	2.90
Tourism & Hospitality Research	770	283	2.72
ASEAN Journal on Hospitality & Tourism	16	7	2.29
International Journal of Hospitality & Tourism Administration	474	208	2.28
Tourism & Hospitality: Planning and Development	188	89	2.11
Journal of Tourism & Cultural Change	173	82	2.11
Anatolia: An Int. J. of Tourism and Hospitality Research	48	23	2.09

Journal of Hospitality Financial Management	12	6	2.00
Tourism: An International Interdisciplinary Journal	46	23	2.00
Tourism Analysis	617	313	1.97
Journal of Hospitality & Tourism Education	212	114	1.86
Asia Pacific Journal of Tourism Research	392	275	1.43
Tourism Review International	230	179	1.28
Journal of Quality Assurance in Hospitality & Tourism	227	181	1.25
Information Technology in Hospitality	15	12	1.25
Journal of Convention & Event Tourism	103	94	1.10
Tourism Review	257	240	1.07
FIU Hospitality Review	67	79	0.85
Journal of Foodservice	98	119	0.82
Journal of Teaching in Travel & Tourism	165	205	0.80
Journal of Foodservice Business Research	161	209	0.77
Journal of Heritage Tourism	46	61	0.75
Journal of Human Resources in Hospitality & Tourism	76	127	0.60
China Tourism Research	22	42	0.52
Acta Turistica	32	75	0.43
Journal of Sport Tourism	12	29	0.41
International Travel Law Journal	3	116	0.02
Consortium Journal of Hospitality & Tourism Management	0	0	0.00
Journal of Hospitality, Tourism, Leisure Science	0	0	0.00

As a whole, findings of this study by and large follow prior studies on ranking tourism and hospitality journals. This is especially true for the big three (ATR, TM, and JTR). What differs this study from prior research is the ranking of TS and JITT. In particular, as a specialized journal, JITT moves up from relatively low positions in lists of findings in prior studies to the fifth position based on the findings in 2009. Due to the specialty nature of the journal, JITT imposes limitations to the type of articles that it publishes. In most cases, researchers are likely to submit their manuscripts to generic journals to ensure wide dissemination. As such, it is not appropriate to directly compare citations of published articles in JITT and the big three tourism journals. While using a more objective approach to evaluate the impact, which is measured by the average number of citations per paper, findings of this research show specialized journals such as JITT do have a significant impact on the research community. A possible reason for the high ranking of JITT could be due to the prevalence of information and communication technologies in tourism.

5 Conclusions

At present, universities in different countries and regions have been, and likely will be, adopting different lists of threshold journals for evaluation purpose. In most cases, these lists of threshold journals are kept for internal use. More importantly, the scientific methods for compiling such journal lists are often unknown, leading to the problem of lack of transparency. Findings of this study are likely to positively contribute to better understand the quality of tourism journals.

It should be mentioned that some journals have changed their names during the data collection period. Examples of these journals include Cornell Hotel & Restaurant Administration Quarterly, Journal of Hospitality & Leisure Marketing, and China Tourism Research. Such changes in journal names should not be a major concern as this study examined the citations per retrieved article. Also, most retrieved articles were published in the journals with the old names.

The study, however, does have some limitations which deserve future research efforts. First, some newly launched journals were not included, which should be incorporated into a future study. As well, this study counts the total number of citations but the channel and quality of citations (i.e. from journals, books, conference proceedings, or trade magazines) were not analyzed. Another limitation of this study is the inclusion of self-citation, which should be excluded in a more accurate way of evaluation to be developed in the future. Also, citation rates are measured by numbers that may not necessarily be related to quality of papers. Lastly, it is unknown if other online tools such as Scopus or JCR return similar findings. Future studies can, and should, take into account of these limitations. After all, with the careful interpretation of findings, this study should be useful to academic researchers and university leaders to better understand the impact of different journals in tourism and hospitality.

Acknowledgement

The author would like to thank Cowoo Chen for data collection and organization. This study was partly supported by a research grant funded by the Hong Kong Polytechnic University.

References

Arendt, S.W., Ravichandran, S., & Brown, E. (2007). Hospitality and Tourism Journal Matrix. *Journal of Hospitality & Tourism Education,* 19(2), 44-50.

Barman, S., Tersine, R.J. & Buckley, M.R. (1991) An empirical assessment of the perceived relevance and quality of POM-related journals by academicians. *Journal of Operations Management*, 10(2), 194-212.

Cobanoglu, C. & Moreo, P.J. (2004). Hospitality Research: Educators' Perceptions. *Journal of Hospitality & Tourism Education,* 16(2), 9-20.

Ferreira, R.R., DeFranco, A.L., & Rappole, C.L. (1998). Hospitality Program Directors' Rating on Hospitality Journals. *Journal of Hospitality & Tourism Education,* 10(1), 46-52.

Frechtling, D.C. (2004). Assessment of Tourism/Hospitality Journals' Role in Knowledge Transfer: An Exploratory Study. *Journal of Travel Research*, 43, 100-107.

Herron, T.L. & Hall, T.W. (2005). Faculty perceptions of journals: quality and publishing feasibility. *Journal of Accounting Education*, 22, 175-210.

Jamal, T., Smith, B., & Watson, E. (2008). Ranking, rating and scoring of tourism journals: Interdisciplinary challenges and innovations. *Tourism Management*, 29, 66-78.

Joseph, K.S. & Hoey, J. (1999). *CMAJ*'s impact factor: room for recalculation. *Canadian Medical Association Journal*, 161(8), 977-978.

Law, R. & Chon, K. (2007). Evaluating Research Performance in Tourism and Hospitality: The Perspective of University Program Heads. *Tourism Management*. 28(5), 1203-1211.

Law, R. & van der Veen, R. (2008). The Popularity of Prestigious Hospitality Journals: A Google Scholar Approach. *International Journal of Contemporary Hospitality Management*, 20(2), 113-125.

Linton, J.D. & Thongpapanl, N. (2004). Perspective: ranking the technology innovation management journals. *Journal of Product Innovation Management*, 21(2), 123-139.

Meier, J.J. & Conkling, T.W. (2008). Google Scholar's Coverage of the Engineering Literature: An Empirical Study. *The Journal of Academic Librarianship*, 34(3), 196-201.

McKercher, B. (2008) A citation analysis of tourism scholars. *Tourism Management*, 29(6), 1226-1232.

McKercher, B., Law, R., & Lam, T. (2006). Rating Tourism and Hospitality Journals. *Tourism Management*. 27(6), 1235-1252.

Murphy, J. & Law, R. (2008). Google Scholar Visibility and Tourism Journals. *Annals of Tourism Research*. 35(4), 1074-1082.

Neuhaus, C., Neuhaus, E., & Asher, A. (2008). Google Scholar Goes to School: The Presence of Goofle Scholar on College and University Web Sites. *Journal of Academic Librarianship*, 34(1), 39-51.

Polonsky, M.J., Jones, G., & Kearsley, M.J. (1999). Accessibility: An Alternative Method of Ranking Marketing Journals. *Journal of Marketing Education*, 21(3), 181-193.

Ryan, C. (2005). The ranking and rating of academics and journals in tourism research. *Tourism Management*. 26(5), 657-662.

Schmidgall, R., Woods, R.H., & Hardigree, C. (2007). Hospitality's most influential scholars: fifteen years of citation analysis. *Journal of Hospitality & Tourism Education*, 19(2), 32-41.

Sheldon, P.J. & Collison, F.M. (1990). Faculty Review Criteria in Tourism and Hospitality. *Annals of Tourism Research*, 17, 556-567.

Walters, H. (2007). Google Scholar coverage of a multidisciplinary field. *Information Processing & Management*, 43(4), 1121-1132.

Vastag, G. & Montabon, F. (2002). Journal characteristics, ranking and social acculturation in operations management. *Omega*, 30(2), 109-126.

Xiao, H.& Smith, S.L.J. (2008). KNOWLEDGE IMPACT: An Appraisal of Tourism Scholarship. *Annals of Tourism Research*, 35(1), 62-83.

Which Overseas Destinations do Chinese Travelers Like to Visit?

Crystal Ip,
ShanShan Qi,
Rosanna Leung, and
Rob Law

School of Hotel and Tourism Management
The Hong Kong Polytechnic University, Hong Kong
{hmcrystal.ip, shan.qi, rosanna.leung, hmroblaw}@polyu.edu.hk

Abstract

While outbound tourism and Internet applications in Mainland China (hereafter known as China) have developed rapidly, understanding the preferred destinations of Chinese travelers is thus crucial. This research investigates the travel preferences of Chinese online travelers by collecting data from Ctrip.com, one of the largest travel websites in China. Research findings show that Australia and Nepal are the most favorable overseas destinations as revealed by Chinese Internet travelers. This research is expected to arouse the influence and impact of electronic Word-of-mouth (eWOM) in Chinese online population.

Keywords: China outbound tourism, Chinese online users, eWOM, travel preferences

1 Introduction

In 1978, the national reform and the open-door policy were introduced in China, during then the Chinese government started to recognize tourism as a generator for economic development and modernization needs (Keating & Kriz, 2008; Lim & Wang, 2008). Along with the increase in disposal income and improvement in living standard among most Chinese citizens, there is a dramatic growth in the Chinese outbound travel as more people are able to pay for the luxury of travel experience. As estimated by the United Nations World Tourism Organization (UNWTO), China will be the fourth largest international tourism market in the world by 2020, corresponding to 6.4% of market share worldwide, and nearly 100 million outbound travelers will be represented by Chinese residents (UNWTO, 2000). This reflected that China has become an important international tourist source-generating market. At the same time, the size of the Chinese Internet users' market is blooming. There were almost 298 million Internet users in 2008 in China, exceeding the United Stated and Japan (227 million and 94 million Internet users, respectively) (Internet World Stats, 2009). According to China Internet Network Information Centre (CNNIC, 2009), Chinese online consumers often use the Internet to read news (78.5%), to communicate (75.3%) and to search for information including travel-related information (68%). These statistics implied that the Internet is being an information source for Chinese travelers as they would like to use the Net to seek for destination information.

With the rapid development of Internet application, the Internet is becoming a new medium for Chinese travelers to seek and share travel information. Ctrip.com, a leading travel website in China, is one of the top popular websites which China needs (Ye, Law & Gu, 2009). It is a free travel community that gathers travel information, allows members to post travel opinions and engage in interactive travel forums. The website is an example of consumer generated media that provides all travel-related information. Although there is an enormous potential of outbound tourism in China, tourism researchers have argued that relatively little research has been conducted into the travel preferences and attitudes of Chinese travelers (Heung, 2000; Kim, Guo & Agrusa, 2005; Mok & DeFranco, 1999; Qu & Li, 1997; Zhang & Chow, 2004). Using the data collected from Ctrip.com, this study makes an initial attempt to investigate the travel preference of Chinese online travelers. Findings are expected to make a meaningful contribution to know where the favorite destinations of Chinese travelers are. Travel agents, government tourism offices and destination management offices would then use the information to attract travelers from this potentially huge market by providing suitable travel-related products and services.

2 Literature Review

In 1983, the Chinese government has managed and regulated some restrictions on the outbound tourism market by introducing Approved Destination Status (ADS) system needs (National Tourism Administration of the People's Republic of China (CNTA), 2009). ADS is based on a bilateral government agreement between China and overseas destinations by the means of which the Chinese residents are permitted to travel to selected countries or regions by joining tour packages from assigned Chinese local travel agencies (ChinaContact, 2009). The ADS agreement is aimed to control the travel balance account and organize local travel agencies and international tour operators in order to secure the standard of travel services to Chinese travelers (ChinaContact, 2009).

Additionally, another breakthrough in outbound tourism appeared in 1997 when the Chinese government had granted the ADS system to Australia and New Zealand, which was carried out in 1999 (CNTA, 2009). Since then, Chinese residents could travel outside Asia for personal and leisure purposes. The number of ADS countries/regions is continually increasing. By the end of September 2008, 96 countries/regions signed the ADS agreements with China, including the United States and Taiwan (ChinaContact, 2009). Since the passport restriction policy is reduced and the number of destination choices increased, Chinese outbound tourism has boosted since 1998 (as illustrated in Table 1). This phenomenon has thus drawn worldwide attention. Countries are now paying a lot of attention to this rapidly emerging market with almost one fifth of the world's population.

Apart from the rapid growth in the number of Chinese outbound tourists, the number of Chinese Internet users has skyrocketed as well. Now, Chinese online population has become the main force in the world with the highest number of Internet users (Internet World Stats, 2009). With the advancements of Internet technologies, increasing numbers of Chinese travelers are using the Internet to seek destination information and to purchase travel products online. According to CNNIC (2009), around 68% of Chinese users have used the Internet for information seeking on destinations, prices or schedules. More importantly, 46% of them have performed online transactions and 5% have made travel reservations online. The Internet has encountered revolutionary changes as it has now become a new communication platform that allows consumers and providers for information sharing, including from business-to-consumer, and from consumer-to-consumer (Litvin, Goldsmith & Pan, 2008). Within these contexts, the concept of electronic word-of-mouth (eWOM) is examined.

Table 1. Number of Chinese Outbound Tourists (1993-2008)

Year	Number of Outbound Tourists	Growth Rate (%)
1993	3,740,000	27.70
1994	3,733,600	-0.17
1995	4,520,500	21.08
1996	5,060,700	11.95
1997	5,323,900	5.20
1998	8,425,600	58.26
1999	9,231,600	9.57
2000	10,468,600	13.40
2001	12,133,100	15.90
2002	16,602,300	39.83
2003	20,220,000	21.80
2004	28,852,900	42.90
2005	31,000,000	7.50
2006	34,520,000	11.35
2007	40,954,000	18.64
2008	45,844,400	11.94

Source: CNTA (2009)

Different from traditional word-of-mouth (WOM), WOM on the Internet is defined as eWOM (Godes & Mayzlin, 2004). Westbrook (1987) stated that the definition of eWOM can be regarded as all information communication channels using Internet-based technologies which provide information about the usage or characteristics of particular products, services, or their sellers. Email, instant messaging, websites, chatrooms, blogs, virtual communities and newsgroups are the examples of eWOM channels (Litvin et al., 2008). Since the characteristics of eWOM are low cost, broad scope, and increasing anonymity, it seems that more consumers would like to seek and be exposed to the advices from these eWOM channels (Hennig-Thurau, Gwinner, Walsh & Gremler, 2004). Also, eWOM can be accessed, linked, and searched easily without time and geographic limitations. Since travelers are paying more attention to search engines for information search, eWOM would change the content of travel information, ease of access in travel information and travelers' knowledge, and perception of travel related products (Litvin et al., 2008). In hospitality and tourism industries, the products are intangible and cannot be evaluated before consumptions. This has raised the importance of eWOM since it creates the virtual relationships and communities between consumers and providers, thereby influencing readers' decisions (Litvin et al., 2008). Also, online travel reviews are the main source of information to travelers (Pan, MacLaurin & Crotts, 2007) as they are recognized as more updated and reliable information than content posted by traditional service providers (Gretzel & Yoo, 2008).

Prior studies stated that Chinese online users are more engaged in eWOM and more likely to search for and respond to eWOM because they encourage information sharing and rely on personal sources of information (Fong & Burton, 2008). Therefore, the influence of eWOM in China should be critical. As previously discussed, China outbound tourism has the tremendous potential in the world, and Chinese travelers devote in higher level of information seeking and higher reliance on eWOM channels. Therefore, it is crucial to analyze the data collected from eWOM channels and evaluate the travel preferences of Chinese travelers.

3 Methodology

This study collected data from Ctrip.com, which is one of the largest travel websites in China. Ctrip.com provides a platform for users to rate and post comments for their visited destinations. Data collection was conducted from February 2009 to April 2009. Based on their preferences, visitors could rate each country/region in terms of scenery, accommodation, food, entertainment, shopping and transportation by using 5-point Likert scale (1=lowest mark; 5=highest mark). Subsequently, an integrated overall score is generated. Based on Ctrip.com, 55 countries/ regions were found including Hong Kong, Macau, Taiwan and Neimenggu (Inner Mongolia). Among these countries/regions, 25 were excluded since some of them have not granted ADS agreements while some of them did not provide any ratings. Therefore, in this study, 30 countries/regions with ADS agreements were selected. According to the overall score, selected countries/regions were prioritized from descending scores as illustrated in Table 2.

4 Findings and Discussions

As indicated in Table 2, 30 countries/regions were divided into three groups based on their integrated overall scores. The first group with the overall score of more than 4.5 included Australia (4.791) and Nepal (4.553). The second group, which includes 25 destinations, scored between 3.5 and 4.5. The third group scored lower than 3.5 includes India (2.406), Vietnam (3.273), and Egypt (3.4). According to the findings, Australia and Nepal received the highest integrated overall scores which reflect these two destinations were the most favorite destinations for Chinese Internet travelers. On the other hand, India, Vietnam, and Egypt received the lowest integrated overall scores. The remaining parts of this research analyze the reasons for Chinese online travelers to rate Australia and Nepal over India, Vietnam, and Egypt as their favorite destinations.

Table 2. Overall Score of the Selected Countries/ Regions

Country/Region	Overall Score	Number of Reviewers	Std.
Australia	4.791	1,440	0.1971
Nepal	4.553	115	0.1095
Special Administrative Region (Hong Kong and Macau)	4.430	5,140	0.1927
Spain	4.375	166	0.1668
Austria	4.356	131	0.1811
Russia	4.208	62	0.3148
New Zealand	4.167	45	0.2384
France	4.156	311	0.4430
Germany	4.097	148	0.0690
Malaysia	4.081	445	0.3110
Thailand	4.048	842	0.1995
Indonesia	4.004	302	0.7352
Singapore	3.981	258	0.0967
Italy	3.980	298	0.1821
United Kingdom	3.928	143	0.1844
United States	3.886	467	0.2514
Philippine	3.885	75	0.5273
Japan	3.878	521	0.3520
South Africa	3.870	54	0.4119
Greece	3.835	40	0.0770
Taiwan	3.821	311	0.3959
Holland	3.750	80	0.4025
Switzerland	3.686	140	0.7657
Cambodia	3.613	135	0.2760
Kenya	3.580	15	0.1521
Korea	3.552	705	0.2695
Neimenggu (Inner Mongolia)	3.524	506	0.2787
Egypt	3.400	107	0.2092
Vietnam	3.273	134	0.6288
India	2.406	128	0.9477

4.1 Australia as the most favored outbound destination

Kim *et al.* (2005) indicated that Chinese travelers prefer to visit democratic cities which have a different cultural background from China together with a long historical background. Also, other important attributes for Chinese travelers choosing a destination are safety and security, as well as beautiful scenery. Their results thus concluded that Australia is perceived as the most attractive destination for Chinese outbound travelers because of its beautiful environment along with a 10-year good relationship with China. In Chinese travelers' minds, Australia has no identical substitute (Kim *et al.*, 2005). Moreover, Australia is the first Western country granted ADS agreement by the Chinese government. It is allowed to promote itself as a leisure destination in China for 10 years, thereby broadening its market base in China. Apart from these factors, Sparks and Pan's (2009) study pointed out that Australia is the desirable destination for Chinese travelers due to its culture and position. The conclusions of prior studies were the same as the result of this study in which Australia had received the highest marks. It is generally known that there are a lot of attractive attractions in Australia such as Great Barrier Reef and Gold Coast. This perfectly matches with one of the most important destination attributes (beautiful scenery) of Chinese travelers. At the same time, cities in Australia, such as Sydney and Melbourne, always dominated surveys about the world's most liveable cities. For example, Sydney ranked top 10 in the Mercer's Quality of Living Survey 2009 in terms of safety, education, hygiene, recreation, political-economic stability, and public transportation (Mercer, 2009). This shows that Australia is perceived as a safe destination for Chinese travelers. Moreover, selected comments of Australia (URL: http://destguides.ctrip.com/oceania/australia/region48/) were collected from the site in order to know more why Australia is the most favored destination of Chinese travelers (Fig. 1).

颖颖真乖 2008-8-4 阳光,海滩,高山,草原...风景优美,气氛和谐,适合渡假.
Janeliu 2004-6-21 澳洲的每一块土地都很漂亮，都有自己的特色，就像在 Gold Coast 里的三个主题公园，以及 VERSACE HOTEL 和一些原始森林等，真的很值得去看看，它的美丽不用说了，世界各地的名人在此花耗资够宅度假就该知道它的魅力了，不过有个小建议给大家，个人认 为 movie world 和 Dream World 只选择去一个就够了，我是都去了，都不错，但是总觉得大家以后去只要选择 movie world 和 Sea world 就可以了，祝大家玩得愉快：）对了到 movie world 后别忘了给自己或家人挑一个正版的长毛绒玩具，虽然当时会觉得贵了些，但是买回来肯定不会后悔的，否则你会留下遗憾的：） 而著名的悉尼的城市是个完全没有工业的城市繁荣而安静，好像在天堂一样，很美也很舒心。 其实澳洲还有一个很漂亮的地方就是 Cairns（凯恩斯）那里有非常漂亮的大堡礁，出船游海，到外海去感受一下蓝天碧海的感觉，靠在建造于海洋之中的平台 上或登上潜水艇或自己背上氧气瓶深入海底，这一份美丽和驰骋是无法用语言来形容的，再看看喂鱼的情景你会爱上这一切的：）~~~~~~~~~ 还有很多地方值得去玩玩，我就不一一列举了，总之澳洲真的很值得去玩玩：）
Joannazuo 2006-2-22 澳洲真是一个好地方.那里的阳光,空气都散发着一种让人舒服的感觉,虽然紫外线异常厉害,但并不妨碍游览的心情.悉尼当然是一座风景优美的城市,很多地方 值得走走,坐坐. 乘着船看歌剧院和海港大桥是必不可少的.还有一个值得推荐的地方是凯恩斯,大堡礁.说它是澳洲最美丽的地方,一点也不错. 如果身体情况允许,一定要去深潜.那海里的美景难以言语.跟三亚的海底比,简直不能相提并论.摸摸海里的活珊瑚,它还能动.非常有趣. 其它的景色就不用再说了,很多网友都有写过.别具光芒的澳大利亚,赶快行动吧.

Fig. 1. Selected Comments from Ctrip.com about Australia

Translation of Fig. 1:

Reviewer A "Sunshine, beach, mountains, grasslands! Beautiful scenery! Australia is suitable for vacation."

Reviewer B "Australia is so pretty. Each city has its own character. Sydney is a prosperous and peaceful city, just like a heaven. Great Barrier Beef in Cairns is wonderful. You can experience it when boating. You will definitely love everything in Australia."

Reviewer C "Australia is great as it is a relaxing country. Sydney is a beautiful city and it is worth to visit, especially Sydney Opera House and Sydney Harbour BridgeClimb. Great Barrier Reef in Cairns is the most beautiful place. The environment is absolutely gorgeous."

In short, the reason why Australia is considered as the most favorable destination for Chinese tourists is largely due to its beautiful scenery and secure environment.

4.2 Nepal as the second most favored outbound destination

It is reasonable that Nepal is the second most favorable overseas destination for Chinese travelers. Based on the selected comments from Ctrip.com, Chinese travelers think that Nepal is a glamorous country which is full of religious atmosphere with a majority of the people being Hindus as illustrated in Fig. 2 (URL: http://destguides.ctrip.com/asia/nepal/region79/).

沙沙公主殿下 2008-8-26 尼泊尔，真是一个让人沉迷又心醉的国度。几年前看了朋友拍的照片，尼泊尔一个 festival 大家盛装出席，翠绿、湖蓝、玫红，什么颜色鲜艳穿什么，还有涂满红色、黃色染料的各种神像，我想我是被那些色彩迷住了，于是认定这是个有意思的地方。事实上，排名世界倒数的经济发展程度，没有让尼泊尔人少一点笑容。尼泊尔堪称一生中值得一去的国度，2000 余万人口和 2000 余万座寺庙相映成趣，加上境内 8 座 8000 米以上的山峰，旅游资源算是优厚。怎么形容尼泊尔人的热情大方，淳朴开朗呢？用相机对准他们，在窗口乘凉的老爷爷会颔首保持 POSE 直到你拍好为止，几个心急的父母，看到镜头甚至急切地告诉孩子要微笑，更不用提那些几乎是冲上前来的小孩子们兴奋地叫着"给我们拍一张，我们是好兄弟！"那嘎阔 hotel view piont，一向以慢著称的当地人问我：why are u so late？那一刻我真是张口结合。博卡拉，我在看 SOHO 小报集结出版的《圈子》，一酒店服务生走过来"我能和你聊天么？"加德满都机场出境处，工作人员笑眯眯地问"觉得尼泊尔怎么样？你为什么不结婚？"还是在博卡拉，一个小姑娘被我拍了以后硬是抢过相机为我拍照。
一路行摄 2008-1-4 尼泊尔一定是你值得去的地方，不论你是哪种类型的人。
I_cookie 2007-11-21 在加德满都随处可见的古老文明印记带给我们震撼的同时，更深深体会了我们眼中的新奇不过就是尼泊尔日常的点滴生活，和我们对柴米油盐的需求一样，平凡而普通。

Fig. 2. Selected Comments from Ctrip.com about Nepal

Translation of Fig. 2:

Reviewer D "Nepal was an attractive and charming country together with the religious atmosphere. It is a valuable visit. People were nice and they showed their hospitality to travelers all the time."

Reviewer E "No matter who you are, Nepal is definitely worth a visit."

Reviewer F "I was shocked by Nepal's ancient civilization."

With the above mentioned reasons, Chinese travelers are dazzled by this religious country for its cultural difference from China. According to Kim et al. (2005), Chinese tourists prefer to visit places whose culture is different from China. Moreover, Nepal has an incredible diversity in natural environment, including mountains, mid hills, valleys, lakes, and plains. The highest mountain in the world, Mount Everest, is another famous attraction in Nepal. Since the landscape in Nepal is very attractive, there is no doubt Chinese travelers enjoy traveling there so much. As Kim et al. (2005) stated beautiful scenery is one of the most important destination attributes of Chinese tourists.

4.3 India, Vietnam and Egypt as the unfavorable destinations

According to the results, India (URL:http://destguides.ctrip.com/asia/india/region80/), Vietnam (URL: http://destguides.ctrip.com/asia/vietnam/region46/) and Egypt (URL: http://destguides.ctrip.com/africa/egypt/region30/) were the most unfavorable overseas destinations of Chinese travelers. In order to prevent any misgivings, three destinations are named as Destination A, Destination B, and Destination C randomly. Selected comments were collected from Ctrip.com in order to evaluate why Chinese travelers dislike these destinations.

Regarding Destination A, Chinese travelers are not satisfied with the standard of infrastructure, environment, transportation system, and terrorism (Fig. 3).

70203732 2008-2-20 这 次春节去了 9天，总的来说景观一流，设施末流，泰姬陵纯洁、琥珀堡的雄伟、恒河岸边的虔诚、红堡的壮观、克拉久霍性爱神庙的开放和精美的雕刻都令人叹为观 止，能够深刻感受到印度历史的悠久、独特的文化特色、过去的辉煌，不过同时也能看到印度的落后一面，自称是世界一流的新德里机场只能与中国西部一些不太发 达身份的机场一比，与北京跟首都机场至少要两三个档次，印度基础设施很差，酒店小、设施明显比国内星级低一个档次，任何餐都是咖喱味且基本上是素食（适合 于减肥），没有高速路，他们称之为高速路是不封闭的双向四车道的（有时是两车道）且因人车混行速度记很难达到 60迈，铁路秩序乱、晚点是很正常的、车厢老 鼠"小强"横行，总之没有一定忍耐能力的朋友去印度旅游最好还是三思而后行，不过印度人感觉良好，本着友谊第一的精神就别摧残他们的自尊心好了。印度是个 感觉复杂无法替代的国家。
And007 2007-12-6 新旧城区差别太大…机场规模太小….
Inveness 2008-10-14 就和这个国家一样，新老德里的反差也是巨大的，新德里的豪华酒店、林荫道和老德里的狭窄极度肮脏的街道房屋形成鲜明的对比。不过和其他地方一样，景点还是保护的很好，像 Red Fort, the Mosque, Humayun Tomb 都很大气，让人眼前一亮。如果要买东西，还是尽量选择去商场，有安检，避免 local market 和拥挤的地方，因为这些地方往往才是恐怖袭击的目标。

Fig. 3. Selected comments from Ctrip.com about Destination A

Translation of Fig. 3:

Reviewer G "The hardware in Destination A were poor, especially the airport. The transportation system was very messy with poor hygiene."

Reviewer H "The size of the airport was too small."

Reviewer I "If you want to go shopping, I suggest choosing shopping malls with security inspection. Otherwise, I am afraid that terrorism will happen in local markets.

On the other hand, Destination B was scored as one of the lowest mark's destinations because of its swindles in transportation, poor hygiene, and unsafe environment (Fig. 3).

颖颖真乖 2008-8-4

出门在外就怕遇到黑出租，上车要警惕，要么谈好价格再上车；当地的水果很多，你能想得到的几乎都有了，可以尽情地吃，街边的咖啡也不错；感觉上城市还是有些落后，不是很繁华，不过去那里也只是想感受一下异域风情，其他的能凑合就凑合。

Loveamy 2008-7-30

在 HCMC，要注意有些黑出租，经常停在大商店或者闹市去，殷勤地拉你上车的。他们的表都是有问题的，好像每 3 秒钟能跳 2200VND，就是 1 块钱。 最好选择那种表被塑料盒封起来的出租车，或者事先谈好价格。

Amywoo 2008-5-8

建议大家带点零食，越南的饮食卫生状况不佳，而且超市极少。我住在他们所谓的法国区，应该市最好的地区了，几天只看到一家超市，还有一类似国内 90 年代初的百货商店的四楼，纯属偶然碰上。街上连像样的便利店也看不到，只在湖边一景点买到过一次可乐，要价 6 元人民币。基本上买可乐不是件容易的事～～～

33075955 2002-12-31

海防的治安好象有点问题，那次我们几个 MM 想在晚上逛街，结果出酒店没几步发现路旁的男人都盯着我们，我们怕得只能赶快拦 TAXI，街上却不见一辆，满街都是自行车，只能赶快逃回酒店。问导游才知道，可以借路边的小店电话请店主帮忙拨号找 TAXI，但导游劝我们不要外出，因为曾经有游客被抢，海防人比较野蛮。

Fig. 4. Selected Comments from Ctrip.com about Destination B

Translation of Fig. 4:

Reviewer J "I am afraid of swindles. It is better for you to deal a price before getting on a taxi.'

Reviewer K "Cheated meters are installed in a lot of taxis."

Reviewer L "I suggest bringing some snacks as the hygiene was poor. Also, it was hard to find a supermarket."

Reviewer M "The public security was unsafe. People were looking attentively at me while I was walking down the street. This made me felt uncomfortable and went back to the hotel as soon as possible.

Apart from these, disorderly transportation systems, swindles and undeveloped infrastructures were the factors why Chinese travelers disfavor Destination C.

Qqkk0017 2008-11-14 埃及与土尔其 8 天.埃及及其差,开罗脏乱差,像 30 年前的中国.汽车破,房屋旧(其实已经不能用"旧"来形容了),所有人都在想骗游客的钱,影响糟糕. 飞机一到土尔其,发现到了另一格天地.比起埃及真是天堂阿!
Scott 2008-10-12 开罗的脏乱差，真是不能用几个字能阐述的。开罗分为旧区和新区。旧区基本是旧的没有修整过的，人还过的去。新区好多了。不过，埃及人很喜欢问你是不是中国人，如果是，就拼命向你要清凉油或是笔。 开罗到处都是为了避税，而没有外立面的楼房。感觉这个城市没有好好规划好，也没有整治。基本在旧区或是郊外，没有红绿灯，人们也没有意识要遵守交通法规。
maomaolu2000 2009-6-19 总觉得亚历山大把地中海给浪费了，那么长的海岸线，却尽是没有饰面的楼房，太可惜了! 很喜欢海岸边谈恋爱的情侣!

Fig. 5. Selected Comments from Ctrip.com about Destination C

Translation of Fig. 5:

Reviewer N "There was chaos in Destination C due to traffic jam. I was cheated when visiting an attraction."

Reviewer O "It seemed undeveloped in this destination. No matter in city or countryside, there were no traffic lights. People, of course, have no sense of safety."

Reviewer P "Undecorated buildings developed along the beautiful long coast. What a waste!"

In terms of the above comments, it is understandable why Chinese travelers rated these three destinations the lowest. Prior research had stated that safety and security as well as beautiful scenery are the most important destination attributes for Chinese travelers (Kim et al., 2005). Also, ACNielsen (2006) performed a survey and found out that Chinese tourists are highly concerned with safety issues in that they are unwilling to take risks in travelling to places which seem to be dangerous. Furthermore, 60% of the Chinese respondents considered that security at the destination is important. By evaluating the comments from these three destinations, it is obvious that Chinese travelers consider these destinations as unsafe and dangerous. Also, swindles took advantages of the visitors during their visits, which is another factor that makes Chinese tourists feel uncomfortable when visiting. Besides, comments pointed out that the development of these destinations were unplanned with poor hygienic problem. This completely deteriorated the travel motivations of Chinese tourists. In short, since Chinese travelers felt that these destinations were unsafe along with poor environment, this simply violated two critical destination criteria in their minds.

5 Conclusion and Implications

This research has investigated the travel preferences in terms of overseas destinations for Chinese travelers on Ctrip.com. As discussed, China outbound tourism is blooming after the introduction of the national reform and open-door policy since Chinese citizens could afford for the luxury travel of experience. At the same time, the number of Chinese online users is growing. Many Chinese travelers like to use the Internet for information search, including destination information, prices and schedules. Also, Chinese online users highly believe in the eWOM while they trust personal sources of information strongly (Fong & Burton, 2008). Therefore, the influence and impact of travel websites cannot be neglected. Using the data collected from a major travel website, findings of this study revealed that Australia and Nepal are the most attractive destinations to Chinese travelers. On the other hand, India, Vietnam, and Egypt showed weakness when attracting Chinese tourists.

Accordingly, hospitality and tourism marketers should understand the travel preferences of Chinese outbound tourists, thereby targeting one of the most important international tourist source-generating markets. At the same time, it is vital to understand that Chinese tourists are going online in increasing numbers and they are more likely influenced by travel websites or online travel forums. Tourism marketers should therefore take the first step in understanding and utilizing the information from travel websites in order to know what their potential customers like and dislike. The website used in this study offers numerous first-hand information and ratings posted by travelers. These reviews can surely provide a strong sense of the destination, and then affect travelers' overall image of a particular destination. As such, it seems that eWOM source is playing an important role in hospitality and tourism industries, in China or in other overseas destinations.

References

ACNielsen (2006). Asia Travel Intentions Survey. http://www.pata.org/patasite/fileadmin/news_pata/060425_ASIA_TRAVEL_INTENTIONS_SURVEY_FINAL.pdf [Accessed on 27 May 2009]

ChinaContact. (2009). *ChinaContact Market Entry for Tourism and Hospitality.* http://www.chinacontact.org/ [Accessed on 24 July 2009].

China Internet Network Information Centre (CNNIC). (2009). *Analysis Report on the 23th Survey Report.* www.cnnic.net.cn [Accessed on 22 July 2009].

Fong, J. & Burton, S. (2008). A Cross-cultural Comparison of Electronic World-of-mouth and Country-of-origin Effects. *Journal of Business Research,* 61(3), 233-242.

Godes, D. & Mayzlin, D. (2004). Using Online Conversations to Study Word-of-mouth Communication. *Marketing Science,* 23(4), 545-560.

Gretzel, U. & Yoo, K. (2008). Use and Impact of Online Travel Reviews. In O'Connor, P., Höpken, W. & Gretzel, U. (Eds.). *Information and Communication Technologies in Tourism 2008*. Spring-Verlag, Wien/ New York, pp.35-46.

Hennig-Thurau, T., Gwinner, K. P., Walsh, G. & Gremler, D. D. (2004). Electronic Word-of-mouth via Consumer-opinion Platforms: What Motivates Consumers to Articulate themselves on the Internet? *Journal of Interactive Marketing*, 18(1), 38-52.

Heung, V. C. S. (2000). Satisfaction Levels of Mainland Chinese Travelers with Hong Kong Hotel Services. *International Journal of Contemporary Hospitality Management*, 12 (5), 308-315.

Internet World Stats. (2009). *Internet Users – Top 20 Countries – Internet Usage.* http://www.internetworldstats.com/top20.htm [Accessed on 23 July 2009].

Keating, B. & Kriz, A. (2008). Outbound Tourism from China: Literature Review and Research Agenda. *Journal of Hospitality and Tourism Management*, 15(2), 32-41.

Kim, S. S., Guo, Y. & Agrusa, J. (2005). Preference and Positioning Analyses of Overseas Destinations by Mainland Chinese Outbound Pleasure Tourists. *Journal of Travel Research*, 44 (2), 212-220.

Lim, C. & Wang, Y. (2008). China's Post-1978 Experience in Outbound Tourism. *Mathematics and Computers in Simulation*, 78(2/3), 450-458.

Litvin, S. W., Goldsmith, R. E. & Pan, B. (2008). Electronic Word-of-mouth in Hospitality and Tourism Management. *Tourism Management*, 29(3), 458-468.

Mercer. (2009). *Mercer's 2009 Quality of Living Survey Highlight.* http://www.mercer.com/qualityofliving [Accessed on 29 July 2009]

Mok, C. & DeFranco, A. L. (1999). Chinese Cultural Values: Their Implications for Travel and Tourism Marketing. *Journal of Travel & Tourism Marketing*, 8(2), 99-114.

National Tourism Administration of the People's Republic of China (CNTA). (2009). China Tourism Statistics. http://www.cnta.gov.cn/ [Accessed on 27 July 2009].

Pan, B., MacLaurin, T. & Crotts, J. (2007). Travel Blogs and the Implications for Destination Marketing. *Journal of Travel Research*, 46(1), 35-45.

Qu, H. & Li I. (1997). The Characteristics and Satisfaction of Mainland Chinese Visitors to Hong Kong. *Journal of Travel Research*, 35(4), 37-41.

Sparks, B. & Pan, G. W. (2009). Chinese Outbound Tourists: Understanding their Attitudes, Constraints and Use of Information Sources. *Tourism Management*, 30(4), 483-494.

United Nations World Tourism Organization (UNWTO). (2000). *Tourism 2020 Vision – A New Forecast*. Madrid: UNWTO.

Westbrook, R. A. (1987) Product/ Consumption-based Affective Responses and Postpurchase Processes. *Journal of Marketing Research*, 24(3), 258-270.

Ye, Q., Law, R. & Gu, B. (2009). The Impact of Online User Reviews on Hotel Room Sales. *International Journal of Hospitality Management*, 28(1), 180-182.

Zhang, Q. H. & Chow, I. (2004). Application of Importance-Performance Model in Tour Guides' Performance: Evidence from Mainland Chinese Outbound Visitors in Hong Kong. *Tourism Management*, 25(1), 81-91.

Egyptian Travel Agents and e-Commerce

Mohamed Abou-Shouk,
Wai Mun Lim

Plymouth Business School
University of Plymouth, UK
mohamed.aboushouk@plymouth.ac.uk

Abstract

The rapid growth of the Internet has provided travel agents with the opportunity to embrace it as an extension of their traditional activities. An effective website could potentially bring the world into the customers' home, and increase their loyalty to the enterprise. The evaluation of websites is one of many ways to benchmark travel agents' websites against their competitors, and to determine their enhancement directions. This research aims to highlight information offered on Egyptian travel agents' websites; and to rank these websites in relation to their readiness for electronic commerce. Surveyed websites showed that the most frequent features are company information and contact details. Websites that have been ranked as practicing 1st phase e-commerce are the majority, while websites supporting the 2nd and the 3rd phases are few, and for between websites ranked as practising 4th phase e-commerce are a minority.

Keywords: e-commerce; websites; travel agencies; Egypt

1 Introduction

The Internet has become an important modern day tool for businesses, especially small and medium size enterprises (SMEs) (Ayeh, 2006; Buhalis, 2002; Khanchouch, 2005; Patricia, 2008; Rosen, 2002; Scarborough & Zimmerer, 2003). Travel agents are typically classified as SMEs (Gammack, Molinar, Chu, & Chanpayom, 2004; Karanasios, 2008; Liu, 2000; Standing, Borbely, & Vasudavan, 1999). Increased number of Travellers make reservations online has motivated travel enterprises to provide their services online (Albuquerque & Belchior, 2002; Lu & Deng, 2007). To support online reservation, the design of websites has become a critical success factor (Hung & McQueen, 2004). The decision makers are continually learning about the factors that affect website and e-business success (Lee & Kozar, 2006). On the other hand, evaluation of websites could help businesses to identify their weaknesses, and the tools for enhancement (Liu & Arnett, 2000; Lu & Deng 2007; Walcott, 2007). In general, the research aims to evaluate the readiness of developing countries travel agencies' websites for e-commerce purposes. Recommendations for further research on e-commerce adoption boundaries in Egyptian travel agents and strategies to enhance their diffusion of such technologies will be discussed.

2 Adoption Strategies of e-Commerce in SMEs

Past studies have divided the stages of e-commerce implementation process into many levels within their models. This study reviews 20 models that examine these stages presented hierarchically. Table (1) shows in details to these models.

Table 1. Review of previous e-commerce adoption models

Researcher	Model description
Moersch, (1995)	In a six sequential level model, level (0) lacks of technology-based tools. Level (1) seeks information dissemination. Level (2) is exploration. Level (3) demonstrates a higher-level of e-commerce adoption. The fourth level includes integration of content processing and in depth examination. Collaboration with other businesses is the fifth level. The last level illustrates refinement, where digital tools for queries and problem-solving tools are used.
Burgess and Cooper (1998)	The first stage is the promotion of products via electronic channels. Provision is the second stage where interaction with customers is achieved. Processing is the third stage where online orders, sales, and payment are conducted.
Allcock, Annette, Webber, & Yeates, (1999)	In a various stage model, the first stage is 'Threshold' where there are computer-based activities. 'Beginner' is the second stage where one or two e-mail addresses and few networked computers are used. In the 'Intermediate' stage, an e-mail contact with suppliers and static websites are processed. At the 'advanced' stage, there is full use of the e-mail, intranet and extranet.
Earl (2000)	The first stage is homepages for external communications. Internal communications is the second stage. Stage three includes online buying or selling. In stage four, there are movements toward e-business to reach the fifth stage of e-enterprise. Continuous reinventing is carried out in the sixth stage.
Heeks (2000)	In a four-step model, the first two steps are precursor activities where simple usage of e-mail and a website moving to a dynamic website. The last two steps are e-commerce based including online transactions and service delivery.
Mckay, Marshall, & Prananto, (2000)	No online presence is the first stage. Static online presence is developed in stage (2). The third stage is interactive online presence. Complete internet transactions are conducted in stage (4). In stage (5), front-back-office internet transactions capabilities are integrated. The last stage is external integration to achieve 'extended enterprise' concept.
Willcocks (2000)	The first stage is developing web pages. Web transacting systems are built in stage (2). Further integration to processes, structures, skills and technologies is constantly undertaken in stage (3). The final stage is e-business.
Wiertz, (2001)	'Access' is the first step. E-procurement' is the second stage. Promotional' websites is the third stage. E-sales are supported in the last stage.
Daniel, Wilson, & Myers, (2002)	A developer using minimal levels of operational e-commerce services is the first cluster. Websites are developed in the second cluster for communication purposes. The third cluster is web presence. 'Transactors' make up the fourth cluster where payment, after sales services are done online.
Levy & Powell, (2002).	E-mail and informative websites are used in the first stage. Then businesses communicate internally and with customers. From 'no plans for growth' stages to 'planned growth', e-mail is used extensively to arrive at the business network stage, and then using electronic data interchange systems (EDI).
Rayport & Jaworski, (2002)	'Broadcast' is the first stage encompassing a webpage with static information. Using the internet to interact with customers is the second stage. The third stage is to 'transact' and internet is used for inter-organisational activities.
Rao, Metts, & Monge (2003).	In a four-strategy model, each strategy has its own benefits and barriers for development. Presence on the web is the first strategy. Two-way communications and e-mail orders are conducted in 'portals' stage. Online transactions are supported in third strategy. Enterprise integration is the fourth strategy where full integration for collaboration is developed.

Chan & Swatman, (2004)	Initial e-commerce adoption amongst departments is the first stage. Implementation becomes company wide in centralized e-commerce stage. Then new technologies are adopted. Finally, is using internet applications to attain e-commerce coverage with an emphasis for customers' satisfaction.
Beck, Wigand, & Konig, (2005)	Online advertising is the first stage, followed by online sales and after sales services, moving on to online procurement. Finally, EDI with suppliers and customers to enable internet based supply chain management is achieved.
Gatautis & Neverauskas (2005)	EDI can be used in the primary stages of e-commerce. The next stages would include centralised e-commerce programs. Then using internet-based technologies to reach global ecommerce comes in the last stage.
Lefebvrea, Lefebvrea, Elia, & Boeck, (2005)	In a six-stage model, e-commerce non-adopters include stage (00) with no interest in e-commerce, and stage (0) is non-adopters but have interested. The first stage for adopters is electronic content creation. The second stage is electronic transactions. Complex electronic transactions are in stage (3), reaching to electronic collaboration in the fourth stage.
Gandhi (2006)	Extensive promotion is used to attract customers, followed by interactions between the business and the customers. The successful interaction would then lead to the act of order processing, delivery and realization of payment. React with customers' feedback and after sales services come lastly.
Al-Qirim, (2007)	Starters (use internet and e-mails) and some adopters use e-mail and passive WebPages are considered low level of e-commerce practices. Using e-mail and websites to sell and collect money online is advanced level adopters. Extended adopters use intranet and extranet.
Chen & McQueen, (2008)	The first level entails information search, e-mail use to communicate with customers and suppliers. Online marketing through static website is the second level. Online ordering with manual payment is the third level. The fourth level supports online transactions and invoice issuing.
NCC, (2009)	In a five-stage model, no use of e-mail, neither internet access is the first stage. Wide use of e-mail and website as a marketing tool is stage (2). Using internet to interact with customers comes in the third stage. The fourth stage includes online relationships with business partners. Online exchange and e-marketplace for customers, suppliers and partners are available in stage (5).

To conclude, these models have some similarities and differences in the number of stages and the features of each stage. In terms of similarities, table (2) shows that the majority of these models share the same stage features.

Table 2. Similarities amongst e-commerce implementation models

Stage	Stage Features
Stage (1)	E-mail interaction with customers and static web site to provide information on the company (Daniel, Wilson & Myers, 2002; Earl, 2000; Heeks, 2000; Levy & Powell, 2002; Rayport & Jaworski, 2002; Rao, Metts & Monge, 2003; Lefebvera, Elia & Boeck, 2005; Al-Qirim, 2007).
Stage (2)	Dynamic websites support negotiation with customers, placing orders and responding to enquiries (Burgess & Cooper, 1998; Heeks, 2000; Mckay, Marshall & Prananto, 2000; Levy & Powell, 2002; Rayport & Jaworski, 2002; Rao, Metts & Monge, 2003; Lefebvrea, Lefebvrea, Elia & Boeck, 2005; Gandhi, 2006).
Stage (3)	Websites enable online orders, sales, and payment integration (Burgess & Cooper, 1998; Earl, 2000; Heeks, 2000; Daniel, Wilson & Myers, 2002; Rayport & Jaworski, 2002; Rao, Metts & Monge, 2003; Chan & Swatman, 2004; Lefebvrea, Lefebvrea,

Elia & Boeck, 2005; Gandhi, 2006).

Stage (4)	ICT- mediated service delivery, after sales services, intranet and extranet to support electronic integration and collaboration with partners (Allcock, Annette, Webber & Yeates, 1999; Heeks, 2000; Daniel, Wilson & Myers, 2002; Levy & Powell, 2002; Rao, Metts & Monge, 2003; Chan & Swatman, 2004; Beck, Wigand & Konig, 2005; Gatautis & Neverauskas, 2005; Lefebvrea, Lefebvrea, Elia & Boeck, 2005; Gandhi, 2006; Al-Qirim, 2007; Chen & McQueen, 2008; NCC, 2009).

On the other hand, some models consider the first stage in implementation process as using computers in daily activities with no use of neither e-mail nor internet access or company website (Moersch, 1995; Allcock, Annette, Webber & Yeates, 1999; APEC, 1999; Mckay, Marshall & Prananto, 2000; Lefebvrea, Lefebvrea, Elia & Boeck, 2005; NCC, 2009). Furthermore, some models expand fifth and sixth stages to achieve the concept of 'extended enterprise' (Moersch, 1995; Earl, 2000; Mckay, Marshall & Prananto, 2000; Chen & McQueen, 2008; NCC, 2009). Based on the features of reviewed models, a proposed four-stage model has been developed and features of each stage have been detailed. Detailed features have been included as detailed in conceptual framework section.

3   Research Gap

To take maximum advantage of e-commerce, businesses often create their websites first (Yao, 2004). Despite this phenomenon, there are many companies that fail to effectively use their websites (Chung & Law, 2003). Furthermore, effective websites have become one of the critical factors supporting business success (Jeong, Oh, & Gregoire, 2003). To evaluate the readiness of these websites for e-commerce purposes in a developing country, it is crucial to identify the implementation stage of e-commerce where organisations have their own websites (Walcott, 2007). This research aims to evaluate Egyptian travel agents' websites and to determine their e-commerce adoption process. One of the key objectives of the research seeks to discover the most frequent features/content found on Egyptian travel agents' websites.

4   Research Objectives

The research aims to:

1   Propose a typology of e-commerce adoption phases amongst Egypt's travel agents sector,
2   Determine features/content offered on Egyptian travel agents' websites through content analysis, and
3   Evaluate Egyptian travel agents' e-commerce readiness by identifying their current level of e-commerce adoption.

5   Conceptual Framework

Based on previous studies of models relating to the adoption strategies of e-commerce in SMEs, this research seeks to develop an adoption model of e-commerce strategies in SMEs. The model is based on models discussed earlier and especially ones were developed by Rao, Metts, & Monge (2003) and and Mckay, Marshall, & Prananto, (2000). The proposed model includes four phases, static web presence, interactive online presence and these two phases are classified as low levels of e-commerce practices. Electronic transactions and electronic integration are the two other phases of the model classified as advanced practices of e-commerce (table 3).

Table 3. Proposed e-commerce adoption strategies model

Phase	Description	Level
Phase (1): static web presence	Using internet to search customers and suppliers; homepage for information dissemination purposes; and using e-mail to communicate customers, suppliers and business partners.	Low-level e-commerce practices
Phase (2): interactive online presence	Two-way interactions via the company portal (company-customers); placing and managing orders with suppliers; using e-mail to receive customers' orders; and digital transfer of documents within the company.	
Phase (3): electronic transactions	Order receiving and processing; online booking; and online payment and digital services delivery.	Advanced-level e-commerce practices
Phase (4): electronic integration	After sales services; full internal and external use of e-mail; intranet; extranet for inter-organisational interaction with business partners; and high level of collaboration.	

Most past studies on e-commerce were focused either on e-commerce strategies or on websites evaluation from an e-commerce point of view (Kim & Lee, 2002; C. Liu & Arnett, 2000; Merwe & Bekker, 2003; Walcott, 2007; WTO, 2001; Yao, 2004; Zafiropoulos & Vrana, 2006). Those studies have assigned the main features of each strategy that could be found in the companies' websites in either stages or levels. Table (4) shows the most frequent features of each strategy in the previous studies.

Table 4. Main online features of each strategy of e-commerce adoption model

Model phases and relevant features

In the first phase 'static web presence', the features are company information: company description; financial facts; photos library; and virtual tours. Services information: packages info; prices; promotions; future packages; and sightseeing areas of the destination. Contact information: address; phone no.; fax no.; e-mail address; distributors' info; and links to other sites. Other information includes currency converter; weather; transportation; and distances.

The second phase is interactive online presence where features are interactive database search facility; virtual brochures; interactive trip planner; online reservation request form; FAQ (Frequent Asked Questions); surveys; feedback forms; chat/forum/e-cards sending; and online finder (hotels, restaurants, flights).

In the third phase 'electronic transactions', features are online booking; online payment receiving; cards accepted; online accounts for buyers; order tracking; and digital delivery of travel documents.

The fourth phase is electronic integration; it includes the third phase features besides after sales procedures; collaboration/alliance member; intranet; and world pay integration.

6 Research Methodology

In order to evaluate the websites, a checklist was designed for content analysis purposes. Examining table (4), about 38 features have been included in the checklist, each feature takes the value of (0) if not found in the website, the value of (1) if it is found and the value of (2) if it cannot be checked. The primary checklist has been used to evaluate 50 websites in order to determine the significant features. Significant features are those that are frequently repeated in the websites. Some other features have been excluded from the checklist for two significant reasons. These features are not found in the 50 pilot websites such as surveys beside some features cannot be checked in the website unless a complete transactions process has been achieved or an account in the company website is done, digital delivery of travel documents, after sales procedures and world pay integration are such examples of these features. Finally, 34 features have been selected to form the final checklist. The initial analysis of the pilot checklist resulted in that the most frequent features are packages information, phone and fax numbers, e-mail addresses, company address, sightseeing areas, company description, and photo gallery. Most of these features are relating to the first phase of the adoption model, and more accurately to the contact information sub-category.

The sample of the study covers category (A) travel agencies that have websites. Category (A), companies are those organising packages for groups or/and individuals, inside or outside Egypt, arranging all items related to these packages and executing planned packages of other tour operators (Ministry of Tourism, 2008). There are 1023 travel agents in category (A). About 418 of these travel agents have their own website (Egyptian Travel Agents Association, 2008). During the evaluation process, out of 418 websites, 62 websites are not found, 17 websites do not work, 22 websites are found under construction, and 317 websites are successfully checked.

To ensure validity, researchers have listed the items of the checklists found in literature review, then some features were replicated, and some others were rephrased to form the final checklist. The initial checklist was piloted to ensure its relevance. This resulted in the exclusion of some items that are not relevant or cannot be checked. Using scaled data for the two levels of e-commerce practices; low-level practices (27 items) and advanced level practices (7 items), a reliability test of the findings revealed a Cronbach alpha of 0.758 and 0.823 respectively.

7 Research results

7.1 Features of websites content

The second research objective aimed to examine features/content offered on travel agents' websites. From the content analysis of the websites (Table 5); it is clear that the most frequent features are classified as the first phase of e-commerce. It can be observed from table (5) that contact information is the most frequently found, with e-mail addresses (81.4%), phone numbers (79.5%), fax numbers (78.2%), and company address (77.3%). For company information, the most frequent feature is company description (75.1%). In terms of services information provision, travel package information (77%), and sightseeing areas of the destination (58.4%), were high on the list of website content. Other information found on websites includes weather forecasts (30.3%), and transportation information (20.5). All the above features are classified as the first phase of e-commerce practices. For the second phase of e-commerce adoption, frequent features are online reservation request form (38.3%), feedback forms (26.5%), and interactive database search box (25.9%). The third phase of e-commerce adoption model includes the features of accepted cards for payments (6.6%), online accounts for buyers (6.3%), order tracking (4.5%), online payment receiving (3.5%), and online booking service (2.8%). The last phase includes features from the third phase and information in relation to the company's membership with an alliance or group (9.2%) and intranet used amongst company staff (1.6%).

Table 5. Statistics of features/content of travel agents' websites

Feature	%	Feature	%	Feature	%
Company Info.	75.1	Transportation	20.5	Feedback forms	26.5
Financial facts	2.5	E-mail	81.4	Chat/forum/	8.5
Photos gallery	37.5	Distribution info.	42.3	e-cards	
virtual tours	4.4	Links to other sites	34.7	Online finder	8.8
Packages info.	77	Currency converter	2.8	Online booking	2.8
Prices	13.6	Weather	30.3	Online payment	3.5
Promotions	20.2	Distances	7.6	Cards accepted	6.6
Future packages	4.1	database search facility	25.9	Online accounts	6.3
Sightseeing areas	58.4	Virtual brochures	0.3	Order tracking	4.5
Address	77.3	Interactive trip planner	0.9	Collaboration/	9.2
Phone numbers	79.5	Reservation request form	38.3	group member	
Fax numbers	78.2	FAQs	4.1	Intranet	1.6

7.2 Travel agents' websites based on proposed model

The following results relate to the third objective of the study, examining the e-commerce readiness of Egyptian travel agents' websites. Some researchers estimated that 60% of the stage's features as the standard percentage to classify the website in each stage depending on their expectation of the importance of the features should be found in websites (Cai, Card, & Cole, 2004). However, from the statistical analysis results in the study, it was found that there are three travel agencies have 100% of the features in both the third and the fourth stages, although they have only 50% of the features in both the first and the second stages. Therefore, it is proposed that the websites are classified into the first or the second phase if it contains at least 50% of the features of each phase. Websites are categorised in the 3rd phase if they include all the features of this phase. The 4th phase should include 100% of its features combined with features from the 3rd phase. The latter two phases are sequential.

Lower levels of e-commerce adoption. About 94 out of 317 surveyed websites were found to have more than 50% of the first phase features; about 29.65% of websites are classified as first phase practitioners of e-commerce. A number of 17 out of 317 websites were found to have more than 50% of the second phase features, and only 5.36% of all surveyed websites includes second phase features. Travel agents' websites classified in the second phase are not necessarily adopting first phase features, as the 2nd phase websites may support less than 50% of the 1st phase features but adopt 50% or more of the second phase features. This is because only 7 out of 17 websites that have been classified as the 2nd phase are already classified as 1st phase websites. The above results indicate that most websites support lower levels of e-commerce adoption.

364

Advanced level of e-commerce adoption. Findings indicated that only 4 out of 317 websites adopts 100% of the features from the 3rd phase, therefore only 1.26% of all websites could be classified as 3rd phase practitioners of e-commerce. Furthermore, a number of 3 out of 317 websites have 100% of both 3rd and 4th phase's features; this translates to 0.95% of all websites is ranked as 4th phase practices of e-commerce. Only four travel agents' websites can be classified as having adopted e-commerce at an advanced level.

7.3 Other statistics

There are seven websites have been classified as 1st and 2nd phases concurrently. Four websites have been classified as 2nd and 3rd phase simultaneously, and three websites have been classified as 3rd and 4th phases in tandem. Three websites can be classified as being in the 2nd, 3rd, and 4th phases (table 6).

Table 6. Cross-tabulation among websites in all phases

	First phase	Second phase	Third phase	Fourth phase
First phase	94	7	0	0
Second phase	7	17	4	3
Third phase	0	4	4	3
Fourth phase	0	3	3	3

About 21.1% of travel agents have been operating for between 21-25 years, only 16.4% have been operating for between 6-10 years while 14.2% have been operating for 16-20 years. Moreover, 10.7% have been operating between 26-30 years (table 7).

Table 7. Years of operation and percentages of surveyed travel agents

Age	%	Age	%	Age	%	Age	%
1-5	12.6	16-20	14.2	31-35	8.5	46-50	1.6
6-10	16.4	21-25	21.1	36-40	2.2	51-60	2.8
11-15	9.1	26-30	10.7	41-45	0.3	71-80	0.3

Measuring the relationship between the travel agents age as the independent variable and online booking enabled in websites. The (b) value in linear regression was (-0.004), indicating a negative relationship between the agencies age and the availability of online booking systems in their website (table 8). Recently established agencies are therefore more likely to apply technology compared to older companies.

Table 8. Regression analysis results for business age and online booking systems

	B	Std. Error	t	Sig.
Constant	.046	.019	2.417	.016
Business Age	-.004	.004	-1.072	.284

However, this effect is not significant (0.284); there is still evidence to accept the alternative hypothesis as 55.6% of websites supports online booking facility are ranging from one to ten years old, about 33.33% of these websites are among 16 to 25 years in age, and 11.11% are within 51 to 60 years old. Finally, correlation measures were conducted amongst some variables; results show that there is a significant correlation at the 0.05 level between websites that have online reservation request form and those with online booking availability. Highly significance correlations at the 0.01 level amongst online booking & online payment receiving; online accounts for buyers & order tracking; and online booking & intranet were also found (table 9). To accurately verify these correlation values, Coefficient of determination (R^2) was determined at (0.627), (0.856), and (0.190) respectively.

Table 9. Correlation analysis results amongst some variables

Variable (1)	Variable (2)	Correlation	Sig. value	R^2
Online reservation request form	Online booking	.136*	.015	.018
Online booking	Online payment	.792**	.000	.627
Online accounts for buyers	Order tracking	.925**	.000	.856
Online booking	Intranet	.436**	.000	.190

**. Correlation is significant at the 0.01 level. *. Correlation is significant at the 0.05 level.

8 Conclusion and Recommendations

This research set out to examine the current adoption levels of e-commerce in Egyptian travel agents category (A) with its own websites. A number of 317 websites were successfully checked against a checklist backed by literature reviews. This study has met its three objectives; proposing a model from extensive literature searches of e-commerce implementation models in SMEs, to determine the level of e-commerce adoption on websites, information features offered on websites, and identifying the readiness of Egyptian travel agents for e-commerce. A four-phase model has been proposed for the study purposes, the most frequent features found in websites of travel agents are contact and company information. Interestingly 29.65% of the surveyed websites are classified as 1st phase adopters of e-commerce, about 5.36% of all websites are classified as 2nd phase adopters. Only 1.26% of websites have been classified as 3rd phase, and 0.95% of all websites are classified as 4th phase adopters.

Comparing these results to other studies on other destinations, as cited by Wan (2002) in his evaluation to websites in Taiwan, only 5 out of 39 websites provide online reservation. Moreover, in their study to the performance of US tour operators focus on Chinese destinations, Cai, Card, and Cole (2004) found that 16 out of 20 websites are classified in the second stage (web service) where they respond to product and service inquiries through e-mail, while only 4 out of 20 websites enabled online reservations and payment (third stage). Furthermore, in their study to evaluate the performance of Chinese travel agencies websites, Lin, Zhou, and Guo (2009) found that 2 out of 30 websites are ranked in the first stage providing basic and promotional information, While 28 out of 30 were in the second stage (provision) supporting interactive communication with customers and offering online booking forms. No agencies were ranked in the third stage supporting online transactions.

The outcome of these studies proves that the majority of travel agencies websites are still not exploiting the full capabilities of the internet. Most websites are providing information about the agency and its services rather than supporting the online transactions and after sales services. The implications of the study could be guided the managers/executives of the tourism websites to consider the features required to move them to the advanced practices of e-commerce in order to enhance the competitive position of travel agencies in the current travel market. To take the full advantages of the Internet and e-commerce technologies, travel agencies have to develop their websites to go beyond the promotional levels towards online transactions. Furthermore, there is a need to consider the features appear in competitors' websites and keep them in line with their competitors. They should focus on consumer-oriented concept. Because the majority of travel agencies are classified on lower levels of e-commerce adoption, they have to take the approach of business process improvement to adopt e-commerce systematically rather than taking the approach of business process reengineering and going to the top adoption level directly. Considering the proposed model in the study, travel agencies can develop their websites step by step to reach the mature stages of e-commerce.

9 Limitations and Suggestions for Further Studies

When reviewing the results of this study, it should be considered that website have dynamic, therefore, these findings could be valid for a short time only. Furthermore, the study records the features availability only in websites and does not consider its quality. One more limitation of this study is excluding the features available only for website registered members or those need complete transaction process to be checked. Because of classifying the majority of travel agencies' websites in Egypt as informative sites, further research should be addressed to understand the barriers that lead to these low adoption rates. These barriers could be internal or external boundaries. Future studies might focus on what those barriers may be and how they can be overcome by investigating them through managers' viewpoint.

References

Al-Qirim, N. (2007). A research trilogy into e-commerce adoption in small businesses in New Zealand. *Electronic Markets, 17*(4), 263-285.

Albuquerque, A., & Belchior, A. (2002). E-commerce websites: a qualitative evaluation. Retrieved 20 May, 2009, from http://www2002.org/CDROM/poster/155.pdf

Allcock, S., Annette, P., Webber, S., & Yeates, R. (1999). Business information and the Internet: Use of the Internet as an information resource for SMEs: final report: Section 18: stages of Internet engagement: proposed model and recommendations. From http://dis.shef.ac.uk/business/BII-18.pdf

Ayeh, J. (2006). Determinants of internet usage in Ghanaian hotels: the case of the Greater Accra Region (GAR). *Journal of Hospitality & Leisure Marketing, 15*(3), 87-109.

Beck, R., Wigand, R., & Konig, W. (2005). The diffusion and efficient use of electronic commerce among small and medium-sized enterprises: an international three-industry survey. *Electronic Markets, 15*(1), 38–52.

Buhalis, D. (2002). E-tourism: Information technologies for strategic tourism management. *Annals of Tourism Research, 31*(3), 461-468.

Burgess, L., & Cooper, J. (1998, September). *The status of internet commerce in the manufacturing industry in Australia: A survey of metal fabrication industries.* Paper presented at the CollECTeR'98, Sydney, Australia.

Cai, L., Card, J., & Cole, S. (2004). Content delivery performance of world wide web sites of US tour operators focusing on destinations in China. *Tourism Management*, 25, 219-227.

Chan, C., & Swatman, P. (2004, January 5-8). *B2B e-commerce stages of growth: the strategic imperatives.* Paper presented at the 37th International Conference on System Sciences, Hawaii, USA.

Chen, J., & McQueen, R. (2008). Factors affecting e-commerce stages of growth in small Chinese firms in New Zealand: an analysis of adoption motivators and inhibitors. *Journal of Global Information Management, 16*(1), 26-60.

Chung, T., & Law, R. (2003). Developing a performance indicator for hotel websites. *International Journal of Hospitality Management, 22*(1), 343-358.

Daniel, E., Wilson, H., & Myers, A. (2002). Adoption of e-commerce by SMEs in the UK: towards a stage model. *International Small Business Journal, 20*(3), 253-270.

Earl, M. (2000). Evolving the e-business. *Business Strategy Review, 11*(2), 33-38.

Egyptian Travel Agents Association. (2008). *Agencies Directory.* Cairo: ETTA, Ministry of Tourism.

Gammack, J., Molinar, C., Chu, K., & Chanpayom, B. (2004). Development needs of small to medium size tourism businesses. APEC international Centre for Sustainable Tourism.

Gandhi, S. (2006). E-commerce and information technology Act, 2000. *Vidyasagar University Journal of Commerce, 11*, 82-91.

Gatautis, R., & Neverauskas, B. (2005, 15-17 August). *E-commerce adoption in transition economies: SMEs perspectives in Lithuania.* Paper presented at the 7th international conference on Electronic commerce Xi'an, China.

Heeks, R. (2000). Analysing e-commerce for Development. Retrieved 7 April, 2009, from http://www.sed.manchester.ac.uk/idpm/research/publications/wp/di/short/di_sp04.pdf

Hung, W., & McQueen, R. (2004). Developing an evaluation instrument for e-commerce web sites from the first-time buyer's viewpoint. *Electronic Journal of Information Systems Evaluation 7*(1), 31-42.

Jeong, M., Oh, H., & Gregoire, M. (2003). Conceptualizing web site quality andits consequences in the lodging industry. *International Journal of Hospitality Management, 22*, 161-175.

Karanasios, S. (2008). *An E-commerce Framework for Small Tourism Enterprises in Developing Countries.* Unpublished Doctorate thesis, School of Information Systems, Faculty of Business and Law, Victoria University.

Khanchouch, A. (2005). E-tourism: an innovative approach for the small and medium-sized tourism enterprises (SMTE) in Tunisia. Retrieved 1 September, 2008, from http://citeseerx.ist.psu.edu/viewdoc/summary?doi=10.1.1.83.5422

Kim, J., & Lee, J. (2002). Critical design factors for successful e-commerce systems. *Behaviour & Information Technology, 21*(3), 185-199.

Lee, Y., & Kozar, K. (2006). Investigating the effect of website quality on e-business success: an analytic hierarchy process (AHP) approach. *Decision Support Systems, 42*, 1383-1401.

Lefebvrea, L., Lefebvrea, E., Elia, E., & Boeck, H. (2005). Exploring B-to-B e-commerce adoption trajectories in manufacturing SMEs. *Technovation, 25*, 1443-1456.

Levy, M., & Powell, P. (2002). *SME internet adoption: towards a transporter model.* Paper presented at the 15th Bled Electronic Commerce Conference eReality: Constructing the eEconomy. Bled, Slovenia.

Lin, D., Zhou, Z., & Guo, X. (2009). A study of the website performance of travel agencies based on the EMICA model. *J. Service Science & Management, 3*, 181-185.

Liu, C., & Arnett, K. (2000). Exploring the factors associated with Web site success in the context of electronic commerce *Information & Management, 38*, 23-33.

Liu, Z. (2000, June 24-26). *Internet tourism marketing: potential and constraints* Paper presented at the Fourth International Conference "Tourism in Southeast Asia & Indo-China: Development, Marketing and Sustainability, ChiangMai, Thailand.

Lu, Y., & Deng, Z. (2007). Analysis and evaluation of tourism e-commerce websites in China. *International Journal of Services, Economics and Management, 1*(1), 6-22.

Mckay, J., Marshall, P., & Prananto, A. (2000). Stages of maturity for e-business: the SOG-e model. Retrieved 9 April, 2009, from http://www.pacis-net.org/file/2000/29-43.pdf

Merwe, R., & Bekker, J. (2003). A framework and methodology for evaluating e-commerce web sites. *Internet Research: Electronic Networking Applications and Policy, 13*(5), 330-341.

Ministry of Tourism. (2008). Law no. 38 (1977) on "Organizing activities of travel companies in Egypt, detailed index. Licensing Department, Cairo: Egypt.

Moersch, C. (1995). Levels of technology implementation (LoTi): A framework for measuring classroom technology use. Retrieved 8 April, 2009, from http://loticonnection.com/pdf/LoTiFrameworkNov95.pdf

NCC. (2009). E-Commerce - exploiting the business to business model. Retrieved 8 April, 2009, from http://www.nccmembership.co.uk/pooled/articles/BF_WEBART/view.asp?Q=BF_W EBART_113141

Patricia, D. S. (2008). The internet, threat or tool for travel agencies? Retrieved 5 February, 2009, from http://steconomice.uoradea.ro/anale/volume/2008/v2-economy-and-business-administration/017.pdf

Rao, S., Metts, G., & Monge, C. (2003). Electronic commerce development in small and medium sized enterprises: a stage model and its implications. *Business Process management Journal, 9*(1), 11-32.

Rayport, J., & Jaworski, B. (2002). *Introduction to e-commerce* (2nd ed.). Boston: Irwin/McGraw-Hill.

Rosen, A. (2002). *The e-commerce questions and answers book* (2nd ed.). USA: AMACOM.

Scarborough, N., & Zimmerer, W. (2003). *Effective small business management: an entrepreneurial approach* (7th ed.). New Jersey: Pearson Education LTD.

Standing, C., Borbely, C., S. & Vasudavan, T. (1999). *A study of web diffusion in travel agencies.* Paper presented at the 32nd Hawaii International Conference on System Sciences, Hawaii.

Walcott, P. (2007). Evaluating the readiness of e-commerce websites. *International Journal of Computers, 1*(4), 263-268.

Wan, C. (2002). The web sites of international tourist hotels and tour wholesalers in Taiwan. *Tourism Management, 23* , 155–160.

Wiertz, C. (2001). The internet adoption decision in small and medium enterprises (SMEs). Retrieved 12 February, 2009, from http://www.bonissen.de/ib/papers/Small%20Biz.pdf

Willcocks, L. (2000). *Moving to e-business: The ultimate guide to effective E-business.* London: Random House Business Book.

WTO. (2001). *E-business for tourism: practical guideline for tourism destination and Business.* Madrid: Spain WTOBC.

Yao, J. (2004). Ecommerce adoption of insurance companies in New Zealand. *Journal of Electronic Commerce Research, 5*(1), 54-61.

Zafiropoulos, C., & Vrana, V. (2006). A framework for the evaluation of hotel websites: the case of Greece. *Information Technology & Tourism, 8*, 239-254.

Acknowledgement

The first author would like to express his gratitude for the sponsor of his research studies (Fayoum University in Egypt).

Service Bundling with seekda! Dynamic Shop

James Scicluna, Nathalie Steinmetz, and
Michal Zaremba

seekda GmbH
6020 Innsbruck, Austria
name.surname@seekda.com

Abstract

The e-Tourism industry has brought incredible benefits to the consumer. A large – and still growing – number of holiday and business travels are today booked via the Internet. With the e-Tourism market becoming larger, consumers are looking beyond the usual travel services like hotel room and flight booking. They are increasingly searching for third party services that fit to their journey (e.g. travel insurances, excursions, renting of equipment). This is however not an easy task as the consumers are obliged to surf through many different websites in order to find and book those services. This paper presents a solution to this problem in form of the *seekda! dynamic shop*. It provides consumers with a single stop-point, e.g., the hotel's website, where they can semi-automatically aggregate hotelier and third party services for their specific travel. The dynamic shop automatically suggests desired services to the consumers that then only need to choose the ones they prefer.

Keywords: e-Tourism, shop, booking, service, composition, parametric design

1 Introduction

The last decade has seen a major development in IT technologies and in the general software landscape, with traditional software systems being more and more replaced or joined by service-oriented architectures (SOAs). Industry in general has widely adopted these new technologies by today, the tourism industry in particular being an important exploiter. The usage of new IT technologies in the touristic sector allows customers to book their holidays and organize their trips (or parts of it) online. This includes the booking of flights, train tickets and hotels, but as well the booking of related things like car rental at the travel destination, concerts, etc. The current state of online booking systems is though not easy and consumer-friendly. Imagine a scenario where a tourist plans a travel to Innsbruck in winter. The tourist books her/his stay online, by doing a reservation over the chosen hotel's website. She/he is arriving by plane, and would like to directly book the transport from the airport to the hotel by choosing either a taxi or a special shuttle service. As the Innsbruck region is a famous winter sports area, she/he would like to combine the stay with some skiing and would therefore be glad to obtain immediately the skinning ticket and rent the equipment. Last but not least she/he would like to buy a travel insurance. To book all these services, the tourist would currently need to visit several websites, search manually for the fitting services and re-enter his data (like name, address, payment details) several times into Web forms, etc. Now imagine all these services would be offered directly on the hotel website: this would allow the tourist to do these bookings in a one-stop manner, i.e., she/he would only need to enter the required details once and choose the services that are relevant for her/him.

In this paper, we present our current ongoing work that aims at overcoming the problems above. Our system – *seekda! dynamic shop* – provides an easy one-stop point for booking third party services, that are suggested to the user, given that the specified constraints are met. These constraints come either from the hotelier, the service provider or the consumer. Our immediate work focuses on integrating this system within seekda's *Internet Booking Engine* (IBE), which is part of the *seekda! connect* system[1]. In the future, we aim at allowing to create templates of services that are semi-automatically refined into concrete service bundles that are ready to be executed and booked. Furthermore, the available services are obtained either from our seekda search engine[2] or from the ones that are directly registered by the service providers. To this extent, we also provide here a brief overview of the search engine.

2 Background

Before it becomes possible to use services within the dynamic shop, several steps need to be done: the provider needs to describe and publish the service; the service consumer needs to discover the fitting service and eventually consume it. As stated, for the needs of the dynamic shop, services are either picked up from the seekda search engine's database or by having the service provider register the service directly. There are several ways to describe and publish (Web) services, but we will concentrate on two approaches: using the Web Service Description Language (WSDL[3]) or using Web APIs (a.k.a. RESTful services [Fielding, 2000]). WSDL is an XML-based language that describes the interface of a Web Service mainly in terms of endpoints, bindings (defining the supported transport protocols and formats), operations and messages. Most often WSDL is used in conjuction with the SOAP[4] protocol. As opposed to WSDL service descriptions, Web APIs do not comply with any standard. Web APIs are actually HTML documents, similar as other Web pages. What differentiates them is only the fact that they expose a functionality that can be invoked over the Internet. In most cases this happens by simply adding a specific query string to a URL that then calls a specific method in the background (e.g. https://api.linode.com/api/?api_key=cakeisgood&action=domainGet&DomainId =45F33). RESTful services, as introduced in [Fielding, 2000], are usually a lot easier to create than WSDL services and are quite understandable for humans. At the same time they are easier to use, as no special client-side code is required to retrieve results. Web APIs are accessible over the Internet using basic HTTP request methods (GET, POST, PUT, DELETE), but as well using SOAP.

As already mentioned in the introduction, Web Services allow all possible functionalities to be exposed on the Web and to be flexibly integrated, either in

---

[1] http://connect.seekda.com
[2] http://webservices.seekda.com
[3] http://www.w3.org/TR/wsdl
[4] http://www.w3.org/TR/soap/

traditional software applications or in Web pages. This way Web Services provide new means for interoperability of business logics, as providers can offer their functionalities in a completely platform- and client-independent way. Another important characteristic of Web Services is the ability to compose them. If, e.g., an atomic service does not yet provide a required functionality, several services can be composed together that then provide a new functionality (that may not have been intended by the single service providers). Between the publishing of a service and its usage – either direct or within compositions – an important step is missing: the service discovery. End-users need to find the service(s) that fit their requirements and that fulfill their conditions (e.g., free service or commercial service, availability, etc.). Section 3 provides an overview on how we approach the task of service discovery while Section 4 presents our approach for composing services, with focus to the e-Tourism domain.

3 Discovering Services

In the scope of the e-Tourism dynamic shop we need to find services that can be composed dynamically to interesting bundles. Such services include to a large part commercial services, as transportation booking (e.g., flight, taxi, shuttle, car rental), insurances, event tickets, sports material renting, etc. But also public free services like weather services, currency converters, maps, etc., are interesting to be embedded in e-Tourism bundles. Both service types – commercial and free – have one thing in common: they need to be discovered before they can be embedded into the dynamic shop. In the beginnings of the Web Service era, UDDI [Bellwood et al., 2002] was proposed as solution to publish and search services. The standard has though not prevailed in the domain of publicly available Web Services, but is today mostly restricted to company internal registries. Three ways to discover services are today pre-dominant: (a) the search on specific portals (e.g., ProgrammableWeb[5]) where services need to be registered manually, (b) the search over standard search engines using keyword search, and (c) the search over vertical search engines focused on Web Services (e.g., seekda Web Service search engine[6]). [Bachlechner et al., 2006] and [Lausen&Haselwanter, 2007] discuss the efficiency of the approaches using specific portals and standard search engines and outline some related problems like outdated or missing data. [Lausen&Steinmetz, 2008] provides moreover a quantitative analysis of Web Service search using these methods.

The approach that we use for the seekda Web Service search engine to discover services is based on focused crawling techniques to automatically detect publicly available services on the Web – both WSDL-based services and Web APIs. The aim of the crawling is to find as much as possible information that is related to the services, such as provider homepages, pricing schemes, terms and conditions, information on whether the services are commercial and/or need authentication, etc. As this paper concentrates on the dynamic shop built on top of the services, we will not go into detail on the service crawling; it is further described in [Steinmetz et al.,

---

[5] http://www.programmableweb.com
[6] http://webservices.seekda.com

2009]. Our approach allows us to find many thousands of services (more than using specific portals or standard search engines as shows [Lausen&Steinmetz, 2008]). The services include both commercial and free services and offer many different functionalities in diverse domains. Surely the free services found via the above described method can be interesting for hoteliers to be embedded on their website, allowing them to improve the service they offer to their customers (e.g. providing the current weather conditions as information to their clients or providing a currency converter to allow clients from different currency areas to see the room prices in their own local currency). The commercial services (as e.g., travel insurance, shuttle service, event tickets) require prior negotiations with the service providers before being embeddable in the dynamic shop. On the one hand business related issues like pricing schemes, terms and conditions, etc. need to be clarified, on the other hand technical constraints and interaction issues need to be settled, like required input data, service availability, etc. The usage of the focused Web Service search engine for discovering interesting services brings many advantages. The services are monitored on a daily basis, a fact that allows us to (partially) judge the quality of the services. Web Services are often underlying quick changes: new services come up, old services drop away, services become temporally unavailable, etc. The fact that we rely on a large repository of available monitored services allows us to quickly react to such changes and to offer new services to the customers when established ones become unavailable.

4 Bundling Services

In the following we will describe our approach for constructing service bundles, i.e. for composing hotelier and third-party services that can be booked in a one-stop-manner by the hotelier clients. As already mentioned before, our immediate work focuses on enabling the dynamic shop with the IBE, followed by a system for creating service templates and refining them into service bundles. Nevertheless, the common core of these subcomponents is a system for suggesting and combining services using the parametric design methodology. Therefore, the dynamic shop finally aims at creating service bundles by leveraging between static and dynamic composition of services. At the static level, it will adopt widely known notations for creating templates; at the dynamic level, it will develop and implement service composition algorithms inspired from parametric design techniques [Motta & Zdrahal, 1998][Teije et al., 2004]. The bundling solution (which we call a Service Bundle) can be characterised by dynamic discovery and binding of third-party services. Fig. 1 shows a conceptual diagram of the service bundling process, as envisioned from the consumer point of view.

Note that the dynamic shop is intended to be used within *seekda! connect*, which allows hoteliers to manage their own hotel booking system (room descriptions, information, availabilities, prices, etc.) and also their presence on hotel distribution channels. Within this system, hoteliers may choose which third-party services can be suggested to the consumers that are booking a room in their hotel. Details of *seekda! connect* are out of the scope of this paper.

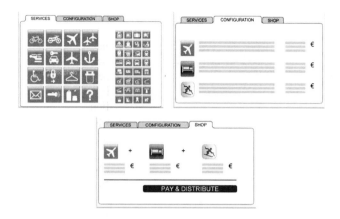

Fig. 1. Conceptual diagram of the service bundling process

In the following of this section, we will give an overview of the general system and the entities involved (Section 4.1) and proceed with further details about the techniques employed by the dynamic shop (Section 4.2), and a small use case (Section 4.3).

4.1 Overview

There are three main entities that interact with the dynamic shop, namely:

- Third party service providers
- Hoteliers
- Consumers

Third party service providers register their services with the system. Currently, such a registration is expected to be done manually by the technical team. In the future, a specific portal will be implemented to perform such a registration. Apart from the description of the services, the providers must register the type of data that is required for booking their service(s), the conditions under which they can be used and the pricing schemes. When setting up a hotel with *seekda! connect*, the hotelier can then choose which third party services can be suggested by the system to the consumers. Finally, consumers can configure the constraints and requirements they desire from their services and the dynamic shop automatically aggregates and/or suggests services that fulfill these constraints. Note that all information is stored using OTA (Open Travel Association[7]) message formats on the *switch*, an entity belonging to *seekda! connect*, which we will not further detail here. Fig. 2 provides an overview of the dynamic shop, the entities that mainly interact with it and the *seekda! connect* environment in which the shop is embedded.

---

[7] http://www.opentravel.org/

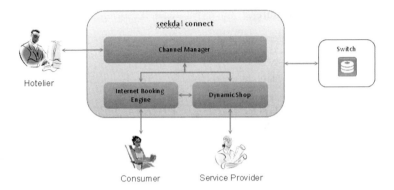

Fig. 2. Entities interacting with the dynamic shop

One of the main advantages of a template based approach for composing several services is reusability. Templates can be stored and reused in similar domains[McIlraith & Cao Son, 2002] [Mandell & McIlraith, 2003]. The changes for templates within the same domain are expected to be minimal and in any cases, this boils down to different settings for constraints and parameters and peculiarities for the specific context in which the bundle has to be executed. Not only the provider of the service platform benefits from it (i.e., seekda) but also the clients (hoteliers and consumers) since skeletons of service bundles (in the form of templates) are readily available and just need to be tailored for specific needs. Again, this results in less effort and consequently less cost burden. Furthermore, the tool itself will be generic enough to handle different kinds of scenarios, i.e. beyond e-Tourism where we envision further applications in the area of e-Conferencing and e-Messaging. This is different from current approaches in industry where generally tools are tailored for specific domains. All in all, we expect to achieve a high degree of flexibility by making the generation of service bundles efficient.

From a scientific perspective, one of the main interesting aspects is how the parametric design methodology will be used for a practical composition of services at a level usable in the industry settings. There has been very little work conducted in this respect, which all does not really cover real world scenarios. Another interesting aspect is the language and data-model used by the system. We stick to XML as the underlying format for describing all the aspects surrounding services. More precisely, we use a subset of the OTA schemas and extend them with support for services. Many of the elements that are required are already modelled in this schema. For example, service providers need to define the conditions that must be met in order for the services to be used. This can be done through the *OfferRules* type in the schemas. However - as said - there is no support for third party services and the managing thereof. We provide these extensions. The advantages brought about by choosing these schemas are two-fold: (1) XML is the de facto standard for message exchange in industry, implying that therefore integration is highly facilitated, and (2) it is a lightweight syntax and therefore does not hamper the performance of the configuration algorithms employed by the dynamic shop.

To summarise, the main features of the dynamic shop for bundling services are:

- It adopts and extends OTA as the standard datamodel for describing the relevant aspects around third party services
- It implements new algorithms for service composition, based on the parametric design methodology
- It automatically suggests services that can be aggregated in the service bundle, based on the consumer requirements and taking into account third party provider and hotelier constraints

4.2 Approach

The main components of the Service Bundler are illustrated in Fig. 3. It is comprised of two main components, namely, the *Graphical Interface* and the *Enactment Engine*. The components will have access to the *Template, Message Mapping* and the *Service repositories*.

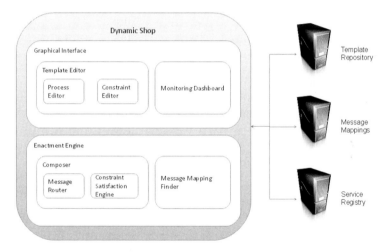

Fig. 3. The Service Bundler Architecture

The *Graphical Interface* is the main entry point for the creation of templates; it is composed of the *Template Editor* and the *Monitoring Dashboard*. The template editor enables to graphically define a classical process (through the *Process Editor*) and additionally to specify constraints (and parameters) that are required to be satisfied by the services (through the *Constraint Editor*). The former typically resembles a normal workflow editor, with additional elements required to fulfill the system's needs; the latter allows the creation and specification of constraints, allowing also actions to be taken in case of constraint violations. The second component of the graphical interface - the monitoring dashboard – allows the selection and configuration of specific monitoring probes as part of the bundle, as well as to monitor service endpoints (for example, for availability). This is useful as it allows us, e.g., not to suggest a service to the consumer that is currently not available. We leave this as part of our future work. The *Enactment Engine* consists of the *Composer* and the *Message Mapping Finder*. The composer is responsible for finding appropriate services that match the required constraints and parameters; this is done through the *Constraint Satisfaction Engine*. If services are required to be connected with one another (especially when one is dependent on the other), then the *Message Router* comes into play to route the appropriate messages between them through the required control flow constructs. The message mapping finder is used to identify the required mappings between the different schema types of the services. The heart of the dynamic shop is the composer component which employs parametric design techniques. This methodology is formalised following [Motta, 1999]. A Parametric Design problem task is characterized as a mapping

$$< P, V_r, C, R, Pr, cf > \rightarrow \{D_1^{sol}, \dots, D_m^{sol}\}$$

such that

- P a set of parameters $\{p_1, \dots, p_n\}$
- V_n a set of value ranges $V_1, \dots, V_n$ s.t. $V_i = \{v_i^1, \dots, v_i^l\}$
- C a set of constraints $\{c_1, \dots, c_k\}$
- R a set of requirements $\{r_1, \dots, r_j\}$
- Pr a set of preferences $\{pr_1, \dots, pr_i\}$
- cf a global cost function

These map to our context as follows:

- parameters are expressed by the service descriptions themselves (e.g., the number of people required for a shuttle transfer)
- value ranges are the actual types of the parameters – since we rely on OTA, these are expressed using XML
- constraints restrict the actual values of the parameters – these are obtained from the service provider (e.g., the service is only available in a given region) or, commonly, by the end user (e.g., the date of when the service is desired).
- preferences define priorities over constraints, namely, it is acceptable that certain constraints can be relaxed, while some of them need to be fulfilled. For integrating with the IBE, all constraints are expected to be fulfilled but within the template creation, these can be given preference values.
- the global cost function is technically a function that aggregates all the cost functions for the preferences.

Essentially, at the heart of each configuration problem are two main tasks, namely, constraint resolution and searching for a solution that satisfies the task. Searching for a solution involves performing the actual constraint resolution. Our immediate work focuses on the constraint satisfaction engine. It is used through the IBE to filter out services that can be suggested to the user, which can eventually be booked by the latter. This is currently being implemented in Java, but will eventually be extended to support more expressive constraints through the integration of a rule engine, (e.g. Jess[8]).

The template editor and bundler, will require also to search over the so called *possible design models* for a solution satisfying the constraints. Therefore, at this stage, it is not enough that constraints are satisfied. Preferences must be evaluated over different design models such as the ones that ore more adequate are selected. This is essentially a search problem, whereby some problem solving methods can be used (e.g., EMR – Extend Model then Revise, CMR-A* - Complete Model then Revise with A*, etc.). We will investigate and optimize a suitable problem solving method to be used within our system. Specifically, we will develop heuristics that enable efficient search within the search space, similar to techniques used in [Börn et al., 2008] [Hoffmann et al., 2008]. This is yet part of our future work. Other aspects like soundness and completeness of the solutions, and transactional issues are still yet to be investigated. Note that the method here differs from traditional AI Planning techniques. The latter generally start with a solution and chain services one after the other in order to satisfy a given goal. The approach used here – parametric design - starts from a proposed template and iteratively refines it into possible design models, until a model satisfies the specified constraints. Nevertheless, the two techniques may share commonalities in their search methodology. For example, the local search method can be used by both AI Planning and Parametric Design.

4.3 Example

We have developed a simple demo that provides the user suggestions for adding third party services after she/he has booked a room in a hotel. In this case, the hotelier enabled an airport shuttle service and a travel insurance agency (see **Fig. 4**). Furthermore, the services are suggested by the system because their location also matches the location of the hotel. In this case, the user is searching for a hotel room through Hotel Erfolg's website. This hotel is situated in the Austrian region of Tyrol. Since Four Seasons travel and also Hanse Merkur Insurance operate in that region, the services are suggested by the system. The user selects the Four Seasons airport shuttle service. Some of the data needed for this third party service is already available from the context of the room booking process and is automatically presented by the system. Note also that some of this data is in fact used as a constraint for the service (e.g., the start and end dates of the travel constraint the service to be available during that period). Now the user only needs to enter the rest of the required data (see **Fig. 5**) and to click 'Purchase'. The service is then booked, with minimal effort from the end user. Note that at the current state, it is the service provider that guarantees to the end user that the service is provided.

---

[8] http://www.jessrules.com/

Fig. 4. Demo of the initial dynamic shop prototype: the user is presented with the available services

Fig. 5. Demo of the initial dynamic shop prototype: the user is selecting the airport shuttle service and inputting missing data

5   Related Work

The *seekda! dynamic shop* will be embedded into a hotel booking management system, *seekda! connect*. In terms of functionality there exist similar systems than seekda! connect, differing mostly from it in terms of scalabily. Major players in this market are: Pegasus Solutions, Synxis, Cultuzz, GlobRes, Booking booster, Live

Link, UniTravel and Hotelupdater & ETPo. While these tools differ partly in terms of available features, their common characteristic is that they can be used for global data exchange between offerers (hoteliers), distributors and marketing executives in the tourism and hotel industries. Nevertheless they do not include a shop as the seekda! dynamic shop that allows the flexible and dynamic bundling of hotelier and third-party services as described in Section 4. The technologies used in the context of the dynamic shop aim to change the sales process for small and mid-size hotels. Service composition within existing e-Tourism products remains a manual and labor-intensive process leading to high costs. In addition operators are integrating third-party services very reluctantly. We develop technologies to ease service composition and configuration to a level that hoteliers and end users can easily modify and adjust usually complex processes.

Parametric design methodologies that are proposed to be used, bridge the gap between static and dynamic composition. We can scale better in environments where services are changing all the time. At the static level, we adopt known notations, especially BPMN (Business Process Modeling Notation)[9], to support designers in defining abstract parametrized processes. At the dynamic level, we will develop and implement composition algorithms inspired from the parametric design techniques allowing for a run-time binding of appropriate services to meet all the constraints as defined by the process. With existing solutions, process composition can be performed at two levels: static and dynamic. Static service composition, which is the current de-facto industry approach to composition, is done manually generally by a process designer prior the execution of the composite process. This usually results in a static process description based on BPEL (Web Services Business Process Execution Language)[10]. Dynamic service composition is performed using some specific algorithms that can automatically search for a chain of services that fulfill a particular requirement (or goal). This type of composition can be done at both design-time and run-time and usually employs AI (Artificial Intelligence) planning techniques [Narayanan & McIlraith, 2002] [Pistore et al., 2005] [Sycara et al., 2003]. Static approaches hamper severely on effort and time spent to design the processes, while fully fledged dynamic approaches cannot scale and cannot produce readily executable composed processes. Our techniques blend both approaches by refining templates and thus limiting the search space and also enabling a readily executable process as a result.

6   Conclusion and Future Work

In this paper we presented the seekda! dynamic shop: a one-stop point for booking third party services when planning holidays. Our current work focuses on extending the IBE with the dynamic shop. More precisely, we are focusing on describing the services within OTA, and on developing the constraint satisfaction engine together with the required graphical presentation elements. Our future work will focus on developing a fully fledged portal for service registration and for the creation of

---

[9] http://www.bpmn.org/
[10] http://www.oasis-open.org/committees/tc_home.php?wg_abbrev=wsbpel

templates. At the core of this portal will be the development of the appropriate problem solving methods for finding bundling solutions which can be readily executed.

References

Fielding R.T. (2000). *Architectural Styles and the Design of Network-based Software Architectures*. University of California, Irvine.

Bellwood T., Clément L., Ehnebuske D., Hately A., Hondo M., Husband Y.L., Januszewski K., Lee S., McKee B., Munter J., & von Riegen C. (2002). UDDI version 3.0.

Bachlechner D., Siorpaes K., Lausen H. & Fensel D. (2006). Web Service discovery – a reality check. 3rd European Semantic Web Conference.

Lausen H. & Haselwanter T. (2007). Finding Web Services. 1st European Semantic Technology Conference.

Lausen H. & Steinmetz S. (2008). *Survey of current means to discover Web Services*. Technical report. STI Innsbruck, University of Innsbruck.

Steinmetz N., Lausen H. & Brunner M. (2009). Web Service Search on Large Scale. 7th International Joint Conference on Service Oriented Computing.

Motta E. & Zdrahal Z. (1998). Parametric Design Problem Solving. Knowledge Media Institute, The Open University, Milton Keynes. Available from: http://ksi.cpsc.ucalgary.ca/KAW/KAW96/motta/pardes-banff.html

ten Teije A., van Harmelen F. & Wielinga B. (2004). Configuration of Web Services as Parametric Design. Proceedings of the International Conference on Knowledge Engineering and Knowledge Management.

McIlraith S. & Cao Son T. (2002). Adapting Golog for Composition of Semantic Web Services. Proceedings of the 8th International Conference on Principles and Knowledge Representation and Reasoning. See: http://citeseer.ist.psu.edu/mcilraith02adapting.html.

Mandell D. & McIlraith S. (2003). Adapting BPEL4WS for the Semantic Web: The Bottom-Up Approach to Web Service Interoperation. Proceedings of the International Semantic Web Conference.

Motta E. (1999). Reusable Components for Knowledge Modelling: Case Studies in Parametric Design Problem Solving. IOS Press. ISBN: 1586030035. Amsterdam, The Netherlands.

Börn M., Hoffmann J., Kaczmarek T., Kowalkiewicz M., Markovic I., Scicluna J., Weber I. & Zhou X. (2008). Semantic Annotation and Composition of Business Processes with Maestro. Proceedings of the 5th European Semantic Web Conference.

Hoffmann J., Weber I., Scicluna J., Kaczmarek T. & Ankolekar A. (2008). Combining Scalability and Expressivity in the Automatic Composition of Semantic Web Services. Proceedings of the 8th International Conference on Web Engineering.

Narayanan S. & McIlraith S. (2002). Simulation, Verification and Automated Composition of Web Services. Proceedings of the International World Wide Web Conference.

Pistore M., Traverso P. & Bertoli P. (2005). Automated Composition of Web Services by Planning in Asynchronous Domains. Proceedings of the International Conference on Automated Planning and Scheduling.

Sycara K., Paolucci M., Ankolekar A. & Srinivasan N. (2003). Automated Discovery, Interaction and Composition of Semantic Web Services. *Journal of Web Semantics*, 2003, vol. 1, nr. 1, pages 27-46.

An Analysis of Search Engine Use for Travel Planning

Daniel R. Fesenmaier[a],
Zheng Xiang[b]
Bing Pan[c], and
Rob Law[d]

[a]National Laboratory for Tourism & eCommerce
School of Tourism and Hospitality Management
Temple University, USA
drfez@temple.edu

[b]School of Merchandising and Hospitality Management
University of North Texas, USA
philxz@unt.edu

[c]School of Business and Economics
College of Charleston, USA
bingpan@gmail.com

[d]School of Hotel and Tourism Management
Hong Kong Polytechnic University, Kowloon, Hong Kong
hmroblaw@polyu.edu.hk

Abstract

Search engines have become a central part of the internet marketing strategy of tourism businesses and, as such, it is essential that destination marketing organizations have a substantial understanding of how search engines are used within the travel planning process. This study proposed a three stage framework for examining how online travellers use search engines and how aspects of the travel planning process shapes this use. A series of key relationships were examined based upon a national survey of American online travel planners. The findings provide significant insight into the role of search engines for travel planning.

Keywords: Search engine marketing; information search; travel planning; destination marketing.

1 Introduction

With the growth of information on all facets of the tourism experience search engines such as Google and Yahoo! have become the "Hubble" of the internet galaxy, enabling travellers to navigate through this space so as to find information that might be useful in the travel planning process (Xiang, Wöber and Fesenmaier, 2008). Recent studies by the Travel Industry Association of America (TIA, 2009) and others have shown that the majority of U.S. travellers use search engines for vacation planning. As a result, search engines have been recognized as the "first step" in the online travel planning process, and therefore, a critical starting point with which destination marketing organizations (DMOs) can communicate through techniques such as search engine marketing (SEM) and search engine optimization (SEO).

Recently, a number of studies focusing on internet search have been conducted within the tourism context (Döring, 2008; Pan & Fesenmaier, 2006; Pan, Litvin, and O'Donnell, 2007; Xiang, Wöber and Fesenmaier, 2008; Xiang, Gretzel and Fesenmaier, 2009). These studies indicate that search engines provide a simplified view of the online tourism domain. Importantly, this view changes on a daily basis and, thus, poses enormous challenges for search engine marketing in tourism. As such, it is argued that search engine marketing is a complex and dynamic process which requires a substantial understanding of how potential visitors use search engines as part of the travel planning process (Moran and Hunt, 2005; Murphy and Kielgast, 2008; Sen, 2005). The goal of this study was, therefore, to build upon this literature to develop a general framework that links together the stages of search and the online travel planning process. It is hoped that this framework will provide a foundation for the development of effective search engine marketing programs for destination marketing organizations.

2   Research Background

The research on search engines and information search has largely been based in computer science, information science, and consumer behaviour. Due to the growing importance of online information search in travel, the use of search engines in the travel planning context has become an increasingly important topic in tourism. This section synthesizes the recent literature on consumers and travellers' use of search engines and then proposes a general framework that describes the various aspects of this process.

2.1 Related Literature

Studies on the use of search engines generally fall into three categories with the focus on the process of search, the nature of user queries, and the interaction between the user and the search interface, respectively. From the process standpoint, using a search engine can be understood as consisting of three distinct steps: 1) query formulation, wherein the user enters a query into the search engine interface (Levene 2006; Slone, 2002); 2) search results generation, wherein the search engine retrieves a number of search results that "match" the query and then displays them in a pre-defined format; and, 3) search results evaluation, wherein the user evaluates the search results and then navigates back and forth between the search engine interface and the web pages linked to those results (Jansen, Spink and Saracevic, 2000; Jansen and Spink 2005; Jansen and Pooch 2001; Marchionini , 1997; Su, 2002).

With respect to user queries, studies by Jansen and his colleagues, and more recently by Xiang et al. (2008) indicate that users' questions tend to be short, consisting of less than four keywords. Studies by Pan et al. (2007) and Hwang, Xiang, Gretzel, &

Fesenmaier (2009) also indicate that searchers usually focus on cities as the geographical boundary instead of states or countries. For example, a search for a city combined with a specific hotel or a hotel brand is one of most common queries that occur when travellers perform accommodation-related searches. In addition, they conclude that travellers often combine their searches for accommodations with other aspects of the trip, including dining, attractions, destinations, or transportation; additionally, many travellers engage in a switching behaviour that varies between broad and focused search strategies (Hwang et al., 2009).

Several studies have focused on users' interaction with the search engine interface, indicating that the rank of web pages significantly influences internet navigation. For example, the majority of search engine users do not look beyond the first three pages of search results (Henzinger, 2007; Pan et al., 2007), which implies that only a relatively small number of search results are relevant from the marketing perspective. Studies also show that users trust more organic listings, which, in turn, have a higher conversion rate (Jansen and Spink, 2006). Recently, Pan et al. (2007) found that the order of search results presented by Google, etc. dramatically affects selection of the respective link; specifically, the subjects were significantly more likely to select the first and second suggested links, that the those links presented 8th – 10th were also likely to be chosen, and those links presented 3rd – 7th were very unlikely to be chosen, due to the scrolling effects. Additionally, Kim and Fesenmaier (2008) suggest that the use of search engines has a significant effect on impression formation, and consequently on the selection and overall evaluation of the website of the tourist firm.

2.2 A General Framework of the Use of a Search Engine for Travel Planning

While past literature in both computer/information sciences and the tourism field has defined a new research area in travellers' use of new technology, most of existing studies have focused on the search process (i.e., the interaction, user queries, search strategies, etc). Building upon this research, a framework is proposed to describe search engine use in relation to the travel planning process. This framework views the use of a search engine for travel planning as a system with its antecedents as well as certain outcomes and feedbacks. As shown in Fig. 1, the first stage, i.e., Pre-Search Conditions, sets the foundation for the actual search process. These conditions include travellers' online information search activities (e.g. searching for a destination, prices for trip, etc.) for travel, the use of various online travel-related tools (e.g. websites provides by airlines, travel agencies, etc.) to find this information, whether or not (yes/no) the traveller will use a search engine as well as the perceived usefulness of the search engine for the current trip planning task. The second stage, i.e., Search Process, describes the basic frames the traveller uses to guide use of the respective search engines within the travelling planning effort. These frames affect the nature of the search query as well as their evaluations of search engine results pages (SERPs). The third stage, i.e., Overall Evaluation, focuses on the overall assessment of search engines as a result of the travel planning process. This stage of search engine use not only results in an overall evaluation (i.e., level of satisfaction), but also attitude formation toward search engine use for future travel planning including the perceived quality of the trip plan, ease of use, as well as whether the search engine was

384

trustworthy. Finally, it is important to note that this third stage provides the feedback to Stage 1 and sets the stage for future use of search engines for trip planning.

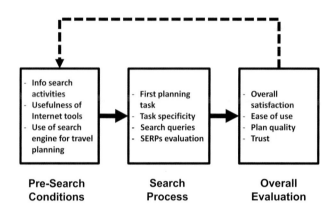

Fig. 1. A General Framework of the Use of a Search Engine for Travel Planning

More specifically, it is hypothesized that two constructs, i.e., the various types of information search activities (Fodness and Murray, 1998; Vogt and Fesenmaier, 1998) and the past use of the various tools/websites on the internet for trip planning (Brandt and Uden, 2003; Hendry and Efthimiadia, 2008; Jansen and Molina 2006; Su, 2002), determine whether or not the traveller regularly will use a search engine as part of the online travel planning process. Thus, it is expected that people who actively seek information about a destination and consider search engines very useful would also consider search engines essential for the specific task of finding information about a particular or alternative destinations.

The search process (the second stage of the framework) describes the sequential aspects of using a search engine including the initial user query, the level of task specificity, and the evaluation of SERPs. The initial user query is conceptualized as the first planning task, i.e., where to begin the search with, e.g., either a destination or accommodation (given a destination has already been chosen). Also, the degree of task specificity (i.e., general vs. specific) is important in that it affects the keywords entered into the search engine as well as the number of search results considered (Jansen and Pooch, 2001). For example, one might expect that when the traveller has already decided the destination and wishes to seek information about places to visit or, perhaps, a hotel at the destination, he/she would use the name of the destination as the keyword within a search engine; and, it might be expected that the number searches he/she would evaluate would be relatively limited.

The third stage, i.e., Overall Evaluation, can be defined using four constructs. First, the traveller forms an overall evaluation of search engines for the use of travel planning, which can be reflected in a general satisfaction measure (Pan and Fesenmaier, 2006; Su, 2002). It is hypothesized that this experience is translated into attitudes towards search engines in terms of trust, ease of use, and their efficacy in supporting the travel planning process (Gefen, Karahanna and Straub, 2003; Gretzel, Fesenmaier and O'Leary, 2006; Nakamura, et al, 2007; Pan and Fesenmaier, 2006; Su, 2002). Thus, it is expected that a person that is very satisfied with their use of search engines would consider search engines as trustworthy, easy to use and the results they provide enable the traveller to make better decisions. Finally, it is hypothesized that these evaluations (and resulting attitudes) shape (or reshape) the mental model that travellers have of the internet (and travel planning tools) as well the use of search engines.

3   Methodology

A national survey was conducted from January 5th – 15th 2009 of Americans that travelled and used the Internet during calendar year 2008. A quota sampling procedure was used whereby 10,000 members of the online panel of Americans maintained by Survey Sampling International (SSI) were invited to participate in the survey, and the first 1,000 respondents (at least) meeting specific conditions were selected. The conditions for participating in this study were that the respondents had to have taken at least one business or pleasure trip (that was at least 50 miles one way from home, or included an overnight stay) and they had used the internet for travel planning including getting information about destinations, checking prices or schedules on the Internet during calendar year 2008. The respective panel members were invited once by SSI to complete the survey with the promise of a small monetary incentive which is established by SSI for all panel members. This effort resulted in a total of 2,508 respondents (representing a 25.1% response rate) completing the initial "filter" questions; 1,288 respondents actually met all conditions of the study and completed the survey.

The online survey was organized into five sections. The first section included a series of "filter" questions relevant to all respondents and focused on their use of the internet, their skills and knowledge of the internet, travel and involvement in the travel planning process. The second section of the survey focused entirely on various aspects of online travel planning including the types of information sought, their attitudes towards various types of websites such as travel agencies, general travel sites and their use of search engines for travel planning. The third section of the survey included questions regarding the respondent's attitudes toward paid listings and other forms of search engine advertising. The next section included a series of questions related to overall satisfaction with the online travel planning process, the use of search engines as well as their attitudes towards search engines in terms of their ability to support the travel planning process. The last section of the survey included a series of questions regarding age, gender, marital status, income and race of the respondent.

Frequency and Chi square analyses were conducted to assess the nature and extent to which online American travellers include search engines as part of their travel planning effort and to assess a set of key relationships within the proposed framework. Chi square analysis was considered appropriate in this exploratory analysis as most of the responses to the questions were discrete, and some questions solicited unstructured responses. Specifically, the analyses focused on testing the following: 1) the relationships between information search activities, evaluation of travel websites and use of search engines for travel planning (Stage 1); that is, this analysis sought to identify the differences between search engine users (SETs) and non users (NSETs) in terms of their online information search activities and the types of websites they use; 2) the relationships between the frames travellers' establish (i.e., first planning task and specificity of search) and the nature of their search query used and their evaluation of SERPs (Stage 2); 3) the relationships between overall evaluation (i.e., satisfaction with the use of search engines as part of the travel planning process) and their attitudes toward search engines including trust, perceived ease of use, and the quality of the trip plan (Stage 3); and, 4) the relationships between the attitudes toward search engines (i.e., trust, perceived ease of use and trip plan quality) and information search activities and evaluation of travel websites.

4 Results

The results of the survey show that the respondents were equally distributed in terms of gender (52% women and 48% men). Many of the respondents considered themselves skilful with using the internet and they were relatively successful in finding what they want on the internet. In addition, the results indicate that most respondents were highly involved in travel planning in that about 50 percent indicated that they tend to devote "a lot of time" to planning a trip.

4.1 Search Engine Use for Travel Planning

The analyses indicate that the huge majority of online American travellers (86%) use general search engines to assist in their travel planning efforts; indeed, 44 percent of the respondents indicated that they used 2 – 3 different search engines while 15 percent indicated that they regularly used 4 or more different search engines to assist in travel planning. Also, a majority (65%) indicated that they use search engines "most of the time" or "almost always" (25%). However, most respondents rated general search engines only somewhat useful for travel planning, and very few considered them an essential travel planning tool. Last, search engines were seen as "essential" for finding maps and/or driving by 35% of the respondents, followed by information about a particular destination (23%).

4.2 Pre-Search Conditions

Descriptive analyses show that most respondents searched for information about a particular destination (76%), searched for hotel prices or places to stay (69%), or searched for airline fares and/or schedules (62%). Relatively few persons searched for 800 numbers (8%), information about stores (24%) or cruises (23%). However, it appears that there is substantial agreement in the degree to which online travel agencies, company websites, destination site and search engines are considered useful in the travel planning process. Specifically, 65% of the respondents indicated that general search engines were very useful or essential to the travel planning process, 62% similarly rated company websites and 57% indicated that online travel agencies such as Expedia and Orbitz were very useful or essential.

It was hypothesized that search engine use can be determined by the types of online information activities as well as evaluations of the usefulness of other types of online planning tools. The results of the Chi Square analyses, as shown in Table 1, indicate that there are consistently significant ($\alpha = 0.05$) differences between SETs (search engine users for travel planning) and NSETs (non users) in terms of their online search activities as well as use of the various online travel planning tools. For example, over 80% of the SETs indicated that they normally search for information about the destination vs. only 56%t of NSETs; 72% of SETs searched for hotel prices or places to stay as compared to 49% of NSETs; and, 59% of SETs search for maps as compared to 35% of NSETs. Also, SETS tend to use many more of the online travel planning tools including online travel agencies (SETs = 69% vs. 42 for NSETs), company websites (64 % vs. 51%), destination websites (47% vs. 33%) and community websites (25% vs. 8%).

4.3 Search Process

The results indicate that online travel search generally starts with one of three tasks: Accommodations (29%), destination selection (29%), or transportation (23%). Very few respondents indicated that they started the online travel planning process by considering shopping alternatives (0.7%), attractions (7.0%), or routes (9.4%). However, the results also indicate that most travellers have some sort of general frame of reference (58.5%) which guides their planning process; that is, 24 percent of the respondents reported that they usually start planning their trip with a specific of where and when they will travel. It appears that, in large part, this frame is defined by a destination as the majority (55%) of respondents reported that they used all (or part) of the name of the destination to initiate the search process. This finding contrasts sharply with that only 10 percent of the respondents indicating that they use the name of an online travel agency (OTA) or that 13 percent that searched for an online travel agency. Last, the results indicate that many (31%) American travellers use only the top three search results; and, an additional 20 percent typically use the results reported in the top page (i.e., the top 10 results). This later finding is consistent with the literature which indicates that many people (50% of the respondents) limit their selection to the first page of search results and an additional 18 percent limit their search to 2 pages (Pan et al, 2008).

Table 1. Information search activities, evaluation of travel websites and use online search engines

Construct:	SETs	NSETs
Types of information searched during 2008 (% yes)	**%**	**%**
Searched for info. about a particular destination	80.4	55.6
Searched for hotel prices or places to stay	72.4	48.9
Searched for airline fares and schedules	63.9	54.5

Searched for and printed out maps, driving instructions	58.6	35.4
Searched for things to do at the destination	56.3	32.0
Searched for any type of travel discount or promotion	49.9	27.5
Searched for potential destinations to visit	46.3	24.7
Searched for dining and entertainment at the destination	45.1	25.3
Searched for rental car prices and availability	38.0	24.2
Searched local event calendars at the destination	36.2	19.7
Searched for travel packages for resorts, etc.	27.4	15.7
Searched for stores or other places to shop	26.3	8.4
Searched for cruises	24.3	14.6
Searched for sites that distribute free travel brochures	16.0	10.7
Searched for 800 numbers	9.0	3.9

(Table 1. Continued)

Types of travel-related websites (% very useful/essential)	%	%
General search engines such as Yahoo!, Google or AOL	72.0	24.7
Online travel agencies (i.e., Expedia, Orbitz, Travelocity)	68.5	42.2
Company sites such as airlines, hotels, rental cars	64.0	50.6
Destination sites such as those provided by a city or state	46.5	33.1
General travel sites that provide free brochures	33.0	24.7
Travel search engines such as Kayak or Sidestep	25.0	12.9
Community sites such as Tripadvisor and Virtual Tourist	24.7	8.4
Travel guidebook sites such as Fodors or Lonely Planet	24.7	11.8
Newspaper/magazine sites such as NY Times/Conde Nast Travelers	17.5	7.3
Consumer content generates sites such as Youtube and Flickr	16.1	6.7
Social Networking sites such as Myspace and Friendster	15.7	5.6

Note: Types of information was measured using a yes/no response format; Types of websites was measured using: 1 = not at all useful, 2 = somewhat useful, 3 = very useful, 4 = essential, and 5 = don't know. Chi-square tests were conducted comparing responses for each item to those not using search engines (NSETs) and those respondents indicating they used search engines for travel planning (SETs). All Chi-squared tests were significant at $\alpha = 0.05$.

Two Chi-Square analyses focused on the relationship between the planning task, task specificity and the keyword they first used to initiate the information search process. As can be seen in Tables 2, there are significant ($\alpha = 0.05$) and meaningful relationships between the keywords one uses and the first task in trip planning that define the search process. Table 2 shows that most people use the name of the destination as the keyword used first but the percentage varies substantially by the initial task within the trip planning effort. In this study 34 percent of those using a destination as a keyword consider the destination as the starting point; however, 30 percent of these online travel planners consider accommodations as the initial planning task, and 18 percent indicated that transportation was their starting point. This finding contrasts sharply with those entering the name of an online travel agency where transportation related issues was the most popular task (36%), accommodations was the second most popular (29%) and destination was the third most frequent starting task (24%). Last, 40 percent of those persons knowing the website address focused first on destination and 25 percent started with transportation-related planning.

An additional analysis considered the relationship between task specificity and the keywords used to initiate the search process. As discussed previously, most respondents use the name of the destination to start the search process; however, the results indicate that the types of keywords used differ significantly ($\alpha = 0.05$) depending upon the search frame. For example, 82 percent of those that searched for an online travel agency had a general idea in terms of travel planning effort, as compared to only 35 percent of those entering the name of a slogan or advertising, or 59 percent of those entering a name of a destination. Almost 30 percent of those searching a travel-related company such as a hotel or airline indicated that they had a specific problem when starting the travel planning process; this compares to 24 percent of those searching for a destination and 22 percent that are searching for an online travel agency.

Table 2. Relationship between First Online
Planning Task and Keywords Used First

Which keywords do you use first?	Aspect of Trip Usually Planned First (%)				
	A*	B	C	D	E
The name (all or part) of a destination	29.8	7.8	34.0	10.2	17.5
The name (all or part) of a travel-related company	27.0	8.1	21.6	9.9	31.5
The name (all or part) of an online travel agency	29.4	4.2	23.8	4.9	35.7
The name (all or part) or an online travel magazine	27.3	9.1	36.4	9.1	9.1
A company (all or part) slogan or advertising	40.0	15.0	10.0	10.0	25.0
The name or address of a website	36.5	3.5	16.5	10.6	27.1

*: A. Accommodation; B. Attraction; C. Destination; D. Route; E. Transportation.
All Chi-squared test was significant at $\alpha = 0.05$.

4.4 Overall Evaluation of Search Engine Use

Generally speaking, online travellers are fairly satisfied with the results provided by search engines. A series of analyses between satisfaction and the twelve items used to measure attitudes toward search engines indicate that those persons that are extremely satisfied with search engines were significantly ($\alpha = 0.01$) more likely to trust the results of search engines, consider them easy to use, and to agree that their use improves the quality of the travel plan. In particular, 41 percent of those extremely satisfied agreed that search engines are reliable (vs. 9% for those somewhat satisfied); 61 percent of those extremely satisfied felt that search engines make travel planning easier to complete as compared to 24% of those somewhat satisfied with search engines; finally, 59 percent of those satisfied strongly agreed that the use of search engines enable them to make better travel decisions vs. 22 percent of those only somewhat satisfied (see Table 3).

Table 3. Relationship between Satisfaction with Search Engines for Travel Planning and Attitudes Toward Search Engines

Attitude construct:	Extremely Satisfied	Somewhat Satisfied
General search engines…(% strongly agree)		
Trust		
are reliable	41.0	9.3
are almost like real experts in assisting me	23.7	4.5
provide quality information needed to plan my trip	33.3	10.8
Ease of Use		
provide easy access to a lot of information about travel	56.1	22.8
Make travel planning easier to complete	61.3	23.7
are easy to use	53.2	18.9
are easy to learn	51.7	17.2
are clear and understandable	45.8	12.9
Plan Quality		
enable me to make better travel decisions	58.8	21.7
enable me to do what I want to do	47.1	15.5
find suitable travel plans	55.0	17.9
improves the quality of my travel planning	45.5	15.1
enable me to make better decisions	56.7	20.0

Chi-square tests were conducted comparing respondents attitudes toward the use of search engines and their overall satisfaction level with the use of search engines for travel planning. All Chi-squared tests were significant at $\alpha = 0.05$.

5 Conclusions and Implications

This study proposes a conceptual framework to describe travellers' use of search engines for travel planning. The results of this study confirm that most Americans use general search engines extensively for travel planning along with many other online tools. The results also show that there are strong and consistent relationships between the respective constructs in that those using search engines tend to be very active and involved travel planners; also, they tend to use a variety of online tools – websites within the overall travel planning effort. Importantly, the search frame (as defined by the first task of the online planning process and the level of specificity) sets the stage for the keywords used to start the search effort, which, in turn, affects the depth of search. Last, the results clearly indicate that most online American travellers differ substantially in terms of their satisfaction with the results of general search engines such as Google and Yahoo! and that this satisfaction is reflected in the extent to which search engines can be trusted, are perceived to provide useful results and the extent to which they enable the traveller to make good travel decisions.

The findings have several implications for the development of an effective program in search engine marketing. First, it is clear from this and past research that search engines are mostly used as the initial tool to support the travel planning process; as such, the design and placement of search engine results is a critical part of the communication process and therefore, considerable effort should be invested to make this a positive persuasive experience. Second, search engine users (SETs) are substantially different from the general online travelling population in that they are much more active and involved in the travel planning process. This suggests that destination marketing organizations can and should employ a variety of strategies with which to engage the travel planning including the use of Web 2.0 (i.e., social communities and consumer generated content) to attract and engage potential visitors. Third, the finding that the many people use destination-oriented keywords regardless of the specific planning problem suggests that destination websites should incorporate a range of functions beyond simply providing information about a destination; these functions might include links to travel agencies, accommodations and transportation providers. However, the differences found in this study suggest that it is important to develop smarter search systems that recognize the goals (and search strategy) of the travel planner. Finally, it is an important finding (and, perhaps not unexpected) that SETs are very positive about the role that search engines play in the overall travel planning process. From this, it seems that DMOs should consider ways to build on this goodwill by co-developing new tools with the search engines to better support tourism products. These tools may include destination-specific recommendation engines, virtual communities, and interactive interpretive systems. However, it must be noted that this exploratory model used constructs that were measured in a variety of formats which limit the use of a variety of statistical analyses and therefore, our ability to assess the relative importance of each component of the model. Thus, future research is needed to better define the constructs and their role(s) within this framework.

References

Brandt, D. S., & Uden, L. (2003). Insights into mental models of novice internet searchers, *Communications of the ACM*, 46(7): 133- 136.

Döring, S. (2008). *Search Processes in Tourism*, Saarbrücken, Germany: VDM Verlag Dr. Müller.

Fodness, D., & Murray, B. (1998). A typology of tourist information search strategies. *Journal of Travel Research*, 37(2): 108-19.

Gefen, D., Karahanna, E., & Straub, D. (2003). Trust and TAM in online shopping: An integrated model. *MIS Quarterly*, 27(1): 51 - 90.

Gretzel, U., Fesenmaier, D. R., & O'Leary, J. T. (2006). The Transformation of Consumer Behaviour. In D. Buhalis and C. Costa (Eds.). *Tourism Business Frontiers*, Elsevier/Butterworth - Heinemann: Burlington, MA, 9 -18.

Hendry, D. G., & Efthimiadia, E.N. (2008). Conceptual models for search engines. In A. Spink and M. Zimmer (Eds.), *Web Search*, Berlin: Spring-Verlag, 277-308.

Henzinger, M. (2007). Search technologies for the Internet. *Science*, 317(5837): 468-71.

Hwang, Y.-H., Xiang, Z., Gretzel, U., & Fesenmaier, D. R. (2009). Assessing structure in travel queries. *Anatolia*, 20(1): 223- 235.

Jansen, B. J., & Molina, P.R. (2006). The effectiveness of Web search engines for retrieving relevant ecommerce links. *Information Processing and Management*, 42(4): 1075-98.

392

Jansen, B. J., & Pooch, U. (2001). A review of Web searching studies and a framework for future research. *Journal of the American Society for Information Science and Technology*, 52(3): 235-46.

Jansen, B.J., & Spink, A. (2005). An analysis of Web searching by European Alltheweb.com users. *Information Processing and Management*, 41(2): 361-81.

Jansen, B. J., Spink, A., & Saracevic, T. (2006). Real life, real users, and real needs: A study and analysis of user queries on the Web. *Information Processing & Management*, 36(2): 207-27.

Kim, H., & Fesenmaier, D. R. (2008). Persuasive design of destination Websites: An analysis of first impression. *Journal of Travel Research*, 47(1): 3-13.

Knight, S. A., & Spink, A. (2008). Toward a Web search information behavior model. In A. Spink and M. Zimmer (Eds.), *Web Search*, Berlin: Spring-Verlag, 209 -233.

Levene, M. (2006). *An Introduction to Search Engines and Web Navigation.* Reading, MA: Addison-Wesley Publishing Company.

Marchionini, G. (1997). *Information Seeking in Electronic Environments.* Cambridge, UK: Cambridge University Press.

Moran, M., & Hunt, B. (2005). *Search Engine Marketing, Inc.: Driving Search Traffic to Your Company's Web Site.* Upper Saddle River, NJ: IBM Press.

Murphy, H. C., & Kielgast, C. (2008). Do small and medium-sized hotels expoloit search engine marketing? *International Journal of Contemporary Hospitality Management*, 20(1): 90-97.

Nakamura, S., Konishi, S., Jatowt, A., Ohshima, H., Kondo, H., Texuka, T., Oyama, S., & Tanaka, K. (2007). Trustworthiness analysis of Web search results. In L. Kovacs, N. Fuhr, and C. Meghini (Eds.), *ECDL 2007, LNCS* 4675: 38 - 49.

Pan, B., & Fesenmaier, D.R. (2006). Online information search: Vacation planning process. *Annals of Tourism Research*, 33(3): 809-32.

Pan, B., Hembrooke, H., Joachims, T., Lorigo, L., Gay, G. & Granka, L. (2007). In Google we trust: Users' decisions on rank, position and relevancy. *Journal of Computer-Mediated Communication*, 12(3): 801-23.

Pan, B., Litvin, S.W., & O'Donnell, T.E. (2007). Understanding accommodation search query formulation: The first step in putting 'heads in beds'. *Journal of Vacation Marketing*, 13(4): 371-81.

Sen, R. (2005). Optimal search engine marketing strategy. *International Journal of Electronic Commerce*, 10(1): 9-25.

Slone, D. J. (2002). The influence of mental models an goals on search patterns during web interaction, *Journal of the American Society for Information Science and Technology*, 53(13): 1152 – 1169.

Su, L T. (2002). A comprehensive and systematic model of user evaluation of web search engines: I. Theory and background, *Journal of the American Society for Information Science and Technology*, 54(13): 1175 – 1192.

TIA (2009). *Travelers' Use of the Internet.* Washington D.C.: Travel Industry Association of America.

Vogt, C. A., & Fesenmaier, D. R. (1998). Expanding the functional information search model. *Annals of Tourism Research*, 25(3): 551-78.

Xiang, Z., Gretzel, U., & Fesenmaier, D.R. (2008). Semantic representatin of the online tourism domain. *Journal of Travel Research*, 47(4): 440-53.

Xiang, Z., & Pan, B. (2009). Travel queries on cities in United States: Implications for search engine marketing in tourism. In *Proceedings of the 16th International Conference on Information and Communication Technologies in Tourism - Enter 2009*. Amsterdam, Netherland: Springer.

Xiang, Z., Wöber, K., & Fesenmaier, D.R. (2008). Representation of the online tourism domain in search engines. *Journal of Travel Research*, 47(2): 137-50.

Web Usage Mining in Tourism – A Query Term Analysis and Clustering Approach

Arthur Pitman[a], Markus Zanker[a],
Matthias Fuchs[b/c] and
Maria Lexhagen[b]

[a] Universität Klagenfurt, Austria
{arthur.pitman,markus.zanker}@uni-klu.ac.at

[b] European Tourism Research Institute (ETOUR), Mid Sweden University, Sweden
{matthias.fuchs, maria.lexhagen}@etour.se

[c]eTourism Competence Center Austria (ECCA),
University of Innsbruck, Austria
{matthias.fuchs}@ecca.at

Abstract

According to current research, one of the most promising applications for web usage mining (WUM) is in identifying homogenous user subgroups (Liu, 2008). This paper presents a prototypical workflow and tools for analyzing user sessions to extract business intelligence hidden in web log data. By considering a leading Swedish destination gateway, we demonstrate how query term analysis in combination with session clustering can be utilized to effectively explore the information needs of website users. The system thus overcomes many of the limitations of typical web site analysis tools that only offer general statistics and ignore the opportunities offered by unsupervised learning techniques.

Keywords: Web usage mining, query term analysis, clustering, destination portal

1 Introduction

Knowledge about the users of a web site, their information needs and search behavior is crucial for ensuring the effectiveness of online marketing (Biswas & Krishan, 2004; Dias & Vermunt, 2007). A web server's log file is one commonly available data source for learning about visitors' information needs, however, it is often left unexploited. Standard analytics tools (e.g. *Google Analytics* or *123loganalyzer*) provide solely descriptive information about page access frequencies, view times, common entry and exit points, referral sites, etc. and thus provide a blurred picture of online behavior. In contrast, web mining aims to discover useful knowledge (i.e. business intelligence) from the structure of hyperlinks (i.e. web structure mining), page content (i.e. web content mining) and usage data (i.e. web usage mining) (Liu, 2008, p. 6). Statistical techniques such as *session analysis* may be applied capture the frequency of page accesses and search words, path lengths, entry and exit points as well as referral sites. Subsequently, the mining methods most frequently applied in web usage mining (WUM) are unsupervised learning techniques and rule mining approaches. *Unsupervised learning* techniques, such as clustering, can be used to discover both user clusters (of sessions or transactions) as well as page clusters (Larose, 2005). This is especially useful when analyzing market segmentation in e-commerce or to provide personalized web content for users with similar interests (Bhatnagar & Ghose, 2004). *Association rule mining* may be used to find groups of items or pages that are commonly accessed or purchased together, thus, organize content more effectively or to cross-sell product items (Mobasher, 2008, p. 471). Finally, *sequential pattern mining* can be applied to capture frequent navigational paths among user trails. In this paper we propose a WUM approach that combines query (i.e. search) term analysis and user clustering. The proposed approach is then empirically tested in the context of a leading online portal of the tourism destination Åre, Sweden. The paper is structured as follows: in Section 2 we examine related work in the area of WUM in tourism. Following this, Section 3 outlines our proposed data mining workflow, including various post processing steps. Section 4 presents results from the analysis of search terms used in referrals and on the site itself as well as results from clustering to identify homogenous web-user groups. The conclusion summarizes the managerial implications and proposed future research.

2 Related Work

Although tourism is dominated by e-business systems and applications (Werthner & Ricci, 2004), to date relatively few attempts have been made to systematically explore the huge potentials of WUM in the e-tourism domain. Some of the few exceptions include: Tichler et al. 1999; Murphy et al. 2001; Cho & Leung, 2002; Olmeda & Sheldon, 2002 and Honda et al. 2006. For the remainder of this section we discuss two recent examples of tourism related WUM. In their attempt to model the navigation behavior of hotel guests, Schegg et al. (2005) analyzed log-files from 15 Swiss hotels. Their findings show that an average visitor stays almost 2 minutes at a site and views 4.7 pages, with the most requested pages being the homepage, information related pages (e.g. hotel information, room information) and transactional pages (e.g. booking, guest book). In half of the cases no referring site was registered, which implies that the visitors typed the domain name directly into their browser, clicked a bookmark, favorite or link in an email, thus suggesting a high degree of website familiarity among users. The authors also identified the top 10 search words (e.g. hotel name, location and tourism activities) and referring search engines as well as tourism websites (e.g. online intermediaries, destination websites, etc.). Similarly, Wolk and Wöber (2009) extracted search words from log files generated by the domain specific search engine 'European Cities Tourism' which is comprised of 186 European touristic cities (www.visiteurope.info). The results revealed 5,550 different search words. Interestingly, the top 100 most frequent search words covered over 75% of all search queries. After transforming the data into a table with the percentages of a specific search word (i.e. columns) and the cities (i.e. rows), search profiles were deduced for a subset of 32 cities, serving as the input for strategic positioning analysis.

3 Methodology

Log files do not permit easy analysis: their sheer volume and simple structure make it difficult to extract business intelligence directly (Liu, 2008). Thus, before applying the unsupervised learning techniques presented in this study we utilized an in-house tool known as *Web Log Analyzer* (WLA) to reconstruct individual user sessions from the raw weblog data and store them in a standard relational database. Its functionality is somewhat equivalent to that described in Mobasher (2008). The advantage of storing extracted data in a database becomes evident when exploring opportunities for further data processing. Business intelligence may be extracted directly from the database using SQL queries or by applying WUM algorithms. In this project we conducted our initial analysis using a series of SQL queries and then further explored the data using *RapidMiner* (http://www.rapid-i.com) and *R* (http://www.r-project.org), two open source packages specializing in data mining and statistics respectively.

The website *www.visitare.se* is a leading tourism portal for the region of Åre, Sweden. It specializes in offering information about skiing, restaurants, accommodation, sightseeing and services, and is available in Swedish, English and German. Importantly, the site does not support bookings or purchases itself, but rather functions as a referrer to partner sites like *Holiday Club* and *SkiStar*, meaning that no obvious conversion ratio is available. Its category-based design is, however, ideal for WUM. The evaluation, illustrated in Figure 1, comprised of examining log data collected from the gateway over an eight month period between August 2008 and March 2009.

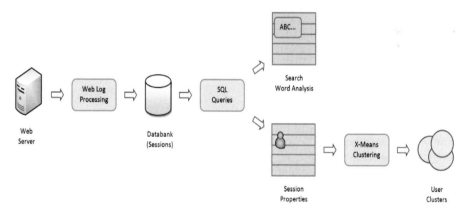

Fig. 1. The web-usage mining workflow

In a first step WLA was used to extract sessions from the raw log files. We specified that requests for images and cascading style sheets should be ignored, focusing instead on sequences of GET and POST requests for HTML files. In addition, we applied patterns to mark key user actions within the sessions, such as search activity, requests for PDF brochures and category-based browsing, as well as ambient information, such as interface language changes. Moreover, of great interest was also how the user entered the site (i.e. through referral from another site or directly via a bookmark or entering the address).

Following this, a series of SQL queries were applied to aggregate this information, producing 106 variables for each session describing temporal aspects (e.g. session duration, start time and day), how the user was referred to the site (e.g. whether the session was the result of a Google search and if so the used search terms and categories) and which areas were viewed (e.g. information categories and subpages), as well as use of special functionality (e.g. search forms or PDF brochures). In addition, we exported search word profiles for Google referrals and the site's internal text search.

We hypothesized that differences in topical variables, such as the categories a user visited or searched for, would be correlated with changes in other variables, particularly in those viewed as success criterion, such as session duration or the number of PDF documents.

4 Findings

The web log analysis revealed a total of 183,728 sessions over the eight month period in which web log data was collected. Of these, 63,648 could be attributed to bots and web crawlers, and a further 28,045 sessions contained negligible activity (i.e. failed to request an actual page) and were thus excluded. Of the remaining 92,035 sessions, 33,981 were referred to the site from Google, the result of searches involving an average of three terms, a figure that fully supports the findings of Orlando and Silvestri (2009). In addition, 13,174 sessions searched the site internally using its internal text search facility with an average of 1.6 words per query and 7,092 used the parametric search form.

Search Term Analysis

The processing of search words presents a number of challenges. Many words may be written in a number of different ways, using multiple spelling, declination or punctuation patterns (Honda et al. 2006; Wolk & Wöber, 2009). In our analysis, we treated search terms in a case insensitive fashion, removed connector words (such as "and" in English and "i" in Swedish), merged multiple spellings or declinations and removed punctuation.

When comparing external search terms used in Google searches to those used in internal searches, it turned out that internal searches are much more specific, usually referring to particular categories or items of interest. Clearly, the top Google referral keyword is the name of the region itself, *Åre*, as it is the key term that differentiates the site from others. Other non-Swedish search terms presumably direct users to other sites, thus, do not appear in the log as frequently. The distribution of referral search terms also basically replicates the results of Wolk and Wöber (2009), with the first 150 terms covering more than three quarters of the search queries (see concentration curve in Figure 2). In contrast, internal searches exhibit much greater diversity with around 250 search terms covering about 75% of all queries.

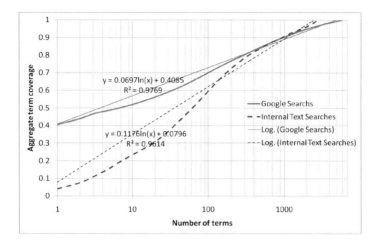

Fig. 2. Coverage of Google and internal search terms

Follow this initial analysis, 290 of the most common search terms were assigned to the eight categories by domain experts with the aim of deriving semantic information to better understand the website's various user groups. The resulting distribution can be summarized as follows: *accommodation* (12%), *activities* (16%), *skiing* (7%), *dining* (7%), *shopping* (3%), *attractions* (7%) and *services* (17%), together with *non-specific* terms (32%).

User Cluster Analysis

Perhaps even more interesting than the general behavior of the site's users is the behavior of homogenous sub groups (Dias & Vermunt, 2007). We explored cluster analysis, a technique which assigns items to subsets according to a similarity criterion to understand how the *VisitAre* gateway serves the interests of different types of visitors to the region. Broadly speaking, *x-means* clustering was applied to a subset variables preselected using *principal component analysis* (PCA). Following this we explored statistically significant differences between the resulting clusters in other variables.

X-means, a variation of *k-means* that determines *k* by optimizing an effectiveness criterion, avoids the difficulty of having to fix the number of clusters beforehand (Pelleg & Moore, 2000; Hastie et al. 2009). PCA, usually employed as a method for transforming potentially correlated variables into a series of uncorrelated components (Jolliffe, 2002), was used to identify which variables were responsible for the majority of variance thus reducing the amount of explicit domain knowledge required.

Seven variables were selected by PCA as clustering input variables, namely category browse actions for *'accommodation'*, *'to do'*, *'to see'*, *'dining'*, *'service'*, *'communications'* and *'program'*. *X-means* clustering carried out for $2 \leq k \leq 30$ revealed four stable clusters. As can be seen in a decision tree constructed using the clustered data, the focus of the clustering was on *accommodation* (Figure 3). A more detailed summary of the properties of each cluster is presented in Table 1.

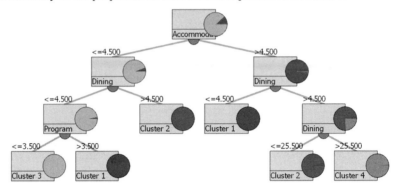

Fig. 3. Decision tree constructed using the clustered data

Cluster 1 contained sessions that were primarily interested in *accommodation* and to some extent *program*. Cluster 2, on the other hand, was made up of sessions that concentrated on *dining* whilst also being interested in most other categories. Sessions in cluster 3, the largest cluster, were focused on *accommodation* and on *to do* to some extent, however were on average significantly shorter than those in cluster 1 and cluster 2, and, with the exception of viewing PDF files, visited fewer areas of the site.

Without additional information it is difficult to pinpoint the cause for this behavior. It is possible, for example that sessions in cluster 3 (i.e. the majority of users) were not particularly interested in any single category, navigated to site in error or found it irrelevant, or even found the required information immediately. On the other hand, sessions in cluster 1 and 2 found the offerings much more useful or encouraging, browsing in specific categories and remaining on the website for significantly longer periods of time, thus, showing a more focused and effective search behavior (Dias & Vermunt, 2007). Sessions in cluster 1 and 2 were also significantly more likely to enter the site through the main page rather than one of the specific pages, presumably then navigating to pages of interest.

Finally, cluster 4, a very small cluster, contained sessions that appeared to have been abnormally interested in all categories. Despite using neither the internal text search nor the search form, they managed to visit most other key components, exhibiting behavior that is typically associated with bots (Liu, 2008). This assumption was confirmed by examining the sessions' user agent strings, which connected all 64 sessions with a Java-based browsing component that is typically used for web spiders.

Table. 1 Site usage by cluster ([1] χ^2 significant p<0.01, [2] χ^2 significant p<0.05)

General properties	Cluster 1	Cluster 2	Cluster 3	Cluster 4
Number of sessions	7989	2839	81143	64
% of all sessions	8.7%	3.1%	88.2%	0.1%
Entered through main page[1]	41.9%	44.9%	34.6%	100%
Session duration (min)	12.6	12.2	2.5	9.1
% of sessions that changed the interface language to…				
Swedish[1]	9.7%	12.5%	5.3%	100%
English[1]	8.5%	8.4%	7.1%	100%
German[1]	2.0%	2.6%	3.1%	100%
% of sessions that browsed…				
Accommodation[1]	80.3%	24.7%	26.5%	100%
To Do[1]	25.8%	33.2%	28.3%	100%
To See[1]	11.7%	20.7%	9.2%	100%
Dining[1]	10.2%	100%	8.0%	100%
Service[1]	6.9%	14.2%	8.5%	100%
Communication[1]	6.0%	7.7%	5.8%	100%
Program[1]	29.2%	17.7%	7.2%	100%
Number of activations (for sessions that browsed a given category)				
Accommodation	6.4	1.0	0.5	14.0
To Do	0.8	1.5	0.7	40.0
To See	0.3	0.8	0.2	51.0
Dining	0.2	8.4	0.2	40.7
Service	0.2	0.8	0.2	18.0
Communication	0.1	0.3	0.1	10.0
Program	1.8	0.8	0.1	13.0
Other key actions - % of sessions…				
Viewing a PDF[1]	2.1%	2.8%	6.8%	0%
Viewing a brochure[1]	5.4%	7.6%	3.4%	100%
Ordering a brochure[2]	0.8%	2.1%	0.6%	100%
Return to main page[1]	18.8%	18.4%	14.5%	100%
Visiting "Congress"[1]	5.3%	7.2%	2.4%	100%
Visiting "Tourism"[1]	11.2%	10.0%	6.7%	100%
Visiting "Åre Summer"[1]	4.6%	5.1%	4.2%	100%

Table. 2 Google referrals among clusters ([1] χ^2 significant at p<0.01)

Google referrals	Cluster 1	Cluster 2	Cluster 3	Cluster 4
% searched with Google[1]	41.4%	44.5%	47.3%	0%
% referred from Google[1]	34.0%	37.8%	37.2%	0%
% referred to home page[1]	21.7%	31.5%	22.4%	NA
Query length (words)	2.9	2.7	3.0	NA
% of Google referrals containing search words that could be associated with…				
Skiing[1]	1.0%	0.6%	3.1%	NA
Activities[1]	3.0%	2.1%	6.6%	NA
Accommodation[1]	10.5%	1.3%	6.0%	NA
Dining[1]	0.9%	13.5%	2.1%	NA
Shopping[1]	0.2%	0.5%	1.4%	NA
Services[1]	17.5%	12.3%	14.0%	NA
Attraction[1]	0.9%	0.7%	1.6%	NA
Non-Specific[1]	91.2%	95.2%	83.9%	NA

Importantly, as shown in Table 2, the analysis of Google referrals to the gateway demonstrates that there is a strong correlation between the categories assigned to search words and the categories visited during the session itself. Both cluster 1 and 2 contained many sessions that were referred on the basis of non-specific search terms and were, thus, more likely to be referred to the main page. It is surprising that sessions in cluster 3 were so short although many of the search terms could be associated with categories corresponding to the information offerings of the website. As expected, no session in cluster 4 was referred to the site by Google.

When examining the use of search functionality offered by the site itself (Table 3), sessions in cluster 3 were found to be significantly more likely to use the internal text search while they were less likely to use the parametric search form.

Tab. 3 Internal search and other functionality among clusters ([1] χ^2 significant p<0.01)

Internal text search	Cluster 1	Cluster 2	Cluster 3	Cluster 4
% sessions that used it[1]	9.4%	9.5%	15.0%	0%
First used after (min)	3.4	3.7	1.3	NA
Query length (words)	1.7	1.6	1.5	NA
% of internal text searches that could be associated with...				
Skiing	5.5%	8.1%	7.9%	NA
Activities	5.1%	4.4%	4.8%	NA
Accommodation[1]	22.1%	17.7%	15.7%	NA
Eating[1]	4.0%	11.1%	2.4%	NA
Shopping[1]	0.1%	2.6%	1.5%	NA
Services[1]	4.9%	7.7%	10.2%	NA
Attraction[1]	2.9%	2.6%	5.1%	NA
Non-Specific	30.2%	25.5%	27.8%	NA
Parametric search form				
% sessions that used it[1]	21.0%	18.8%	6.0%	0%
First used after (min)	5.0	4.3	1.5	NA
Average number of uses	4.4	4.9	1.9	NA

In both instances, sessions in cluster 3 that used search functionality were more likely to do so earlier in the session (see the *first used after* variables). Interpretations of this difference could include that these sessions had difficulty locating relevant information using category-based site structure or that the information offerings of the parametric search facility (that allows users to specify specific search criteria like type of accommodation or activities) did not match their actual information needs. Given that once again most of cluster 3's internal text search terms could be associated with a category, it is reasonable to assume that this is an indication that the site would benefit from additional content, particularly in the areas of *skiing*, *accommodation* and *service*.

We complete our analysis by returning to the search terms used for both Google referrals and internal text searches. Figure 4 lists the 50 most common key terms used in Google searches for each cluster, with size indicating a term's relative frequency. Non-differentiating terms were excluded since such terms (e.g. *åre*) are a de facto requirement for referrals to the site (Wolk & Wöber, 2009). Interestingly, each cluster contains a number of topical terms specific to that cluster. For example, cluster 2, clearly interested in dining, contains terms such as *pub*, *konditori* and *restaurang*.

Turning our attention to the terms used in internal text searches (Figure 5), it is obvious that the terms refer to more specific needs and are in general more diverse.

a. Cluster 1

accommodation accomodation afterski areturistbyra åreturistbyrå att bo boende bröllop camping com
fiske fjällby fjällgård göra händer holiday höstmarknad hotel hotell hyra in inn jämtland karta lägenhet lägenheter
nattliv och övernattning pensionat personer privatstugor rum ski skidstuga storulvån stuga stugby stugor timmervillan
turistbyra turistbyrå turistbyrån turistinformation uthyres uthyrning vad vandrarhem vecka

b. Cluster 2

affärer armfeldts äta att bar bistro black cafe café club dahlboms dds fjällby göra helpension hotell ica janne
julbord kabinbana kabinbanan karta knuten konditori krog mat meny morsel oliven på pub raw
restaurang restauranger runt schaffer sheep stormköket supper tännforsen taxi timmerstugan toppstugan
tts turer turistbyrå turistbyrån turistinfo våfflor xc3

c. Cluster 3

anjans att bibliotek bo boende buss camping com fiske fjällby fjällstation från göra holiday höstmarknad
hotel hotell hyra ica inn islandshästar jämtland julfirande kabinbanakabinbanan karta kyrka
längdåkning längdspår och öppettider på restaurang restauranger shop skalstugan skiduthyrning skoter skoterleder skoteruthyrning
stuga stugor till transfer turistbyrå turistbyrån turistinformation vandra vandrarhem vandring

Fig. 4 Dominant Google search terms by cluster

a. Cluster 1

afterski alpina åregårdarna åregården åresjön äta bastu bergbanan bjørnen bo boende bygget club diplomat
fiskecamp fjallby fjällby fjällbyn fjällbys fjällgård fjällgården fjällhotell fjällstuga fjällvärlden gästhuset holiday
hotel hotell internet jope kabinbanan karta kommunikationer kvm kyrka liftkort mörviksgården
oviksfjällen pistkarta radio renen röding rum rustika service ski skidliftar snasahögarna tännforsen
toaletter

b. Cluster 2

after anaris åregården åresjön armfeldts äta bädds bar bastu bastuanläggning bergbanan
blåhammarens bo bustamoen butiker bykrog bykrogen club continental edhsgården fäviken fiskefiskecamp fj fjällbys
fjällgården fjällhotell grappa hummelstugan inn julbord kabinbanan karta kläppen knuten
krog liftkort lillåstugan rautjoxa renfjället restaurang restauranger service shopping skoteruthyrning
sträcker timmerstugan tottebo våfflor worsens

c. Cluster 3

afterski alpina åregården åresjön äta bastu bergbanan bo bubbelpooler churchill club dammån fj fjällbyn
fjällbys fjällgård fjällhotell fjällstationer fjällstugor hälsocentral hälsocentralen heliski hotell hundspann
kabinbanan karta klockstapeln kommunikationer kvisslesträmmarna kvm lägenhet
liftkort monte oviksfjällen röding service sevärdheter skalstugan ski skidliftar skoter skoteruthyrning slalom
storulvåns tännforsen toaletter totto väder villa winston

Fig. 5. Dominant internal search terms by cluster

The dominating types of search words used by cluster 1 in internal text searches are associated with accommodation. Search terms such as *fjällbyn* and *åregården* are names of hotels, while *bo* and *hotel/hotell* refer to accommodation category more generally. Similarly, in cluster 2 the dominating search terms refer to the dining category, either by using the names of restaurants (e.g. *worsens, fjällgården)* or by using more generic search words (e.g. *restauranger, äta, julbord)* associated with this information category. Summarizing, the different clusters clearly represent user groups with distinct information needs. However, the fact that the vast majority of users (i.e. cluster 3) remained on the site for such a short period of time, particularly in comparison to the presumably more successful clusters (i.e. clusters 1 and 2), is an indication that the site may need to be reorganised and expanded to fit different customer groups and information needs. Typically, in an e-marketing context the customer initiates a search for information on products and services for which they have already formed an interest (Biswas & Krishnan, 2004). Consequently, it is important to satisfy customer needs once they are using a web site. Failure to do this may reflect badly on the destination brand or signify lost business opportunities.

5 Conclusions

This paper introduced a workflow for utilizing standard web server log data in WUM. In order to show how such a workflow might be applied to a real-world website, we considered the example of the *visitare.se* tourism destination gateway and demonstrated how usage data can be extracted and processed. In particular we focused on examining search terms as well as identifying differences between homogenous user groups revealed by unsupervised learning techniques. When examining the results of our investigation, it is evident that different user groups approach the site with significantly differing information needs (Bhatnagar & Ghose, 2004).

More precisely, our results indicate that the majority of users (i.e. cluster 3) spend rather little time on the site, perhaps signifying that their specific information needs have not been met. Admittedly, at such an early stage in our research it is not possible to ascertain the causes for the differences between the clusters, something that remains for future work. Nevertheless, knowledge about specific user groups is crucial for understanding the relationships between (potential) tourism products, users and related information categories. Finally, the diversity of search words and the value of Google as a source of referrals strongly underline the importance of proper search engine management.

References

Biswas, A. & Krishan R. (2004). The Internet's impact on marketing, *Journal of Business Research*, 57 (7): 681-684.
Bhatnagar, A. & Ghose, S. (2004). Segmenting consumers based on the benefits and risks of Internet shopping, *Journal of Marketing Research*, 40 (2): 235-243.

Cho, V. & Leung, P. (2002). Towards using knowledge discovery techniques in database marketing for the tourism industry, *Journal of Quality Assurance in Hospitality & Tourism*, 3(3): 109-131.

Dias, J. G. & Vermunt J. K. (2007). Latent class modeling of website users' search patterns: Implications for online market segmentation, *Journal of Retailing and Consumer Services*, (14): 359-368.

Hastie, T., Tibshirani, R. & Friedman, J. (2009). The elements of statistical learning – Data mining, inference and prediction (2nd ed.), New York, Springer.

Honda, T., Yamamoto, M. & Ohuchi, A. (2006). Automatic Classification of Websites based on Keyword Extraction of Nouns, In, Hitz, M., Sigala, M., Murphy, J. Eds.), *Information and Communication Technologies in Tourism 2006* NY: Springer: 263-272

Jolliffe, I. T., (2002). Principal Component Analysis. Springer-Verlag. USA.

Larose, D.T. (2005). *Discovering knowledge in data – An introduction to data mining*. John Wiley & Sons, New Jersey.

Liu, B. (2008). *Web Data Mining - Exploring hyperlinks, contents and usage data* (2nd ed.), Springer, New York.

Mobasher, B. (2008). Web Usage Mining, In: Liu, B. (ed.) *Web Data Mining- Exploring hyperlinks, contents and usage data* (2nd ed.) Springer, New York, pp 449-483.

Murphy, J., Hofacker, C.F., & Bennett, M. (2001). Website-generated Market-Research data: Tracing the tracks left behind by visitors, *Cornell Hotel and Restaurant Administration Quarterly*, 42(1): 82-91.

Olmeda, I. & Sheldon, P.J. (2002). Data Mining Techniques and Applications for Tourism Internet Marketing, *Journal of Travel & Tourism Marketing*, 11(2/3): 1-20.

Orlando, S. & Silvestri, F. (2009) Query Log Analysis for Enhancing Web Search, IEEE/WIC/ACM International Conference on Web Intelligence, Milano, Italy.

Pelleg, D., Moore, A.W. (2000). X-means: Extending K-means with Efficient Estimation of the Number of clusters, *Proceedings of the Seventeenth International Conference on Machine Learning*. pp727 – 734. USA.

Pyle, D. (1999). *Data preparation for data mining*. New York, Morgan Kaufmann Publishers.

Scharl, A., Wöber, K. & Bauer, Ch. (2004). An integrated approach to measure web site effectiveness in the European hotel industry, *Journal of Information Technology and Tourism*, 6(4): 257-271

Schegg, R., Steiner, Th., Gherissi-Labben, T. & Murphy, J. (2005). Using Log-File Analysis and Website Assessment to Improve Hospitality Websites, Frew, A.. (Ed.) *Information and Communication Technologies in Tourism 2005*. New York, Springer, 566-576.

Tichler, G., Grossman, W. & Werthner, H. (1999). Using Data Mining in Analysing Local Tourism Patterns. In Buhalis, D. & Schertler, W. Eds., *Information and Communication Technologies in Tourism 1999* Vienna: Springer: 1-11.

Werthner, H. & Ricci, F. (2004). E-commerce and tourism. *Communications of the ACM*, 47(12): 101-105.

Wolk, A. & Wöber, K. (2009). A Comprehensive Study of Info Needs of City Travellers in Europe, *Journal of Information Technology and Tourism*, 10(2): 119-131.

Acknowledgement

Parts of this work have been financed by the ÖNB grant no. 13.000 of the Austrian National Bank Jubilee Foundation and by the EU Structural Fund objective 2 project no. 39736, Sweden.

Assessing the Dynamics of Search Results in Google

Bing Pan[a]
Zheng Xiang[b]
Heather Tierney[c]
Daniel R. Fesenmaier[d] and
Rob Law[e]

[a] Department of Hospitality and Tourism Management
School of Business and Economics
College of Charleston, USA
bingpan@gmail.com

[b] School of Merchandising and Hospitality Management
University of North Texas, USA
philxz@unt.edu

[c] Department of Economics and Finance
School of Business and Economics
College of Charleston, USA
tierneyh@cofc.edu

[d] National Laboratory for Tourism & eCommerce
School of Tourism and Hospitality Management
Temple University, USA
drfez@temple.edu

[e] School of Hospitality and Tourism Management
Hong Kong Polytechnic University, HK SAR
hmroblaw@inet.polyu.edu.hk

Abstract

Search engine marketing requires a substantive understanding of the dynamics of the search system in the travel information search context. The goal of this study is to explore the dynamic nature of online information space through Google as well as its direct impact on the traffic of a destination website. Utilizing a computer program to track Google search results, Google Trends, and a Destination Marketing Organization's (DMO) website traffic data, this study identified the variation in information space as reflected by different queries related to Charleston, South Carolina. The results of regression analysis indicates that the web traffic of the Charleston Convention and Visitors Bureau website was strongly correlated with search volumes for certain queries and the ranking of some queries in Google.

Keywords: travel information search; search engines; Search Engine Result Page; ranking; travel queries; destinations; search engine marketing.

1 Introduction

Today, more and more travellers are using the Internet in general search engines in specific to plan their trips (TIA, 2005, 2008). Findings of a few recent studies have documented that the majority of online U.S. consumers use search engines as the number one information source for their vacation planning (eMarketer, 2008; Prophis-Research, 2007). Search engines have, thus, become the battleground for tourism businesses and organizations for the purpose of attracting, engaging, and converting potential visitors (Google, 2006; Xiang & Fesenmaier, 2006). As such, search engine marketing (SEM) plays an increasingly important role in tourism organizations' online marketing programs.

It is argued that a successful SEM program requires substantive understanding of the dynamic nature of online information. Search engines, users, and online tourism information space may keep changing frequently, making SEM potentially a moving target. The goal of this study was to identify and substantiate the dynamics of online information search by focusing on the changes of search result rankings in Google over time. In addition, this study intended to examine the extent to which these dynamics can be directly linked to a DMO's website traffic.

2 Research Background

A search engine, search engine users, and online information space can be seen as a system wherein the search engine mediates the interaction between the other two "players" (Pan & Fesenmaier, 2006; Xiang, Wöber, & Fesenmaier, 2008). In order to successfully connect and communicate with potential customers through search engines, marketers must keep abreast of the development of each of the components in this search triad. This section reviews the literature on the dynamic relationships existing in the search triad to establish the rationale for this study.

2.1 Dynamics in Online Travel Information through Search Engines

It is argued that the three components of the search triad, i.e., the search engine, search engine user, and online tourism information space, are constantly evolving. In general, a number of factors could contribute to this phenomenon. First, a search engine may change its algorithms on a continuous basis to fight against search engine spam and misuse of search engine optimization (SEO) (Bar-Ilan, 1999). For example, when a search engine detects keyword spamming or keyword stuffing, the weight applied to each keyword will be reduced. On the other hand, online information space continues to change on a daily basis. Everyday new web pages appear and old pages vanish and get updated (Bar-Ilan, 2007). For instance, one study showed certain existing web pages may appear or disappear from search engines without any apparent reasons (Tatum, 2005). Another study indicates that the results from AltaVista, one of the main search engines, fluctuate greatly in 21 weeks without any major changes on the actual web pages (Bar-Ilan, 2007). Bar-Ilan (2004) attributed these changes to many factors, including the changes of search engine servers, frequency of search algorithm updates, and frequency of web index updates in search engine crawlers. Importantly, businesses and organizations tweak their web pages and adopt SEO techniques to increase their ranking in major search engines, sometimes with illegitimate means such as Google "bombing" (manipulating Google results through collective hyperlinking behaviour) or keyword stuffing (Bar-Ilan, 2004). Finally, search engine users may change their search behaviour by using, for example, more keywords in the queries, viewing fewer pages on search engines, and changing the topics of search (Jansen, Spink, & Pedersen, 2005; Wu & Davison, 2005). As a result, the information space on the Internet is extremely dynamic and ephemeral. Arguably, within the context of using the Internet for travel planning purposes this search triad is even more dynamic, considering that travel planning is a complex process requiring the assembly of many trip "facets" and, potentially, numerous businesses and organizations that may be involved and actively participate in this contest. Consequently, tourism information space is a very dynamic and hyper-competitive and SEM becomes a challenging task.

2.2 Research Rationale

Because search engines are the systems through which potential customers access the tourism information space about a destination, whether or not a result shown in the search engine is viewed or clicked will determine how likely a tourism business and organization can attract and convert their potential visitors. Many factors may influence how the searchers view and access different alternatives on a typical search engine result page (SERP). Among them, the ranking of a particular page is extremely important. Studies have shown that users have tremendous trust in the ranking of Google. This trust even exceeded their own judgments on the relevance of results (Pan, et al., 2007). Specifically, the first three results on a Google SERP are much more likely to be clicked than others. Also, Kim and Fesenmaier (2008) demonstrated that the text included in search engine results significantly influence one's impression toward tourism websites. However, studies have shown that tourism businesses and organizations have not yet achieved high visibility in search engines. For example, Wöber (2006) revealed low rankings of many individual tourism businesses. A recent study by Xiang et al. (2008) discovered that it is the "big players", e.g. tourism aggregators that dominated the prominent positions in Google, and thus, left little visibility for small and medium-sized businesses.

While these studies have documented the disadvantageous position of many tourism businesses and organizations in search engines, they do not accurately reflect the dynamic nature of travel information search. This is because these studies used a "snapshot" approach by examining a part of online tourism information space represented by a search engines at one time and, thus, the changing nature of travel information search is not well understood. Therefore, it is important to develop viable means to describe the dynamics in using search engines for travel purposes.

3 Research Questions

The primary goal of this study was to document the dynamic nature of travel information search as reflected through search engines. A set of research questions were raised which direct this study including: What is the size of the tourism information space as represented by the estimated in the number of results for a search query? To what extent do the sizes vary across different queries? To what extent does the size change over time? And, to what extent do the rankings of top websites change over time in a search engine given a specific search query? The secondary goal of the study was to examine the extent to which the variation in search volumes and rankings relates to the website traffic of a DMO. Specifically, the goal was to find out, based upon a set of predefined queries, whether there is any relationship among the search volumes of these search queries, rankings of the DMO website in the search engine, as well as the traffic volumes on the DMO website.

4 Methods

In order to answer the above research questions, Google was chosen as the focal search engine because it is the largest search engine in the United States with 65% of market share by visits and 71% by search volumes (Hitwise, 2009). The city of Charleston, South Carolina, USA was chosen as the destination in focus due to one of the authors' affiliation. Five queries related to the destination were selected based on the most popular queries on Google AdWords Keyword Tool (Google, 2009b) and also considering the various aspects of travel planning tasks.

4.1 Data

Three types of data were used in this study and include:

Google Ranking Data The ranking of all the web pages for certain queries for Charleston, SC, were captured through a custom-built computer program which tracks and downloads daily Google results for the five queries for Charleston, SC. The tracking period lasted more than one year. The time period is from January 19, 2008 to March 9, 2009. Some of the queries were captured 3 or 4 times a day in order to get a better idea on the changes during one day; others were captured twice a day (see Table 1). For these five queries, the top 500 results in Google SERPs were recorded. For each session, the program downloaded the top 500 results for that query; for each result, the program captured the time of downloading, the webpage's rank in the result page, the text snippets displayed in Google interface. In addition, the estimated number of search results was also downloaded for each query in order to show the estimated size of the information space over time.

Table 1. Charleston Related Queries and Frequency of Capturing

Query	Starting Time (2008)	Ending Time (2009)	Total Number of Days	Times per Day	Results Captured per Day
charleston sc	January 19	March 16	422	2	399
travel charleston	January 19	March 5	411	2	282
charleston tourism	January 20	December 21, 2008	336	3	247
charleston hotels	January 19	March 8	414	4	303
charleston restaurants	January 19	March 8	414	2	261

Search Volume Data The daily and weekly search volume data for the same five queries listed in Table 1 were retrieved through Google Trend (Choi & Varian, 2009). As a public tool provided by Google, Google Trend "shows how often a particular search-term is entered relative to the total search-volume across various regions of the world, and in various languages (Google, 2009a; Wikipedia, 2009). The search volume data reported are normalized and scaled (Google, 2009a). Those search volumes include volumes for all types of queries and also those specifically categorized as travel queries by Google.

DMO Website Traffic Data Google Analytics was used to download the daily traffic for Charleston Area Convention and Visitors Bureau (CACVB) website (http://www.charlestoncvb.com/). Four types of traffic were reported, including All Visits, New Visits, Search Traffic, Nonlocal Visits, and Local Visits. Search Traffic is used in this study since they are most relevant.

4.2 Data Analysis

Google ranking data were analyzed using SQL (Structural Query Language) queries to describe the changes over time. Regression analyses were then conducted to assess the correlation between search volumes, rankings of the site on Google, and the web traffic for CACVB website.

5 Results

This section details the results of the data mining and regression analyses on website traffic of Charleston CVB site with search volumes and rankings of certain search queries.

5.1 Size of the Information Space in Google

Comparing the statistics of those queries along one year's time frame (see Table 2), it is clear that the daily numbers vary greatly and, thus, the medians will be more meaningful. The query of "charleston sc" has the biggest estimated numbers of results compared to the rest, since it is a general query rather than travel-specific query. Interestingly, "charleston hotels" has more estimated results than "charleston travel", "charleston restaurants", or "charleston tourism", indicating fierce competition among accommodations on the tourism information space. Interestingly, little commonalities seem to exist between the five queries across one year. According to Bar-Ilan (2004), this fluctuation could be attributed to many factors, including accessing of search engine servers, search algorithm updates, and web index updates in search engine crawlers. As such, the estimated number of results for a specific day provided by Google may not be used as an appropriate indicator of the size of visible information space since it is not consistent from day-to-day.

Table 2. Daily Estimated Number of Results for Five Queries (in Thousands)

Statistics	charleston sc	travel charleston	charleston tourism	charleston hotels	charleston restaurants
N	422	301	285	340	286
Mean	8,960	578	243	1,062	361
Median	10,700	350	198	689	330
Mode	12,400	348	156	1,070	340

Changes in the estimated number of results within one day for certain queries were also examined. The system captured Google results for "charleston tourism" and "charleston hotels" three times in a day. Among valid 787 records, the estimated numbers remain the same only in 486 cases. About one third (38.2%) of records changed their numbers. Next, the authors looked at the changes of the estimated results during half a day. Table 3 shows the percentages of changes. Among the five queries, "charleston sc" has the biggest amount changes while "travel charleston" has the lowest amount. The analyses on the estimated numbers of results clearly showed the size of the tourism information space changes varies significantly between the queries and over time.

Table 3. Changes of Estimated Number of Results Changes within 11-14 Hours

Query	N	Average Percentage of changes
charleston sc	739	4.5%
travel charleston	514	0.6%
charleston tourism	419	1.2%
charleston hotels	263	1.6%
charleston restaurants	526	0.4%
Total	**2461**	**1.8%**

5.2 Changes in the Rankings of Top Website in Google

First, changes of the rankings of the top 100 results in Google were examined. Table 4 and Figure 1 show the number of newly added URLs (i.e., web page addresses), which is also equal to the number of newly removed URLs, on the top 100 results. Among the top 100 results, smaller tourism information space such as "charleston restaurants" are relatively more stable, whereas larger tourism information spaces such as "charelston sc" seem more dynamic. The averages are around five new URLs every 11-14 hours among the top 100 results. Daily changes also showed that on average around 30% of URLS will change their locations; they may move up or move down (Table 5).

Table 4. Newly Added URLs in 11-14 Hours for Top 100 Results

Query	N	Average Numbers of Changes
charleston sc	820	5.6%
travel charleston	816	5.0%
charleston tourism	819	5.4%
charleston hotels	1364	4.5%
charleston restaurants	819	3.9%
Total	**4638**	**4.8%**

Table 5. Daily Changes of URLs among Top 100 Results

Query	stayed the same**	Moved Up	Moved Down*
charleston sc	27.5	32.5	32.9
travel charleston	31.8	31.0	29.4
charleston tourism	28.7	32.1	30.4
charleston hotels	28.4	33.6	30.2
charleston restaurants	33.5	31.7	28.8
Average	**30.0**	**32.2**	**30.3**

** significant at 0.01 level; *significant at 0.05 level.

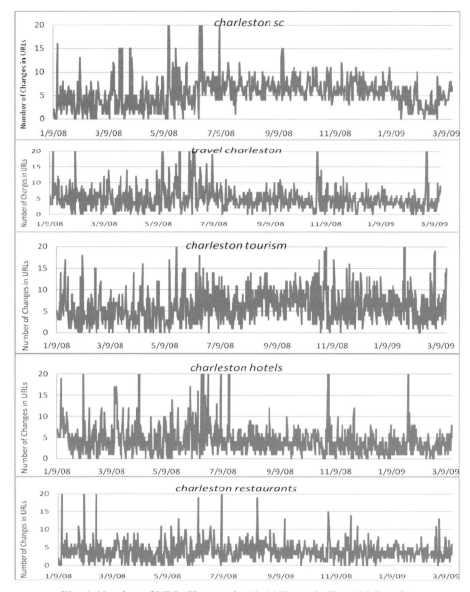

Fig. 1. Number of URL Changes in 11-14 Hours in Top 100 Results

Since the first SERP has by default 10 search results and most users only looked at the first page (Henzinger, 2007), websites which are in the top 10 results were analyzed. Similar to the top 100 results, the analysis shows the competition is fierce. Table 5 shows those websites which are always in the top 10 positions for the five queries. There are only on average 2 websites which are always in the top 10 positions. Those websites include the local DMO site (charelstoncvb.com), local news site (charleston.net), commercial search site (yahoo.com), web 2.0 site (tripadvisor.com), and commercial tourism sites (10best.com and hotelguides.us). There is not a single site which stayed in the top 10 for the query "charelston sc" over the course of this study.

Table 6. Number of domain names in the top Results for 433 days

Query	Number of Domains	Number of Domains been on #1 position	Sites Stayed Top 10
charleston sc	57	2	*None*
travel charleston	22	3	10best.com, charlestoncvb.com
charleston tourism	29	4	Tripadvisor.com, charlestoncvb.com,Charleston.net
charleston hotels	28	3	Yahoo.com and Hotelguides.us
charleston restaurants	32	3	Sciway.com, tripadvisor.com, Fordors.com and "citysearch.com
Average	32.4	3	2.2 sites

5.3 Impact of Search Dynamics on the DMO Website

Three sets of daily data for about one year were captured during this analysis: Charleston CVB website traffic, search volumes for five queries, and the ranking of the CVB website on those queries. Since weekly data could be obtained on the same scale through Google Trend, regressions on weekly data were performed. Since search volumes, web traffic, and rank data are all count data which only takes non-negative values, Poisson quasi-maximum likelihood estimator (QMLE) is considered appropriate (Cameron & Trivedi, 1998). Regression was used to predict the search traffic of the DMO site with a significance threshold of 0.05 for the 60 week data. The regressors are five search volume variables for those queries in all categories and the 5 ranking variables of the site on those 5 queries. The results in Table 6 show that search volume for "charleston sc", "charleston hotels" and "charleston restaurants" and ranking of the site for queries "charleston sc", "charleston hotels" and "travel charleston" are all significant. The Adjusted R square for the overall model is 0.876, indicating a high degree of correlation and high degree of predictive power for website search traffic. Interestingly, the coefficient for ranking for "charleston sc" and "charleston hotels" are positive, indicating that a higher ranking is correlated with lower search traffic for the DMO. It means that high rankings in more relevant queries (such as "travel charleston") are more important for the DMO rather than the higher ranking in any queries. However, the small coefficients for "charelston hotels" and "travel charelston" indicate that search volumes play a more important role than the actual rankings.

Table 7. QMLE Regression Model on Search Traffic of DMO Site

	Estimated Coefficients	Z Stats	p-value
Intercept	3.824	5.160	0.000**
Search volume for "charleston sc"	1.395	9.040	0.000**
Search volume for "charleston hotels"	0.436	5.524	0.000**
Search volume for "charleston restaurants"	-0.159	-2.261	0.024*
Ranking for "charleston sc"	0.016	2.039	0.042*
Ranking for " charleston hotels"	0.002	4.211	0.000**
Ranking for "travel chareleston"	-0.098	-3.094	0.002**

**Significant at 0.01 level; * Significant at 0.05 level.

6 Conclusions and Implications

It is argued that tourism marketers must understand the dynamic nature of travel information search using search engines in order to develop a successful SEM program. The results of this study clearly demonstrate that the size of tourism information spaces change on a daily, or even hourly, basis. The results also revealed that there is a strong correlation between search traffic for a DMO site, the rankings of the site for certain queries, and the search volumes on Google for those queries.

The dynamic space of tourism information calls for continuous monitoring and changes in SEM strategies. Since the dynamics during a day or a few hours are not controllable, any ranking or estimated results from a certain time should not be adopted as the performance of one's website; instead, tourism businesses should use the medians or averages across a certain period of continuous monitoring. As a DMO or tourism businesses, one needs to contiguously anticipate the changes in the tourism information space, monitor those new and disappearing competitors, and change their strategies accordingly. To study the significant queries for one's DMO site could also predict and inform the future visitor volumes to one's site.

In addition, the results showed different levels of competition among various queries. More general queries seem more competitive and dynamic than niche-based queries. Thus, it is important for tourism businesses and organizations to target at those long tail keywords. In other words, targeting at "charleston restaurants" will be cheaper and easier than "charleston sc". Furthermore, not all high rankings are good: rankings for relevant queries are more beneficial than others. Thus, it is important to rank higher for relevant queries rather than non-relevant queries.

References

Bar-Ilan, J. (1999). Search engine results over time: a case study on search engine stability. Cybermetrics, 2(3), 1.

Bar-Ilan, J. (2004). Search engine ability to cope with the changing web. Web Dynamics. Berlin: Springer-Verlag.

Bar-Ilan, J. (2007). Google bombing from a time perspective. *Journal of Computer-Mediated Communication,* 12(3), 910-938.

Cameron, A., & Trivedi, P. (1998). *Regression analysis of count data*: Cambridge University Press.

Choi, H., & Varian, H. (2009). Predicting the Present with Google Trends. Retrieved from http://google.com/googleblogs/pdfs/google_predicting_the_present.pdf

eMarketer (2008). First Summer Vacation Stop: The Internet Retrieved June 2, 2008, from http://www.emarketer.com/Article.aspx?id=1006344&src=article1_newsltr

Google (2006). Seattle's Convention and Visitors Bureau found 30% ROI with Google AdWords Retrieved December 15, 2006, from http://www.google.com/ads/scvb.html

Google (2009a). About Google Trends Retrieved August 30, 2009, from http://www.google.com/intl/en/trends/about.html

Google (2009b) Google AdWords Keyword Tool Retrieved July 1, from https://adwords.google.com/select/KeywordToolExternal

Henzinger, M. (2007). Search technologies for the Internet. Science, 317(5837), 468-471.

Hitwise (2009). Top 20 Sites & Engines Retrieved August 24, 2009, from http://www.hitwise.com/datacenter/main/dashboard-10133.html

Jansen, B. J., Spink, A., & Pedersen, J. (2005). A temporal comparison of AltaVista Web searching. *Journal of the American Society for Information Science and Technology*, 56(6), 559-570.

Kim, H., & Fesenmaier, D. R. (2008). Persuasive design of destination Websites: an analysis of first impression. *Journal of Travel Research*, 47(1), 3-13.

Pan, B., & Fesenmaier, D. R. (2006). Online Information Search: Vacation Planning Process. *Annals of Tourism Research, 33(3), 809-832.*

Pan, B., & Tierney, H.L.R. (2009). A Poisson Regression Examination of the Relationship between Web Traffic and SearchEngine Queries. Technical Report, available at http://www.ota.cofc.edu/pan/PoissonRegressionOfWebTraffic.pdf

Pan, B., Hembrooke, H., Joachims, T., Lorigo, L., Gay, G., & Granka, L. (2007). In Google We Trust: Users' Decisions on Rank, Position, and Relevance. *Journal of Computer-Mediated Communication*, 12(3), 801-823.

Prophis-Research (2007). 2006 US Online Travel Process Report: Prophis Research and Consulting, Inc.

Tatum, C. (2005). Deconstructing google bombs: A breach of symbolic power of just a goofy prank? First Monday, 10(10). Retrieved from http://www.firstmonday.org/issues/issue10 10/tatum/

TIA (2005). Travelers' Use of the Internet. Washington, DC: Travel Industry Association of America.

TIA (2008). Travelers' Use of the Internet. Washington D.C.: Travel Industry Association of America.

Wikipedia (2009). Google Trends Retrieved August 30, 2009, from http://en.wikipedia.org/wiki/Google_Trends

Wöber, K. (2006). Domain specific search engines. In D. R. Fesenmaier, K. Wöber & H. Werthner (Eds.), Destination Recommendation Systems: Behavioral Foundations and Applications. Wallingford, UK: CABI.

Wu, B., & Davison, B. D. (2005). Identifying link farm spam pages. Paper presented at the Special interest tracks and posters of the 14th international conference on World Wide Web.

Xiang, Z., & Fesenmaier, D. R. (2006). Assessing the initial step in the persuasion process: Meta tags on destination marketing websites. *Information Technology & Tourism*, 8(2), 91-104.

Xiang, Z., Wöber, K., & Fesenmaier, D. R. (2008). Representation of the online tourism domain in search engines. *Journal of Travel Research*, 47(2), 137-150.

Acknowledgements

The authors would like to thank the support from Hong Kong Polytechnic University with an international grant. Part of support came from the Office of Tourism Analysis, Department of Hospitality and Tourism Management, College of Charleston, USA. Sincere thanks go to Wei Ding, Brian Muller, and Matthew Gregg for their hard work on developing the data collection system and helping with data analysis; thanks to Kevin Smith for thorough copy-editing work.

A Sociological View of the Cybertourists

Valérie Guex

Sociology department
Geneva University, Swiss
Valerie.guex@unige.ch

Abstract

The article aims to consider from a social point of view the tourist's use of the web, examining these practices themselves but also their social functions and repercussions. The social functions will be dealt with by focusing on the individual taking part in "tourist surfing". We will see that using the Internet allows individuals not only to "escape social constraints" but also to create social links or bonds. The social repercussions will be analysed by centring our attention on the professionals in tourist communications. We will show that it is important for professionals in tourist communications to pay very close attention to the opinions of those on the receiving end of their messages.

Keywords: cybertourism/cybertourist/web/tourism/social function/ social repercussion

1 Introduction

This article intends to consider tourism and, more particularly, the use of the web by individual tourists. It will not so much be a matter of analysing these as of demonstrating that looking for tourist information on the web has itself social functions and that these online tourist practices affect the professionals in tourist communications. In order to better deal with social practices, it is necessary to understand the reasons for their emergence as well as their functions and effects. At first, the tourist's use of the web to seek tourist information will be investigated. Subsequently, the social functions of these practices will be discussed. And, finally, it seems appropriate to deal with the social repercussions of these practices on the professionals in tourist communications.

2 The individual tourist's use of the web

This part will be interested in the uses made of the web by tourists looking for information. But, previous to this, it seems of interest, on the one hand, to consider the medium Internet[1] from a historical and statistical standpoint. And, on the other hand, to consider E-tourism[2].

---

[1] The Internet is considered to be a "medium", as it fits the limited definition of the tern, i.e. " a technical support for communications" (Maigret E.   (2006:256)). In fact, it is an example of multimedia, as it has the text, the image (still or animated) and the sound.
[2] Literally means online tourism

2.1 Facts and figures about the web

The web as we know it today made its appearance at the beginning of the 1990s. This new medium redefined the limits of time and space and made information from anywhere in the world available at any time. Hervé Fisher (1995) speaks in this connection of "the conquest of a new space: time" (Fisher 1995:45). Dominique Jorand (2002) emphasizes that "the broadening of society's horizons brought about by the Internet surpasses the technical, political and economic conditions of its existence" (Jorand 2002:55). In the space of about ten years, the web has become more and more democratic[3] because of its very low cost and ease of transmission[4]. In Europe, nearly half of the population makes use of it[5], while in North America this is already the case for 74.4% of the population[6]. This difference in percentage illustrates that there is still a large potential for growth in Europe.

2.2 The web and e-tourism[7]

Before e-tourism, the future tourist had at his disposal diverse sources of information in order to form a picture of his destination: on the one hand, sources inside the tourist industry such as advertising campaigns, prospectuses, catalogues and tourist guides, and, on the other hand, sources outside the industry such as word-of-mouth, articles in the press, television reports, videos and books about tourist destinations, etc. But the tourist could also obtain information indirectly, for example, by watching a film or a TV series or by reading a novel which takes place in the specific area he is interested in. This multiplicity of sources demonstrates that, already in the early Internet period, professionally produced tourist information was not the only source where would-be tourists could acquire knowledge.

With the arrival of e-tourism, a fundamental change lies in the fact that potential tourists have much greater autonomy with respect to tourist information. This can be seen, for example, in the phase preceding the trip when a potential tourist is researching several places in order to choose a destination. It is true that the research done by an individual can be influenced by advertisements, posters, etc., published by professional tourist communicators. However, the future tourist will not leave it at that. He will look for information on the web and form his own opinion.

The coming of e-tourism has provoked a quick evolution in professional tourist communications.

---

[3] The term "democratic" is used in the sense of: becoming available to all social classes
[4] Taking up Patrice Flichy's idea (1991), we think that, although the Internet has become democratic, it will not replace the other media. Thus we do not consider the Internet to be THE medium which will eventually supplant the others. From now on, it is not the goal of this article to praise a new era of communications. The article will study the impact of the medium Internet on tourism.
[5] 48.9%. Taken from http://www.internetworld stats.com/stats.htm. (Consulted on 12 May 2009).
[6] From http://www.internetworldstats.com/stats.htm. (Consulted 12 May 2009).
[7] Literally means online tourism

It is not a matter of only communicating as before[8], but also in new ways.

Professional tourist communicators have been obliged to adapt to this changed public and their new practices. To respond to these new trends, tourist communicators have adopted the web, putting official sites for their destinations on the Internet, creating e-magazines or newsletter or proposing their services online (travel agencies)[9]. Thus, the web and the appearance of e-tourism have produced important changes in the tourism field. There is now a new way of perceiving tourism, which has led to a "profound evolution in the relationship between producer and consumer." (Fabry 2008:12) This change has had a direct influence on the two social actors in tourism: the creators of the communication and the receivers (the tourists). This evolution can be seen in the practices of the actors. "Nearly 50% of European Internet users say they used the web for travel information in the preceding three months[10]. And the tourism sector has become the first sector worldwide for online sales." (Bannwarth 2007:42)

According to Jean-Luc Boulin (2008): «35% of European online tourists use tourism 2.0 once a month, 26% once a week, and 10% every day! They use this service mainly to read other consumers' notes, commentaries and blogs and, on average, two out of three European tourists use the Internet at one point during their holiday (before, during, after)." (Boulin, 2008:30). Thanks to e-tourism, the relationship between the potential tourist and tourist communications has evolved. The web offers the individual more information which allows him to become "more of a comparer, "more of a discoverer", "more of a social actor". (Raffour 2003:34).

2.3 Tourist practices on the web

In the framework of an analysis of tourist usage of the Internet, it is important to take into account the timeframe of a trip. The idea that will be used here comes from the tourist historian, Marc Boyer (1999). He proposes a timeframe in three phases: the "dreamed trip", the "experienced trip" and the "prolonged trip". (Boyer 1999:166-167)[11]

During the "dreamed trip" phase, the person wanting to leave on vacation will have recourse to the web, for example, to choose his future destination or to buy tourist services online. He will find formal information on the web: prices, most favourable seasons, etc. He will also be able to find informal information such as "social representations" or "images"[12] from other individuals concerning one destination or another.

---

[8] Via advertising posters, catalogues, prospectuses, etc.

[9] The list is of course not exhaustive

[10] 47% Source: Statistics in Brief (Statistiques en bref – Industrie, commerce et services / Population et conditions Sociales / Science et technologie – 20/2006 Eurostat. http://.epp.eurostat.ec.europa.eu/cache/ITY-OFFPUB/KS-NP-   06-020-FR.PDF)

[11] This idea of the timeframe of a voyage was also put forward by the sociologist Graham M.S. Dann who distinguishes 3 times: pre-trip, on-trip and post-trip. (M.S. Dann 1996:142-144)

[12] In the framework of this article, we will consider "social representations" and "images" to be synonyms.

With e-tourism, several means of obtaining information are available. For formal information the would-be tourist will be able to consult official and unofficial sites regarding his destination or use search engines or "social media"[13] (such as blogs and forums (Voyageforum.com, E-voyageur). Concerning informal aspects, he will have the opportunity to look for them via search engines (Google, Yahoo), or by surfing the "web 2.0" via blogs, forums and video sharing sites (Youtube, Dailymotion) and photos (Flickr). These social media, true places for exchanging «social representations», will help the tourist to create his own image of his destination.

It is also important to state that, for some would-be tourists, the trip will never become reality. For these people, surfing becomes a means of travelling without moving physically. Bruce Prideaux (In: Graham M.S. Dann 2002:335) speaks of surfing as a "substitute" for physical travel.

For the "experienced trip", the use of the Internet can diverge slightly[14]. The vacationer will certainly consult it as usual to obtain practical information via official sites, search engines or social media, but he will not use it solely for that purpose. As the Internet does not have the same constraints of space and time as the real world, it will permit people to stay in contact during their vacation with the world they have left. Thus, the Internet becomes a provider of long-distance social links. This perspective has also been developed by Jean-Claude Morand and Brice Mollard (2008), who declare in their book:"Rare are the travelers who nowadays go on a trip without staying in contact with friends and family." (Mollard, Morand 2008:21).

Tourists can now become transmitters of tourist communications by sharing their travel experiences via the social media such as forums, video or film sharing sites, etc. Some people will wait for the "prolonged trip" phase to become transmitters of tourist communications on the web. This idea was conceptualised by Philippe Fabry (2008) who emphasized that «Internet users are passing from the status of passive consumers of information to that of active creators of information». (Fabry 2008:13). By becoming a tourist information transmitter and by sharing his vacation experiences on the web, the individual will create "buzz", word-of-mouth (Morand 2008:22) in order to transmit his travel experiences to his fellow tourists.

3   Social functions of tourist research on the web 2.0[15]

In this part, a micro-socialogical point of view will be adopted in order to understand the social functions of tourist surfing on the web 2.0. and the actors who practice it. This treatment of the subject does not pretend to be exhaustive. Its purpose is to demonstrate that it is possible to consider the tourist images on the web 2.0 from a social point of view.

---

[13] The social media are, according to Jean-Claude Morand (2008) "multiple supports which permit meeting and sharing on the Internet".
[14] It should be noted that certain tourists would like to consult the web during their vacation but are unable to do so due to non-existent or bad connections.
[15] The web 2.0 is defined as an interactive community web.

3.1 Tourist surfing and «escape» from social constraints

Jost Krippendorf, a Swiss specialist in tourism research, noted in his book, "Holidays and After" published in 1987, that tourism was a response to the desire for "escape" felt by individual people: "This thesis, the most widely held of all, maintains that the human being travels especially under the impulse of a desire to escape. This would even be the principal raison d'être of tourism today." (Krippendorf 1987:47). Travel has been adopted to "escape" the daily grind because it represents the opposite. The author defines it as the "anti-daily grind". (Krippendorf 1987:22): "Tourism appears more and more to be an escape en masse from daily realities to the imaginary kingdom of freedom." (Krippendorf 1987:47). This idea of "escape" had already been conceptualised by John Crompton in 1979, as part of the concept of "push"[16] in his article regarding "the motivations for pleasure trips", he points out that one of the motivations for leaving on a trip can be the desire to flee an environment considered banal (Crompton 1979:409). Thus, a trip becomes a temporary change of environment. (Crompton 1979:416).

Certainly, as Jost Krippendorf (1987) and John Crompton (1979) suggest, travelling can constitute an "escape", but isn't the desire to flee already alive when the actors undertake tourist research on the Internet? From that point on, it could already be a question of "social evasion" during the "dream trip" phase. Tourist research on the web could constitute a way for the actors to "flee" social constraints, to "escape" the daily grind during a few minutes of surfing.

This need for "social evasion", whether on the level of the act of travelling or of surfing the web, is a response to social ill feelings, to social dissatisfaction. As the words of Jost Krippendorf illustrate (1987): "The human being avoids confronting his unsatisfactory situation by developing a tendency to escape." (Krippendorf 1987:47). The author explains this need to "flee" from the regulated professional environment, which can be perceived by the actors as a "prison". (Krippendorf 1987:47). The sociologist Robert Lanquar Le sociologue Robert Lanquar (1990 1985) sees tourism as a «refuge from certain frustrations and unsatisfied desires...» (Lanquar 1990 1985:26). This idea can also be found in writing by Marc Boyer and Philippe Viallon (1994), who declare: "Tourists leave without really knowing why, pushed by a kind of bitterness or anger which seems to be the illness of the century." (Boyer, Viallon 1994: 13). Rachid Amirou (1994) does not see the desire to travel negatively (desire to "escape"). He believes it is necessary to stop considering the tourist phenomenon from the traditional point of view of "escape", as this neglects a more important aspect of travel as "a search for meaning" (Amirou 1994:20).

A person passing from the world of work to that of holidays passes from "fancied necessity" towards a universe characterised by a "perfect availability to oneself" (Amirou 1994:20). From that point on, tourism represents an "uncoupling" which allows an individual to "reconnect to the social rhythm and, what is more, to the search for a lost sociability which he has, in reality, never really known (la

---

[16] "Push" in the sense of pushing the individual to leave on a trip (Crompton 1979:412).

communitas)" (Amirou 1994:20).   The vacation period becomes "a utopia of togetherness" (Amirou 1994:20).

If we follow the thinking of Rachid Amirou (1994) that means that vacationing would be a practice, which permits a person to fend off the mounting individualism of our current society. Thus, if we associate this idea with the practice of tourist surfing, it is possible to declare that tourist surfing could be a practice which responds to this "search for a lost sociability" and that it would constitute in its way an "uncoupling" favourable to the creation of social links and an acceptance of individual differences. This idea will be taken up again in the following section where it will be shown that tourist surfing permits the creation of social links.

Tourist surfing and the creation of social links

Tourism is an excellent opportunity for social actors to create social links or bonds. Jost Krippendorf (1987) talks in this connection about the "vacation community" (Krippendorf 1987:48). This facet can also be identified on the web. In fact, by making use of social media such as forums, blogs or others before, during and after their trip, individuals can enter into contact with other users. The Internet has an ambivalent status because it permits "community individualism". This means that a single user, facing his screen, can create, if he wishes, social links around the world. Domique Wolton (2000) speaks in this regard of a new "era of interactive solitude" (Wolton 2000:106). This definition is echoed by Patrick Flichy (2004), who talks about "connected individualism" (Flichy 2004:19).

Concerning the question of social links, four social functions of tourist use of the web can be counted: the mixing of socially divergent categories, a gathering together around common interests (nationality, types of vacation), the creation of an atmosphere of respect[17] and a contribution to the positive "identity" of the individual.

First, tourist usage of the Internet allows for a real mixing of socially different categories and for the creation of social links beyond the social "borders" such as sociocultural adherence. In our society, the individual identifies himself socially and is identified by his job. Thus, each individual will tend to associate with people sharing the same habitus[18]. However, vacation time can be favorable to the creation of social links or bonds between categories. Edgar Morin's play on words picks up this idea: «La vacance des valeurs fait la valeur des vacances» (in Lanquar 1990, 1985:45). (The vacancy (= absence) of values makes the value of a vacation.) Nonetheless, holidays remain a stratified space: very often those who belong to the same socio-cultural group choose the same destination (object of distinction) and find themselves in the same places (five-star hotels or youth hostels, etc.). Lanquar (19901985) also mentions this fact: "There is an obvious segregation regarding leisure time and holidays and the differences between individuals in their daily existence,

---

[17] Recognition of each individual and acceptance of his difference.
[18] "Habitus" in the bourdieusien sense.

their working conditions, their style of life and the level of their education lead to segregation during their vacation. The essential reason is their standard of living." (Lanquar 1990̞1985:48).

It seems, however, that tourist surfing on the web is capable of removing the borders between socially divergent groups. The trip having been defined as "anti-daily grind", the users of social media are not going to emphasize their revenue or job in order to distinguish themselves socially. Not mentioning these would favour an exchange and the creation of inter-group social links. However, we are aware that at least one distinction will persist on the web because of tourist practices concerning the type of holiday (camping versus safari) or the choice of destination. Trips to Bhutan, for example, are accessible to certain social categories only. Bhutan has a very restrictive tourist policy. Visitors must pay a tax of €180 per day, in order to limit their number.

The social networks dealing with travel also allow linkage within cultural communities, such as the French, the Swiss, the Germans, etc. On tourist forums, the user's nationality is almost always mentioned in his profile. Thus, the individual can identify himself with a virtual group, having the feeling of socially belonging to a «virtual community". But this feeling of group adherence can also express itself in relation to common interests such as the type of voyage, destination, activity, etc.

Tourist surfing on the web 2.0 also facilitates entry into contact with the inhabitants of the country the tourist wishes to visit. In fact, it happens that tourists travelling in their own country also make use of the web to obtain information. While gathering this information, some of them take advantage of the occasion to give information to other users. In this case, tourist usage of the Internet makes for easier contact with local people. When the trip then takes place, this is bound to have a positive impact on the relationship between the travelers and the local inhabitants. In this way, tourist surfing can help to create good rapport between individuals. The following extracts come from a travel forum (http://voyageforum.com/destinations/suisse/), and aim to illustrate this exchange between future tourists about to leave for Switzerland and local Swiss residents:

"Fredgirl75
France
19 janvier 2009 à 17:05
Bonjour tout le monde!
Je m'appelle Frédérique, j'ai 22 ans et je suis étudiante en journalisme.
J'ai l'idée de parcourir ce magnifique pays qu'est la Suisse cet été! Je pense que le système d'Interrail (billet pour tout le réseau ferré) est une bonne occasion de découvrir de beaux paysages tout en voyageant simplement.
Je recherche donc des compagnes et compagnons de voyage pour participer à ce rail trip!
Je n'ai pas d'idées précises pour le moment des endroits à voir, de la durée et des coûts (l'idée du train est tout de même de limiter les frais). Deux ou trois semaines seraient bien, je pense.
Si des aventuriers sont partants pour partager ce périple, faites moi signe et donnez moi toutes vos merveilleuses idées!!!
A très bientôt...Sourire? "

"Dynastarider
Suisse

24 janvier 2009 à 21:15
Salut,
En effet, le voyage en train est très intéressant en Suisse. Le réseau est dense et très bien conçu.
En plus des grandes lignes InterCity, tu trouveras des petits trains ou des cars postaux pour te
mener partout, même jusque dans les vallée les plus reculées des Alpes ou du Jura !
Attention juste aux suppléments qui pourraient t'être demandé pour certaines parcours sur des
lignes très touristiques ainsi que pour prendre le bateau.
En 2 ou 3 semaines tu pourras voir pas mal du pays... Si tu as des questions précises, je me ferai
un plaisir de te répondre ! Clin d'oeil "

"carovoyage51
Suisse, Suisse
25 février 2009 à 17:47
Salut, salut !!!
Et bien voila ici une très belle idée, que de visiter mon pays !!Clin d'oeil
J'habite dans la campagne de Genève, je réponds à ton annonce juste pour te dire que si tu as
besoins de quoi que se soit, infos, conseils, lieux pour dormir, etc.. je serai ravie de t'aider! ainsi
que pour les lieux A NE PAS MANQUER, qui ne sont pas forcément connu et reconnu...
Je travaille aussi dans le tourisme, ce qui peut apporter un peu plus d'aide..
A bientôt peut être sur nos routes suisses!! Clin d'oeil
Caroline"

This creation of social links, by permitting the exchange of tourist information, will also have an impact on the "social representations" that the social actors form of a destination. This tourist surfing will give the individual a chance to construct his "image" of a destination. Thus, the image the user forms of a destination can change as he makes contact with other users. This exchange allows the user to form a picture which could be quite different from the polished "postcard image" published by tourist communicators.

In addition, the social interaction and exchange of social representations[19] can contribute to the building of a positive "identity" for the individual. By telling others about his vacation on the web or by answering other users' questions, the person can feel "socially useful". This identity building through contact with the web is even more positive as it happens in an area where culture is less important. In this way, most Internet users will feel capable of airing their opinions on a subject such as travelling.

4 Repercussions of tourist surfing on the publishers of tourist communications

Almost fifteen years ago, Louise Guay thought that this new technological age would affect the tourist industry in more important ways that did "the appearance of jet planes" (1995:23). She even predicted that "access to the tourist market will (would) from now on be of an electronic nature..." (Guay 1995:23). Nowadays, however, access to the tourist market is not limited to electronic means; but it is true that the web has acquired immense importance inside the tourist industry. In fact, according

---

[19] "Social representation: Way of seeing and thinking socially acquired" (Champagne 1998:5).

to Jean-Luc Boulin (2008) ˝(...) nearly half of European Internet users prepare their holidays online by using the web. 2.0.˝ (Boulin 2008:30).

According to Isabelle Bourgeois (2006), adolescents between the ages of 12 and 19 are ˝the Internet generation˝. Knowing this, we can sense the importance of the web as a tool to communicate with the tourists of tomorrow. E-tourism and the new Internet practices constitute important stakes for tourist communicators and necessitate, as Claude Bannwarth emphasizes (2007), ˝a new approach to the production of tourist communications ˝ (2007:40). Thus, as Eric Maigret states (2006), the Internet medium permits, contrary to other media, ˝individual and group expression˝ (Maigret 2006:267). The real stakes are at the level of the ˝image˝ of a tourist destination. Although tourist communication publishers did not have total control of the ˝image˝ of a potential tourist destination before the web era, now that ˝image˝ is becoming more and more difficult to control, due to the multiplicity of sources available via the Internet. Claude Bannwarth (2007b) states that: ˝from now on, the battle of the destinations is raging in the virtual world. ˝ (Bannwarth 2007b:40).

It is by having clients who are satisfied with their trip that the tourist communication publishers will best be able to control this ˝image˝. For, as has already been mentioned, every former client becomes a potential tourist communication transmitter. In accordance with his degree of satisfaction, he will criticise or sing the praises of his destination. At that moment, the web will constitute one means of publishing his opinion. Claude Bannwarth (2007a) takes up this idea, stating that: ˝ before the Internet, it was possible to promote a dreamed-up image which did not mirror the reality of the offer. This has become more difficult in an era where rapidly-multiplying personal tourist blogs describe without hesitation the slightest crack in a hotel which had been labelled as "charming"... (Bannwarth 2007a:42-43).

Before, tourist marketing concentrated on the departure. People had to be convinced to leave on a trip to one place or another. Today, it is not only a question of selling a ˝dream˝, but the dream must correspond to the tourist's ˝experienced, lived-through trip˝ and it must fulfil his expectations. The ˝on-trip˝ must be as close as possible to the ˝pre-trip˝. This is, therefore, a new era which is opening up for tourist communications, for it is not just a question of adopting the status of transmitter or publisher to sell, but the communicator must also become a receiver, always interested in the tourists' opinions concerning their trip. This idea was conceptualised in the marketing field, using the term ˝mass individualisation˝[20] (Poupard 2003:1). This type of individualization aims for: ˝a larger consideration of the particularities of each individual˝, concentrating on ˝his tastes˝ and ˝his preferences˝ (Poupard 2003:2).

---

[20] Jean-Marc Poupard (2003) defines mass individualisation as follows: ˝ We define mass individualisation as the possibility, on the one hand, to deliver a large quantity of individualised messages to a great number of individuals, and, on the other hand, to produced individualised products in large numbers. ˝ (Poupard 2003:2).

However, we must not think that the web has an inordinate influence on the "image" the tourists have of a destination, because "this image" is not formed only with this tool, it is co-constructed in connection with the social and psychical universe of the individual.

5 Conclusion

This article has attempted to deal with tourist usage of the web from a new point of view, by regarding tourist surfing as a social object. This undertaking meant that it was necessary to surpass normal usage[21] by also analysing functions and effects. It has been shown that tourist surfing involves social functions, especially because it has permitted an escape from social constraints, but also because it has favoured the creation of social links or bonds. It has also been established that these tourist practices on the web have also affected the professionals working in tourist communications and that they have had to redefine their practices accordingly.

In the face of these new practices, the professional tourist communicators took the big step onto the web. It is not sufficient, however, just to be present on the web; one must take into account the specificities of the Internet medium. In fact, the Internet has not just improved the means of communication, it has turned them upside down. This has necessitated a considerable rethinking of the methods of professional tourist communicators, in order to take into account the social specificities of the Internet.

It has now become necessary to be receivers, paying careful attention to the expectations and needs of individuals written on the web, for, nowadays, we are dealing with what Dominic Wolton (1997) called a "massively individualistic" society. (Wolton 1997:95). In fact, for numerous people, the web has become an "Ersatz" for human presence. Web usage has been able to answer a social need which has appeared in response to a "social ill feeling" and dissatisfaction following the rise of individualism.

Thus, in this time of "interactive solitude", the web has become for many a "travel companion" who gives "good advice" and has an "attentive ear". Patrick Flichy (2004) speaks in this regard of: "network individualism" (Flichy 2004:30). As a consequence, professional tourist communicators would be well advised to listen with an "attentive ear" to the requirements and expectations of individuals[22] .

---

[21] Many articles have been written about tourism and usage of the web – whether about professional communicators or tourist practices – but without surpassing them.
[22] This can be done, for example, by carrying out quality studies on satisfaction during and after the trip.

The article by Philippe Laublet, Chantal Reynaud and Jean Charlet (2002) on the "semantic web[23]" ("web 3.0") leads one to imagine that his future web will also have an impact on the practices of transmitters and receivers of tourist communications.

In fact, according to these authors, this new web should see, in contrast to the web we know today, "the users liberated from a large part of their research tasks, from constructing and combining results, thanks to increased capacities of the machines to access resource content and to carry out reasoning and calculation using these." (Laublet, Reynaud, Charlet 2002:60). This new web will increase the visibility of professional tourist communicators, but it will also provide receivers with greater possibilities for comparison. Hence, the importance for professional tourist communicators to pay attention more than ever to those on the receiving end of their communications.

Reference

Amirou, R., 1994. Le tourisme comme objet transitionnel. *Espaces,* 76, 149-164. Edition électronique à partir de http://classiques.uqac.ca/contemporains/amirou_rachid/tourisme_objet_transitionnel/tourisme.html [Consulté le 11 mai 2009].

Bannwarth, C., 2007a. Internet renouvelle le combat identitaire. *Espaces*, 245, 41- 44.

Bannwarth, C., 2007b. L'e-révolution des destinations touristiques. *Espaces*, 247, 40-44.

Boulin, J.-L., 2008. L'e-tourisme institutionnel n'échappe pas au web 2.0. *Espaces*, 265, 30-34.

Bourgeois, I., 2009. *12-19 ans: la génération Internet* [online]. Regards sur l'économie allemande. A partir de http://rea.revues.org/index739.html. [Consulté le 11 mai 2009].

Boyer, M., Viallon Ph., 1994, *La communication touristique*. Paris: PUF.

Boyer, M., 1999. *Histoire du tourisme de masse*. Paris: PUF.

Charlet, J., Laublet, Ph., Reynaud Ch., 2002. *Sur quelques aspects du Web sémantique*. Actes des deuxièmes assises nationales du GdR I3. A partir de *http://enssibal.enssib.fr/autres-sites/RTP/websemantique/octobre/programme0209.html.* [Consulté le 12 mai 2009].

Crompton, J., 1979. Motivations for pleasure vacation. *Annals of Tourism Research,* 6(4), 408-424.

Fabry, Ph., 2008. Le web 2.0 s'installe au coeur des stratégies touristiques. *Espaces*, 265, 12-18.

Fisher, H., 1995. Tourisme virtuel. *Téoros*, 14, 45-47.

Flichy, P., 2004. L'individualisme connecté entre la technique numérique et la société. *Réseaux*, 124, 19-51.

Flichy, P., 1991. *Une histoire de la communication moderne. Espace public et vie privée*. Paris: La Découverte.

M.S. Dann, G., 1996. *The language of tourism. A sociolinguistic perspective.* Oxon: CAB publishing.

M.S. Dann, G., 2002. *The tourist as a metaphor of social World.* New York: CAB publishing.

Guay, L., 1995. Le tourisme au pays du multimédia pour s'y rendre comment s'y prendre? Quoi faire? *Téoros*, 14, 22- 25.

Jorand, D., 2002. Entre utopie et catastrophisme un témoignage sur quelques pratiques actuelles de l'Internet. *Loisir et Société*, 25, 55-76.

Krippendorf, J., 1987. *Les vacances et après?* Paris: Editions Harmattan.

Lanquar, R., 1990. *Sociologie du tourisme et des voyages*. Paris: PUF.

---

[23] "The semantic web, (…), is at first a new infrastructure permitting software technicians to help different types of user more effectively to access web resources (information sources and services)." (Laublet, Reynaud, Charlet 2002:59).

428

Maigret, E., 2006. *Sociologie de la communication et des médias.* Paris: Armand Colin.

Mollard, B., Morand, J.-C., 2008. *Tourisme 2.0, Préparer son voyage, préparer son offre de tourisme.* Paris: M21 Editions.

Morand, J.-C., 2008. Les médias sociaux sur Internet outils de marketing touristique. *Espaces,* 265, 19-23.

Poupard, J., 2003. *De l'individualisation de masse l'industrialisation de la commercialisation. Le rôle des TIC dans la recomposition de la chaîne de distribution* [online]. Revue du Gresec. Les Enjeux de l'information et de la communication. A partir de http://w3.u-grenoble3.fr/les_enjeux/ [Consulté le 11 mai 2009].

Raffour, G., 2003. *E-tourisme les enjeux des infomédiations sur l'offre et la demande touristique.* La Paris: La Documentation Française.

Wolton, D., 1997. *Penser la communication.* Paris: Flammarion.

Wolton, D., 2000. *Internet et après? Une théorie critique des nouveaux médias.* Paris: Flammarion.

A Comparative Analysis of Content in Traditional Survey versus Hotel Review Websites

Roland Schegg[a]
Michael Fux[b]

[a] Ecole Suisse de Tourisme, Institut Economie & Tourisme, HES-SO Valais, Switzerland, roland.schegg@hevs.ch

[b] Institut für Tourismuswirtschaft, Hochschule Luzern – Wirtschaft, michael.fux@hslu.ch

Abstract

Increasingly customers publish their opinions or observations regarding tourism products on the internet. Review websites allow customers to express their opinion regarding the service offered during their stay by awarding points to pre-selected criteria or by publishing their comments. This feedback can provide valuable information to service providers. Whether these alternative sources of marketing research fulfil the quality criteria of classical marketing research has not yet been fully explored. In this contribution, the question asked is whether there are significant differences between the results provided by traditional marketing surveys and those provided by more alternative surveys using the web. The explorative analysis of the Swiss tourism destination Saas-Fee shows that the customers' appraisals of the offers does not differ fundamentally between classical marketing research and the evaluations on review websites. However, anonymous forms of assessment on customer evaluation portals or online questionnaires seem to lead to more critical results compared to classical face-to-face marketing research.

Keywords: user-generated content, hotel review platforms, marketing research, TripAdvisor, HolidayCheck, Switzerland

1 Introduction

The importance of the internet as a source of information for travellers is already well- known. According to a study, conducted in 2008, 50% of Germans used the internet to help make their travel plans (F.U.R., 2008). Travellers increasingly discover new sources of information when they share experiences and appraisals with other customers. Along with classical sources of information, such as accommodation and travel agency website, new websites are taking on a more important role. Included amongst these alternative sources of information are social networking sites such as Facebook and MySpace, online communities such as Virtual tourist and TravBuddy, and opinion and evaluation portals such as TripAdvisor, HolidayCheck (Forrester, 2008). Various studies, e.g. Shea et al., 2004 or Litvin et al., 2006, show that more and more customers rely on recommendations of other customers and no longer blindly trust information given by the hotel service providers. It is also observed that there is a new participative or collaborative paradigm by which the classical word-of-mouth communication is increasingly being shifted to the internet.

Nowadays, contents published online by individual customers can reach millions of members of the public within seconds thus increasing market transparency. With regard to the quality of information, studies show that online communities are not inferior to classical travel guides in paper form. In an empirical study it was proven that customers who searched for travel information such as addresses, contact details, or prices in online communities obtained valid information (Prestipino et al., 2007).

Meanwhile, not only customers but also tourism service providers recognize and use such collaborative evaluation platforms. An empirical examination of over 300 enterprises in Switzerland (Schegg et al., 2008) shows that tourism service providers increasingly use travel review platforms for market research purposes. For more than half of the interviewees, for example, platforms such as TripAdvisor or HolidayCheck are rated as being indispensable to very important and 60% see a great opportunity in these portals. 75% still check their image and customers' opinions regarding services provided on the internet manually and do not take advantage of instruments providing automatic notification such as e-mail alerts or RSS feeds. However, it is astounding that almost every other enterprise checks the various websites with customers' opinions and evaluations at least once per week. On the basis of these numbers it can be presumed that tourism service providers use collaborative review websites for marketing research purposes and obtain information about how customers perceive their own services. In the context of web 2.0 this behaviour has also been understood as the use of collective intelligence on the internet (Kilian et al., 2007).

In spite of widespread acceptance of these portals by hotel service providers, the question can be asked whether they fulfil the quality criteria of marketing research and thereby are trustworthy sources for operational decisions. It is critical to question whether the results are reliable because currently, in Europe, only a third of the population actively evaluates offers and publishes opinions; whereas, in North America this behaviour is already observed in more than 50% of the population (Forrester Research, 2008). Against this background, the criticism is occasionally expressed that opinions on the internet do not correspond to reality and, therefore, can be ignored by hotel service providers. The authors are unaware of any authoritative research that substantiates how decision makers appraise the representativeness of data in the hotel industry. On the basis of general misgivings concerning the representativeness of online studies it can be assumed that there is also scepticism regarding other forms of internet-based data acquisition (Withers and Matzat, 2008).

2 Marketing Research Approaches

Marketing research concentrates generally on the systematic acquisition, processing, and analysis of market information which is especially relevant to marketing. Some of the central quality criteria of marketing research are reliability (reliability of the used instruments regarding data acquisition), objectivity, and validity. Whilst with conventional marketing research data are collected by means of questioning or observation, new approaches use user-generated content in social media as the data source. User-generated content is to be understood as content that is published online by internet users, usually end-users. With this form of marketing research no data are actively collected; rather, content available on the internet is used.

While attempting to describe the specific advantages and disadvantages of this new form of marketing research, this contribution concentrates upon the use of hotel review websites. What is not considered, are opinions of customers in online forums or social networks which are characterized by unstructured communication and discussion; whilst with customer review portals a part of the data is presented in a structured form. Marketing research based on user-generated content generally uses qualitative methods such as Netnography or Webnography to gain relevant information (Bartl, 2007).

Table 1. Advantages and disadvantages of marketing research with user-generated content

Advantages	Disadvantages
▪ Real time: Negative messages and dissatisfaction can be recognized early. ▪ Cost: The infrastructure of websites can be used and data are already available electronically. ▪ Competitor analysis: Information regarding the competition is easily available. ▪ No interviewer bias: The anonymous data input results in more unbiased answers and evaluations.	▪ Representativeness: The composition (demography) of the user sample does not correspond to the target group. ▪ Individualization: Marketing research contents cannot be defined independently. ▪ Lack of experience: The research approaches (processes, structures, metrics) have not yet matured.

3 Profile of the Destination Saas-Fee

Saas-Fee is one of the top destinations in the Swiss Alpine tourism industry. The destination is located at the end of one of the numerous north-south oriented valleys in the canton of Wallis. The high Alpine mountain environment, the Fee glacier, which is used as a summer skiing area, together with reliable snow conditions due to the altitude of the village (1,800 m) and the skiing area (1,800-3,600m) are important natural factors which favour the development of the tourism sector. Other important characteristics are the authentic, intact, compact, and car-free village. Saas-Fee offers 57 hotels with 1274 available rooms with approximately 2670 beds. Luxury class hotels (1 five-star hotel and 7 four-star hotels) have a market share in terms of room capacity of approximately 20%; while three star hotels, which seem to be predominant, offer almost 50% of the rooms available. The hotel industry generates approximately 420,000 overnight stays per year, with approximately two- thirds of the bookings generated during the winter season. The occupancy rate for available hotel beds in Saas-Fee during the winter season 2007/2008 was 56% and 32% during the summer season 2008. The most important markets for the hotel industry in Saas-Fee are Switzerland with 41% of guests in 2007-2008, England (18%), Germany (14%), and Holland (5%).

4   Methodical Approach

Saas-Fee was chosen as a case study for the comparison of the results of classical marketing research with data from hotel review websites because we had access to the current data of two classical surveys for the destination. Both surveys also look into customers' satisfaction with the hotels. In one of the surveys, in summer 2007 in the framework of a research project, 362 overnight guests in Saas-Fee were questioned in face-to-face interviews. Although the focus of the study lay more in the general appraisal of the guests concerning the destination itself, satisfaction with the accommodation was investigated in one of the questions. However, satisfaction with a specific accommodation facility cannot be determined. However, for the second poll, we could also obtain internal marketing research data from Saas-Fee tourism (SF). All guests who book directly through the reservation centre of the destination are contacted by e-mail and requested to answer a web-based customer survey following their stay. The guests evaluate the hotel where they stayed and other aspects of the destination such as atmosphere and infrastructure on a scale from 1 to 6 with regard to various factors (see table 2). For the present study, the answers of 458 guests during the observation period from December 2006 to July 2008 were included.

The data from TripAdvisor (TA) and HolidayCheck (HC) were manually entered into a databank for further processing. All evaluations of the hotels in Saas-Fee up to July 2008 were considered. It is critical for the evaluation that customers' evaluations on TripAdvisor are based upon a 5-point Likert scale whilst HolidayCheck as well as the poll from Saas-Fee tourism uses a 6-point Likert scale, which is typical for German-speaking countries. To guarantee comparability, a scale transformation of the TripAdvisor data to a 6-point Likert scale was carried out in accordance with the Dawes' approach (2008).

Table 2. Applied marketing research instruments and data sources in overview

	Trip Advisor (TA)	Holiday Check (HC)	Field survey in Saas-Fee	Online survey Saas-Fee tourism
Topics covered on review websites / in questionnaire				
Hotel in general	•	•	•	•
Room	•	•		•
Service	•	•		•
Hotel location	•	•		•
Catering		•		•
Sport / entertainment		•		•
Cleanliness	•			
Atmosphere				•

Value for money	•	•		
Check-in / reception	•			
Open comments	•	•		
Socio-demographics	•	•		•
Number of items	5	6	6	6
Additional information on questionnaire and data				
Evaluation scale	Very well – not at all	Extremely well - very badly	Very enthusiastic - disappointing	
Observation period	01/03 – 07/08	01/06 – 07/08	07/07 – 08/07	12/06 – 07/08
Number of evaluations	146	227	362	458
Number of hotels reviewed	31	29	No information	53

5 Results and Analysis of the Hotel Evaluations

In all 152 evaluations of 31 hotels on TripAdvisor and 227 evaluations of 29 hotels on HolidayCheck were analysed. Although Saas-Fee can register more than 400,000 overnight stays annually, the number of the evaluations is rather modest and shows that the image of the hospitality sector in Saas-Fee on these portals is determined by a small group of guests.

It is also striking that the number of customer evaluations per hotel is extremely variable. On HolidayCheck four hotels attracted between 26 and 41 evaluations, which makes up more than 60% of all evaluations of the destination at that time. The situation is more balanced on TripAdvisor where 5 hotels received 11 to 15 evaluations which amounted to slightly more than 40% of all evaluations for Saas-Fee. Remarkably, however, no hotel had more than 10 evaluations on both customer evaluation portals. 18 hotels had less than 5 evaluations on TripAdvisor and HolidayCheck, respectively. A large majority of the hotels in Saas-Fee are not present on these portals at all or only have a few evaluations. In extreme cases, individual evaluations could affect in a significant manner the image regarding the quality of a hotel and this could represent a potential danger for the hotels.

The socio-demographic characteristics of the customers on both portals are rather different, first of all, concerning origin. Whilst on TripAdvisor guests from the UK dominate with almost 70% of feedback; the evaluations on HolidayCheck are distributed amongst Swiss (50%), German (25%) and English (10%) customers. The composition of those making evaluations on HolidayCheck corresponds roughly to the composition of guests in Saas-Fee where Swiss and German hotel guests make up approximately 55% of the clientele. However, the age distribution of the guests is similar on both platforms and covers all age groups, with the 35-49 age group being predominant.

Table 3 gives the first elements of answers to our principal research question concerning differences in the assessment of hotels on the internet as compared to classical marketing research studies. Table 3 shows a global comparison of customer evaluations in terms of an average of all scores collected for the hotels in Saas-Fee based on the evaluations of TripAdvisor (TA) and HolidayCheck (HC) as well as the data from the online survey of Saas-Fee (SF) tourism. It should be noted that the calculated average marks can be regarded as good in the evaluated quality dimensions with values of around 5. Although the average values of the review websites and the questionnaire are relatively close to one another – particularly the values from TripAdvisor and Saas-Fee tourism – the variance analysis proves that the evaluations on HolidayCheck are statistically significantly higher by up to 0.5 points. An analysis of data from the winter season 07/08 shows no fundamental differences compared to this overall evaluation: results for HolidayCheck are still significantly higher and nearly identical to the results of the overall sample. The analysis of the results of the classical face-to-face marketing research from the summer of 2007 reveals that 69% of the questioned hotel guests (n=157) were very enthusiastic and that 22% were enthusiastic. The resulting average mark is 5.5 and is much higher than on the customer evaluation portals and in the online survey of the destination management organisation.

Table 3. Global comparison of hotel evaluations on HolidayCheck (HC), TripAdvisor (TA) and from online survey of Saas Fee (SF) tourism for selected dimensions

	Average	Standard deviation	Median	Observations	ANOVA
Hotel HC	5.11	0.93	5.3	227	
Hotel TA	4.77	1.38	4.75	146	**p = <0.001** F = 14.9
Hotel SF	4.68	0.79	5	457	
Room HC	*5.08*	*1.1*	*5.5*	*227*	
Room TA	*4.45*	*1.26*	*4.75*	*109*	**p = < 0.001** F = 13.72
RoomSF	*4.6*	*2.48*	*4.5*	*457*	
Service HC	5.3	1.06	5.7	227	
Service TA	4.82	1.39	4.75	109	**p = <0.001** F = 8.81
Service SF	4.73	0.96	5	457	
Hotel location HC	*5.21*	*0.76*	*5.3*	*227*	
Hotel location TA	*5.17*	*1.12*	*6*	*78*	**p = <0.001** F = 23.53
Hotel location SF	*4.87*	*0.84*	*5*	*457*	
Total opinion	*4.86*	*1.33*			

The explorative analysis of the data concerning the hotel category (see Table 4) shows a statistically significant relationship between the aspects evaluated and the classification of the hotels. First of all, evaluations from HolidayCheck are much higher with regard to hotel, room, and service in five-star hotels than in budget hotels. With TripAdvisor the customers' satisfaction does correlate to the hotel category. These inconsistent relationships offer empirical evidence for the plausible assumption that there is no link between quality categories and evaluations.

Table 4. Comparison of hotel evaluations on HolidayCheck (HC), TripAdvisor (TA) and from online survey of Saas Fee (SF) tourism as a function of the hotel category

Dimension		1-2*	3*	4-5*	Others	Total	ANOVA
Hotel	HC	4.81	5.24	5.35	4.29	5.11	$p = <0.001$ $F = 6.78$
	n	44	148	22	13	227	
	TA	4.35	4.8	4.75	4.96	4.77	$p = 0.717$ $F = 0.46$
	n	11	74	43	18	146	
	SF	4.59	4.59	5.04	4.73	4.67	$p = <0.001$ $F = 6.86$
	n	96	254	72	25	447	
Room	HC	5.06	5.12	5.38	4.23	5.08	$p = 0.022$ $F = 3.26$
	n	44	148	22	13	227	
	TA	4.44	4.59	4.16	4.58	4.45	$p = 0.49$ $F = 0.82$
	n	8	54	32	15	109	
	SF	4.87	4.49	4.68	4.49	4.6	$p = 0.638$ $F = 0.57$
	n	96	254	72	25	447	
Service	HC	5	5.41	5.53	4.68	5.3	$p = 0.013$ $F = 3.66$
	n	44	148	22	13	227	
	TA	5.06	4.87	4.67	4.83	4.82	$p = 0.883$ $F = 0.22$
	n	8	54	32	15	109	
	SF	4.69	4.64	4.93	4.84	4.71	$p = 0.143$ $F = 1.81$
	n	96	254	72	25	447	
Location	HC	5.13	5.25	5.32	4.8	5.21	$p = 0.176$ $F = 1.65$
	n	44	148	22	13	227	
	TA	3.97	5.5	5.07	5.22	5.17	$p = 0.004$ $F = 4.80$
	n	8	35	27	8	78	
	SF	4.78	4.89	4.95	4.78	4.87	$p = 0.495$ $F = 0.80$
	n	96	254	72	25	447	

In the evaluations and discussions above, comparisons were conducted with the knowledge that the observational units are composed of different hotel portfolios, i.e. the sample of hotels on TripAdvisor is different than that on HolidayCheck. In order to increase the relevance of the comparisons, analyses at the level of individual hotels were also performed. The problem here is that it is difficult to find hotels that have sufficient evaluations on both customer evaluation portals and the online survey of Saas-Fee tourism. Our analyses show (Table 5) that the overall results of the different hotel evaluations seem to converge; statistically significant differences can only be observed in a few cases. The different evaluation systems seem to lead to comparable results at the individual hotel level.

Table 5. Comparison of the Customers' Evaluations for selected individual hotels

	HC	SF	TA	Total	ANOVA
Hotel 1 (Bed and breakfast)					
Hotel	4.29	4.6	4.33	4.36	F = 0.15, 1-p = 0.14
Room	4.23	4.6	3.68	4.15	F = 0.63, 1-p = 0.45
Service	4.68	4.8	4.04	4.53	F = 0.58, 1-p = 0.43
Location	4.8	4	4.44	4.54	F = 1.51, 1-p = 0.75
N	13	5	9	27	
Hotel 2 (3*)					
Hotel	5.14		5.55	5.2	F = 1.91, 1-p = 0.83
Room	4.99		5.29	5.03	F = 0.53, 1-p = 0.52
Service	5.47		5.82	5.52	F = 0.83, 1-p = 0.63
Location	4.93		6	5.08	F = 14.62, 1-p = 0.999
N	41		7	48	
Hotel 3 (4-5*)					
Hotel	4.16	5.1	4.25	4.74	F = 2.74, 1-p = 0.91
Room	4.4	4.48	3.19	4.25	F = 2.77, 1-p = 0.92
Service	4.16	5.07	4.13	4.72	F = 2.62, 1-p = 0.91
Location	5.6	5.2	4.75	5.25	F = 1.57, 1-p = 0.77
n	5	15	5	25	
Hotel 4 (4-5 *)					
Hotel	5.25	5.75	4.07	4.6	F = 1.95, 1-p = 0.82
Room	4.75	4.75	3.5	4.08	F = 0.74, 1-p = 0.50
Service	6	5.75	3.5	4.58	F = 6.67, **1-p = 0.99**
Location	5.75	5.5	4.5	5.09	F = 2.39, 1-p = 0.85
n	2	4	11	17	

6 Analysis of free text comments

Along with the analysis of the evaluation criteria, the individual free text comments on the portals are also examined. As the research was of explorative nature, no weights have been assigned to the categories. The majority of evaluations regarding hotels in Saas-Fee are recorded in a very neutral and authentic context. Thereby, many guests use the opportunity to fundamentally praise the hotel for its services but also to point out operational weaknesses. Of course, there are also extreme comments, both positive and negative. The main and most frequently mentioned topics regarding the hotels in Saas-Fee are comments concerning the friendliness and the helpfulness of the staff – so-called 'soft factors'. Important secondary topics are catering, the wellness offer, as well as the beautiful view and location of the hotels.

7 Discussion und conclusions

It can be assumed that customers in the future will increasingly exchange their experiences online in various digital forms such as text, audio, photographs, or video. A consequence of this trend is that, amongst other things, customer evaluation portals will have increasing influence on the perception of hotels by customers. The digitalization of word-of-mouth recommendations is changing the balance of power. Whilst previously tourism suppliers could push their marketing messages by means of mass media and direct communication channels, today customers have the possibility to affect the image of an enterprise by simply publishing reviews on the internet. For tourist service providers the question arises as to whether this type of data is reliable regarding customer satisfaction research. Moreover, it is uncertain whether the analysis of data from various sources results in consistent conclusions. To check validity, data from hotel review sites (TripAdvisor, HolidayCheck) were compared with the data of classical marketing research, supposing that the data basis of classical marketing research fulfils all quality criteria.

Our results suggest that the assessment of hotels via an online questionnaire does not differ fundamentally from customer evaluations on websites such as HolidayCheck and TripAdvisor. Satisfaction with accommodation in the classical customer survey in the summer of 2007, however, proved to have much more positive results. Therefore, the question arises whether "anonymous" evaluations, administered either through an online questionnaire or on hotel review sites, are generally more critical. In both cases, customers can express themselves freely which is not so easy in "face-to-face" evaluations.

As the statistical comparison of the various electronic data sources shows, the evaluations on one platform, i.e. HolidayCheck, turn out, on average, to be significantly higher. Due to the inadequate data basis, the reasons for this observation could not be explained in detail. As the origin of the users on the hotel review sites differs significantly, this differentiating characteristic could be a determinant of the variation. The generally higher evaluations on HolidayCheck may simply reflect the fact that the expectations of the guests from the German-speaking countries (Switzerland, Germany, and Austria) which dominate this review site are better fulfilled. However, the guests from other countries possibly simply arrive with different expectations, and this is what is reflected in the differing level of satisfaction for hotels in Saas-Fee on TripAdvisor.

8 Implications for Research

Within the framework of the present explorative study, it could be shown that generally only small, but still significant differences exist between the different data sources. In order to support the statements and answer the research question, statistical analyses based on a greater data volume would be necessary. Future research efforts should direct their focus towards the identification of the variables influencing the evaluation of tourism services and offers. The origin of the guests could be one of these determining factors as discussed above. It is also possible, that the different evaluation scales have an influence on the result. Occasionally, the question is raised whether the real world can be portrayed by processes and events in the virtual world. So, attempts are made, for example, on the basis of online reviews of new films to predict the future revenues that will be generated (Dellarocas, 2007). Whether similar forecasting mechanisms also lead to the desired results in the tourist context could be the subject of future research projects.

9 Implications for Practice

One of the weak points which has been highlighted by our study is the small number of evaluations on review sites for a majority of the hotels in Saas-Fee. Therefore, the customers should be encouraged by the hotels to give their feedback on review portals. To do so, mechanisms should be implemented which motivate customers to publish their opinions on the internet. As the comparison with classical marketing research has shown, hotels need not fundamentally fear negative evaluations. With a proactive system of steering the customers to specific portals, evaluations would concentrate primarily on selected platforms which would simplify monitoring. This activation of customers can have two positive effects. On the one hand, potential customers obtain undistorted information, and the hotel service providers acquire feedback for the improvement of their services. This is an interesting starting point for the creation of added value for customers (Prahald & Ramaswamy, 2004). The feedback process regarding customer evaluation portals can also be helpful for quality management of hotels and supply important input for future service offers. Committed managers, who transform such deficits into strengths with new products or improvement measures can, thereby, create competitive advantages. If customers repeatedly point out the urgent need for refurbishment of specific facilities, e.g. massage rooms, the relaxing of rules regarding nakedness in the wellness areas, the enforcement of a general smoking ban, or ambiance enhancement in dining areas, then one should act. Soft factors such as lack of friendliness and the helpfulness of the staff are also popular topics in customers' comments. Such topics should be discussed seriously within the team, and if necessary, appropriate training measures should be taken.

In the case of very negative comments, direct contact with the customer should be made in order to clarify what exactly led to service failure. Several of the leading hotel review sites offer the hotels a place to post a comment under a written evaluation. Therefore, transparency can be increased with the complaint management system and the confidence of potential guests can be gained by a positive handling of criticism as well as by showing that customers' opinions are valued. Compensation strategies, e.g. a discount on the next stay, should be considered because negative verbal comments by deeply disappointed customers are very damaging for the enterprise. Thereby, it is made clear that a proactive use of customer evaluation platforms is an opportunity rather than a risk for the hotels - particularly, in the areas of quality management, product development, and customer relationship management (CRM). However, this potential can only be put to good use if the monitoring of the evaluations and opinions on the internet takes place systematically. Amongst other things, professional monitoring requires the inclusion and survey of different platforms. Market intelligence tools are available today which make the monitoring of different hotel review sites much easier and valuable. With these systems, data collection, aggregation, and processing can be automated.

Hotels should collect both primary data and also secondary data from review websites to know customer needs better and improve quality. In order to optimally use synergies between both forms of data acquisition, new scenarios for the combination of both types of market research need to be developed. A complementary consideration of both data source types appears to be sensible to the authors because by focusing on only one type, valuable information is likely to be lost. Integration of other data from the social media context such as blogs, online communities, or social networks can increase awareness of customers' needs and also aid enterprises in becoming aware of their own strength-weakness profiles.

References

Bartl, M. (2007): Netnography, Einblicke in die Welt der Kunden. In: *Planung & Analyse*, 5, S. 83-87.
Dawes, J. (2008): Do data characteristics change according to the number of scale points used? An experiment using 5-point, 7-point and 10-point scales. *International Journal of Market Research,* 50 (1), 61-104.
Dellarocas, C., Zhang, X., & Awad, N. F. (2007): Exploring the Value of Online Product Ratings in Revenue Forecasting: The Case of Motion Pictures, *Journal of Interactive Marketing, 21(4), 23-45.*
Forrester Research (2008): Forrester's Technographics Benchmark Study Q2 2008, http://www.forrester.com/Groundswell/profile_tool.html
F.U.R. (2008): Reiseanalyse, http://www.reiseanalyse.de/
Kilian, T., Hass, B. H., & Walsh, G. (2007): Grundlagen des Web 2.0. In: Kilian, T., Hass, B. H., Walsh, G.(Hg.), *Web 2.0, Neue Perspektiven für Marketing und Medien*, Berlin: Springer, S. 3-21.
Prahald, C. K., & Ramaswamy, V. (2004): *The Future of Competition: Co-Creating Unique Values with Customers*, Harvard Business School Press. Boston.
Prestipino, M., Aschoff, R., & Schwabe, G. (2007): How up-to-date are Online Tourism Communities? An Empirical Evaluation of Commercial and Non-commercial Information Quality, *Proceedings of the Hawaii International Conference on System Sciences* (HICSS) 2007.
Saas Fee Tourismus (2008): *Geschäftsbericht Saas-Fee Tourismus* 2007/2008. Online: http://www.saasfee.ch [15.03.2008]
Schäfer, F. (2008): Comparison of "Frames of References" for Tests in the Customer Research Sector. GOR 08 Research Paper. Online:

http://www.gor.de/conftool08/index.php?page=browseSessions&form_session=77 & presentations=show&abstracts=show [15.03.2008]

Schegg, R., Scaglione, M., Favre, R., & Délétroz, N. (2008): Schweizer Tourismus im Mitmach-Internet - was wird bereits gemacht? Vortrag am *Forum "Web 2.0 - das Mitmach-Internet! Chancen und Risiken für die Tourismusbranche"*, IFITT Switzerland, 3. September 2008, http://www.ifitt.ch [15.03.2008]

Shea, L., Enghagen, L., & Khullar, A. (2004): Internet diffusion of an e-Complaint: a content analysis of unsolicited responses, *Journal of Travel & Tourism Marketing*, 17 (2/3), 145-165.

Litvin, S.W., Goldsmith, R.E., & Pan, B. (2006): Electronic Word-of-Mouth in Hospitality and Tourism Management. In: *Tourism Management* 29, 458-468.

Welker, M., & Matzat, U. (2008): Online-Forschung: Entwicklungslinien, Defizite und Potentiale. In: Jackob, N., Schoen, H., & Zerback, T. (Hg.): *Sozialforschung im Internet. Methodologie und Praxis der Online-Befragung*. VS Verlag. Wiesbaden. 33-48.

Acknowledgement

The authors would like to thank the University of Applied Sciences of Western Switzerland (HES-SO) for financing this research. Thanks also to Leonard Adkins from Ecole Suisse de Tourisme for the final English editing.

An Investigation of Leapfrogging and Web 2.0 Implementation

Miriam Scaglione[a]
Ahmad Fareed Ismail[b]
Jean-Philippe Trabichet[c],
Jamie Murphy[d],

[a]École Suisse de Tourisme
University of Applied Sciences Western Switzerland, Sierre
miriam.scaglione@hevs.ch

[b]University of Western Australia/Universiti Putra Malaysia
aismail@biz.uwa.edu.au

[c]Geneva School of Business Administration
University of Applied Sciences Western Switzerland
jean-philippe.trabichet@hesge.ch'

[d]University of Western Australia
jmurphy@biz.uwa.edu.au

Abstract

This paper investigates the leapfrog phenomenon, particularly late adopters of the Internet bypassing early Internet adopters in the implementation of Web 2.0 in tourism. Even though the Diffusion of Innovation theory covers many aspects of innovation adoption and implementation, implementation stage research remains sparse and perhaps no research has investigated the leapfrog phenomenon across different adopter categories. Thus, this study used a software robot to generate reports on Web 2.0 and User Active Features (UAF) by Swiss tourism websites. Moreover, this study used the Wayback Machine to classify website adopter categories and then investigate the leapfrogging phenomenon across adopter categories. The results suggest a link between adopter categories and the odds of implementation of at least one UAF or Web 2.0 feature. However, the findings only showed a slight leapfrogging phenomenon between Laggards and the Late Majority in the UAF model. This research helps fill the gap on implementation stage research by the analysis of Web 2.0 features implemented in tourism.

Keywords: Leapfrogging, Internet, Implementation stage, Diffusion of Innovations.

1   Introduction

Research of website evolution often uses Rogers' (2003) Diffusion of Innovations (DOI) theory. His theory offers multiple perspectives on the organizational adoption of innovations and innovation effectivenes (McGrath & Zell, 2001). Additionally, defining the diffusion stage – adoption or implementation – is vital, as different stages portray different diffusion findings (Carter, Jambulingam, Gupta, & Melone, 2001). Most Internet diffusion studies focus on the adoption stage, and factors related to website adoption such as perceived benefits, organizational compatibility, technical compatibility, organizational features and social pressure (Dholakia & Kshetri, 2004). These abundant adoption findings enhance diffusion research, but there is a need for implementation stage research

(Fichman, 2004). Implementation stage studies often cover the post-adoption effectiveness of an innovation throughout the organization (Fichman, 2000; Hashim & Murphy, 2007). Website implementation usually progresses from basic to comprehensive sophistication (Beatty, Hsim, & Jones, 2001; Hashim & Murphy, 2007) such as adding website features over time that progress from providing basic information towards interactivity and personalization (Hashim, Olaru, Scaglione, & Murphy, 2006). A recent study suggests Malaysian hotels late to adopt websites leapfrogged the early adopters in their addition of website features (Hashim, Kassim, & Murphy, 2008).

Research explores leapfrogging – bypassing early adopters in the use of a technology – in various fields (Amir, 2004; Gallagher, 2006). For example, a study of East Asian electronic technology producers suggested the latecomer firms tended to leapfrog in developing strategies (Hobday, 1995). The latecomers leapfrogged to a minor product innovations strategy based on incremental improvements to the manufacturing process rather than starting with research and development. The leapfrog phenomenon seems crucial for organizations to gain competitive advantage (Gallagher, 2006). Yet to the authors' knowledge, Internet leapfrogging research is limited. Despite growing numbers of website feature studies (Beatty, et al., 2001; Hashim & Murphy, 2007; Law & Hsu, 2006; Murphy, Olaru, & Schegg, 2006), none examine Rogers' (2003) five adopter categories – innovators, early adopters, early majority, late majority, and laggards – in general or in relation to implementation.

For academia, this study helps fill gaps in the adopter categorizations (Rogers, 2003) and Internet implementation literature (Fichman, 2004). For industry, investigating the leapfrog phenomenon in Internet implementation should shed insights on successful Internet use. To help address these research gaps, this paper focuses on Web 2.0 features (O'Reilly, 2005) in the tourism sector. The term Web 2.0, coined by Tim O'Reilly in 2004, "... is the business revolution in the computer industry caused by the move to the internet as a platform, and an attempt to understand the rules for success on that new platform. Chief among those rules is this: build applications that harness network effects to get better the more people use them" (O'Reilly, 2005). These Web 2.0 technologies suggest going beyond adoption and implementation of the World Wide Web (Graham, 2005; IBM developerWorks Interviews, 2006).

2 Literature Review and Theoretical Framework

2.1 Diffusion of Innovations Theory (DOI)

Innovations are new ideas, techniques, practices, objects, or strategies (Tornatzky & Fleischer, 1990). Innovations are subjective and depend on individual, group or organizational perceptions that an innovation is a new means of solving problems or exploiting opportunities (Brancheau & Wetherbe, 1990; Rogers, 2003). The Diffusion of Innovations (DOI) is a fundamental theory to explain innovation use (Fichman, 2000; Rogers, 2003). Two DOI streams are individual and organizational (Agarwal & Prasad, 1997; Hashim & Murphy, 2005; Rogers, 2003; Wolfe, 1994). Organizational diffusion examines innovation adoption and use throughout the organization (Choudrie & Dwivedi, 2005; Hashim & Murphy, 2007). Compared to individual diffusion, the organization-innovation decision is more complicated due to complex organizational structures (Rogers, 2003). It is crucial to define organizational diffusion stages as adoption or implementation; different stages portray different findings (Carter, et al., 2001). For instance, adoption stage research often emphasizes factors related to the adoption of an innovation (Brancheau & Wetherbe, 1990; Hwang, Ku, Yen, & Cheng, 2004). In the implementation stage, innovation continuity and effects on organization performance is a major concern (Cooper & Zmud, 1990). The implementation stage relates to innovation use and organizational performance (Brynjolfsson & Hitt, 2000; Carter, et al., 2001; Zhu & Kraemer, 2005). For example, a construction organization's successful implementation of a virtual reality system for internal design review related to consistent and good user-developer communications (Whyte, Bouchlaghem, & Thorpe, 2002). Furthermore, a study on enterprise resource planning implementation suggested that consensus in organizational objectives and competitive pressure relate to organizational performance (Bradford & Florin, 2003). Implementation also covers organizational implementation rates of an innovation (Cooper & Zmud, 1990). For example, the implementation rate of material resource planning by US manufacturers relates to compatibility with current systems (Cooper & Zmud, 1990). Due to few studies, researchers call for findings related to the implementation stage (Fichman, 2000). For example, post-adoption investigation should examine the effectiveness of innovation adoption throughout the organization (Fichman, 2000; Hashim & Murphy, 2007). In the hospitality industry, Internet studies examine the successful implementation of email and websites (Frey, Schegg, & Murphy, 2003; Hashim & Murphy, 2005). Yet there seems no attempt to relate the implementation stage of an innovation with adopter categorizations.

2.2 Adopter Categorization

Rogers (2003) five-adopter categories are innovators (2.5% of adopters), early adopters (13.5%), early majority (34%), late majority (34%), and laggards (16%). This study relies upon a coupled Bass (1969) and Rogers diffusion model (Mahajan, Muller, & Bass, 1990, pp. 4-7; Mahajan, Muller, & Srivastava, 1990), hereafter the BR model. This model has the dual advantages of allocating adopter categories based on actual data and reflecting two coefficients – innovation and imitation – that drive adoption, respectively internal communication such as word of mouth and external communication such as mass-media. Equation 1 shows the Bass function (1969) that captures new product growth. N(t) is the cumulative number of adopters at time t; m is the total market potential for new products. Parameters p and q are the coefficients of innovation and imitation, respectively.

$$\frac{dN(t)}{dt} = p(m - N(t)) + q\frac{N(t)}{m}(m - N(t)) \quad (1)$$

Three points – the peak T and inflection points T1 and T2 – determine the BR categories. Up to T1, the adoption rate increases rapidly and delineates the Early Adopter and Early Majority categories. From T1 to the peak T the growth rate slows, indicating the time of maximum adopters and separating the Early Majority and Late Majority. Finally, from T the adoption rate decreases until T2, which separates the Late Majority and Laggards (Mahajan, Muller, & Bass, 1990; Mahajan, Muller, & Srivastava, 1990). Different adopter categories often reveal different innovation implementation patterns (Stafford, 2003). For example, a 2000-2006 longitudinal US study found varied attitudes, opinions and behaviors across adopter categories of individual Internet users (Lunn & Suman, 2008). Similarly, different American Online adopter categories showed different behaviors (Stafford, 2003). For example, innovators preferred technological content in their early Internet use and laggards exhibited significantly lower content gratifications for online services than innovators. Organizational innovation studies also suggest different adopter category finding. For instance, research of medium-large US firms' adoption of corporate websites showed that early adopters were more concerned on the Web's compatibility with existing technology and organizational norms than were the late adopters (Beatty, et al., 2001). Another example is a disruptive innovations study suggesting the importance to seek niche markets based on adopter categories with different needs and characteristics (Slater & Mohr, 2006). Therefore, it is important to understand different adopter categories and their implementation of evolving Internet technologies. The categorization of organizations based on the five-adopter categories could help predict outcomes in Internet implementation and help fill gaps in the literature on the implementation stage and leapfrog phenomenon.

2.3 Internet Implementation and Leapfrogging

Internet use studies suggest similar implementation stages (Doolin, Burgess, & Cooper, 2002; Hanson & Kalyanam, 2007; Teo & Pian, 2003). These implementation stages tend to portray website and email use on a development continuum (Kowtha & Choon, 2001) and usually progress from providing information to personalized services (Hashim & Murphy, 2007; Murphy, et al., 2006). However, recent research of Malaysian hotels suggests that the website features of late adopters leapfrogged the features of early adopters (Hashim, et al., 2008). For instance, the late adopters used personalized and loyalty building features in their websites in addition to providing information. The findings suggest that Malaysia's hotel industry contradicts the normal sequence of Internet implementation. In other words, Malaysian hoteliers late to adopt the Internet leapfrogged early adopters in their Internet implementation. Yet a Swiss hospitality study of BR adopter categories and customer benefits showed that except for early adopters, most hotels failed to prioritize technologies that add customer value (Perruchoud-Massy, Scaglione, Schegg, & Murphy, 2005). The proportion of hotels providing Internet access to customers and using advanced Customer Relationship Management tools was significantly higher for early compared to later adopter hotels. Laggards and non-adopters implemented websites simply as a new information channel. Leapfrogging and ICT implementation studies cover issues such as supporting infrastructures, requirements and solutions, challenges, safety, and successful implementation (Gray & Sanzogni, 2004). Yet none discusses leapfrogging and Internet implementation, nor relates leapfrogging with Rogers' (2003) five innovation-adopter categories. Web 2.0 enables users more so than businesses and facilitates social interaction that emphasizes user generated content (O'Reilly, 2005). Web 2.0 implementation includes features of three different categories. The first facilitates asynchronous web communications such as AJAX, and consolidation via a Javascript such as XMTML, Atom and CSS. These techniques enable retrieving and displaying data into web pages via asynchronous requests without reloading the whole web page (Potthast & Rowe, 2007). The result is minimal technical constraints to get content so that users can focus on the content itself. The second category of features is a group of applications/services to enrich the users' interface such as RSS, del.icio.us and Folksonomie. Finally, the third category of features allows users to up/download content such as podcasts, blogs and videoblogs − Users Generated Content (UGC). The latter two categories interrelate in that they empower social interaction. On one hand, marketers consider UGC as word-of-mouth. On the other hand, features related to the repeated use such as Really Simple Syndication (RSS) let readers subscribe to a UGC source such as blogs or podcasts (Hanson & Kalyanam, 2007, p. 80). Finally, the folksonomie offers a collaborative, spontaneous and decentralized classification and the del.icio.us website assists online bookmarking. From hereafter, this paper refers to features belonging to these two categories as User Active Features (UAF). This paper analyses leapfrogging phenomena by modeling the probability of implementing at least one Web 2.0 feature across adopter categories. The analysis of Web 2.0 features in this research falls into two groups. The first group is the implementation of Web 2.0 features belonging to the three categories and the second group focuses on UAF.

3   Data and research Methods

3.1 Data

Table 1 describes the sample and sources. Besides Swiss restaurants, the other categories used a website database (Schegg, Liebrich, Scaglione, & Syed Ahmad, 2008). The samples, except restaurants, originated from trade association member lists and represented over 90% of the population. Restaurant data from the 2008 of Swisscom digital telephone directory using the filter "Café, Restaurant", represents around 10% of all Swiss restaurants.

3.2 Analysis of Web 2.0 features

The study used a software robot (softbot) with exploratory and parsing capacities that runs automated tasks over the Internet (Steiner, 1999). Softbots are common in information technology (Bradshaw, 1997). A proprietary softbot from a prior study (Evéquoz, Favre, Herzog, Luthi, & Probs, 2007) was optimized for this research and ran during November-December 2008. The softbot processed all static and semi-dynamic HTML pages, starting at the top URL and then following all links in that website, but ignoring links in graphics or behind dynamic scripting techniques. The softbot then generated a report containing the counts for each criterion. Table 2 lists the features, their definitions and the code searched by the softbot.

Table 1. Study websites sample

Sector	Abbreviation	n (URL)	n (website age)	Source
Swiss cable car companies.	cable CH	190	190	Seilbahnen Schweiz (www.seilbahnen.org)
Swiss destination management organizations	DMO CH	128	128	myswitzerland.ch
Swiss hotels	hotel CH	1813	1765	(Scaglione, Steiner, Schegg, & Murphy, 2005)
Swiss travel agencies	TA CH	244	251	Schweizerischer Reisebüro-verband (www.srv.ch)
Int. hotel chains	hotel chain	262	251	www.hotelsmag.com (July 2006)
European tour operators.	TO Europe	107	107	(www.etoa.org), www.european-travel-market.com
Swiss restaurants	Rest CH	1858	1573	Swisscom Directories
Total		4602	4265	

Table 2. Web 2.0 technologies and softbot search criteria

Name	Description	Search code
AJAX	AJAX (Asynchronous Javascript and XML) integrates technologies to make user information retrieval experiences smoother and faster, such as applications in Google Maps and Flickr (Laudon & Traver, 2007, p. 229)	XMLHttpRequest(); ActiveXObject("Msxml2.XMLHTTP; ActiveXObject("Microsoft.XMLHTTP");
XHTML	The Extensible HyperText Markup Language, or XHTML, sits between the basic HTML used for building web pages and the advanced XML for adding context/structure to web pages (Turban, King, Viehland, & Lee, 2006, p. 380)	<html xmlns="http://www.w3.org/1999/xhtml"
Javascript	"A scripting language developed by Netscape to enable web authors to design interactive sites. Although it shares many of the features and structures of the full Java language, it was developed independently. JavaScript can interact with HTML source code, enabling web authors to spice up their sites with dynamic content." http://publications.europa.eu/vademecum/vademecum/9313fdfe-c49e-119e-45c6a6441e63e066 en.html]	<script;language='javascript'; type="text/javascript"
CSS	Cascading Style Sheets (CSS) is a simple mechanism for adding style (e.g. fonts, colors, spacing) to Web documents. (http://www.w3.org/Style/CSS/)	type="text/css" .css
RSS	Really Simple Syndication (RSS) provides subscribed users with notification, (RSS feeds), when content changes for chosen websites (Hanson & Kalyanam, 2007, p. 80) .	<rss /rss+xml /rss+xml;feeds

ATOM	The Atom Syndication Format is an XML language for web feeds, while the Atom Publishing Protocol is a simple HTTP-based protocol for creating and updating Web resources. (http://tools.ietf.org/html/rfc4287)	xmlns:atom=http://www.w3.org/2005/Atom .atom
del.icio.us	The del.icio.us website assists online bookmarking with users able to gather, share and find websites on topics of interest (http://del.icio.us/about/[September 10, 2007])	del.icio.us/html/;http://del.icio.us/post
Folksonomie	A neologism from "taxonomy" for a collaborative, spontaneous and decentralized classification. The prefix "folk" signifies contributors can ignore predefined classification and have the freedom for classifying the resources. It is equivalent to "keyword" or "tag" and "etiquette" in French (O'Reilly, 2005).	/tag; tagcloud
podcasting	A digital audio or video program that is available for download. They may be free and may be downloaded manually or by automatic subscription. They are playable through a computer or digital player including Ipod and mp3 players (Hanson & Kalyanam, 2007, p. 600).	Podcast /podcast ;xmlns :itunes=" viewPodcast?
blog	Website with frequent postings, often focused on a certain topic, and typically organized chronologically. Blogs may be individual or collaborative (Hanson & Kalyanam, 2007, p. 594)	Blog ;/blog ;blog.
videoblog	A blog that consists of videos.	/vblog ;vblog ;videoblog ;/videoblog ;movie ; /video

3.3 Analysis of Bass Rogers' diffusion of innovation per sector

To classify the organizations into adopter categories, the study relied upon the Internet archive (www.archive.org), a non-profit organization that began archiving websites in 1996 (FAQs, 2007). Dates available through the Wayback Machine (WM) in the Internet archive suggest when a website first went on World Wide Web (Murphy, Hashim, & O'Connor, 2007). The WM, however, has problems archiving dynamic or password-protected sites (Veronin, 2002) and index sites that decline indexing through robot exclusion commands (FAQs, 2007). In order to calculate the BR website adoption categories (Mahajan, Muller, & Srivastava, 1990) the algorithm stems from Lilien and Rangaswamy (2002) as explained in Scaglione, Steiner, Schegg, & Murphy (2004). Table 3 shows the BR parameters for each sector. The first sector to peak in website adoption rate was Swiss destination organizations in February 1998, followed 18 months later by Swiss cable car companies. The international hotel chains' website adoption rate peaked in September 2000, followed one month later by European tour operators. Swiss hotels peaked in their adoption rate 17 months later in April 2002, over four years after the Swiss destination organizations and the Swiss travel agencies reached peak adoption. The Swiss restaurants sector deserves a separate discussion. The estimated value for m through the BR model, which represents the total potential market, is 1,645. As a result, the sample under study contains 96% of the potential market. Therefore, for restaurant, even though its process is the second to peak

(January 1999), only preceded by Swiss destination organizations (February 1998), the total ultimate adopters only reaches 10% of all Swiss restaurants.

Table 3. Bass model coefficients and adoption dates across seven tourism sectors.

	T1 inflection point	peak maximum	T2 inflection point	p innovation	q imitation	q/p
DMO CH	jan. 1997	febr. 1998	nov. 2001	0.0052	0.0416	8.0
cable CH	aug. 1998	aug. 1999	oct. 2002	0.0000	0.0875	nill (∞)
hotel chain	june 1998	sept 2000	nov. 2002	0.0043	0.0455	10.7
TO Europe	dec. 1996	oct. 2000	dec. 2003	0.0001	0.0693	746.1
hotel CH	jan. 1997	feb. 2001	nov. 2002	0.0038	0.1381	36.8
TA CH	sep. 2000	avr. 2002	dec. 2003	0.0063	0.0676	10.7
rest CH	dec 1997	jan. 1999	sept.2001	0.0035	0.0392	11.19

4   Research Results

This research uses logistics models to examine the link between the probability having at least one feature, in either all Web 2.0 features or UAF features, across the BR categories. These models have as an endogenous dichotomus variable whether the website adopted at least one Web 2.0 feature in the first model and a UAF feature in the second model. Both models have two categorical explanatory variables: BR categories and the tourism sector. Rather than the probabilty, the logistic model yields the log-odds or the log of the ratio between the probabiltiy of having of at least one features over the probability of not having for each obervation. The BR reference category is Laggards in order to investigate if laggards leapfrog earlier BR categories. The tourism reference sector is Swiss hotels as they have the lowest level of Web 2.0 implemenation (Scaglione, Johnson, & Trabichet, 2009). The calculations used the routine *Proc logistic* of SAS Institut Version 9.2 (Allison, 2003).

Table 4. Results of logistic models (against Laggards and Swiss hotels) and tests of goodness of fit. Lower and upper limit's Confidence interval of Odds Ratio Estimates, Wald Chi-Square at 95% level.

	UAF				Web 2.0			
	Lower limit	Upper limit	Exp Coeff	Logistic coeffs p-values	Lower limit	Upper limit	Exp Coeff	Logistic coeffs p-values
Intercept			0.224	<.0001			1.049	0.3321
Innovators +EA	1.221	1.888	1.334	<.0001	0.974	1.489	1.042	0.5469
EM	0.976	1.526	1.073	0.3209	1.088	1.731	1.188	0.0235
LM	0.758	1.08	0.795	<.0001	0.903	1.288	0.933	0.2248
DMO	3.447	7.433	5.062	<.0001	2.191	5.434	3.451	<.0001

CH								
Rest CH	2.464	3.45	2.916	<.0001	4.005	5.582	4.728	<.0001
TA CH	2.377	4.302	3.198	<.0001	3.518	7.611	5.175	<.0001
TO Europe	3.487	7.915	5.253	<.0001	2.947	8.735	5.074	<.0001
cable CH	2.045	3.879	2.816	<.0001	1.913	3.78	2.689	<.0001
hotel chain	5.045	8.939	6.715	<.0001	4.392	9.594	6.492	<.0001

Goodness of fit test	stats	p-values		stats	p-values
Likehood ratio ch2 df=9 statistics	355.98	<.0001		510.9	<.0001
Hosmer and Lemeshow chi2 df=7 statistics	0.973	0.9953		0.701	0.7011
BR categories Type 3 effects Wald chi2 df=3 statistics	26.9	<.0001		4.662	0.0442
Sectors Type 3 effects Wald chi2 df=6 statisitics	298.8	<.0001		448.9	<.0001

Table 4 shows the results for each sector and the odds ratio. To ensure the validity of the method, the authors merged the Innovator and Early Adopter categories in order to include in this merged category a number of observations greater than five. First, the model's goodness of fit based on the likelihood ratio statistics, which is significant, and therefore it rejects the hypothesis of coefficients to be simultaneously nulls. Second, the Hosmer and Lemeshow test was not significant in both models, reflected that there are not enough evidence of lack of fit in any of both models. Finally, the type 3 analysis of effects showed enough evidences that BR category and sector influence the odds of implementation in both Web 2.0 and UAF features. Table 4 shows the exponential of the coefficient, which if greater than one and its corresponding p-value significant, means the corresponding odds of BR category (sector) of having one feature is greater than the contrast BR category, namely, Laggards (Swiss hotels). If there is leapfrogging effects for Laggards, the exponential of the coefficient should be smaller than one and its corresponding p-value significant. The only case with this situation is Late Majority in the UAF model. Nevertheless, the corresponding upper 95% confidence interval for the odds ratio is around one (1.08). This shows that either Laggards leapfrogged the Late Majority category or at similar levels of implementation. This latter case is an extreme one as it corresponds to the upper limit of the confidence interval. For sectors and in both models, odds of having at least one feature are greater for all of them compared to Swiss hotels which resembles findings on Swiss (Scaglione, et al., 2009). In conclusion, even though there is evidence of a link between BR categories and the odds of implementation of at least one Web 2.0 or UAF feature, the analysis shows evidence of a slight leapfrog effect for Laggards against Late Majority in the UAF model.

5 Implications and Conclusion

Academically, this study helps fill a gap in the innovation diffusion literature, especially in the implementation of Internet technology (Fichman, 2004). The findings of this study support the leapfrog effect observed in the adoption of Internet technology in Malaysia's hotel sector (Hashim, et al., 2008) . Moreover, the study added to the body of knowledge especially in understanding the different adopter categories perspectives in the Internet implementation. The used of Web 2.0 features and UAF as the main characteristics in determine the implementation of Internet would suggest a new paradigm of investigating the leapfrog phenomenon in the current Web 2.0 environment. At large, this result exemplifies and justifies the need to investigate the leapfrogging in Internet implementation. Additionally, limited literature discusses the leapfrogging in the Internet diffusion compared to the other technologies. For industry, the findings on the leapfrogging in Internet implementation should shed insights on current Internet use in tourism sector. Practitioners should consider having enough information and knowledge about Web 2.0 specifically the UAF. Subsequently, they should starts to identify the impact of leapfrogging their competitors in having certain features of Web 2.0 or UAF. This point leads to future research possibility in leapfrog studies, such as successful Internet implementation.

References

Agarwal, R., & Prasad, J. (1997). The Role of Innovation Characteristics and Perceived Voluntariness in the Acceptance of Information Technologies. *Decision Sciences, 28*(3), 557-582.

Allison, P. D. (2003). *Logistic Regression Using the SAS (r) System . Theory and Application* (4th Edition ed.). Cary, NC: SAS Institut

Amir, S. (2004). The Regime and the Airplane: High Technology and Nationalism in Indonesia. *Bulletin of Science Technology Society, 24*(2), 107-114.

Bass, F. M. (1969). A New Product Growth Model for Consumer Durables. *Management Science, 15*(5), 215-227.

Beatty, R. C., Hsim, J. P., & Jones, M. C. (2001). Factors Influencing Corporate Web Site Adoption: A Time-Based Assessment. *Information and Management, 38*(6), 337-354.

Bradford, M., & Florin, J. (2003). Examining the role of innovation diffusion factors on the implementation success of enterprise resource planning systems. *International Journal of Accounting Information Systems, 4*(3), 205-225.

Bradshaw, J. (1997). *Software Agents.* Cambridge MA: AAAI / MIT Press.

Brancheau, J. C., & Wetherbe, J. C. (1990). The Adoption of Spreadsheet Software: Testing Innovation Diffusion Theory in the Context of End-User Computing. *Information Systems Research, 1*(2), 115-143.

Brynjolfsson, E., & Hitt, L. M. (2000). Beyond Computation: Information Technology, Organizational Transformation and Business Performance. *The Journal of Economic Perspectives, 14*(4), 23-48.

Carter, F. J., Jambulingam, T., Gupta, V. K., & Melone, N. (2001). Technological innovations: a framework for communicating diffusion effects. *Information & Management, 38*(5), 277-287.

Choudrie, J., & Dwivedi, Y. K. (2005). Investigating the Research Approaches for Examining Technology Adoption Issues. *Journal of Research Practice, 1*(1), 1-12.

Cooper, R. B., & Zmud, R. W. (1990). Information Technology Implementation Research: A Technological Diffusion Approach. *Management Science, 36*(2), 123-139.

Dholakia, R. R., & Kshetri, N. (2004). Factors Impacting the Adoption of the Internet among SMEs. *Small Business Economics, 23*(4), 311-322.

Doolin, B., Burgess, L., & Cooper, J. (2002). Evaluating the use of web for tourism marketing: A case study from New Zealand. *Tourism Management, 23*(5), 557-561.

Evéquoz, R., Favre, F., Herzog, A., Luthi, J., & Probs, S. (2007). HWebBot: application de mining pour Web 2.0. realised by students of HES-SO Valais under the direction of Prof. T. Steiner. Sierre: HES-SO Valais.

FAQs. (2007). The Wayback Machine: Frequently Asked Questions. Retrieved 5 April, 2007, from www.archive.org/about/faqs.php

Fichman, R. G. (2000). The Diffusion and Assimilation of Information Technology Innovations. Framing the Domains of IT Management. In R. W. Zmud (Ed.), *Projecting the Future through the Past* (pp. 105-128). Cincinnati, Ohio: Pinnaflex Publishing.

Fichman, R. G. (2004). Real Options and IT Platform Adoption: Implications for Theory and Practice. *Information Systems Research, 15*(2), 132-154.

Frey, S., Schegg, R., & Murphy, J. (2003). E-mail Customer Service in the Swiss Hotel Industry. *Tourism and Hospitality Research, 4*(3), 197-212.

Gallagher, K. S. (2006). Limits to leapfrogging in energy technologies? Evidence from the Chinese automobile industry. *Energy Policy, 34*(4), 383-394.

Graham, P. (2005). Web 2.0. Retrieved from http://www.paulgraham.com/web20.html

Gray, H., & Sanzogni, L. (2004). Technology Leapfrogging in Thailand: Issues for the Support of eCommerce Infrastructure. *The Electronic Journal on Information Systems in Developing Countries, 16*(3), 1-26.

Hanson, W., & Kalyanam, K. (2007). *Internet Marketing and e-Commerce* (1st ed.). Mason City, OH: Thomson South-Western.

Hashim, N. H., Kassim, A., & Murphy, J. (2008). *Investigating the relationship between business strategic types and website use.* Paper presented at the 6th Asia Pacific CHRIE (APacCHRIE) 2008 Conference & THE-ICE Panel of Experts Forum 2008, Perth, Australia.

Hashim, N. H., & Murphy, J. (2005). *The Diffusion of Websites and Email among Malaysian Hotels.* Paper presented at the International Conference on Tourism and Hospitality, Penang, Malaysia.

Hashim, N. H., & Murphy, J. (2007). Branding on the Web: Evolving Domain Name Usage among Malaysian Hotels. *Tourism Management, 28*(2), 621-624.

Hashim, N. H., Olaru, D., Scaglione, M., & Murphy, J. (2006). A Theoretical Framework of Factors Relating to Internet Adoption by Malaysian Hotels. In M. Hitz, M. Sigala & J. Murphy (Eds.), *Information and Communication Technologies in Tourism 2006, proceedings of ENTER 2006* (pp. 196-208). Vienna, Austria: Springer Verlag.

Hobday, M. (1995). East Asian latecomer firms: Learning the technology of electronics. *World Development, 23*(7), 1171-1193.

Hwang, H.-G., Ku, C.-Y., Yen, D. C., & Cheng, C.-C. (2004). Critical factors influencing the adoption of data warehouse technology: a study of the banking industry in Taiwan. *Decision Support Systems, 37*(1), 1-21.

IBM developerWorks Interviews. (2006). BM developerWorks Interviews: Tim Berners-Lee. Retrieved from http://www.ibm.com/developerworks/podcast/dwi/cm-int082206txt.html

Kowtha, N. R., & Choon, T. H. I. (2001). Determinants of website development: a study of electronic commerce in Singapore. *Information & Management, 39*(3), 227-242.

Laudon, K. C., & Traver, C. G. (2007). *E-commerce: Business, Technology, Society.* Boston:MA: Pearson Addison-Wesley.

Law, R., & Hsu, C. H. C. (2006). Importance of Hotel Website Dimensions and Attributes: Perceptions of Online Browsers and Online Purchasers. *Journal of Hospitality &Tourism Research, 30*(1), 295-312.

Lilien, G. L., & Rangaswamy, A. (2002). *Marketing Engineering.* New Jersey: Pearson Education.

Lunn, R. J., & Suman, M. W. (2008). A Longitudinal Examination of Internet Diffusion and Adopter Categories. *Observatorio (OBS) Journal, 6*(1), 97-110.

Mahajan, V., Muller, E., & Bass, F. M. (1990). New Product Diffusion Models in Marketing: A Review and Directions for Research. *Journal of Marketing Education, 54*(1), 1-26.

Mahajan, V., Muller, E., & Srivastava, R. (1990). Determination of Adopter Categories by Using Innovation Diffusion Models. *Journal of Marketing Research, XXVII*(February), 37-50.

McGrath, C., & Zell, D. (2001). The Future of Innovation Diffusion Research and its Implications for Management: A Conversation with Everett Rogers. *Journal of Management Inquiry, 10*(4), 386-391.

Murphy, J., Hashim, N. H., & O'Connor, P. (2007). Take Me Back: Validating the Wayback Machine as a Measure of Website Evolution. *Journal of Computer-Mediated Communication, 13*(1), article 4.

Murphy, J., Olaru, D., & Schegg, R. (2006). Investigating the Evolution of Hotel Internet Adoption. *Information Technology and Tourism, 8*(3/4), 161-178.

O'Reilly, T. (2005). What is the Web 2.0? Design Patterns and Business Models for the Next Generation of Software. *O'Reilly Radar*. Retrieved from http://www.oreilly.de/artikel/web20.html

Perruchoud-Massy, M.-F., Scaglione, M., Schegg, R., & Murphy, J. (2005). Category of adopters and customer values of on-line services in Swiss hotels. In P. Keller & T. Bieger (Eds.), *Innovation in tourism : Add customer value, Proceeding 54th AIEST Conference, Petra Jordan* (Vol. 47, pp. 171-188). St Gallen: AIEST Publications.

Potthast, S., & Rowe, M. (2007). *An Analysis of Approaches for Asynchronous Communication in Web Applications*. Paper presented at the Midwest Instruction and Computing Symposium 2007 40th Anniversary: A Celebration of Midwest Computing Heritage. Retrieved from www.micsymposium.org/mics_2007/papers/Potthast.pdf

Rogers, E. M. (2003). *Diffusion of Innovations* (Fifth ed.). New York, New York: Simon & Schuster.

Scaglione, M., Johnson, C., & Trabichet, J.-P. (2009). How Tourism sector is managing the change to Web 2.0. In P. Keller & T. Bieger (Eds.), *Management of Change in Tourism* (pp. Forthcoming). Berlin: Erich Schmidt Verlag.

Scaglione, M., Schegg, R., Steiner, T., & Murphy, J. (2004). Internet Adoption by Swiss Hotels: The Dynamics of Domain Name Registration. In A. J. Frew (Ed.), *Information and Communication Technologies in Tourism 2004* (pp. 481-490). New York: Springer-Verlag.

Scaglione, M., Steiner, T., Schegg, R., & Murphy, J. (2005). Investigating Domaine Name Diffusion across Swiss Acommodation Entreprise. In A. J. Frew (Ed.), *Information and Communication Technologies in Tourism Enter 2005*. Wien, New York: Springer-Verlag.

Schegg, R., Liebrich, A., Scaglione, M., & Syed Ahmad, F. S. (2008). An Exploratory Field Study of Web 2.0 in Tourism In P. O'Connor, W. Höpken & U. Gretzel (Eds.), *Information and Communication Technologies in Tourism 2008. Proceedings of the International Conference in Innsbruck, Austria, 2008* (pp. 152-163). Vienna: Springer

Slater, S. F., & Mohr, J. J. (2006). Successful Development and Commercialization of Technological Innovation: Insights Based on Strategy Type. *The Journal of Product Innovation Management, 23*(1), 26-33.

Stafford, T. F. (2003). Differentiating between adopter categories in the uses and gratifications for Internet services. *IEEE Transactions on Engineering Management, 50*(4), 427-435.

Steiner, T. (1999). Distributed Software Agents for WWW-based Destination Information System, *PhD Thesis*. Lausanne: Universty of Lausanne.

Teo, T., & Pian, Y. (2003). A Contingency Perspective of Internet Adoption and Competitive Advantage. *European Journal of Information Systems, 12*(2), 78-92.

Tornatzky, L. G., & Fleischer, M. (1990). *The process of technological innovation.* New York: Lexington Book.

Turban, E., King, D., Viehland, D., & Lee, J. (2006). *Electronic Commerce 2006: A Managerial Perspective.* Upper Saddle River, NJ Pearson Prentice Hall.

Veronin, M. A. (2002). Where Are They Now? A Case Study of Health-related Web Site Attrition. *Journal of Medical Internet Research, 4*(2), www.jmir.org/2002/2002/e2010/.

Whyte, J., Bouchlaghem, D., & Thorpe, T. (2002). IT implementation in the construction organization. *Engineering Construction & Architectural Management (Blackwell Publishing Limited), 9*(5/6), 371-377.

Wolfe, R. A. (1994). Organizational Innovation: Review, Critique and Suggested Research Directions. *Journal of Management Studies, 31*(3), 405-431.

Zhu, K., & Kraemer, K. L. (2005). Post Adoption Variations in Usage and Value of E-Business by Organizations: Cross-Country Evidence from the Retail Industry. *Information Systems Research, 16*(1), 61-84.

Backpacker Use of User-Generated Content: A Consumer Empowerment Study

Luiz Mendes-Filho[ab],
Felix B Tan[a], and
Simon Milne[b]

[a]Business Information Systems, [b]New Zealand Tourism Research Institute
Auckland University of Technology, New Zealand
{luiz.mendesfilho; felix.tan; simon.milne}@aut.ac.nz

Abstract

This study examines the importance of the proposed components of Consumer Empowerment through User-Generated Content (UGC) in the travel industry. Researchers have argued that a single common conception of Empowerment is not appropriate across all disciplines and across all contexts. By employing the Uses & Gratifications and Dual-Process Theories, we propose that Consumer Empowerment in the context of UGC can be formed through Content Empowerment, Social Empowerment and Process Empowerment. A focus group discussion session with international tourist backpackers was conducted to gather qualitative data and to verify the importance of the proposed components of Consumer Empowerment. Results indicate that international backpackers identified with all three proposed components of Consumer Empowerment in the context of UGC: Content, Social, and Process.

Keywords: Consumer Empowerment, User-Generated Content, Uses & Gratifications Theory, Dual-Process Theory

1 Introduction

User-generated content (UGC) constitutes the data, information, or media produced by the general public (rather by professionals) on the Internet (Arriga & Levina, 2008). UGC is changing the dynamics of the travel industry profoundly using its global word-of-mouth forces (Laboy & Torchio, 2007). Travellers are getting in touch directly with other travellers who have similar destination interests through social networking in the online travel world (Laboy & Torchio, 2007). Gretzel & Yoo (2008) assert that consumer-generated content such as online travel reviews written by tourists on virtual communities are more available and used frequently to transmit travel-related decisions.

A web-based survey carried out by Gretzel and Yoo (2008) showed that 97.7% of Internet users who travel said they read other travellers' reviews during the process of planning a trip. Examples of websites that help tourists to interact and offer peer to peer advice on the Internet are TripAdvisor.com, IgoUgo.com, and Virtualtourist.com (Xiang & Gretzel, 2009). Approximately 20 million travellers planned trips through TripAdvisor by September 2007 (Schegg, Liebrich, Scaglione, & Ahmad, 2008).

The content generated by the Internet users is empowering online travellers in the planning and buying processes of their trips (Schegg et al., 2008; Sigala, 2007). Constantinides (2007) states that UGC applications have contributed to an increasing consumer empowerment. Therefore, consumers that use these applications do not depend on website owners to publish the information they look for, but they just rely on information provided by their own peers (O'Connor, 2008).

Although UGC has increasingly been seen as one of the vital information sources to web users and has brought an increased impact on electronic commerce (Forman, Ghose, & Wiesenfeld, 2008), little theoretical work has been done on understanding this new technology phenomenon in the scientific community (O'Connor, 2008). Of interest is how consumers are empowered by UGC.

Empowerment tends to mean different things to different people (Quinn & Spreitzer, 1997). Sehgal and Stewart (2006) argue that a single common conception of empowerment is not appropriate across all disciplines and across all contexts. Following Rappaport (1987), Consumer Empowerment is defined in the context of this study as "a process by which tourists gain control over their own destiny using the user-generated content to help booking an accommodation".

Despite the increasing influence of UGC within the travel and tourism sectors (Daugherty, Eastin, & Bright, 2008), there has been no prior research that explores how UGC empowers online consumers in the travel industry. By employing the Uses & Gratifications and Dual-Process Theories, we propose that Consumer Empowerment in the context of UGC can be formed through Content Empowerment, Social Empowerment and Process Empowerment. The Uses & Gratification Theory (Stafford, Stafford, & Schkade, 2004) is used to unify the components of Consumer Empowerment under one theory. Also, the theoretical lens of Dual-Process Theory (Deutsch & Gerard, 1955) is used to help determine the Content and Social Empowerment dimensions of the Consumer Empowerment construct. This study attempts to verify the proposed components of Consumer Empowerment through UGC in the travel industry through a focus group.

2 Uses & Gratification Theory (U&G)

Due to less social presence and less information richness, UGC is described as the data produced by individuals on the Internet, where they exchange opinion/information about a specific content as well as fulfil their social interaction needs (Shao, 2009). As well, UGC is immensely gratifying people who consume its content (Shao, 2009). Since inconsistent results of social presence and media richness theories were found for the new media, other researchers recommend other factors to assess and select new media, for example: assessment of need fulfilment, social norms and peer evaluations of media (Flanagin & Metzger, 2001).

Fulk et al. (1990) proposed the Social Influence Model of Technology Use, where individuals' media perception and use are socially constructed subjective, and assessment of media influences its usage. Authors pointed out that social influences can both positively and negatively influence people attitude toward the use of new media.

Flanagin and Metzger (2001) claim that Uses and Gratifications theory (U&G) is consistent with Social Influence approaches. This theory perspective states that people select media based on needs (Flanagin & Metzger, 2001). Derived from mass communications research, the Uses and Gratifications theory refers to users who are keenly involved in media usage and interact with the communication media (Luo, 2002). U&G research is helpful for explaining the social and psychological motives that influence people to choose a specific media to gratify a set of psychological needs (Katz, Blumler, & Gurevitch, 1974). Uses and Gratifications theory is also useful for understanding motivations for using the Internet, largely because its characteristics of active choice of media and user-centered perspective on the relation between users and media (Guo, Cheung, & Tan, 2008). In addition, Stafford (2003) claims that U&G theory is very useful for diagnosis Internet-making decisions.

Recently Internet research using U&G theory has examined three components related to consumer motivation for using the Internet: process gratifications, content gratifications, and social gratifications (Stafford et al., 2004). When people use media just for the content carried by a medium, such as information, knowledge or research, this is considered content gratifications. However, when people use a media just for the simple experience, such as browsing or playing with the technology, this is process gratifications. Whereas social gratifications are characterized by a social dimension of U&G, such as chatting, friends, interaction and people. The dimensions from these three U&G components seem very broad and might relate to any content on the Internet. For the purpose of this research, in order to be related to the UGC context the dimensions from content and social gratifications come from the Dual-Process Theory, and the dimensions from process gratifications comes from other U&G studies. Since UGC is affected by informational and normative factors, the informational and normative influence dimensions from Dual-Process theory seem more appropriate in the UGC context.

3 Dual Process Theory

A reader's information evaluation is really affected by informational factors (Wathen & Burkell, 2002). However, since user-generated content is submitted by strangers on the Internet, informational elements would not be enough to evaluate its content. In that case, including normative factors would complement the evaluation of the content due the UGC social aggregation capacity.

Dual-Process theory is used to view how different types of influences (normative and informational) affect the persuasiveness of information (Deutsch & Gerard, 1955). Dual-Process theory not only considers the informational social influence, but also the normative power influence from other audiences (Burnkrant & Cousineau, 1975). In other words, informational influence is based on the content of the received information, whereas normative influence is based on the other people's opinions about the received information and how these opinions would affect others' choice preferences (Kaplan & Miller, 1987). The Dual-process approach is useful to explain communication effectiveness when group opinions/discussion is present (Sia, Tan, & Wei, 2002). Thus, this theory is suitable for applying in UGC studies.

Dual-Process theory is used in this study to understand how and to what extent both types of influence (informational and normative) affect the persuasiveness of user-generated content. Informational social influence and normative social influence come from the Social Influence approach (Bearden, Calcich, & Netemeyer, 1986). Therefore, both U&G theory and Dual-Process theory are consistent with the Social Influence theories. These two theories have similarities that make them helpful to conceptualise the UGC issue using the Consumer Empowerment concept.

4 Consumer Empowerment

Various definitions of empowerment exist in literature (Sehgal & Stewart, 2004) and no consensus occurs regarding this concept (Ergeneli, Arl, & Metin, 2007). For this study, empowerment is defined as a motivational construct and is viewed as an enabling process (Conger & Kanungo, 1988). According to Conger and Kanungo (1988, p. 474), "enabling implies creating conditions for heightening motivation for task accomplishment through the development of a strong sense of personal efficacy". In order to understand empowerment in motivational terms, Bandura (1986) defines it as a process whereby an individual's belief in his self-efficacy is enhanced.

Empowerment can be defined on an individual level, as the process by which people acquire the necessary psychological resources enabling them goal achievement (Amichai-Hamburguer, McKenna, & Tal, 2008). As well, empowerment can be viewed as a process by which individuals gain control over their own destiny as well as participation with others to achieve goals (Rappaport, 1987). Consequently, processes involving empowerment are influencing the decisions that affect people's lives (Zimmerman, 1995).

Consumer empowerment has been related to changes in the travel and entertainment industries (Freedman, 2007). For example, before booking trips 61% of travellers consult online search engines (Conrady, 2007). As a consequence, tourists are becoming empowered. Hjalager (2001, p. 289) points out that "a truly empowered tourist is a person who, without much pain or intellectual effort, is able to make an informed choice of services and products in accordance with his/her own preferences". Indeed, the Internet enables tourists to receive and pass on recommendations of tourist experiences (Hjalager, 2001).

Although empowerment is discussed with increasing regularity (Harrison, Waite, & Hunter, 2006), there is a lack of a clear definition of a type of empowerment specific to a context (Sehgal & Stewart, 2006). No other study has explored the role of empowerment in the UGC context. With the aim of understanding how UGC empowers online consumer in the travel industry, the Consumer Empowerment construct is proposed and verified in this study.

For this study, the research model on Consumer Empowerment will be grounded on Uses and Gratification Theory (Stafford et al., 2004) and Dual-Process Theory (Deutsch & Gerard, 1955). The three components of U&G theory (Content, Social, and Process) are proposed to form the concept of Content Empowerment, Social Empowerment and Process Empowerment, respectively in the Consumer Empowerment construct. Dual-Process Theory is used to help determine the Content Empowerment dimensions (argument quality, source credibility, information consistency, and information framing), and Social Empowerment dimensions (recommendation consistency, and recommendation rating). Process Empowerment dimensions are derived from U&G's process gratifications studies (medium and entertainment). Consumer Empowerment construct proposed in this study is then shown in figure 1.

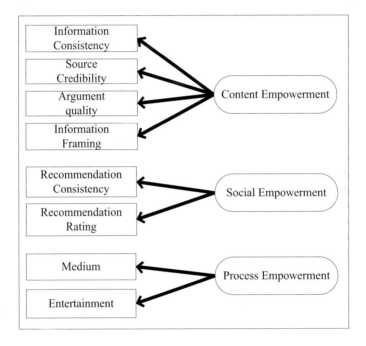

Fig. 1. Consumer Empowerment construct

4.1 Content Empowerment

Content gratifications from U&G theory (Stafford et al., 2004) is characterized as related to information content, and is derived from the use of mediated messages for their intrinsic value for the receiver (Cutler & Danowski, 1980). For the purpose of this study, content gratifications is conceptualised under empowerment theory, and is utilizing informational influence determinants (source credibility, argument quality, information consistency, and information framing) to help define its construct as Content Empowerment.

- Source Credibility. People are more acceptable with information that comes from highly credible source, and consequently less likely to accept it when the source has low credibility (Grewal, Gotlieb, & Marmorstein, 1994). Lim, Sia, Lee and Bensabat (2006) claim that source credibility can be applied to the online environment.
- Argument Quality. Concerns the quality or strength of the received information (Cacioppo, Petty, & Morris, 1983). According to Cheung et al. (2009), when the received information has strong arguments, receivers will develop a positive attitude towards the information.
- Information Consistency. Indicates the extent to which the current message is consistent with the prior knowledge of the member accessing it (Zhang & Watts, 2003). Hence, when people read online recommendations that have advice which confirms the reader's existing belief, they will be more likely to believe the information (Cheung et al., 2009).
- Information Framing. Refers to the content of the message, if it is positively framed or negatively framed (Cheung et al., 2009). Positively framed information is related to product's strengths, whereas negatively framed information is associated to product's weakness/problems (Grewal et al., 1994).

4.2 Social Empowerment

Social gratifications from U&G theory is characterized by chatting and interacting with people over the Internet, and is generally in the form of normative forces (Stafford et al., 2004). For the purpose of this research, social gratifications is conceptualised under empowerment theory, and is utilizing social influence determinants (recommendation consistency and recommendation rating) to help define its construct as Social Empowerment.

- *Recommendation Consistency.* Refers to the extent to which the current recommendation is consistent with other contributors' experiences regarding the same product/service evaluation (Zhang & Watts, 2003). People likely rate the credibility of the recommendation highly when there is consistency between the recommendations (Cheung, Luo, Sia, & Chen, 2007).
- *Recommendation Rating.* Refers to the overall rating provided by other people on a recommendation (Cheung et al., 2007). Online consumers can mark a high or low rating depending on the perception of the message (Cheung et al., 2009).

4.3 Process Empowerment

Process gratification is derived from the use of mediated messages for extrinsic values, in contrast to a specific interest in its content (Cutler & Danowski, 1980), where people surfing the web are motivated by the process of browsing for enjoyment (Stafford et al., 2004). For this study, process gratifications is conceptualised under empowerment theory, and is utilizing dimensions (medium and entertainment) derived from U&G's process gratifications studies (Stafford & Stafford, 2001; Stafford et al., 2004) to help define its construct as Process Empowerment.

- *Medium.* Process gratifications concern actual use of the medium itself (Cutler & Danowski, 1980). Variables such as "web sites", "search engines", and "technology" can be considered part of the dimension of Internet usage process gratifications (Stafford et al., 2004).
- *Entertainment.* When people obtain gratifications by taking advantage of entertainment offered on the web, it can be considered as a process-motivated gratification (Stafford & Stafford, 2001). Entertainment refers to the extent to which the web media is fun to media users (Eighmey & McCord, 1998).

5   Research Methodology

A focus group discussion session was conducted to gather qualitative data from backpackers in the travel industry and to verify the importance of the proposed components of Consumer Empowerment in the UGC context. Focus group interview involves between eight to twelve people in order to discuss a particular topic in depth, and gain a better understanding of their response (Stewart, Shamdasani, & Rook, 2007).

The focus group was moderated by the researcher and was managed in accordance with standard procedures (Lunt & Livingstone, 1996). There was a structured discussion guide with thirteen questions which were asked to participants during the discussion. The focus group session debated significant issues relating to the three proposed components of Consumer Empowerment. Recordings of the focus group comments were transcribed and analyzed by the researchers line by line to confirm the importance of the proposed components through UGC in the travel industry.

The researcher was capable of moderating and participating in the discussion without providing biased or leading the focus group participants into a desired response. Also, a perceived advantage of focus group is that participants generate rich and believable data, and then compensate for their lack of reliability with greater validity (Lunt & Livingstone, 1996).

Participants of the discussions were international tourist backpackers staying at Auckland YHA (Youth Hostels Association) hostel, New Zealand. The focus group interview was advertised by the YHA receptionists. Participants were randomly selected, but only international backpackers who speak sufficient English to communicate properly participated in the focus group. The focus group session was held in June 2009, and lasted 75 min. In return for their participation, backpackers received one free night of accommodation at YHA Auckland. As well, if requested, each participant will receive a copy of the results at the end of this research.

A total of ten international backpackers participated in the focus group discussion session. There were seven females and three males. The participants were all aged over 20 years. Ninety percent of the participants had at least undergraduate degree. Most participants had more than six years of computer experience. Participants came from six different countries: England, Ireland, Wales, Australia, Germany, and Korea.

6 Results and Discussion

The discussion results suggest that participants are using consumer-generated content on the Internet to help them to book accommodation. The results support the existence of the three proposed components of Consumer Empowerment and their dimensions: Content Empowerment (Source Credibility, Argument Quality, Information Consistency, and Information Framing); Social Empowerment (Recommendation Consistency and Recommendation Rating); and Process Empowerment (Medium and Entertainment). We discuss below the focus group findings. Participant comments are presented within parenthesis and within double quotation marks.

6.1 Content Empowerment

- *Source Credibility.* Participants are concerned with the user-generated content on the Internet because they do not know who they are dealing with ("You have to be careful with the user comments"). One participant gave an example of a user who posted several good comments about an accommodation. This person may be one of the accommodation employee or perhaps friend of the owner ("Good comments can come from people who work on there"). Another participant prefers going through TripAdvisor.com to read comments rather than hostel websites. She said that there are generally positive comments on hostel websites. So these comments do not look trustable, and that is why she prefers reading online comments on TripAdvisor.com.
- *Argument Quality.* All participants consider argument quality important. For example, update information is quite relevant to make the accommodation decision ("If the review is from two years ago, the hostel may be deteriorated by now"). Also, the amount of reviews makes difference too ("people will be more influenced if they read a reasonable amount of reviews rather than just one good or bad comment"; "If it is just one person comment, it doesn't make my decision about the accommodation. I need to get information from different people, not just one person").
- *Information Consistency.* Many participants are keener to accept information that is similar to their own. One participant gave an example saying that she is more likely to believe the advice from a review on the web about an accommodation if this information confirms her own opinion. She mentioned that she stops researching accommodation when the information confirms her opinion ("When I read the first comment about a hostel on the web and it has the same opinion as me, I stop researching and go for it"). Participants are more willing to trust information from people with same opinion.
- *Information Framing.* Participants feel more confident to make the decision to book accommodation if they have both positive and negative comments in their hands ("Looks more believable when there are both positive and negative

comments. When there are just positive comments, you wondering where are the negative ones?"). One participant made an analogy between UGC and a review magazine ("It is like a review magazine. The reviewer writes both negative and positive things about the magazine. If you take into consideration UGC, you believe that person is going to take a more measureable view of the place been reviewing to. So, I will be more inclined to follow that view "). Another participant is skeptical if there is just one negative comment related to a hostel ("Depends how bad the comment is, and perhaps it is just a minor incident"). However, if he sees several bad comments for the same hostel, this can make an impact in his decision to book an accommodation there.

6.2 Social Empowerment

- *Recommendation Consistency.* Most participants believe that if similar experiences are repeatedly posted by different people on the web, the likelihood of backpackers trust in that experience is higher ("When comments are consistent, you know exactly what you will have in the accommodation"). One participant said that when the comments are consistent among them, you know better about the hostel before you book it. For instance, when there are several negative comments from different people complaining about small rooms or bad Internet connection, this helps you not to surprise when you get into the accommodation.
- *Recommendation Rating.* Recommendation ratings are considered quite important for the backpackers participants ("Ratings from user-generated content on accommodation really influences me to make the decision to book"). A backpacker gave an example of her experience with ratings ("I think definitely it helps. When I used hostelworld.com looking for information about Auckland. I looked at anything above 60% rating first. I never use low rating regarding accommodation and its facilities"). Other participant is cautions if just few people rate the hostel ("It is better when many people have been rated for that accommodation"). Backpackers feel more confident before booking if several people rate the accommodation and its facilities.

6.3 Process Empowerment

- *Medium.* All participants agree that medium such as technology, websites, search engines are essential for them to use before booking accommodation. One backpacker mentioned that UGC websites are more accurate and updated than books like Lonely Planet ("Websites are more updated than books. You can read a review posted yesterday from hostelworld.com, for instance. Books take time to do the research and get published. By the end of the day, books are outdated if you compare with the websites, but be careful if website is reliable or not"). Other participant said that hostel website helps promote itself on the web showing pictures, prices, sales and other relevant information about the accommodation. They are fast and quick to access in a few minutes.
- *Entertainment.* Most participants feel entertaining by reading review comments on the Internet. They feel excited surfing on the websites to get opinions about the accommodation and its facilities. Participants have fun through the process to get

the comments ("If I search for some accommodation, I type in hostel in the particular city, I generally use Google...the results come up, quite often, there will be databases like hostel.com, they have a list of the relevant hostels, and then I pick the cheapest and read UGC review comments").

7 Conclusions

The purpose of this paper is to report the preliminary results of a study designed to examine the concept of Consumer Empowerment through User-Generated Content context in the travel industry. We argue that it is important for researchers to clearly define Consumer Empowerment in the UGC context since a single conception of Empowerment is not appropriate across all disciplines and across all contexts. The results of focus group discussion confirm the importance of three components of Consumer Empowerment: Content Empowerment, Social Empowerment, and Process Empowerment. The findings contribute to a more comprehensive understanding of the Empowerment concept.

Although there are clearly limitations in relation to the small sample size of the focus group as well the inability of generalizing the findings from the focus group session, the research moves current research into a new direction. The future outlook of this research is to undertake a more rigorous study to validate the model using surveys with international backpackers. In order to achieve this larger objective, a theoretical framework using the Theory of Planned Behavior as its basis will be employed to test quantitatively hypotheses using the measures developed in this study.

This study shows the importance of UGC to empower travellers to book accommodation. From a practical standpoint, these findings will help the competitiveness of the accommodation section, which is a cornerstone to broader tourism development, and will support the growth of tourism in New Zealand. Finally, this study will be valuable to web researchers and travel practitioners interested in designing their websites.

References

Amichai-Hamburguer, Y., McKenna, K. Y. A., & Tal, S.-A. (2008). E-empowerment: Empowerment by the Internet. *Computers in Human Behavior, 24*(5), 1776-1789.

Arriga, M., & Levina, N. (2008). *Social dynamics in online cultural fields.* Paper presented at the 29th International Conference on Information Systems (ICIS'08), Paris.

Bandura, A. (1986). *Social foundations of thought and action: a social cognitive theory.* Englewood Cliffs, NJ: Prentice-Hall.

Bearden, W. O., Calcich, S. E., & Netemeyer, R. (1986). An exploratory investigation of consumer innovativeness and interpersonal influences. *Advances in Consumer Research, 13*(1), 77-82.

Burnkrant, R. E., & Cousineau, A. (1975). Informational and normative social influence in buyer behavior. *Journal of Consumer Research, 2*(3), 206-215.

Cacioppo, J. T., Petty, R. E., & Morris, K. J. (1983). Effects of need for cognition on message evaluation, recall, and persuasion. *Journal of Personality and Social Psychology, 45*(4), 805-818.

Cheung, M.-Y., Luo, C., Sia, C.-L., & Chen, H. (2009). Credibility of Electronic Word-Of-Mouth: Informational and Normative Determinants of On-line Consumer Recommendations. *International Journal of Electronic Commerce, 13*(4), 9-39.

Cheung, M. Y., Luo, C., Sia, C. L., & Chen, H. (2007). *How do people evaluate electronic word-of-mouth? Informational and normative based determinants of perceived credibility of online consumer recommendations in China.* Paper presented at the 11th Pacific-Asia Conference on Information Systems (PACIS'07), Auckland, NZ.

Conger, J. A., & Kanungo, R. N. (1988). The empowerment process: integrating theory and practice. *Academy of Management Review, 13*(3), 471-482.

Conrady, R. (2007). Travel technology in the era of Web 2.0. In R. Conrady & M. Buck (Eds.), *Trends and Issues in Global Tourism 2007* (pp. 165-184). New York: Springer.

Constantinides, E. (2007). *Web 2.0 and marketing issues.* Retrieved 17/12/2007, from www.ebusinessforum.gr

Cutler, N. E., & Danowski, J. A. (1980). Process gratification in aging cohorts. *Journalism Quarterly, 57*(2), 269-276.

Daugherty, T., Eastin, M. S., & Bright, L. (2008). Exploring consumer motivations for creating User-Generated Content. *Journal of Interactive Advertising, 8*(2), 1-24.

Deutsch, M., & Gerard, H. B. (1955). A study of normative and informational social influence upon individual judgment. *Journal of Abnormal and Social Psychology, 51*, 629-636.

Eighmey, J., & McCord, L. (1998). Adding value in the information age: uses and gratifications of sites on the world wide web. *Journal of Business Research, 41*(3), 187-194.

Ergeneli, A., Arl, G. S., & Metin, S. (2007). Psychological empowerment and its relationship to trust in immediate managers. *Journal of Business Research, 60*(1), 41-49.

Flanagin, A. J., & Metzger, M. J. (2001). Internet use in the contemporary media environment. *Human Communication Research, 27*(1), 153-181.

Forman, C., Ghose, A., & Wiesenfeld, B. (2008). Examining the relationship between reviews and sales: The role of reviewer identity disclosure in electronic markets. *Information Systems Research, 19*(3), 291-316.

Freedman, J. B. (2007). *What motivates voluntary engagement in cooperative information systems.* Paper presented at the 40th Annual Hawaii International Conference on System Sciences (HICSS'07).

Fulk, J., Schmitz, J. A., & Steinfield, C. W. (1990). A social influence model of technology use. In J. Fulk & C. Steinfield (Eds.), *Organizations and communication technology* (pp. 117-140). Newbury Park, CA: Sage.

Gretzel, U., & Yoo, K. H. (2008). Use and impact of online travel reviews. In P. O'Connor, W. Höpken & U. Gretzel (Eds.), *Information and Communication Technologies in Tourism 2008* (pp. 35-46). New York: Springer Wien.

Grewal, D., Gotlieb, J., & Marmorstein, H. (1994). The moderating effects of message framing and source credibility on the price-perceived risk relationship. *Journal of Consumer Research, 21* (1), 145-153.

Guo, Z., Cheung, K., & Tan, F. B. (2008). *Motivations for using CMC and Non-CMC media in learning contexts: A Uses and Gratifications approach.* Paper presented at the 29th International Conference on Information Systems (ICIS'08), Paris.

Harrison, T., Waite, K., & Hunter, G. L. (2006). The internet, information and empowerment. *European Journal of Marketing, 40*(9/10), 972-993.

Hjalager, A.-M. (2001). Quality in tourism through the empowerment of tourists. *Managing Service Quality, 11*(4), 287-295.

Kaplan, M. F., & Miller, C. E. (1987). Group decision making and normative versus informational influence: Effects of type of issue and assigned decision rule. *Journal of Personality and Social Psychology, 53*(2), 306-313.

Katz, E., Blumler, J. G., & Gurevitch, M. (1974). Utilization of mass communication by the individual. In J. G. Blumler & E. Katz (Eds.), *Current Perspectives and Gratifications Research* (pp. 19-32). Beverly Hills: Sage.

Laboy, F., & Torchio, P. (2007). *Web 2.0 for the travel marketer and consumer.* Retrieved 17/12/2007, from www.esitemarketing.com/web2-travel-marketing.php

Lim, K. H., Sia, C. L., Lee, M. K. O., & Benbasat, I. (2006). How do I trust you online, and If so, will I buy?: An empirical study of two trust building strategies. *Journal of Management Information Systems, 23*(2), 233-266.

Lunt, P., & Livingstone, S. (1996). Rethinking the focus group in media and communications research. *Journal of Communication, 46*(2), 79-98.

Luo, X. (2002). Uses and gratifications theory and e-consumer behaviors: a structural equation modeling study. *Journal of Interactive Advertising, 2*(2), 44-54.

O'Connor, P. (2008). User-Generated content and travel: A case study on TripAdvisor. In P. O'Connor, W. Höpken & U. Gretzel (Eds.), *Information and Communication Technologies in Tourism 2008* (pp. 47-58). New York: Springer Wien.

Quinn, R. E., & Spreitzer, G. M. (1997). The road to empowerment: Seven questions every leader should consider. *Organizational Dynamics, 26*(2), 37-49.

Rappaport, J. (1987). Terms of empowerment/exemplars of prevention: toward a theory for community psychology. *American Journal of Community Psychology, 15*(2), 121-148.

Schegg, R., Liebrich, A., Scaglione, M., & Ahmad, S. F. S. (2008). An exploratory field study of Web 2.0 in tourism. In P. O'Connor, W. Höpken & U. Gretzel (Eds.), *Information and Communication Technologies in Tourism 2008* (pp. 152-163). New York: Springer Wien.

Sehgal, R., & Stewart, G. (2004). *Exploring the relationship between user empowerment and enterprise system success measures.* Paper presented at the Tenth Americas Conference on Information Systems (AMCIS), New York.

Sehgal, R., & Stewart, G. (2006). Using qualitative analysis for deriving evidence based construct definition: A case narrative of User Empowerment. In A. Ruth (Ed.), *Quality and Impact of Qualitative Research* (pp. 116-128). Gold Coast: Griffith University.

Shao, G. (2009). Understanding the appeal of user-generated media: a uses and gratification perspective. *Internet Research, 19*(1), 7-25.

Sia, C. L., Tan, B. C. Y., & Wei, K. K. (2002). Group polarization and computer-mediated communication: Effects of communication cues, social presence, and anonymity. *Information Systems Research, 13*(1), 70-90.

Sigala, M. (2007). *Use, management and impact of the Social Web (Web 2.0) on business operations and strategies in the tourism and mass media sectors.* Retrieved 17/12/2007, from www.ebusinessforum.gr

Stafford, T., & Stafford, M. R. (2001). Identifying motivations for the use of commercial web sites. *Information Resources Management Journal, 14*(1), 22-30.

Stafford, T. F. (2003). Differentiating between adopter categories in the uses and gratifications for Internet services. *IEEE Transactions on Engineering Management, 50*(4), 427-435.

Stafford, T. F., Stafford, M. R., & Schkade, L. L. (2004). Determining uses and gratifications for the Internet. *Decision Sciences, 35*(2), 259-288.

Stewart, D. W., Shamdasani, P. N., & Rook, D. W. (2007). *Focus Groups: Theory and Practice* (2nd ed.). California: Sage Publications.

Wathen, C. N., & Burkell, J. (2002). Believe it or not: Factors influencing credibility on the Web. *Journal of the American Society for Information Science and Technology, 53*(2), 134-144.

Xiang, Z., & Gretzel, U. (2009). Role of social media in online travel information search. *Tourism Management, doi:10.1016/j.tourman.2009.02.016*, 1-10.

Zhang, W., & Watts, S. (2003). *Knowledge adoption in online communities of practice.* Paper presented at the 24th International Conference on Information Systems (ICIS'03), Seattle.

Zimmerman, M. A. (1995). Psychological empowerment: issues and illustrations. *American Journal of Community Psychology, 23*(5), 581-599.

An Investigation of Motivation to Share Online Content by Young Travelers - Why and Where

Hilary Catherine Murphy[a],
Elia Adriana Centeno Gil[a] and
Roland Schegg[b]

[a]Ecole Hotelière de Lausanne (EHL), HES-SO (University of Applied Sciences Western Switzerland), Lausanne, Switzerland,
hilary.murphy@ehl.ch, elia.centenogil@ehl.ch

[b]Ecole Suisse de Tourisme, HES-SO Valais (University of Applied Sciences Western Switzerland Valais), Sierre, Switzerland,
roland.schegg@hevs.ch

Abstract

Social networks and social media channels have experienced phenomenal growth and influence over the last few years and provide a platform where consumers share video clips, pictures and texts to express their opinions and experiences of products and services. This raises major issues for hotels and travel firms, when consumers resort to instantly available, online and unmanaged information to choose destinations, accommodation and travel suppliers. This paper examines the phenomenon of shared "content" online and particularly investigates, why, when, where and what type of content (young) travel consumers share online in the context of a recent "trip". The method used is an online survey with mostly quantitative data gathered from nearly 450 respondents. The preliminary results reveal that most respondents post content within a week of completing a trip, that they mostly post text and photos and that they are more likely to post content on their "own" social media website (e.g. Facebook, MySpace) than on a commercial supplier/intermediary website. Recommendations are made for marketers in the context of promoting post-purchase behaviour, e.g. in terms of the timing and content, and offers conclusions that support further examination of this phenomenon.

Keywords: social media, user-generated content, post-purchase behaviour, UGC, online

1 Introduction

Technologies that facilitate sharing text, photos, and videos continue to grow with the volume of user generated content (UGC) consequently rising. Social networks and social media channels disrupt the influence of marketing when consumers prefer collective expression in video clips, blogs and ratings of their peers to form opinions of products and services and to share experiences post purchase via electronic word of mouth (Trusov et al., 2008). This willingness to express oneself in public seems to mark a generational shift in attitudes to privacy and sharing with digital generations having fewer qualms about revealing their habits, purchases and opinions online. This raises major issues for destinations, hotels and travel firms as consumers exploit instantly available, online, and unmanaged information to overcome any perceived risk they have in choosing destinations, accommodation and travel suppliers and share purchase experiences, both during and after consumption.

Traditional word of mouth (WOM), particularly from reference groups, has long served to give orientation points to customers to reduce uncertainty and risk, particularly in high service content products and research reveals social interaction utility as one of the most important motivation to propagate WOM (Hennig-Thurau et al., 2004). Additionally, marketers have struggled to profit from the exploitation of, what appears to be, free customer advocacy, improved search engine visibility and the opportunity to harness customer opinion and feedback.

This paper examines the phenomenon of shared "content" online (UGC) and particularly investigates the post purchase stage of buyer behaviour and focuses on why, when, where and what type of content consumers share online in the context of a recent "trip". It further investigates if this form of electronic word of mouth can be managed with this "peer- to peer" sharing of content, experiences and knowledge, particularly at post- purchase stage of consumption. Understanding the motivation, timing, content preferred and which websites are preferred would provide deeper marketing insights in order to exploit social media content in a more effective way.

2 Literature Review

2.1 The rise of social media

Several researchers have investigated the replacement of real communities with virtual communities (e.g. Fernback, 2007; Soukup, 2006). The increase in high-speed and high-bandwidth internet access around the world (Internet World Statistics, 2009) and the ubiquity of computers and internet in the civilized world is another factor which supports the growth of online social network participation, "with more people living more of their lives online, new kinds of relationships [...] have appeared" (Sebor, 2007, p. 34). This may be partly due to globalization, "individuals have become increasingly detached from traditional structural, institutional and communal sources of collective identity" (Hodkinson, 2007, p. 627). Clearly, the increasing individualization of today's society are closely interlinked to the rise of social media and Rheingold claims that "perhaps, cyberspace is one of the informal public places where people can rebuild the aspects of community that were lost when the malt shop became a mall" (Rheingold, 1993 as cited in Soukup, 2006, p. 422). Soukup (2006) further develops this theory of 'third places', places between home and work, where people primarily gather to enjoy each other's company and which represent a context for sociability, spontaneity, community building and emotional expressiveness. Apart from it being a sociological phenomenon, it is clear that social network websites would appear to be a fertile ground for marketers who can target groups of similarly minded customers and this has resulted in some recent attention from marketing academics. Trusov et al. (2008), for example, propose a model that helps to identify those social media members who are likely to be influential and therefore important to the business, particularly for new customer acquisition. They reveal that "elasticity for

WOM is approximately 20 times higher than that for marketing events and 30 times that of media appearances" i.e. that volume of WOM may have an inflated impact on demand. However, specific investigation at an academic level is sparse and requires further investigation into specific sectors.

2.2 Consumer behaviour and the role of word of mouth

When making a product or services purchase, a buyer usually follow certain steps. These steps have been modeled by many authors, including Solomon (2006) as follows (Figure 1):

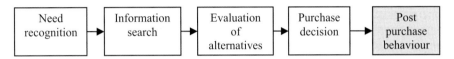

Fig. 1. Purchase Steps

They identify four stages before the actual purchase and one after the purchase, further defined as; post-experience evaluation, WOM referral and brand loyalty stages. There is ample theoretical support for the idea that WOM impacts consumers' actions, e.g. Banerjee (1992) presents a model that suggest that people are influenced by others' opinions, particularly in the context of "herd behaviour" and that information from previous consumers impact on consumption patterns. Söderlund & Rosengren (2004, 2007) also highlight the importance of word of mouth in the service profit chain which links satisfaction to word of mouth and word of mouth to profitability. IAB (2008) found that "30 percent of frequent social networkers trust their peers' opinions when making a major purchase decision, but only 10 percent trust an advertisement". Moreover, "40% of all social networkers said they use social networking sites to learn more about brands or products they like" and also found that "77% of online shoppers read consumer product reviews and ratings before making a purchase" (TNS, 2007). Nevertheless, there is a difference in importance between negative and positive online feedback: a study found that 43.5 % of consumers 'always' or 'mostly' refrain from a purchase after reading a negative comment, but only 28% 'always or 'mostly' buy after reading a positive comment (Hennig-Thurau & Walsh, 2003). Consumer to consumer (C2C) relationships on social networks can thus critically influence brand choice in both online and offline purchases (Hennig-Thurau & Walsh, 2003) and while this C2C influence can be either positive or negative for the suppliers, they will always be positive for consumers (Farquhar & Rowley, 2006), if only for the "reward" of being better informed. Besides which, consumers read not only for functional reasons directed to purchase but also for pleasure and hedonic reasons (Goldsmith & Horowitz, 2006).

Murray (1991 cited in Bansal & Voyer, 2000) argues that interpersonal sources, i.e. WOM, represent the most important source of risk-reducing information for services. Dissonance reducing behaviour is also a critical factor in high risk consumptions where consumers seek reassurance at post purchase stage to validate their consumption choices (Sweeney et al, 2000). This is further supported by Solomon (2006), who argues that novices who face the highest risk tend to rely more on other's opinions.

2.3 The impact of reference groups on consumer behaviour

All word of mouth transactions occur within some social relationship, Bansal & Voyer, (2000) and other researchers have tried to measure the determinants and characteristics of these relationships and their normative influence on the receiver. Two main notions of interpersonal relations have emerged from this: *tie strength and homophily* (Brown & Reingen, 2001). The strength of tie between two people in a community can range from strong primary to weak secondary and they are determined by the importance attached to the social relation, the frequency of social contact and the type of social relation (Brown & Reingen, 2001). The *expertise of the sender* however, also impacts how actively his message will be sought and a message which is "actively sold" again will have greater influence on the receiver than one which is passively attained (Brown & Reingen, 2001).

An important type of interpersonal relations and a platform for word of mouth are *reference groups*, who serve as orientation points for consumers (Solomon, 2006). Another important factor is the *decreased presence of contextual social cues in online environment,* which represents a challenge to readers (Dellarocas, 2003). Online social networks can play a major role as reference groups with the electronic channels (word of mouse) having several distinct differences from offline, such as the increased anonymity and confidentiality, the larger number of evaluators available compared to offline word of mouth as well as the asynchronicity, which allows for comments to be read long after they have been posted (Pitta & Fowler, 2005; Vilpponen et al. 2006). Moreover, people raising their voice about products or services in specialized forums are often attributed a sort of *"expert power"* and increased informational influence (Gelb & Sundaram, 2002; Solomon, 2006). Edwards (2006) summarises the disadvantages of taking opinions online as it being less personal, less immediate and less disinterested, more significant reach, its increased credibility in print, its accessibility by people who are interested and receptive and its occurrence closer to the purchase decision. Dellarocas (2003) states that a major advantage of online word of mouth is in the ability of the web to collect and aggregate the information to construct large-scale WOM networks.

2.4 The motivation to engage in word of mouth

Despite the *strong link between sending and receiving of word of mouth*, there are nevertheless important differences in the motivations to engage in either one. Since the reception of word of mouth in the pre-purchase stage is part of the information search stage, it is mainly motivated by the desire to decrease risk associated with an intended purchase (as mentioned above). In the post-purchase stage, or in the stage where word of mouth is actively sent, the sender has already experienced the purchase and is thus facing less risk. The motivations to send word of mouth are consequently entirely different. For example, Rimé et al. (1991) suggest that many who experience an "emotional event" feel a sense of urgency to connect with others; i.e. "*social sharing of emotion*". This phenomenon occurs when individuals communicate frankly with others about the circumstances of the emotion-eliciting event and about their feelings. However, Fou (2008, p13) comments that "WOM is just something that happens naturally when customers are thrilled by an extraordinary product/service" and further criticises exploitation of these social networks by commercial marketing activities.

2.5 Social interaction utility and word of mouth

Balasubramanian and Mahajan (2001, as cited in Hennig-Thurau et al., 2004) stated *social interaction utility* as the most important motivation in the context of post purchase behaviour. They further differentiated this social interaction utility into several sub-categories: (1) focus-related utility, which is motivated by adding value to the community through the word of mouth contribution, (2) consumption utility, which is motivated by obtaining value through direct consumption of the contributions of other community members and (3), approval utility, which is motivated by obtaining satisfaction when others consume and approve of contributions. Hennig-Thurau et al. (2004) add another utility to this list, which is (4) homeostase utility and which is explained by the desire for some form of balance in life. He argues that a dissatisfying (purchase) experience can harm this balance and commenting/reporting can help to restore it. Sundaram et al. (1998, as cited in Hennig-Thurau et al., 2004) allege that there are different motivations for sending either positive or negative word of mouth. For positive word of mouth, they list *altruism, product involvement, self-enhancement, and helping the company.* As motivations for negative word of mouth, they list *altruism, anxiety reduction, vengeance and advice seeking.*

There is also an aspect of self-enhancement, *or gaining expert status* by opining on subjects (Dellarocas, 2004) as one of the most important factors determining word of mouth solicitation. Due to the specific characteristics of the online environment, this factor gains even more strength, since the anonymity in online environments allows senders to assume authority which they could not as easily claim in an offline situation (Brown & Reingen, 2001). This may distort word of mouth as publishers are disproportionately likely to consider themselves as experts and are also more likely to have strong opinions than offline word of mouth senders. Moreover, the online environment and the lack of personal contact often result in an increased willingness to publish negative feedback (Brown & Reingen, 2001).

Though much of the literature is focused on traditional word of mouth in the context of post purchase behaviour, very little research is available which empirically investigates if this can be translated to *online* consumer behaviour, particularly in pragmatic terms of why, when, what and where this post purchase opinion is shared. The "referral effect" is almost impossible to gauge in the offline world, i.e. to investigate what/when/why people engage in post purchase behaviours, and relies on "referral tracking" from marketers, e.g. feedback forms, coupon redemption etc. In an online world where individuals can be tracked and post purchase behaviour can be monitored and stimulated, it would appear easier to measure post purchase activity with "cookies" and other behavioural tracking software.

The *main aim of this paper* is to explore the social media behaviour at the post-purchase stage of those having taken a recent trip. This paper attempts thus to explain WHERE content is shared (specifically looking a 4 types of UGC; social media websites, supplier websites, hotel review websites, and video/picture sharing websites) in relation to post-purchase experience sharing pattern expressed through motivation (WHY), type of content (WHAT) and timing of posting (WHEN). Specifically, in this paper, the following research question is examined: *Is there is a relationship between post-purchase experience sharing motivation (WHY) and the type of UGC site utilized (WHERE)?*

3 Methodology

3.1 Research instrument

A questionnaire using mostly closed, Likert-scale statements, is designed to investigate; demographic factors, the "motivation to engage in sharing/posting content online" (both positive and negative), the type of UGC that is posted (text, video, pictures), the timing of posting UGC (during, after, within certain times frames after) and to identify where the UGC was posted. Such sites are categorised into 4 types: social media sites like Facebook or Bebo etc (UGC category 1), travel supply sites like websites of destinations, hotels or airline (UGC category 2), commercial travel review sites such as TripAdvisor, HolidayCheck (UGC category 3) and video/picture sharing websites such as Flickr, YouTube or Picasa (UGC category 4). Hence certain key dimensions are established that explored the relationship between "motivation to engage in sharing/posting content online" which could include both positive and negative dimensions and where these respondents engage in sharing/posting content.

This is a purposive sample of young, recent European travellers. A link to an online survey was sent by e-mail to 1500 recent alumni and final year students from 3 European universities who represent a wide geographical European background, in September/October 2008. The introduction explains the context and rationale for the survey, asking them to voluntarily complete the questionnaire in the context of their most recent trip and guaranteed anonymity.

The survey instrument is reasonable short; completion takes 10-15 minutes and includes mostly simple statements related to all the variables to be tested in the research. Behavioural variables (what, when and where they post) are assessed with a frequency measure (5-point Likert scale from 1=never to 5=always), whereas motivational variables (why they post) are evaluated with an agreement scale (1=totally disagree to 5=totally agree). Of the 1500 emails sent, 446 questionnaires are completed, giving an acceptable response rate of 29.7%. A response rate >20% and reminder emails help to minimise non- response bias.

3.2 Data analysis

Descriptive statistics are employed and presented in tables 1 & 2 below. Cross-tabulations are additionally performed in order to observe Spearman's correlations, since all variables are ordinal, and thus discover any significant relations between key variables in the study with the most significant results in table 3 below. Anova (F) tests are additionally used to discover significant differences between groups in the research.

4 Results

4.1 Sample description and behavioural characteristics

A socio-demographic description shows that respondents are mostly (58%), female, 84% are between 15 to 25 years old, more than a half of them live in urban areas and most (87%) of them are students. In terms of travel preferences and Internet usage, two thirds of the respondents take less than 5 trips in a year and one out of four takes between 6 and 10 trips per year. These respondents book mainly through supplier websites (48%) and Internet travel agencies (28%) and more than 60% spend more than 10 hours a week on the web and define themselves as experts at online searching. The internet technology proficiency of respondents is also underlined by the fact that more than 50% consider themselves expert at social media interaction and think that a "virtual presence" (e.g. a profile on Facebook) is valid and important.

Table 1. Descriptive analysis of UGC behaviour (what, where, when)

What type of content do you post mainly?	never	rarely	occasionally	rather frequently	very frequently
3D content	88%	9%	2%	0%	1%
Podcasts	85%	12%	2%	1%	0%
Videos	53%	31%	13%	2%	1%
Pictures	12%	17%	32%	29%	10%
Comments or texts	8%	13%	30%	33%	15%
Websites I use to share content (Where)					
UGC cat 1(social media sites e.g Facebook)	14%	9%	20%	34%	23%
UGC cat 2 (review sites of travel suppliers)	63%	23%	12%	1%	0%
UGC cat 3 (commercial review sites e.g.Tripadvisor)	69%	17%	11%	3%	0%
UGC cat 4 (picture / video sharing site e.g YouTube)	64%	19%	12%	5%	1%
When do you share/post content?					
during my trip	55%	23%	14%	5%	2%
within 24h of completing the trip	44%	24%	19%	10%	3%
continually during and for several weeks afterwards	48%	19%	18%	11%	3%
within a week of completion of trip	18%	16%	25%	27%	14%

4.2 Online UGC sharing behaviour

Concerning their posting attitudes, some 40% of respondents frequently share text and photos, only 3% post videos frequently whereas other forms of content (e.g. podcast) are posted rarely (see table 1). Respondents are more likely (nearly 60% do it rather/very frequently) to post content on their "own" social media website (UGC category 1, e.g. Facebook, Myspace) than on a media sharing (UGC category 4, e.g. YouTube) or review site (UGC category 2 & 3 e.g. travel supplier site, TripAdvisor).The results show that respondents tend to post content more frequently after than during the trip.

4.3 Motivation to share UGC regarding a trip (WHY)

Table 2. Descriptive analysis of UGC sharing behavior (why)

The reason **why** I post content	totally agree	agree	neither agree nor disagree	disagree	totally disagree
I want to share my experiences with friends	20%	52%	15%	5%	8%
I want to express my satisfaction with trip	15%	52%	17%	8%	8%
I want to promote the experience that I have had	12%	42%	23%	12%	11%
I want to reflect-relive my trip experience	8%	46%	22%	10%	14%
I want to warn others of a bad experience	11%	36%	29%	11%	13%
I want to compare and share	5%	41%	28%	13%	13%
It is more convenient than writing or emailing directly	17%	34%	23%	12%	15%
I want to "display my knowledge " about the trip/destinatiom	3%	23%	33%	23%	18%
I do not know why I post	4%	5%	30%	15%	46%
I seek "status" in being associated with a brand/product	1%	9%	22%	24%	44%
I want to seek reassurance and approval from others	3%	9%	18%	26%	44%
I want to confirm my purchase/spend on my trip	2%	6%	21%	27%	45%
I want to be recognised as an expert	2%	4%	19%	29%	46%
I seek revenge	2%	3%	17%	18%	60%
The reason **why I do NOT** post content					
I do not have time	19%	42%	19%	11%	9%
I do not want to share	5%	20%	23%	28%	25%
I do not think people are interested in reading my comments	6%	24%	27%	26%	18%
I fear that that this infringe on my privacy & security	11%	26%	20%	22%	22%
I feel my "identity" would be jepoardised/stolen	6%	18%	21%	29%	27%
I would want to keep the trip/destination a secret	6%	16%	20%	26%	32%
I do not have the confidence to post	2%	12%	16%	29%	42%
I fear retribution if I post	1%	7%	20%	25%	47%

The results also reveal (table 2) that most respondents "totally agree/agree" to post content to "share experiences with friends" (72%), "express their satisfaction with trip" (67%), "promote the experience" (54%) and "reflect-relive experience" (54%) but also because it is more convenient than writing e-mail (51%). They do not want to be recognized as experts (only 6% totally agree/agree), neither do they "seek revenge" (5%), for "reassurance" or "approval from others" (12%) or "confirmation for their purchase/spend on their trips" (8%). They do not seem to seek "status" in being associated with a brand/product (10%) and they largely disagree with "not knowing why they post" (9%) i.e. they mostly "know". Reasons why they do NOT post are mainly because they have no time (61%) and, to a minor extent, due to privacy and security reasons (37%).

Females demonstrate a significant higher motivation "to express their satisfaction" than males (Anova: F=4.24, p=3.8%), whereas males tend to post content for functional/purposive reasons as they want to be recognized somewhat more as experts than females (Anova: F=3.0, p=8%).

Table 3. Most Significant Spearman correlations between motivation to post (WHY) and UGC sites (WHERE)

Spearman Correlation		
UGC category 1 [Posting on social media websites such as facebook]	Value	Sig.
I want to reflect-relive my trip experience	.28	***
I want to compare and share	.26	***
I want to express my satisfaction with the trip	.24	***
I want to promote the experience that I have had	.23	***
I want to "display my knowledge " about the trip/destinatiom	.23	***
It is more convenient than writing or emailing directly	.22	***
I want to share my experiences with friends and like-minded people	.19	***
UGC category 2 [Posting on the review sites of destinations/ airlines/ travel suppliers]		
I want to warn others of a bad experience	.19	***
I want to promote the experience that I have had	.16	**
UGC category 3 [Posting on commercial travel review sites such as TripAdvisor]		
I want to warn others of a bad experience	.24	***
UGC category 4 [Posting on picture/ video sharing websites such as YouTube]		
I want to promote the experience that I have had	.16	**

'**' p<0.001, '***' p<0.0001

4.4 Correlation analysis

Motivational variables have highly significant correlations with posting on all 4 UCG sites examined in this study. "I want to share and compare" and "I want to promote the experience that I have had" are motivations which are shared by all the 4 categories of UGC websites researched in this study. It is clear, in table 3, that those posting on UCG category 1 (social media websites such as facebook) have the strongest motivation to extend and share the travel experience with "I want to reflect/relive my experience", "I want to compare and share" and "I want to compare and share" the most significant responses.

By contrast, the respondents motivation to post on UGC category 2 (the travel/supplier) and UGC category 3 (commercial review sites) reveal "the warning others of bad experiences," with the most significant correlation. Finally, respondents motivation to post on UGC category 4 (picture or video sharing websites) focuses on the convenience of promoting and reliving experiences, with "promoting the experience that I have had" being the most significant correlation.

5 Discussion and Conclusions

Potentially, in terms of timing, there is scope to extend the actual service experience for some time after consumption, particularly within the travel sector, with sharing of content continuing over the weeks after a trip. Additionally, sharing of experiences online at post purchase stage also has an impact at pre-purchase stage for other consumers. Not only can positive content extend the affirmative effects of a trip but also, individually and collectively, heavily influence future consumers. This impact will increase as consumers spend more time on user generated (social) content sites (here characterized as UGC category 1) and less on other more commercial sites (e.g. UGC category 2, 3). It is clear that there are different drivers that motivate sharing of experiences on their social media sites to those on the other categories of UGC. The motivations expressed (for commercial sites) are more explicit and functional in terms of "warning, comparing & sharing, promoting and expressing satisfaction" perhaps exhibiting characteristics that Hennig-Thurau et al. (2004) might describe as consumption or focus-related utility. This may be because these more blatantly commercial sites limit the scope of feedback (via scoring/ranking, text limitation, censoring) and consumers conform to the norms of accepted practice there.

On social media sites (i.e. UGC category 1, Facebook, Bebo, Myspace) a larger range of significant motivations which are mostly functional and hedonic dominate. Hennig-Thurau et al. (2004) might characterize them as approval and/or homeostase utility, reflecting in part the nature of these "social" media websites, where more intimate expressions of feelings are shared, social positions are already established, groups of "friends" are already connected and where sharing is limited to those permitted into a closer inner group based on some form of reciprocity. This "source attractiveness" (Gatignon & Robertson, 1986) is more clearly displayed on social media sites and can enhance the influence of communication sources, particularly in contexts where "benefits" between members of the group are expected to be exchanged/shared.

6 Recommendations

For marketers, recommendations may be made in the context of promoting post-purchase behaviour e.g. by encouraging customers to engage in   trustworthy online word of mouth (WOM) systems which may help both their potential customers reduce the perceived risk of purchase and extend the positive purchase experience for recent customers. It is proposed that a direct appeal to the "social utility" associated with positive WOM from other consumers, who already have real experience related to the product or service, may be a valuable marketing tactic. Specifically, the timing, location of sharing content and the type of content shared could be actively promoted by marketers. As most of the young travelers in our study share content within weeks, then encouraging, facilitating and reminding customers within that time frame would be expedient. Dependent on the type of UGC that is "worth" eliciting (deeper content that is both functional and hedonic versus quick scoring/ranking which is mostly functional) marketers should promote sharing on specific sites (e.g. Facebook for the deeper,social content and TripAdvisor for quick scoring) and may consider providing direct links to these sites in their post purchase/follow up activities and make direct appeals to customers based on identifiable motivations. In terms of type of content preferred for their social media website (text, pictures, video etc.,) facilitating content generation, (e.g. narrative discussion, picture taking or video-logging which may be self-managed or directed), throughout consumption (e.g. via competitions, incentives, providing photo opportunities/settings) would at least ensure that the preferred content format is generated for post purchase sharing. Furthermore, this volume of aggregated user content could then be integrated into a more holistic view of the trip, not only for future consumers at pre-purchase stage, but also would form valuable insights to consumer and markets for travel related companies.

7 Limitations and future research

Though this research is insightful, as a purposive sample it is therefore subject to selection bias and limited to a population of young travelers which, although perhaps representative somewhat of social media users, may not be representative of the entire traveler population. Additionally, further examination and analysis of this data set is still to be completed and qualitative work instigated that will examine and probe further the factors underlying sharing content online, e.g. perceived risk, characteristics of social media expertise etc., and within a wider demographic context (e.g. all age groups, extended geographic reach etc).In a research area where established accepted empirical models and frameworks are just emerging, this field of investigation is a challenge. However, in the context of travel where there continues to be a growth in online consumption, and given the relentless growth and influence of online social networks, both the pragmatic implications and wider contexts merit further investigation.

References

Banerjee, A.V. (1992). A Simple Model of Herd Behavior, The Quarterly *Journal of Economics,* 107(3) (Aug), 797-817

Bansal, H.S. & Voyer, P.A. (2000). Word-of-mouth processes within a services purchase decision context. *Journal of Service Research*, 3(2), 166-177.

Brown, J.J. & Reingen, P.H. (2001). Social ties and word-of-mouth referral behavior. *Journal of Consumer Research,* 14(3), 350-362. [Retrieved September 24, 2009 from Ebsco database].

Dellarocas, C. (2003). The digitalization of word of mouth: promise and challenges of online feedback mechanisms. *Management Science*, 49(10), 1407-1424.

Edwards, S. (2006). From the guest editor: Special issue on electronic word-of-mouth and its relationship with advertising, marketing and communication. *Journal of Interactive Advertising*, 6(2), 1-2. [Retrieved April 4, 2009 from Ebsco database.]

Farquhar, J. & Rowley, J. (2006). Relationships and online consumer communities, *Business Process Management Journal,* 12(2), 162-177.

Fernback, J. (2007). Beyond the diluted community concept: a symbolic interactionist perspective on online social relations, *New Media & Society,* 9(1), 49-69. [Retrieved April 4, 2007 from Sage Communication Studies database]

Fou, A. (2008). WOM: Just Don't Do It. Adweek, 49(3), 13.

Gatignon, H. &Robertson, T.S. (1986) An exchange theory model of interpersonal communication, *Advances in Consumer Research,* 13(1), 534-538.

Gelb, B. D., & Sundaram, S. (2002). Adapting to "word of mouse." *Business Horizons*, 45(4), 15-20.

Goldsmith, R. E. & Horowitz, D. (2006). Measuring motivations for online opinion seeking, *Journal of Interactive Advertising,* (Spring), 6(2), 1-16.

Haythornthwaite, C. (2002). Strong, weak and latent ties and the impact of new media, The Information Society, 18, 385-401.

Hennig-Thurau, T., Gwinner, K.P., Walsh, G. & Gremler, D.D. (2004). Electronic word-of-mouth via consumer opinion platforms: what motivates consumers to articulate themselves on the internet? *Journal of Interactive Marketing*, 18(1), 38-52.

Hodkinson, P. (2007). Interactive Online Journals and Individualization. New Media Society, 9(4), 625-650.

IAB (2008). IAB Platform Status Report:User Generated Content, Social Media,and Advertising — An Overview April 2008.[Retrieved 15th December, 2008 from http://www.iab.net]

Internet World Stats (2009). Internet World Stats- Internet Usage, population and Statistics. [Retrieved 30th June , 2009 from http: www.internetworldstats.com/stats.htm]

Pitta, D.A. & Fowler, D. (2005). Internet community forums: an untapped resource for consumer marketers. *Journal of Consumer Marketing*, 22(5), 265-374.

Rimé, B. Mesquita, B. Philippot ,P. & Boca, S. (1991). Beyond the emotional event: Six studies on the social sharing of emotion, Cognition and Emotion 5, 435–465

Sebor, J. (2007). Mercurial Marketing, *Customer Relationship Management*, 02/2007 [Retrieved February 23, 2007 from Ebsco database]

Söderlund, M., & Rosengren, S. (2004). Dismantling positive effect and its effects on customer satisfaction: An empirical examination of customer joy in a service encounter, *Journal of Consumer Satisfaction, Dissatisfaction and Complaining Behavior*, 17, 27-35.

Söderlund, M. & Rosengren, S. (2007). Receiving Word-of-mouth from the Service Customer: An Emotion-based Effectiveness Assessment, *Journal of Retailing & Consumer Services,* 14(2), 123-132

Solomon, M.R. (2006). Consumer Behavior, 7th edition. Pearson Prentice Hall, Upper Saddle River, NJ, USA

Soukup, C. (2006). Computer-mediated communication as a virtual third place: building Oldenburg's great good places on the world wide web. *New Media & Society*, 8(3), 421-440.

Sweeney, J.C., Hausknecht, D., & Soutar, G.N. (2000). Measuring cognitive dissonance: A multidimensional scale, *Psychology and Marketing*, 17(5), 369-386.

TNS, (2007). Making the Case for a Social Media Strategy, [Retrieved October25[th], 2008 formhttp://www.nedma.com/pdfs/]

Trusov, M & Bucklin, R.E. & Pauwels, K. (2008). Determining influential users in internet social networks, working paper, Robert H Smith School of Business, University of Maryland.

Vilpponen, A., Winter, S. & Sundqvist, S. (2006). Electronic word-of-mouth in online environments: exploring referral network structure and adoption behavior, *Journal of Interactive Advertising*, 6(2), 71-86.

Acknowledgement

The authors would like to thank the University of Applied Sciences of Western Switzerland (HES-SO) for financing this research

ICT and its Role in Sustainable Tourism Development

Alisha Ali[a]
Andrew J. Frew[b]

[a]Sheffield Business School
Sheffield Hallam University, UK
Alisha.Ali@shu.ac.uk

[b]School of Business, Enterprise and Management
Queen Margaret University, UK
afrew@qmu.ac.uk

Abstract

The paper discusses an investigative study into the uses and applications of information and communication technology for sustainable tourism development. It develops the proposition that use of such technologies can be a practical approach which destinations may use to mitigate some of tourism's negative impacts. Adopting a destination-focused perspective and through the undertaking of a worldwide study, this research examined how ICT can be used in the management of sustainable tourism. It presents an array of ICT-based tools/applications for use by destination managers and discusses the opportunities in destination management for applying ICT to Sustainable Tourism Development.

Keywords: computer-mediated sustainability, eTourism, ICT, sustainable tourism

1 Introduction

Tourism, like any economic activity, has arguably produced detrimental environmental and socio-cultural impacts, some of which may be irreversible. Balancing economic growth and protection of the environment is a challenge which tourism professionals continue to grapple with. The increasing threat of climate change for the tourism industry will no doubt intensify these already present problems. Taken collectively, the tourism industry has responded to these challenges by applying the concept of sustainable development to tourism policy and planning i.e. Sustainable Tourism Development (Choi & Sirakaya, 2006). This research proposes that sustainable tourism development (STD) can become an effective concept in destination management through the application of ICT. STD is a positive, comprehensive and integrated approach to tourism development, which involves resource management and working together with stakeholders for the long-term viability and quality of the social, economic and environmental resources (Miller & Twining-Ward, 2005). Attempts have been made to develop destinations in a sustainable fashion by using indicators, monitoring, eco-labelling, codes of conduct, educating the tourist and other best practices. However, many of these approaches have been documented as having a "lack of quality, technical content, reliability, maturity, equity and effectiveness" (van der Duim & van Marwijk, 2006, p. 449).

Most of the research on STD has focused on theorising and policy formulation with challenges still existing on finding viable ways of translating this theory into practical actions for tourism professionals (J. Swarbrooke, personal communication, October 1, 2008). Given the existing difficulties with the current approaches and tools used for STD, this paper therefore introduces the proposition that STD can become an effective concept in overall destination management through the application of information and communication technology (STD$_i$). For ease of reference within this paper, the term STD$_i$ will be used to denote the application of ICT to sustainable tourism development.

2 Background

A literature search revealed that opportunities do exist for STD$_i$. These are information management, tourist satisfaction, interpretation, enabling partnerships, community participation and energy consumption and each will be discussed subsequently. It was observed by Fuchs & Höpken (2005) that there is only weak use of information for decision making and the potential for ICT in supporting tourism managerial decision making is largely unexplored and unexploited. At the heart of STD lies the process of decision-making which is focused on the best allocation of resources in a limited period of time that satisfies all stakeholders involved. If a destination manager has sound methods of monitoring and analysing environmental data (El-Gayar & Fritz, 2006), the routes tourists use, the frequency of use and timings and how tourists account for time, space and place (Lew & McKercher, 2005), they can better support planning to ensure tourism is more sustainable for destinations. The literature reveals several key ICT-based tools/applications that can be used for *information management*; Computer Simulation, Destination Management Systems (DMS), Economic Impact Analysis Software, Environment Management Information Systems (EMIS), Geographical Information Systems (GIS), Global Positioning System (GPS), Tourism Information System (TIS) and Information Management of Weather, Climate and Ocean Changes. *Tourist satisfaction* is another opportunity for STD$_i$. The United Nations World Tourism Organisation (2004) identified tourism satisfaction as a baseline issue for STD. One of the most important determining elements of satisfaction is receiving accurate and comprehensive tourist information (Buhalis & O'Connor, 2006). Some indicative ICT-based tools/applications which can be used for fulfilling tourist satisfaction include; DMS, Location Based Services (LBS) and Intelligent Transport Systems (ITS). *Interpretation* too plays an important role in STD (Moscardo, 1998). Improving the visitor experience, knowledge, understanding and helping with the protection and conservation of places and cultures have been identified as the main functions of interpretation with regards to achieving STD (Moscardo & Walker, 2006). One ICT-based tool/application which can aid in interpretation is LBS which can be used at the destination to push messages to tourists to create awareness and familiarise them with the culture and customs of a destination. Involving different stakeholders in tourism planning is now being seen as an essential (Bramwell & Lane, 2000; Tourism Sustainability Group, 2007) since tourism is heavily dependent on *effective partnerships* (Buhalis & O'Connor, 2006) which are linked to the sustainability of tourism (Milne & Ateljevic, 2001). *Community participation* has been indentified as a critical issue for STD (Hardy & Beeton, 2001). There has been a lot of discussion that tourism should reap benefits for the local community but there has been limited means of explaining how this can be accomplished (Din, 1996). Mowforth & Munt (1998) observed that community involvement in tourism planning and decision making can be important for allowing the host population more control in tourism development decisions. Involving the local community would also lead to increased environmental awareness and maximise local economic benefits (Milne, 1987). Some indicative ICT-based tools/applications which can be used in support of community participation include; Community Informatics (CI), GIS and Computer Simulation. *Energy usage* has become a major concern for tourism especially with global warming and climate change. The tourism industry requires large amounts of energy for transportation to, from and at the destination, as well as providing the facilities and services required at the destination (Becken, 2002). From a global point of view, transport is the most relevant sector in terms of the environmental sustainability of tourism, accounting for an estimated 75%–90% of all greenhouse gas emissions caused by tourism (Gössling, 2002; Ceron & Dubois, 2003). Managing the uses and impacts of energy is beyond a destination manager's control (Kelly & Williams, 2007), however, there are still some ICT-based tools that they can adopt to enhance their destinations such as Virtual Tourism, ITS and Carbon Calculators. The use of ICT in tourism is not new of course; rather the tourism industry has been influenced by ICT for the past thirty years (European Commission, 2006). It continues to be one of the greatest influences fuelling dramatic changes within the tourism industry (Gratzer et al., 2004) and it does possess the potential to mitigate tourism's negative impacts at the destination level (Liburd, 2005). Mention has been made of the use of STD_i (Gilbert et al., 1998) however; there has been little research on the applications for *destination managers*.

3 Purpose

The motivation for this current research stems from the realisation that developing research in the ICT and STD domain can be invaluable for destinations as they strive to become more holistically sustainable. The main aim of this research was to investigate the uses of information and communication technology (ICT)-based tools/applications in destination management in support of STD. The populations deemed relevant for investigation in this study were Destination Management Organisations (DMOs) and eTourism experts.

4 Research Approach

An interpretivist perspective was considered the most appropriate to this research. The relative novelty of STD_i as a research field and exploratory nature of this study aligns to a more flexible and open research design rather than one that was highly structured and rigid. An interpretive stance would allow elicitation of data that was not constrained by fixed analytical categories and allow the researcher to visit and re-visit the linkages between the data and the theory and explore the respondents' viewpoints on STD_i. Primary research was conducted in two complementary phases, online questionnaires and semi-structured interviews. The first phase involved administering online questionnaires to destination managers and to eTourism experts with a separate questionnaire being customised for each distinct population. The responses to the questionnaires provided the foundation for the type of questions to be asked in the interviews and served as a means of adding validity and reliability to the interview questions. It was also felt that combining these methods would improve the confidence of the findings and enhance the generalisations of the results (Bryman & Bell, 2007). These questionnaires were administered during the period of July-October 2008 with the interviews taking place December 2008- February 2009. For each of the populations being surveyed, a database was obtained that was agreed to be representative of them. From the 434, DMOs surveyed, 37 valid responses were received, yielding a response rate of 9%. Of the 202, eTourism experts, 23 responses were received producing a response rate of 11%. This response rate was considered acceptable for the nature and scope of this study. Sequential sampling was used to identify participants for the semi-structured interviews. This sampling approach was felt to be most appropriate for this phase because the selected interviewees would possess greater knowledge about the uses of ICT for STD and make a valuable input into accomplishing the aims and objectives of this work. Cooper & Schlinder (2003) commented that this approach is best matched to exploratory research and when the researcher wants to discriminate the type of respondents that are required. Thirteen experts' interviews were conducted and this number was based on reaching a saturation point.

5 Results and Discussion

This section presents the results of the questionnaires and the interviews conducted as well as provides an interpretation of these results. Just under half of these DMOs (47%) were located in Europe, whilst one fifth (19%) were located in Australia and 16% in North America. The remaining DMOs were located in Africa (8%), Asia (5%) and South America (5%). Of the 23 eTourism experts surveyed, almost half (48%) were located in Europe. About one-fifth (17%) was located in Australia whilst 13% was each situated in North America and Asia and the remaining were based in South America. The interviewed experts were a subset of these two groups. Of the thirty-seven DMOs that responded with valid data, most (20%) were local DMOs whilst the least were continental DMOs (5%) and coastal DMO (5%) as seen in Figure 1.

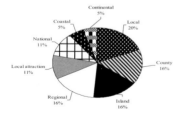

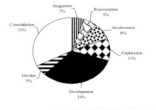

Fig. 1. Distribution of the Types of DMOs Surveyed

Fig. 2. Stage of Tourism Development

DMOs were asked to identify their destination's stage in the tourism development process. Responses provided for this question were based on the classifications identified in Butler's (1980) Tourism Area Life Cycle of a Destination. This has been widely discussed in the literature (see Butler, 2006) and destination managers were familiar with using this terminology. One-third was developing tourism destinations (33%) and one-third was in the consolidation stage (33%) as depicted in Figure 2. All respondents surveyed identified that ICT can be used for STD. Despite over two-thirds of eTourism experts attributing that ICT can be used for sustainable tourism, in actuality, only 4% of eTourism experts stated that ICT is currently being used to a great extent for sustainable tourism. Just under half (44%) identified that ICT is being somewhat used for sustainable tourism. None of these eTourism experts stated that ICT is being used universally by DMOs for sustainable tourism. Comparing these results to the DMOs surveyed, almost half (46%) of DMOs indicated that ICT was used somewhat whilst a little over a quarter (27%) stated that it was used very little. Five percent of DMOs identified that ICT was used universally for STD whilst 11% stated it was not used at all. Table 1 indicates identified specific uses of ICT for sustainable tourism development.

The *stage* of tourism development was seen as being important in the selection of these ICT-based tools/applications. Despite no statistically significant relationship existing between the stage of tourism development and ICT usage for sustainable tourism, the general consensus from the experts interviewed was that ICT would be used more at the development and consolidation stage for sustainable tourism development. This was confirmed with the results of the destination managers' survey. Even though it would have been better for destinations to use ICT during the early stages, it was during the development and/or consolidation stages where difficulties due to improper tourism planning and over-development were realised (Martin & Uysal, 1990). This provided greater justification for use in the earlier phases as tourism's negative impacts becomes more advanced in the later stages of a destinations' tourism development. Moreover, in the early stages of development, destinations many have problems in adopting ICT for sustainable tourism due to funding. Their priority would be on marketing, promotion and getting the destination known rather than on STD. An example of such a destination is Aruba which is a well established destination but only recently has begun to develop a sustainable tourism plan since they have now realised the problems of over-development. If destinations at the beginning of their tourism development plan and grow their industry in a sustainable manner then they can prevent many of the problems which occur later on in the destination's life cycle (Manning & Dougherty, 2000). ICT can help in this process. From the responses, one group felt that there would be wider usage the more local the level of the DMO. This is demonstrated from the general usage of ICT-based tools/applications by the local level DMOs surveyed. Taking the above into consideration, it was concluded that DMOs will use these ICT-based tools/applications based on the sustainability goals of their destinations. So if both a local attraction DMO and a Continental Tourism Organisation were experiencing problems of selecting appropriate areas for tourism development they would both consider the use of a GIS.

Table 1. Uses of ICT-based Tools/Applications for Sustainable Tourism

Opportunity	Sustainability Goal	ICT- based tools/applications
Information Management	Inventory of tourism resources	GIS
	Identifying suitable locations for tourism development	CS ,GIS
	Identifying damaged areas at the destination	GIS
	Managing the destination's resources	DMS, EMIS, GIS, LBS
	Managing sites and attractions	GIS, LBS, TIS, VT
	Zoning	EMIS
	Measuring changes in indicators	GIS, CS
	Identifying indicators	GIS, CS
	Measuring indicators	CS GIS
	Data integration from a variety of sources	DMS, EMIS, GIS
	Determining the economic impact of tourism	EIAS
	Determining climate, weather and ocean change	WCOCFS
	Monitoring emissions	CC, EMIS
	Monitoring solid waste	EMIS
	Tourist statistics	TIS
Energy Consumption	Reducing energy usage at the destination	CC, EMIS, ITS, LBS, VT
	Marketing the destination	DMS, GIS, LBS, VT
	Reduce print material	CC, DMS, GPS, LBS, VT
Interpretation	Tourist education	CI, DMS, LBS, VT
	Influencing tourist behaviour	CC CI, DMS, LBS, VT
	Preserving culture and heritage of the destination	CI, LBS, VT
Community Participation	Involving the community in the tourism process	CI, CS, GIS
	Providing information to the local community	CS, DMS, GIS, VT
Tourist Satisfaction	Providing safety and security information to tourists	DMS, GPS, LBS, ITS
Enabling Partnership	Collaboration with local businesses at the destination	DMS
Energy Consumption Information Management	Visitor management	EMIS, GIS
	Managing tourist flows	GIS, LBS, TIS, VT
	Tracking tourist movements	CS, GIS, GPS
Energy Consumption Tourist Satisfaction	Identifying market segments	DMS,GIS, LBS, VT
Community Participation Information Management	Producing realistic images of what proposed developments would look like	CS, GIS
	Scenario testing and modelling	CS, GIS

Opportunity	Sustainability Goal	ICT- based tools/applications
Interpretation Tourist Satisfaction	Engaging with the tourists	DMS, GPS, LBS, ITS, VT
	Sensitising tourists about the destination	CI, DMS, LBS, VT
Information Management Interpretation Tourist Satisfaction	Profiling visitors	GIS, GPS, VT
Energy Consumption Interpretation Tourist Satisfaction	Location identification for tourists	GIS, GPS, LBS
Energy Consumption Information Management Tourist Satisfaction	Providing real time transport information	ITS
	Planning transport routes for optimising protection of the natural environment and reducing tourist traffic in sensitive areas	CS, GIS, GPS, LBS, ITS
Energy Consumption Information Management Tourist Satisfaction Interpretation	Providing information to the tourists	DMS, GPS, LBS, ITS, VT

CC	Carbon Calculator	GPS	Global Positioning System
CI	Community Informatics	ITS	Intelligent Transport System
CS	Computer Simulation	LBS	Location Based Services
DMS	Destination Management System	TIS	Tourism Information System
EIAS	Economic Impact Analysis Software	VT	Virtual Tourism
EMIS	Environment Management Information System	WCOCFS	Weather, Climate and Ocean Change Forecasting Software

Table 2. Ranking of ICT-based Tools/Applications for Sustainable Tourism

DMO Ranking	eTourism Ranking	ICT-based tools/applications
1	5	Destination management system
2	7	Intelligent transport system
3	4	Tourism information system
4	6	Environment management information system
5	3	Location based services
6	2	Global positioning system
7	1	Geographical information system
8	11	Community informatics
9	10	Economic impact analysis software
10	13	Carbon calculators
11	9	Virtual tourism
12	8	Weather, climate and ocean change forecasting software
13	12	Computer simulation

Both destination managers and eTourism experts were asked to rank the ICT-based tools/applications considering their level of importance to STD as illustrated in Table 2. It is interesting to note that the tools destination managers considered as being important for them were not the same as those of the eTourism experts. In the literature it is argued that despite the growth in tourism research there has been poor dissemination and usage by tourism businesses (Cooper, Ruhanen, & Craig-Smith, 2004). This may be attributed to the fact that there are inadequate linkages between industry and academia (Stamboulis & Skayannis, 2003) with tourism businesses viewing this research as being difficult to access and irrelevant to their needs (Ruhanen, 2008). Tourism stakeholders such as DMOs view such research as being very complex and highly advanced when rather they are searching for uncomplicated techniques and easily applied solutions (Xiao, 2006). From the list presented to respondents in the survey, no additional tools/applications were identified. It was thus concluded that the initial list of ICT-based tools/applications presented was comprehensive. Destination managers and eTourism experts were asked to rank the areas where they felt ICT would be most useful for STD based on the findings in the literature. Both groups ranked information management as the most important area of STD_i as evidenced in Table 3.

Table 3. Ranking of Areas ICT would be Most Useful

Area	DMO Ranking	eTourism expert Ranking
Information management	1	1
Tourist satisfaction	2	4
Transportation	3	2
Sustainable consumption	4	7
Enabling partnership	5	6
Interpretation	6	8
Energy consumption	7	5
Community participation	8	3

Destination managers recognised tourist satisfaction as the second area where ICT-based tools/applications can be most useful. Transport was ranked as third important as interest in this area has increased due to the climate change agenda. eTourism experts identified transportation as the second area where ICT would be most useful for STD. In contrast to the destination managers, eTourism experts identified community participation as the third most useful are. Destination managers ranked this as their area of least importance. eTourism experts may have ranked this area highly because in the literature there has been much discussion on involving community in the tourism development process and the necessity of accomplishing this. However in reality this is rarely happening and destinations may have more other concerns rather that getting the community involved in the tourism planning process. All respondents identified a wide array of barriers and critical success factors for the uptake of STD_i, some of which were similar. Instead of separating these factors, the researchers will address them as factors influencing the uptake of ICT for sustainable tourism. All parties surveyed identified cost as an important factor. They felt that if DMOs did not have the finances to support the implementation of these tools then there would be little or no use of ICT (Nodder, Mason, Ateljevic, & Milne, 2003) for STD. DMOs need to be fully aware of the value derived from implementation as well as understand if these ICT-based tools/applications were fit for purpose in meeting the

STD objectives of destinations. It might be feared that in times of economic uncertainty that the investment in tools/mechanisms needed for promoting and maintaining the sustainability of the tourism industry will be limited. Bramwell & Lane (2009) commented that cost savings to be realised from such investment might be more appealing to organisations during times of economic recession. It was also felt that government support was important in enhancing uptake.

Another influencing factor identified was the lack of knowledge and understanding of these ICT-based tools/applications and how it can help (Yuan, Gretzel, & Fesenmaier, 2006) with managing the sustainability of their destination. Not only did DMOs need to understand the technology but the it was felt that they should have someone on staff who needed to have expertise in these tools and how to use them for the best purposes of the destination. Other concerns expressed were that many destination managers have a limited view of what STD entails. They saw these destination managers as only viewing STD from a natural environment viewpoint, they were uncertain how to apply the principles to practice (Ruhanen, 2008) and were unsure whose responsibility the management of STD was at the destination level. Stakeholder buy-in and support for using these tools by DMOs was also recognized as an influencing factor. If DMOs are supportive of STD_i, they will become champions and find the necessary funding to implement the tools. From the results and the literature, it was seen that ICT can be used to create partnerships for managing STD. The creation of partnerships and co-operation was also seen as being important (Milne & Altejevic, 2001; Buhalis & O'Connor, 2006) in the implementation of these tools. Some of these tools have multiple applications and can benefit more than one stakeholder therefore forming partnerships would be integral for its success. Popularity of these ICT-based tools/applications was seen to be another influencing factor. If these tools were being used by other DMOs then there would be greater uptake since the general feeling amongst DMOs is that they must keep up with the technology that the other DMOs are using. Employee resistance was also important to the uptake of ICT for STD. It was felt that lack of training on the use of these tools would prevent them from being used accurately and might lead to staff resistance (Nodder et al., 2003). Therefore these tools needed to be user-friendly. Other factors influencing the uptake of STDi are lack of data at the destination to feed into the models, lack of confidence by destinations to engage in use of these ICT-based tools/applications, consumer demanding the use of technology (Buhalis & O'Connor, 2006), these tools needs to target the destination's problem, rapid changes in technology making the existing technology obsolete, accurate interpretation of data, producing measurable outputs which were easily interpreted and the generation of timely results. Taking these factors into consideration as well as the factors that would influence destination managers' selection of these ICT-based tools/applications, from the researchers' understanding it was felt that the sustainability goal of the destination would outweigh these influencing factors in the use of ICT for sustainable tourism. Once destination managers understand that ICT can help alleviate some of their sustainability concerns and the way in which this can be accomplished then they would argue for greater use of the technology.

Just under half (45%) of DMOs indicated that ICT will be very important in the future management of STD whilst 41% indicated that it would be important. Eight percent of DMOs felt it would be moderately important, 3% felt it would be of little importance whilst 3% felt it would be unimportant. Respondents were asked how they envisage destinations using these ICT-based tools/applications if they became readily available. The general feeling was that if ICT was used properly it can offer great tools for STD. It will provide DMOs with the information required to make informed decisions through improved information sharing for planning a suitable course of action for managing STD. These ICT-based tools/applications would aid in improving a destination manager's ability to search and measure the dispersion of information related to STD. These tools also aid in developing platforms around communities sharing their interests related to tourism development. It helps DMOs participate in existing social networks and build relationships by ensuring stakeholders at the destination can contribute and listen to the others on sustainable tourism-related matters. Community and stakeholder involvement is important in a destination's approach to implementing the principles of sustainable tourism since tourism is a diverse and fragmented sector. Through the use of ICT, DMOs can create and enhance networks (Milne & Ateljevic, 2001) as well as provide a means of enabling destination stakeholders in becoming more efficient in their communication strategies and support greater cooperation in the delivery of the tourism products and services (Buhalis & O'Connor, 2006). DMOs also visualised ICT being used for increased marketing, better management of the destination, waste management, energy monitoring, information comparison and integration and fostering better decision–making. Using ICT for STD will also lead to better communication with the visitor and tourism businesses regarding sustainable business management and enhanced monitoring of STD measures. It will make it easier to understand the responsibility to diversified stakeholders and make them more aware of what to do and what not to do.

6 Conclusion and Areas for Future Research

Significant pressures are being placed on destinations today to account for the environment in their business operations (Moore & Bordeleau, 2001). Destinations need to adopt ICT and become technology experts, eco-efficient and environmentally innovative in their operations with reference to STD. Not doing this may lead to economic and environmental deterioration of destinations. A contribution to knowledge was made through the identification of a collection of ICT-based tools/applications and their respective uses in destination management as depicted in Table 1. This table showed that ICT can have wide-ranging uses for STD as well as it can be used to progress the already existing approaches for STD such as visitor management techniques and indicator development. In the literature, there has been published research on these ICT-based tools/applications and their uses but they have not been specifically looked at from the overall goal of sustainable tourism. They have been looked at from specific applications such as the use of Geographical Information System for tracking tourist movements (Lau & McKercher, 2007) and marketing (Elliott-White & Finn, 1998) or from specific case studies such as the use of Computer Simulation in managing Acadia National Park (Manning, 2005). Therefore this work helps to draw some perspective on the ICT-STD domain. It serves as a reference point where both academics and industry can identify and build on the uses of these ICT-based tools/applications tools in destinations management.

This research has practical applications for industry and tourism stakeholders. Destination managers can identify their problems associated with tourism and select the ICT-based tools/applications can be best use for helping them. A starting point for advancing this research would be to use the results presented to determine the suitability, applicability and feasibility of these ICT-based tools/applications for destination managers. Additional channels such as the undertaking targeted studies within destination will be employed in order to boost response rates for progressing this research. The results of this work will be used for refinement of Table 1. Future research could look at each of these ICT-based tools/application in–depth and their specific uses for STD. Climate change and transport are currently "hot" topics and areas where ICT can have a valuable contribution to lessening tourism negative impacts but they were largely under-researched in the tourism literature. Added to these, other potential areas of research for STD$_i$ are sustainable production, energy management, water availability and consumption, and wastewater management. The research also sought to look at the use and applications of ICT from the perspective of DMOs and a further area of research would be to look at the application of ICT from the perspective of the individual tourism businesses at the destination. Consumer perspectives and their motivations to visit a destination engaging with technology for making the destination more sustainable could profitably be considered. It might also be worthwhile to explore how consumers make use of the Internet in promotion of the principles for STD. Additionally, this work specifically focused on the use of ICT. It did not focus on the use of clean technology in the STD process. Other types of technology such as wind power, geothermal, small scale hydro, bio energy and solar cells/ solar photovoltaic and its applications to the tourism industry are warranted futher research. Building from this research, a longitudinal study could be developed which focuses on specific destinations which engage in the uptake of ICT for STD and using the theory of innovation diffusion (Rogers, 1983) determine how these innovations are applied. Research could focus on testing destination managers' use of this technology and determining how it works in managing STD and truly assessing their approach in applying ICT for sustainable tourism.

Despite STD and eTourism being core subjects in research, the knowledge transfer to tourism practitioners has been limited (Garrod & Fyall, 1998; Ruhanen, 2008). The hope is that the knowledge presented here will be diffused to industry and they use ICT for the better management of the industry hence curing many of the ills destinations have long suffered. The researchers hope that this work has painted a representative landscape of the current ICT-STD research, laid the foundation for future research efforts to enhance this body of knowledge and the theoretical progression of ICT and sustainable tourism. This research broadens the existing knowledge and understanding of mechanisms for STD of destinations by applying ICT, with the anticipation that the results will be used by destination managers and DMO as part of their strategy in dealing with the sustainability concerns of tourism destinations.

490

References

Becken, S. (2002). Analysing international tourist flows to estimate energy use associated with air travel. *Journal of Sustainable Tourism*, 10(2), 114-131.

Bramwell, B., & Lane, B. (2000). Collaboration and partnerships in tourism planning. In: B. Bramwell & B. Lane (Eds.), *Tourism collaboration and partnerships: politics, practice and sustainability* (pp. 1-19). Clevedon: Channel View Publications.

Bramwell, B., & Lane, B. (2009). Economic cycles, times of change and sustainable tourism. *Journal of Sustainable Tourism*, 17(1), 1-4.

Bryman, A., & Bell, E.(2007). *Business research methods 2nd ed*. Oxford: Oxford University Press.

Buhalis, D., & O'Connor, P. (2006). Information communication technology - revolutionizing tourism. In: D. Buhalis & C. Costa (Eds.), *Tourism management dynamics: trends, management, tools (pp. 196-209)*. Oxford: Elsevier Ltd.

Butler, R. W. (2006). *The tourism area life cycle*. Clevedon: Channel View Publications.

Ceron, J.P., & Dubois, G. (2003). Tourism and sustainable development indicators: The gap between theoretical demands and practical achievements. *Current Issues in Tourism* 6(1), 54-75.

Choi, H., & Sirakaya, E. (2006). Sustainability indicators for managing community tourism. *Tourism Management*, 27(6), 1274-1289.

Cooper, D. R., & Schindler, S. P. (2003). *Business research methods*. New York: McGraw-Hill/Irwin.

Cooper, C., Ruhanen, L., & Craig-Smith, S. (2004). Developing a knowledge management approach to tourism research. Paper presented at *The Tourism State of the Art II Conference*. Glasgow: University of Strathclyde.

Din, H. K. 1996. Tourism development: still in search of a more equitable mode of local involvement. *Progress in Tourism and Hospitality Research*, 2(3&4), 273–281.

El-Gayar, O. F., & Fritz, B. D. (2006). Environmental management information systems (EMIS) for sustainable development: a conceptual overview. *Communications of the Association for Information Systems*, 17, 756-784.

Elliott-White, M., & Finn, M. (1998). Growing in sophistication: the application of geographical information system in post-modern tourism marketing. *Journal of Travel & Tourism Marketing*, 7(1), 65-84.

European Commission. (2006). *A pocketbook of e-business indicators: A portrait of e-business in 10 sectors of the EU economy*. Bonn: eBusiness W@tch.

Fuchs, M., & Höpken, W. (2005). Towards @Destination: a DEA-based decision support framework. In: A.J. Frew (Ed.), *Information and Communication Technologies in Tourism 2005 (pp. 57-66)*. New York: Springer.

Garrod, B., & Fyall, A. (1998). Beyond the rhetoric of sustainable tourism? *Tourism Management*, 19(3), 199-212.

Gilbert, A., Hoa, N., & Binh, V. (1998). A strategic model for using information technology in developing strategic tourism. *Journal of Vietnam Studies*, 1(1), 1-17.

Gössling, S. (2002). Global environmental consequences of tourism. *Global Environmental Change*, 12(4), 283–302.

Gratzer, M., Werthner, H., & Winiwarter, W. (2004). E-business in tourism. *International Journal of Electronic Business*, 2(5), 450-459.

Hardy, L. A., & Beeton, S. (2001). Sustainable tourism or maintainable tourism: managing resources for more than average outcomes. *Journal of Sustainable Tourism*, 9(3), 168-192.

Kelly, J., & Williams, P. W. (2007). Modelling tourism destination energy consumption and greenhouse gas emissions: Whistler, British Columbia, Canada. *Journal of Sustainable Tourism*, 15(1), 67-90.

491

Lau, G., & McKercher, B. (2007). Understanding tourist movements patterns in a destination: A GIS approach. *Tourism and Hospitality Research*, 7 (1), 39-49.

Lew, A., & McKercher, B. (2005). Modeling tourist movements: a local destination analysis. *Annals of Tourism Research*, 33(2), 403-423.

Liburd, L. J. (2005). Sustainable tourism and innovation on mobile tourism services. *Tourism Review International*, 9(2), 107-118.

Manning, R. (2005). The limits of tourism in parks and protected areas: managing carrying capacity in the U.S. National Parks. In C. Ryan, S.J. Page & M. Aicken (Eds.), *Taking tourism to the limits: issues, concepts and managerial perspectives (pp. 129-139).* Oxford: Elsevier Ltd.

Manning, E.W., & Dougherty, T.D. (2000). Planning sustainable tourism destinations. *Tourism Recreation Research*, 25 (2), 3–14.

Martin, S. B., & Uysal, M. (1990). An examination of the relationship between carrying capacity and the tourism lifecycle: Management and policy implications. *The Journal of Environmental Management*, 31(4), 327–333.

Milne, S. (1987). The Cook Islands tourist industry: Ownership and planning. *Pacific Viewpoint* 28(2), 119–38.

Milne, S., & Ateljevic, I. (2001). Tourism, economic development and the global-local nexus: theory embracing complexity. *Tourism Geographies*, 3, (4), 369-393.

Miller, G., & Twining-Ward, L. (2005). *Monitoring for a sustainable tourism transition: the challenge of developing and using indicators.* Wallingford: CABI Publishing.

Moore, M., & Bordeleau, D. (2001). The environmental management information system (EMIS) of the intelligent environmental management system. Available from: http://www.eco-web.com/editorial/00044.html [Accessed May 3 2007].

Moscardo G. (1998). Interpretation and sustainable tourism: functions, examples and principles. *The Journal of Tourism Studies*, 9(1), 2–13.

Moscardo, G., & Walker, K. (2006). The impact of interpretation on passengers of expedition cruises. In R.K. Dowling (Ed.), *Cruise Ship Tourism* (pp. 105-114). London, CABI Publishing.

Mowforth, M., & Munt, I. (1998). *Tourism and sustainability: new tourism in the third world.* London: Routledge.

Nodder, C., Mason, D., Ateljevic, J., & Milne, S. (2003). ICT adoption and use in New Zealand's small and medium tourism enterprises: a cross sectoral perspective. In A.J. Frew, M. Hitz, & P. O'Connor (Eds.), *Information and Communication Technologies in Tourism 2003* (pp. 355-363). New York: Springer.

Rogers, E. M. (1983). *Diffusion of innovations 3rd ed.* London: Collier Macmillan Publishers.

Ruhanen, L. (2008). Progressing the sustainability debate: a knowledge management approach to sustainable tourism planning. *Current Issues in Tourism*, 11(5), 429-455.

Stamboulis, Y., & Skayannis, P. (2003). Innovation strategies and technology for experience-based tourism. *Tourism Management*, 24(1), 35-43.

Tourism Sustainability Group. (2007). *Action for more sustainable European tourism: report of the Tourism Sustainability Group.* Geneva: European Commission.

United Nations World Tourism Organisation. (2004). *Indicators of sustainable development for tourism destinations: a guidebook.* Madrid: United Nations World Tourism Organisation.

van der Duin, R., & van Marwijk, R. (2006). The implementation of an environmental management system for Dutch tour operators: an actor-network perspective. *Journal of Sustainable Tourism*, 14(5), 449-472.

Xiao, H. (2006). Towards a research agenda for knowledge management in tourism. *Tourism and Hospitality Planning & Development*, 3(2), 143–157.

Yuan, Y., Gretzel, U., & Fesenmaier, D. (2006). The role of information technology use in American convention and visitors bureaus. *Tourism Management*, 27(2), 326-341.

Exploratory Study on Contributions of ICTs to Sustainable Tourism Development in Manchester

Kabiru Touray[a]
Timothy Jung[a]

[a]Department of Food and Tourism Management
Manchester Metropolitan University, UK
kalimerok2000@yahoo.com; t.jung@mmu.ac.uk

Abstract

Despite the potential of ICTs and its revolution in the contemporary tourism industry, very little academic research has been carried out on the contribution of ICTs to Sustainable Tourism Development (STD). This study aims to explore various different stakeholders' perception on the contribution of ICTs to sustainable tourism development in Manchester. Semi-structured interviews were conducted with various different stakeholders who are involved in sustainable tourism development in Manchester area. Findings revealed that ICTs can offer platform to facilitate sustainable tourism development and emerging ICTs can be utilized to maximize tourism's positive impacts and minimize negative impacts at tourism destination. The research also identified a number of barriers to the implementation of ICTs in sustainable tourism development. Limitations of the study which should be addressed in future research are discussed and some recommendations for further research are provided.

Keywords: ICTs, Sustainable Tourism Development, Destination Management

1 Introduction

Tourism plays a significant role for world economy (UNWTO, 2008) and similarly, tourism is becoming an increasingly significant sector for destination's economy. In Greater Manchester, tourism sector contributes around £5.6 billion to the local economy and sustaining nearly 80,000 full time jobs (The Manchester Tourist Board, 2009). Despite the potential of tourism to destinations' economy, previous studies in tourism literature revealed that protection and preservation of environments are considered as increasingly important issue by tourists (Holden, 2000) and furthermore tourism growth could be stagnant without addressing the major tourism impacts (Berry and Ladkin, 1997; Swarbrooke, 1999). In this view, WTO (1993) strongly emphasised that tourism must be environmentally sustainable in order to be economically sustainable. The concept of sustainability is an essential approach to tourism development and many attempts have been made in order to plan and develop tourist destinations in more sustainable manner (Miller and Twining-Ward, 2005). Along with sustainability issue, another area which contributes the growth of tourism economy is ICTs. The emergence of ICTs and recent digital technologies revolutionised entire tourism industry (Poon, 1993; O'Connor, 1999; Buhalis; 2003) and, in particular, it has deeply affected destination management, marketing and promotion (Buhalis, 1998; Werthner & Klein, 1999; Buhalis & Licata, 2002;

Schwanen & Kwan, 2008). In addition, it is evident that ICTs have the potential to provide strategic tools to facilitate sustainable tourism development at destination (Buhalis, 1997; Go and Govers, 1999; Buhalis, 2003; Liburd, 2005; Ali and Frew, 2008). However, despite the potential of ICTs and its revolution in relation to sustainability issue in the contemporary tourism industry, very little academic research has been carried out on the strategic contribution of ICTs to sustainable tourism development (Ali and Frew, 2008; Buhalis and Law, 2008). Therefore, the aim of this research is to investigate the perceived role of emerging ICTs in planning and development of sustainable tourism at tourism destination and further evaluate the benefits and implications of ICTs from the perspective of various different stakeholders of Marketing Manchester, Destination Marketing Organisation (DMO) of Greater Manchester.

2 Sustainable Tourism

It is evident that tourism is a significant component of production in many economies (Garcia and Servera, 2003) and tourism has a major effect on the value of production on, and levels of employment in destination areas. Tourism redistributes income between different areas within a national economy. It further provides the opportunity to create employment and income in areas with limited alternative sources. Despite the prevailing perception that economic benefits accrue to tourism destinations, which creates employment opportunities and stimulates the development process in resorts and localities, on the other hand it could be argued that tourism also has a major negative impact upon the physical environment and society in which it takes place (Cooper *et al.* 2006). In practical terms, this raises the challenge for planners of balancing tourism demand and supply and recognising the emerging or future effects of tourism if the concept of sustainable tourism is not considered (Page, 2003).

It has been established that the concept of sustainability in tourism development has resulted from a global speculation of concern with the future impact of economic activity, with growing attention to environment and ecological issues (Simpson, 2001). One of the main consequences of the increasing awareness and significance of sustainable tourism is the fact that tourism growth could no longer be continued at the present rate without mitigating or addressing the major tourism impacts (Berry and Ladkin, 1997). In this context, Butler (1993) suggests that sustainable tourism has been a key concept for the tourism industry and there is a strong consensus that tourism should be sustainable. It has been further argued that the principle of sustainability and sustainable tourism should be central to any programme within the tourism landscape (Bramwell *et al.* 1996). The concept of sustainability was suggested by the World Commission on Environment and Development (WCED, 1987). WCED defined sustainable development practices as those which meet the goals of the present without compromising the ability of future generations to meet their own needs. Sustainable tourism, however, has been described as a form of tourism in which there is greater equity of outcomes for stakeholders in tourism which means not just the developers, tourism industry and the tourist but also the wider community whose destination is being consumed (Hall, 2000).

In spite of economic potential of tourism in destinations economies, tourism also has a major negative impact upon the physical environment and society in which it takes place (Cooper *et al.* 2006) such as sound and noise pollution, crime, overcrowding and congestion (Lumsdon, 2000, p.362). In practical terms, this raises the challenge for planners of balancing tourism demand and supply and recognising the future effects of tourism if the concept of sustainable tourism is not considered (Page, 2003). Whilst the tourism industry becomes more vulnerable to the potential negative impacts of tourism activities, sustainable tourism concept emerged as a desirable outcome of necessary change to current tourism consumption pattern, an essential strategic alternative to the perceived short-term economic growth at the expense of environmental and socio-cultural resources (Simpson, 2001). On the contrary, despite the increasing importance of sustainable tourism, one of the barriers to successful implementation of sustainable tourism practices is lack of adequate understanding of the concept of sustainability. Berry and Ladkin (1997) looked at stakeholders' perception of sustainable tourism and they concluded that some tourism stakeholders do not have clear perception of sustainable tourism or its implementation. Further, Swarbrooke (1999) asserted that if sustainable tourism is to be implemented into workable practices it is imperative for involved stakeholders to know what sustainable tourism is and also they should have the strong intention to take action and develop effective techniques to achieve sustainable tourism.

3 Stakeholders' Involvement in STD

Stakeholder participation as a contributor to sustainable tourism planning is an appropriate framework within which stakeholder driven development activity can occur (Simpson, 2001). In essence, the arguments developed on the planning of tourism in a sustainable manner suggest that sustainable tourism in practical form is about stakeholders (the residents, visitors, the private sector businesses, public sector and agencies) leading to organise, plan and control tourism development in relations to policies in each destination area (Page, 2003). However, Bramwell (1994) described stakeholder participation as the terminology used when all individuals, organisations and groups, whose lives are affected by tourism development, play at least some part in determining the nature of the developmental direction selected. Bramwell and Sharman (1999) noted that stakeholders driven approach can help to avoid conflicts, resulting in policies that are more politically legitimate and improve the coordination of policies by promoting consideration of the wider-ranging effect of tourism. In addition, the significance of stakeholders' participation in sustainable tourism development was stressed by Marien and Pizam (1997) and they mentioned that sustainable tourism can not be successfully implemented without the direct support and involvement of those who are affected by it. Therefore, evaluating a community's sensitivity to tourism development is imperative in planning for sustainable tourism development (Miller and Twining-ward 2005).

Studies on the basis of stakeholder participation as a contributor to sustainable tourism development contended that the mechanism in any strategic planning in any given situation will be strongly influence by the stakeholder values (Hall, 2000). Hall (2000) underlined that tourism strategy development cannot realistically be conducted

496

in isolation manner, it is therefore necessary for planners/DMOs to adopt a holistic approach to tourism as a component of a regional open system. Thus, 'the scope of stakeholder participation' domain measured the degree to which the subject planning process was conducted within a framework which recognised the overall regional business environment as an appropriate setting' (Simpson, 2001). Simpson (2001) highlighted a range of legitimate stakeholder groups to be involved in all stages of tourism planning and development. Figure 1 shows an outline of stakeholder groups in the tourism development process. However, it has been argued that the effectiveness of all stakeholders participation or collaborative process in tourism planning remain questionable and Simpson (2001) asserted that the concept of overall host community participation in the tourism planning process is an idealistic proposition with little chance of effective implementation. Whilst Gilbert (1993) noted the problems related to a lack of industry knowledge to support informed comment, a mistrust of participation by external experts, and inadequacy of access to development funds and tourism industry expertise.

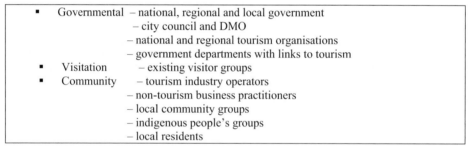

Fig. 1. Stakeholder Groups for Consultation (Simpson, 2001)

4   ICTs and Sustainable Tourism Development

As Swarbrooke (1999) propounded, if DMOs want to achieve sustainable tourism, it is imperative for them to develop some frameworks or tools to achieve goals of sustainable tourism. In order that tourism can continue to be a key sector of regions or destinations economy for the long-term rather than short-term, it is essential that DMOs deliver truly sustainable tourism. However, this cannot be achieved in an isolation manner. In fact, ICTs have been used to develop a range of techniques to facilitate sustainable tourism development including Destination Management System (DMS), and Geographical Information Systems (GISs). Archdale *et al.* (1992) have indicated that DMS can create more efficient internal and external networks, which can have sustainable positive effects on the local economy in achieving competitive advantage. In addition, DMS, as a destination management strategic tool, contributes to the sustainable planning of tourism at destinations and enabling the host community to maximise the positive impacts of tourism by drawing the attention of both visitors and locals to vulnerable ecosystems and resources (Buhalis, 1997). In other words, DMS offers a platform to enhance the economic, ecological and socio-cultural structures of destination areas, for instance, management of tourism demand by supporting the visitor experience before, during, and after the visit (Sheldon,

1993). Similarly, Bahaire and Elliott-white (1999) asserted that GIS is useful instrument for the achievement of sustainable tourism development, for example, auditing environment conditions, examining the sustainability of locations for proposed developments, identifying conflicting interests and modelling relationships. Further, Hasse and Milne (2005) explored how participatory approaches and GIS can be blended to provide framework that can facilitate a better understanding of attitudes toward tourism and enhance participation and stakeholder interaction in tourism planning. Recently, there are growing interests in using ICTs to sustainable tourism development and efforts were made by researchers for the development of approaches or tools in order to manage and develop destinations in a more sustainable manner such as eco-labelling, codes of conducts, monitoring and educating the tourist as having lack of quality, reliability and effectiveness. (Ali and Frew, 2009). Ali and Frew (2008) proposed the ICTs framework for the role of ICTs in sustainable tourism and they identified tourism planning, tourist satisfaction, tourist experience, host community benefits, information management, sustain consumption, partnerships, local participation, location satisfaction, transport, climate change and interpretation as areas in which ICTs can be used to accomplish sustainability. Furthermore, Gretzel (2009) proposed a model of sustainability issues which directly supported by ICTs. Within this model, the concept of Green IT, which supports planning, marketing, development, operation, monitoring and interpretation, was introduced.

From the previous study, it is apparent that ICTs contribute in planning sustainable tourism development at tourism destination level. Buhalis (2003) mentioned that the rapid progress of ICTs has clearly manifested that organisations have more powerful tools for enhancing their efficiency and sustainable competitive advantage. In addition, the development of ICTs has a profound effect on the operation, structure and strategy of organisations. It has also become clear that dynamic capabilities of ICTs enhance interactivity, flexibility, efficiency, productivity and competitiveness (Poon, 1993; Buhalis, 2003). Within the context of sustainable tourism development, Ekins (2002) asserted that if the population doubles and consumption quadruples (2-3%) per annum by 2050, then emerging technologies must reduce impact to halve, as required to make meaningful movement towards sustainability. Further, recent Internet developments revolutionised the entire tourism industry and as a result, it is becoming a major tool not only for planning and purchasing and consumption of tourism products and services (Buhalis and Laws, 2001) but also for sustainable tourism development. Brynjolfsson and Hitt (2000) pointed out that ICTs are transforming the way Destination Management Organisations (DMOs) are operating and managing destinations more effectively and in sustainable manner. In addition, Liburd (2005) clarified that the emerging ICTs have the potential to minimise tourism's negative impacts at destination level. There has been much focus on DMSs and GISs in relation to sustainable tourism development research, however, there is little empirical research on the contribution of more recent digital technologies including E-mail, Short Message Service (SMS), audio guide, Social Media Networks and User Generated Contents (UGC) (Buhalis and Law, 2008) in connection with DMSs to sustainable tourism development from the multi-stakeholder approach. Therefore, this study explores various different stakeholders' perception on the contribution of more recent emerging ICTs to sustainable tourism development in Manchester area.

5 Research Method

Semi-structured interviews were conducted with various different stakeholders who are directly or indirectly involved in sustainable tourism development in Manchester area. In order to gain broader understanding of the strategic contribution of ICTs on sustainable tourism development, a qualitative research method in conjunction with case study approach has been used to conduct this research. Participants are selected from the entire legitimate tourism stakeholder groups in Manchester tourism destination based on Simpson's (2001) framework of stakeholder groups as there is a strong consensus that sustainable tourism development is a stakeholder' driven approach. The research was carried out in July and August 2009 with the tourism stakeholders in Manchester. Overall, a total of 30 people from the various stakeholder groups were participated. Table 1 shows different interviewees groups and they are from local government (MM1, MM2, MM3, TIC1, TIC2, and TIC3), visitors (V1, V2, V3, V4 and V5), local residents (R1, R2, R3, R4, R5, R6, R7 and R8), and local tourism businesses (H1, H2, H3, H4, H5, RO1, RO2, RO3, TG1, TD1 and TD2). Generally, the interview questions focused on the contribution of ICTs to sustainable tourism development in order to explore stakeholders' perception. The questionnaire was split into three main sections and the first part examines whether stakeholders understand the concept of sustainable tourism. The second part looked at the use of various ICTs for sustainable tourism development and the third part considered the contribution of ICTs to sustainable tourism development in Manchester in order to examine what extent the emerging ICTs can enhance the development of sustainable tourism at destination level.

Table 1. Tourism Stakeholders Participated in the Study

Interviewees	Stakeholders
MM1, MM2 and MM3	Marketing Manchester IT Manager Marketing Manchester Marketing Manager Marketing Manchester Tourism Development Manager
TIC1, TIC2, and TIC3	Members of Staff at the Manchester Tourist Information Centre
H1, H2, H3,H4 and H5	Hoteliers
RO1, RO2 and RO3	Restaurant Operators
TG1	An official Tourist Guide
V1, V2, V3, V4 and V5	Visitors/Tourists
R1, R2, R3, R4, R5, R6, R7 and R8	Residents of Greater Manchester–Host population
TD1 and TD2	Taxi Drivers

6 Research Findings

This study revealed a number of interesting findings on the contribution of ICTs to sustainable tourism development in Manchester. Following section will report main findings from qualitative analysis. Firstly, the contribution of ICTs to sustainable tourism development is examined. Secondly, various technologies which used for the enhancement of sustainable tourism development are reviewed. Finally, barriers to the implementation of ICTs in sustainable tourism development are discussed.

6.1 Contribution of ICTs to STD

In terms of whether emerging ICTs can contribute to sustainable tourism development in Manchester, the empirical findings lead to conclusion that ICTs offer strategic tools to maximise the positive impact of tourism and minimise its negative impact at destination level. Majority of participants suggested that ICTs are strategic contributor to enhancing sustainable tourism development (MM1, MM2 TIC1, TIC2, TIC3, H1, H2, H3, H4, H5, RO1, RO2, RO3, TG1, V1, V2, V3, V5, R1, R2, R3, R4, R6, R7, TD1 and TD2). Some respondents (MM1, TIC1, H1, H2, R4 and R5) pointed out that, ICTs, in particular, Internet reengineered the way consumers search for tourism product and information from traditional paper based method to internet empowered self interactive method. In the context of Manchester as a tourism destination, a number of ICTs have been used in a range of operational activities such as sustainable tourism planning and development, marketing campaigns to promote Manchester at an international level, promotion of competitions and special offers to raise interest in Manchester. It has been revealed that over 80% of tourist researching for a holiday or visit Manchester use the internet to plan their trip (MM1). With regard to ICT applications in sustainable tourism development in Manchester, participants from local government (MM1, MM2 and TIC1) were asked to identify ICT tools which they use in potential socio-cultural or environmental impact assessment. Findings revealed that despite the potential of ICTs infrastructures namely GIS and DMS in monitoring and assessing environmental impact of tourism, Marketing Manchester has no particular ICTs techniques or applications in place in conducting environmental impact assessment for example carrying capacity. Furthermore, the findings revealed that Marketing Manchester do not use any ICT tools or infrastructures in monitoring and evaluating socio-cultural impact of tourism. The findings show that ICT tools which are commonly used in tourism planning project or sustainable tourism development in Manchester include mobile phone, SMS, social media, audio guide, user generated content and demographic or customer profiling tools such as Arkenford as well as DMS.

6.2 ICT Applications

Short Message Service (SMS). With regard to the question whether SMS, as an ICT application, can enhance sustainable tourism development, it has been postulated that SMS text service is especially significant in terms of sustainable tourism development. Half of respondents (MM1, TIC1, TIC2, TIC3, RO1, V1, V2, V3, V4, R1, R2, R3, R7, TD1 and TD2) indicated that they are aware of potential of SMS in finding out information on the events happening or where to go in Manchester. It was suggested that SMS provides visitors with a quick, inexpensive and easy way of finding out where to go and what is on.

Arkenford. It was shown that Arkenford (demographic or customer profiling system) is a significant ICT application which used by Marketing Manchester (MM1, MM2 and MM3). It is particularly useful in assessing visitor market to a particular tourist destination. From the organization point of view, it was noted that it has been used by Marketing Manchester for strategic segmentation of existing visitor data, accurate report management and provision for pre and post visit e-correspondence.

Audio Guide. It was found that audio guide helps to raise visitor awareness through interpretation and communication (MM1, TIC1, TIC2, TG1, V2, V4 and V5). In the context of sustainable tourism, the research shows that audio guides as ICT infrastructure are particularly useful in sustainable tourism development. For example, for visitor interpretation at tourist attraction, visitor and queue management and minimising environmental impact such as overcrowding. This view is supported by Dunlop (2006) that the potential of ICT applications have enabled tourism destinations and attractions to develop audio guide in order to enable them to achieve the balance at the management and operations level (Dunlop, 2006). She argued that audio guides aid to enhance product quality and therefore have a significant impact on organisational and environmental risk management. Moreover, it was indicated that for the sake of visitor interpretation and sustainable tourism, Destination Manchester introduced audio guides in some of its heritage attractions.

Social Media Networks and User Generated Contents. Another interesting finding from the interview with stakeholders is that participants indicated that social media networks and user generated contents are commonly used by visitors in planning their trip to a particular destination. Twenty per cent of the interviewees (MM1, TIC1, V1, V2, V4 and R8) indicated that social media is useful tool for finding additional information. In terms of diversification and planning of sustainable tourism, it was reported that these technologies help to provide channel for engagement and encouraging principle of sustainability. It was indicated that these ICT applications increase the richness of information and content specific or relevant to what visitors are looking for. The participants from Marketing Manchester (MM1, TIC1 and TIC2) further stated that social media networks and user generated contents help coordinating and improving visitor awareness from the marketing perspective. It was noted that the ICT innovations permit visitors to have certain amount of experiential information in place and to hear the truth or authentic information about the destination not what the tourist board is providing. For example, comments, reviews and audio files posted by bird watchers. The research suggests that in terms of destination image, social media and user generated content play a very significant role in tourism decision making and behaviour. As these technologies will reduce the level of perceived risk and profoundly help tourist to gain more confidence in emotional responses.

E-Mail. From the organizational point of view, the study revealed that E-mail is playing a major role in planning of sustainable tourism development in Manchester.

IT manger of Marketing Manchester (MM1) indicated that they have been using email as a strategic distribution channel to target customers and to disseminate information and newsletter to stakeholders and strategic partners in order to promote and spread the goals of sustainable tourism development. From the marketing perspective, some interviewees (MM1, TIC, TIC3 H1, H2, H3, RO3, R4 and R5) clearly pointed out that E-mail is a significant marketing tool as it is cost effective and easy way of communication and achieving a number of marketing objectives such as enhancing visitor awareness programme. The findings concluded that E-mail helps to send destination information to visitors and stakeholders about destinations for instance to encourage visitors contribution to local environment and understanding of the benefit of sustainable tourism.

Strategic Networks. With regard to strategic cooperation, respondents from Marketing Manchester and Tourism Information Centre (MM1, MM2, MM3, TIC1, TIC2, and TIC3) noted that Destination Management System (DMS) helps empower both Marketing Manchester and Tourist Information Centres (TICs) to link website to regional or national DMO website such as VisitBritain. It was also found that DMS plays a crucial role in facilitating B2B communication and in order to facilitate ICT applications in sustainable tourism development, it is imperative to have a partnership between public and private sector. Some participants (MM1, MM2 and TIC1) mentioned that the development of alliances, joint ventures and partnerships through ICTs will facilitate the development of sustainable tourism (Peatie and Moutinho, 2000; Dale, 2003).

Despite the recognition and consensus that ICTs can play a strategic role in sustainable tourism development, it was shown that currently ICT applications do not play a major role in sustainable tourism in Marketing Manchester. However, the issue becomes much more important for Marketing Manchester in the near future and Marketing Manchester will promote sustainable alternatives through ICTs for green communication rather than traditional communication methods.

6.3 Barriers to the Implementation of ICTs in STD

Despite the acceptances of ICT as a strategic tool for sustainable tourism development, the research found out that there are a number of potential barriers to successful implementation of ICTs in sustainable tourism development such as lack of expertise in ICTs functionality. In addition, some respondent (MM1, TIC1 and H2) expressed concerns about the substantial capital cost involved in installing and operating ICT applications such as database driven DMS. This result indicated that high procurement cost is one of the reasons of avoiding emerging technologies (McAdam, 1999). It was also noted that a Destination Marketing Organization (DMO) like Marketing Manchester generate the majority of its funding from external bodies and therefore sustainable tourism development has to be high on their agenda for investments in order to develop ICT applications in line with sustainable tourism development.

7 Conclusions, Recommendations and Limitations

Despite the assumption that sustainable tourism development is a complex and ambiguous term, it is clear that planning and developing tourism in a sustainable manner is a growing concern for DMOs. This study has sought to investigate whether ICTs can significantly contribute to sustainable tourism development at tourism destination, Manchester. Furthermore, in light of the empirical findings and conceptual reviews the research demonstrated the strong relationship between ICTs and sustainable tourism development. It has also outlined some ICT applications or tools which can enable the establishment of platforms for facilitating sustainable tourism development at destination level. The primary objective of this study was to investigate the contribution of ICTs to sustainable tourism development. Particular focus on emerging ICT applications including SMS, E-mail, audio guide, Arkenford, Social media and user generated contents in connection with DMS were considered in order to examine the empirical evidence of accomplishing successful sustainable tourism development. Based on the review of existing literature and in-depth semi-structured interviews with the tourism stakeholders, it is concluded that ICTs can serve various sustainable goals at destination level. In addition, the study identified that there are some potential challenges or barriers associated to the implementation of the ICTs applications in sustainable tourism development. From the analysis, it is evident that applying ICTs to facilitate or enhance sustainable tourism development is profoundly becoming beneficial and significant for tourism destinations.

The research suggests several key implications for Destination Marketing Organizations (DMOs) in Manchester. Firstly, in order to make the best use of the emerging technologies, Marketing Manchester should adopt proper ICT benefit evaluation strategies to enable them to sustain long term benefit and competitive advantage and to maximize the success of ICT applications in sustainable tourism development. Research conducted by Melville *et al,* (2004) revealed that organizations that adopt proper IT evaluation practices tend to achieve better business performance. Therefore, it is imperative for Marketing Manchester to monitor and evaluate the success of ICTs implementations for sustainable tourism development. Secondly, this study suggests that the ICT innovations in contemporary tourism industry need to be supplemented with stakeholders' involvement if the ICT applications in sustainable tourism are to become successfully implemented. In addition, despite the potential of ICTs in sustainable tourism development, Marketing Manchester and stakeholders should be prepared to embrace or adopt the emerging and high potential technologies in order to deliver improvements to business and/or organisational performance. Thirdly, in terms of translating sustainable tourism principles into workable practice, the goal of sustainable tourism development could be achieved through the proper development of policy and planning incorporating all stakeholders both within the public and private sector in order to act in a sustainable manner through effective use of ICTs (Simpson, 2001). The research concluded that there need to be more partnership and participation among tourism stakeholders at destination level as well as partnership between the public and private sector in order to maximize ICTs contribution to sustainable tourism development.

This study has several limitations and suggestions for future research. One of the main limitations of this research is the fact that research on ICTs and sustainable tourism is still at its very early level of development (Ali and Frew, 2008; Gretzel, 2009). While there has been a lot of research undertaken on ICTs and tourism, there has been a very little empirical research carried out in the area of ICTs and sustainable tourism development. In addition, as noted by a number of previous studies in tourism literature, sustainable tourism is a complex, broad and somewhat ambiguous subject encompasses a wide range of information, concept, principles, practices and techniques for helping to achieve sustainable tourism. In addition, little empirical data exists to support some arguments and suggestions. Due to the fact that sample used in this study is various stakeholders of one specific destination region, Manchester, therefore, caution should be taken in terms of generalization of these findings. In terms of future research, the results of this research could be taken forward by developing the scope of the questions and widening the scale of potential response. For example, an exploration into the strategic impacts of ICTs on sustainable tourism development at Northwest regional level could be considered. Further, quantitative approach in order to investigate contribution of ICTs to sustainable tourism development is suggested.

References

Archdale, G., Stanton, R. & Jones, G. (1992) *Destination databases: Issues and Priorities*. San Francisco: Pacific Asia Travel Association.

Ali, A. & Frew, J.A. (2008). ICT for Sustainable Tourism Development – An Emergent Framework. In: Sigala, M. (Ed.), *Proceedings of the 2nd International Scientific Conference of the e-Business Forum: E-Business in Travel, Tourism and Hospitality 2008*. Athens: University of Aegean.

Ali, A. & Frew, A. (2009). ICT and sustainable tourism development: An analysis of the literature. Queen Margaret University, UK, SITI Research Centre.

Bahaire, T. & Elliott-White, M. (1999). The Application of Geographical Information Systems (GISs) in Sustainable Tourism Planning: A Review, *Journal of Sustainable Tourism*, 7(2), pp. 159-174.

Berry, S. & Ladkin, A. (1997) Sustainable tourism: a regional perspective. *Tourism Management* 18 (7), pp. 433-440.

Bramwell, B. (1994) 'Rural tourism and sustainable rural tourism'. *Journal of Sustainable Tourism*. 2, pp.1-6.

Bramwell, B. & Sharman, A. (1999). Collaboration in local tourism policymaking, Annals of Tourism Research, 26 (2), pp. 392-415.

Bramwell, B., Henry, I., Jackson, G., Prat, A., Richards, G. & Van der Straaten, J (1996). *Sustainable Tourism Management: Principles and Practices*. Tilburg: Tilburg University Press.

Brynjolfsson, E. & Hitt, L.M. (2000) "Beyond computation informational   technology, organization transformation and business performance". *Journal of Economic perspectives* 14(4), pp.23-48.

Buhalis, D. (2003) *eTourism: Information Technology for Strategic Tourism Management*. London: Prentice Hall.

Buhalis, D. (1998) 'Strategic Use of Information Technology in the Tourism Industry'. *Tourism Management* .19(5), pp.409-421.

504

Buhalis, D. (1997) 'Information Technology as a Strategic Tool for Economic, Social, Cultural and Environmental Benefits Enhancement of Tourism at Destination Regions'. *Progress in Tourism and Hospitality Research,* 3, pp. 71-93.

Buhalis, D. & Law, R. (2008). 'Progress in information technology and tourism management: 20 years on and 10 years after the Internet – The state of eTourism Research'. *Tourism Management*, 29, pp. 609-623.

Buhalis, D. & Law, E (2001) *Tourism distribution enhance practice, issues and transformations.* London: continuum.

Buhalis, D. & Licata, M. C. (2002). The Future of eTourism Intermediaries, *Tourism Management*, 23, pp. 207-220.

Butler, R. (1993) Tourism: An Introductionary Perspective. In: Nelson, J.G., Butler, R. & Wall, G. Eds. *Tourism and sustainable development: Monitoring, planning, managing publication series, 37, University of Waterloo*: Department of Geography.

Cooper, C., Fletcher, J., Fayall, A., Gilbert, D. & Wanhill, S. (2006). *Tourism Principles and Practice, 3rd ed.* Harlow: Pearson Education Ltd.

Ekins, P. (2002) *Sustainable Development and the work of policy studies institute's environment group.* Presentation given at University of Westminster, London, 4th December. In: Miller, G. & Twining-Wand, L. (2005) *Monitoring for a sustainable tourism transition: The challenge of developing and using indicators.* Oxford: CAB Publishing.

Garcia, C. & Servera, J. (2003). Impacts of Tourism Development on Water Demand and Beaches Degradation on the Island of Mallorca, *Geogratiska Annaler,* 85 (3-4), pp. 287-300.

Gilbert, D. (1993) 'Issues in appropriate rural tourism development for Southern Ireland.'*Leisure Studies.*12, pp.137– 46.

Go, F.M. & Govers, R. (1999) Integrated quality management for tourist destinations: A European perspective of an achieving competitiveness. *Tourism Management,* 21 (1), pp. 79-88.

Gretzel, U. (2009). The Role of ICTs in Sustainable Tourism Development: Proceedings of the 2009 Chungnam International Tourism Conference, 66th, OSOK Academic Symposium & Research Presentation. Chungnam, Korea, July 3, 2009, pp. 100-109. Seoul, Korea: *Tourism Sciences Society of Korea.*

Hall, C.M. (2000) *Tourism: planning: policies, processes and relationships.* Hallow,Essex: Pearson Education Limited.

Hasse, J. & Milne, S. (2005). Participatory Approaches and Geographical Information Systems in Tourism Planning, *Tourism Geographies,*7 (3), pp 272-289.

Holden, A. (2002). *Environment and Tourism,* London: Routledge

Liburd, J. (2005). Sustainable Tourism and Innovation on Mobile Tourism Services, *Tourism Review International*, 9, pp.107-118.

Lumsdon, L. (2000) Cycle tourism - A mode for sustainable development. *Journal of Sustainable Tourism.*8 (5), pp.361-377.

Marien, C. & Pizam, A. (1997) *Implementing sustainable tourism development through citizen participation in the planning process.* In: Miller, G. & Twining-Ward, L. (2005) Monitoring for a sustainable tourism transaction. *The Challenge of developing and using indicators.* Wallingford: CABI Publishing.

McAdam, D. (1999) 'The Value and Scope of Geographical Information System in Tourism Management'. *Journal of Sustainable Tourism,* 7(1), pp.77-92.

Miller, G. & Twining-Wand, L. (2005) *Monitoring for a Sustainable Tourism Transition: The Challenge of Developing and Using Indicators.* Oxford: CAB Publishing.

O'Connor, P. (1999*) Electronic Information Distribution in Tourism and Hospitality.* Wallingford, Oxon: CABI Publishing.

Page, S.J. (2003) *Tourism Management: Managing for Change.* Oxford: Butterworth-Heinemann.

Poon, A. (1993) *Tourism technology and competitive strategies.* Oxford: CAB International.

Schwanen, T., & Kwan, M. (2008). The Internet, Mobile Phone and Space-time Constraints, *Geoforum,* 39 (3), pp 1362-1377.

Sheldon, P. (1997). Destination Information Systems, *Annals of Tourism Research* 20 (4), pp. 633-649.

Sheldon, P. (1993) 'Destination information systems'. *Annals of Tourism Research*, 20 (4), pp. 633-649.

Simpson, K. (2001) 'Strategic Planning and Community Involvement as Contributors to Sustainable Tourism Development'. *Current Issues in Tourism*, 4 (1), pp. 3-41.

Swabrooke, J. (1999) *Sustainable Tourism Management*. Wallingford: CAB Publishing.

The Manchester tourist Board (2009) *Tourism for Greater Manchester* [Online] Available from http://www.visitmanchester.com/ [Accessed] 1/09/2009.

UNWTO (2008). Tourism Highlights 2008 Edition, [on-line] Available from http://www.unto.org/facts/eng/pdf/highlights/UNWTO.

Werthner, H. & Klein, S. (1999) *Information Technology and Tourism: A Challenging Relation.* Vienna: Springer-Verlag.

Werthner, H. & Klein, S. (1999) 'ICT and the Changing Landscape of Global Tourism Distribution', *Electronic Markets*, 9 (4), pp.256-262.

WCED (1987) The Brundtland Report: *Our common future – World Commission on Environment and Development*. Oxford: Oxford University Press. In:

WTO (1993) *Sustainable tourism development: Guide for Local Planners*. Madrid, Spain: WTO Publication, Tourism and Environment.

eTourism for All? Online Travel Planning of Disabled People

Wolfgang Drews[a],
Christiane Schemer[a]

[a] University of Trier
Chair for Organisation and Strategic Management
{drews;schemer}@osm.uni-trier.de

Abstract

Online communities, social networks and social media in general have been recognised as important information resource for consumers and are more and more influencing the travel planning of consumers nowadays (Gretzel & Yoo, 2008; Arsal et al, 2008). Consumers cannot only receive content from the Internet, but also generate their own content in form of travelogues, photos, videos, reviews or even tweets and status updates on social networks like Facebook or Twitter. This so called User Generated Content (UCG) often is perceived more reliable than information provided by the destination or tourism service provider and subsequently considered as substitute for word of mouth (Niininen et al, 2006). While particular attention was given to studying the online travel planning and booking behaviour of the overall population, less attention was paid to this behaviour when it comes to disabled travellers. The survey results presented in this paper therefore provide interesting insights regarding this issue as well as the general trip planning behaviour of people with impairments.

Keywords: tourism for all, accessible travel, travel planning, online travel reviews, online communities, social media

1 Introduction

According to the OSSATE-Report, in the European Union there are 127.5 million people suffering from limitations of their mobility (Buhalis et al, 2005). About two thirds of them plus accompanying people – a total of about 200 million people - are potential customers for the tourism industry, disposing of some 83 to 166 billion Euros that might be spent in tourism. Even though this is a huge market that will continue to grow due to the increased expectation of life and a decline in mortality, people with impaired mobility are still considered a niche market by the tourism industry. If they are addressed at all, it is only by means of special offers or specialized tour operators.

Today, the Internet plays an increasing role when the focus is on obtaining travel information, sharing of experiences or purchasing travel-related products and services. Almost every travel-phase is supported online: in the pre-phase one can search for information and/or book directly; in the during-phase one can publish weblog entries, search for information like "pubs nearby" via location based services on their mobile or write status updates on Twitter or Facebook. Finally one can review accommodations, share travel experiences or upload photos and videos from their trips in the post-phase. Many travellers already use this user-generated content as reliable source of information in order to plan their trips and therefore community-driven content has been identified to be of major importance to tourism service provider. Yet, only little effort was put in online tourism information systems that meet the requirements of accessibility and the needs for online user participation (Drews, 2008). Thus, this research aims to find out, if and how handicapped people use the Internet for travel planning and booking in the pre-phase, during the trip and in the post-phase.

2 Theoretical Issues: Disability and Touristic Demands

In general, the term disability is used and interpreted in many different ways. Definitions range from purely medical understanding, which considers disability as a biological deficiency, to the notion of disability as a social construct, which does not realise it as a person's individual characteristic, but as an impairment caused by social circumstances. Likewise, there are many types of disabling condition that can arise from a variety of impairments. To cope with this complexity and to be able to deduce categories of touristic demands, this paper refers to the International Classification of Functioning, Disability and Health (ICF) of the World Health Organisation (WHO) (see Fig.1). This organisational framework is divided into two parts and describes situations with regard to human functioning and disability: the first supplies a bio-psycho-social model of the components of health (body functions and structures, activities and participation), while the second part describes environmental and personal factors. These so-called context factors can both positively and negatively affect the components of functioning and disability and thus are in an interactive relationship (World Health Organisation, 2005). Consequently the ICF represents an open, dynamic and interactive model of disability and offers a multi-perspective access to the term disability. The component of activity is central to these relations and expresses that any occurrence of the other components can have an effect on the possibilities of being active, which is - in this case - an important fact for tourism.

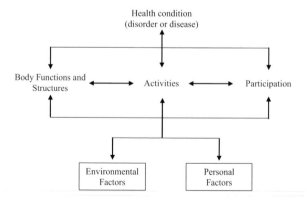

Fig. 1. International Classification of Functioning, Disability and Health.

For the tourism industry, the following classes, which have the same or similar needs with regard to the tourism infrastructure and which refer to the same or similar restrictions in the activities of the disabled persons, can be deduced from:

- Limitations on the musculoskeletal system
- Visual limitations
- Limitations on hearing and speech impediments
- Mental limitations, i.e. people with a mental or learning disability
- Chronic diseases

These categories could be confirmed within the framework of the survey; most of the impairments stated by the disabled respondents could be assigned to one of the predefined categories.

3 Methodology

The survey was realised as a Web-based online survey, as it focused on disabled people already using the Internet. It was conducted in a three-month period between February 1 and April 30, 2009. A drawing for one of two stays in accessible hotel accommodations in Austria was used as incentive.

The questionnaire itself was divided into six parts and covered the topics online behaviour, travel behaviour, travel organisation (preparation, information, booking), travel accomplishing, travel recapitulation and confirmation as well as a section with questions regarding demographic characteristics.

The Web-based survey was conducted on a range of German-speaking websites through links on specific platforms dealing with all kind of disabilities (37), newsletters (49) and different forums (29). In addition, the study was covered in different offline publications (7) and sent by email to various organisations (e.g. universities, associations), which forwarded the link of the survey online and offline to their members. The media were selected by the criterion disability, whereby the covering of all dimensions of disability was warranted.

The online character of the study implies also several limitations. First, the phenomenon of self-recruiting represents a problem that online surveys have to cope with. That means that mainly intensive surfers and persons interested in the topic or in the incentives participate in the study. So, the respondents decide for themselves being part of the target group or not (Theobald et al, 2003). The lack of representativeness is another disadvantage of online surveys. Representativeness postulates that all units of a predefined population have a predictable chance to be chosen for the sample (Berekoven et al, 2009). This would only be the case, if theoretically all people could be reached via Internet. In presence, only approximately 70 percent of the private households in Germany are reachable over the Internet (Initiative D21, 2009), which implies that there is no representativeness given. On the other hand, this number of "Onliners" is growing continuously (even a four percent growth in Germany in 2009 (Initiative D21, 2009)). Moreover only the online method made it possible to get such a high participation rate with limited resources what, in turn, induced a higher representativeness. Furthermore, participants of online surveys are likely to answer in a more honest and critical way than participants of offline surveys (Berekoven et al, 2009). In addition, every effort has been made to reach all "groups" of disabled people to be as representative as possible.

4 Results

4.1 Profile of Sample

1.286 persons filled in the questionnaire; 879 questionnaires were filled in completely and therefore were used in the analysis.

74.8 percent of the respondents reported to have personal experience of a disability, 23.0 percent had no handicap and 2.2 percent were not specified. Most of the persons without a handicap participated in the survey because they were relatives (46.5 percent), because of interest (26.7 percent) or because their jobs were related to the topic of disability or tourism for all (25.2 percent).

The reported impairments of the disabled respondents can be divided into limitations on the musculoskeletal system (80.9 percent), visual limitations (14.6 percent), limitations on hearing and speech impediments (6.2 percent), mental limitations (i.e. mental or learning disability, 6.7 percent), chronic diseases (29 percent) and other impairments (14 percent) (see Fig. 2). About 73 percent of the participating people with a disability got their handicap in the course of their lives and 26.2 percent were natural disabled. 31.7 percent of them declared to have multiple disabilities.

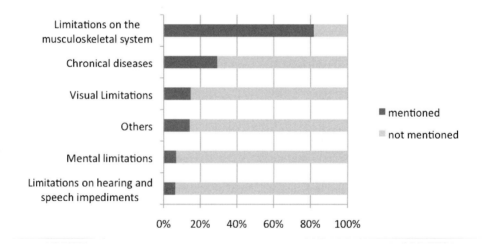

Fig. 2. Distribution of impairments within the sample.

Slightly more females (54.1 percent overall, 51.4 percent of the disabled respondents) than males (45.9 percent overall, 48.6 percent of the disabled respondents) completed the survey.

The following results, if not stated otherwise, are given for the group of respondents with impairments only. 91.7 percent of the sample came from Germany, 3.8 percent from Austria and 3.2 percent from Switzerland. Only 1.4 percent came from other countries, which can be derived from the fact, that the survey was mainly publicised in Germany and the German-speaking area.

The average age of the sample amounts to approximately 48 years, whereby it ranges from 13 to 88 years. The largest age group comprises those who are between 40 and 49 years (28.7 percent), directly followed up by the group of those, who are between 50 and 59 years of age (27.8 percent). About 17 percent are between 30 and 39 years old, 14.5 percent are between 60 and 69 years and 4.2 percent are 70 years or older. Quite surprisingly, only 7.3 percent of the respondents are between 20 and 29 years old and only 0.9 percent is under 20 years. On average there are 2.27 persons living in a household, indicating travelling with children plays a less important role. Indeed only about 8 percent of all respondents have one or more children.

About 32 percent of the respondents have a tertiary education, 17 percent an upper secondary or post-secondary non-tertiary education and 30.5 percent a secondary education first stage (cf. United Nations Educational, Scientific and Cultural Organization, 1997 for more information about the educational classification ISCED). About 40 percent draw a (invalidity) pension, another 40 percent are employees and 6.1 percent are freelancer. The majority (29.3 percent) has a monthly household income (after tax) between EUR 500 and 1.500. 28.0 percent of the respondents have between EUR 1.501 and 2.500, 18.8 percent between EUR 2.501 and 3.500 and 6.7 percent between EUR 3.501 and 4.500. Only 4.5 percent have more than EUR 4.500.

4.2 General Travel Behaviour

Most of the disabled respondents (79.2 percent) went on a journey in the last twelve months. According to research done in Germany back in 2003, only 54.3 percent of disabled people actually travel (Forschungsgemeinschaft Urlaub und Reisen, 2003). That is 21 percent less than people without a disability. The high ratio of travellers with impairments in our study suggests, handicapped persons who use the Internet generally travel more often, because the Internet makes travel planning easier for them. In comparison with the persons without impairment it could be determined, that disabled persons do not travel less. The main reasons for not going on a journey are financial factors (60.1 percent). This is less surprising taking into account what has been said about the average monthly household income and the fact, that 46.2 percent of disabled people say their handicap is causing additional expenditure (on average at about EUR 715). Besides financial reasons respondents name healthy factors (51.4 percent), professional reasons (15 percent) and missing information about the accessibility of the destination and the accommodation (15 percent), a deficit of

512

assistance or a total lack of handicapped accessible services as reasons for not travelling.

People with a disability go on average 2.2 times on a short trip (less or equal 4 days). The number of voyages that take more than four days averages 1.7. This reveals that there is not much of a difference in comparison to the overall population. Rather, the number of voyages that takes more than four days averages 1.3 within the group of persons without impairment and is therefore 0.4 points less than the value within the group of handicapped in our study (Forschungsgemeinschaft Urlaub und Reisen, 2008). In context of travel duration there is not much of a difference in comparison to the overall population. Disabled people travel on average for 12.6 days and within the overall population the average travel duration amounts to 13.5 days (Bundesministerium für Wirtschaft und Technologie, 2004). They travel on average with one accompanying person and with few or no children (on average 0.38 children).

Regarding the accommodation, 31.4 percent of disabled people choose a holiday apartment respectively a cottage. 20.6 percent go for a middle class hotel, 17.5 percent decide in favour of a hotel of the upper class. Concerning the choice of an accommodation, the following features are of particular importance:

- Accessibility of sanitary facilities (85.1 percent)
- Accessibility of the dining hall / breakfast room (84.1 percent)
- Accessibility of the rooms / room equipment (82.7 percent)
- Friendly, trained staff (81 percent)
- Access of the accommodation (79.8 percent)
- Accessibility of the corridors (78.3 percent)
- Parking (68.9 percent)

With reference to the seasonality of their journeys, most of the respondents start their journey in the summer months from May until September, whereas the climax is reached in August and September (about 16 percent) (see Fig. 3).

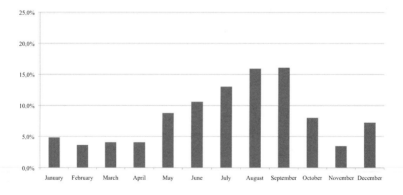

Fig. 3. Seasonality of journeys.

About 88 percent of the handicapped persons say that their handicap has an influence on the choice of their holiday resort. Furthermore 52.5 percent stated that their impairments affect their travel capabilities very strong. Within the sample, wheelchair users see themselves mostly restricted in their travel capabilities. 46 percent of the German respondents spent their last holiday in Germany. In comparison to the overall population (30.5 percent, cf. Forschungsgemeinschaft Urlaub und Reisen, 2003) this documents a much higher loyalty to the home-destination even though this is caused by the impairment and not necessarily a free decision. Many disabled people report to feel less uncertain and risky when spending their holiday in their home country, as there are less communication difficulties otherwise occurring due to a foreign language or foreign medical health system.

Taking again all disabled respondents into account, 43.7 percent chose Germany as holiday destination, 6.5 percent went to Austria and 1.7 percent to Switzerland. 36.3 percent went to another European country (e.g. Italy, Spain). Globally, 2.6 percent chose Africa for their holiday country, 3.3 percent Asia and 4.7 percent North America.

4.3 General Internet Usage

Since the survey was carried out online, the respondents are more likely to use the Internet than the overall population. Therefore it is not surprising, that about 80 percent of the handicapped respondents quote to use the Internet daily and about 90 percent use it at least on 5 days per week. 85.9 percent of the respondents are not in need of any assistive technology to surf the Internet. Assistive technologies are of particular importance especially for persons with a visual impairment and for blind people.

The main Internet functions used by the respondents are: email and instant messenger / VoIP-tools like ICQ, AIM, MSN or Skype (82.9 percent), followed up by looking for travel information with about 71 percent. Other types of usage are reading news online (70 percent), searching for medical information (61.8 percent), looking for product information (58.7 percent), buying products and services online (58.4 percent) or using social networks (51.1 percent).

Almost 77 percent visit platforms aiming at a specific kind of impairment and about 40 percent confirm a membership in a dedicated online-community where they provide content to other users. Even though this degree of organisation is lower than the degree of organisation in the offline world (62.1 percent confirmed to be member of an association, club or network regarding an impairment), it nevertheless is quite high and suggests their addressability over the Internet.

4.4 Online Travel Planning

The main travel information resources for disabled people are the Internet (92.6 percent) and friends (56.9 percent) (see Fig. 4).

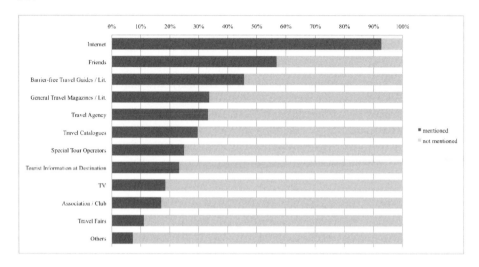

Fig. 4. Travel information resources for disabled people.

52.4 percent of the disabled quote that they have already surrendered a holiday in a certain destination because of a lack of information concerning the accessibility of the destination or accommodation. In addition 45.4 percent of the disabled people would travel more often if there existed more information concerning the accessibility of the accommodation and/or the destination itself. Therefore information about the accessibility of the accommodation is not only the most important type of resource when planning a travel trip, but also the kind of information respondents will generally require much more in the future (see Fig. 5). Second most disabled travellers request more information about the accessibility of the destination, the so-called mobility-factor. Next, information on handicapped accessible arrival and departure, cultural facilities and entertainment locations is of high importance and needs to be enhanced in future. Catering and shopping facilities are still of high importance, but respondents do not feel to have a lack of information in this respect. The same applies to medical assistance, sport facilities or information on the personnel's skills.

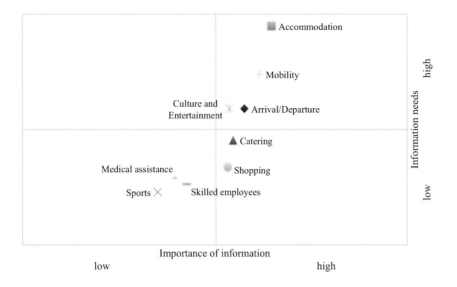

Fig. 5. Importance of information and information needs.

When using the Internet to achieve suitable travel information, handicapped people use particular search engines (80.7 percent), official websites of the destination (74.7 percent), provider websites (72.7 percent) and portals dedicated to accessible travel (54.2 percent). With reference to the usage of Web 2.0 sites or tools for travel planning, about 34 percent are using wikis, 16 percent social networks like Facebook, 14 percent photo-communities like Flickr, 9.6 percent video-communities like YouTube and 8.2 percent weblogs. Surprisingly only 20.6 percent of the respondents are using travel review sites like TripAdvisor or Holidaycheck.

55.6 percent of the handicapped consider evaluations, opinions and travelogues on travel platforms (e.g. TripAdvisor) as at least relatively reliable. In the group of those, who use this kind of review platforms, even 80.1 percent think this way. Moreover, about 85 percent in this group state, user-generated content has at least a mean (29 percent) or even a significant (55.9 percent) influence on the decision in which destination one will spend their holiday. Differences exist regarding the gender of the respondents that use travel review sites for gaining travel information. Females (94.2 percent) are more likely to think that reviews influence the decision making process than males (74.6 percent) do. This kind of gender differences for travel information search for the overall population has already been found before (Kim, Lehto & Morrison, 2007).

4.5 Booking Behaviour

Concerning the booking behaviour of handicapped people it can be stated that the majority (33.7 percent) organises its holidays itself and books directly at the destination or accommodation. Tour operators, which are specialised in accessible

516

holidays, have only a share of 6.7 percent, which is almost the same as for common tour operators (6.2 percent). While TUI (22.4 percent) and Neckermann (20.7 percent) are leading in the group of common tour operators, RfB Touristik (13 percent), BSK Reisedienst (11.6 percent) and Mare Nostrum (10.1 percent) are the most mentioned specialised tour operators.

Another big proportion (28.4 percent) of disabled people books via the Internet. It can be assumed that there is a big range of online booking sites from which disabled people choose to book their holidays. Leading organisations are HRS.de (16.7 percent), Hotel.de (14 percent), Expedia.de (10.2 percent) and Opodo.de (10.2 percent). Some of these sites offer information about the accessibility of the services (e.g. hotels) but there cannot be observed a correlation between their positions and the offerings of information. Therefore, it would be a vague assumption that their leading positions in this segment would be the result of these facts. Moreover, it is more likely that disabled people do not want to be treated like handicapped and therefore do not emphasize the availability of information about accessibility on such websites.

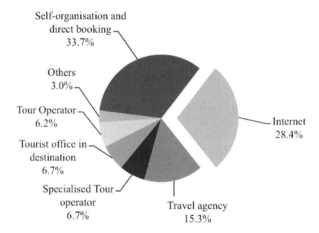

Fig. 6. Booking behaviour of disabled travellers.

4.6 Use of the Internet during and after a Travel-Trip

Concerning the use of Internet during a holiday, 33.8 percent of the handicapped quoted that they used the Internet during their last holidays. 47.4 percent think about using the Internet during a future holiday while 39.6 percent cannot imagine. If they use the Internet during their holidays, disabled traveller mainly use it for sending emails (87 percent), searching for events, tips to go out or insider tips (35.4 percent), calling up meteorological data (46.2 percent) and using city maps and location based services (36.3 percent). After their holidays disabled people use the Internet mainly to share photos and videos (44.2 percent), to share travel experiences (37.5 percent) and to stay in touch with new friends (15 percent). Only 21.9 percent review their accommodation online. Moreover, 38.1 percent of the respondents quoted not using the Internet after their holidays to share their experiences, whereby 20.7 percent of these could imagine an online travel recapitulation in the future.

5 Conclusion

First of all the study shows the relatively high degree of organisation and networking of disabled people – offline as well as online. This leads to the assumption, that they are extremely well addressable by marketers. Furthermore disabled travellers using the Internet for travel planning have a relatively high income (over 60 percent have an income above EUR 1.500) and a high education and thus represent an attractive target group for tourism service provider. Another important finding of this study is that the Internet seems to enable people with an impairment to travel, as it facilitates the search for suitable and reliable information about (accessibility issues of) a destination or an accommodation in particular. Respondents state that their impairment has a very high impact on the decision in favour or against a holiday destination as well as on the ability to travel at all. Taking this into account a lower travel frequency could be expected compared to the overall population and indeed research already found a significant difference of 21 percent. Anyhow, the study showed that there is almost no difference. Rather disabled travellers using the Internet for travel planning and/or booking are even travelling 0.4 times more frequently than the overall population.

Nevertheless, there are a considerable proportion of respondents that have already surrendered a holiday because of a lack of appropriate information. And an almost equally big group stated to be willing to travel more often, if there only was more suitable information. Quite interesting that 71 percent of the disabled travellers use the Internet for travel preparation and focus (beside search engines) on the official destination and accommodation websites. In addition they are also gaining travel information by watching videos and photos on Web 2.0 communities like Flickr or YouTube and use social networks as well as wikis. This substantiates the possibility for destinations and tourism service provider to capture profitable market segments of the growing market of travellers with impairments and gain competitive advantages by providing the required information at the right place on the Internet. Primarily they are requested to offer more information about the accessibility of the destination on their websites, as over 70% of the respondents are using the official websites of a destination or service provider to accomplish their informational needs. In particular it is crucial to supply information about the accessibility of the accommodations, the arrival and departure, the cultural facilities as well as the general accessibility of the environment of the destination. Without this information, travellers with disabilities are unsure if their requirements can be met and may as a consequence abstain from travelling into a desired destination or from staying in an accommodation in favour of a competitor. In addition it will become increasingly important for tourism service provider, to take action in social media and Web 2.0 respectively. Over 50% of the respondents stated, that they are using social media like travel review platforms, photo- and video sharing platforms or social networks in order to gather trustworthy (accessible) travel information. Future research will focus on the challenges, pitfalls and possibilities of an involvement in Web 2.0 and social media for destinations and tourism service provider regarding this highly interesting target audience.

References

Arsal, I., Backman, S. J., & Baldwin, E. D. (2008). Influence of an Online Travel Community on Travel Decisions. In P. O'Conner, W. Höpken, U. Gretzel (ed.) Information and Communication Technologies in Tourism, Proceedings of the International Conference in Innsbruck, Austria, 2008, Springer, Wien - New York, 82-93.

Berekoven, L., Eckert, W. & Ellenrieder, P. (2009): *Marktforschung : methodische Grundlagen und praktische Anwendung*, Wiesbaden: Gabler, 107-109.

Buhalis, D., Eichhorn, V., Michopoulou, E., & Miller, G. (2005). *OSSATE Accessibility Market and Stakeholder Analysis*. Retrieved on August 12, 2009 from http://www.ossate.org/library_news_002.jsp.

Bundesministerium für Wirtschaft und Technologie (2004). *Ökonomische Impulse eines barrierefreien Tourismus für alle. Eine Untersuchung im Auftrag des Bundesministeriums für Wirtschaft und Technologie. Kurzfassung der Untersuchungsergebnisse* (No. 526). Retrieved on June 22, 2009 from http://www.bmwi.de/BMWi/Redaktion/PDF/Publikationen/Dokumentationen/oekonomi sche-impulse-eines-barrierefreien-tourismus-fuer-alle-dokumentation-526,property=pdf,bereich=bmwi,sprache=de,rwb=true.pdf.

Drews. W. (2008). *A Web 2.0 Tourism Information System for Accessible Tourism*. In P. O'Conner, W. Höpken, U. Gretzel (ed.) Information and Communication Technologies in Tourism, Proceedings of the International Conference in Innsbruck, Austria, 2008 Springer 2008, Wien - New York, 164-174.

Forschungsgemeinschaft Urlaub und Reisen (F.U.R.) (2003). *33. Reiseanalyse 2003.* Hamburg/Kiel.

Forschungsgemeinschaft Urlaub und Reisen (F.U.R.) (2008). *Erste Ergebnisse der 38. Reiseanalyse RA 2008.* Hamburg/Kiel. Retrieved on January 22, 2009 from http://www.reiseanalyse.de/downloads/Reiseanalyse_2007.pdf.

Gretzel, U., & Yoo, K.H. (2008). *Use and Impact of Online Travel Reviews*. In P. O'Conner, W. Höpken, U. Gretzel (ed.) Information and Communication Technologies in Tourism, Proceedings of the International Conference in Innsbruck, Austria, 2008, Springer 2008, Wien - New York, 35-46.

Initiative D21 (2009). (N)ONLINER Atlas 2009. *Eine Topographie des digitalen Grabens durch Deutschland.* Retrieved on November 1, 2009 from http://www.nonliner-atlas.de/.

Kim, D.Y., Lehto, X. Y., & Morrison, A. M. (2007). *Gender differences in online travel information search: Implications for marketing communications on the Internet.* Tourism Management, 28 (2), 423-433.

Niininen, O., March, R. & Buhalis, D., 2006. *Consumer Centric Tourism Marketing.* In: Buhalis, D. and Costa, C., eds. Tourism Management Dynamics : Trends, Management and Tools. London: Buttterworth Heinemann, 175-186.

Theobald, A. (2003). *Online-Marktforschung: Theoretische Grundlagen und praktische Erfahrungen*. Wiesbaden: Gabler, 31ff.

United Nations Educational, Scientific and Cultural Organization (1997). *International Standard Classification of Education ISCED 1997*. Retrieved on September 15, 2009 from http://www.uis.unesco.org/ TEMPLA TE/pdf/isced/ISCED_A.pdf.

World Health Organisation (2005). *ICF. Internationale Klassifikation der Funktionsfähigkeit, Behinderung und Gesundheit*. Retrieved on August 10, 2009 from http://www.dimdi.de/dynamic/de/klassi/downloadcenter/icf/endfassung/icf_endfassung-2005-10-01.pdf.

Destination Marketing through User Personalised Content (UPC)

Joanna Matloka[a]
Dimitrios Buhalis[b]

[a] Bournemouth University, England
i7845925@ bournemouth.ac.uk

[b] ICTHR, Bournemouth University, England
dbuhalis@bournemouth.ac.uk

Abstract

The emergence of Social Media has already started revolutionising the tourism industry. User Personalised Content (UPC) appears as a new Web 2.0 form of customised information access and streaming, based on content aggregators and widgets. This study explores emerging opportunities originating from the development of UPC tools for destination marketing and the need for its leveraging. It investigates the range and value of widgets and assesses the potential of UPC for marketing destinations. The findings demonstrate that there is a great opportunity to deliver customised information that addresses personal needs and preferences to travellers. They also imply that in order to advance destination marketing through UPC, destination database should be created and a more systematic and efficient technique of widget search, selection and download shall be developed. Joining these two innovations together allows creation of an Open Global Destination Marketing System (OGDMS) which is suggested as solution to destination marketing challenges.

Keywords: widgets, user personalised content, destination marketing, information search

1 Introduction

Information search, being the essential part of travel decision making process, was revolutionised with the emergence of Internet (Fodness & Murray, 1997, Werthner & Klein, 1999). The Information Communication Technologies (ICTs) have enabled travellers to access reliable and accurate information on a variety of tourism products and services (Buhalis, 1998). Despite that, the online vacation planning may be a frustrating experience because of the excess of information available (Radoshevich, 1997; Stoltz, 1999). Additionally, both Destination Marketing Organisations (DMOs) (Gretzel, Yuan & Fesenmaier, 2000) and Small and Medium Tourism Enterprises (SMTEs) (Buhalis & Main 1998) encounter numerous challenges to ICT integration and, as a result, to taking advantage of the opportunities of online marketing. Effectively, destinations and tourists struggle to successfully communicate their offers and needs to each other online. However, Web 2.0 developments, can greatly save time and tackle the information overload problem (Litvin, Goldsmith & Pan, 2008). Content aggregators, i.e. websites like iGoogle or MyYahoo provide content based on users' preferences (Ho, 2006) by allowing users to fully personalise the content they wish to access (Constantinides & Fountain, 2008). The preference set happens through widgets - small bundles of software which can easily be downloaded, personalised and forwarded (King, 2008). Content aggregators together with customisable widgets constitute User Personalised Content (UPC), since widgets are pieces of personalisable software, that add value for customers. UPC has not been researched extensively in tourism yet. This study aims to discover the way in which UPC can be used to advance destination marketing. The need for leveraging destination marketing through UPC is discussed in the conceptual model whilst the type and value of widgets in destination marketing is researched and assessed. The joint analysis of the exploratory research findings and the conceptual model recommends the creation of Open Global Destination Marketing System (OGDMS) built on open source destination database and accessed by users through UPC.

2 Literature Review

Destinations are amalgams of all the tourist products, services and experiences such as: attractions, accessibility, amenities, available packages, activities and ancillary services provided locally (Buhalis, 2000). They are the most difficult tourism sector to market (Fyall & Leask, 2006), because of their numerous stakeholders and complex product offer (Palmer & Bejou, 1995). DMOs are usually regarded as the main bodies held responsible for the destination's marketing (Buhalis, 2000) and they determine its competitive advantage (Ritchie & Crouch, 2005). Decision to visit a tourism destination relies heavily on information available to tourists (Rita, 2000; Vogt & Fesenmaier, 1998). Therefore many opportunities to address the destination marketing challenges lay in ICTs integration - providing new marketing tools and empowering consumers who are now more independent, well informed, and look for new experiences (Buhalis, 2003). Although the demand for specific, niche destinations is increasing (Lew, 2008), tourists find it difficult to filter out the relevant information they really require (Hwang & Fesenmaier, 2001). Online travel planning can be a very frustrating experience due to excess of information (Radosevich, 1997; Stoltz, 1999). On the supply side, destinations and enterprises commonly lack resources, experience and marketing skills to take full advantage of ICTs. As a result the Internet is not fully used as the marketing tool to reach prospective tourists with travel offers (Gretzel *et al*, 2000). For the last 20 years the development of Destination Management Systems (DMSs) has been one of the most popular solutions to address these issues. The basic version of DMS consists of Product Database, Customer Database and a mechanism connecting the two (Buhalis, 2008). Not only DMSs enable coordination of whole range of products and services offered by the local suppliers and promote them on the global scale but also allow travellers to create a personal destination experience (Buhalis, 2003).

The recent emergence of Web 2.0 with its ideology of openness, sharing and cooperation gives hope that there might be more affordable and easy to use marketing/information search tools. If the right information could be found by the right consumer, the sales of destinations and their enterprises could increase. Out of the five main types of Web 2.0 applications described by Constantinides and Fountain

(2008) the content aggregators (allowing automatisation and customisation of information access and streaming) are the only ones that had not been researched in the tourism context so far. Content aggregators, as opposed to the rest of Web 2.0 developments which can be grouped under the term of User Generated Content (UGC), offer unique functionality for complete customisation of the accessed content through widget technology. UPC offers great marketing potential for destinations due to the multi-functionality of widgets and its ability to tackle information overload problems (Litvin et al, 2008), and to provide content based on users' preferences (Ho, 2006). Widgets can be selected, aggregated in one interface page and allow users to do what normally is done by visiting many different pages (Litvin et al, 2008). They are defined as small bundles of software, which can easily be downloaded, personalised and forwarded (King, 2008); or portable and lightweight applications which can be embedded into HTML based page (Lawton, 2007). Widgets are codes embedded into website that let users do something and give users information access efficiency (Woody, 2009). They can be found and downloaded on websites such as Widgetbox, Widgipedia, Yahoo!Widgets or Google Gadgets (Zangirolami, 2008). Woody (2009) suggests that widgets scattered the Web into 'unimaginable numbers of semi-autonomous tools which on one hand are suspended in a vacuum waiting to be picked by the users and on the other hand are able to do what they were built for regardless of the location'. Amongst others widgets can: display news alerts, sport scores, maps, database statistics, weather reports, and RSS (Really Simple Syndication) feeds, technology personalising stream of information for website viewers (Lawton, 2007). Not only can they be picked to meet specific user's needs and interests, but also, depending on their purpose, they can be personalised to accurately filter the information to the exact requirement of users. The personalisation in terms of UPC happens on three levels. Firstly, the interface of the content aggregator can be customised with preferred theme, colours etc. available from the aggregator's gallery. Secondly, only the widgets of interest are selected and downloaded to build the personal page. Finally, further personalisation is possible by setting the individual preferences for the specific widget. For example the weather forecast widget is picked only by these users that have interest in weather reports. The final stage of customisation happens once the widget is downloaded, when the user specifies the city or cities he or she wants the weather reports for.

The marketing potential of widgets was spotted when Facebook enabled building them into the social network, where they can be shared and passed among users and spread virally. In March 2008 there were over 14000 widgets competing on Facebook only (Kuntz, 2008) even though the ad-related market of widgets was only at its infancy (King, 2008). Although companies primarily invest in advertising widgets (Lawton, 2007), some use widgets for customer relationship building (O'Connor, 2008). A popular example of a travel widget is 'Cities I've Visited' by TripAdvisor which took 3 days and 2 people to create and has been installed by 7.8 million users (O'Connor, 2008). Although, as in case of any personalisation tools, there are privacy but also malware concerns about using widgets, many investors are convinced that the widgets will become very important in the future (Lawton, 2007).

3 Methodology

The primary purpose of this research was to discover how UPC can be used to advance destination marketing. The method chosen for that purpose was web analysis using a qualitative online exploratory study. Since it is the widgets that users personalise their content with, they were chosen as the research objects. The presence of travel and tourism related widgets online was investigated by O'Connor (2008) and the findings suggested that the biggest sample of those could have been found among Google Gadgets, designed for the iGoogle content aggregator.

A GoogleMail account was created for the purpose of the research and used to sign up for the iGoogle account. In July 2009 the personalised homepage was used for the download of the widgets representing tourism destinations, which were searched for using four keywords: 'destination', 'travel', 'holidays' and 'vacations' and downloaded. The widgets which came up as the search results but were not representing tourism destinations in any way; were not in English or had already been included to the page were omitted. As a result 170 widgets matched the research needs and were explored in detail. The analysis of the collected widgets took place in order to meet the second objective of the study: researching the actual, present value of widgets and assessing the potential of UPC for destination marketing. The actual, present value of widgets in destination marketing was examined with use of six research questions: **R1**: Does the widget represent long tail or/and short head destination(s)?; **R2**: Which tourism sector does the organisation/individual that uploaded the widget come from?; **R3**: What was the purpose of the widget creation?; **R4**: What function does the widget offer to the content aggregator users?; **R5**: What form is the widget presented in?; **R6**: Which stage(s) of the travel information search does it facilitate? Each of the questions was asked with regards to each of the downloaded widgets. The results gave grounds to answer the final research question: **R7**: How can UPC be used to advance marketing of destinations? The potential of UPC for destination marketing was assessed and the second research objective was fully met.

The classification of the destination(s) presented in the widgets according to the long tail vs. short head position (R1) was done following the criteria suggested by Lew (2008). The smaller (in terms of number of visitors, facilities, revenues or attractions), the less known (with exception of bad reputation which pushes destinations further down the long tail) and the more geographically isolated a destination was, the more it belonged to the long tail. Hence, the mass tourism destinations fell therefore into the short head while the niche destinations were the long tail. In case of R2, R3, R4 and R5 the criteria for classification of the widgets were created as they emerged during the research process. For the analysis of the collected widgets according to the R6, the model suggested by Gretzel, Fesenmaier and O'Leary (2006) was used. Following this framework there are three stages of the travel information search: 1) pre-consumption stage where information is used for decision making, planning, transaction, expectation and anticipation of the trip; 2) consumption stage where information is required to make connections with people, facilitate en-route and on-site navigation, support short term decision making and carry out on-site transactions;

and 3) post-consumption stage where the information from the trip is documented, stored and shared with other people. R7 was the final question and was answered basing on the results of the analysis of R1-R6 and was only approached once the analysis of R1-R6 was completed. Finally, the exploratory research findings were analysed together with the conceptual model and allowed meeting the primary study objective – discovering how UPC could be used to advance destination marketing.

There are several limitations to the method. The keywords used to search for the widgets were rather popular ones, thus belonging to the short head of keywords. The research by Xiang, Gretzel and Fesenmaier (2009) found however, that while tourism domain is mostly represented in search engines by small amounts of keyword, there is also a long tail of words reflecting unique experiences offered at destinations which also represent individual and specific needs of tourists. The same might be assumed in case of widget search engine, where there might have been more widgets relevant to the study which have not been collected as they did not come up under the keywords used. Furthermore, data collection and analysis was carried out by one researcher only. Hence, some functions, values or attributes of the widgets with response to the seven research questions might have been unnoticed or misread during the classification and exploring the widget potential.

4 Results

4.1 The actual present use of widgets for destination marketing

The research has shown that the top five destination related widget providers (R2) in order of extent are: OTAs, content aggregator (Google), travel information/reviews/blogs aggregator, meta-search engines and travel guides. Other widget providers included: attractions, car hire companies, online press, accommodation providers, tour operators and UGC networks/communities. DMOs were found to be providers of only three of the 170 researched widgets. Long tail destinations (R1) in particular have very low online representation through widgets. Short head destinations have higher widget presence yet the overwhelmingly biggest proportion of widgets represent a mix of long tail and short head destination. The main purpose of widget creation (R3) of the widgets was informational, or transactional, followed by promotion of destinations or other products. Few organisations used widgets purely to add value for customers, while Google used them in order to redirect users to customised search engines and to increase targeting accuracy. The most common type of widgets (R4)is tourism product search engines, followed by photo galleries or individual photos, travel news and deal updates. More innovative forms of widgets included: price calendar on a selected flight route, best fares graphs, web camera transmissions from selected destinations, promotional videos from destinations, interactive underground maps, driving direction finders, journey planners for London transport and holiday countdowns. Text followed by pictures as the most popular form of information communication in widgets (R5). More unique forms included: video, map, or calendar. Widgets are useful not only for all three stages of travel information search (R6) but occasionally are also designed to provide information relevant to locals, which can also be used by tourists. The overall analysis suggests that destination marketing can be advanced (R7) through UPC in three ways: by facilitating destination information search, increasing destination online presence, and by providing the visitors with tools which add value and might be applicable to any destination.

4.2 The potential use of widgets in destination marketing

The UPC seems to be the most sophisticated form of personalisation, perfectly meeting its main goals indicated by Albert, Goes, and Gupta (2004); and Pitkov, Schutze, Cass, Cooley, Turnbull, Edmonds, Adar and Breuel, (2002) namely: control of purposeless Web surfing and delivering highly focused and relevant content that matches users' needs. Following Park and Gretzel (2007) who suggested that personalisation increased customers' satisfaction with DMO websites, and Gretzel *et al* (2000) who claimed that success of online marketing is relating to users through customised interactions, it can be assumed that destination online presence in the form of widgets should also be appreciated by potential visitors. The privacy issues, inseparably related to personalisation (Manber, Patel & Robison, 2000), can be resolved in the widget context, since the widgets can be downloaded and disposed of without any strings attached.

The travel related UPC is the next step in tourist empowerment as pointed out by Buhalis (2003) and Buhalis and O'Connor (2005) and happens on three levels. Firstly, travellers are empowered to access accurate and relevant information (Buhalis, 1998) - including those designed for destination locals (e.g. traffic updates). Secondly the empowerment comes through further interface customisation and increased user friendliness, and finally through even stronger control of promotional messages and incentives (King, 2002) which thanks to UPC tourist can filter and select to allow to be reached by. Once the relevant widgets are found and downloaded the user gets easy access to relevant information for each of the three stages of information search (Gretzel *et al,* 2006). More efficient pre-consumption search includes access to sources such as UGC, and meta-search engines, which increase price transparency, reduce the risk of purchase and offer great assistance in travel decision making and choices – both in terms of inspiration and finding products and information that meet customers' needs. During the consumption stage, UPC can assist in en-route, dynamic packaging of tourism products at the time of consumption (Buhalis, 2003). They can provide highly relevant location-based information such as mash-up of map, reviews and travel guides, including pictures and text, enhancing customer satisfaction. Finally, at the post-consumption stage, UPC allows to share information gained during the travel with other users (R6) but also can be used for building relationship between destinations and visitors through providing updates that the tourist might be interested in after the travel. The access to the accurate and relevant information on domestic and international destinations can encourage travellers to decide to choose new places to discover, inspire and help to realise new needs, allow more full exploration of destinations. Therefore it can increase sales within the destination and build relationships with customers by 'staying in touch' even after travelling. Other widgets may not necessarily increase sales, but help the tourists during the travel (e.g.

weather forecast or currency converter) making the trip more pleasant and as the result increasing the satisfaction with the destination. Widgets were found to be extremely user friendly in terms of their design as well as functionality. They can be organised according to users' wishes and imagination and the whole UPC page can be further personalised by adding different colourful themes. The UPCs are very easy to use which makes them accessible to all market targets. Hence the Internet can support a pull-marketing strategy, where users go online and look for the information when they want to. This form is more innovative than disrupting ads on TV (Gretzel *et al*, 2000) thus has more potential to bring competitive advantage. The UPC in particular guarantees even stronger control of the messages, since tourists choose only those widgets that provide the offers and updates they are specifically interested in. Personalised marketing used by widget providers works on one-to-one terms. The marketing message is tailored to the specific preferences of the user whilst undesired and irrelevant messages are filtered and omitted.

5 Discussion and Recommendations

Currently only few destinations use widgets for marketing purposes. Those that do seem to be scattered across different unrelated widgets coming from different providers and having different purposes; which makes a comprehensive and systematic use of the widgets still difficult. Several destinations are represented by widgets assisting pre-consumption information search, yet they tend to offer very little for the other two stages. While the short head destinations increase their widget presence on the large scale through databases and experience of technology savvy Online Travel Agencies (OTAs) specialising in the mass tourism sales (R3), no widget was found focusing on aggregated sales or promotion of less popular destinations. The reason behind it might be the fact that destinations which are not sold by intermediaries do not exist in any database. Due to the obstacles of DMOs to ICTs integration (Buhalis, 2003) no such database seems to exist for the long tail of destination managed only by DMOs. Therefore, for a widget to represent a group of independent destinations, a database must emerge. More travel widgets would have to be created in order to execute this technique, which seems rather paradoxical, as proliferation of widgets shall strip the widgets off the value they add through information search efficiency. Very few users would be willing to spend hours on selecting and downloading widgets that could help the pre-consumption search and then, spend even more time looking for widgets providing information on the selected destination. Therefore, a more systematic and efficient technique of widget management, search, selection and download is required.

5.1 Creation of destination database

The recent phenomenon of gigantic database creation is connected with social networking, where users upload their profiles to communicate with friends. However, no such database exists for organisations. If a B2C User Generated Content database was created for tourism enterprises and DMOs and SMTEs were given the same tools as individual users, they could upload their profiles, share their experiences and content, and present themselves to the online world for free. It could have a great potential to grow as the social networks do. Building an open and innovative Web 2.0 database, where the information on destinations and suppliers is represented may create a centralised marketplace. If the network was proliferated as efficiently as the social networks have proved to spread, it could lead to the emergence of an open global destination database. Hitherto, in the absence of anything else, Tripadvisor.com has systematically managed information of nearly all hotels and destinations around the world. From the tourist point of view, additional value could be added if users were allowed to review the destinations and the SMTEs and if they could download widgets to personalise their information requirements. The size of the database together with the standardised profile format and richness of all forms of content could make the network attractive to browse through in search of holidays. Assuming that the potential customers would be willing to provide their basic details in exchange for the access to the database, soon the consumer database would exceed the supplier one. All in all, the most basic type of DMS consisting of supplier and customer databases and the technology connecting the two (Buhalis, 2003), could emerge in Web 2.0 era in the global, open source version. An Open Global Destination Marketing System (OGDMS) could be created to facilitate the connectivity between all players in the marketplace.

5.2 Widget search, selection and download

Standard widgets could be built to represent each type of organisations (DMOs, SMTEs) which upload their profile to the database of the OGDMS. I.e. in case of meta-search engine widgets, one should be created for each of the key types of SMTEs (e.g. restaurants, accommodation, clubs, etc.) and then automatically adjusted according to the selected destination, once the destination of interest was set by the user. The same would happen for photo gallery widgets, UGC widgets, video postcard widgets, etc. The adjustment of the content according to the destination can be assisted by using a default 'master widget', which would be a piece of software coordinating all the downloaded widgets. The master widget would automatically switch the destination of interest for all the other widgets to adjust the content to the personalised needs. This could allow the user personal preferences and interests to be set once, but provide the customised information relevant only to the destination in question. The widgets should also allow further personalisation in order to present more precise and accurate information. Using a meta-search engine widget as an example, not only should the user be able to pick the widget representing the right type of business, e.g. restaurant; but also to further personalise it by choosing the preferred type of restaurants (e.g. 'romantic', Italian or Chinese). Each destination and tourism enterprise would have to define themselves in the profile, simply by ticking the boxes best matching their brand and product offer. Apart from the OGDMS related widgets, the users could also systematise and personalise their content with other widgets such as OTAs search engines or calendar fares, currency converter, etc. Already existing destination specific widgets such as e.g. London Tube Travel Planner could be uploaded to the DMOs profiles in the OGDMS and delivered to the users through the master widget, if a universal 'tube' widget (e.g. Underground Travel

Planner) was downloaded. An illustration of the mechanisms of communication between the destinations and the users through OGDMS is presented in Figure 1.

5.3. The User Personalised Content (UPC) structure

The UPC could be divided into four (or more if required) tabs: 1) myTown, 2) myDestination, 3) myDestinationSearch and 4) myTravelSearch. The first two tabs would be personalised by users with widgets serving their interest. These would help to explore the users' own towns and cities more effectively and facilitate the pre-consumption and consumption stage of travel information search. Tab labelled myDestinationSearch would allow download of chosen meta-search engine widgets and setting the preferences within them in order to find the destination that best matches the selected criteria. Finally, myTravelSearch could invite companies

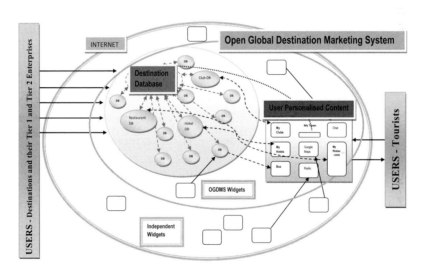

Fig. 1. Open Global Destination Marketing System

providing transport between destinations (e.g. airlines) to include their widgets helping the users to find means of transport for the dream holidays, and even OTAs and TOs, to offer packages for the less independent travellers. The users could set their pages choosing from: a) OGDMS widgets: 1) myDestination master widget – set as default for the myDestination tab, where the destination and dates of travel would be entered. The widget would work as software that adjusts the other downloaded widgets (OGDMS as well as independent ones) to search for the same personalised content regarding specific destination selected. 2) myDestinationSearch search engine widget (set as default for myDestinationSearch tab) working as a software searching for ideal destinations best fitting the set preferences in each of the selected meta-search widget of interest by matching them with destinations' profiles. 3) Topic specific meta-search engine widgets (e.g. myRestaurants) – that would search the content uploaded to the database profiles by DMOs and tourism enterprises. They could provide users with filtered information regarding the products/services available within the Town/Destination that the users set in their interests in the profile. 4) Destination/Town specific widgets (e.g. London tube interactive map) – existing widgets, which are not provided by the OGDMS but could be uploaded by DMOs into their profiles and automatically searched for in the database and downloaded to the UPC by the master widget. 5) Region specific service widgets (e.g. coach/train service widgets) – existing widgets, which are not provided by the OGDMS but could be uploaded by DMOs into their profiles and automatically searched for in the database and downloaded to the UPC by the master widget. b) Independent transport/travel provider widgets. Independent push widgets (e.g. OTAs, airline widgets, etc.) – which could be uploaded on the myTravelSearch tab and would update their offers depending on destination set in the 'outbound' or 'inbound' and finally c) Independent general gadgets. 1) General information providing widgets (e.g. weather forecast) – that would be automatically modified according to the destination chosen, by the master widget. 2) General tool widgets (e.g. currency converter).

6   Conclusion

The findings of this research imply that UPC can be utilised for the efficient management of the information online and the personalisation of products and services. In order to advance destination marketing through UPC, a global destination database should be created and a more systematic and efficient technique of widget search, selection and download shall be developed. The suggested solution in the form of a OGDMS consisting of UPC and an open source destination database has the clear potential to create an environment of equal opportunities for all destinations and enterprises, where the competition would happen on the level of best customer service, value and tourist experience provision, rather than access to financial resources and marketing skills. The destinations and SMTEs could be effectively pulled by customers instead of being pushed by the suppliers and intermediaries, while their value would be defined by the users themselves through user reviews. Although creation of such system would certainly be a costly and challenging undertaking, the research has proved that there are technology based organisations and companies which have interest in promoting long tail of destinations online. For example Google uses destination photo widgets to achieve more accurate customer targeting or to redirect users to their services such as customised search engines. Presumably, it is not the very service of creating and uploading destination widget that generates profits for Google but increased accuracy of targeting the users who expressed their interested in that destination by downloading the widget. Assuming the system would become popular, the targeting accuracy for the long tail of tourism related AdWords could be so significantly improved that sponsoring the technology even without charging destinations and their players should bring high ROI for the company. Indeed, Joyce (2009) reported on his blog that in June 2009 Google had launched a new application called 'City Tours' which consists of points of interest added to Google Maps, yet allows all destination enterprises to add their locations and content on the site. Joyce suggested that there is a great potential hidden behind this simple site – the creation of an enormous database. The data handled by different devices, can bring unimaginable effects. Xiang, Wober and Fesenmaier (2008) argued that identifying innovative ways to represent tourism information to travellers in search of experiential encounters and new solutions to improve the visibility of the tourism industry on the Internet was imperative for the competitiveness of the industry. The suggested solution in form of the OGDMS could be considered as such, yet it would also certainly require further investigation. There are not many corporations which could benefit from sponsoring such system and even if OGDMS structure was created, DMOs and SMTEs would still have to be willing to take advantage of it. Therefore, a comprehensive market research is required. Potential demand for such system, both from the tourist and the tourism industry needs to be investigated together with possible ROI for the system providers.

References

Albert, T. C., Goes, P. B. & Gupta, A. (2004). 'GIST: A Model for Design and Management of Content and Interactivity of User-Centric Websites', *MIS Quarterly* 282: 161–82.

Buhalis, D. (1998). Strategic use of information technologies in the tourism industry. *Tourism Management*, 195, 409-421.

Buhalis, D. (2003). *eTourism: Information Technology for Strategic Tourism Management.* Prentice-Hall, Upper Saddle River, New Jersey.

Buhalis, D. (2000). Marketing the Competitive Destination of the Future. *Tourism Management.* 211, 97-116.

Buhalis, D. (2008). E-Tourism and Destination Management Organisations. *Tourism Insights* [online]. Available from:
http://www.insights.org.uk.libezproxy.bournemouth.ac.uk/articleitem.aspx?title=e-Tourism+and+Destination+Management+Organisations [Accessed on: 15 May 2009]

Buhalis, D. & O'Connor, P. (2005). Information Communication Technology Revolutionizing Tourism. *Tourism Recreation Research*, 303, p. 7-16.

Buhalis, D. & Main, H. (1998). Information technology in small and medium hospitality enterprises: strategic analysis and critical factors, *International Journal of Contemporary Hospitality Management,* 105, 198-202.

Constantinides E. & Fountain, S.J. (2008). Web 2.0: Conceptual foundations and marketing issues. *Journal of Direct, Data and Digital Marketing Practice*, (9), 231-244.

Fodness, D. & Murray, B. (1997). Tourist information search. *Annals of Tourism Research* 372, 108– 119.

Fyall, A. & Leask, A. (2006). Destination marketing: Future issues — Strategic challenges. Tourism and hospitality research, 71, 50-63.

Gretzel, U., Fesenmaier, D. R. & O'Leary, J. T. (2006). The transformation of consumer behaviour. In: D. Buhalis and C. Costa eds., *Tourism business frontiers.* Oxford, UK: Butterworth-Heinemann, 9-18.

Gretzel, U., Yuan, Y. L. & Fesenmaier, D. R. (2000). Preparing for the new economy: Advertising strategies and change in destination marketing organizations. *Journal of Travel Research*, 39, 146–156.

Ho, S.Y. (2006). The Attraction of Internet Personalization to Web Users. *Electronic Markets*, 161, 41-50.

Hwang, Y. H. & Fesenmaier, D. R. (2001). Collaborative filtering: Strategies for Travel Destination Bundling. In: Sheldon, P. Wöber, K. and D. R. Fesenmaier eds. *Information Technology and Communication Technologies in Tourism. ENTER2001*, Berlin: Springer, 167-175.

Joyce, S.A. (2009, June 29). Why Google City Tours is Important to Tourism., *T4 BLOG – Travel & Tourism Technology Trends.* Available from:

530

http://tourismtechnology.rezgo.com/2009/06/why-google-city-tours-is-important-to-tourism.html [Accessed on 9 July 2009]

King, B., (2008). Building a Brand with Widgets. *Business Week*, 3 March, Available from: http://www.businessweek.com/technology/content/feb2008/tc20080303_000743_page_2.htm [Accessed on 15 May].

King, J., (2002). Destination marketing organizations: Connecting the experience rather than promoting the place. *Journal of vacation marketing*, 82, 105-8.

Kunz, B. (2008). CEO Guide to Widgets, Why Widgets Don't Work., *Business Week*, 3 March, Available from: http://www.businessweek.com/technology/content/feb2008/tc20080229_131531.htm. [Accessed on: 15 May 2009].

Lawton, G. (2007). These Are Not Your Father's Widgets. *Computer*, 407, 10-13.

Lew, A. (2008). Long tail tourism: new geographies for marketing niche tourism products. *Journal of Travel & Tourism Marketing*, 253/4, 409-419.

Litvin, S. W., Goldsmith, R. E. & Pan, B. (2008). Electronic word-of-mouth in hospitality and tourism management, *Tourism Management* 29, 458-468

Manber, U., Patel, A. & Robison, J. (2000). Experience With Personalization On Yahoo! *Communications of the ACM*, 438, 35-39.

O'Connor, P. (2008). Online Social Media and Travel, *Mintel Oxygen*. Available from: http://academic.mintel.com/sinatra/oxygen_academic/search_results/show&/display/id=387948 [Accessed on 30 May 2009]

Palmer, A. & Bejou, D. (1995). Tourism destination marketing alliances. *Annals of tourism research*, 223, 616-29.

Park, Y.A. & Gretzel, U. (2007). Success Factors for Destination Marketing Web Sites: A Qualitative Meta-Analysis. *Journal of Travel Research*, 46(1), 46-63.

Pitkov, J., Schutze, H., Cass, T., Cooley, R., Turnbull, D., Edmonds, A., Adar, E. & Breuel, T. (2002). Personalized Search, *Communications of the ACM*, 459, 50–5.

Radosevich, L. (1997). Fixing web-site usability. *InfoWorld*. 1950, 81– 82.

Rita, P., 2000. Web marketing tourism destinations. *Proceedings of the 8''' European Conference on Information System*, Vienna, Austria.

Ritchie, J. R. B. & Crouch, G. (2005). *Competitive destination : A sustainable tourism perspective*. 2nd ed. Wallingford, Oxon: CABI Publishing.

Stoltz, C. (1999). Each year, a bit less. *Washington Post*, 11 November.

Vogt. C. A. & Fesenmaier, D.R. (1998). Expanding the functional information search model. *Annals of Tourism Research*, 253, 551-578.

Werthner, H. & Klein, S. (1999). *Information Technology and Tourism – A Challenging Relationship*. Springer, Vienna.

Woody, E. (2009). Searching The Widgetized Web. *Searcher*, 171, 10-47.

Xiang, Z., Wöber, K. & Fesenmaier, D. R. (2008). The representation of the tourism domain in search engines. *Journal of Travel Research,* 472, 137-150

Zangirolami, G. (2008). Understanding the possibilities: Web widgets for beginners. *Public Relations Tactics*, 157, 11.

The Role of Social Media in Promoting Special Events: Acceptance of Facebook 'Events'

Cody Morris Paris,
Woojin Lee, and
Paul Seery

School of Community Resources & Development
Arizona State University, USA
{Cody.Paris; Woojin.Lee.1; Paul.Seery}@asu.edu

Abstract

This study examines Facebook 'events' as a medium for promoting special events to consumers. This study proposes a Social Technology Acceptance Model, an extension of the TAM model, to examine the influence of trust, expected relationships and perceived enjoyment in forming consumer attitudes towards Facebook and consumers intentions to attend an event. Data was collected through an online survey administered through special event organizer's Facebook 'Pages'. Findings of the study suggest that users' trust and expected relationship through Facebook had a significant effect on users' acceptance of Facebook and their intended offline behaviour to attend the event. Practical and theoretical implications are discussed.

Keywords: Social Capital, Web 2.0, Marketing, Consumer Behavior

1 Introduction

The virtualization of human social interactions can be attributed to the development of Web 2.0 technologies and individual's acceptance of those technologies. Recently, CGM(consumer generated media) and peer-to-peer applications known as Web 2.0 or social networking media have been perceived as a new form of word-of-mouth communication that occurs beyond the traditional social circles of consumers. (Gretzel, Kang & Lee, 2008). Social Media has gained substantial popularity in the context of online travellers' use of the Internet, as travellers can share their experiences with friends, family, tourism business, and strangers by posting their stories, comments, photos and videos (Xiang & Gretzel, 2009). Social Media or Web 2.0, also referred to as "Travel 2.0" in tourism has introduced a wide range of new advanced technology applications including media, content syndication, tagging, blogging, web forums, customer ratings and evaluation systems, virtual worlds, podcasting and online videos and so forth (Xiang & Gretzel, 2009). In other words, the term "Web 2.0" refers to a perceived second generation of web development and design, that aims to facilitate communication, secure information sharing, interoperability, and collaboration on the World Wide Web (O'Reilly, 2005). There seems to be a consensus that social media is an innovative feature of the World Wide Web (Dippelreiter, 2008; Eyrich, 2008; Subrahmanyam, 2008; Gorringe, 2009). The core idea of social media is defined as: *"information content created by people using highly accessible and scalable publishing technologies that is intended to facilitate communications, influence and interaction with peers and with public audiences, typically via the Internet and mobile communications networks."* (Wikipedia, 2009)

Tourism, as stated by Werthern & Klien (1999), is a hybrid industry that is dominated by information yet at the same time has a very real and physical service. This illustrates how unique of an industry tourism is and suggests that the application of technology in the virtual world can be as effective as marketing in the physical world. The technology and globalization push from the 1990s has changed the way markets now interact, *"Markets are becoming faster, bigger, more uniform as well as segmented, and more competitive"* (Werthern & Klien, 1999). By examining how technology is utilized by consumers through the assimilation of information, researchers get a better view of the effectiveness of online marketing as well as how consumer created content effects consumer decision making.

According to Complete.com (2009) their most recent July 2009 ranking of social networking sites Facebook has become the most used social networking site world wide, with 122 million unique visits during that month. Facebook has shown a +220.52% yearly growth and has twice as many unique visits compared to MySpace, the second ranked social networking site with 59 million unique visitors in the same month. Along with the increase of traffic to Facebook the site's interactive features have also been adapted for commercial purposes. New individualized "pages" allow for companies, non-profits, and special interest groups, as well as organizers of special events and festivals. These pages allow them to showcase their products and reach out to consumers. Facebook is a powerful online social media tool to reach countless individuals.

Hsu & Lin (2008) claimed that trust and expected relationships influence blog participants' attitude and behaviour. They identified the expected relationship as the degree that a person believed he or she could develop mutual relationship through knowledge sharing. and trust as the tendency to believe in others and in their online posted material. Additionally, Valenzuela, Park, & Kee's (2008) study shows how the social networks solidify a person's relationship and even strengthens the individuals trust of old and new acquaintances. In this study the participants social trust is taken into account on whether the person is more likely to attend a special event by either seeing if someone they know is going, if someone they trust invites them, or if the event is presented by an organization they can trust. Recent study by Chow & Chan (2008) confirmed that a social network significantly contributed on the positive attitude toward knowledge sharing and intention to share knowledge, which can lead to enhance users' mutual relationship.

Research on the marketing implications of social media, especially within the fields of tourism and special events, have recently started to take root in response to the proliferation of information technologies and the surge in new users. Most of the recent studies have been broad in focus, examining the most popular social media sites and briefly examining their potential (Todi, 2008; McGrath, 2008; O'Connor, 2008; Subrahmanyan, 2008; Gumpert, 2007). Taking a more focused approach this study examines the role Facebook has on actual marketing of special events primarily though the use of Facebook's "Events" features. This study uses an extended Technology Acceptance Model (TAM) to examine the role of trust and the expected relationship with special events' organizers on Facebook in the formation of consumer attitudes' towards Facebook as a medium for finding out about special events, and consumers intentions to attend the events.

2 Literature Review

With the rapid growth in the number users frequently logging-on to Facebook, the Technology Acceptance Model (TAM)_can provide insight for special event organizers and marketers into the full potential and capabilities of Facebook in building relationships and promoting events to users. This builds upon the TAM by examining the roles of Trust, Expected Relationships, and Perceived Enjoyment in forming Attitudes towards Facebook and influencing intentions to attend an event.

The TAM includes the variables Perceived Usefulness (PU), Perceived Ease of Use (PEOU) and Attitude. The TAM model assumes that people are likely to adapt a new technology to the extent that they believe it would be helpful for them to perform the job better, which refers to PU. With regard to PEOU, it is the degree to which an individual believes that using a new technology would be free of cognitive effort (Zhang, Zhao & Tan, 2008).

A user's enjoyment is one of the most important aspects contributing to a Websites success (Liu & Arnett, 2000). The intrinsic motivation of enjoyment has also been added as a predictor in technology acceptance behaviour (Zhang, Zhao & Tan, 2008). The extended TAM presented in this study includes a perceived enjoyment variable, which refers to the enjoyment of the experience using Facebook. Dong (2009) employed an extended TAM, with the use of intrinsic and extrinsic motivation variables, on Second Life users. The results of the study suggest that a users' several intrinsic and extrinsic motivations contribute to the enjoyment of participating in Second Life and that empathy is a key component for the enjoyment for intrinsic users while synchronicity was found to have the same importance for extrinsic users. All the while, self-efficacy was found to be equally important to both group of users. The study also suggests that the community interactions associated with Second Life have an affect on the participation. While Dong's (2009) study focuses on the "love of the game" and coercion motivations, the study itself sets up a fundamental bases for this study of how an individual's relationships and trust add on to what is already known about user acceptance of new technologies and in turn their attitude and intentions.

Additionally, the current study examines the Perceived Usefulness and Perceived Ease of Use associated with the influences of an individual's emotional response through their level of perceived enjoyment in using social media tools. Previous studies have investigated how an individual's emotional response influences Perceived Use and Perceived Ease of Use in the context of the individual's job environment, educational endeavours and using World Wide Web by indicating that positive and/or negative emotions such as; anxiety, joy, distaste and pleasure could predict overall technology acceptance (Saade & Kira, 2006; Venkatesh, 2000; Wu & Lee, 2006). The present study proposes that individuals' Perceived Enjoyment level will influence their Perceived Usefulness and Perceived Ease of Use while using Facebook, and in turn will result in a higher attitudes towards Facebook and greater intentions to attend a special events promoted through Facebook. Sas, Dix, Hart, & Su (2009) study shows that individuals using Facebook are more engaged in communication to other individuals they are familiar with and as such provide emotional support to each other increasing their enjoyment of online social media tools. This exchange of ideas creates a virtual social support system in which the individuals are able to build upon the trust already established and thus reflecting a positive perception of Facebook.

Social media and related technologies can be facilitators of social capital as they allow individuals to maintain sustained interactions with a large and diverse network of contacts. Although people often accumulate social capital as a result of their daily interactions with friends, co-workers, and strangers, it is also possible to make conscious investments in social interaction (Resnick, 2002).

Valenzuela, Park, & Kee's (2008) study indicated that there is a positive relationship between social media, specifically Facebook, and social capital as related to behaviors and attitudes. Their study focuses on how individuals interact with other individuals and how these interactions are perceived. Further, they suggest that social media can solidify a person's relationship and/or strengthen the person's trust of old and new acquaintances. Dwyer, Hitlz, & Passerini (2007) examined the relationship between trust, both in Facebook and other Facebook users, and the development of new relationships. Their findings suggest that trust is not necessary in developing new relationships on social networking sites, rather that trust is an important factor in the amount of information shared and the type/depth of a relationship. The social capital resulting from the relationships between people can contribute to knowledge sharing (Chow & Chan, 2008). More specifically, the social capital coinciding with social networks, social goals and social trust can influence the attitude and subjected norm about knowledge sharing and affect individual's intentions to knowledge sharing (Chow & Chan, 2008).

A Trust and TAM model has been well studied in the area of online shopping (Gefen, Karahanna, & Straub, 2003) and the adoption of on-line tax systems (Wu & Chen, 2005). They model used in those studies conceptualizes trust from a social exchange theory (Kelley, 1979) perspective, where trust, as a antecedent to a successful business transaction is influenced by the Perceived Ease of Use of an online vendor. Trust in turn then influences the Perceived Usefulness and Intended Use of the online vendor. The model presented in the present study suggests that Trust is and Antecedent to Perceived Usefulness and Perceived Ease of Use as mediated through Expected Relationships and Perceived Enjoyment. Trust is a precursor to strong social capital and strong relationships, which in the context of social media can both influence the perceived level of enjoyment.

As a result of the literature review the hypothetical model is presented in Figure 1. The Social TAM model is an extension of the TAM model (Lee, Kozar, & Larsen, 2003), and incorporates social constructs of trust, expected relationship and Perceived enjoyment. Further the model seeks to explain both attitude towards social media, and the offline behaviour intentions of individuals as a reflection of their acceptance of the technology. This study tests the model within the context of Facebook users intention to attend special events that they were invited to by Special events organizers through Facebook 'Pages' and Facebook 'Events'. The following sections explore the methods employed and the testing of the model. Implications and conclusions from the research are then examined.

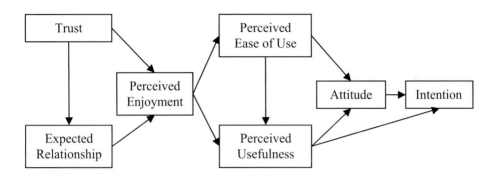

Fig. 1. Proposed Hypothetical Social TAM (** p<.01)

3 Methods

Data for the study was collected using a web-based survey that was administered throughout a 4-week period during and after selected special events held in Phoenix in spring 2009. An online survey was sent to 800 individuals who were invited to the events through Facebook. More specifically, surveys were sent out through Facebook to fans of the different special event Facebook 'Pages'. The Facebook pages consisted of Phoenix Metro area special events; The Great Arizona Beer festival and Phoenix Pride celebration, as well as undergraduate students at Arizona State University, who had been to other events promoted through Facebook. The response rate was about 20 percent, which resulted in 155 usable responses.

All the items used to measure the constructs were adapted from prior studies with modifications to fit the specific context of the social networking media (in this case, Facebook) Those who were invited to events promoted through Facebook in Phoenix were asked to indicate whether they have been invited to an event using Facebook before, the usefulness of Facebook, the ease of use and enjoyment of Facebook for sharing and finding out about events. Perceived usefulness and perceived ease of use were operationalized with three items respectively, which were derived from previous research (Lai & Li, 2005; Shih, 2004). Additionally, perceived enjoyment was measured using three items from Venkatesh, Speier & Morris (2002).Respondents were also asked to indicate how their level of trust of the information on provided by event organizers on Facebook and their expected relationship through Facebook. The scale items for trust and expected relationship were adapted and modified from Hsu & Lin (2008). Finally, respondents needed to indicate the intention to attend the events that they were invited to through Facebook. Users' attitudes toward using Facebook to get the information of events were measured with three items adapted from Hsu & Lin (2008), and the scale items for the participants' intentions to go to the event were adapted and modified from Morosan & Jeong (2008). Each item was measured on a seven-point Likert scale, ranging from "strongly disagree" (1) to "strongly agree" (7). Descriptive analyses, Discriminant Validity, Reliability and Path analyses were used to test the proposed relationships of the extended TAM model including trust and expected relationships variables.

4 Results

4.1 Reliability and Validity

The internal consistency reliability (ICR) of each construct was measured by computing the composite reliability coefficients. According to Bagozzi and Yi (1988), it was suggested that all composite reliabilities should be above the .60 benchmark. As shown Table 1, the internal consistency reliability values ranged from .85 (Intention) to .95 (Attitude). Since none of the values for all seven constructs including Trust, Expected Relationships, Perceived Usefulness, Perceived Ease of Use, Perceived Enjoyment, Attitude and Intention were less than .6, the reliability of the scales could be accepted.

Discriminant validity of the constructs, presented in Table 1, can be confirmed when the estimated correlations of the constructs are not excessively high (> .85) or excessively low (<.10) (Kline, 1998). Based on the value of all the correlation estimates between the associated constructs, all values fell in the acceptable range, which indicated that the discriminant validity of the constructs was supported. At the same time, the convergent validity was also evaluated by the average variance extracted (AVE). According to Fornell & Larcker (1981), it was recommended that AVE values higher than .5 are acceptable. The average variance extracted for all seven constructs exceeded the threshold value of .5, thus it can be claimed that discriminant validity was justified. Furthermore, for a satisfactory degree of discriminant validity, it was argued that the square root of AVE of an each construct should exceed the inter-construct and the other constructs in the model (Gefen & Straub, 2005). With regard to this research, even though some of the variables present relatively high inter-correlations, the convergent and discriminant validity of this model were satisfactory, showing all the AVE square roots are above .8

Table 1. Discriminant Validity of Constructs

	Trust	Relate*	Enjoyment	Ease of Use	Usefulness	Attitude	C.R	A.V.E.
Trust							.88	.85
Relate*	.68**						.92	.89
Enjoyment	.69**	.62**					.91	.88
Ease of Use	.62**	.47**	.67**				.88	.85
Usefulness	.69**	.55**	.73**	.82**			.86	.82
Attitude	.69**	.64**	.77**	.64**	.68**		.95	.93
Intention	.63**	.68**	.67**	.57**	.59**	.75**	.85	.81

Note: Relate* stands for Expected Relationship, C.R. is Composite Reliability, A.V.E. is Average Variance Extracted, ** p<.01

4.2 Path Analysis

A path analysis was conducted to validate the hypothetical Social Technology Acceptance Model (Figure 1), which adds the social constructs of trust, expected relationship variable, and perceived enjoyment to the TAM model. The basic assumption of this study is that users' trust of information about an event on Facebook can influence the strength of the relationship between users on Facebook, and then it can affect perceived usefulness, ease of use, and enjoyment of using the Facebook, which can lead to their favourable attitude toward using Facebook and finally influence the intention to go to the event.

SPSS Amos 16.0 software using the ML estimation method (Arbuckle, 2007) was used to perform the path analysis with all the casual relationships being tested simultaneously. In the context of reasonable fit for the model, it is recommended that X^2/df should not exceed 3 (Bentler & Bonett, 1989) while GFI should be greater than the recommended value of .8 (Seyal, Rahman and Rahim, 2002). It was also suggested by Bentler & Bonett (1989) that NFI and CFI should be the scores of .9 or higher as the evidence of good fit and RMSEA needs to be around 0.1 (Browne & Cudeck, 1993). All of the goodness-of-fit measures in the study fell into acceptable ranges with scaled X^2/df =1.2, CFI=.99, GFI=.98 NFI=.99; RMSEA=.04, thus it can be acclaimed that the path model for this study provided an excellent fit to the data.

Furthermore, the regression coefficient of each proposed path was positive and significant as shown in Figure 2. Accordingly, it indicated that all hypothesized relationships between constructs (Figure 1) are supported in this study. As the result of the analysis, 40% of the variance of the Intention to go to the event after having looked at Facebook is explained by the specified explanatory constructs. First of all, trust and expected relationships explained 51% of variance in perceived enjoyment.

538

Perceived enjoyment and perceived ease of use together explained 70% of the variance in perceived usefulness. Also, perceived ease of use and perceived usefulness explained 27% of variance in attitude toward to use Facebook.

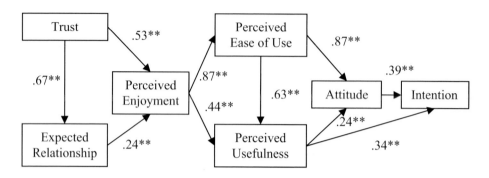

Fig. 2. Results of Path Analysis (** p<.01)

This study was able to establish trust of the event information on Facebook users' expected relationship on Facebook as an important and valid construct and its effects on favourable attitude toward using Facebook and intention to go to the event. More specifically, trust of event information on Facebook had a significant effect on the strength of the relationship between users on Facebook (β=.67, p<.01) and the trust and strength of relationship variables had a significant impact on perceived enjoyment (β=.53, p<.01, β=.24, p<.01). Interestingly, perceived enjoyment not only had a direct effect on perceived usefulness (β=.44, p<.01) but also indirectly affected perceived usefulness through perceived ease of use (β=.87, p<.01). Similarly, Perceived usefulness also not only directly influences the intention to go to the event (β=.34, p<.01) but also indirectly affects intention to go to the event through favourable attitude toward using Facebook (β=.24, p<.01) for sharing and viewing events. In addition, perceived ease of use itself has a strongly impact on attitude toward using Facebook.

5   Conclusions and Implications

Consequently, as expected, the core hypotheses of the Social TAM model were satisfied from this study, which is consistent with previous studies. The results also contributed to the literature suggesting that users' trust and expected relationship through Facebook had a significant effect on users' acceptance of Facebook and their actual offline behaviour. While previous extensions of the TAM model focused on the acceptance of technologies, especially user's adoption of information systems and information technologies, this study focused on the social implications associated with user's acceptance of social media. The findings of this study are important for businesses and organizations as they increasingly adopt marketing strategies focused around social media and consumer generated media. Understanding the social concepts inherent to social media, such as social capital and the related concepts of trust and relationships, and the influence of these concepts on the attitudes towards the technologies being utilized and the influence on consumer behaviour will allow for more successful marketing strategies. The results of this study suggest that businesses should actively seek to build trust with their consumers using their Facebook pages, and that their efforts should be made to focus on making their Facebook Events straightforward and entertaining to be most effective. The findings of this study suggest that user's acceptance of Facebook Events can influence their actual intentions to attend an event.

Future studies should test the Social TAM model proposed by this study in different situations. The model could be further validated by testing it on other social media, like Twitter and Youtube in order to explore any differences in the relationship between acceptance of social media and off-line behaviour intentions. Further, the implications for purchasing behaviour or destination choice of reviews and social relationships/interactions on sites like TripAdvisor or information on sites like Wikitravel, could further be understood. Some limitations of this study could also be overcome through future research. Larger sample sizes would allow for robust statistical methods like structural equation modelling to be used to examine relationships. As this study has a small sample size, the results should not be generalized without future testing of the model will a larger sample.

References

Arbuckle, J.L,(2007). *Amos 16.0 User's Guide*, Amos Development Corporation USA.

Bagozzi, R.P. & Yi, Y. (1989). On the Evaluation of Structural Equation Models. *Journal of Academy Marketing Science*. 16, 74-94

Bentler, P.M. & Bonett, D.G. (1989). Significance Tests and Goodness of Fit in the Analysis of Covariance Structures. *Psychology Bulletin*. 88, 588-606

Browne, M. & Cudeck, R. (1993). Alternative Ways of Assessing Model Fit, in: K.A. Bollen, J.S. Long (Eds.), *Testing Structural Equation Models*, Sage, Newbury Park, CA.

Chow, W.S. & Chan, L.S. (2008). Social Network Social Trust and Shared Goals in Organizational Knowledge Sharing. Information & Management. 45, 458-465

Compete.com (2009). "Social Networks: Facebook Takes Over Top Spot, TwitterClimbs" Retrieved 8/31/2009 from http://blog.compete.com/2009/02/09/facebook-myspace-twitter-social-network/

Dippelreiter, B., Grün, C., Pöttler, M., Seidel, I., Berger, H., Dittenbach, M., et al. (2008). Online tourism communities on the path to web 2.0: An evaluation. *Information Technology and Tourism, 10*(4), 329-353.

Dong, H. S. (2009). The evaluation of user experience of the virtual world in relation to extrinsic and intrinsic motivation. *International Journal of Human-Computer Interaction, 25*(6), 530-553.

Dwyer, C., Hiltz, S., & Passerini, K. (2007). Trust and privacy concern within social networking sites: A comparison of Facebook and Myspace. *Proceedings of the Thirteenth American Conference on Information Systems, Keystone, Colorado*, August 9-17.

Ellison, N. B., Steinfield, C., & Lampe, C. (2007). The benefits of Facebook "friends:" Social capital and college students' use of online social network sites. *Journal of Computer-Mediated Communication, 12*(4), 1143-1168.

Fornell, C.R. & Larcker, D.F. (1981). Structural Equation Models with Unobserved Variables and Measurement Error. *Journal of Marketing Research*. 18, 39-50

Gefen, D., Karahanna, E., & Straub, D. (2003). Trust and TAM in online shopping: An integrated model. *MIS Quarterly, 27(1)*, 51-90.

Gefen, D. & Straub, D. (2005). A Practical Guide to Factorial Validity Using PLS-Graph: Tutorial and Annotated Example. *Communications of AIS.* 16(1): 182-217.

Gorringe, H. (2009). New ways to communicate: The development of web 2.0 and social media; paper presented at the UK national farm management conference, oxford, UK, November 2008. , *13*(8) 587-592.

Gretzel, U., Kang, M & Lee, W.J. (2008). Differences in Consumer-Generated Media Adoption and Use: A Cross-National Perspective. *Journal of Hospitality and Leisure Marketing,* 17(1-2).

Xiang, Z. & Gretzel, U. (2009). Role of Social Media in Online Travel Information Search. *Tourism Management*, in press.

Gumpert, D. E. (2007). *What entrepreneurs need to know* McGraw-Hill Companies, Inc. Business Week Online.

Hendrickson, A. R., Massey, P. D., & Cronan, T. P. (1993). On the test-retest reliability of perceived usefulness and perceived ease of use scales. *MIS Quarterly*, 17, 227-230.

Hsu. C.L., & Lin, J.C. (2008). Acceptance of blog usage: The role of technology acceptance, social influence and knowledge sharing motivation. *Information & Management, 45*, 65-74.

Kelley, H. H. (1979). *Personal relationships: Their structure and processes.* Mahwah, NJ:Lawrence Erlbaum Associates.

King, W. R., & He, J. (2006). A meta-analysis of the technology acceptance model. *Information & Management, 43*(6), 740-755.

Kline, R.B. (1998). *Principles and practice of structural equation modeling.* New York: The Guildford Press.

Lai, V.S., & Li, H. (2005). Technology acceptance model for Internet banking: An invariance analysis. *Information & Management*, 42, 373-386.

Lee, Y., Kozar, K., & Kai, L. (2003) The technology acceptance model: Past, present, and future. *Communications of the Association for Information Systems*, 12, 752-780.

Liu, Chang., & Arnett, Kirk. (2000). Exploring the factors associated with Web site success in the context of electronic commerce. *Information and Management*, 38 (1), pp. 23-33.

McGrath, Michael G. (2008). Employing 'Social Networking Analysis' to Influence Tourism Events Decision-Making: A Pilot Study. Centre for Hospitality and Tourism Research.

Morosan, C. & Jeong, M. (2008). Users' perception of two types of hotel reservation Web sites. *International Journal of Hospitality Management*, 27, 284-292.

O'Connor, P. (2008). Online social media and travel - international. *Travel & Tourism Analyst,* , 1-33.

O'Reilly, Tim (2005). "What Is Web 2.0" O'Reilly Network. Retrieved 8/26/2009 from http://oreilly.com/web2/archive/what-is-web-20.html

Saade, R. G., & Kira, D. (2006). The emotional state of technology acceptance. *Issues in Informing Science and Information Technology, 3*, 529-539.

Sas, C., Dix, A., Hart, J., & Su, R. (2009) Emotional experience on Facebook site. *Conference on Human Factors in Computing Systems, 27*, 4345-4350

Seyal, A.H., Rahman, M.N. & Rahim, M.M. (2002). Determinants of Academic Use of the Internet: A Structural Equation Model. *Behavior and Information Technology.* 21(1): 71-86.

Shih, H.P. (2004). Extended technology acceptance model of Internt Utilization behaviour. *Information & Management*, 41 (6), 719-729.

Subrahmanyam, K., Reich, S. M., Waechter, N., & Espinoza, G. (2008). Online and offline social networks: Use of social networking sites by emerging adults. *Journal of Applied Developmental Psychology, 29*(6), 420-433.

Szajna, B. (1994). Software evaluation and choice: predictive evaluation of the Technology Acceptance Instrument. *MIS Quarterly*, 18(3), 319-324.

Todi, Mrinal. (2008) Advertising on Social Networking Website. *Wharton Research Scholars Journal*

Valenzuela, S., Park, N., & Kee, K. F. (2008) Lessons from Facebook: The Effect of Social Network Sites on College Students' Social Capital. *9th International Symposium on Online Journalism, 2008*

Venkatesh, V. (2000). Determinants of perceived ease of use: integrating control, intrinsic motivation, and emotion into the technology acceptance model. *Information Systems Research, 11*(4), 342-365.

Venkatesh, V., Speier, C., & Morris, M.G. (2002). User acceptance enablers in individual decision making about technology: toward an intergrated model. *Decision Sciences*, 33(2), 297-315.

Werthern, H., & Stefan, K. (1999) *Information technology and tourism : a challenging relationship,* Wien, New York : Springer, 1999.

Wikipedia.org (2009). "Web 2.0". Retrieved 6/31/2009 from
   http://en.wikipedia.org/wiki/Web_2.0

Wu, I. & Chen, J. (2005). An extension of Trust and TAM model with TPB in the initial adoption of on-line tax: An empirical study. *International Journal of Human-Computer Studies*, 62, 784-808.

Wu, W. & Li, C. (2006). A contingency approach to incorporate human, emotional, and social influence into a TAM for KM programs. *Journal of Information Science, 33*(3), 275-297.

Xiang, Z. & Gretzel, U. (2009). Role of Social Media in Online Travel Information Search. *Tourism Management*, in press.

Zhang, S., Zhao, J. & Tan, W. (2008). Extending TAM for online learning systems: An intrinsic motivation perspective. Tsinghua Science and Technology, 13(3), 312-317.

Shared Arabian Muslim Travel Photos

Dayangku Ida Nurul-Fitri Pengiran-Kahar[ab],
Sharifah Fatimah Syed-Ahmad[ac]
Sharifah Hayaati Syed Ismail[d] and
Jamie Murphy[a]

[a]Business School,
University of Western Australia, Australia
syedas01@student.uwa.edu.au
jmurphy@biz.uwa.edu.au

[b]Faculty of Business and Information Technology
Institute of Technology, Brunei
ida.kahar@itb.edu.bn

[c]Faculty of Business and Accountancy
University of Malaya, Malaysia
sfsa@um.edu.my

[d]Academy of Islamic Studies
University of Malaya, Malaysia
sashsiaq@um.edu.my

Abstract

This paper investigates user generated Muslim travel photos in the understudied Arab World. In June 2009, Flickr had over 8,000 Muslim travel photos for Arab countries. Content analysis on 589 photos revealed that males surpassed females in posting photos and nearly two-thirds of the photos showed human presence. The North African region had more photos with human presence than the Middle East region. Most Arab countries had more male than female presence, with four in five female photos containing females wearing a headscarf. Countries with more or equal female presence to males could suggest investment opportunities by female business entrepreneurs with Arab Muslim women.

Keywords: user-generated content, photo, Arab League, travel, Muslim

1   Introduction

A common view of the Arab Muslim world seems limited to portrayals by Western media, movies, and tourism organizations (Govers & Go, 2004; Hudson, 2006; Shaheen, 2006). A new trend, user-generated content (UGC), shifts some control of this view away from these traditional media as anyone with Internet access can upload and view images of the Arab World. With UGC, individuals create and share photos, text, video and audio of a country or destination that potential travellers could use (Choi, Lehto, & Morrison, 2007; Daugherty, Eastin, & Bright, 2008). As one in two tourists view photos via UGC (Yoo, Lee, Gretzel, & Fesenmaier, 2009), UGC photography sites such as Flickr (flickr.com) could shape Arab countries' images.

From an applied perspective, tourist and local portrayals of the increasingly important Muslim and Arab tourism destinations (Al-Hamarneh & Steiner, 2004) can accentuate or attenuate the world's interest. Furthermore, these portrayals differ within the Arab World – Middle Eastern and North African countries – due to varying tourist arrivals and Muslim populations (Central Intelligence Agency, 2009; World Tourism Organisation, 2007a, 2007b). For example, Arab countries' differing tourist and Muslim populations could shape the tourist gaze of Muslim and local customs such as Arab women with varying headscarf styles. In addition, as the posters of UGC can shape viewers' gaze for a destination, examining the posters of Arab World photos and their portrayals could increase understanding of photo-based UGC as possible destination recommenders.

Academically, as the West dominates mainstream tourism studies including technology research (Hashim, Murphy, & Hashim, 2007), this study add to the research of tourism and technology in Muslim countries. Furthermore, while studies focus on tourist photos, few if any studies examine destination portrayal via photo-based UGC such as Flickr.com. This paper helps tackle these research gaps by examining Flickr for Muslim travel photos from the League of Arab States' 22 countries, and addresses three research questions:

- How does the gender of Flickr posters relate to the portrayal of humans in Arab countries?
- How do Muslim travel Flickr photos portray human presence for Arab countries?
- How do Flickr photos for Middle Eastern and North African regions differ?

2 Literature Review

2.1 Photography and User-generated content

UGC photos are important to tourists, with one in two tourists viewing them (Yoo et al., 2009). Users can view and post photos on Flickr, its main attraction, through photo features on social networks sites such as Facebook, MySpace and Friendster, as well as on travel review sites such as TripAdvisor (Cantoni, Tardini, Inversini, & Marchiori, 2009; Cormode & Krishnamurthy, 2008; Syed-Ahmad, Hashim, Horrigan, & Murphy, 2009). Users can also control privacy settings for their posted photos and identities (Cox, Clough, & Marlow, 2008; Lange, 2008). For example, users could post public photos while keeping their identities anonymous or post private photos accessible just for selected friends and family. Flickr, ranked 33rd of all Internet sites in September 2009, enables users to share artistic, family, friend and travel photos with friends, family, contacts and the general public (Alexa, 2009; Cox et al., 2008).

Aside from depicting objects and environments, photos can inform and reveal photographer beliefs about objects and environments (Banks, 2007). While studies focus on tourist photos, few if any studies examine travel photos on UGC websites. Flickr photos can portray what locals enjoy and how tourists perceive destinations as well as what destinations offer. As part of their gaze on destinations, tourists take and share photographs (Urry, 1990) offline and online to inform, show and possibly recommend selected destinations. For instance, tourists in Muslim countries could encounter and capture photos of cultural and religious norms such as praying in public and women wearing headscarves.

As tourism is increasingly important in the Muslim and Arab World (Al-Hamarneh & Steiner, 2004), what tourists and locals portray could shape viewer's destination gaze and promote that destination. Yet while travellers photograph locals (Urry, 1990), tourists to Arab countries cannot freely capture locals, namely Muslim women. For example, tourist brochures warn tourists not to "photograph or point and stare at Muslim women" (Webb, 2007, p. 176) and to request permission before photographing Muslim women (Dunston & Monaghan, 2008).

2.2 The League of Arab States and Muslim Culture

Established in 1945, the 22 League of Arab States member countries in the Middle East and North Africa (MENA) are: Bahrain, Iraq, Jordan, Kuwait, Lebanon, Oman, Palestine, Qatar, Saudi Arabia, Syria, United Arab Emirates and Yemen in the Middle East, and Algeria, Djibouti, Egypt, Libya, Mauritania, Morocco, Somalia, Sudan and Tunisia in North Africa.

The MENA region has similarities in language, identity and culture (Otterman, 2009), but differences in economic policy (Dervis & Shafik, 1998), political and social structures (Gray, 2000). The geographic advantages also differ, particularly North Africa benefitting from its tourism industry (Gray, 2000). Egypt typifies this advantage, "the most modernized and populous country in the Arab world" in the early twentieth century (Yousef, 2004, p. 91). With its "historical and natural attractions" (Gray, 2000, p. 406), Egypt is the top Arab tourist destination followed by Saudi Arabia and United Arab Emirates (World Tourism Organisation, 2007b). In general, Egypt accounts for the greatest population in North Africa (Internet World Stats, 2009a, 2009b) and has a slightly higher Muslim population at 95% (Central Intelligence Agency, 2009) compared to the Middle Eastern region.

The Arab States have a high Muslim population, 89% on average (Central Intelligence Agency, 2009) reflecting the prominence of Muslim culture, albeit differing across countries. The unique cultures stem from many factors including Muslim beliefs and practices, and local traditions inherited from the norms and influences of Mongol, Persian, Turkic, Berber, Indian and Indonesian cultures. Muslim beliefs and practices originate from the Quran (revelations from God to the Prophet Muhammad), and the *hadith* (a compilation of Muhammad's traditions and statements) (Nigosian, 1987). In acknowledging Muslim culture, one should distinguish between Islamic teaching and practices, and local culture; Islam may forbid some local customs.

2.3 Headscarves and Arab Muslim women

Wearing a headscarf or *hijab* is an interpretation of a command in the Quranic verse al-Nur (24:31): "And say to the believing women that they should lower their gaze and guard their modesty; that they should not display their *zeenah* (charms, or beauty and ornaments) except what (must ordinarily) appear thereof" (Al-`Ak Abdul Rahman, 1998). Yet in practicing this command, each Muslim woman or community group may perform the Quranic injunction according to their country's cultural background.

A Muslim woman's identity may be seen from the headgear, headscarf or veil (Insoll, 1999), which indicates the country of origin (Ruby, 2006). Arab Muslim women wear an *abaya*; Persian women a *chedor*; Afghani women a *Burqa*; Indo-Pakistani women a *niqab* or *purdah*; Malaysian/Indonesian women a *tudung* or *kerudung*; and the *buibui* in East Africa (Imam Reza, 2009). These headscarf variations, observable and photographable, appear in UGC photographs.

These variations create interesting and distinct regional representations of Arab Muslim women (Zuhur, 2003). Used as a physical garment, the headscarf may be worn in many combinations from covering the head to covering part or all of the face or body (El Guindi, 1999). For example, Tunisian women wear a long scarf covering their head and shoulder (Charrad, 1998) and Yemeni women wearing a *lithma* that covers the hair, forehead and whole face (El Guindi 1999). The variety in styles shows a dynamic aspect of *syari`a* or Islamic law.

3 Methodology

To investigate photographs of women in the Arab states, this study employed content analysis, which is prevalent in tourism, photography, website and UGC studies (Cox et al., 2008; Garrod, 2009; Hashim et al., 2007). Critical steps in content analysis include sampling, operationalizing the variables and establishing coding reliability (Neuendorf, 2002).

Prior to sampling, the researchers examined keywords; visitors can search Flickr photos using keywords. Flickr searches in June 2009 returned more photos for the keywords 'Muslim' and 'travel' than for 'Islam' and other tourism terms respectively. The three chosen keywords, using the Boolean 'and', were the Arab country, Muslim, and travel. Researchers chose Flickr result listings according to relevance, instead of the two other possible criteria, recent or interesting, in order to focus on Muslim travel photos in the Arab countries.

The first column in Table 1 shows the 18 June 2009 number of Flickr photos by three keywords "country, Muslim, and travel". The second column indicates this study's quota sampling to analyze up to the first 30 returned photos, or 589 photos across 23 countries and emirates. Sampling for the United Arab Emirates was for all seven emirates – Abu Dhabi, Ajman, Dubai, Fujairah, Sharjah, Ras al-Khaimah, and Umm

al-Quwain − due to each emirate's autonomy and diversity (UAE Government, 2006).
The Comoros and four emirates had no photos with all three keywords.

Table 1. Arab Countries' Flickr Photos and Human Presence

Country	Country Muslim travel photos	Studied Country Muslim travel photos	% of Studied Photos				% Female Headscarf
			Human	Male	Female	Headscarf	
Bahrain	133	30	43	20	27	17	63
Iraq	85	30	87	80	30	17	66
Jordan	920	30	73	57	30	23	78
Kuwait	26	26	69	50	8	8	100
Lebanon	187	30	63	43	33	23	70
Oman	39	30	67	30	37	33	91
Palestine	600	30	63	33	23	13	57
Qatar	14	14	43	29	21	21	100
Saudi Arabia	104	30	60	27	13	13	100
Syria	792	30	63	50	27	23	88
Dubai (UAE)	171	30	33	20	13	10	75
Abu Dhabi (UAE)	38	30	40	40	10	3	33
Sharjah (UAE)	92	30	20	10	0	0	n/a
Yemen	874	30	67	33	27	20	75
M.E. Total	4,075	400	57	38	22	16	74
Algeria	18	17	65	35	29	29	100
Djibouti	4	4	25	25	0	0	0
Egypt	2,280	30	53	33	33	33	100
Libya	10	12	58	50	50	33	67
Mauritania	21	21	71	52	19	19	100
Morocco	1,615	30	90	57	37	33	91
Somalia	30	30	83	53	63	53	84
Sudan	15	15	67	60	7	0	0
Tunisia	348	30	57	37	20	17	83
N.A. Total	4,341	189	68	46	33	29	87
Overall Total	8,416	589	357	237	148	118	80
% of studied photos	-	100	61	40	25	20	

Pre-testing with two non-Arab Muslim countries, Malaysia and Turkey, aided
operationalising human and gender presence variables as in Table 2, as well as the
poster's gender and presence of headscarves, totalling eight variables. Three variables

548

of human presence, four for female headscarf variations and one for poster gender assisted with the first research question *'How does gender of Flickr posters relate to portrayal of humans in Arab countries?'* Human presence photos may portray either male, female, both gender and general human presence due to distance (Table 2), assisting the second research question *'How do Muslim travel Flickr photos portray human presence for Arab countries?'* Human presence and headscarves aided the third research question *'How do Flickr photos for Middle Eastern and North African regions differ?"* While female headscarf had four variations, the variables were grouped to reflect a general category of females wearing headscarves.

Table 2. Human Presence on Flickr Photos

MALE	FEMALE	MALE AND FEMALE	HUMAN
Praying by Jungle_Boy	Mother and Daughter by Whippeltree	A man and his child by moniwe1	March of the Pilgrims by Shabbir Siraj

Two Muslim postgraduate students at an Australian university, authors of this paper, refined and managed the coding process from April to June 2009. A second set of pre-tests with Iran, Pakistan and Turkey familiarized coders with the variables, helped revise variables and test coding reliability. The pre-test on Turkey had a Scott's pi intercoder reliability coefficient (Neuendorf, 2002, p. 150) of .76 for the most disagreed variable. Coders disagreed on 8, or 7%, of the 120 (15 photos x 8 variables) coding entries for Turkey. The main study ran from 15 May to 2 June 2009, on 589 Flickr photos posted before 12 May 2009. Reliability increased for the main study; Scott's pi ranged from .88 to 1.0. Both coders agreed on 230 coding entries, or 96% of the 240 Egyptian entries (30 photos x 8 variables).

4 Results

4.1 Flickr Posters and Arab Human Portrayal

Of the 589 photos, almost two-thirds had human presence, and males dominated as both photo subjects and posters. As Table 3 shows, human presence was visible in 357 photos (61%); 237 (40%) photos had male subjects and 148 (25%) contained females. Male posters shared the highest number of photos (65%), female (18%), while some concealed their identities (18%), as reported in Table 3.

Poster's gender had no significant relationship with human presence and a small relationship, as measured through Cramer's V for the three categories of male, female and headscarf portrayal (Pallant, 2007). For male presence, all poster categories had more photos of male subjects than no male subjects. For female presence however, male and anonymous posters had more photos without female presence, while female posters had more photos with female subject than without. All posters had fewer photos with women's headscarves than without the headscarf.

Table 3. Poster's Gender with human, male and female presence

Categories	Poster's Gender			Total Photo	Chi-Square Tests for Independence for Poster's Gender		
	Male (%)	Female (%)	Not given (%)		Chi-square (χ^2)	Sig. (p)	Cramer's V
Posters	65	18	18	589			
Human presence							
	(% within poster's gender)			Photos	Relationship		
Human	59	70	56	357			
No human	41	30	44	232	4.81	.09	.09
Total	100	100	100	589			
Male presence							
	(% within poster's gender)			Photos	Relationship		
Male	41	37	42	237			
No male	19	33	15	120			
No human	41	30	44	232	13.70	.008	.108
Total	101	100	101	589			
Female presence							
	(% within poster's gender)			Photos	Relationship		
Female	21	37	27	148			
No female	38	33	29	209			
No human	41	30	44	232	12.83	.012	.104
Total	100	100	100	589			
Headscarf presence							
	(% within poster's gender)			Photo	Relationship		
With headscarf	17	30	22	118			
Without headscarf	43	40	34	239			
No human	41	30	44	232	12	.02	.101
Total	101	100	100	589			

Note: Percentages do not tally to 100% due to rounding of numbers.

4.2 Human Presence and Country

All the Arab countries had human presence, ranging from 20% to 90% of the posted photos. Morocco and Iraq had the highest human presence, respectively at 90% and 87%. Both countries were also the top countries with high male presence in their Flickr photos. Most countries (77%) had more male than female presence. Libya and Egypt had equal numbers of Flickr photos of male and female presence. Three countries – Somalia Oman and Bahrain – had more female than male presence.

Countries with the highest female presence were Somalia (63%) and Libya (50%). Public photos for Djibouti and Sharjah (UAE) had no female presence.

4.3 Comparison of Middle East and North African (MENA) regions

A comparison between the Middle East and North African regions showed the Middle East photos had a wide distribution across countries. Yet two countries – Egypt and Morocco – dominated the North African Muslim travel photos. While both regions had similar numbers of photos, this study's focus on country/emirate's quota sampling created more Middle East studied photos due to higher number of Arab states (14) compared to North Africa (9).

Of the studied photos, a higher percentage of human presence (68%) was from the North African region than from the Middle East (57%). North Africa also had more male (46%) and female (36%) photos compared to the Middle East region, 38% and 22% respectively.

Females with headscarves were also higher in North Africa, accounting for 29% compared to 16% in the Middle East. Public Flickr photos in six countries – Algeria, Egypt, Saudi Arabia, Mauritania, Qatar and Kuwait – showed all females wearing headscarves. Egypt and Libya were the only countries with equal number of male and female photos but contrasted in females wearing headscarves, 100% and 67% respectively.

5 Discussions

This study supports findings that males dominate UGC photo postings (Meyer, Rosenbaum, & Hara, 2005), unlike social network sites such as Facebook and MySpace that are more popular with females (Hargittai, 2007). This study also found nearly a fifth of posters not revealing their gender, supporting anonymity in posting UGC (Lange, 2008).

While tourists cluster the Arab World together (Winckler, 2007), the results in this study differentiated Arab countries through varying Flickr photo presence and content. Three countries – Somalia, Libya and Morocco – had higher female than male presence, perhaps suggesting the females' engagement in public community groups (TakingITGlobal, 2002). While most countries with more male than female subjects suggests low female presence in the public sphere, low female images could also stem from adherence to warnings to not photograph women. Egypt's equal male and female presence may reflect women empowerment as Egypt ranks amongst the highest within the Arab countries for female participation in economic and political activity (Sonmez, 2001).

The North African region had proportionally more human, male, female and headscarf presence than the Middle East. Perhaps posters portray Middle Eastern attractions, buildings and nature due to attractions or current situations. For example,

United Arab Emirates' Abu Dhabi, Dubai and Sharjah scored the lowest human presence across all Arab states, possibly as posters focused on images portraying country development (Govers & Go, 2004).

6 Implications

This study identified portrayals of Arab countries' posters and human subject presence, filling knowledge gaps for UGC in general and within the Arab World. This paper also contributes to the limited UGC photos studies. As users prefer recommendations from others over formal sources (Cheong & Morrison, 2008), tourism organisations could study the posted images to understand posters' gaze on destinations, as these images represent the destinations to potential consumers. Arab tourism organisations could possibly seek and promote images that best represent their countries.

Arab tourism organisations could use results from this study to change travel decisions and tourist behaviours in the Arab World. For example, countries with female dominated photos could align Flickr photos with their country's promotion to target female tourists and family travellers. Females and families may visit these countries after viewing female dominated photos, possibly creating a more welcoming impression compared to countries with male dominated Flickr presence. In addition, business women might consider travelling to these countries to look for investment opportunities (Leiper, 1979).

7 Future Research

Future studies could examine Arab World content across other UGC sites such as YouTube for videos and TripAdvisor for text reviews. As YouTube ranks 4th and TripAdvisor 349th of all websites (Alexa, 2009), these UGC websites have global reach and could influence travel decisions (Gretzel & Yoo, 2008; Tussyadiah & Fesenmaier, 2009). Other studies could focus on official Arab country images via destination websites and brochures. While travel photos on official websites for other world regions highlight the best of what destinations offer including nature and culture (Hashim et al., 2007) or project images such as wealth, power and patriotism (Huang & Lee, 2009), Arab countries may portray different images. Consequently, another study could compare what UGC and official images portray.

Flickr and other UGC sites offer new opportunities to study tourism in general and in Arab destinations. Two future studies could assist Arab tourism organisations understand tourists and target potential groups. One study could examine the types of images Flickr posters portray, such as landscapes, locals, family members and mundane images (Haldrup & Larsen, 2003; Urry, 1990). These images may be useful to depict tourist behaviour and the main purpose for travelling to these Arab countries. Another study could explore travellers' profiles, gathering information such as demographics and interests, to understand the various tourist segments. Results from both studies could assist tourism organisations plan and execute tourism programs and promotions.

References

Al-'Ak Abdul Rahman, K. (1998). *Syakhsiyyah al-Mar'ah al-Muslimah fi Dhauk al-Quran wa al-Sunnah*. Beirut: Dar al-Ma'rifah.

Al-Hamarneh, A., & Steiner, C. (2004). Islamic Tourism: Rethinking the Strategies of Tourism Development in the Arab World After September 11, 2001. *Comparative Studies of South Asia, Africa and the Middle East, 24*(1), 173-182.

Alexa. (2009). Top Sites. Retrieved 23 September, 2009, from www.alexa.com/topsites

Banks, M. (2007). *Using Visual Data in Qualitative Research*. London: SAGE Publications Ltd.

Cantoni, L., Tardini, S., Inversini, A., & Marchiori, E. (2009). *From Paradigmatic to Syntagmatic Communities: A Socio-Semiotic Approach to the Evolution Pattern of Online Travel Communities*. Paper presented at the Information and Communication Technologies in Tourism (ENTER) 2009, Amsterdam, the Netherlands.

Central Intelligence Agency. (2009). The World Factbook. Retrieved 29 April 2009, from www.cia.gov/library/publications/the-world-factbook/index.html

Charrad, M. M. (1998). Cultural Diversity Within Islam: Veils and Laws in Tunisia. In H. L. Bodman & N. Tohidi (Eds.), *Women in Muslim Societies*. Colorado: Lynne Rienner Publishers Inc.

Cheong, H. J., & Morrison, M. A. (2008). Consumers' Reliance on Product Information and Recommendations Found in UGC. *Journal of Interactive Advertising, 8*(2), //jiad.org/article103.

Choi, S., Lehto, X. Y., & Morrison, A. M. (2007). Destination Image Representation on the Web: Content Analysis of Macau Travel Related Websites. *Tourism Management, 28*(1), 118-129.

Cormode, G., & Krishnamurthy, B. (2008). Key Differences between Web 1.0 and Web 2.0. *First Monday, 13*(6), www.uic.edu/htbin/cgiwrap/bin/ojs/index.php/fm/article/view/2125/1972.

Cox, A. M., Clough, P. D., & Marlow, J. (2008). Flickr: A First Look at User Behaviour in the Context of Photography as Serious Leisure. *Information Research, 13*(1).

Daugherty, T., Eastin, M. S., & Bright, L. (2008). Exploring Consumer Motivations for Creating User-Generated Content. *Journal of Interactive Advertising, 8*(2), //jiad.org/vol8/no2/daugherty/index.htm.

Dervis, K., & Shafik, N. (1998). The Middle East and North Africa: A Tale of Two Futures. *Middle East Journal, 52*(4), 505-516.

Dunston, L., & Monaghan, S. (2008). *Top 10: Dubai and Abu Dhabi*. London: Dorling Kindersley Limited.

El Guindi, F. (1999). *Veil. Modesty, Privacy and Resistance*. Oxford: Berg.

Garrod, B. (2009). Understanding the Relationship Between Tourism Destination Imagery and Tourist Photography. *Journal of Travel Research, 47*(3), 346-358.

Govers, R., & Go, F. M. (2004). Projected Destination Image Online: Website Content Analysis of Pictures and Text. *Journal of Information Technology & Tourism, 7*(2), 73-89.

Gray, M. (2000). The Political Economy of Tourism in North Africa: Comparative Perspectives. *Thunderbird International Business Review, 42*(4), 393-408.

Gretzel, U., & Yoo, K. H. (2008). Use and Impact of Online Travel Reviews. In P. O'Connor, W. Hopken & U. Gretzel (Eds.), *Information and Communication Technologies in Tourism 2008* (pp. 35-46). Innsbruck, Austria: Springer-Verlag Wien.

Haldrup, M., & Larsen, J. (2003). The Family Gaze. *Tourist Studies, 3*(1), 23-45.

Hargittai, E. (2007). Whose Space? Differences Among Users and Non-Users of Social Network Sites. *Journal of Computer-Mediated Communication, 13*(1), jcmc.indiana.edu/vol13/issue11/hargittai.html.

Hashim, N. H., Murphy, J., & Hashim, N. M. (2007). Islam and Online Imagery on Malaysian Tourist Destination Websites. *Journal of Computer-Mediated Communication, 12*(3), jcmc.indiana.edu/vol12/issue13/hashim.html.

Huang, W.-J., & Lee, B. C. (2009). *Capital City Tourism: Online Destination Image of Washington, DC.* Paper presented at the Information and Communication Technologies in Tourism (ENTER) 2009.

Hudson, M. C. (2006). Washington vs. Al Jazeera: Competing Constructions of Middle East Realities. In *Arab Media in the Information Age* (pp. 229-248). Abu Dhabi: The Emirates Center for Strategic Studies and Research.

Imam Reza. (2009). Imam Reza (A.S.) Network. Retrieved 29 September 2009, from http://www.imamreza.net/eng/

Insoll, T. (1999). *The Archaeology of Islam.* Oxford: Blackwell Publishers Ltd.

Internet World Stats. (2009a). Internet Usage in the Middle East. Retrieved 11 September 2009, from www.internetworldstats.com/stats5.htm#me

Internet World Stats. (2009b). Internet Usage Statistics for Africa. Retrieved 11 September 2009, from www.internetworldstats.com/stats1.htm

Lange, P. G. (2008). Publicly Private and Privately Public: Social Networking on YouTube. *Journal of Computer-Mediated Communication, 13*(1), 361-380.

Leiper, N. (1979). The Framework of Tourism: Towards a definition of tourism, tourist and the tourist industry. *Annals of Tourism Research, 6*(4), 390-407.

Meyer, E. T., Rosenbaum, H., & Hara, N. (2005). *How Photobloggers are Framing a New Computerization Movement.* Paper presented at the Internet Generations 6.0: Annual Conference of the Association of Internet Researchers (AoIR).

Neuendorf, K. A. (2002). *The Content Analysis Guidebook.* Thousand Oaks: Sage Publications

Nigosian, S. A. (1987). *Islam: The Way of Submission.* Great Britain: Crucible.

Otterman, S. (2009). Arab League. *The New York Times* Retrieved 22 June, 2009, from topics.nytimes.com/topics/reference/timestopics/organizations/a/arab_league/

Pallant, J. (2007). *SPSS Survival Manual: A Step by Step Guide to Data Analysis Using SPSS.* Crows Nest, Australia Allen & Unwin

Ruby, T. F. (2006). Listening to the voices of hijab. *Women Studies International Forum, 29*(1), 54-66.

Shaheen, J. G. (2006). The New Anti-Semitism: Hollywood's Reel Bad Arabs: Impacting Public Opinion and Policy. In *Arab Media in the Information Age* (pp. 323-362). Abu Dhabi: The Emirates Center for Strategic Studies and Research.

Sonmez, S. (2001). Tourism Behind the Veil of Islam: Women and Development in the Middle East. In Y. Apostolopoulos, S. Sonmez & D. J. Timothy (Eds.), *Women As Producers and Consumers of Tourism in Developing Regions.* Westport: Praeger Publishers.

Syed-Ahmad, S. F., Hashim, N. H., Horrigan, D., & Murphy, J. (2009). *Travel Research and Sharing through User-Generated Content.* Paper presented at the 7th Asia Pacific CHRIE (APacCHRIE) 2009 Conference

TakingITGlobal. (2002). A look at Women in Somalia - Panorama - TakingITGlobal. Retrieved 31 October 2009, from http://www.tigweb.org/express/panorama/article.html?ContentID=865

Tussyadiah, I. P., & Fesenmaier, D. R. (2009). Mediating Tourist Experiences: Access to Places via Shared Videos. *Annals of Tourism Research, 36*(1), 24-40.

UAE Government. (2006). About UAE. *UAE Federal e-Government Portal* Retrieved 26 Jun 2009, 2009, from www.government.ae/gov/en/general/uae/country.jsp

Urry, J. (1990). *The Tourist Gaze: Leisure and Travel in Contemporary Societies.* London: Sage.

Webb, M. (2007). *Dubai, Abu Dhabi & the UAE*. London: Time Out Group Ltd.

Winckler, O. (2007). The Birth of Oman's Tourism Industry. *Tourism, 55*(2), 221-234.

World Tourism Organisation. (2007a). Tourism Market Trend: Africa. Retrieved 28 August 2009, from www.unwto.org/facts/eng/pdf/indicators/ITA_Africa.pdf

World Tourism Organisation. (2007b). *Tourism Market Trends: Middle East*. Madrid: World Tourism Organisation.

Yoo, K. H., Lee, Y., Gretzel, U., & Fesenmaier, D. R. (2009). *Trust in Travel-Related Consumer Generated Media*. Paper presented at the Information and Communication Technologies in Tourism (ENTER) 2009.

Yousef, T. M. (2004). Development, Growth and Policy Reform in the Middle East and North Africa since 1950. *Journal of Economic Perspectives, 18*(3), 91-116.

Zuhur, S. (2003). Women and Empowerment In The Arab World. *Arab Studies Quarterly, 25*(4), 17-38.

Acknowledgements

The authors thank the four Flickr posters for giving permission to use their photographs and Ali Medabesh for the paper's production.

The Impacts of Virtual Experiences on People's Travel Intentions

Yu-Chih Huang[a],
Sheila J. Backman[a], and
Kenneth F. Backman[a],

[a]Department of Parks, Recreation and Tourism Management
Clemson University, USA
{yhuang; back; frank}@clemson.edu

Abstract

As a virtual revolution in emerging media environments, it is believed that the 3D virtual world environment of Second Life will gain more attention and become more pervasive as a new marketing tool in business and tourism industries. The purpose of this study is to investigate flow theory in understanding the impacts of virtual experiences of Second Life on people's travel intentions. Undergraduate college students at Clemson University were chosen as participants and data was collected in April, 2009, entailing 42 usable surveys. The study results demonstrated that the antecedents of flow and flow experiences in 3D virtual destinations positively associated with people's intentions to take an actual trip. By engaging in a virtual tourism destination site and experiencing enhanced flow, customers can develop consideration and awareness in their potential destination choice. More systematic research is needed to investigate the virtual experience and its effects on the traveler's decision making process.

Keywords: Second Life; virtual experiences; travel intentions; flow theory

1 Introduction

Middleton (1994) pointed out that the process of travel decision-making is sequenced and affected by stimulus inputs, which are comprised of formal communication like advertising, internet, and sale promotion as well as informal channels of information. Montinho (1987) indicated that mass communication creates a favorable attitude that will lead to positive feelings toward a product in the travel decision-making process. Surfing the travel destination in the virtual world provides consumers with a source of vicarious experience, as well as vital information for making a travel decision (Crotts, 1999). The search for information is undertaken at different stages of the decision-making process (Murphy, Mascardo & Benckendorff, 2007) and the information gathered from the websites contributes to the development of destination image and travel decisions (Kokosalakis, et al., 2006; Prentice, 2006).

Nowadays, tourists are interested in seeking information that enables them to experience the destination rather than simply obtaining objective facts about it (Cho & Fesenmaier, 2001). Cho, Wang, and Fesenmaier (2002) declared that the emergence of the Internet and virtual reality systems enable tourists to choose what they want to experience, being active virtual participants, so that they can better assess the destination. Cheong (1999) claimed that virtual reality systems afford consumers the opportunity to experience the atmosphere of destinations, and that the customers would be in a better position to make an informed decision and thus initiate travel arrangements. When the web sites of destinations offer interactivity, the virtual experience is greatly enhanced for the customer (Cano & Prentice, 1998; Gretzel et al., 2000). Park et al. (2008) declared that virtual worlds, such as Second Life, are a natural extension of the existing Internet, potentially increasing the richness of virtual experience and social interaction.

Second Life, Created by Linden Lab in 2003, provides a social network service where people can interact, chat, talk and meet with each other. Second Life not only focuses on social interaction but also offers a variety of different forms of entertainment, including socializing, playing, and shopping (Martin, 2008). To date, the total number of residents in Second Life has reached 16 million people (Linden Lab, 2009). With the exponentially increasing population in the virtual world, businesses are participating in these environments because they see significant potential and opportunities (Schwarz, 2006). Residents of Second Life spend, in real world currency and virtual Linden dollars, the equivalent of more than 30 million US dollars a month on user to user transactions for in-world products and services (Linden Lab, 2009). Due to the attractiveness and potential of the online virtual environment for promoting products and services, companies are presenting themselves in virtual worlds to provide services (Park et al., 2008). Such companies include IBM, Toyota, Dell, Best Buy, Adidas, Cisco systems, Coca-Cola, and Sony. The business applications and economic implications generated in the virtual world of Second Life are significant.

In the tourism industry, numerous tourism destinations have invested substantially to claim virtual real estate in this three-dimensional online world. People who experience virtual destinations such as the St. Louis Arch, Galveston in Texas, Chichen Itza in Mexico, London, or Paris, for example, may become interested in visiting those destinations in person. Moreover, a number of national tourism organizations consider the virtual environment as an effective emerging tool for destination marketing. For instance, the Netherlands Board of Tourism has opened the world's first virtual national tourism board in Second Life to provide information about travel to Holland (www.hollandsecondlife.com). The tourism department of Ireland has also launched a marketing campaign in Second Life to market a real holiday destination, Dublin city (www.dublinsl.com). In addition, Starwood Hotels built a prototype of their new concept for a hotel, aloft, in Second Life to test their hotel design; the feedback received from customers was then used to help Starwood develop their design (retrieved from businessweek.com). The ultimate goal of the aloft project is to attract youthful, tech-savvy customers to the brand of Starwood Hotels. Similarly, STA Travel, the largest travel agency in the world with a focus on students, allows avatars to visit exotic locales in-world and interact with other students who may be past or potential customers, thus building social networks (Goel & Mousavidin, 2007). From a marketing point of view, the virtual world of Second Life can also become an optimal marketing platform for tourism businesses to provide travel information and to develop consideration and awareness for potential customers in their destination choice.

Tourism markets are utilizing the immersive virtual environment to enrich customers' experiences, enhancing interactions with customers at specific tourism destinations through hands-on activities and events. Hemp (2006) pointed out that online virtual worlds offer marketing potential for real-world products and services, because of their ability to generate sustained consumer engagement with a brand. Hay (2008) stated that tourism businesses who want to change their destination images can use the virtual sites to bring new products to the attention of hard-to-reach consumers. But because tourism markets are not familiar with the new medium of virtual worlds, and do not know with certainty what they can offer, not all tourism providers are ready to launch marketing campaigns to market a real holiday destination in the virtual world of Second Life. Thus, if tourism service providers could determine the needs and expectations of target markets in the virtual environment and deliver the desired satisfaction effectively to enhance the consumer's virtual experience, then tourists will create travel intentions and desires in their trip decision-making process.

2 Literature review

In the past, the concept of flow has been applied by a number of researchers to understand the interaction between consumer experience and online environments (Ghani, Supnick & Rooney, 1991; Koufaris, 2002; Novak & Hoffman, 1996; Trevino & Webster, 1992). It has been established that consumers do experience flow while navigating web sites (Novak, Hoffman & Yung, 2000). Flow has been described as "the process of optimal experience" (Csikszentmihalyi, 1977; Csikszentmihalyi & LeFevre, 1989; Csikszentmihalyi & Csikszentmihalyi, 1988) and defined as "the holistic sensation that people feel when they act with total involvement" (Csikszentmihalyi, 1975, p36). Flow activities on the web facilitate deep concentration and intense participant involvement, especially network navigation, because they are distinct from the "paramount reality of everyday life" (Csikszentmihalyi, 1990, p.72). Based on flow theory, Hoffman & Novak (1996) proposed a conceptual model of consumer navigation behavior in the hypermedia computer mediated environment to understand human and computer interactions. They asserted that the flow experience will lead to numerous positive marketing consequences like increased learning, increased perceived behavior control, increased exploratory and participatory behavior, and positive subjective experience. Koufaris (2002), applying flow theory to examine online consumer behavior, declared that the emotional and cognitive components of flow experiences include intrinsic enjoyment, concentration, and perceived control; these components also influence online consumers' purchasing behaviors. Hausman & Siekpe (2009) investigated the effects of web interface features on consumer online purchase intentions and found that intentions to return to, and purchase from, the website are positively related to the perceived level of flow. Looking at flow experience in web/Internet surfing from a leisure perspective, Mannell, Zuzanek & Aronson (2005) examined the relationship between internet/computer use and flow experience of adolescent leisure behavior and found that when adolescents engage in web/Internet surfing, the state of flow was experienced. In their study, they asserted that Internet/Web surfing and computer game playing do appear to displace other forms of leisure such as physical activity, socializing, reading, and television viewing. Skadberg & Kimmel (2004) indicated that in the Web environment, the flow experience enhanced visitors' engagement and led to changes of attitude and behavior including taking positive actions. However, travel consumer researchers do not have a comprehensive understanding of the flow experience of consumers in the 3D virtual world.

Although travel researchers have examined travellers decisions in the context of web communities to determine if the web presence is related to travellers' intentions to visit a destination, this question has not received much attention from researchers interested in Second Life. This is an important question, which should be addressed. Thus, the purpose of this study is to investigate flow theory in understanding the impacts of virtual experiences of Second Life on people's travel intentions. Two main research questions motivate this study: 1) examining the impacts of antecedents of flow and flow experiences on travel intentions when experiencing the virtual world of Second Life; 2) examining the associations between antecedents and consequences of flow experiences during a consumer's navigation of the virtual world. To elaborate the research questions, five hypotheses are proposed in this study.

Flow has been used as a central construct in the studies of consumer behavior and computer mediated environments, and it has proven a useful construct for describing online consumer experience (Hoffman et al., 2000; Hausman & Siekpe, 2009; Richard & Chandra, 2005). The study by Hoffman, Novak & Yung (2000) examined the effect of flow variables on consumer behavior in online environments, and it indicated that flow experience strongly related to repeat visits and online purchases. Moreover, Chang & Wang (2008) revealed that flow experience is positively correlated with behavioral intention. In addition, Richard & Chandra (2005) pointed out that when consumers surf the web, flow is positively related to pre-purchase intentions. Hausman & Siekpe's (2009) study found that flow has a significant impact on consumers' purchase intentions and return intentions. Moreover, Skadberg & Kimmel (2004) found that flow experience has a positive impact on people's learning about the place presented in virtual environments and, in turn, directly affects people's intentions to take a trip. Hence, we believe that people who experience a flow state in the virtual world are more likely to make a leisure trip to the destination.

Hypothesis 1: the flow experience in virtual destinations will be significantly related to people's intentions to take an actual trip.

Hypothesis 2: the antecedents of flow experiences will be significantly associated with people's travel intentions.

Hoffman & Novak (1996) proposed a flow model to examine the antecedents and consequences of flow experiences during consumers' navigation of Web. In their model, they asserted that perceived congruence of skills and challenges, presence of focused attention, interactivity and tele-presence are necessary for the flow state to be experienced. In online consumer behavior, individual skills and challenges presented by an activity are the most important predictors of flow experience (Ghani & Deshpande, 1994; Trevino & Webster, 1992; Hoffman et al., 2000, Koufaris, 2002). Hoffman et al., (2000) pointed out that skill refers to an online consumer's ability to act during the navigation process; greater skill at using the Web thus relates to greater flow while using the Web. In addition, when consumers perceive congruence of skill and challenges, flow can potentially occur (Csikszentimihalyi & Csikszentimihalyi, 1988). Positive challenges in online environments will affect how consumers respond to that experience (Koufaris, 2002). Hoffman et al. (2000) found that greater challenges correspond to greater flow. Hoffman & Novak (1996) also introduced tele-presence as one the antecedents of flow. Tele-presence is the perception of virtual environment where "presence" is the natural perception of actual physical environment (Steuer, 1992). Hoffman et al.'s study (2000) found that greater tele-presence related to greater flow. Thus, this study also tests the hypotheses of the association between antecedents of flow and flow experience in 3D virtual world.

Hypothesis 3: greater skills at experiencing 3D virtual worlds associate with greater flow.

Hypothesis 4: greater challenges at experiencing 3D virtual worlds relate to greater flow.

Hypothesis 5: greater tele-presence at experiencing 3D virtual worlds corresponds to greater flow.

3 Methodology

Quantitative methods of research were used to investigate the relationships between people's virtual experience in Second Life and their intention of destination choice, by examining the concepts of antecedents and consequences of flow experiences. A self-administered survey questionnaire was utilized to collect the information from participants. The undergraduate college students at Clemson University were chosen as participants. Data was collected in April 2009. This study entailed 42 usable surveys. The participants took part in a virtual trip on the basis of their interests to visit two tourism destination spots in Second Life. This virtual field trip provides opportunity for participants to experience the atmosphere of destinations and to collect travel information about the attractions and facilities of destinations. The top-themed social networking Sims in Second Life, the Sister Cities and Friends, were selected for participants to navigate and experience. The Sister Cities and Friends networks, a Resident Managed chamber of commerce (board of trade)-type program, operate to promote and support selected Second Life Sims including the virtual destinations of Africa, Croatia, Czech and Slovak Republics, France, Germany, Ireland, Italy, Luxembourg, Netherlands, Poland, Portugal, Switzerland, Romania, Spain, UK, and US (www.sistercitiessl.com). The activities in those sites comprise of arts, museums, music, nature, romance, sailing, and sightseeing. Participants taking the virtual trip to destination spots in Second Life also completed a questionnaire.

The questionnaire, which used closed-ended question to indicate participants' virtual experiences and travel intentions, consisted of the constructs of flow and intention to visit. In assessing flow, three major approaches have been taken in empirical research. The first one is the narrative approach, which asks respondents to provide a narrative description of a flow experience and uses surveys to evaluate the flow experience (Privette & Bundrick, 1987; Lutz & Guiry, 1994). Second, the activity approach is to ask respondents who participated in a selected activity to evaluate their experience by using a survey instrument (Trevino & Webster, 1992; Ghani & Deshpande, 1994; Hoffman et al., 2000). A third approach, the experience sampling method (ESM) has been used in leisure studies to quantify flow experience (Csikszentmihalyi & LeFevre, 1989; Decloe, Kaczynski & Havitz, 2009; Ellis, Voelkl & Morris, 1994). Hoffman & Novak (1997) pointed out that the activity approach method is useful for specific events for either concurrently or retrospectively determining the experience of flow. Therefore, this study employed the activity approach to measure participants' flow experience in the virtual world.

Hoffman & Novak (1996) declared that antecedents and consequences of the flow experience need also to be measured. The measurement of antecedents of flow scale developed by Hoffman & Novak (2000) was adapted for this study. The scale contained 21 items for measuring challenge, control, focused attention, skill, time distortion, interactivity and tele-presence on seven-point Likert-type scale and ranged from Definitively Disagree to Definitively Agree (strongly disagree =1 to strongly agree =7). Although Hoffman & Novak (2000) measure the flow experience by directly asking participants to describe whether they have flow experience, this study was concerned that participants may not well understand the definition of flow experience. Thus, the construct of flow was adapted from Trevino & Webster's (1992) study, which was operated in a four item scale: 1) the online user finds the interaction intrinsically interesting; 2) the online user feels in control of the computer interaction; 3) the online user's attention is focused on the interaction; and 4) the online user's curiosity is aroused during the interaction.

4 Results

Prior to hypotheses testing, the 28 items of antecedents and consequences of the flow experience and travel intentions were subjected to factor analysis using principal components analysis with varimax rotation to validate the multi- items scale of flow experience and travel intentions as seen in Table 1. The criterion used to identify factors was that each item should have a factor loading greater than 0.5. The final factors solution was comprised of five factors, namely Tele-Presence, Skills, Challenges, Travel Intentions and Flow, with an eigenvalue exceeding 1 and explaining 84.78% of the total variance. The Kaiser-Meyer-Olkin Measure for the data was 0.77, exceeding the recommended minimum value of 0.60 (Kaiser, 1974) and the Bartlett's Test of Sphericity (Bartlett, 1954) reached statistical significance (p <.001), supporting the factorability of the correlation matrix (Field, 2000). The Kaiser's criterion indicated that a five factor-solution is appropriate for these data.

The reliability analysis was conducted on the five factors and Cronbach's alpha coefficients ranged from 0.80 to .88.

Table 1. Factor analysis for antecedents of flow, and flow variables

Dimensions and items	Factor loadings	Cronbach 's alpha	Eigen-value	Explained variance%
Tele-Presence		0.801	2.833	18.888
Experiencing Second Life makes me forget where I am	.862			
After experiencing Second Life, I feel like I come back to the real world after a journey	.801			
When I experience Second Life, my body is in the room, but my mind is inside the world created by Second Life I visit	.685			
Skills		0.856	2.597	17.312
I am very skilled at using Second Life	.907			
I know how to find what I want on Second Life	.818			
I find Second Life easy to use	.804			
Challenges		0.861	2.569	17.124
Using Second Life challenges me to perform to the best of my ability	.813			
I find that using Second Life stretches my capabilities to my limits	.799			
Using Second Life challenges me	.748			
Travel Intentions		0.888	2.457	16.380
After the virtual tour, I gained an interest in visiting the place in person	.875			
After the virtual tour, I will try to visit the place in the future	.721			
After the virtual tour, I want to find out more information about the place	.606			
Flow	.862	0.884	2.261	15.070
During my visit to Second Life, my attention was focused on the activity				
When experiencing Second Life, I lose track of time	.786			
Experiencing Second Life is intrinsically interesting	.602			
Total explained variance %				84.78

Following the factor analysis, Pearson's correlations were used to identify relationships between antecedents of flow, and the flow experience. The key constructs' scores were computed on the basis of the result of factors analysis. Table 2 provides a correlation matrix of all key constructs. Correlation analysis revealed that during navigation of the virtual world, skills, challenges, tele-presence and flow experiences were significantly correlated to people's intentions to take an actual trip. All the relationships are highly significant ($p < 0.01$). People's travel intention was positively correlated with the tele-presence dimension ($r = .609$, $p < .001$), skills dimension ($r = .486$, $p < 0.01$), challenges dimension ($r = .636$, $p < .001$), and flow experiences ($r = .607$, $p < .001$). In general, these analyses indicated the strong relationships between people's behavioral intention to go on a trip, and the antecedents and consequences of flow experiences. In addition, highly significant relationships were observed between the antecedents and consequences of flow experiences during navigation virtual world of Second Life. The achievement of flow experience in 3D virtual world was positively related to tele-presence dimensions (r = .675, p < .001), skills dimensions (r = .454, p < .001), and challenge dimension (r =.656, p < .001).

Table 2. Correlation Matrix among the constructs

	1	2	3	4	5
1. TelePresence	—				
2. Skills	.335	—			
	(0.43)				
3. Challenges	.484	.48	—		
	(.002)	(.003)			
4. Travel Intentions	.675	0.454	0.656	—	
	(<0.01)	(<0.06)	(<0.01)		
10.Flow	.609	0.486	0.636	0.607	—
	(<0.01)	(.002)	(<0.01)	(<0.01)	

(P values are in parentheses)

5   Discussions and implications

The immersive nature of 3D virtual worlds presents marketing implications in promoting tourism such as attractive visualization of tourism products, interactive events planning, virtual customer relationship management, the consulting role of travel agents, and the social networking and information exchange between travellers who can develop constructive destination image (Berger et al, 2007; Goel & Mousavidin, 2007; Hay, 2008). This study was designed to investigate the impacts of virtual experiences of Second Life on people's behavioral intentions to take an actual trip. One contribution of this study is to validate the notion that flow is a useful and practical instrument to understand users' experiences while navigating the 3D virtual world of Second Life. The quality of engaging and pleasant experiences is influenced by three factors: the navigational challenge of 3D virtual environments, the skills available to tackle on challenging tasks, and the degree of presence sensation perceived by customers. Further, the results demonstrated that when engaging the virtual world of Second Life, the antecedents and consequences of optimal experiences were positively associated with people's behavioral intentions that stimulated people's interests in acquiring more information and an explicated desire to take actions to visit a tourism destination.

The scale used in this research revealed that the underlying dimensions had considerable reliability. Using factor analysis, a set of underlying dimensions for the key constructs was revealed in this study: travel intentions, skills, challenges, tele-presence, and flow. The study also investigated how the antecedent factors of flow can influence on online users' optimal experiences when experiencing the virtual world of Second Life. The study indentified three antecedent factors of flow experiences while navigating virtual world: skills, challenges, and tele-presence. As expected, the results showed that people's skills, challenges, and tele-presence were positively related to flow experiences while navigating on 3D virtual worlds. In comparison with prior studies, the result was consistent with works of Ghani & Deshpande (1994), Trevino & Webster (1992), Skadberg & Kimmel (2004), Koufaris (2002) and Hoffman et al. (2000). Hoffman et al. (2000) indicated that greater users' perception of their ability to navigate through the virtual environment correspond with greater opportunity to achieve flow. Moreover, this study found that greater challenge positively related to reaching the state of flow that is incidental to Ghani & Deshpande (1994), Trevino & Webster (1992), and Skadberg & Kimmel (2004)'s studies that found that skill and challenge had a positive association with flow experience. In addition, Hoffman et al. (2000) revealed that higher level of perception of telepresence can enhance flow experiences. Thus, skills, challenges and tele-presence were key factors leading to the experience of flow while navigating the virtual world environment of Second Life.

From the standpoint of virtual tourism site development practitioners, this study has demonstrated that the structure of flow experience is an important attribute for marketing tourism destinations in Second Life and that optimal experience in the context of 3D virtual communities is related to travellers' intentions to visit an actual destination. By enhancing people's flow experiences in a virtual tourism destination site, customers are more likely to enjoy and interact with the virtual destination sites to the extent that they perceive positive destination images and, in turn, develop consideration and awareness in their potential destination choice. In addition, the markets that are interested in designing an enjoyable and compelling virtual experience in virtual world need to take the aspects of navigational challenges, skill and tele-presence sensations into consideration. The results suggested that virtual world design must provide enough challenge to arouse the consumers, and if the virtual tourism destination sites do not provide enough challenge for people to engage, the potential customer will become bored and leave the sites quickly (Hoffman et al., 2000). Moreover, markets need to consider consumers' capacity to perform actions during the navigation process in virtual worlds. Finally, virtual tourism sites designers should pay attention to the significance of the presence experience that people perceived, not only of the real surroundings where they are physically present, but also of the environment defined by virtual world.

The virtual world environment provides new business opportunities for building destination images that allow customers to make an informed decision and initiate travel arrangements. With rapid growth and change in today's Internet and 3D virtual world environment economy, tourism markets should develop new models to market their destinations. This study has proposed a framework to explain how the 3D virtual world of Second Life can be used by tourism markets to enhance people's travel intentions. We believe that tourism marketers should improve tourists' virtual experiences, allowing individuals to engage in flow and to highly involve themselves with virtual sites, which can then create a favorable attitude that will lead to positive feelings toward the destination. Park et al., (2008) stated that due to the reduced geographic boundaries and increased accessed to specific target markets, acquiring new customers through a virtual world could be low-cost. Destination markets should pay attention not only to the effects of flow experience but also to the impacts of antecedents of flow such as the skills, challenges, and tele-presence. In addition, to create a flow experience in people's virtual tour, markets should take the antecedents of flow into consideration.

As a virtual revolution is emerging in media environments, it is believed that the 3D virtual world environment will gain more attention and become more pervasive as a new marketing tool in business and tourism industries. This study is a starting point in investigating the new marketing media, exploring the virtual world of Second Life, and providing a framework for understanding the notion of 3D virtual experiences and their impact on tourism destination marketing. More systematic research is needed to investigate the virtual experience and its effects on the traveller's decision-making process. For future research, it is likely that the construct of involvement will be important. An examination of the relationships between consumer involvement and Second Life flow will, for example, move the research forward in this area.

6 Limitations

This study is subjected to several limitations. The first limitation is relevant to the generalizability issue. Because the data were collected in only one university and mainly among college students, it may not well represent broader populations. It is suggested that further study should be expanded to conduct cross-validated diverse populations and longitudinal research in multiple countries. Second, due to the exploratory nature of this study, this study entailed small samples, and it is suggested that future study should be devoted to validate all scales by larger samples and to secure the construct validity. Moreover, future research should build upon structure model and employ structure equation modelling/regression analysis to examine the causal relationships between multiple indicators of the antecedents of flow, state of flow and travel intentions. In addition, there are many other factors that can influence people's behavioral intentions to choose a destination, and future research can study the impacts of other variables such as social, cultural, individual, and psychological perspectives to continually investigate the relative influences of these factors.

References

Bartlett, M. S. (1954). A Note on the Multiplying Factors for Various Approximations. *Journal of the Royal Statistical Society* 16(2), 296-298.

Cano, V., & Prentice, R. (1998). Opportunities for Endearment to Place through Electronic 'Visiting': WWW Homepages and the Tourism Promotion of Scotland. *Tourism Management,* 19(1), 67-73.

Chang, H.H. & Wang, I. C. (2008). An Investigation of User Communication Behavior in Computer Mediated Environments. *Computers in Human Behavior*, 2336-2356.

Cheong, R. (1995). The Virtual Threat to Travel and Tourism. *Tourism Management*, 16(6), 417-422.

Cho, Y. & Fesenmaier D. R. (2001). A New Paradigm for Tourism and Electronic Commerce: experience Marketing Using the Virtual Tour, in *Tourism Distribution channels:*

Practices, Issues and Transformations, Eric Laws and Dimitrios Buhalis (Editors), CAB International.

Cho, Y.-H., Wang, Y., and Fesenmaier, D. R. (2002). The Web-Based Virtual Tour in Tourism Marketing, *Journal of Travel & Tourism Marketing,* 12 (4), 1-17.

Crotts, J. C. (1999). Consumer decision making and prepurchase information search. In Pizam A. & Mansfeld, Y. (Ed.) *Consumer Behavior in Travel and Tourism* The Haworth Hospitality press, 149-184.

Csikszentmihalyi, M. (1997). *Finding Flow: The Psychology of Engagement with Every-Day Life.* Basic Books.

Csikszentmihalyi, M. (1975). *Beyond Boredom and Anxiety.* San Francisco: Jossey-Bass.

Csikszentmihalyi, M., & Lefevre, J. (1989). Optimal Experience in Work and Leisure. *Journal of Personality and Social Psychology*, 56(5), 815-822.

Csikszentmihalyi, M. (1977). *Beyond Boredom and Anxiety, Second Printing.* San Francisco: Jossey-Bass.

Csikszentmihalyi, M. (1990). *Flow: The Psychology of Optimal Experience,* New York: Harper and Row.

Csikszentmihalyi, M. and Csikszentmihalyi, I. S. (1988). *Optimal Experience: Psychological studies of flow in consciousness*, Cambridge: Cambridge University Press.

Decloe, M. D., Kaczynski, A. T., & Havitz, M. E. (2009). Social Participation, Flow and Situational Involvement in Recreational Physical Activity. *Journal of Leisure Research*, 41(1), 73-90.

Ellis, G. D., Voelkl, J. E., & Morris, C. (1994). Measurement and Analysis Issues with Explanation of Variance In Daily Experience Using The Flow Model. *Journal of Leisure Research,* 26(4), 337-356.

Field A. (2000). *Discovering statistics using SPSS for windows.* London: Sage Publications.

Ghani, J. A., & Deshpande, S. P. (1994). Task Characteristics and the Experience of Optimal Flow in Human-Computer Interaction. *Journal of Psychology*, 128(4), 381-391.

Ghani, J. A., Supnick, R. & Rooney, P. (1991). The Experience of Flow in Computer-Mediated and in Face-To-Face Groups, *Proceedings of the Twelfth International Conference on Information Systems*, New York, NY.

Goel, L & Mousavidin, E. (2007). vCRM: Virtual Customer Relationship Management. *The DATA BASE for Advances in Information Systems*, 38(4), 56-60.

Gretzel, Y.-L. Yuan and D.R. Fesenmaier (2000). Preparing for the new economy: advertising strategies and change in destination marketing organizations. *Journal of Travel Research* 39, 146–156

Hausman, A. V., & Siekpe, J. S. (2009). The Effect of Web Interface Features on Consumer Online Purchase Intentions. *Journal of Business Research*, 62(1), 5-13.

Hay, B. (2008). Where the Bloody Hell Are We? Fantasy Tourism and Second Life. *Proceedings of the CAUTHE 2008 Conference.*

Hemp, P. (2006). Avatar-based marketing. Harvard Business Review, 84(6), 48-+.

Hoffman, D. L., & Novak, T. P. (1996). Marketing in Hypermedia Computer-Mediated Environments: Conceptual Foundations. *Journal of Marketing*, 60(3), 50-68.

http://us.holland.com/secondlife.php

http://www.dublinsl.com

Kaiser, H. F. (1974). An Index of Factorial Simplicity. *Psychometrika*, 39(3), 31-36.

Kokosalakis, C., Bagnall, G., Selby, M. & Burns, S. (2006) Place Image and Urban Regeneration in Liverpool. *International Journal of Consumer Studies,* 30, 389–397.

Koufaris, M. (2002). Applying the Technology Acceptance Model and Flow Theory to Online Consumer Behavior. *Information Systems Research*, 13(2), 205-223.

Linden Lab (2009) Retrieved from http://blog.secondlife.com/2009/01/15/q42008/#more-3487

Lutz, R.J., & Guiry, M. (1994). Intense consumption experiences: Peaks, performances, and Flow. *Proceedings of the Winter Marketing Educators' Conference*, St. Petersburg, FL.

Mannell, R., Zuzanek, J., & Aronson, R. (2005). Internet/Computer Use and adolescent Leisure Behavior, Flow Experiences and Psychological Well-Being: The Displacement Hypothesis. *Proceedings of the Eleventh Canadian Congress on Leisure Research*

Martin, J. (2008). Consuming Code: Use-Value, Exchange-Value, and the Role of Virtual Goods in Second Life, *Journal of Virtual Worlds Research*, 1 (2). Retrieved from https://journals.tdl.org/jvwr/article/view/300/262

Middleton, V. T. C. (1994). *Marketing in Travel and Tourism.* Oxford; Boston: Butterworth-Heinemann. Retrieved from WorldCat

Montinho, L. (1987). Consumer Behaviour in Tourism. *European Journal of Marketing*, 21 (10), 5.

Murphy, L., Mascardo, G., & Benckendorff P. (2007). Exploring Word-of-Mouth Influences on Travel Decisions: Friends and Relatives vs. Other Travelers. *International Journal of Consumer Studies*, 31 (5), 517-527.

Novak, T. P., Hoffman, D. L., & Yung, Y. (2000). Measuring the customer experience in online environments: A structural modeling approach. Marketing Science, 19(1), 22-42.

Novak, T. P., Hoffman, D. L., & Duhachek, A. (2003). The Influence of Goal-Directed and Experiential Activities on Online Flow Experiences. *Journal of Consumer Psychology*, 13(1-2), 3-16.

Park, S. R., Nah, F. F.-H., DeWester, D. & Eschenbrenner, B. (2008). Virtual World Affordances: Enhancing Brand Value. *Journal of Virtual Worlds Research*, 1 (2), Retrieved from https://journals.tdl.org/jvwr/article/view/350/267

Prentice, R. (2006) Evocation and Experiential Seduction: Updating Choice-Sets Modelling. *Tourism Management,* 27, 1153–1170.

Privette, G., & Bundrick, C. M. (1987). Measurement of Experience - Construct and Content Validity of the Experience Questionnaire. *Perceptual and Motor Skills*, 65(1), 315-332.

Richard, M. O., & Chandra, R. (2005). A Model of Consumer Web Navigational Behavior: Conceptual Development and Application. *Journal of Business Research*, 58(8), 1019-1029.

Schwarz, J. (2006). *Bold new opportunities in virtual worlds. iMedia Connection.* Retrieved from http://www.imediaconnection.com/content/8605.asp

Skadberg, Y. X., & Kimmel, J. R. (2004). Visitors' Flow Experience while Browsing a Web Site: Its Measurement, Contributing Factors and Consequences. *Computers in Human Behavior,* 20(3), 403-422.

Steuer, J. (1992). Defining Virtual Reality - Dimensions Determining Telepresence. Journal of Communication, 42(4), 73-93.

Trevino, L. K., & Webster, J. (1992). Flow in Computer-Mediated Communication - Electronic Mail and Voice Mail Evaluation and Impacts. *Communication Research*, 19(5), 539-573.

Wang, Y., Yu, Q., & Fesenmaier, D. R. (2002). Defining the Virtual Tourist Community: Implications for Tourism Marketing. *Tourism Management*, 23(4),

Webster, J., Trevino, L. K., & Ryan, L. (1993). The Dimensionality and Correlates of Flow in Human-Computer Interactions. *Computers in Human Behavior*, 9(4), 411-426.

Gastronomy and Tourism in Turkey: The Role of ICTs

Aysegul Surenkok[a],
Rodolfo Baggio[a], and
Magda Antonioli Corigliano[a]

[a]Master in Economics and Tourism
Bocconi University, Milan, Italy
aysegul.surenkok@gmail.com
{rodolfo.baggio, magda.antonioli@unibocconi.it}

Abstract

Food has an undeniable importance for holiday makers. As such, food tourism has gained an enormous potential in recent years. A high percentage of travellers, consider dining and food as relevant activities during their travels. On the other hand, Internet has shown to be a powerful means for promoting a destination and all its resources. Studies on the uses of ICTs and the Internet with regards to tourism, and food tourism in particular, have mainly focused so far on European and Western countries. This exploratory investigation deals with Turkey and how food and wine are represented online and examines the behaviour of website visitors when searching information. The findings indicate a good, yet niche, demand against low levels of supply for gourmet tourism with lack of sufficient understanding of tourism by the governing institutions. The latter finding becomes more evident when considering online offerings.

Keywords: Turkey; food and wine tourism; online promotion; cross cultural diversity.

1 Introduction

Food has an undeniable importance for life. Increasingly, food is also becoming a central factor driving travellers' choice with regards to the purpose of their trips. Destinations are no longer competing only in terms of their vast natural resources and cultural heritage, but also in their food offering. Talbot Inn at Knightwick in U.K. serves as an epitome of food related destination marketing and travel since the late 14th century (Hall et al., 2003). An increasing number of other studies also show that a high percentage of travellers care about what they eat while travelling or make journey decisions by well valuing food. Hall and Sharples (2003) enumerate a number of statistics on business and leisure travellers and their attitude towards food in their travels. For instance, as of 2000, 87% of all US travellers had eaten out at a restaurant. In this process Internet has shown to be able to provide many benefits for both suppliers and customers. Most importantly, it can reduce barriers across countries, making food culture of one country visible to another. Many travel agencies and operators utilise these benefits to effectively market their products online. Most investigations into these issues, up to now, have been directed to European and Western countries showing only limited interest in other areas of the World.

This work stems out of a wider investigation on the Turkish travel market and specifically on food tourism in Turkey. Aim of this paper is to complete the analysis by assessing both demand and supply side attitudes towards ICTs when considering food tourism.

2 Food and Food Tourism

Food has always been an essential component of a society and an essential motivation for most human activities (social eating, meetings, weddings, journeys, celebrations etc.) (Antonioli Corigliano & Baggio, 2003). The link existing between food and tourism is also widely established and food is recognised to be an essential part of any tourist experience (Brown et al., 2006; Hall et al., 2000). Food has been often conceived as part of an all-inclusive tourism package, but today the changing dynamics of the business and consumers' preferences and sophistication have affected the way that food is conceived during holidays. Today's consumers demand more than just something to eat. They ask for good taste, more frequently local taste as part of their cultural experience, and often demand good service with it (ref food tourism). As noted by Larcombe (2007) in his online report on food tourism for the World Travel Market: "Like never before, holidaymakers are choosing where they go by what they can put in their stomachs - and catering for them is now top of the menu for tour operators and destinations."

Research also confirms that food has become a central component of travel, accounting for large parts of travellers' expenditures (Brown et al., 2002; Hjalager & Richards, 2002). As a consequence, it is not surprising that the restaurant business is thriving today with a multitude of offers -from sophisticated or exotic meals to "cook yourself - eat yourself" offers. Restaurants, nevertheless, are only one example in the multitude of businesses that are leveraging from food tourism and the growing essence of food for the tourism industry in general. Other examples abound: from wine or food tasting at the production sites or wineries to cooking workshops, to the whole production sector involved into the typical food and beverage products. There is of course a radical distinction in demand for these offers and industries. For instance, the restaurant business differs from a food trail tour, even though both offers have food as their core element. The restaurant business prevails with or without a customer's genuine interest in food. Eating out may indeed result from a genuine interest in the local cuisine, but it may also follow a celebratory, business or some other formal event. A food trail tour, on the other hand, is not conceivable without customers whose sole interest is in the food. This understanding highlights the need to differentiate 'food and tourism' and 'food tourism'.

Food tourism or gourmet tourism are forms of travel in which the primary motivation is food along with a strong interest in local products. This high interest group travels to a destination with the primary motive to visit a specific restaurant, eat a specific dish, or go to a certain food market or a winery. Both types of tourism -gourmet tourism and gastronomic tourism- reflect consumers whose interest in food and wine is a form of "serious leisure" (Hall et al., 2000)

2.1 Food and wine in Turkey

Turkish gastronomy has its roots in the Ottoman cuisine, a combination of the influences of Central Asian, Middle Eastern and Balkan traditions. It has then influenced other Mediterranean cuisines with which it shares today many ingredients and recipes. As in other areas, it also exhibits a vast array of regional and local variations. The food offering varies immensely from north to south and east to west. In the south-eastern region of Turkey, for instance, the local cuisine is dominated by heavy spices and meat. On the contrary, vegetable dishes, various grasses and grass roots seasoned with virgin olive oil along with seasonal fish dishes constitute the fine print of the Agean coastal parts. This feature tends to make olive and olive oil cultivation a dominant farming activity in the Agean area of Turkey, allowing also for attracting visits and gastronomy tourism. Nevertheless, substantial demand and supply lack to date. Despite its richness, food is not used as a cultural marker in the promotion of Turkey as a tourism destination, and its advertising has a low visibility. Turkey is, in the perception of international tourists, almost exclusively a sea-sun-sand destination (Okumus et al., 2007).

The condition of wine is even more peculiar. Grapes have been cultivated in Turkey for at least 6000 years and the country, according to the available FAO statistics (www.fao.org), is one of the largest producers. More than half a million hectares of vineyards put Turkey at the fourth place in the World as for extension of cultivation, and 3.6 million tons grant the country the sixth place among the grapes producers. However (FAO data), only less than 5% of this goes into wine making and the local consumption is very low (almost 1 liter/person/year). Low quality of the grapes and cultural barriers are commonly invoked by the experts interviewed to explain this situation (Gumus & Gumus, 2008; Var et al., 2006). Raki (the Turkish ouzo, also produced from fermenting grapes), which is the more traditional alcoholic beverage consumed by the Turkish people, has similarly not been able to generate enough interest for generating food tourism either.

2.2 The role of ICTs

Internet and the Web have provided features that are highly relevant to the marketing of tourism, and they are indeed powerful drivers for the growing significance of food tourism and food. Buhalis (2003) provides an in-depth coverage of online information, reviews and online reservation systems, as well as more sophisticated ICT systems used in the tourism industry. As such, online information and reservation systems to restaurants or food tours are only a small part of the attractive picture that the Internet is able to create for those interested in food tourism.

The hospitality business includes hotels and similar accommodation establishments, *as well as* restaurants and catering services. Nevertheless, up to now the literature has focused more often on the ICT usage in accommodation establishments, rather than analysing food-related services.

When this has been done, studies have highlighted a kind of separation between more general 'tourism' and food and wine contents and information. In the case of Italy, for example, despite the renown and large gastronomic production, very little is done online to use this as tourism attraction, and only a few websites belonging to food and wine producers seem to realise the importance of the tourism resources of the territory in which they are located (Antonioli Corigliano & Baggio, 2003).

3   Methodology and Background Data

The overall objective of the study is to understand the role of food in Turkish people's travel decisions made by Turkish travellers and to assess possible cross-cultural differences with tourists of other nationalities with respect to the use of online resources and the Internet. To this end, a qualitative survey was conducted on a sample of tourists divided into two groups: Turkish and International (mainly Europeans and Americans). The questions focused on four main indicators: vacation preferences, interest in food, Internet usage and demographic information. Questions were designed to group people in terms of their cultural, gastronomic, all-inclusive or sportive orientations with respect to their travel motivation. The primary idea was to understand the frequency of people, whose vacation preferences could be correlated with their interest for food. Then the argument was taken further to assess whether people with a genuine interest in food are also likely to search in advance for niche or special places where they can get a taste of the local food or beverages. The demographic information allowed for an investigation into the Internet usage patterns in order to determine which segments are more likely to use Internet resources for their informational needs. The research analysed the supply side as well. To this extent, a qualitative exploratory comparison was performed on the online offer made available by producers. A few Turkish websites have been scrutinised to assess how much they emphasise and leverage the opportunities available for promoting food tourism.

The Turkish sample is composed of 102 people, aged 15 and more and living in a major city. The International sample consists of 69 people chosen among foreign tourists visiting Turkey. In order to ensure validity of research and to overcome any possible biases induced from data gathering, a sub-Turkish sample was generated to serve as a control element. Data for the questionnaire were gathered by using both e-mail and face-to-face interviews. The supply side was studied by conducting eight in-depth, non structured interviews. Interviewees were field specialists (a Turkish wine brand manager, a tour operator and food producers) attending tourism fairs (EMITT in Turkey and BIT in Italy) and a wine-tasting seminar. All data were collected in early 2009.

Finally, a 'mystery shopping' approach was adopted for an online investigation. Tour operators' and agencies' websites were visited to explore their connections to local wine or other food producers' websites. User-friendliness and quality and accuracy of information were qualitatively evaluated (methodology followed that of Antonioli Corigliano & Baggio, 2003; Antonioli Corigliano & Baggio, 2004). Attention was given to any tour package involving some kind of gastronomic activity or interest. Same analyses were conducted on producers' websites and their relations with tour operators or agencies.

What stated above concerning the image of Turkey as a tourism destination has been verified in the general results of the survey conducted (Fig. 1)

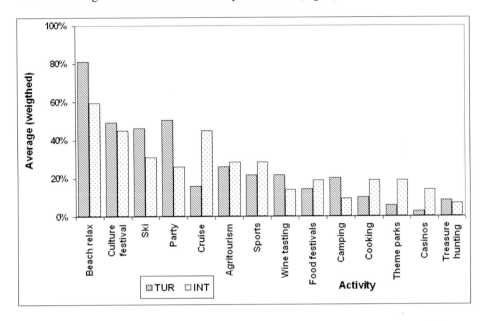

Fig. 1. Preferences stated by Turkish (TUR) and International (INT) tourists visiting Turkey

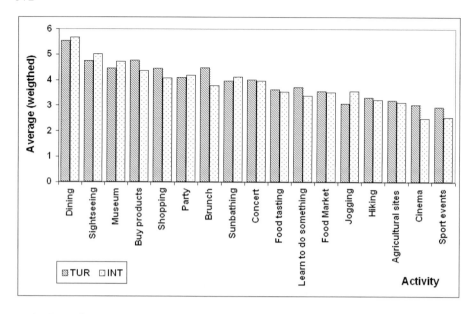

Fig. 2. Preferred activities at destination by Turkish (TUR) and International (INT) tourists. Average evaluations are weighted on the number of respondents which have chosen an activity.

Then, as it also happens in many other cases, the most satisfying activities at the destination are related to food and wine (Fig. 2). This leaves space to a much better exploitation of these themes for promoting Turkey on both the internal and international tourism markets.

4 The ICT Role in the Turkish Food and Wine Market

As seen in the preceding section, the general view emerging from the main investigation is that, when considering Turkey as a destination, food-related tourism is not among the most preferred choices. This section reports the results of the investigations conducted by analysing the role of Internet in general as a source of information for the tourists and specifically as a means to create awareness and promote enogastronomy products.

In both the Turkish and the International sample, the travellers have shown a positive attitude towards eating well. This attitude is also confirmed by the intention to look for specific information by using different sources. While 22.55% of the Turkish people and 33.33% of the International would consult a friend, 33.33% and 31.88 respectively, would conduct some kind of further research before their trip. Besides that, the surveyed sample has also shown some intention to provide information to others via online social networking facilities (see Table 1).

Table 1. Attitude towards online social networking functions

	Turkish	International
Read reviews		
Yes	51.96%	40.58%
No	48.04%	59.42%
Write reviews		
Yes	13.73%	4.35%
No	86.27%	95.65%

The use of Internet for searching food related information does not seem to be very widespread. It looks that, even if dining or drinking are favourite activities for travellers to Turkey (Fig. 2), only few of them seem to go beyond their friends and relatives as immediate sources of information.

Reviews read online may have, as known, a credibility problem (Metzger, 2007; Zhang et al., 2009). This is reflected also in the results of the survey. The main elements considered important by the interviewees are consistent with what the general literature reports, as shown in Fig. 3. No large differences seem to exist between Turkish and International travellers.

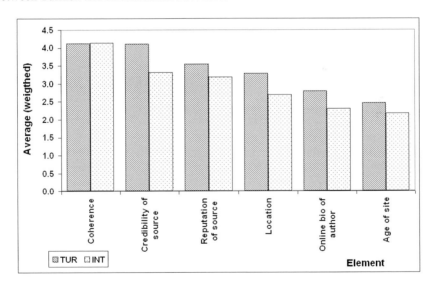

Fig. 3. Elements considered in assessing the credibility of online sources

The lack of interest in online sources may be due to a general lack of interest in ICTs, but it may also be also due to the fact that online sources are not considered to be providing adequate information. Turkish online sources definitely need to work on increasing their credibility and making their sites more attractive and useful for the readers. The qualitative analysis, in fact, of online gourmet tourism websites in the

Turkish market shows their inadequacy, mainly if compared to the International market.

As an example we report an analysis of two websites. One of the most prominent organisations, also a pioneer in the sector, is Oasis Travel (www.oasis.com.tr). Together with the Istanbul Culinary Institute, Oasis Travel organises different expeditions to both prominent Turkish and international cities. It also provides a wider range of special interest and regular tours. Their special interest tours are "tailor-made itineraries [that] contain surprising 'off the beaten path' escapades" (form the Oasis Web site) and they include art, history, archaeology, religious heritage, folk dances and music, sports and hobby related tours, as well as culinary heritage. Nevertheless, Oasis Travel is different from the mainstream tour operators in the way that they reach out for their customers. They do not post their tours online; they rather mail out the itineraries to their customers. In this way, they try to maintain a certain level of quality. Unfortunately, this makes their Web site look very unprofessional and poor when compared to other operators' sites.

Web sites that are considered to be the best in their segment do not improve this perception. Travel Turkey (www.travelturkey.us) is a tour operator that provides a variety of special interest services and tours including pilgrimage, wedding, honeymoon, yachting, meditation, Aegean Cruises and gourmet travels. However, their gourmet travel section covers four basic tours only, all of which have Istanbul as destination. Table 2 provides more details on these websites.

Table 2. A comparison between two websites

	Oasis Travel	**Travel Turkey**
Reference to hotels within the destination	Yes, but only their own hotel (Adatepe)	Yes, to many hotels in many different cities
Reference to restaurants within the destination	Only in tour descriptions	Not specifically
Reference to other tourism related sites	No	To their own sites
User friendliness	Fine	Fine
Accuracy	Not enough information to make an assessment	Some general information on Turkey, limited information on different cities
Updates	Yes	Provides the current day's date on each entry

Site structure and organisation	Bad and very simple. Not very attractive for visitors. Lacks marketing perspective	Good
Provision of transportation	Yes	Says yes, but not visible on Web site
Scope of website	Not touristic, not niche either. Operates for major corporate events only.	Niche
Provision of accommodation	Yes	Sometimes
Combination of active holiday and food	No	Yes

Other operators and agencies, which have gained themselves fame and trust from their customers through their high quality operations and the longevity of their presence in the sector, do not provide special interest tour packages. Setur (www.setur.com.tr), one of the most renown and trusted agencies in Turkey, do not only handle reservations, but also help customers with the outbound operations such as getting a visa or exchanging currency. Nevertheless, tours organised by Setur are more likely to fall into the main demand categories such as beach holidays, cruises and ski holidays.

Specialised websites, acting as hubs or collectors of different interest groups in the gourmet sector do not perform much better. One example is Gurme Guide (www.gurmeguide.com). Although rich in specific content (cuisine, wines, specialties etc.), Gurme Guide does not provide a list of gourmet tours or gastronomic activities by city or area. No integration of information seems to exist. The website is rigidly partitioned into sections that offer, for example, detailed information on different kinds of gourmet foods and beverages and, separately, lists of restaurants in different cities. It may be useful for residents in Turkey, but an international traveller would not be very attracted by this layout. Moreover, it does not offer or suggest packaged gastronomic tours.

The website Web site Lezzet Duraklari (www.lezzetduragi.net) is a known and important source of information on Turkish cuisine. It is a complement to the TV program by Mehmet Yaşin, a Turkish gourmet traveller, journalist and writer who has undertaken several initiatives to promote the local Anatolian cuisine and the unique and local taste of many small and big cities in Turkey other than Istanbul. For more than 20 years, he has been writing gourmet articles describing the places he has visited and the food he has eaten. Recently, he has also started a popular TV program called "Yol Üstü Lezzet Durakları" (Delicious Stops on the Road) that features the finest places in Turkey where to eat samples of regional cuisine. His contribution to regional culinary tourism is therefore quite important. The Web site includes a list of restaurants and city guides. The city guides feature only places where to eat good food. Thus, depending on the level of the city's culinary appeal, a city guide may be half a page or two pages long. Still, Yaşin's contributions do not go beyond introducing the tastes of regions and cities and, unfortunately, few agencies or operators or entrepreneurs actually pay attention to his recommendations and consider to organise tours to those regions. More importantly its last update dates back to 2007. On the other hand, the regions featured in his program recognise their potential and start to hang posts and slogans on their store windows to receive recognition from incoming visitors as "place visited by Mr. Yaşin", but do not actively promote this fact as a tourism attraction.

Time Out Istanbul, Istanbul.net and IstanbulRestaurants.com are typical and good examples of restaurant directories. Time Out Istanbul (www.timeoutistanbul.com) is regularly updated and filled with information on restaurants, cafes, upcoming festivals, concerts etc. Istanbul.net (www.istanbul.net.tr) is similar to Time Out Istanbul, featuring a restaurant and café guide along with listings of cultural events, information for shopping, maps and more. IstanbulRestaurants.com (istanbulrestaurants.com) contains gastronomy and food related articles, along with a restaurant guide, recommendations for places to host an event and information on different types of cuisines from around the world. However, they are designed for frequent users and residents (only Istanbul). No mention of tourism facilities is made for travellers coming from different cities or different countries.

5 Concluding Remarks

The limitations of the work presented here are evident. It is only an exploratory qualitative review of some aspects connected with the online representation of food and wine as tourism attractions. Nonetheless, the outcomes provide some interesting insights. Turkey, as other destinations studied from this point of view, does not seem to value much its culinary resources when promoting its image to tourists. The importance of the food element as part of a holiday itinerary and the impact of this on travellers' choice and (mostly) satisfaction of a destination, have been treated extensively in literature (see for example Hall et al., 2000).

Yet, in many cases there seems to exist a curious attitude towards these elements. They are cited often, and correctly considered as important part of the culture and the traditions of the local communities, but when it comes to tourism marketing, they are somehow neglected.

Beyond many and deep cultural differences, tourists of any country, travelling to any destination (Turkey in the present case) care for eating good food during a trip or a vacation. They also express a genuine interest in the diversity of the local culinary heritage and normally value this experience as the most important when leaving the place where they spent some time.

This, however, in the case of Turkey, does not mean that gastronomy can be taken as a major motivation for a trip. Probably heavily influenced by the way the destination is presented, cuisine related activities are a nice segment. This segment, furthermore, does not show large national or cultural differences. Everyone likes to eat and drink well. The demand seems to be solid, but, as it many times happens, the supply side looks to be a little 'hard of hearing'. One of the reasons can be found, as in other countries, in the governance of these topics. Food and wine are typically managed by agricultural authorities, which usually do not exhibit an excessive interest or understanding of tourism issues.

Internet and the Web, despite their huge diffusion and their recognised importance for the tourism field, do not offer much help to those interested in gastronomy tourism to Turkey. A chasm exists between tourism organisations and culinary operators. Apart from some restaurant suggestions or food advices, not many opportunities exist for planning gourmet tours online to Turkey. Relevant organisations or prominent tour operators prefer, evidently, to use traditional media for their marketing strategy. As the technological opportunities already abound, and are quickly developing, it is hopeful to believe that the situation may change soon.

The International market, in comparison, utilises more effectively the online resources for the topics that may interest and attract a 'good eater', including a large number of hubs that put together relevant tour operators, agencies and information on food, cooking holidays or wine tasting.

Turkish operators lack all of this, and they may be missing out on a wealth of opportunities. Limited vision with too much emphasis on profits seems to be the main concern of the Turkish operators, which ultimately causes them to foster the image of their country as a sea-sun-sand destination.

The limited extent of the investigation presented here, does not allow for definite conclusions, but what commented above seems to be, at least qualitatively, a faithful representation of the current situation. More and deeper analyses are already under way to better assess these results and to improve our knowledge of the relations between gastronomy and tourism in Turkey.

References

Antonioli Corigliano, M., & Baggio, R. (2003). Italian culinary tourism on the Internet. In J. Collen & G. Richards (Eds.), *Gastronomy and Tourism, Proceedings of ATLAS Expert Meeting, Sondrio (Italy), 21-23 November 2002* (pp. 92-106). Antwerpen: Academie voor de Streekgebonden Gastronomie.

Antonioli Corigliano, M., & Baggio, R. (2004). Italian Tourism on the Internet - New Business Models. In K. Weiermair & C. Mathies (Eds.), *The Tourism and Leisure Industry - Shaping the Future* (pp. 301-316). New York: The Haworth Press.

Brown, G. P., Havitz, M. E., & Getz, D. (2006). Relationship Between Wine Involvement and Wine-Related Travel. *Journal of Travel & Tourism Marketing, 21*(1), 31-46.

Brown, M. D., Var, T., & Lee, S. (2002). Messina Hof Wine and Jass Festival: An economic impact analysis. *Tourism Economics, 8*(3), 273-279.

Buhalis, D. (2003). *eTourism: information technology for strategic tourism management.* New York: Prentice Hall.

Gumus, S. G., & Gumus, A. H. (2008). The Wine Sector in Turkey: Survey on 42 Wineries. *Bulgarian Journal of Agricultural Science, 14*(6), 549-556.

Hall, M.C., Mitchell, R. & Sharples, L. (2003). Consuming places: the role of food, wine and tourism in regional development. In Hall, M.C., Sharples, L., Mitchell, R., Macionis, N., Cambourne, B. (Eds.). (2003). *Food tourism around the world: development, management and markets* (pp. 25-60). Amsterdam: Butterworth Heinemann

Hall, M.C. & Sharples, L. (2003). The consumption of experiences or the experience of consumption? An introduction to the tourism of taste. In Hall, M.C., Sharples, L., Mitchell, R., Macionis, N., Cambourne, B. (Eds.). (2003). *Food tourism around the world: development, management and markets* (pp. 1-24). Amsterdam: Butterworth Heinemann

Hall, M. C., Sharples, L., Cambourne, B., Macionis, N., Mitchell, R., & Johnson, G. (Eds.). (2000). *Wine tourism around the world: development, management and the markets.* Oxford: Butterworth Heinemann.

Hjalager, A. M., & Richards, G. (Eds.). (2002). *Tourism and Gastronomy.* London: Routledge.

Larcombe, J. (2007). Food Tourism is on the Boil. Retrieved March, 2009, from http://www.wtmlondon.com/page.cfm/link=59.

Metzger, M. J. (2007). Making Sense of Credibility on the Web: Models for Evaluating Online Information and Recommendations for Future Research. *Journal of the American Society for Information Science and Technology, 58*(13), 2078-2091.

Okumus, B., Okumus, F., & McKercher, B. (2007). Incorporating local and international cuisines in the marketing of tourism destinations: The cases of Hong Kong and Turkey. *Tourism Management, 28*, 253-261.

Var, T., Kaplan, M. D., & Yurt, O. (2006). Challenges and Opportunities of Developing Wine Tourism in a Small Community in Turkey. *e-Review of Tourism Research (eRTR), 4*(1), 9-18.

Zhang, L., Pan, B., Smith, W., & Li, X. (2009). Travelers' Use of Online Reviews and Recommendations: A Qualitative Study. *Information Technology and Tourism, 11*(2), in press.

Attitudes towards e-Solutions in a Small Destination

Jarmo Ritalahti[a]
Jarmo Sarkkinen[a]

[a]HAAGA-HELIA University of Applied Sciences, Finland
{jarmo.ritalahti, jarmo.sarkkinen}@haaga-helia.fi

Abstract

The regional research and development project ITU reacts to an ongoing change in the service infrastructure of the Finnish tourism industry. Finnish Tourist Board decided to renew its VisitFinland site (visitfinland.com) and change it to satisfy the demands of the present day. The target destination in this research and development project is the province of Eastern Uusimaa that lies about 50 kms east of Helsinki, the capital of Finland. The province with 90 000 inhabitants is a cultural destination with about 1 million annual visitors. The tourism industry in the province of Eastern Uusimaa is a network of small or micro companies that operate with minimal resources for development such as new products and target groups, networking and digital solutions or more sophisticated applications in the Internet. A web-based study explored the regional suppliers' attitudes towards e-commerce and business supported by electronic facilities and portals. Based on the results of the study, tourism suppliers seem to know and understand that e-commerce enables business growth and new customers. But we could not get any clear answer to what type of portal (a regional one or one covering the whole country) respondents would prefer. Discussions in the future and the ITU project are to pave the way for e-solutions in this small destination.

Keywords: Tourism Portal, Digital Business Solution, Small Destination, Change

1 Introduction

A small tourist destination and its service providers are facing an ever harder competition in spite of the growing number of tourists. New emerging destinations and information and reservation systems in the Internet that are available 24/7 demand new actions. A small destination needs a functional and effective electronic service infrastructure in order to remain competitive. Furthermore, tourism suppliers must change their operational models to be able to improve the businesses.

The ITU project was found to ease seeking of new digital business solutions for small destinations and their suppliers. The abbreviation ITU stands for IT uses in Itä-Uusimaa (Eastern Uusimaa). It also means the word "sprout". It symbolizes something that is growing up and, finally, producing something useful, that is, new e-solutions in this case. The aim of this project is to upgrade destinations' and suppliers' competitiveness and business to generate benefits in the global tourism market. The project will pave the way for the needed change in the chosen province by promoting and using new technologies that allow customer and company profiling, networking and service co-development. In this study we needed to understand what the attitudes of the local actors towards use of ICT and its potential impacts on business are in more detail.

2 Issues

The target destination in this research and development project is the province of Eastern Uusimaa that lies about 50 kms east of Helsinki, the capital of Finland. The province with 90 000 inhabitants is a cultural destination with about 1 million annual visitors. The tourism revenue per capita is the second highest in Finland after Lapland. The main attractions are culture and nature based. Most of the visitors are domestic day-trippers who stay in the destination no more than two, three hours and arrive from the neighboring provinces and metropolitan area. Furthermore, visitors are repeaters who use mainly cafeteria and restaurant services during their stay. The use of the Internet in the information search prior to the visit to the destination is not very high, only about 15% of the visitors use the destination website mainly to acquire information (Taipale 2007).This far there are only two hotels in the region with an option for on-line bookings. International visitors receive information on the destination mainly in the Internet or e.g. the tourist information bureau in Helsinki.

The tourism industry in the province of Eastern Uusimaa is a network of small or micro companies that operate with minimal resources for development such as new products and target groups, networking and digital solutions or more sophisticated applications in the Internet. Tourism businesses in the province of Eastern Uusimaa are at the lowest level of digitalization (after Gratzer et al. 2002) even though digitalization could be seen as a motor of development or transformation for tourism actors in the age of Internet economy. The challenge is not only among tourism suppliers: Destination management organization should also change from an information supplier to a value enhancer (Kothari & Fesenmaier 2007, 193).

Passive and infrequently updated product and venue information is quite a normal state of affairs for many of the small and micro companies in the province of Eastern Uusimaa. Some of the entrepreneurs could even be called life-style entrepreneurs who are happy to live in an idyllic or picturesque region, and are not looking for bigger revenues. Of course, they would be happy to get more customers but are not willing or interested in investing in it.

Trends in tourism today show an interest in shorter but more frequent holidays or visits. Furthermore, the decision making is more spontaneous and short-termed as well as bookings. Tourists are more sophisticated, critical and less loyal than before. This all leads to the fact that destinations and service providers must provide customers with access to relevant information and booking anytime and anywhere, before, during and after the visit. Access must be allowed for different devices, and received content adapted according to the profiles and preferences of the users in their current location, time, etc. (Werthner and Klein 1999).

To fulfill the requirements above tourism information systems or in our case a destination management system must enable a very adaptive and personalized behavior. It has to be able to filter information and activities according to customer profiles and preferences. (i.e. Ricci et al. 2005).

A destination with no customer access to an online travel market place or shop facilitating information, bookings, purchasing, social networking and co-creating misses the ever growing market share of on-line business (Buhalis 2003). Furthermore, the "information bundling" requires from the tourism industry actors an implementation of an alternative strategy which includes the use of an integrated network and mutual co-operation from all service providers (Ritchie et al. 2002). A network thus comprises entrepreneurs and enterprises that have a common interest to develop new products together. They cooperate because resources and objectives that they have, complement each other, and because they might find it very difficult, if not impossible, and in any case time consuming to create new products without any partners (cf. Harrigan 1985).

As pointed out above, the province of Easter Uusimaa and its tourism industry are in the lowest level of digitalization even though digitalization is said to be the motor of transformation for the tourism industry in the age of the Internet economy. According to Gratzer et al. (2002) digitalization can be defined according to the intensity of the use. The first level is a pure presentation and information in website. The e-commerce level will be reached through a sales channel function, and the e-business through business process integration and new business models with virtual products and services.

The research and development project ITU reacts to an ongoing change in the service infrastructure of the Finnish tourism industry. Finnish Tourist Board decided to renew its VisitFinland site (visitfinland.com) and change it to satisfy the demands of the present day. The site was finally launched on August 2009, and it will bring a remarkable change in the national tourism marketing and visibility. It will be quite a comprehensive tourism portal combined with Web 2.0 features. It has been marketed as a unique business opportunity for small and medium-sized tourism suppliers, offering, for example, booking facilities (Starry 2009). It has also been marketed as the travelers' first touchpoint to Finland (Starry 2009). Customers are provided by a set of tools making it easier to book and buy enticing products. They can also be part of something bigger by participating, socializing and creating own content in the platform, as Starry (2009) mentioned.

Good as it is, however, it brings with it challenges to be overcome by tourism actors in some of the small destinations in Finland. One of those destinations is the province of Eastern Uusimaa. In that region, DMO, tourism service providers and the representatives of the key municipalities have operated with each other mainly locally. This tradition makes a transition to a bigger scale Finnish portal a giant leap that may be too big. However, a move to some direction needs to be made now when many Finnish suppliers and regions are making their own decisions. The actors in the region need to decide whether they choose the VisitFinland portal or a local e-solution as their key operational e-platform.

The ITU project helps to decide what should be done next. The project proceeds in two phases. The first phase has already been executed in the spring 2009. The aim was to explore the regional suppliers' attitudes towards e-commerce and businesses supported by electronic facilities and portals. This was carried out as a web-based study. The results of this study have been summarized later in this working paper. The decision was finally made to have a local e-solution which, however, would be integrated with the VisitFinland portal.

The second phase of the project started with planning sessions in Porvoo and Loviisa towns on June 2009. The more concrete steps will be taken during the fall 2009 and from that time forward. The general aim is to do research and development work in order to find out ways to increase the use of e-solutions in providing and developing tourism services and products as well as other services and products. The aim is also to find out best ways to integrate these local e-solutions with the VisitFinland portal.

3 Procedures

The research model used in this study is presented in Figure 1. It is called E-Business Intensity-Readiness-Impact framework, and it has been further adapted from Fuchs et al. (2009) and Fux & Myrach (2009). The original version of the model is from Zhu & Kramer (2005). The model is used here because it is composed of key elements of business on which use of ICT could have effect. Every company needs sales. They also have to be efficient and fulfill customer needs. Finally, business relationships and well functioning business processes enable sales, efficiency and customer satisfaction.

The model is composed of e-business readiness, e-business intensity and e-business impact. The first element is *e-business readiness,* under which term several contextual indicators were originally enumerated. These contextual indicators can be used to describe the characteristics of the studied organization as well as its environment and so on, each having an effect on how intensively different information systems and platforms are used in the company. The *e-business intensity* element describes ICT use. It is about what systems are used and to what extent and how intensively they have been used in the company. The added value coming from ICT use then leads to impact on business (*e-business impact*). The areas of business that can be examined from this viewpoint are sales, efficiency, business relationships, customer satisfaction and business processes. The last area, business processes, has been added to the framework from Buhalis (2003). To sum up, the framework can be used to explain contexts of business, ICT use and impacts of ICT on business.

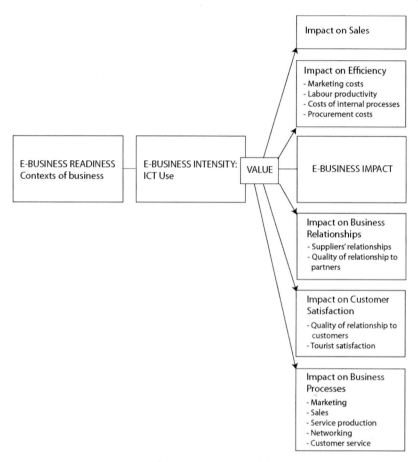

Fig. 1. Research model

The questionnaire was built up to understand the regional entrepreneurs' attitudes towards the transition to e-business and the impacts of ICT. The E-Business Intensity-Readiness-Impact framework provided the structure, themes and sub-themes for the questionnaire. However, we decided to examine e-business impact only. This is because, as was mentioned earlier, tourism businesses in the province of Eastern Uusimaa are at the lowest level of digitalization. For this reason, we decided we should not dig into the current situation too much merely to underline its shortcomings (e.g. a low intensity of using ICT). It was natural that not only e-business readiness but also e-business intensity remained out of scope. Instead, we took a more positive and future oriented viewpoint. That is, we wanted to understand the entrepreneurs' attitudes towards how they see their potential future in the era of ever growing digitalization from their perspective. We wanted to understand whether they agree with the potential impacts of ICT.

In the questionnaire, there were 29 facts taken from the literature (ie. Buhalis 2003; Schegg, Scaglione, Liebriech & Murphy 2007; Tseng & Hsu 2007). With these facts, the aim was to point out what benefits e-solutions may offer and how they might change the operational environment. That is, there is an educational dimension built in the questions, as well. The respondents could have otherwise faced major difficulties to answer the statement. They just do not know enough about ICT. There was a practice oriented and, to some extent, provocative statement after each fact. The respondents were asked to commit themselves particularly on the statement instead of the fact itself. The fact was merely background information. The respondents were asked to be either for or against the statement on a scale from 1 to 5. The option 3 means that "one cannot answer". One option was 6. It means that "one does not know the issue sufficiently to answer it". The respondents were also provided with an empty space in which they could tell their most daunting, e-business related concern.

Each fact/statement pair (F/S) is linked to the corresponding e-business impact theme or its sub-theme (links have been presented in table 1). Each F/S can be linked to at least one of these themes and sub-themes. One F/S can also be linked to more than one single theme/sub-theme. In these borderline cases, the closest option was chosen as a corresponding theme or sub-theme. However, a couple of these F/S pairs were linked to the two closely related options. They could not be separated.

Table 1. Survey themes

Theme	F/S
Impact on Sales	1,2,3,4,5,6
Impact on Efficiency	
Marketing costs	7
Labour productivity	8
Costs of internal processes	10
Procurement costs	9
Impact on Business Relationships	
Suppliers' relationships	12
Quality of relationship to partners	11
Impact on Customer Satisfaction	
Quality of relationship to customers	14,15
Tourist satisfaction	13,16
Impact on Business processes	
Marketing	19,25,29
Sales	17,19,22,25,29
Service production	20
Networking	18,21,23,24,26
Customer service	27,28

Main themes are impact on sales, impact on efficiency, impact on business relationships, impact on customer satisfaction and impact on business processes.

Nevertheless, one needs to remember that the purpose of this study is not to examine the *actual impacts* of implemented ICT, for example, on sales, but the aim, instead, is to understand regional entrepreneurs' attitudes towards changes, for example, in sales, caused by possible future implementations of ICT.

The analysis is based on the distribution of the answers in percentage values. We thus measured how many of the respondents felt positively and negatively towards the potential impacts of ICT. We also wanted to know how many of the respondents are not aware of how ICT could help their business to grow. There was no need for a more complex measurement instrument and analysis based on the numbers due to the low number of repliers.

The study was carried out on the Web. Web based study was chosen because it is the easiest way to reach every known tourism actor in the province of Eastern Uusimaa. An email link to the questionnaire was sent by the regional DMO to 315 regional tourism and other related enterprises and entrepreneurs. We did not want to create a certain type of sample structure. This is because we wanted to mobilize every local actor regardless of what their backgrounds are. As mentioned earlier, we did not pay too much attention to e-business readiness. It was not meaningful to know for our purposes, for example, what information systems had been installed and which of them are used.

The local actors we contacted had one week to answer the questionnaire and they were reminded of the deadline after a couple of days. We were able to get 31 respondents in total. This yielded a participation rate of about 10 % only. The low participation rate might be an indication of negative attitudes or even disregard. We can speculate that only those who are already on the digitalization map answered the questionnaire. We cannot, however, prove these arguments, but the general attitude in the region supports them. The results, for this reason, are not reliable in the whole population but they should be understood as indicative of the general attitudes of the region. At least, we were able to mobilize 10% of people who are not advanced users of ICT.

4   Results

The theme *Impact on Sales* includes the six first questions in the survey. The conclusion is that most of the repliers understand the growth potential in Web based selling. They are also willing to change their business processes in order to promote sales as well as welcome new and more spending customers. This far, a direct contact with the customers before the arrival has been an important detail in business processes of the micro and small tourism enterprises in the region. A big part of the repliers would be willing to give up with this habit in order to welcome customers booking on-line. Over one fifth of the repliers are very satisfied with their business of today (March-April 2009). They are not willing to change their processes, nor receiving new customers. They are also happy with the existing pricing. There are also question marks or topics difficult to answer to: Customer spending in the enterprises, personnel contacts with the customers before arrival, and pricing of products.

The next theme, *Impact on Efficiency* consists of four next questions. The main result is that most of the enterprises would like to operate in a more efficient way. This means that there is a need to reach customers better and want to save in procurement. The repliers also doubt if they are operating in an efficient way in general. But they also want to keep a personnel contact when communicating with the staff members.

Two next questions relate to *Impact on Business Relationships*. The replies were a bit paradoxical. Most of the enterprises would like to have a wider range of tools for communication but anyway, they preferred face-to-face contacts. There were also a lot of "I can't say" or "I don't know the theme well enough" answers.

Questions 13-16 focus on *Impact on Customer Satisfaction*. Most of the enterprises want to have more feedback from the customers. They also emphasized the importance of other media than a brochure or telephone. There were also repliers who relied or wanted to rely on the old tools, and found that an oral feedback is enough. Some of the enterprises admitted that they don't have always time to react to the given feedback.

The rest of the questions (17-29) are linked to *Impact on Business Processes*. The individual topics are marketing, sales, service production, networking and customer service. The changes in marketing and sales processes do not frighten the repliers because they find enough flexibility in their operations and staff. They also see challenges in Net sales that are related to costs, but these challenges are not regarded insurmountable. Once again, about one fifth of the repliers are uncertain. The flexibility in business operations allows staff members to produce up-to-date information in the Net. The role of the on-line shop keeper or responsible tour operator is not always seen very clear. Furthermore, technical issues are a bit equivocal. There is no agreement on the sufficiency of existing hard-, nor software. There is no opposition for non-tourism organizations to join the network. Tourism is regarded as a wide industry with options for i.e. creative and wellness enterprises. Comments on regional or national portal were equivocal, but there were also a lot of "I can't say" or "I don't know the theme well enough" replies.

Based on the results of the study, tourism suppliers seem to know and understand that e-commerce enables business growth and new customers. Majority of the respondents prefer increase in sales. Approximately every fifth of them, however, is satisfied with the current amount of sales. The enterprises' and entrepreneurs' willingness to face the changing operational environment and change operations and adapt to the changing environment were also examined. Majority of the respondents are willing to develop their operations, but again, about 20 percent of them are satisfied with the current situation. In corporate communications, personal contacts are still important. This is, however, not an obstacle to using e-solutions in business. According to the responses, e-business enables customer contacts of better quality and use of customer information. It seems to be that the respondents are already ready to enter the realm of e-commerce. This is despite the fact that they are willing to develop their operations. Company personnel are competent enough, and in many case, they have enough resources to act on the Net. One challenge involved in committing to e-commerce is possible increase in expenses due to investing money in new technology and payments to an intermediary.

We could not get any clear answer to what type of portal (a regional one or one covering the whole country) respondents would prefer. The portal was still under development during our research effort. For this reason, we could not achieve enough background information for the respondents about the country portal. However, it became evident that the respondents do not have any preferences to operate only locally or in one province only. Those who responded also understand tourism industry as something bigger, for example, including also arts and crafts. However, one must remember that the results are only indicative. The results include a lot of responses such as "one cannot answer" and "one does not know the issue sufficiently" which might mean that the subject matter is rather new to the entrepreneurs of the province. They only give an impression of how 10 percent of the target population feels. It is impossible to say how the rest of the population feels. Maybe they do not understand e-solutions at all or maybe they even resist new e-solutions.

5   Following Steps

The results of the study were presented in Tourism Parliament of the Eastern Uusimaa on April 2009. The aim of this one day seminar was to present the newest news in the tourism industry, disseminate information and enable creation of new contacts and fruitful discussions with colleagues. The target group is tourism professionals of the province of Eastern Uusimaa and other people interested in tourism.

In addition to the results of the web-based study, Finnish Tourist Board answered to the VisitFinland related questions that covered issues such as the visibility of single enterprises in the portal, resources to be allocated for the maintenance of content, B2B networking and uses of customer feedback and information in the product development. The results of the whole study were summarized as a matrix. It presented the pros and cons of both the country portal and a hypothetical local portal. This aimed to give the audience more background information about the country portal to be discussed after the presentation. After the presentation and discussion, the audience was asked to vote for which option of the two they would commit to. Voting was only informal. A local portal won but narrowly. Once again it was not possible to say clearly what should be done next.

After discussions with the key representatives of the province (those from Porvoo and Loviisa) and with DMO, the decision was made not to go straight to the country portal. The participants in the session were finally more willing to have a local solution which would be integrated with the VisitFinland portal. Of course, it is still possible in the future that service providers go straight to the VisitFinland portal. HAAGA-HELIA University of Applied Sciences acts as a catalyst and facilitator in forthcoming sessions, whether they be planning or design oriented. The actual construction of a local e-solution is out of focus of HAAGA-HELIA. On June 2009, HAAGA-HELIA organizes first two workshops in Porvoo and Loviisa. The aim is to discuss the following themes.

- How do regional enterprises and other tourism actors understand a local portal?
- What are regional enterprises' and other actors' hopes and needs concerning this local portal?
- What is the role of HAAGA-HELIA in this change process?
- What is the role of regional enterprises in this change process?
- What are the aims of the development project, how will it be scheduled and how resources will be allocated?

Topical issues after the project are the roles and tasks of the individual tourism operators in the province. Where the resources come from, and emphasis be? It is very easy, and perhaps Finnish to concentrate on the technology but according to Daniele and Frew (2008, 242) there can be a gap between the technology and ability to use it in a proper way in small tourism enterprises.

HAAGA-HELIA will be one of the key partners as a facilitator during the whole process. One of the most potential issues to start with is to describe sales and marketing processes of the chosen enterprises and DMO, study them in great depth and to find out ways to support the processes with e-solutions that could be pieced together to construct a portal. Discussions in the future are to pave the way for e-solutions in this small destination.

6 Conclusions

This web-based study explored the regional suppliers' attitudes towards e-commerce and business supported by electronic facilities and portals. Based on the results of the study, tourism suppliers seem to know and understand that e-commerce enables business growth and new customers. But we could not get any clear answer to what type of portal (a regional one or one covering the whole country) respondents would prefer. What is successful in our research effort is that we were able to mobilize 10% of the regional tourism actors. Discussions in the future and the ITU project are to pave the way for e-solutions in this small destination. This should be easier now that we have mobilized the mentioned 10% of the local actors. However, the way forward may still be a rocky one.

References

Buhalis, D. (2003). e-Tourism: Information Technology for Strategic Tourism Management. Harlow: Prentice Hall.

Daniele, R. & Frew, A.J. (2008). Evolving Destination Systems: VisitScotland.com. In P. O'Conner, W. Höpken & U. Gretzel (eds.) Information and Communication Technologies in Tourism 2008 (pp. 232-243). Wien: Springer.

589

Fuchs, M., Witting, C.& Höpken, W. (2009). E-Business Readiness, Intensity and Impact – An Austrian Hotel Study. In W. Höpken, U. Gretzel & R. Law (eds.) Information and Communication Technologies in Tourism 2009 (pp. 431-442). Wien: Springer.

Fux, M. & Myrach, T. (2009). Adaption of a Destination-Wide CRM Approach: An Empirical Analysis of the Determinants in the Swiss Hospitality Industry. In U. Gretzel & R. Law (eds.) Information and Communication Technologies in Tourism 2009 (pp. 506-517). Wien: Springer.

Gratzer, M., Winiwarter, W. & Wertner H. (2002). State of the art in eTourism. In Proceedings of the 3rd SouthEastern European Conference on E-commerce. Nikosia.

Harrigan, K. (1985). Strategic flexibility: a management guide for changing times. Lexington, MA: Lexington Books.

Kothari, T. & Fesenmaier, D. R. (2007). Assessing eBusiness Models and U.S. Destination Marketing Organisations. In M. Sigala, L. Mich & J. Murphy (eds.) Information and Communication Technologies in Tourism 2007 (pp. 185-194). Wien: Springer.

Ricci, F., Wöber K. & Zins A. (2005). Recommendations by collaborative browsing. In A. Frew (ed.), Information Technologies in Tourism (pp. 172-182). Wien: Springer.

Ritchie, R. & Ritchie B. (2002). A Framework for an industry supported destination marketing information system. Tourism Management, 23(5): 439-454.

Schegg, R.; Scaglione, M; Liebriech, A. & Murphy, J. (2007). Internet use by Hospitality SMEs in Alpine Destinations. In Sigala, M.; Mich, L and Murphy, J. Information and Communication Technologies in Tourism 2007 (pp. 469-480). Wien: Springer.

Starry, I. (2009). Shifting to 2.0. Presentation in the 16th Information and Communication Technologies in Tourism Conference (ENTER 2009).

Taipale, I. (2007). Itä-Uudenmaan matkailijatutkimus. Helsinki: HAAGA-HELIA ammattikorkeakoulu.

Tseng, C-Y. & Hsu, Y-L. (2007). Employment Performance in the Hospitality Business. In Proceedings of TTRA Europe Conference.

Werthner, H. & Klein S. (1999). Information Technology and Tourism – A Challenging Relationship. Wien: Springer.

Zsu, K. & Kraemer, L. (2005). Post-Adaption Variations in Usage and Value of e-Business by Organisations: Cross-Country Evidence from the Retail Industry. Information Systems, 16(1): 61-84.

Arabian Photos: Investigating User-Generated Content

Sharifah Fatimah Syed-Ahmad[ab],
Dayangku Ida Nurul-Fitri Pengiran-Kahar[ac],
Azlinda Lahadzir[d] and
Jamie Murphy[a]

[a]Business School,
University of Western Australia, Australia
syedas01@student.uwa.edu.au
jmurphy@biz.uwa.edu.au

[b]Faculty of Business and Accountancy
University of Malaya, Malaysia
sfsa@um.edu.my

[c]Faculty of Business and Information Technology
Institute of Technology, Brunei
ida.kahar@itb.edu.bn

[d]Faculty of Economic and Muamalat
Islamic Science University of Malaysia, Malaysia
azlinda@usim.edu.my

Abstract

This paper focuses on User-Generated (UG) photos in the understudied Arab Muslim World. Over four million public photos on Flickr.com represent Arab countries' UG presence, with Egypt and Palestine the top countries for the respective keywords of *travel* and *Muslim*. The findings also reveal varied United Arab Emirates' presence, with ten times more Dubai photos than the next highest emirate Abu Dhabi and two hundred times more than three emirates. At the country level, the results of hypotheses testing showed significant relationships between the presences of public Flickr photos with Arabian Internet connectivity, tourist arrivals and Muslim population.

Keywords: user-generated content, Arab League, photo, travel, Muslim.

1 Introduction

The Western image of Arabia is primarily negative, projected through the news and mass media such as CNN and Hollywood films (Hudson, 2006; Shaheen, 2006). Another Arab image emerged with the Al-Jazeera news channel 1996 debut. Al-Jazeera's reach, however, seems limited to Arabs and special interest groups (AbiNader, 2006; Hudson, 2006). A third source of Arab country images stem from tourism marketing organisation promotions, websites and brochures (Govers & Go, 2004). Yet a new trend, user-generated content (UGC), shifts control of the image away from the traditional media and official organisations, Western or Arab. With this new technology, anyone with Internet access can present or view images of the Arab World. UGC lets individuals create and share photo, text, video, and audio that could interest past and potential travellers to Arab countries. Travel UGC studies centre primarily on tourism sites such as TripAdvisor, ranked 366 by Alexa, with few examining tourism on popular non-tourism UGC websites such as YouTube (videos, ranked 4th) and Flickr (photos, ranked 32nd) (Alexa, 2009; Cantoni, Tardini, Inversini, & Marchiori, 2009; Gretzel & Yoo, 2008; Tussyadiah & Fesenmaier, 2009; Vermeulen & Seegers, 2009; Ye, Law, & Gu, 2009). As one in two tourists view photos via UGC, and photo viewing is the most popular UGC activity (Alexa, 2009; Daugherty, Eastin, & Bright, 2008; Yoo, Lee, Gretzel, & Fesenmaier, 2009), Flickr is an avenue where users and visitors can access the myriad shared photos, such as artistic, family, friend and travel photos (Cox, Clough, & Marlow, 2008).

While many embrace UGC sites, several constraints could stop individuals from sharing photos. Pre-requisites to posting photos are available Internet connectivity as well as available destination travel photos to post. In addition, posters determine the images to capture and post, such as a destination's religion and culture. Although tourists cluster the Arab World together (Winckler, 2007), Flickr photos could project and differentiate Arab countries to viewers. As tourism is increasingly important in the Muslim and Arab World (Al-Hamarneh & Steiner, 2004), UGC of this religion and region is relevant for Arab destinations. And, as the West dominates mainstream tourism and technology research (Hashim, Murphy, & Hashim, 2007), this study adds to the dearth of Islamic tourism and technology research. Thus, this paper extends the burgeoning UGC travel research stream by addressing two research questions:

- How do Arab countries vary in public travel, Muslim and general Flickr postings?
- How do public Flickr photos relate to Arab countries' Internet connections, users, visitors and Muslim population?

The results of this study should assist governments and tourism organisations, particularly in Arab and other Muslim countries, understand the photo sharing trend and Arab countries' UGC presence. This understanding could lead to future decisions regarding official portrayals of their countries, as well as aligning this channel with the official destination image.

2 Literature Review

2.1 Photography, Travel and User-generated content

The world's fascination with photography began in 1839 with human portraits, previously only available through paintings (Freund, 1980). Photographers captured images for realistic portrayals, artistic expression and commercial mass-production. After five decades, photography bloomed thanks to Kodak cameras that let amateur photographers capture everyday events and travels (Freund, 1980; Lowry, 1999). For example, tourists photograph unique landscapes, locals (Urry, 1990), family members and mundane images (Haldrup & Larsen, 2003). Tourists keep the photos for remembrance (Haldrup & Larsen, 2003) and share them (Cox et al., 2008; Urry, 1990). The Internet facilitates photo sharing, such as via instant messaging and UGC websites (Syed-Ahmad, Hashim, Zubairi, & Murphy, 2008). UGC lets users share travel photographs, videos and opinions, with personal contacts and the public (Cox et al., 2008; Tussyadiah & Fesenmaier, 2009). Travel visuals, such as on YouTube and Facebook, help viewers imagine, intend, and plan destination visits (Syed-Ahmad, Hashim, Horrigan, & Murphy, 2009; Tussyadiah & Fesenmaier, 2009). Users can view and post photos on Flickr, a website focused on photos, and through social networks websites such as Facebook, MySpace and Friendster (Cantoni et al., 2009; Cormode & Krishnamurthy, 2008). Furthermore, photo-based UGC websites are popular, ranked by (Alexa, 2009) in the top 64 of all sites: Flickr (32), Photobucket.com (42) and ImageShack.us (64).

Flickr.com. Established in 2004, Flickr features photo sharing with the ability to network and socialise with family, friends, contacts and the public (Boyd & Ellison, 2007). Viewing these photos is a motivation to take and possibly post photos (Cox et al., 2008). On Flickr, users post many photo types from artistic to the mundane. In searching for public photos, Flickr visitors specify keywords according to their interests. To seek UGC travel content for a country, visitor searches include the country name and travel associated keywords. For example, a YouTube study of New York travel posts employed combinations of the city's name variations, as well as *travel* as keywords (Tussyadiah & Fesenmaier, 2009). Public Flickr photos serve as possible travel recommendations with tens of millions of country photos in October 2009 – USA (7 million), UK (5 million) and Australia (4 million). Muslim countries also have public Flickr photos, such as Turkey (1.6 million), Malaysia (1.3 million), Egypt (1.2 million) and Jordan (0.7 million). Aside from having global popularity, Flickr's reach includes the Arab League; Flickr was within 12 Arab countries' top 100 websites in October 2009 (Alexa, 2009), as shown in Table 1 later.

2.2 The League of Arab States

Established in 1945, the League of Arab States 22 countries – Algeria, Bahrain, Comoros, Djibouti, Egypt, Iraq, Jordan, Kuwait, Lebanon, Libya, Mauritania, Morocco, Oman, Palestine, Qatar, Saudi Arabia, Somalia, Sudan, Syria, Tunisia, United Arab Emirates, and Yemen – in the Middle East and North Africa share a common language, identity and culture (Otterman, 2009). The World Travel and Tourism Council forecasts annual travel and tourism growth until the year 2019 of 4.3% and 5.1%, respectively for the Middle East and North Africa, higher than the global average of 4.0% (World Travel and Tourism Council, 2009a, 2009b). Another growing area in Arab countries is Internet adoption, which has bloomed this century, with over 1,000% user growth, higher than the rest of the world's 350% growth (Internet World Stats, 2009a, 2009b). The growth rate is different among the countries, for instance from 2007 to 2009, countries such as Egypt and Morocco recorded big increases in Internet users while some remained static (Central Intelligence Agency, 2009; Internet World Stats, 2009a, 2009b), shown in Table 1. Arab Internet users can consume and share thoughts online (Al-Jassem, 2006), yet governments such as Saudi

Arabia limit and monitor their citizen's Internet use, such as content contradicting Muslim culture (Kraidy, 2006). As Arab countries have high Muslim populations, 89% on average (Central Intelligence Agency, 2009), Muslim culture is prevalent in their daily life. Muslim culture comes from the holy book Quran, the revelations from God to Muhammad, and *hadith*, a compilation of Muhammad's actions and sayings (Nigosian, 1987). Muslims embrace five obligatory actions – *shahada*, prayer, alms-giving, fasting and pilgrimage (Mawdudi, 1985; Nigosian, 1987). First, Muslims believe and voice the *shahada,* a sentence declaring that Allah is the only God and Muhammad as God's messenger. Second and third, Muslims pray five times a day to worship God and give alms according to their wealth. Fourth, from sunrise to sunset in the month of Ramadan, Muslims abstain from activities that would nullify their fast. Lastly, able Muslims perform the *hajj* pilgrimage in Saudi Arabia. Only some of these Islamic practices, such as praying as opposed to fasting, are observable in UGC photographs. Flickr photos could depict Muslim culture, as well as travel in a country.

3 Conceptual Development

This study examines Arab countries' UGC presence on public Flickr photographs. Due to the increasing importance of UGC and Arab tourism, visuals portraying the region could interest or deter tourists from visiting. This paper hypothesizes relationships between Flickr photo presence and Arab countries' Internet adoption, tourist arrivals, and Muslim images. A country's Internet adoption and connection, and tourist arrivals should relate positively to that country's public Flickr photos. Similarly, the presence of Muslim images should relate positively to the proportion of Muslims in a country.

3.1 Internet Hosts and Users with Flickr postings

UGC sites are popular in the Arab region with YouTube, Facebook, and Wikipedia in the top 30 most popular sites for most Arab countries (Alexa, 2009). In addition, three photo-based sites − Photobucket, ImageShack and Flickr − are amongst the top 100 websites in many Arab countries. Internet adoption and connection should support UGC participation. With Internet users increasing in this region, Arab Internet users' participation in UGC activities, such as viewing and posting on Flickr, should also increase. Furthermore, as a country's Internet hosts indicate Internet connectivity (Central Intelligence Agency, 2009; Turban, King, Viehland, & Lee, 2006, p. 674), Internet hosts assist UGC participation. Thus, countries with higher Internet connectivity and adoption should have more public Flickr photos,

H1a: The number of Internet hosts in an Arab country has a positive relationship with the country's public Flickr photographs.

H1b: The number of Internet users in an Arab country has a positive relationship with the country's public Flickr photographs.

3.2 Tourist arrivals and Flickr travel postings

Tourists can share travel photos with just friends or the public (Cantoni et al., 2009; Cox et al., 2008; Syed-Ahmad et al., 2009). When sharing photos on Flickr, tourists could specify keywords for the posted Flickr photos to indicate their trip and assist viewers searching for travel photos. Countries with more visitors should have more travel photos,

H2: The number of tourists in an Arab country has a positive relationship with the country's public Flickr travel photographs.

3.3 Muslim population and Flickr Muslim postings

As Flickr users share many types of photos (Cox et al., 2008) including norms and culture, Arab Internet users could post photographs that share their Muslim culture. In addition, taking and posting photos of Muslim norms in these countries could interest Western tourists (Urry, 1990). Thus the stronger a country's Muslim culture, the more opportunities to capture and post photographs of Muslim norms. For instance, Mauritania, Saudi Arabia, Somalia and Yemen are 100% Muslim, while Egypt is 90% Muslim and Lebanon is 60% (Central Intelligence Agency, 2009). Thus, the number of public Flickr photos of Muslim images in Arab countries should relate positively to the percentage of Muslims in each country.

H3: The percentage of Muslims in an Arab country has a positive relationship with the country's public Flickr photographs of Muslim images.

4 Methodology

As visitors search Flickr photos using keywords, this study used keywords to represent travel, Muslim and general photos. Flickr searches in June 2009 for travel returned over nine million photos, the highest among other tourism words such as vacation, holiday, tour, tourist and tourism. A search for *Muslim* returned nearly 192 thousand photos and *Islam* returned over 154 thousand photos, making Muslim the prominent keyword for Muslim photos on Flickr. The addition of the country name specifies photos for the country; *country* on its own represents general public photos. The final keywords for this study were the Arab *country*, *country and travel*, as well as *country and Muslim*, as shown in Table 1. The United Arab Emirates (UAE) search was for the country's seven emirates – Abu Dhabi, Ajman, Dubai, Fujairah, Sharjah, Ras al-Khaimah, and Umm al-Quwain – due to each emirate's autonomy and diversity (UAE Government, 2006). The search used the Boolean 'AND' so that a search for *Egypt* and *travel* returned photos tagged with both keywords.

5 Results

Table 1 shows the number of Flickr photos by three keyword searches, listing all Arab countries and the seven UAE emirates in descending order for the keyword "country".

Table 1. Arab Flickr Photo Results (18 June 2009) and Country Statistics

	H1a,b	H2	H3	H1a	H1b	H1b	H2	H3
	Country	Country + Travel	Country + Muslim	Internet host[a] (2008) (thou)	Internet users[a] (2006/ 2007) (million)	Internet users[b] (2009) (million)	Tourist arrivals[c] (2004 /2005) (thou)	Muslim[a] (%)
Egypt	**1,143,702**	77,441	8,271	175.34	**8.62**	**12.57**	8,244	90
Jordan*	676,124	20,973	1,688	21.15	1.13	1.50	2,987	92
Morocco	649,199	47,939	5,716	275.89	7.30	10.30	5,843	99
UAE (7 emirates total)	490,472	14,731	1,931	**381.92**	2.30	2.86	n/a	96
Dubai (UAE)	428,332	12,966	1,307	n/a	n/a	n/a	n/a	n/a
Iraq*	276,940	2,127	2,660	.003	.05	.28	n/a	97
Lebanon*	214,952	5,410	14,430	36.68	.95	1.57	1,140	60
Tunisia*	181,764	12,479	1,030	.38	1.72	2.80	6,378	98
Palestine	148,159	3,657	**18,181**	n/a	.36	.36	88	75
Syria*	145,696	10,337	13,854	7.86	3.47	3.57	3,368	74
Kuwait*	114,565	1,593	652	3.29	.90	.90	91	85
Oman*	102,958	2,344	1,358	4.79	.34	.47	1,195	75
Qatar*	95,278	2,179	382	.56	.35	.44	732	78
Bahrain*	75,751	2,017	420	2.62	.25	.25	3,514	81
Sudan	55,190	2,359	580	.03	1.50	3.80	61	70
Saudi Arabia*	50,455	2,871	1,355	141.23	6.20	7.20	**9,100**	100
Libya*	50,075	1,715	276	.03	.26	.29	149	97
Yemen*	49,783	5,411	1,753	.17	.32	.32	336	100
Abu Dhabi (UAE)	40,505	1,306	439	n/a	n/a	n/a	n/a	n/a
Algeria	36,063	1,483	489	.48	3.50	3.50	1,443	99
Mauritania	15,295	646	1,049	.03	.03	.05	n/a	100
Sharjah (UAE)	13,454	321	164	n/a	n/a	n/a	n/a	n/a
Somalia	10,046	438	188	.001	.10	.10	n/a	100
Djibouti	7,846	244	25	.16	.01	.01	30	94
Fujairah (UAE)	4,472	41	14	n/a	n/a	n/a	n/a	n/a
Ajman (UAE)	1,759	39	4	n/a	n/a	n/a	n/a	n/a
Ras al-Khaimah(UAE)	1,729	58	3	n/a	n/a	n/a	n/a	n/a
Comoros	1,483	20	5	.01	.02	.02	18	98
Umm al-Quwain (UAE)	221	0	0	n/a	n/a	n/a	n/a	n/a
Total	4,591,796	218,414	76,293	1,052.62	39.68	53.16	44,717	-
% of total country photos	100	4.8	1.7	-	-	-	-	-

* Arab countries with Flickr in the top 100 websites in the country (Alexa, 2009),
[a] (Central Intelligence Agency, 2009) , [b] (Internet World Stats, 2009a, 2009b),
[c] (World Tourism Organization, 2007a, 2007b), **Bold** numbers represent column leaders

Flickr users displayed over four million photos for the League of Arab States. Egypt led with over one million photos. The top three countries for *travel* keyword photos were Egypt, Morocco and Jordan, while the top *Muslim* photos were for Palestine, Lebanon and Syria. There were more *travel* than *Muslim* photos in total and within each country, except in five countries − Palestine, Lebanon, Syria, Iraq and Mauritania. UAE's Dubai had nearly half a million *travel* photos, surpassing all but three Arab countries.

As Table 1 shows, United Arab Emirates had the most Internet hosts and Egypt the most Internet users. Saudi Arabia had the most 2004/2005 tourist arrivals, over nine million, followed by Egypt (8.2 million), Tunisia (6.4 million) and Morocco (5.8 million). Comoros, an island nation in the Indian Ocean, had the least tourist arrivals at 18,000. Four Arab countries − Mauritania, Saudi Arabia, Somalia and Yemen − had 100% Muslim population; Lebanon had the lowest proportional Muslim population (60%).

Calculations for the correlation for the hypothesized relationships used Table 1's Flickr photo keyword results and the Arab country statistics. Spearman's rho measured the correlations due to non-normal data distributions (Meyers, Gamst, & Guarino, 2006) with one-tailed test due to hypothesized relationships. As shown in Table 2, the results supported H1 and H2, with strong and positive relationships, but did not support H3.

Table 2. Hypotheses Testing

		Spearman's rho	Significance	Sample size	Result
H1a: Internet host and Flickr country photos		.681	< .001	21	Supported
H1b: Internet users and Flickr country photos	Internet users (2006/2007)	.598	.002	22	Supported
	Internet users (2009)	.602	.002	22	
H2: Tourist arrivals and Flickr travel photos		.637	.002	18	Supported
H3: Muslim population and Flickr Muslim photos		-.294	.092	22	Not supported

6 Discussions and Implications

6.1 Tourists and Arab countries

Flickr user postings differentiated Arab countries through varying photo presence. The significant positive relationship between tourist arrivals and Flickr travel photos suggests that Arab tourists post photos with the keyword *travel*. Arab countries' Flickr travel photos reflect tourism in the region. The top six Arab countries – Egypt, Morocco, Jordan, UAE, Tunisia and Syria – with over 10 thousand travel photos listed in Table 1, had among the highest tourists in the region.

Consistent with its position as a top Arab destination, Egypt dominated Flickr results for two searches, *country*, and *country and travel*. This big lead could stem from Egypt's high number of Internet users. While Egypt did not receive the highest tourist arrivals, Egypt's popularity as a tourist destination and photographic spot since the 19th century could motivate tourist postings (Levine & Jensen, 2007). Amongst the UAE, Dubai travel photos surpassed countries such as Tunisia, Syria and Saudi Arabia. The emirates' differing Flickr coverage could reflect emirate-level tourism activities (Sharpley, 2002, p. 221), with three emirates – Dubai, Abu Dhabi and Sharjah – having the most Flickr travel presence.

Flickr photos also reflected situations within the countries. Millions travel to Saudi Arabia for religious visits and the *hajj*, the once in a lifetime mandatory pilgrimage to Mecca and Medina (Organisation of the Islamic Conference, 2005; Smith, 2008). While Saudi Arabia had the most tourists, its limited travel posts could indicate that travellers concentrated on religious responsibilities and not on tourist activities such as taking photos. Another example of Flickr's close association with reality emerged as four countries near each other – Palestine, Lebanon, Syria and Iraq – had more Muslim than travel photos, suggesting lower tourism than Muslim associations, possibly due to unstable situations in Palestine and Iraq (Gregory, 2004; Sirriyeh, 2007). Palestine had the highest Muslim photos suggesting Flickr posters associate Palestine with Muslims.

Arab countries could use these Flickr results to assist planning and budgeting for the development and promotion of destinations, especially for countries with less Flickr presence indicating untapped tourism potential. Within UAE for instance, tourism organisations could plan to widen Dubai's popularity to other emirates such as the lowest Flickr presence emirate Umm Al-Quwain, by pairing the two states in tour packages. Tourism organisations within less popular Arab countries could collaborate and introduce inter-country tour packages based on selected locations shown in Flickr. This effort could increase tourism revenue for each Arab country, minimise promotional costs and possibly increase the countries' user-generated presence.

Flickr photos seem an avenue to represent a country as UGC photo viewing – generally and amongst tourists – is popular (Daugherty et al., 2008; Yoo et al., 2009). As UGC users rely on photos to plan their trips (Syed-Ahmad et al., 2009), tourism organisations could collaborate with Flickr users as well as use posted Flickr photographs of their countries to encourage tourist visits. As posters might not add specifics in photos, Arab tourism organisations could assign a staff to monitor and add keywords/tags and notes for their countries' photos. For example, additional keywords regarding the depicted region, street, buildings and festivities could assist viewers' search for photos and add knowledge about the country. Furthermore, tourism organisations could select popular Flickr photos and use them for online and offline travel brochures. Aside from able to easily target and use popular shots of their countries, by employing these photos, tourism organisations only incur the costs to gain the rights to use the photographs from Flickr posters. In addition, these photos should have more credibility compared to official portrayals as consumers favour others' over formal sources (Cheong & Morrison, 2008).

6.2 Internet Adoption and Muslim population

The Internet connectivity and adoption in Arab countries had positive relationships with Flickr country photos, suggesting that Arab countries' Internet users have Flickr memberships and posts. While a 2005 study found 70% of sampled Flickr members were from North America and Europe and none from Arab nations (Meyer, Rosenbaum, & Hara, 2005), the rapid regional growth of Internet users should increase Arab Flickr users' global presence.

The proportion of Muslim population had no relationship with the 76 thousand Muslim photos for Arab countries, failing to support the third hypothesis. At least four possibilities help explain this result. Firstly, posters could post Muslim images but did not tag the photos with the word *Muslim*. Secondly, Flickr Muslim photos could include images that do not equate to Muslims. Third and fourth reasons related to low local posts due to Internet connection and low tourist posts due to low tourist numbers in 10 highly populated Muslim countries, more than 95% Muslim population (Central Intelligence Agency, 2009). For instance, the majority (73%) of high Muslim countries have less than a thousand Internet hosts, while a majority (64%) of countries with less than 95% Muslims have more than a thousand Internet hosts. Additionally, only 36% of the high Muslim countries have more than half a million tourists (Central Intelligence Agency, 2009; World Tourism Organization, 2007a, 2007b).

This study identified Arab countries' Flickr presence, filling knowledge gaps for UGC within the Arab World. This paper also contributes to the limited UGC photos studies. Furthermore, the result suggests that Arab tourism organisations should widen the scope of the usual tourism development plans to include Internet connectivity to support more photo posts. For example, the Internet infrastructure at hotels within a city could assist or deter tourists from posting travel photos of a destination as some tourists might prefer to post photos during their holidays.

7 Limitations and Future Research

At least four limitations exist in this study and illustrate fruitful future research avenues. Firstly, this study examined only three keyword combinations. Future studies could explore keywords to capture tourist attractions or festivals. Secondly, the number of photos returned for a particular keyword might not reflect those keywords in actual photos. For example, aside from indicating holiday trips, Flickr travel photos could also refer to the transportation during journeys. Thirdly, only the 2004/2005 tourist arrivals data were available, with data for some countries unavailable (World Tourism Organization, 2007a, 2007b). Lastly, not every traveller or Internet user becomes a Flickr member, and not all Flickr members post photos or equal numbers of photos. Different users have their own motivation behind posting photos and further studies should examine reasons why individuals post travel photos.

Qualitative studies could unearth posters' travel posting motivations, such as injunctive and descriptive norms (Lapinski & Rimal, 2005). Seeing others post photos, descriptive norm, and others' expectations for photos, injunctive norm, could affect posts. Other motivations could revolve around the destinations' descriptive norm or popularity.

Future studies could benefit from differentiating locals and tourists as they might have different views of a country, as well as the images to photograph. As many tourists access user-generated photos, another study could explore the types of representations that viewers enjoy by their comments and favourite awards. For example, studies found an aversion for destination photos containing crowds, food and commercial buildings (Dewar, Li, & Davis, 2007; Fairweather & Swaffield, 2001). Results could assist destination organisations understand and use popular photo types to attract potential visitors.

A final research area could examine other regions of the world, such as developing Muslim countries in Asia – Brunei, Indonesia and Malaysia. Due to the limited studies in developing countries (Hashim et al., 2007), studies could shed light on how tourists and locals view these countries. These countries also have strong Flickr presence in September 2009 with Malaysia (1,315,652) Indonesia (777,887), and Brunei (73,606).

References

AbiNader, J. (2006). The Role of the Arab Media in Shaping the Western Perspective of Arabs. In *Arab Media in the Information Age* (pp. 281-297). Abu Dhabi: The Emirates Center for Strategic Studies and Research.

Al-Hamarneh, A., & Steiner, C. (2004). Islamic Tourism: Rethinking the Strategies of Tourism Development in the Arab World After September 11, 2001. *Comparative Studies of South Asia, Africa and the Middle East,* 24(1), 173-182.

Al-Jassem, M. (2006). The Impact of the Electronic Media on Arab Socio-Political Development. In *Arab Media in the Information Age* (pp. 169-182). Abu Dhabi: The Emirates Center for Strategic Studies and Research.

Alexa. (2009). Top Sites. Retrieved 28 October 2009, from www.alexa.com/topsites

Boyd, D. M., & Ellison, N. B. (2007). Social Network Sites: Definition, History, Scholarship. *Journal of Computer-Mediated Communication,* 13(1), jcmc.indiana.edu/vol13/issue1/boyd.ellison.html.

Cantoni, L., Tardini, S., Inversini, A., & Marchiori, E. (2009). *From Paradigmatic to Syntagmatic Communities: A Socio-Semiotic Approach to the Evolution Pattern of Online Travel Communities.* Paper presented at the Information and Communication Technologies in Tourism (ENTER) 2009, Amsterdam, the Netherlands.

Central Intelligence Agency. (2009). The World Factbook Retrieved 29 April, 2009, from www.cia.gov/library/publications/the-world-factbook/index.html

Cheong, H. J., & Morrison, M. A. (2008). Consumers' Reliance on Product Information and Recommendations Found in UGC. *Journal of Interactive Advertising,* 8(2), //jiad.org/article103.

Cormode, G., & Krishnamurthy, B. (2008). Key Differences between Web 1.0 and Web 2.0. *First Monday,* 13(6), www.uic.edu/htbin/cgiwrap/bin/ojs/index.php/fm/article/view/2125/1972.

Cox, A. M., Clough, P. D., & Marlow, J. (2008). Flickr: A First Look at User Behaviour in the Context of Photography as Serious Leisure. *Information Research,* 13(1).

Daugherty, T., Eastin, M. S., & Bright, L. (2008). Exploring Consumer Motivations for Creating User-Generated Content. *Journal of Interactive Advertising*, 8(2), //jiad.org/vol8/no2/daugherty/index.htm.

Dewar, K., Li, W. M., & Davis, C. H. (2007). Photographic Images, Culture, and Perception in Tourism Advertising: A Q Methodology Study of Canadian and Chinese University Students *Journal of Travel & Tourism Marketing* 22(2), 35-44.

Fairweather, J. R., & Swaffield, S. R. (2001). Visitor Experiences of Kaikoura, New Zealand: An Interpretative Study using Photographs of Landscapes and Q Methods. *Tourism Management*, 22(3), 219-228.

Freund, G. (1980). *Photography & Society*. London: David R. Godine.

Govers, R., & Go, F. M. (2004). Projected Destination Image Online: Website Content Analysis of Pictures and Text. *Journal of Information Technology & Tourism*, 7(2), 73-89.

Gregory, D. (2004). Palestine and the "War on Terror". *Comparative Studies of South Asia, Africa and the Middle East*, 24(1), 183-195.

Gretzel, U., & Yoo, K. H. (2008). Use and Impact of Online Travel Reviews. In P. O'Connor, W. Hopken & U. Gretzel (Eds.), *Information and Communication Technologies in Tourism 2008* (pp. 35-46). Innsbruck, Austria: Springer-Verlag Wien.

Haldrup, M., & Larsen, J. (2003). The Family Gaze. *Tourist Studies*, 3(1), 23-45.

Hashim, N. H., Murphy, J., & Hashim, N. M. (2007). Islam and Online Imagery on Malaysian Tourist Destination Websites. *Journal of Computer-Mediated Communication*, 12(3), jcmc.indiana.edu/vol12/issue3/hashim.html.

Hudson, M. C. (2006). Washington vs. Al Jazeera: Competing Constructions of Middle East Realities. In *Arab Media in the Information Age* (pp. 229-248). Abu Dhabi: The Emirates Center for Strategic Studies and Research.

Internet World Stats. (2009a). Internet Usage in the Middle East. Retrieved 11 September, 2009, from www.internetworldstats.com/stats5.htm#me

Internet World Stats. (2009b). Internet Usage Statistics for Africa. Retrieved 11 September, 2009, from www.internetworldstats.com/stats1.htm

Kraidy, M. M. (2006). Hypermedia and governance in Saudi Arabia. *First Monday,* Special Issue(7), http://www.uic.edu/htbin/cgiwrap/bin/ojs/index.php/fm/article/view/1610/1525.

Lapinski, M. K., & Rimal, R. N. (2005). An Explication of Social Norms. *Communication Theory*, 15(2), 127-147.

Levine, B., & Jensen, K. M. (2007). *Around the World: The Grand Tour in Photo Albums*. New York: Princeton Architectural Press.

Lowry, J. (1999). Photography, Video and the Everyday. In D. Brittain (Ed.), *Creative Camera: Thirty Years of Writing* (pp. 278-283). Manchester: Manchester University Press.

Mawdudi, S. A. A. l. (1985). *Let Us be Muslims*. Leicester, United Kingdom: The Islamic Foundation.

Meyer, E. T., Rosenbaum, H., & Hara, N. (2005). *How Photobloggers are Framing a New Computerization Movement*. Paper presented at the Internet Generations 6.0: Annual Conference of the Association of Internet Researchers (AoIR).

Meyers, L. S., Gamst, G., & Guarino, A. J. (2006). *Applied Multivariate Research: Design and Interpretation*. Thousand Oaks: Sage Publications, Inc.

Nigosian, S. A. (1987). *Islam: The Way of Submission*. Great Britain: Crucible.

Organisation of the Islamic Conference. (2005). About OIC. Retrieved 30 June, 2009, from www.oic-oci.org/page_detail.asp?p_id=52

Otterman, S. (2009). Arab League. *The New York Times* Retrieved 22 June, 2009, from topics.nytimes.com/topics/reference/timestopics/organizations/a/arab_league/

Shaheen, J. G. (2006). The New Anti-Semitism: Hollywood's Reel Bad Arabs: Impacting Public Opinion and Policy. In *Arab Media in the Information Age* (pp. 323-362). Abu Dhabi: The Emirates Center for Strategic Studies and Research.

Sharpley, R. (2002). The Challenges of Economic Diversification Through Tourism: The Case of Abu Dhabi. *International Journal of Tourism Research*, 4(3), 120-130.

Sirriyeh, H. (2007). Iraq and the Region Since the War of 2003. *Civil Wars,* 9(1), 106-125.

Smith, P. A. (2008, May). Opening the Door to Foreign Investment in the Arab World. *The Middle East, 389,* 28-31.

Syed-Ahmad, S. F., Hashim, N. H., Horrigan, D., & Murphy, J. (2009). *Travel Research and Sharing through User-Generated Content.* Paper presented at the 7th Asia Pacific CHRIE (APacCHRIE) 2009 Conference

Syed-Ahmad, S. F., Hashim, N. H., Zubairi, Y. Z., & Murphy, J. (2008). *An Exploratory Study of Digital Word of Mouth in Travel by Malaysian Women.* Paper presented at the 6th Asia Pacific CHRIE (APacCHRIE) 2008 Conference and THE-ICE Panel of Experts Forum 2008, Perth, Australia.

Turban, E., King, D., Viehland, D., & Lee, J. (2006). *Electronic Commerce: A Managerial Perspective 2006* Upper Saddle River: Pearson Education Inc.

Tussyadiah, I. P., & Fesenmaier, D. R. (2009). Mediating Tourist Experiences: Access to Places via Shared Videos. *Annals of Tourism Research,* 36(1), 24-40.

UAE Government. (2006). About UAE. *UAE Federal e-Government Portal* Retrieved 26 Jun 2009, 2009, from www.government.ae/gov/en/general/uae/country.jsp

Urry, J. (1990). *The Tourist Gaze: Leisure and Travel in Contemporary Societies.* London: Sage.

Vermeulen, I. E., & Seegers, D. (2009). Tried and Tested: The Impact of Online Hotel Reviews on Consumer Consideration. *Tourism Management,* 30(1), 123-127.

Winckler, O. (2007). The Birth of Oman's Tourism Industry. *Tourism,* 55(2), 221-234.

World Tourism Organization. (2007a). Tourism Market Trend: Africa. Retrieved 28 August, 2009, from //unwto.org/facts/eng/pdf/indicators/ITA_Africa.pdf

World Tourism Organization. (2007b). Tourism Market Trend: Middle East. 2006. Retrieved 28 August, 2009, from //unwto.org/facts/eng/pdf/indicators/ITA_ME.pdf

World Travel and Tourism Council. (2009a). *Travel and Tourism Economic Impact 2009: Middle East.* London.

World Travel and Tourism Council. (2009b). *Travel and Tourism Economic Impact 2009: North Africa.* London.

Ye, Q., Law, R., & Gu, B. (2009). The Impact of Online User Reviews on Hotel Room Sales. *International Journal of Hospitality Management,* 28(1), 180-182.

Yoo, K. H., Lee, Y., Gretzel, U., & Fesenmaier, D. R. (2009). *Trust in Travel-Related Consumer Generated Media.* Paper presented at the Information and Communication Technologies in Tourism (ENTER) 2009.

Semantic-Based Contextual Computing Support for Human Mobility

Carlos Lamsfus,
Aurkene Alzua-Sorzabal,
David Martín, and
Zigor Salvador

mugiLab - Laboratory for Studies on Human Mobility and Technology
Competence Research Centre in Tourism, CICtourGUNE, Spain
carloslamsfus@tourgune.org

Abstract

This paper presents a Contextual Computing Framework (CONCERT) that uses a rule-based filtering system built on top of a context modelling network of ontologies to provide visitors with the kind of information and services they require while on the move. The tourism domain is very well suited to make use of the recent advances in mobile devices and connectivity technologies, enabling visitors to access context-based services and information, which can greatly enhance their tourism experiences. To achieve this goal, the representation and use of context information are key aspects that need to be carefully addressed. Despite the recent proliferation of context-aware applications and the existence of some mobile tourism guides that partly incorporate this concept, no widespread adoption of such technologies has taken place. The main goal of this paper is to propose a different conception of the notion of context and provide an extensible, ontology-based model of context that filters incoming tourism information based on the context of visitors.

Keywords: Tourism, Semantic Web, Ontologies, Push, Contextual-Computing, Digital Broadcasting.

1 Introduction

This paper presents the CONCERT framework: an approach to contextual computing in the framework of human mobility. Some studies and research show that context-based applications represent an opportunity for future services within the travel and tourism industries (Gretzel & Wöber, 2004; Bernardos et al., 2007; Grün et al., 2008) and the possibility to better understand human behaviour in the future digital society. By 2015 there will be around 3 billion people moving around the world (SITA, 2009) and regional and international visitor flows will be multiplied by three (Lamsfus & Alzua-Sorzabal, 2009c). Most of these people, i.e. visitors according to official established nomenclature (UNWTO International Recommendations for Tourism Statistics, 2008, p.10), will have lived the majority of their (adult) lives in the digital era and their behavioural patterns with their environment will be significantly different from today's standards. Time will continue to be a very scarce resource and this new type of travellers will require anytime, anywhere, personalized kinds of services, i.e. context-dependent services (Höpken et al., 2008).

Since Mark Weiser enunciated his vision of a new interaction paradigm with computers (Weiser, 1991), intensive research has been conducted within the so-called context-awareness area. However, despite all the effort invested, these types of systems have not yet been made available to the general public and they only exist in certain laboratory environments (Lamsfus et al., 2009a). At the same time, location and context-based information systems still have to get off the ground in the field of tourism (Buhalis & Pistida, 2009).

There are a number of reasons for this. Firstly, there is no sufficient consensus on a conceptual framework for context-based systems (Dey et al., 2001; Gu et al. 2004; Ay, 2007) and thus, there is no operative definition of the notion of context. Secondly, context has never been studied as such, but as a tool for other research disciplines such as, human-computer interaction (Dey, 2000), intelligent software agents (Chen et al., 2003) or distributed systems (Strang & Linnhoff-Popien, 2004). These works show an oversimplified approach to context and authors use contextual information to enhance their systems' functionalities but not for the sake of studying context itself. Thirdly, most context-aware applications require populating areas of interest with sensors to gather contextual information. Nonetheless, the dramatic evolution of mobile devices and connectivity technologies are setting the path for context-based services. Functionalities and computing capabilities of mobile devices have grown considerably (G. Chen & Kotz, 2001). Moreover, latest generation devices such as Apple's iPhone, Google's Android G1, the Nokia E series or new device types such as Netbooks are being widely accepted in society to the extent that they will very likely support the primary access to online services (Want, 2009). Moreover, connectivity technologies, such as 3G, UMTS, Wi-Fi, WiMAX (G. Chen & Kotz, 2001; Buhalis & Pistida, 2009) have evolved rapidly enabling people to be continuously connected to online services following the promises of the Ubiquitous Computing paradigm. The fast adoption of these kinds of devices and technologies by everyday users in today's society is producing new behaviour patterns and changing tourism consumer habits. People increasingly demand new services that are hardly implementable with current scientific and technological state of the art. There are a number of scientific challenges amongst which semantic technologies, automatic-learning algorithms, development of connectivity technologies, optimization algorithms, human device interaction and persuasive computing are significantly important. Based on all of the above, the objectives of this new framework are the following: provide a new approach to the notion of context, by focusing on the visitor and provide an integrated definition of the notion of context within the framework of human mobility. Another important goal is to make this framework independent from external sensors and thus, gather contextual information from the Web. This information together with tourism information will be distributed through digital broadcasting. Lastly, provide an ontology-based context model that filters the information according to the values of context at a given moment of time providing just relevant information to the visitor.

Since research on context-awareness began almost 20 years ago, two different trends can clearly be distinguished. The first trend covers the 1990s decade. The work carried out during those years basically focused on defining the theoretical and conceptual foundations of context-awareness. Researchers developed a number of applications that managed context information primarily to assist users in their interaction with electronic devices. The theoretical work carried out was so intense that the most relevant definitions of 'context' were put forward throughout those years (Want et al., 1992; Schilit et al., 1994; Dey, 2000). However, this first generation of researchers did not reach consensus on delimiting the scope of context-awareness and neither did they agree upon a unique methodology or model to manage context information. Besides, none of the context-aware systems initially put forward suggested the use of semantic technologies to manage contextual information. At that time (1990s), the potential and functionalities of ontologies (Gruber, 1994) were still not clearly specified and therefore researchers did not even consider them an alternative for context information management and thus, they used different context management methodologies (Strang and Linnhoff-Popien, 2004). At the end of the 90s and early years of the new century, the work carried out by the Artificial Intelligence (AI) community since the early 70s on Knowledge Representation (Newell, 1980) showed evidence that formal ontologies could be used as a way to specify content-specific agreements for sharing and re-using knowledge among software entities (Gruber, 1994). Nowadays ontologies are considered (within computer science) a commodity that can be used for the development of large number of applications in different fields such as knowledge management, eCommerce, intelligent integration of information and information retrieval (Corcho et al., 2007).

The second trend, which started back in 2000, was characterized by the use of semantic technologies to approach context. In these last 9 years, ontologies have extensively been used in Pervasive Computing environments as a tool for realising context-aware systems (Chen et al., 2003; Strang and Linnhoff-Popien, 2004; Gu et al. 2004). Researchers within this trend have been more concerned in finding alternatives to more efficiently manage contextual information rather than working on its conceptualization, aiming at establishing a standard context management method. In fact, authors within this decade have provided no new definitions of context and have mostly used the one put forward by Dey (Dey, 2000). An exhaustive analysis of context management methods (Strang and Linnhoff-Popien, 2004) indicates that ontologies are the most adequate tool for context information management. Thus, several authors working on context-awareness converged upon a fact: context information and context models could well be handled using semantic technologies. This would set the way for systems to more easily share and re-use context and moreover, it would support to not only check the model's consistency, but also to infer implicit context knowledge by the reasoning capabilities of ontologies. Several examples of such context ontologies covering different aspects of context can be found in the literature (Chen et al., 2003; Gu et al., 2004; Chen et al., 2005; Strimpakou et al., 2006; Preuveneers et al., 2006). However, none of these ontologies fully copes with the requirements of the tourism domain, since assisting humans on the move was not within the specific objectives of the projects in which they were developed. Moreover, these ontologies did not implement tourism specific established vocabulary (UNWTO, 2008). A deep review of mobile tourist guides (Grün et al., 2008) shows that most of the mobile tourist services either provide location-based information or concentrate on delivering personalized information. One of the major drawbacks of all these systems is the amount of (active) interaction they require from the user point of view. There are just some few examples of a combination of both (Höpken et al., 2006; Beer et al., 2007; Höpken et al., 2008). Interestingly, the CAIPS system (Beer et al., 2007) provides rule-based push information, however, it fails to provide a general framework to support mobility, since it is more focused on creation of rules for information delivery.

None of the aforementioned context-aware systems (tourism guides or any other kind) use digital broadcasting technology. This technology is however extensively used for traffic information applications, such as Traffic Message Channel (TMC), or applications proposed by the Transport Protocol Experts Group (TPEG) (http://www.tisa.org). One of the main characteristics of this connectivity technology is its "push" nature, which makes it particularly interesting for the tourism domain (Beer et al., 2006) relieving the visitor from having to actively search and browse for information (Gretzel & Wöber, 2004).

2 Research Work: Contextual-Computing in Tourism

The CONCERT framework has three main characteristics: Firstly, within the framework of human mobility the objective is to study the context of visitors as such in order to more precisely determine the information that formally describes that context. Context is a main entity, not an auxiliary variable for studying something else. Under these circumstances the difficulty lies in determining what information is necessary to define a visitor's context, what the minimum amount of information is needed, where it (the information) is and how it can be obtained. In addition, the information has to be translated into a consistent computing model so that it can effectively assist visitors in their mobility, enhance and improve their tourism experience. Secondly, populating cities, regions or open areas in general with networks of sensors would not be affordable. In order to tackle this barrier, the CONCERT framework gathers (contextual and tourism) information from the Internet as well as from mobile embedded sensors and does not require further complex infrastructures. This way the use of the CONCERT framework is not limited to certain sensor-populated areas. Thirdly, a network of ontologies shall be used in order to model the visitor. This network of ontologies considers visitor related information in terms of motivation, preferences-demographics and role according to standard parameters established by the tourism scientific community (UNWTO, 2008). A rule-based information engine built on top of the ontology will filter the incoming tourism information and will select the one that best matches with visitors' context.

2.1 Definitions

Considering the previous approach, some definitions are provided in order to establish the framework of context-based applications in tourism.

Definition of Context in the tourism domain. A new definition of Context is needed to suit the requirements of visitors (UNWTO, 2008) and to delimit the scope of the CONCERT framework. The intention is to adapt and integrate already existing definitions and make them more operative for the tourism domain application. Thus, based upon Dey's definition (Dey, 2000) the following new definition is put forward: *"Context is any relevant information that characterizes the situation of a visitor. A visitor is a traveller taking a trip outside his/her usual environment and her situation is specified by data concerning a) the individual itself, b) the individual's environment (and surroundings) and c) the individual's objective at a particular moment of time. This information can be of use for a computing-application in order to support the visitor's mobility"* (Lamsfus et al., 2009a).

Three different categories of information can be found in the definition of Context put forward earlier:

- Information about the visitor such as the role, preferences-demographics, motivation, context history, device, etc.;
- Information about the environment: location, network, environmental conditions, tourism services offered in that environment;
- Information about the objective of the visitor at a certain moment, i.e. data about the immediate Context.

Contextual computing in Tourism. Most of the literature in Computer Science utilizes the term context-awareness to allude to systems that make use of information that originates within the context in which they run. These applications have been programmed to automatically react (in various ways) to changes that occur in their environment without explicit human intervention. However, this way of operating does not make these systems either fully aware of their context or intelligent, as awareness is an eminently human capacity. On the contrary, these (context-aware) systems have been enabled to detect, gather, manage and process contextual information under certain system governing parameters or rules. They just process information. This is the reason why this paper refers to contextual (information originated in the context) computing (processed through information systems) rather than to context-awareness. Since the domain application is tourism, therefore the paper refers to contextual-computing in tourism. Accordingly, *"Contextual computing in Tourism is the scientific approach that studies and observes the context of an individual on the move and pursues to generate knowledge out of that observation in terms of how to model and manage the information originated in that context. It also explores how that information can be processed in a way that is useful to assist the visitor through an application. Furthermore, it provides the foundational means to study the way visitors will interact in future complex (digital) environments".*

2.2 Context ontology: ContOlogy

One of the core elements of the CONCERT framework is the context ontology called ContOlogy (Lamsfus et al., 2009b). It represents the translation of the conceptual notion of context presented above into a computing model through an ontology language capable of providing relevant information through rule-based reasoning. Despite the fact that there are already various context modelling ontologies (Chen et al., 2005; Gu et al., 2004; Wang et al., 2004; Preuveneers et al., 2005; Strimpakou et al, 2005), they are still in an early experimental phase. As is the case with most of the work on context-awareness up to now, those ontologies have been developed for different specific uses and cover different domains, but they are hardly extensible. Thus, a new ontology structure needs to be found. A possible approach to overcome this obstacle is to use networks of ontologies (Haase et al., 2006). A network of ontologies is a collection of ontologies that are related by properties. Therefore, this approach is different from others in that it does not have a double ontology conception of context consisting of a core ontology and other domain ontologies that align to the core ontology. Rather, it focuses on the different constituents of context and develops an ontology for each of them. Networks of ontologies enhance ontologies' modularity and flexibility and hence make their interoperability and re-use much simpler and less dependent on the specific purpose of the ontology.

In order to proceed with the development of the ContOlogy context network of ontologies, a number of methodologies for building ontologies have been reviewed (Gruber 1994; Grüninger et al. 1995; Uschold et al. 1996; Noy et al. 2001; Gómez-Pérez et al. 2003). However, these methodologies lack guidelines for both building networks of ontologies and re-using already existing ontological resources. Due to these two reasons, the NeOn methodology for building networks of ontologies (Suárez-Figueroa et al., 2008) shall be used. Since the ontology building process is iterative, following the NeOn methodology guidelines the ContOlogy network of ontologies shall be implemented in three consecutive iterations. Each of them will provide a working prototype of the network of ontologies suitable for model validation purposes. At the moment of writing this paper the first iteration of the ontology network has been completed. The components of the network of ontologies, i.e. context constituents, have been determined considering the definition of the notion of context put forward earlier in the paper and its architecture (presented in the following Section). Based upon the objective pursued by the framework, the relationship among them will be determined.

Table 1. Results of the first iteration of the ContOlogy building process

Ontology	Definition
Visitor (UNWTO, 2008)	Characteristics of the human being in mobility
Preferences (UNWTO, 2008)	Information that describes the visitor's personal characteristics, demographics, etc.
Role (UNWTO, 2008)	The role a visitor plays in a given moment.
Activity (Strimpakou et al., 2005)	What the visitor is doing at a given moment. This information can be taken from the mobile device's agenda. (COMANTO)
Environment (Preuveneers et al., 2005)	Represents the surroundings of the visitor (CoDaMoS) as well as the weather conditions at the location of the visitor.
Device (W3C, 2004a)	Physical object the visitor carries with him.
Network (Cadenas et al., 2009)	Infrastructure to connect devices and convey information
Motivation (UNWTO, 2008)	Represents the reason why the visitor is travelling.
Location (Preuveneers et al., 2005)	Coordinates that define where a visitor is at a given time.
Time (W3C, 2006)	Physical dimension that measures spam between facts.
Tourism Services	Represents the services provided in a certain environment.

The network of ontologies integrates at the moment 11 ontologies. All together there are 86 classes, 41 object properties, 22 datatype properties and 43 restrictions. The following table shows the ontologies that configure the network. The language used to specify each of the ontologies has been OWL (W3C, 2004b) in its DL sublanguage. The level of expressivity shown by the network of ontology is SHOIN(D). This first version of the ContOlogy network represents core context elements in the CONCERT framework. Its structure will not change, but the individuals (instances of the ontologies) expressing the values of context at a given moment of time will be changing. As argued in the literature, the insufficient involvement of final users (visitors in this case) during the ontology development phase is one of the most significant causes for the current shortage of and the unsatisfying coverage found in domain ontologies (van Damme et al., 2007). Thus, the results of the user evaluation of this first iteration of the context network of ontologies will be used together with other information sources (e.g. empirical data, brainstorming sessions, etc.) in future iterations.

2.3 System architecture

Building contextual computing systems implies a number of challenges and therefore an adequate architecture plays a major role. Contextual computing systems need to efficiently gather, model, store, manage and process contextual information to fulfil the requirements of visitors. Thus, the various components of the system as well as interactions among them need to be clearly defined. This justifies the need for an architectural support in order to provide the Semantic-based Contextual-Computing framework with an efficient infrastructure. The validation of the context approach and semantic model built upon it could be carried out by use of any of the traditional connectivity technologies. However, the price of data-transfer on mobile devices is relatively high, especially under roaming conditions. For this reason, the system proposed in the paper experiments using digital broadcasting (push) technology. Figure 1 shows the overview of a typical broadcasting service architecture. The server side gathers information from heterogeneous distributed sources. This information contains data about tourism sightseeing offers as well as other context information, such as weather information, etc. These sources can be simple (unstructured) Web sites, structured databases, XML (W3C, 2009) files, etc. The information is then structured in a specified XML format file and uploaded to the Content Server (IIS, 2008). The structure of the XML file has to be compliant with the defined Journaline schema (ETSI, 2008), so that it can be first formatted into the JML (Journaline Markup Language) (ETSI, 2008) and then broadcasted via MDI (Multimedia Distribution Interface) (ETSI, 2008). This has to be done in this way, since broadcasting bandwidth is often limited by the configuration of the Content Server's carousel. The Journaline module located on the client receives the information that is being continuously broadcasted by the Content Server. It implements two functionalities: first, it decompresses the information that has been received in JML format back to XML in the decoder module. Then, the resulting XML file is further transformed into HTML information and it is ready to be browsed in a typical Web navigator located in the visitors' mobile device. This way, the information displayed in browser would be all of the information that has been previously broadcasted by the Content Server, so to say, all the raw-information without any further processing. So, it would provide visitors with all kinds of information (relevant and non-relevant) and they would have to actively browse the application to find relevant information.

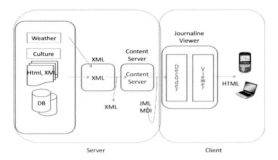

Fig. 1. A general architecture for broadcasting services

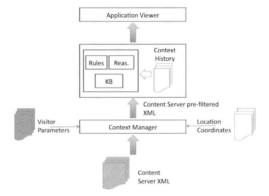

Fig. 2. Contextual-Computing layer

Figure 2 presents the Contextual-Computing layer which sits on top of the previous architecture on the client side. This layer acts as a filter over the decompressed XML file received by the Journaline module and through semantic processing automatically provides visitors with context dependent information. The components of the Contextual-Computing module are (some have been omitted for clarity):

- Context Manager: this is the central component of the Contextual-Computing layer. The software module is a background process that runs on mobile devices (client). The Context Manager receives information from the Context Providers (information input), such as the location sensor embedded in the mobile device, the wireless broadcast source and the repository of user preferences. The Context Manager pre-processes all of the gathered information and consequently feeds the Knowledge Base with that information triggering the flow of events, which are necessary to provide visitors with the most relevant information for their needs.
- Context Providers: context providers are software adapter modules, which specialise in a specific type of context information and manage the capture,

treatment and final insertion of that information into the contextual computing system. So far, three context information providers have been devised and implemented. One of them interfaces with the location hardware present in the mobile device and feeds the system with visitor location information. Another context provider is in charge of maintaining an up-to-date list of user preferences that visitors are expected to provide to the system via the mobile device. Finally, a third context Provider handles the reception of Journaline XML information provided by means of digital broadcasting. context providers gather this information and feed the context manager for its pre-processing and aggregation in the knowledge base of the contextual computing system.

- Knowledge base: comprises the network of ontologies and instance data, which models visitors' context. Initially, the knowledge base is populated with static information regarding the environment and the services offered in that environment. Gradually, as the dynamic flow of context information reaches the context manager, it is sent to the knowledge base after pre-processing. There are three other components that handle and interact with the knowledge base, namely, an inference and a rule engine and the context history repository. As dynamic context information reaches the network of ontologies, the reasoning engine filters tourism information based upon the rules that govern its behaviour and uses the specific values of context constituents at that moment in order the filtering to match the user's requirements at a given time.

- Context history: the context history contains data about past values of context. This information can be of use to predict future situations as well as supporting and enhancing the filtering process.

- Application Module: the application layer consists of the presentation logic that interfaces between the contextual computing system and the user. The application features an embedded web browser where the result of the filtering (an output HTML file containing only context-based information) is displayed (Figure 3).

3 Use Case Validation

A use case validation has been developed to evaluate the CONCERT framework. Three main tools have been used in the development phase. The ContOlogy network of ontologies has been developed using the Protégé open source ontology editor (http://protege.stanford.edu/). The context manager and the ontology manager have been developed in Java. The Jena API (http://jena.sourceforge.net/) has been used in order to handle the ontology, manage the instances of the ontology (which give the value of context –situation- at a given moment of time) and to write the rules that filter the information by the values of context. Finally, a Content Server (IIS, 2008) has been used in order to simulate digital broadcasting DRM standards. The use case considers a visitor is located in the city of San Sebastian, on the seashore. For simplicity, let us suppose the individual is a visitor whose role is "HolidayLeisureVisitor", i.e., that individual is visiting San Sebastian for holidays. The visitor is looking for a beach where to stay for a while and turns on his/her mobile device. The application's Context Manager requests the visitor's coordinates to the mobile device. The coordinates have been gathered from GPS or A-GPS like sensors in the device. The Context Manager then queries the location and determines that the visitor is located close to La Concha beach, in the city of San Sebastián. Through a digital broadcasting receiver plugged or embedded in a mobile device, the context manager receives tourism information about San Sebastián and other areas of interest. However, given that the context manager already knows the location of the visitor, it filters information related to San Sebastián, more precisely to La Concha beach area. This information, together with the visitor's location and personal preferences, role, motivation and some user input feeds the ContOlogy network of ontologies. The resulting information is processed through rule-based reasoning and is able to obtain relevant information for visitors. For example, considering weather conditions, time of the day and knowing that the visitor is a vegetarian, the context manager displays information about vegetarian restaurants at the location's environment. The following picture shows a screen shot of the application.

Fig. 3. Snapshot of the Semantic-based Contextual-Computing application

4   Conclusions

eTourism represents nowadays an active field of research within Computer Science. This paper presents the CONCERT framework and discusses a new approach to the notion of context and context-awareness within human mobility. Although the stress is put in creating a new vision of context in the framework of human mobility and a particular example is provided to deliver tourism services through digital broadcasting, most general aspects of this paper aim to provide new discussion issues within the Ubiquitous Computing and Semantic Technologies communities. A thorough review of the relevant literature shows that (i) neither does consensus exist on a definition for the notion of context nor do existing ones suit the requirements to support Human mobility, (ii) a sufficiently agreed model for context and methods for contextual information management do not exist, (iii) the existing works reveal the need of a scientific approach to study context as a scientific discipline on its own right and (iv) the use of sensors to gather contextual information poses serious limitations and pre-requisites for making Contextual-Computing systems universally utilized. The specific contributions of this piece of research tackle these problems from three different perspectives. Firstly, a new definition of context aiming at integrating and making the notion of context more operative is provided. This adapted definition of context is human-centred and contextualizes the visitor and the visitor's location. It observes the nature of human mobility and opens new chances to study complex scenarios in highly digitalized and hybrid spaces. Secondly, this approach does not use networks of sensors to capture contextual information in addition to the ones that are already embedded in mobile devices. It is argued that a visitor may be contextualized according to certain existing (well established) criteria (UNWTO, 2008) and Web based distributed and heterogeneous information sources, instead of contextualizing a system or a particular environment. As a consequence, the amount of imposed preconditions with regard to existing research approaches is greatly reduced, since the use of the CONCERT framework is not restricted to the existence of networks of sensors. This is one step forward to making contextual computing applications available to everyday users. Thirdly, by using networks of ontologies to model context, a framework for interoperability for other kinds of systems is provided, since ontologies have shown to be an appropriate tool for data exchange and integration. Besides, ontologies provide reasoning capabilities, which are particularly interesting for data inference, consistency checking and detection of data duplicity. The rule-based reasoning engine built on top of the network of ontologies allows filtering tourism information received by the values of the context constituents at a given moment of time (situation) and avoids the visitor having to actively search on the Web for the appropriate piece of information.

The model presents however a number of limitations. As most contextual information is gathered from Web repositories, the application has to rely on the fact that data is accurate and that it is being continuously updated. Furthermore, the data obtained this way presents some limitations since there is some information that cannot be obtained, like noise or lighting level, for example. Having stated that, early surveys reveal that this information is not strictly relevant for a tourism application. Several experiments in other sectors indicate that digital broadcasting is an adequate technology to provide push-based information. However, this technology is in its early stages and presents some issues to tackle. Firstly, the amount of information that can be broadcasted is not high. Nonetheless, by means of the information filtering process and reasoning capability of ontologies this is not an obstacle to provide context-based information. Secondly, typical mobile phones are not yet equipped with digital broadcast receivers, and therefore, these experiments haven been carried out in a conventional laptop. Lastly, digital broadcasting does not provide an uplink communication channel. How this framework can work with other connectivity technologies at the same time is also an open issue. More research is necessary as well on middleware technologies and platforms to find out to what extent they can support contextual computing applications efficiently, for example, using Wi-Fi, RFID or Bluetooth as uplink channel and processing part of the reasoning in a remote server. Also, considering that the main contextual information source is the Internet, it is essential to understand how the Future Internet will impact on the CONCERT framework. Real visitors shall be involved in an experimental phase of the ontology development. This will allow finding out more about intentions and motivations of visitors en route in order to include them into the network of ontologies. This is something that has not yet been considered in other context ontologies and as it has previously been stated, the participation of real users may improve the usefulness of the final (network of) ontologies.

References

Beer, T., Fuchs, M., Höpken, W., Rasinger, J., & Werthner, H., (2007). CAIPS: A Context-Aware Information push Service in Tourism. In Sigala, M., Mich, L. and Murphy, J. (eds) Information and Communication in Tourism, pp. 129 – 140.

Bernardos, A. B., (2007). Servicios y aplicaciones en movilidad para el sector turístico. CITIC 2007.

Buhalis, D., & Pistidda, L., (2008). The impact of WiMAX on Tourist Destinations. In Proceedings of the ENTER 2008 Conference. Innsbruck, Austria, pp. 383 – 394.

Chen, G. & Kotz, K., (2001). A Survey on Context-Aware Mobile Computing Research. Dartmonth College.

Chen, H., Finin, T., & Joshi, A., (2003). An ontology for Context-Aware Pervasive Computing Environments.

Chen, H., Finin, T. & Josh, A. (2005). The SOUPA Ontology for Pervasive Computing. In Ontologies for Agents: Theory and Experiences, pp. 233-258.

Corcho, O., Fernández-López, M., & Gómez-Pérez, A., (2007). Ontological Engineering: What are ontologies and how can we build them? Chapter III, pp. 44 – 70.

van Damme, C., Hepp, M. & Siorpaes, K., (2007). FolksOntology: An Integrated Approach for Turning Folksonomies into Ontologies. In Proceedings of the ESWC Workshop "Bridging the gap between Semantic Web and Web 2.0".

Dey, A. K., (2000). Providing Architectural Support for Building Context-Aware Applications. Georgia Institute of Technology, Ph.D. Thesis.

Dey, A.K., & Abowd, G.D., (2001). Towards a better understanding of context and context awareness. Proceedings of the workshop on the What, Who, Where, When and how of Context Awareness, ACM Press, New York. 2000.

ETSI – European Telecommunications Standards Institute (2008). Digital Radio Broadcasting, Journaline.

Gómez-Pérez, A., Fernández-López, M., & Corcho, O., (2003). Ontological Engineering. ISBN 1-85233-551-3. *Springer Verlag*.

Gretzel, U. & Wöber, K., (2004). Intelligent Search Support: Building Search Term Associations for Tourism specific Search Engines. In Frew (Ed.), Information and Communication Technologies in Tourism, pp. 239 – 248.

Gruber, T. R., (1994). Toward Principles for the Design of Ontologies Used for Knowledge Sharing. In Formal Ontology in Conceptual Analysis and Knowledge Representation. Kluwer Academic Publishers. 1994

Grün, C., Pöll, B., Werthner, H., Retschitzegger, W., & Schwinger, W., (2008). Assisting Tourists on the Move: An evaluation of Mobile Tourist Guides. 7th International Conference on Mobile Business, pp. 171 – 180.

Grüninger, M., & Fox, M., (1995). Methodology for the Design and Evaluation of ontologies.

Gu, T., Pung, H. K., & Zhang, D. Q., (2004). A service oriented middleware for building context-aware services. Journal of Network and Computer Applications, pp. 1 – 18.

Haase, P., Rudolph, S., Wang, Y., Brockmans, S., Palma, R., Euzenat, J. & d'Aquin, M., (2006). NeOn Deliverable D1.1.1 Networked Ontology Model.

Höpken, W., Fuchs, M., Zanker, M., Beer, T., Eybl, A., Flores, S., Gordea, S., Jessenitschning, M., Kerner, T., Linke, D., Rasinger, J. & Schnabl, M., (2006). etPlanner: An IT Framework for Comprehensive and Integrative Travel Guidance. In Hitz, Sigala and Murphy (Eds.) Information and Communication Technologies in Tourism, pp. 125 – 134.

Höpken, W., Scheuringer, M., Linke, D. & Fuchs, M., (2008). Context-based Adaptation of Ubiquitous Web Applications. In Tourism Information and Communication Technologies in Tourism, pp. 533 – 544.

Fraunhofer Institut für Integrierte Schaltungen, (2008). DRM User Manual. Content Server.

Lamsfus, C., Alzua-Sorzabal, A., Martín, D., Salvador, Z., & Usandizaga, A., (2009a). Contextual computing based Services in Tourism. Mediterranean Conference on Information Systems. Athens, Greece. September 24-27.

Lamsfus, C., Alzua-Sorzabal, A., Martín, D., Salvador, Z., & Usandizaga, A., (2009b). Human-Centric Semantic-based Context Modelling in Tourism. International Conference on Knowledge Engineering and Ontology Development, KEOD. Madeira, October 5-8 2009b.

Lamsfus, C., & Alzua-Sorzabala, A., (2009c) Computación Contextual basada en Tecnologías Semánticas en el Marco de la Movilidad Humana. CIC Network Magazine, pp. 50 - 54.

Newell, A., (1980). The Knowledge Level. AI Magazine.

Noy, N., F., & McGuinness, D. L., (2001). Ontology Deveopment 101: A guide to creating your first ontology. *Stanford University*.

Preuveneers, D., Van den Bergh, J., Wagelaar, D., Georges, A., Rigole, P., Clerckx, T., Berbers, Y., Connix, K., Jonckers, V. & de Bosschere, K., (2004). Towards an Extensible Context Ontology for Ambient Intelligence.

Schilit, B. N.; Adams, N. W. R., & Roy, W., (1994). Context-Aware Computing Applications.

SITA, (2009). Ten technology advances that will change air Travel.

Strang, T., & Linnhoff-Popien, C., (2004). A Context-Modelling survey. First International Workshop on Advanced Context Modelling, Reasoning and Management. UbiComp.

Strimpakou, M. A., Roussaki, I. G. & Anagnostou, M. (2006). Context Ontology for Pervasive Service Provision*Proceedings of the 20th International Conference on Advanced Information Networking and Applications.*

Suárez-Figueroa, M. C., Aguado de Cea, G., Buil, C., Dellschaft, K., Fernández-López, M., García, A., Gómez-Pérez, A., Herrero, G., Montiel-Ponsoda, E., Sabou, M., Villazón-Terrazas, B. & Yufei, Z., (2008). NeOn D5.4.1: NeOn Methodology for Building Contextualized Ontology Networks. NeOn project.

Uschold, M., & Grüninger, M., (1996). Ontologies: Principles, Methods and Applications. *Knowledge Engineering Review, vol. 11*, pp. 93 – 155.

Vázquez, I., (2007). A behavioural model for Context-Aware Semantic Devices. Ph.D Dissertation. Universidad de Deusto.

Want, R., Hpper, A., Falcao, V., & Gibbons, J., (1992). The Active Badge Location System. ACM Transactions on Information Systems, pp. 91 – 102

Want, R., (2009). When Cell Phones Become Computers. Pervasive Computing. In IEEE CS, pp. 2 – 5.

Weiser, M., (1991). The Computer of the 21st Century. SIGMOBILE, Mobile Computing and Communications Review, 3(3):3-11.

United Nations World Tourism Organization, (2008). International Recommendations for Tourism Statistics. ST/ESA/STAT/SER.M/83/Rev.1

W3C, World Wide Web Consortium, (2004a). Composite/Capability/Preference Profiles (CC/PP): Structures and Vocabularies 1.0. W3C Recommendation 15 January 2004 http://www.w3.org/TR/CCPP-struct-vocab/

W3C, World Wide Web Consortium (2004b), OWL Web Ontology Language Guide. W3C Recommendation, 10th February 2004. http://www.w3c.org/TR/

W3C, World Wide Web Consortium, (2004c), SWRL: A Semantic Web Rule Language Combining OWL and RuleML. W3C Member Submission 21st May 2004. http://www.w3c.org/Submission/SWRL.

W3C, World Wide Web Consortium, (2008). Delievery Context ontology. W3C Working Draft 15 April 2008. http://www.w3.org/TR/dcontology/

W3C, World Wide Web Consortium, (2006). Time Ontology in OWL. W3C Working Draft 27th September 2006, http://www.w3c.org/TR/owl-time.

W3C, World Wide Web Consortium (2009). Main page for World Wide Web Consortium XML activity and information. http://www.w3c.org/XML

Dynamic Packaging Semantic Platform for Tourism Intermediaries

Sonia Bilbao,
Adelaida Lejarazu, and
Jesús Herrero

INFOTECH
Robotiker-Tecnalia, Spain
{sbilbao; alejarazu; jesus}@robotiker.es

Abstract

Dynamic packaging is one of the most important technological trends in tourism. Intermediaries need e-Business solutions to offer the growing demand of personalised products and services. This paper describes a semantic e-Business platform for tourism package intermediaries that allows: adaptation and customisation of tourism products and services to the desires and restrictions of the tourist at any time; negotiation and coordination among different business partners; a digital collaboration environment of entities to carry out the business processes of the tourism intermediary; enough flexibility to adapt to future market demands and trends; enough flexibility to adapt to future tourist's needs, business opportunities and restrictions.

Keywords: Dynamic packaging; e-Business, Tourism information systems; Semantics.

1 Introduction

Traditionally, tourism intermediaries (travel agents, tour operators, etc.) were the main link between tourism suppliers and potential customers. However, ICT and e-Business adoption have had a deep impact on intermediaries. Internet offers a wide choice of tourism suppliers so customers now have the means to access them directly and obtain lower prices. Hence, intermediaries need to reinvent themselves and to offer added value services to the customer (Longhi, 2005; Fitzgerald, 2005; Buhalis, 2002, 2003, 2008).

According to (e-W@tch, 2006), "considering ICT adoption and size of companies, the most outstanding result is that small tourism companies are more active users of e-Business compared to their counter-parts from other industries".

Additionally, current individualisation trends are reaching the tourism market. Customers no longer want traditional packages provided by tour operators or travel agencies with limited flexibility. They request their own package customised to their wishes, restrictions and personal profiles. Therefore, intermediaries' business model must change and offer flexible and dynamic packaging (Cardoso et al, 2007; Solutions, 2005).

(e-W@tch, 2006) mentions that "traditional packages offered by tour operators and travel agencies tend to be effective in bundling separate products, but only with limited flexibility. However, the increasing trend towards individualisation of tourism demand requires more flexible, dynamic packages".

The latest semantic technologies are crucial in the development of this kind of ICT solutions due to the heterogeneity of tourism products and services; the lack of standards to define customers' wishes and profiles; the need to correctly interpret messages; and the definition of the common entities, concepts and relationships between all the business actors that participate in a tourism scenario (Cardoso, 2006).

This paper presents an e-Business semantic platform for dynamic packaging. The solution tries to offer new personalised products and services through the integration of the information in the back-end systems, with the information offered by third-parties that is available through Web services and with the e-Business processes of tourism suppliers.

2 Background

All studies reveal that tourism is a growing sector, at least in the most industrialized countries. According to the World Tourism Organization, tourism is, in fact, the fastest growing industry in the world.

In line with these predictions the World Travel & Tourism Council suggests that the demand for travel and tourism will continue growing at an annual rate of 4.3% over the next 10 years.

Current initiatives for tourism promotion and development are aware that tourism activity should be focused on the tourist. Therefore any conception of the future tourism must consider the adaptation and customisation of tourism products and services to the desires and restrictions of the tourist at any time.

Due to these trends, participation and coordination among different agents becomes increasingly important for the configuration and provision of the packages demanded by the tourist. These packages result from a (dynamic and customised) combination of simple tourism products and services provided by each agent.

According to ISTAG (IST Advisory Group, 2008), "one of the emerging visions for the Internet is the vision for the Internet of Services. To realize this vision, an open platform for tradable, composable, value-added services on the Internet is required. Such a platform will need to build upon and extend: Web 2.0 concepts to allow for community-driven service innovation and engineering on a large scale; global repositories for value-added services; and, semantic support to enable automatic composition of value-added services".

2.1 E-Business

In relation to e-Business there are two major trends:

- **Traditional B2B relationships,** which corresponds to the life cycle of commercial transactions between two entities, buyer and seller, and their integration in the internal processes of each entity.
- **Collaboration among network enterprises,** which corresponds to an environment of "n" collaborating entities, mainly digitally, through telecommunication networks over which they become visible and develop the processes of the company, even those that have traditionally been carried out internally.

This second mode of collaboration is the basis of the dynamic composition of complex tourism products and services and takes into account the following issues:

- Identify tourist's needs, business opportunities, restrictions bearing in mind the context
- Discover, analyse and evaluate composition possibilities
- Identify, evaluate and select potential business partners
- Dynamic negotiation at individual product (B2B) and complex product (B2C) levels
- Commercial transactions
- Simple product/service provision to generate complex product/service
- After-sales services

In addition, the platform described in this paper should be useful for the future e-Business scenarios of Tourism Package Intermediaries. Hence, it must be flexible and seamlessly adaptable to the future trends that will influence the sector:

- New tourism segments and profiles
- New relevant e-Business partners
- Economic, social, political and technological conditions where tourism activity will be performed
- New value chains of the tourism product/service
- Future tourism e-Business processes

2.2 Semantic composition of services

In order to offer a dynamic and customised package it is necessary to compose products and services offered by different tourism partners: accommodation services, information services, rental services, air travel products, etc. (Herrero et al, 2009)

Web Services standards did not allow to specify the semantic meaning of the data. Hence, specific agreements had to be reached between the provider and the consumer of the Web service which made automatic Web service composition very difficult.

Semantic Web Services technologies (OWL-S, WSMO and SAWSDL) came into place to provide a layer of semantic meaning that would facilitate discovery, selection and composition of services that match the customers' wishes or goals (Lara et al, 2004;Kopecký, 2007)

WSMO's conceptual model is based on 4 top level elements that are: ontologies that provide the terminology; goals that describe aspects related to user desires with respect to the requested functionality; Web services that represent computational entities able to provide access to services that, in turn, provide some value in a domain; and mediators that handle interoperability problems between different WSMO elements. (Domingue et al, 2005)

OWL-S has 4 main elements to describe a service: the process model that describes how a service performs its tasks; the profile that provides a general description of a Web Service intended to be published and shared to facilitate service discovery; the grounding that specifies how a service is invoked; and the service that binds the other parts together into a unit that can be published and invoked.(Elenius et al, 2004)

SAWSDL (Semantic Annotations for WSDL) is agnostic to semantic representation languages and it enables semantic annotations for Web services not only for discovering Web services but also for invoking them. SAWSDL defines three new extensibility attributes to WSDL 2.0 elements to enable semantic annotation of WSDL components: "modelReference" to specify the association between a WSDL component and a concept in some semantic model; "liftingSchemaMapping" and "loweringSchemaMapping" for specifying mappings between semantic data and XML. (http://www.w3.org/2002/ws/sawsdl/) (Akkiraju, 2007)

The platform described in this paper uses SAWSDL to describe the tourism package.

2.3 Collaborative environments

There are different initiatives in the field of digital collaborative environments or ecosystems that try to define and formalise the actors and business processes of the tourism sector. These initiatives fall into two categories: strategic and technological.

Technological strategies define the current actors that participate in the digital collaborative environment and suggest technological solutions to facilitate interoperability between them. To do so, they define, on the one hand, common semantic data models that allow information exchange in a standardised way and, on the other hand, a service-based model and solutions to compose services in the new business scenarios. Models tend to be generic so they can be applied in any region.

In these strategies, tourist characterization is based only on preferences on the actors' characteristics such as type of hotel, facilities available, type of food in restaurants, etc. not taking into account other factors such as preferences on the activities performed by tourists during their stay.

Among these initiatives we can point out:

- Harmonise, HARMO-TEN and HarmoNET projects (Jentzsch, 2005) that worked on harmonization of data interchange in tourism.
- SATINE project (http://www.srdc.metu.edu.tr/webpage/projects/satine/) realized a secure semantic-based interoperability framework for exploiting Web service platforms in conjunction with Peer-to-Peer networks in tourism industry.
- DERI's e-Tourism initiative is working on an advanced e-Tourism Semantic Web portal which will connect the customers and virtual travel agents from anywhere at anytime with any needs and requests.
- The standardisation efforts in tourism, for instance by the Open Travel Alliance (OTA) or the IFITT Reference Model Special Interest Group (RMSIG).

Strategic initiatives often refer to specific regions and are more focused on making the most of the region's tourism resources. These initiatives take into account a wider range of actors and resources such as natural resources like beaches and mountains, cultural resources, entertainment, and so on. Among the actors considered, we can mention providers of tourism information, museums or exhibitions.

The work described in this paper considers both technological and strategic factors with the aim of offering the most appropriate tourism product or service package as well as a customised offer that includes activities and information not covered in current packages.

3 Methodology

The objective was to design a semantic e-Business platform for tourism package intermediaries that would allow:

- adaptation and customisation of tourism products and services to the desires and restrictions of the tourist at any time;
- negotiation and coordination among different business partners;
- a digital collaboration environment of "n" entities to carry out the business processes of the tourism intermediary;
- enough flexibility to adapt to future market demands and trends; and
- enough flexibility to adapt to future tourist's needs, business opportunities and restrictions.

The steps followed to achieve the objective were: identify different tourist profiles and contexts; identify new business partners; define possible future business processes of tourism intermediaries and their requirements; design the e-Business platform and identify technologies.

Different social groups were identified according to the tourism activities they carry out. Among them we can point out: retired people (due to time and economic restrictions), elderly and disabled people (due to their additional care needs), youth

622

(due to their economic and activity types restrictions), families (especially with children) or on business tourists.

In addition, strategic factors were included in the definition of the data models for profiles and contexts: type of tourism activity (adventure, nature, cultural, historical, sports); combination of time and economic resources (weekend, on business).

The purpose was to be able to formalise a wide range of requests, e.g.:

- I would like to spend 15 days in a city and I look for a hotel with certain characteristics regarding price, facilities, and so on.
- I would like to spend 15 days in this region doing trekking in routes of a particular difficulty
- I travel to a country I have never visited before and I would like information about its history, culture, currency and mandatory documentation
- I travel to this city on business and I would like to spend one additional day if an event of this type took place

In order to offer a tourism package that responds to such a wide range of requests, it is necessary to include new business partners and that those involved collaborate in a standardised way. Hence, semantic models are needed.

Next figure shows a high level view of the platform's architecture.

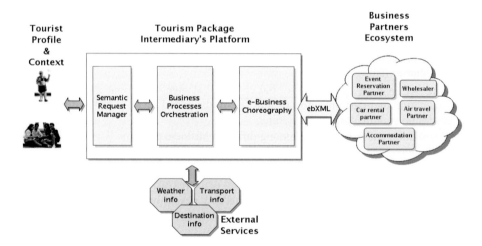

Fig. 1. High level architecture of the e-Business platform

Some of the information that is useful to build this complex tourism package can be obtained by the intermediary using external web services, e.g. documentation required at the destination, trekking routes in a region, history information…

However, other information needs to be negotiated with the business partners in the ecosystem through ebXML messages, e.g. accommodation price and availability.

4 Results

Next figure shows in more detail the modules that are part of the tourism package intermediary's platform.

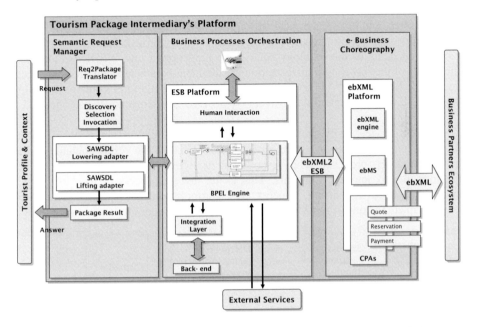

Fig. 2. Low level architecture of the Tourism Package Intermediary's Platform

4.1 Semantic Request Manager

This module deals with the requests of the tourists. The first step is to translate the request as well as the profile and context of the tourist into concepts of the semantic models. These semantic models are useful to share information among the business partners in a common vocabulary; to define a standard classification of the products, services and resources from the tourism domain; to translate the tourist's preferences and wishes into a tourism package; to facilitate the discovery and invocation of the products and services offered by third-parties; for the correct interpretation of messages.

The semantic model proposed allows storing both static and dynamic information about the tourist and the trip.

Information about the tourist includes, among others, age range, social group (youth, retired, elderly, disabled), limitations (disabilities, gluten free food) and preferences (type of events, monuments, resources, cuisine).

Information about the trip covers the duration, reason for the trip (leisure, business), number of travellers (on its own, family, group), budget range and preferred type of activity (enjoy nature, trekking, visit interest point, attend events, do sports).

Once, the request is translated into a package request, the execution environment will discover, select and invoke the most appropriate Web services. If these Web services are semantic a "lowering" transformation needs to be performed. This means that the semantic concepts of the ontology need to be transformed into WSDL parameters. The results of the lowering transformation are the input parameters and the address of the WSDL file of the Web service to be executed. The platform contains a set of predefined lowering adapters for different types of tourism semantic Web services.

These Web services will start the business processes defined in ESB platform (orchestration processes) and once performed will return the result containing the tourism package proposal. The response is a SOAP message that has to be transformed into semantic concepts. This is the inverse process of the "lowering" process and is called "lifting" process. The platform contains a set of predefined lifting adapters to convert the XML data into different types of tourism packages.

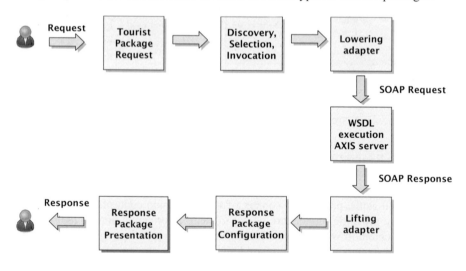

Fig. 3. Lowering and lifting adaptations.

It is important to point out that given the same request by two different tourist profiles or contexts, the package suggested by the platform will be different. This is due to the fact that the platform processes both the information explicitly provided by the tourist about the trip as well as information about the profile or context which is not supplied explicitly. This information determines the criteria that govern the discovery and selection of the products and services.

4.2 E-Business Model

The e-Business Model is based on three pillars:

- Business messages, which are sent between the different business partners in the ecosystem that provide a product or service of the tourism package,
- Internal business processes, which define the tasks to be done internally in a tourism intermediary company when a message is received. Some of these tasks can be calls to back-end systems through the integration layers or calls to external services.
- External services, which provide information without a negotiation process, e.g. documentation required at the destination, trekking routes in a region or history information.

The BPMN (Business Process Modelling Notation) descriptions of the business processes contain the configuration and workflows for:

- the internal orchestration that is supported or runs on a BPEL engine (Juric, 2006). Orchestration covers ESB platform communications and web service calls.
- the external collaboration (choreography) that is described in the ebBP (ebXML Business Process) (Patil, 2003). Choreography takes the node-to-node communication part between business entities.

The ebXML2ESB adapter provides integration functionalities between ebXML and ESB in order to communicate and synchronise the business process orchestration and choreography.

The platform's e-Business components can be grouped by:

- **Security layer**: responsible for access control, customer profiles and provides authentication to the platform. Security can be provided on transport (IP, HTTP) level, message level (SOAP, WS-Security, ebMS) or inside the service itself (passwords, signatures, proprietary payload security).
- **BPEL Engine**: executes the tourism business scenarios defined using the BPEL Standard
- **Human Interaction layer**: allows a person to interact and participate in the workflow in two ways. On the one hand, when participating in decisions points, it allows accepting or rejecting an action. On the other hand, it allows the person to be informed about actions and situations regarding any step of the business process (Balčiūnaitis et al, 2008).
  In general, human interaction is needed when the running business process workflow is too complex and some non-automated decisions (validation of non-computable information and decision-making) are required and when unexpected

problems appear (elapsed time for response without any answer, specific error handling is required etc.).

- **Integration layer**: responsible for the integration with the back-end systems (CRM, ERP, and Document Management System) of the intermediary.

5 Benefits

The approach described in this paper benefits the whole tourism chain: potential customers, tourism suppliers and intermediaries.

Customers avoid having to visit different Web sites to build their trips. Just by registering in one site, they can get a complete offer of products and services that suit their needs and context. Additionally, certain requirements are not covered in traditional web sites or complex searches have to be performed in order to get a result, e.g. looking for a hotel that serves gluten free meals and offers cradles for babies.

Tourism suppliers can increase their market share as their product or service is offered jointly with other tourism products and services, e.g. a hotel can offer horse riding services and leisure activities to attract potential customers.

There are other solutions that allow bundling of tourism services. For instance, the etPackaging project (http://www.ecca.at) supports web-based interactive bundling of tourism services by tourists. In (Zanker, 2007) a personalized approach for bundling of tourism products is proposed. However, the innovation in the solution proposed is about integrating services bundling with business processes orchestration and choreography needed to obtain the services in the tourism package.

Finally, intermediaries have to differentiate from competitors offering added value to customers. This platform provides a technical solution to automate the negotiation process and the flexibility to create dynamic packaging based on customer's preferences. Besides, the connection to external services is designed to add useful information to the tourism package not covered in traditional systems. E.g. tourists could be very interested in obtaining jointly with the trip, information about documentation required at the destination, currency or emergency telephones if travelling to a new country.

6 Conclusions and Future Research

ICT and e-Business processes adoption have forced tourism intermediaries to change their business model. While rigidly packaged tours are in decline, dynamic packaging is one of the most important technological trends in tourism. Intermediaries need e-Business solutions to offer the growing demand of personalised products and services.

Semantics and semantic Web services technologies are crucial in the development of this kind of ICT solutions due to the heterogeneity of tourism products and services;

the lack of standards to define customers' wishes and profiles; the need to correctly interpret messages; and the definition of the common entities, concepts and relationships between all the business actors that participate in a tourism scenario.

The e-Business platform described in this paper assumes that there will be a collaboration and negotiation process between the tourism intermediary and the business partners in the ecosystem in order to offer the customer with a personalised tourism package. For this reason, the technological solution is based on standards and open source components. Still future research needs to be carried out to define standards to communicate and synchronise the business process orchestration and choreography as well as to define human interaction in connection with the workflow engine (BPEL).

In addition, further research is needed regarding security when customer profiles are handled. Serious privacy and data protection as well as legal issues could arise if mistreated.

The approach selected benefits the whole tourism chain, that is, potential customers, tourism suppliers and intermediaries. Customers avoid having to visit different Web sites to build personalised trips. Tourism suppliers can increase their market share as their product or service is offered jointly with other tourism products and services. Intermediaries can offer added value to customers and flexible tourism packages based on customer's preferences and context.

References

Akkiraju, R. & Sapkota, B. (2007). Semantic Annotations for WSDL and XML Schema - Usage Guide, W3C Working Group, http://www.w3.org/TR/sawsdl-guide/.

Balčiūnaitis, G., Čiumanovas, V. & Gricius, R. (2008). Human interaction implementation in workflow of construction & building SMEs. ECPPM 2008, eWork and eBusiness in Architecture, Engineering and Construction, Alain Zarli & Raimar Scherer (eds), CRC Press, 2008, ISBN: 978-0-415-48245-5 (pages 729-734)

Buhalis, D., & Licata, M. C. (2002). The future eTourism intermediaries. Tourism Management, 23(3), 207–220.

Buhalis, D. (2003). eTourism: Information Technology for Strategic Tourism Management, Prentice Hall

Buhalis, D., & Law, R. (2008). Progress in information technology and tourism management: 20 years on and 10 years after the Internet – The state of eTourism research. Tourism Management, 29 (4), 609-623.

Cardoso, J. (2006). Developing Dynamic Packaging Systems using Semantic Web Technologies. Transactions on Information Science and Applications, Vol. 3(4), pp. 729-736, ISSN: 1970-0832.

Cardoso, J. & Lange, C. (2007) A Framework for Assessing Strategies and Technologies for Dynamic Packaging Applications, in: Journal of Information Technology & Tourism, Vol. 9 (1), pp. 27-44.

Domingue, J., Cabral, L., Stollberg, M. & Galizia, S. (2005). WSMO tutorial, DIP and WSMO tools. DIP Training Workshop.
http://stadium.open.ac.uk/stadia/preview.php?s=35&whichevent=542

E-Business W@tch (2006). The European e-Business Market Watch, Sector Reports No. 08/2006, "ICT and e-Business in the Tourism Industry", European Commission, Enterprise & Industry Directorate General.

Elenius, D., Denker, G. , Martin, D., Gilham, F., Khouri, J. , Sadaati, S. & Senanayake, R. (2004). The OWL-S Editor – A Development Tool for Semantic Web Services. SRI International, http://owlseditor.semwebcentral.org/documents/paper.pdf

Fitzgerald, C. (2005). Dynamic Packaging: The impact of technology on the sale of commodity products, both online and offline, http://www.solutionz.com/pdfs/01-Dynamic_Packaging.pdf. The Solutionz Group International, Inc.

Herrero, J., Bilbao, S., Herrero, G., González, J.S. & Lladó, E. (2009). Flexible Creation of Virtual Companies to Satisfy the New Market Demands in the Tourism Sector. Expanding the Knowledge Economy: Issues, Applications, Case Studies, Paul Cunningham and Miriam Cunningham (Eds), IOS Press.

IST Advisory Group (2008). Working Group Report on Future Internet Infrastructure. ftp://ftp.cordis.europa.eu/pub/ist/docs/future-internet-istag_en.pdf

Jentzsch, A. (2005). Tourism Standards. Technical Report XML Clearinghouse Report 12, Freie Universität Berlin, Humboldt-Universität zu Berlin.

Juric, M. B. (2006). Business Process Execution Language for Web Services Second Edition. Packt Publishing.

Kopecký, J., Vitvar, T., Bournez, C. & Farrell, J. (2007). Sawsdl: Semantic annotations for wsdl and xml schema. IEEE Internet Computing, 11(6).

Lara, R., Roman, D., Polleres, A. & Fensel, D. (2004). A conceptual comparison between WSMO and OWL-S. The European Conference on Web Services (ECOWS'04), Erfurt, Germany.

Longhi, C. (2005). Usages of the Internet and e-tourism. Towards a new economy of tourism. Working Paper, GREDEG, Sophia Antipolis, France, 2005

Patil, S. & Newcomer, E. (2003). ebXML and web services. Internet Computing, IEEE 74-82.

Solutions, T. (2005). Making sense of dynamic packaging. http://www.triseptsolutions.com/Dynamic_Packaging.pdf.

Zanker M., Aschinger M., & Jessenitschnig M. (2007). Development of a Collaborative and Constraint-Based Web Configuration System for Personalized Bundling of Products and Services. In: 8th International Conference on Web Information Systems Engineering, Nancy, France., (LNCS, 4831), pp. 273-284.

Semantic Online Tourism Market Monitoring

Norbert Walchhofer[a], Milan Hronský[a],
Michael Pöttler[b],
Robert Baumgartner,[c] and
Karl A. Fröschl[d]

[a]EC3 – Electronic Commerce Competence Centre, Austria
{norbert.walchhofer,milan.hronsky}@ec3.at

[b]Institute of Software Technology and Interactive Systems, EC Group
VUT Vienna Technical University, Austria
michael.poettler@ec.tuwien.ac.at

[c]Lixto Software GmbH, Austria
robert.baumgartner@lixto.com

[d]Dept. of Scientific Computing
University of Vienna, Austria
karl.anton.froeschl@univie.ac.at

Abstract

SEMAMO (SEmantic MArket MOnitoring) is a research project seeking to make use of the increasingly growing information available at Web-based sales and marketing channels for continuous market research. Assuming that online channels indeed mirror salient market developments faithfully, SEMAMO implements a nearly fully automatic adaptive data capture and analysis process delivering customer-defined market reports on demand. The paper describes the SEMAMO prototype implementation and exemplifies the functionality and utility of the approach in the domain of e-tourism, with a focus on the type of reports and visualisations the software, albeit not completely finished yet, can already deliver based on real-world data. Additionally, the role of formal domain description in SEMAMO is emphasized.

Keywords: online market intelligence, domain model, e-tourism, data aggregation

1 Introduction

In the Internet-based economy, traditional market research (Marder, 1997), including methods of market segmentation and price discrimination, no longer work the way they used to. In particular, the transparency of e-markets and the speed of market movements call for an increasingly comprehensive and efficient monitoring of markets and competitor behaviour (e.g., cf. Doorenbos et al., 1997). More specifically, in a tremendously competitive environment such as online tourism, the continuous observation of market behaviour is vital for every market participant: offers vary more dynamically, prices are set more frequently, and are quite often changed even on the spot. As a consequence, e-markets are much more volatile and sensitive due to the relative simplicity to put such changes in place. Accordingly, e-businesses need a concise, recent and comprehensive picture of online markets to guide their product marketing strategy, particularly including pricing decisions. Advanced information technologies – and particularly semantic technologies (Sheth & Ramakrishnan, 2003) – provide a means to intensify and accelerate market observation by reducing the cost of information procurement, thereby expanding the scope of competitive decision-making. Addressing this issue, the SEMAMO (SEmantic MArket MOnitoring) project, presented in this paper, explores an approach to continuous online market monitoring which extends current business intelligence methodologies and solutions by linking established statistical methods of market research to the mechanised collection of online market data. The SEMAMO system gathers business information available at Web-based sales and marketing channels, using semi-automated analysis processes driven by an (interchangeable) semantic model of the application domain.

Assuming that the Web indeed truly maps market developments in terms of product descriptions, distribution, promotions, and price developments in a timely and sufficiently accurate manner, SEMAMO implements a flexible modular framework of online market intelligence. The following sections, in turn, describe the main architecture components of SEMAMO (Sect. 2), highlight some of the market reports derivable form gathered online data (Sect. 3), and provide methodological details on the modelling and use of domain semantics (Sect. 4). A brief summary of the current state of the SEMAMO project concludes the paper.

2 SEMAMO Architecture

SEMAMO monitors target markets, represented through a set of – pre-selected – Web portals, over time to detect changes in features declared relevant in a defined business context. To this end, a directed data flow from portals to customer-specified business reports is periodically cycled through, as shown in Figure 1: The active data harvesting stage uses Web wrappers realised with Lixto (Baumgartner et al., 2009) to collect data from portals – the SEMAMO sampling methods decide the optimal amount of data from the Web that is needed for a representative market picture without trying to be too exhaustive. Gathered data is rectified for subsequent processing and aggregation in a data transformation stage, and forwarded to the stage of statistical analysis and reporting.

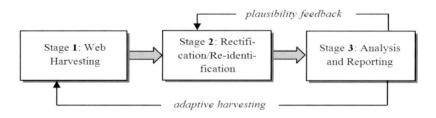

Fig. 1. Main SEMAMO processing schema

While this cardinal data flow is modelled in generic terms and thus basically application-independent, the semantics of a particular market monitoring application is captured in a separate *semantic domain model* component (cf. Sect. 4) also controlling the respective data processing flow. The transformed (validated and cleansed) data is accumulated in a permanent internal repository delivering aggregate information to both, adaptive process control and the preparation of markets reports. The data repository distinguishes between (i) *offer* data, recording time-dependent market features (in particular, offer price tags), and (ii) *registry* data, storing pivotal economic entities such as products (e.g., package tours, hotel rooms) and sellers/distributors (e.g., tour operators, hotels). Both types of data holdings are cyclically updated based on harvested Web portal data, involving entity recognition methods for the accurate (though probabilistic) re-identification of entities already registered.

SEMAMO conceptualises monitored markets in terms of individual products, observed over time. Figure 2 illustrates the generic internal representation of (online) market structures, using an excerpt of an e-tourism application. While products are monitored, market aggregators or distributors actually offer them through one or more online portals. Accordingly, any product may in fact appear on several portals offered by the same or different sellers or intermediaries. This gives rise to a three-tier representation, consisting of a set of SAMPLER populations gathering products by type, a set of SWITCH populations gathering the product distributors or aggregators (intermediaries) as well as an artificial set of SENSOR populations. The latter is linking individual members of matched SWITCH and SAMPLER populations with one portal at a time, respectively, to represent a unique product offer named, for the sake of genericity, a *sensor*. Actually, each sensor inherits all defined and recorded attributes of the portal, switch and sampler instances it is a composition of (Walchhofer et al., 2009b).

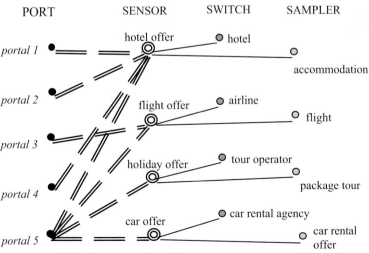

Fig. 2. SEMAMO market structure representation

SEMAMO operates cyclically; in each harvest cycle (e.g., every 6 hours), a subset of registered sensors is accessed online. Every time a sensor is accessed, or harvested, an observation value is generated (and stored) which is assumed to represent a valid price tag of the offer observed. Thus, repeated observation of a sensor generates a portal-dependent price history for the offer it tracks. In the online context, quite specific observation conditions prevail. Most critically, wrapping from Web portal induces server traffic which must not exceed certain levels, in order to prevent access denials to the wrapper demons. In general, sensors cannot be accessed individually but rather as whole classes of sensors as expressible by the query logic of the respective portals. Moreover, accessing a portal may not always produce the sensor data wished for. Finally, offer prices exhibit a more or less dynamic behaviour. SEMAMO seeks to account for these inherent peculiarities by an adaptive data harvesting strategy (cf. Fig. 1): based on previous evidence of harvest performance and, more importantly, the observed price dynamics of sensors, harvest samples are prepared allotting larger shares of the sensor population to market segments exhibiting more dynamic behaviour as opposed to less volatile market segments. On the individual sensor level, a sensor observing price changes more often or of larger magnitudes, is sampled more frequently compared to other sensors, and vice versa (Walchhofer et al., 2009a). Thus, while restricting the overall effort of online data procurement, market coverage and reporting timeliness can be improved substantially without compromising the statistical accuracy of analyses and forecasts.

The offer data repository of SEMAMO accumulates individual sensor price histories for statistical aggregation and analysis. Customer requests specifying certain market reports make use of this data holding by extracting relevant price histories. While possibly being processed on an ad hoc basis, it is assumed that, in general, monitoring requests entail a rather continuous observation of certain market segments, or features, to be reported on periodically. Reports may be composed either in a pull or push mode; pull requests specify a desired reporting periodicity while push requests generate reports triggered by predefined market events (e.g., price changes above a certain threshold). A set of typical reports that can be derived from SEMAMO offer data through pre-configured requests by choosing interactively from several statistical analysis, break-down, and visualisations options, is presented below.

3   Sample Market Reports: The Tourism Domain

As a trial application, SEMAMO uses the domain of hotel room prices, with a geographic focus on offers in Germany. Accordingly, the market structure reflects the top row of Fig. 2, with hotels in German cities and regions as instances of a SWITCH population "hotels" and hotel rooms to book as instances of the SAMPLER population "hotel accommodation". The Web portals used for data harvesting are concealed for presentation purposes, but the data shown are real, and collected during 2009. Obviously, the restriction to German-based hotel accommodations provides a fairly limited view of (global) tourism markets; yet, the example is considered comprehensive enough to highlight the virtues of both, adaptive harvesting and timely online reporting/visualisation of monitoring results.

In illustrating (a small selection of) the reporting capabilities of SEMAMO in terms of three representative, yet contrasting use cases, attention is restricted deliberately to the market reporting dimensions of price levels, price variation, and price distribution, broken down with respect to attributes such as

- time, also incorporating seasonality, seasons, workdays, or weekdays;
- geography, with its hierarchical political decomposition (such as country, state, and city) as well as subdivisions into tourism destinations, including the relationship between both political and tourism regions;
- other attributes defining an offer, like hotel ratings, number of beds in the hotel room/room type, and so on.

Clearly, it is also feasible to draw comparisons, with respect to any of dimensions mentioned, between portals as well as between distributors (intermediaries), in order to explore structural market properties and their dynamics, respectively. Actually, because of the built-in flexibility regarding the selection of the price histories in SEMAMO, customers are fairly free to define "their" market segments of interest, provided these can be expressed in terms of available and recorded offer (that is, sensor) attributes. The data harvesting strategies can also be modified over time, based on the primary interests of customers, such as sampling interesting market segments more frequently. Data selections, then, may be combined flexibly with a wide range of statistical analysis methods, from simple data description through model-based price estimation (such as sector price indexes) to market segmentation and forecasting.

3.1 Use Case: Market Overview

Tourism stakeholders – e.g., hotel chains, tourism boards, or tourism institutes – have a natural interest in overall price levels in the hotel room market, its structural composition and development. For the sake of a specific illustration, assume a Bavarian tourism institute representing several hundred of members throughout the state. One of the institute's main tasks consists in providing a centralised marketing hub. Now, in order to make an informed pricing decision, all the recorded room bookings with the prices actually paid are demanded. Most hotels participate in international reservation systems displaying vacant rooms with their price tags, hence there are several (online) channels to book a room, very often at varying rates for each of the channels. At this point, SEMAMO provides the required data by monitoring the (most) relevant Web portals the pertinent Bavarian hotels use as their preferred sales channels. Figure 3, left-hand side, exhibits a chart of price levels of double rooms for all German states and nearly 200 of the largest cities, including state capitals (marked by squares). The actual price levels can be gleaned from the grey-shaded scale next to the price map, with the scale to the left referring to states, and the scale to the right to cities. The right-hand side of Figure 3 presents the price development of double room offers in Bavaria during summer of 2009, with the abscissa denoting the week of advance booking one month ahead of time. Besides the overall and Bavarian average price levels as juxtaposed to those of four major Bavarian cities, the dotted lines indicate the standard deviation of prices. By the way, in week 38 (mid-September), the city of Munich displays a markedly deviant price behaviour (at least for double rooms),

634

signifying a major event of tourism relevance taking place. Having at its disposal such kind of market information (which, by the way, can still be drilled down considerably), the considered tourism organisation is in a good position to adjust marketing decisions to both market state and dynamics. Furthermore, these reports can be carefully aligned to local specialties or events (such as folklore events, art festivals, etc.), or used to watch the performance of one's own, or the competitors', marketing campaigns. Apparently, by using such a market monitor, a tourism stakeholder cannot only observe her home market but has, in principle, equally easy access to the market data of competing tourism destinations.

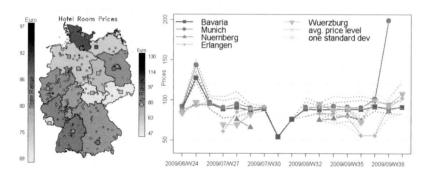

Fig. 3. Price map of German hotel room prices and their temporal development for Bavaria and four selected major Bavarian cities

3.2 Use Case: Peer Group Analysis

Another very interesting use case is about observing micro markets with only a few players acting in a tight regional competition. Often, peer group comparison is interesting to business entities to watch their strongest rivals.

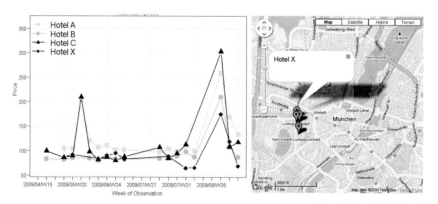

Fig. 4. Peer group analysis of four hotels located near the main station of Munich with a Google map view attached (prices one month before departure)

Hence, if a particular hotel located, say, in the centre of Munich, as illustrated through the Google Maps mashup in Figure 4, is about to set a price of double rooms, there are several factors to account for, such as current room capacity, season, economic conditions, and price arrangements with cooperating business partners. Many of these can be dealt with by fairly standard internal business intelligence tools; however, the additional usage of competitive information on relevant peers as offered by SEMAMO contributes crucially to making well-informed business decisions.

In order to highlight the flexibility offered by SEMAMO, in Figure 4 an exemplary *peer group analysis* is shown for some 3* 'Hotel X' and three of its nearest neighbours. On the left-hand side of the exhibit, the price development for double rooms of these 3* hotels is depicted from June to October. As can easily be seen from the chart, 'Hotel X' is acting in the lower price segment, which makes it even more essential to know its competitors' prices. Assuming that the three "peer" hotels depicted are X's only local competitors, it becomes apparent that X might easily raise the price to about € 20 higher, from end of June to the beginning of August, without exceeding competitor offers. The steep rise in prices towards September (bookings for October), by the way, is reflecting the collective annual price adjustment anticipating the popular 'Oktoberfest' in Munich, as already alluded to in Sect.3.1. Furthermore, the chart illustrated in Figure 4, if combined with geographical data, can easily boost a hotel's pricing decisions without doing any further market research on its own.

3.3 Use Case: Market Structure Analysis

The adaptive data harvesting process decides which offer (i.e., sensor) classes to observe how frequently. For harvesting, selected sensors are mapped to values of a deep web search, consisting of attributes acting as search and filter criteria on attached Web portals. As a result, a number of harvest records are returned for each such query. For the adaptive data harvesting procedure to operate properly, there are three phases to pass through: market exploration and calibration of offer behaviour as initial phases, followed by the actual continuous monitoring operation

Market Exploration Phase. As a first step, the target market, or market segments, have to be defined. In the tourism domain, the market characterisation includes (i) the geographical focus and (ii) several offer selection criteria, together defining the queries (i.e., search and filter parameters) and their instantiations submitted to the attached Web portal wrappers. Accumulated query responses – some of which may remain empty, even after several re-trials, and entail a cancellation of involved sensor classes – provide the *effective* coverage of the target market, with its accuracy and structural distribution depending on the overall market variability. Upon convergence of iterative market exploration, in this phase all accessible domain entities (such as hotels, hotel rooms on offer, etc.) have been extracted and registered.

Parameter Calibration Phase. After the exploration phase has generated an initial market coverage, sensor price histories are gathered. Since, in the beginning, neither the frequency nor the magnitude of price changes are known, another couple of harvest iterations is required to stabilise estimates. To this end, a *market census* including virtually all sensors collected in the market exploration phase, is taken repeatedly. Apparently, market census processing may encounter further domain entities not yet registered, e.g., because of constraints on Web server access quotas, implying a continuous update of the registry. Provided that estimates of price dynamics (price change rates) stabilise eventually, the initial parameter values necessary to run the routine adaptive data harvesting are available.

Adaptive Monitoring Phase. After calibration, the monitor enters the regular sequence of harvest cycles. In each cycle, a *harvest sample* (i.e., a random set of sensors) is generated from wrapper queries based on previous evidence adaptively governing the heuristic selection of sensors depending on the sensors' recorded price histories or, rather, the parameters estimated thereof in the calibration phase (cf. Sect. 4.2, below). During the adaptive monitoring phase, still new domain entities will be encountered, while others perhaps may vanish, entailing a continued update and maintenance of registry data.

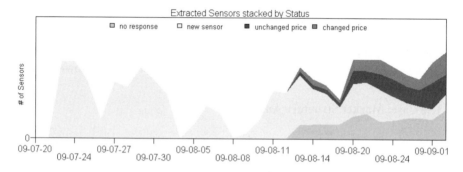

Fig. 5. Market exploration and beginning of the calibration phase of SEMAMO

The reports generated during these successive phases are, on the one hand, interesting for the SEMAMO operator to better understand and monitor the progress in each phase; on the other hand, they also shed light on general market dynamics, e.g., the frequency of price changes and of new offers occurring. Figure 5 illustrates the market exploration and calibration phases, and depicts the number of new hotel offers in each cycle as well as surveyed sensors not available or responding temporarily. Moreover, on entering the calibration phase, offers with both changed and stable prices are visualised for already registered sensors. While the adaptive harvest heuristic seeks to spot *changing* offers with priority, a nearly constant share of about half of the responding sensors signals changed prices, indicating a highly dynamic market indeed.

4 Incorporating Domain Semantics

In SEMAMO, the *automation* of data collection, statistical analysis, and market report generation processes is emphasized while a maximum of flexibility and general applicability of the core system is still preserved: the specific properties of market monitoring applications are apportioned to a dedicated configuration layer, called the *semantic domain model* (SDM, for short) which comprises, among configurations of minor relevance:

- the wrappers tapping Web portals of interest (e.g., online hotel booking sites);
- SWITCH, SAMPLER, and SENSOR populations characterising the application domain (cf. **Fig.2**), including the variables to observe with value domains attached;
- the coupling of SENSOR populations to portal wrappers through virtual data *sources* abstracting the particular query logic of the wrapped portals;
- analytical markets, representing excerpts of the offer data repository used for statistical analyses and report generation, alongside with their dimensional structure for roll-up and grouping (that is, data warehousing; cf. Kimball & Ross, 2002) operations;
- report and order structures governing content and periodicity, or triggering conditions, of reports to generate;
- mapping functions converting (i) raw harvest data into internal, rectified offer data structures, (ii) the latter into analytical market data structures, and (iii) harvest samples to queries on Web portals.

In favour of a modular set-up, the SDM is split into two representation layers, viz. a (single and generic) *system* layer, and a *domain* layer capturing the semantics of the respective SEMAMO application; the latter explicitly represents applications (such as hotel bookings) in terms of (i) data models and mappings as well as (ii) domain-dependent processing parameters, as discussed in the following subsections.

4.1 Ontology-based Application Modelling

In terms of a *domain structure description*, the elements of a domain ontology comprise the specific data models used by SEMAMO sources (i.e., portals) and registries, both linked to the ontology structures predefined on the system layer in order to make the general data harvesting and order processing logic applicable to the respective application domain instances. To this end, both representation layers are expressed in OWL-DL (W3C, 2004) using SPARQL (W3C, 2008) as query language.

For example, in the hotel price monitoring case, referring to **Fig. 2**, a hotel data schema comprising attributes relevant for describing individual hotels becomes linked to the SWITCH class of the system layer; likewise, a room description data schema could be chosen for assignment to its SAMPLER class. Ideally, structurally compliant domain ontologies – such as the *ebSemantics* accommodation ontology (http://www.ebsemantics.net/doc/acco.owl [Sept. 4, 2009]) – can be utilised to simply "plug-in" established models into the SEMAMO domain layer. However, it must be remarked that standard domain models (such as the ones of the Open Travel Alliance; http://xml.coverpages.org/openTravel.html [Sept. 7, 2009]) generally do not specifically fit analytical purposes such as market research. For example, price quotes for the very same hotel room may (and will) differ if booked the day before, the month before, or the season before – but, in general, in the standards there will not be such a room attribute accounting for different booking leads. Hence, manual extensions and adjustments of the domain layer become inevitable.

Actually, in linking a variety of online data sources to a single central data model, a *schema integration* task (Ziegler & Dittrich, 2004) has to be solved effectively. As a consequence, in addition to the central domain model of a market monitoring application providing a hub for the harmonisation of source data, the partial source data models linked to individual Web portals are mapped to the respective domain model. Since Web portals rarely publish their internal data models, even if these comply to one of the established models or data exchange standards, both the domain model and the associated source mappings of an application have to be handcrafted most of the time before they can be inserted into the SDM and connected to the respective system layer structures. Once arranged, the mappings are included in the generic SEMAMO processing schema for feeding harvest data from accessed portals automatically to the successive SEMAMO processing stages, as discussed next.

4.2 Domain Processing Data

A second component of the SDM provides domain-dependent information controlling the processing of harvest data. Particularly data rectification processes resist simple standardisation, entailing almost inevitably an application-specific configuration of portal wrappers, data cleansing routines, and entity recognition (as part of record linkage) methods. Again, however, these tasks depend on domain knowledge represented in dedicated SDM structures. In brief, stage 2 of the SEMAMO processing schema (cf. Fig. 1) can be conceived as a compound function

$$ reid_D \left(\bigcup_p reg_p \left(ret_p \left(Q_p \right) \right) \right) $$

where

- p denotes a portal (i.e., a data source) attached to SEMAMO;
- Q_p denotes a set of queries (i.e. instantiated binding patterns) submitted to portal p, i.e. $Q_p \subseteq dom(A_1) \times \cdots \times dom(A_k)$, letting $dom(A_j)$ denote the value domain of the j-the attribute of the query space of portal p;
- ret_p denotes the retrieval function (i.e., a configured wrapper) returning a harvest sample, including offer prices, according to the source data model of portal p;
- reg_p denotes the function which rectifies harvest samples towards the central sensor data model (applying schema mappings, data cleansing operations and further value pre-processing, possibly using ancillary domain-specific lookup up data (such as thesauri, etc.) or depending on distributional properties of entity populations (entailing yet another information link back from the statistical analysis stage of a SEMAMO instance; cf. Fig. 1), resulting in a split of harvest

records into sensor registry data and sensor price histories (i.e., time-dependent offer data);

- the union of all regularised harvest data is pooled across all portals involved in a central transient *staging area*;
- D denotes a set of domain-dependent discriminating rules used for entity re-identification, derived from a domain-specific learning sample; and, finally,
- $reid_D$ denotes the function which partitions the staging data for re-identifying individual SWITCH and SAMPLER entities, respectively, against the current registry.

In doing so, the re-identification function also detects (particularly during the market exploration phases, cf. Sect. 3.3, but occasionally also later on) new domain entities – e.g., cities, or hotels, etc. – not yet registered and, thus, left unassigned. In this case, the registries as well as the query/sensor relations are updated accordingly (sometimes asking for the operator's assistance, though), as illustrated in Figure 6. Generally, with respect to the hotel booking application of SEMAMO, hotel data harvested from different portals are pooled first in the staging area (lower part of the figure); after matching harvest records found to belong to the same hotels (dashed ovals) these hotel entities are matched with entries in the hotel registry. Likewise, harvested room descriptions are matched with entries in the accommodation registry. The upper part of the figure shows the query/sensor relation used for linking cyclically selected random samples of harvest sensors to portal queries. If a new entity is encountered in the staging area during the re-identification process – in the case shown, a new hotel offer (i.e., room description) of a re-identified hotel – the hotel offer registry is updated with a new sensor assigned to the wrapper query bringing forth this new hotel offer.

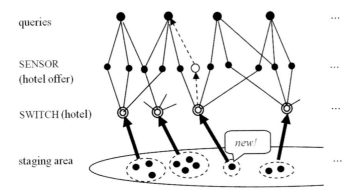

Fig. 6. SEMAMO entity re-identification

Although not yet implemented in SEMAMO, the predictive model markup language (http://sourceforge.net/projects/pmml/ [Oct. 27, 2009]) is considered a promising choice for the representation of domain processing knowledge such as data transformations and re-identification functions.

As a side effect, the SDM incrementally gathers also application-relevant knowledge from staging area data such as, e.g., the link of cities to tourism destinations other than predefined political regions, by tracking co-occurrences of attribute values in connection with specifically tuned (density) estimation procedures to recognize the geographic extension of tourism destinations.

5 Summary

The SEMAMO project pursues research in online market intelligence by coupling methods of online data collection from Web-based sales channels with statistical tools of market research to generate timely and accurate aggregate information about online markets and their dynamics. Based on semantically rich models of monitored markets using dedicated representation standards and tools, a generic framework for data capture, storage, analysis, and reporting according to customer orders has been conceived and prototypically implemented. Moreover, the statistical functionality of SEMAMO has been designed adaptive in order to optimise the market monitoring effort without compromising market coverage, data quality, and accuracy. The SEMAMO solution is composed modularly, so that it is applicable quite easily to different domains by exchanging the formal representations of the respective market models.

As a test case, SEMAMO is applied to the domain of online hotel booking portals. Because of its rather complex product and service structures, the tourism domain provides an ideal candidate for proving the benefits of semantic technologies (Staab & Werthner, 2004). In this paper, use cases and sample reports drawn from this particular domain highlight (some of) the capabilities of the system to tourism marketers and decision makers whereas salient technical issues were indicated only in brief.

References

Baumgartner, R., Gottlob, G., & Herzog, M., (2009) Scalable Web Data Extraction for Online Market Intelligence. VLDB 2/2, 1512-1523.

Doorenbos, R.B., Etzioni, O., & Weld, D.S. (1997) A scalable comparison-shopping agent for the World-Wide-Web. In: Proc. AAMAS, 39-48.

Kimball, R. & Ross, M. (2002) *The data warehouse toolkit: the complete guide to dimensional modeling*. Wiley & Sons, 2nd ed.

Marder, E. (1997) *The laws of choice – predicting customer behavior*. The Free Press/Simon and Schuster.

Sheth, A.P., & Ramakrishnan, C. (2003) Semantic (web) technology in action: ontology driven information systems for search, integration and analysis. *IEEE Data Engineering Bulletin*, Vol. 26, No. 4.

Staab, S. & Werthner, H. (2002) Intelligent systems for tourism – Introduction. IEEE Intelligent Systems 17/6, 53-55.

W3C (2004) OWL Web ontology language use cases and requirements. W3C Recommendation. http://www.w3.org/TR/webont-req/ [Sept. 4, 2009]

W3C (2008) SPARQL query language for RDF. W3C Recommendation. http://www.w3.org/TR/rdf-sparql-query/ [Sept. 4, 2009]

Walchhofer, N., Froeschl, K.A., Hronský, M., & Hornik, K. (2009a) Dynamic population segmentation in online market monitoring. Proc. IFCS 2009 (Dresden, Germany), to appear. (preprint available at http://www.ec3.at/semamo)

Walchhofer, N., Hronský, M., & Froeschl, K.A. (2009b) The online market observatory: A domain model approach. In: Karagiannis, D. & Jin, Z. (eds.) Proc. KSEM 2009, 229-240. (preprint available at http://www.ec3.at/semamo)

Ziegler, P. & Dittrich K.R. (2004) Three decades of data integration – all problems solved ? In: Proc. WCC 2004, 3-12.

Acknowledgements

The SEMAMO project is supported through Fit-IT "Semantic Systems and Services" grant No. 815.135 of the Austrian Research Promotion Agency (FFG).